Jeep Cherokee Automotive Repair Manual

by Jeff Killingsworth

Models covered:
Jeep Cherokee
2014 thru 2019

ABCDE
FGHIJ
KLMNO
PQR

Haynes Publishing Group
Sparkford Nr Yeovil
Somerset BA22 7JJ England

Haynes North America, Inc
859 Lawrence Drive
Newbury Park
California 91320 USA
www.haynes.com

Acknowledgements

Technical writers who contributed to this project include Demian Hurst and Scott "Gonzo" Weaver. Mechanical work and photography was provided by Mark Henderson.

A book in the Haynes Automotive Repair Manual Series

Printed in Malaysia

ISBN-13: 978-1-62092-365-8
ISBN-10: 1-62092-365-3

Library of Congress Control Number: 2019945997

While every attempt is made to ensure that the information in this manual is correct, no liability can be accepted by the authors or publishers for loss, damage or injury caused by any errors in, or omissions from, the information given.

Contents

Haynes mechanic and photographer with a 2016 Jeep Cherokee

About this manual

Its purpose

The purpose of this manual is to help you get the best value from your vehicle. It can do so in several ways. It can help you decide what work must be done, even if you choose to have it done by a dealer service department or a repair shop; it provides information and procedures for routine maintenance and servicing; and it offers diagnostic and repair procedures to follow when trouble occurs.

We hope you use the manual to tackle the work yourself. For many simpler jobs, doing it yourself may be quicker than arranging an appointment to get the vehicle into a shop and making the trips to leave it and pick it up. More importantly, a lot of money can be saved by avoiding the expense the shop must pass on to you to cover its labor and overhead costs. An added benefit is the sense of satisfaction and accomplishment that you feel after doing the job yourself.

Using the manual

The manual is divided into Chapters. Each Chapter is divided into numbered Sections, which are headed in bold type between horizontal lines. Each Section consists of consecutively numbered paragraphs.

The reference numbers used in illustration captions pinpoint the pertinent Section and the Step within that Section. That is, illustration 3.2 means the illustration refers to Section 3 and Step (or paragraph) 2 within that Section.

Procedures, once described in the text, are not normally repeated. When it's necessary to refer to another Chapter, the reference will be given as Chapter and Section number. Cross references given without use of the word "Chapter" apply to Sections and/or paragraphs in the same Chapter. For example, "see Section 8" means in the same Chapter.

References to the left or right side of the vehicle assume you are sitting in the driver's seat, facing forward.

Even though we have prepared this manual with extreme care, neither the publisher nor the author can accept responsibility for any errors in, or omissions from, the information given.

NOTE

A **Note** provides information necessary to properly complete a procedure or information which will make the procedure easier to understand.

CAUTION

A **Caution** provides a special procedure or special steps which must be taken while completing the procedure where the Caution is found. Not heeding a Caution can result in damage to the assembly being worked on.

WARNING

A **Warning** provides a special procedure or special steps which must be taken while completing the procedure where the Warning is found. Not heeding a Warning can result in personal injury.

Introduction

These models feature either a transversely mounted 2.0L in-line four cylinder engine with double overhead camshafts (DOHC), roller rockers and hydraulic lash adjusters, a 2.4L in-line four cylinder engine with single overhead exhaust camshaft (SOHC) and a Variable Valve Actuator Assembly (VVAA), with roller rockers and hydraulic lash adjusters, or a 3.2L V6 engine with double overhead camshafts and mechanical cam followers. These engines have four valves per cylinder, Variable Valve Timing (VVT) and electronic multi-port fuel injection.

The engine drives the front wheels through a nine-speed automatic transaxle via independent driveaxles. All-wheel drive is available on all models, in which a transfer case, driveshaft, rear differential and rear driveaxles deliver power to the rear wheels.

The fully independent front suspension consists of coil spring/strut units, control arms and a stabilizer bar. The rear suspension uses a multi-link design that consists of a knuckle, stabilizer bar, upper control arms, trailing arms, toe links, lower control arms and coil springs and shock absorbers.

The Electric Power-Assisted (EPS) rack-and-pinion steering unit is mounted on the front suspension crossmember.

Front and rear brakes are disc-type. Power brake assist is standard, as is an Anti-lock Brake System (ABS).

Vehicle identification numbers

Modifications are a continuing and unpublicized process in vehicle manufacturing. Since spare parts manuals and lists are compiled on a numerical basis, the individual vehicle numbers are essential to correctly identify the component required.

Vehicle Identification Number (VIN)

This very important identification number is stamped on a plate attached to the left side of the dashboard just inside the windshield (see illustration). The VIN also appears on the Vehicle Certificate of Title and Registration. It contains information such as where

and when the vehicle was manufactured, the model year and the body style.

VIN year and engine codes

Two particularly important pieces of information located in the VIN are the model year and engine codes. Counting from the left, the engine code is the eighth digit and the model year code is the 10th digit.

On the models covered by this manual the engine codes are:

N	2.0L engine
B	2.4L engine
S	3.2L engine (2017 and earlier)
X	3.2L engine (2018 and later)

On the models covered by this manual the model year codes are:

E	2014
F	2015
G	2016
H	2017
J	2018
K	2019

Safety Certification label

The Safety Certification label is affixed to the end of the left front door (see illustration). The label contains the name of the manufacturer, the month and year of production, the Gross Vehicle Weight Rating (GVWR) and the safety certification statement. This label also contains the paint code. It is especially useful for matching the color and type of paint during repair work.

Engine identification number

On four-cylinder engines, the engine serial number is stamped into a machined pad on the rear of the cylinder block just below the cylinder head (see illustration).

On V6 engines, the engine serial number is located on the left end of the cylinder block near the transmission.

Transaxle identification number

The ID number on the automatic transaxle is stamped into a pad on the bottom of the transaxle housing (see illustration).

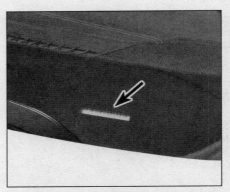

The VIN plate is visible from outside of the vehicle, through the driver's side of the windshield

The Vehicle Safety Certification label is affixed to the end of the driver's door

2.4L engine identification number location

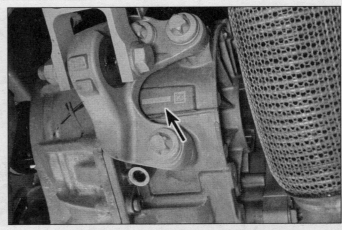

Automatic transaxle identification number location

Recall information

Vehicle recalls are carried out by the manufacturer in the rare event of a possible safety-related defect. The vehicle's registered owner is contacted at the address on file at the Department of Motor Vehicles and given the details of the recall. Remedial work is carried out free of charge at a dealer service department.

If you are the new owner of a used vehicle which was subject to a recall and you want to be sure that the work has been carried out, it's best to contact a dealer service department and ask about your individual vehicle - you'll need to furnish them your Vehicle Identification Number (VIN).

The table below is based on informa-tion provided by the National Highway Traffic Safety Administration (NHTSA), the body which oversees vehicle recalls in the United States. The recall database is updated constantly. For the latest information on vehicle recalls, check the NHTSA website at www. nhtsa.gov, www.safercar.gov, or call the NHTSA hotline at 1-888-327-4236.

Recall date	Recall campaign number	Model(s) affected	Concern
June 4, 2014	14V293000	2014 Cherokee	On some models equipped with rear disc brakes, the length of the rear wheel hub mounting bolts may prevent actuation of the park brake. This could allow unintended movement of the vehicle under certain conditions and cause a crash.
July 02, 2014	14V392000	2014 Cherokee	On some models, due to an insufficient weld, the rear shocks may detach from the vehicle at one end and possibly damage other chassis components, the tire or result in reduced braking. Damage to the tire or reduced braking increases the risk of a vehicle crash.
January 28, 2015	15V041000	2014, 2015 Cherokee	Some models may experience unintended side curtain and seat airbag deployment during vehicle operation. If the airbags deploy unexpectedly during vehicle operation, it can increase the risk of personal injury and increase the risk of a crash..
June 22, 2015	15V393000	2014, 2015 Cherokee	Chrysler is recalling certain vehicles equipped with a Power Liftgate option. In the affected vehicles, water may enter the Power Liftgate Control Module and cause a high resistance short circuit in the module. A short circuit in the liftgate control module may result in a fire.
July 23, 2015	15V461000	2014, 2015 Cherokee	Some models may have vulnerabilities that can allow third-party access to certain networked vehicle control systems. Exploitation of the software vulnerability may result in unauthorized remote modification and control of certain vehicle systems, increasing the risk of a crash.

Recall date	Recall campaign number	Model(s) affected	Concern
August 12, 2015	15V509000	2014 Cherokee	On some models, the use of the front windshield wipers on dry glass may cause damage to the body control module (BCM). BCM damage may result in the failure of the windshield wipers, impairing the driver's vision and increasing the risk of a crash.
October 19, 2015	15V676000	2015 Cherokee	Some models may have a misrouted air conditioning suction/discharge hose. If the line is misrouted, it may contact the exhaust manifold, increasing the risk of a fire.
December 9, 2015	15V826000	2015, 2016 Cherokee	On some models equipped with the power liftgate option, water may leak into the Power Liftgate Control Module and result in a high resistance short circuit. A short circuit in the module increases the risk of a fire.
May 11, 2016	16V284000	2016 Cherokee	On certain models, the right driveaxle may have been incorrectly manufactured causing it to break, which woud increase the risk of a crash.
July 12, 2016	16V529000	2014, 2015 Cherokee	Jeep is recalling certain models equipped with 9-speed automatic transmissions. The transmission sensor clusters may have insufficient crimps in the transmission wire harness, and as a result, the transmission may unexpectedly shift to neutral. If the vehicle unexpectedly shifts to neutral, there is an increased risk of a crash.
August 10, 2016	16V590000	2014, 2015, 2016 Cherokee	On some models, the seat fasteners on the first or second row seats may not have been tightened to the proper torque specification. Loose fasteners may allow the seats to move, increasing the risk of injury to the seat occupants in the event of a crash.
November 2, 2016	16V799000	2017 Cherokee	On certain models, improper welds on the driver's knee airbag inflator may prevent the air bag from properly inflating. If the driver's knee airbag does not inflate, there is an increased risk of injury in the event of a crash.
August 31, 2017	17V543000	2017, 2018 Cherokee	On certain models, the tire and rim size information required to be on the Certification label was omitted during manufacturing, which may result in an incorrect tire and rim combination being installed on the vehicle. The missing tire and rim designation information may lead to an incorrect combination being installed on the vehicle, increasing the risk of a crash.
October 24, 2017	17V670000	2018 Cherokee	On certain models equipped with 2.4L engines. The engines may have a cracked oil pump housing that can result in oil pump failure. If the oil pump fails, the engine will stall, increasing the risk of a crash.

Recall date	Recall campaign number	Model(s) affected	Concern
December 21, 2017	17V824000	2014, 2015, 2016, 2017, 2018 Cherokee	Chrysler is recalling certain models equipped with a Kidde Plastic-Handle or Push Button 'Pindicator' Fire Extinguishers. These extinguishers may become clogged, preventing the extinguisher from discharging as expected or requiring excessive force to activate the extinguisher. Additionally, in certain models, the nozzle may detach from the valve assembly with enough force that it could cause injury and also render the product inoperable. If the fire extinguisher does not function properly, it can increase the risk of injury in the event of a fire.
May 1, 2018	18V282000	2018 Cherokee	Some models equipped with a 2.4L engine may leak fuel into the engine compartment. A fuel leak in the presence of the ignition source can increase the risk of a fire.
May 17, 2018	18V332000	2014, 2015, 2016, 2017, 2018 Cherokee	Chrysler is recalling certain models to address a defect that could prevent the cruise control system from disengaging. If, when using cruise control, there is a short circuit within the vehicle's wiring, the driver may not be able to shut off the cruise control either by depressing the brake pedal or manually turning the system off once it has been engaged, resulting in either the vehicle maintaining its current speed or possibly accelerating. If the vehicle maintains its speed or accelerates despite attempts to deactivate the cruise control, there would be an increased risk of a crash.
May 25, 2018	18V344000	2019 Cherokee	On certain models equipped with 2.0L engines, the engine may be missing valve stem keepers, which can allow the valve to drop into the engine cylinder causing engine damage. These engines may also have a reversed camshaft cap that can damage the camshaft bearing causing camshaft failure. Cylinder damage or camshaft failure can cause the engine to stall, increasing the risk of a crash.
July 26, 2018	18V492000	2018 Cherokee	On certain models, a component in the transmission may not have been welded properly, possibly causing the transmission to not transmit engine power to the wheels. If the transmission weld fails, the vehicle will stop moving, increasing the risk of a crash.
July 26, 2018	18V494000	2018 Cherokee	On certain models equipped with all-wheel-drive, the bearing cage for the right front driveaxle assembly may not have been properly heat treated, possibly resulting in the bearing cage breaking and a potential driveaxle failure. If the driveaxle bearing cage breaks, the driveaxle may not be able to transmit engine power, causing a loss of driver or it can allow the vehicle to move while in the "Park" position. Either condition may increase the risk of a crash.

Recall date	Recall campaign number	Model(s) affected	Concern
August 9, 2018	18V523000	2018, 2019 Cherokee	On certain models, the rear brake caliper pistons may have an insufficient coating causing gas pockets to form, potentially reducing rear brake performance. A reduction of braking performance can increase the risk of a crash.
August 9, 2018	18V524000	2018, 2019 Cherokee	On certain models, the powertrain control module may be equipped with a voltage regulator chip in the circuit board that may fail, causing a stall or a no start condition. A vehicle stall can increase the risk of a crash.
October 19, 2018	18V739000	2019 Cherokee	On certain models equipped with 2.4L engines, improper transmission calibration may result in a stall. A vehicle stall can increase the risk of a crash.

Buying parts

Replacement parts are available from many sources. Our advice concerning them is as follows::

Retail auto parts stores: Good auto parts stores will stock frequently needed components which wear out relatively fast, such as clutch components, exhaust systems, brake parts, tune-up parts, etc. These stores often supply new or reconditioned parts on an exchange basis, which can save a considerable amount of money. Discount auto parts stores are often very good places to buy materials and parts needed for general vehicle maintenance such as oil, grease, filters, spark plugs, belts, touch-up paint, bulbs, etc. They also usually sell tools and general accessories, have convenient hours, charge lower prices and can give you knowledgeable answers to your questions. To be sure of obtaining the correct parts, have engine and chassis numbers available and, if possible, take the old parts along for positive identification.

Authorized dealer parts department: This is the best source for parts which are unique to the vehicle and not generally available elsewhere. Prices for most parts tend to be higher than at retail auto parts stores.

Auto recyclers or salvage yards: Auto recyclers and salvage yards are good sources for components that are specific to the vehicle and not subject to wear, such as fenders, bumpers, trim pieces, etc. You can expect substantial savings by going this route, and self-service salvage yards offer still more savings if you're willing to bring your own tools and pull the part(s) yourself.

Warranty information: If the vehicle is still covered under warranty, be sure that any replacement parts purchased - regardless of the source - do not invalidate the warranty! In most cases, replacement parts, even from aftermarket suppliers, are designed to meet manufacturer specifications. If in doubt, check with the parts supplier.

Because of a Federally mandated extended warranty that covers the emissions control system components, check with your dealer about warranty coverage before working on any emissions-related systems.

To be sure of obtaining the correct parts, have engine and chassis numbers available and, if possible, take the old parts along for positive identification.

Maintenance techniques, tools and working facilities

Maintenance techniques

There are a number of techniques involved in maintenance and repair that will be referred to throughout this manual. Application of these techniques will enable the home mechanic to be more efficient, better organized and capable of performing the various tasks properly, which will ensure that the repair job is thorough and complete.

Fasteners

Fasteners are nuts, bolts, studs and screws used to hold two or more parts together. There are a few things to keep in mind when working with fasteners. Almost all of them use a locking device of some type, either a lockwasher, locknut, locking tab or thread adhesive. All threaded fasteners should be clean and straight, with undamaged threads and undamaged corners on the hex head where the wrench fits. Develop the habit of replacing all damaged nuts and bolts with new ones. Special locknuts with nylon or fiber inserts can only be used once. If they are removed, they lose their locking ability and must be replaced with new ones.

Rusted nuts and bolts should be treated with a penetrating fluid to ease removal and prevent breakage. Some mechanics use turpentine in a spout-type oil can, which works quite well. After applying the rust penetrant, let it work for a few minutes before trying to loosen the nut or bolt. Badly rusted fasteners may have to be chiseled or sawed off or removed with a special nut breaker, available at tool stores.

If a bolt or stud breaks off in an assembly, it can be drilled and removed with a special tool commonly available for this purpose. Most automotive machine shops can perform this task, as well as other repair procedures, such as the repair of threaded holes that have been stripped out.

Flat washers and lockwashers, when removed from an assembly, should always be replaced exactly as removed. Replace any damaged washers with new ones. Never use a lockwasher on any soft metal surface (such as aluminum), thin sheet metalor plastic.

Fastener sizes

For a number of reasons, automobile manufacturers are making wider and wider use of metric fasteners. Therefore, it is important to be able to tell the difference between standard (sometimes called U.S. or SAE) and metric hardware, since they cannot be interchanged.

All bolts, whether standard or metric, are sized according to diameter, thread pitch and length. For example, a standard 1/2 - 13 x 1 bolt is 1/2 inch in diameter, has 13 threads per inch and is 1 inch long. An M12 - 1.75 x 25 metric bolt is 12 mm in diameter, has a thread pitch of 1.75 mm (the distance between threads) and is 25 mm long. The two bolts are nearly identical, and easily confused, but they are not interchangeable.

In addition to the differences in diameter, thread pitch and length, metric and standard bolts can also be distinguished by examining the bolt heads. To begin with, the distance across the flats on a standard bolt head is measured in inches, while the same dimension on a metric bolt is sized in millimeters (the same is true for nuts). As a result, a standard wrench should not be used on a metric bolt and a metric wrench should not be used on a standard bolt. Also, most standard bolts have slashes radiating out from the center of the head to denote the grade or strength of the bolt, which is an indication of the amount of torque that can be applied to it. The greater the number of slashes, the greater the strength of the bolt. Grades 0 through 5 are commonly used on automobiles. Metric bolts have a property class (grade) number, rather than a slash, molded into their heads to indicate bolt strength. In this case, the higher the number, the stronger the bolt. Property class numbers 8.8, 9.8 and 10.9 are commonly used on automobiles.

Strength markings can also be used to distinguish standard hex nuts from metric hex nuts. Many standard nuts have dots stamped into one side, while metric nuts are marked with a number. The greater the number of dots, or the higher the number, the greater the strength of the nut.

Metric studs are also marked on their ends according to property class (grade). Larger studs are numbered (the same as metric bolts), while smaller studs carry a geometric code to denote grade.

It should be noted that many fasteners, especially Grades 0 through 2, have no distinguishing marks on them. When such is the case, the only way to determine whether it is standard or metric is to measure the thread pitch or compare it to a known fastener of the same size.

Standard fasteners are often referred to as SAE, as opposed to metric. However, it should be noted that SAE technically refers to a non-metric fine thread fastener only. Coarse thread non-metric fasteners are referred to as USS sizes.

Since fasteners of the same size (both standard and metric) may have different strength ratings, be sure to reinstall any bolts, studs or nuts removed from your vehicle in their original locations. Also, when replacing a fastener with a new one, make sure that the new one has a strength rating equal to or greater than the original.

Tightening sequences and procedures

Most threaded fasteners should be tightened to a specific torque value (torque is the twisting force applied to a threaded component such as a nut or bolt). Overtightening the fastener can weaken it and cause it to break, while undertightening can cause it to eventually come loose. Bolts, screws and studs, depending on the material they are made of and their

thread diameters, have specific torque values, many of which are noted in the Specifications at the beginning of each Chapter. Be sure to follow the torque recommendations closely. For fasteners not assigned a specific torque, a general torque value chart is presented here as a guide. These torque values are for dry (unlubricated) fasteners threaded into steel or cast iron (not aluminum). As was previously mentioned, the size and grade of a fastener determine the amount of torque that can safely be applied to it. The figures listed here are approximate for Grade 2 and Grade 3 fasteners. Higher grades can tolerate higher torque values.

Fasteners laid out in a pattern, such as cylinder head bolts, oil pan bolts, differential cover bolts, etc., must be loosened or tightened in sequence to avoid warping the component. This sequence will normally be shown in the appropriate Chapter. If a specific pattern is not given, the following procedures can be used to prevent warping.

Initially, the bolts or nuts should be assembled finger-tight only. Next, they should be tightened one full turn each, in a criss-cross or diagonal pattern. After each one has been tightened one full turn, return to the first one and tighten them all one-half turn, following the same pattern. Finally, tighten each of them one-quarter turn at a time until each fastener has been tightened to the proper torque. To loosen and remove the fasteners, the procedure would be reversed.

Component disassembly

Component disassembly should be done with care and purpose to help ensure that the parts go back together properly. Always keep track of the sequence in which parts are removed. Make note of special characteristics or marks on parts that can be installed more than one way, such as a grooved thrust washer on a shaft. It is a good idea to lay the disassembled parts out on a clean surface in

Grade 1 or 2   Grade 5   Grade 8

Bolt strength marking (standard/SAE/USS; bottom - metric)

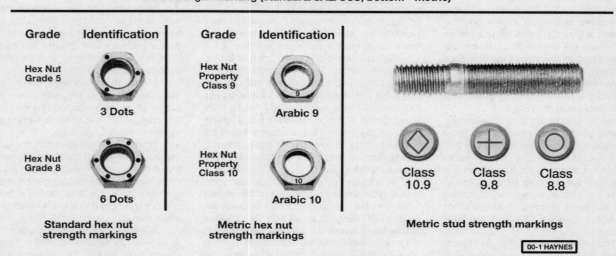

Standard hex nut strength markings   **Metric hex nut strength markings**   **Metric stud strength markings**

00-1 HAYNES

the order that they were removed. It may also be helpful to make sketches or take instant photos of components before removal.

When removing fasteners from a component, keep track of their locations. Sometimes threading a bolt back in a part, or putting the washers and nut back on a stud, can prevent mix-ups later. If nuts and bolts cannot be returned to their original locations, they should be kept in a compartmented box or a series of small boxes. A cupcake or muffin tin is ideal for this purpose, since each cavity can hold the bolts and nuts from a particular area (i.e. oil pan bolts, valve cover bolts, engine mount bolts, etc.). A pan of this type is especially helpful when working on assemblies with very small parts, such as the carburetor, alternator, valve train or interior dash and trim pieces. The cavities can be marked with paint or tape to identify the contents.

Whenever wiring looms, harnesses or connectors are separated, it is a good idea to identify the two halves with numbered pieces of masking tape so they can be easily reconnected.

Gasket sealing surfaces

Throughout any vehicle, gaskets are used to seal the mating surfaces between two parts and keep lubricants, fluids, vacuum or pressure contained in an assembly.

Metric thread sizes

	Ft-lbs	Nm
M-6	6 to 9	9 to 12
M-8	14 to 21	19 to 28
M-10	28 to 40	38 to 54
M-12	50 to 71	68 to 96
M-14	80 to 140	109 to 154

Pipe thread sizes

1/8	5 to 8	7 to 10
1/4	12 to 18	17 to 24
3/8	22 to 33	30 to 44
1/2	25 to 35	34 to 47

U.S. thread sizes

1/4 - 20	6 to 9	9 to 12
5/16 - 18	12 to 18	17 to 24
5/16 - 24	14 to 20	19 to 27
3/8 - 16	22 to 32	30 to 43
3/8 - 24	27 to 38	37 to 51
7/16 - 14	40 to 55	55 to 74
7/16 - 20	40 to 60	55 to 81
1/2 - 13	55 to 80	75 to 108

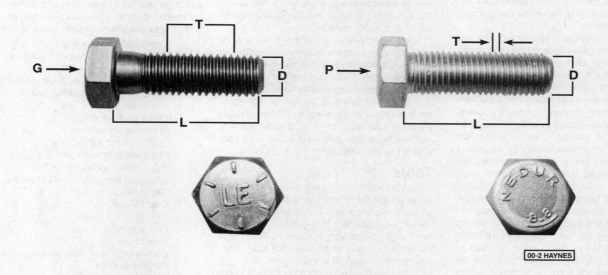

00-2 HAYNES

Standard (SAE and USS) bolt dimensions/grade marks

G   Grade marks (bolt strength)
L   Length (in inches)
T   Thread pitch (number of threads per inch)
D   Nominal diameter (in inches)

Metric bolt dimensions/grade marks

P   Property class (bolt strength)
L   Length (in millimeters)
T   Thread pitch (distance between threads in millimeters)
D   Diameter

Micrometer set

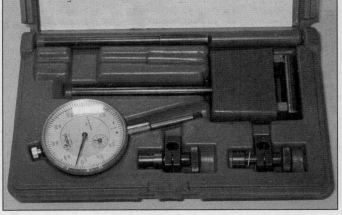

Dial indicator set

Many times these gaskets are coated with a liquid or paste-type gasket sealing compound before assembly. Age, heat and pressure can sometimes cause the two parts to stick together so tightly that they are very difficult to separate. Often, the assembly can be loosened by striking it with a soft-face hammer near the mating surfaces. A regular hammer can be used if a block of wood is placed between the hammer and the part. Do not hammer on cast parts or parts that could be easily damaged. With any particularly stubborn part, always recheck to make sure that every fastener has been removed.

Avoid using a screwdriver or bar to pry apart an assembly, as they can easily mar the gasket sealing surfaces of the parts, which must remain smooth. If prying is absolutely necessary, use an old broom handle, but keep in mind that extra clean up will be necessary if the wood splinters.

After the parts are separated, the old gasket must be carefully scraped off and the gasket surfaces cleaned. Stubborn gasket material can be soaked with rust penetrant or treated with a special chemical to soften it so it can be easily scraped off. **Caution:** *Never use gasket removal solutions or caustic chemicals on plastic or other composite components.* A scraper can be fashioned from a piece of copper tubing by flattening and sharpening one end. Copper is recommended because it is usually softer than the surfaces to be scraped, which reduces the chance of gouging the part. Some gaskets can be removed with a wire brush, but regardless of the method used, the mating surfaces must be left clean and smooth. If for some reason the gasket surface is gouged, then a gasket sealer thick enough to fill scratches will have to be used during reassembly of the components. For most applications, a non-drying (or semi-drying) gasket sealer should be used.

Hose removal tips

Warning: *If the vehicle is equipped with air conditioning, do not disconnect any of the A/C*

hoses without first having the system depressurized by a dealer service department or a service station.

Hose removal precautions closely parallel gasket removal precautions. Avoid scratching or gouging the surface that the hose mates against or the connection may leak. This is especially true for radiator hoses. Because of various chemical reactions, the rubber in hoses can bond itself to the metal spigot that the hose fits over. To remove a hose, first loosen the hose clamps that secure it to the spigot. Then, with slip-joint pliers, grab the hose at the clamp and rotate it around the spigot. Work it back and forth until it is completely free, then pull it off. Silicone or other lubricants will ease removal if they can be applied between the hose and the outside of the spigot. Apply the same lubricant to the inside of the hose and the outside of the spigot to simplify installation.

As a last resort (and if the hose is to be replaced with a new one anyway), the rubber can be slit with a knife and the hose peeled from the spigot. If this must be done, be careful that the metal connection is not damaged.

If a hose clamp is broken or damaged, do not reuse it. Wire-type clamps usually weaken with age, so it is a good idea to replace them with screw-type clamps whenever a hose is removed.

Tools

A selection of good tools is a basic requirement for anyone who plans to maintain and repair his or her own vehicle. For the owner who has few tools, the initial investment might seem high, but when compared to the spiraling costs of professional auto maintenance and repair, it is a wise one.

To help the owner decide which tools are needed to perform the tasks detailed in this manual, the following tool lists are offered: *Maintenance and minor repair, Repair/overhaul* and *Special.*

The newcomer to practical mechanics should start off with the *maintenance and minor repair* tool kit, which is adequate for the simpler jobs performed on a vehicle. Then, as

confidence and experience grow, the owner can tackle more difficult tasks, buying additional tools as they are needed. Eventually the basic kit will be expanded into the *repair and overhaul* tool set. Over a period of time, the experienced do-it-yourselfer will assemble a tool set complete enough for most repair and overhaul procedures and will add tools from the special category when it is felt that the expense is justified by the frequency of use.

Maintenance and minor repair tool kit

The tools in this list should be considered the minimum required for performance of routine maintenance, servicing and minor repair work. We recommend the purchase of combination wrenches (box-end and open-end combined in one wrench). While more expensive than open end wrenches, they offer the advantages of both types of wrench.

Combination wrench set
  (1/4-inch to 1 inch or 6 mm to 19 mm)
Adjustable wrench, 8 inch
Spark plug wrench with rubber insert
Spark plug gap adjusting tool
Feeler gauge set
Brake bleeder wrench
Standard screwdriver
  (5/16-inch x 6 inch)
Phillips screwdriver (No. 2 x 6 inch)
Combination pliers - 6 inch
Hacksaw and assortment of blades
Tire pressure gauge
Grease gun
Oil can
Fine emery cloth
Wire brush
Battery post and cable cleaning tool
Oil filter wrench
Funnel (medium size)
Safety goggles
Jackstands (2)
Drain pan

Note: *If basic tune-ups are going to be part of routine maintenance, it will be necessary to purchase a good quality stroboscopic timing light and combination tachometer/dwell*

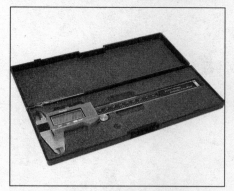

Dial caliper

Hand-operated vacuum pump

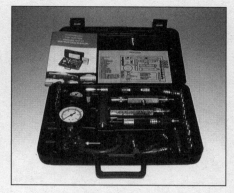

Fuel pressure gauge set

Trouble code reader

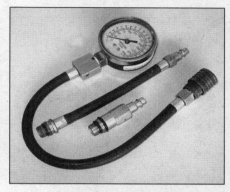

Compression gauge with spark plughole adapter

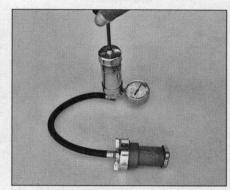

Cooling system pressure tester

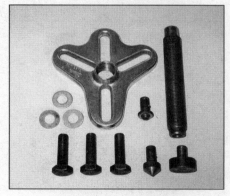

Damper/steering wheel puller

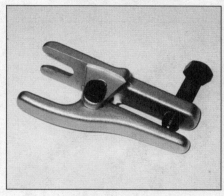

Balljoint separator

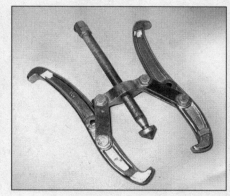

General purpose puller

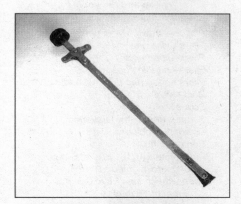

Hydraulic lifter removal tool

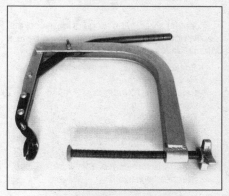

Valve spring compressor

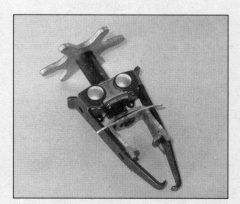

Valve spring compressor

Ridge reamer

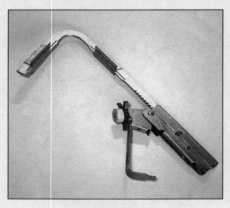

Piston ring groove cleaning tool

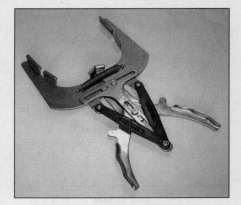

Ring removal/installation tool

Ring compressor

Cylinder hone

Brake hold-down spring tool

Torque angle gauge

Clutch plate alignment tool

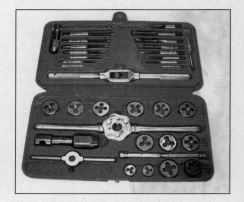

Tap and die set

meter. Although they are included in the list of special tools, it is mentioned here because they are absolutely necessary for tuning most vehicles properly.

Repair and overhaul tool set

These tools are essential for anyone who plans to perform major repairs and are in addition to those in the maintenance and minor repair tool kit. Included is a comprehensive set of sockets which, though expensive, are invaluable because of their versatility, especially when various extensions and drives are available. We recommend the 1/2-inch drive over the 3/8-inch drive. Although the larger drive is bulky and more expensive, it has the capacity

of accepting a very wide range of large sockets. Ideally, however, the mechanic should have a 3/8-inch drive set and a 1/2-inch drive set.

Socket set(s)
Reversible ratchet
Extension - 10 inch
Universal joint
Torque wrench
    (same size drive as sockets)
Ball peen hammer - 8 ounce
Soft-face hammer (plastic/rubber)
Standard screwdriver (1/4-inch x 6 inch)
Standard screwdriver
    (stubby - 5/16-inch)
Phillips screwdriver (No. 3 x 8 inch)

Phillips screwdriver (stubby - No. 2)
Pliers - vise grip
Pliers - lineman's
Pliers - needle nose
Pliers - snap-ring (internal and external)
Cold chisel - 1/2-inch
Scribe
Scraper (made from flattened
    copper tubing)
Centerpunch
Pin punches (1/16, 1/8, 3/16-inch)
Steel rule/straightedge - 12 inch
Allen wrench set (1/8 to 3/8-inch or
    4 mm to 10 mm)
A selection of files

Wire brush (large)
Jackstands (second set)
Jack (scissor or hydraulic type)
Note: *Another tool which is often useful is an electric drill with a chuck capacity of 3/8-inch and a set of good quality drill bits.*

Special tools

The tools in this list include those which are not used regularly, are expensive to buy, or which need to be used in accordance with their manufacturer's instructions. Unless these tools will be used frequently, it is not very economical to purchase many of them. A consideration would be to split the cost and use between yourself and a friend or friends. In addition, most of these tools can be obtained from a tool rental shop on a temporary basis.

This list primarily contains only those tools and instruments widely available to the public, and not those special tools produced by the vehicle manufacturer for distribution to dealer service departments. Occasionally, references to the manufacturer's special tools are included in the text of this manual. Generally, an alternative method of doing the job without the special tool is offered. However, sometimes there is no alternative to their use. Where this is the case, and the tool cannot be purchased or borrowed, the work should be turned over to the dealer service department or an automotive repair shop.

Valve spring compressor
Piston ring groove cleaning tool
Piston ring compressor
Piston ring installation tool
Cylinder compression gauge
Cylinder ridge reamer
Cylinder surfacing hone
Cylinder bore gauge
Micrometers and/or dial calipers
Hydraulic lifter removal tool
Balljoint separator
Universal-type puller
Impact screwdriver
Dial indicator set
Stroboscopic timing light
(inductive pick-up)
Hand operated vacuum/pressure pump
Tachometer/dwell meter
Universal electrical multimeter
Cable hoist
Brake spring removal and
installation tools
Floor jack

Buying tools

For the do-it-yourselfer who is just starting to get involved in vehicle maintenance and repair, there are a number of options available when purchasing tools. If maintenance and minor repair is the extent of the work to be done, the purchase of individual tools is satisfactory. If, on the other hand, extensive work is planned, it would be a good idea to purchase a modest tool set from one of the large retail chain stores. A set can usually be bought at

a substantial savings over the individual tool prices, and they often come with a tool box. As additional tools are needed, add-on sets, individual tools and a larger tool box can be purchased to expand the tool selection. Building a tool set gradually allows the cost of the tools to be spread over a longer period of time and gives the mechanic the freedom to choose only those tools that will actually be used.

Tool stores will often be the only source of some of the special tools that are needed, but regardless of where tools are bought, try to avoid cheap ones, especially when buying screwdrivers and sockets, because they won't last very long. The expense involved in replacing cheap tools will eventually be greater than the initial cost of quality tools.

Care and maintenance of tools

Good tools are expensive, so it makes sense to treat them with respect. Keep them clean and in usable condition and store them properly when not in use. Always wipe off any dirt, grease or metal chips before putting them away. Never leave tools lying around in the work area. Upon completion of a job, always check closely under the hood for tools that may have been left there so they won't get lost during a test drive.

Some tools, such as screwdrivers, pliers, wrenches and sockets, can be hung on a panel mounted on the garage or workshop wall, while others should be kept in a tool box or tray. Measuring instruments, gauges, meters, etc. must be carefully stored where they cannot be damaged by weather or impact from other tools.

When tools are used with care and stored properly, they will last a very long time. Even with the best of care, though, tools will wear out if used frequently. When a tool is damaged or worn out, replace it. Subsequent jobs will be safer and more enjoyable if you do.

How to repair damaged threads

Sometimes, the internal threads of a nut or bolt hole can become stripped, usually from overtightening. Stripping threads is an all-too-common occurrence, especially when working with aluminum parts, because aluminum is so soft that it easily strips out.

Usually, external or internal threads are only partially stripped. After they've been cleaned up with a tap or die, they'll still work. Sometimes, however, threads are badly damaged. When this happens, you've got three choices:

1) *Drill and tap the hole to the next suitable oversize and install a larger diameter bolt, screw or stud.*
2) *Drill and tap the hole to accept a threaded plug, then drill and tap the plug to the original screw size. You can also buy a plug already threaded to the original size. Then you simply drill a hole to the specified size, then run the threaded*

plug into the hole with a bolt and jam nut. Once the plug is fully seated, remove the jam nut and bolt.
3) *The third method uses a patented thread repair kit like Heli-Coil or Slimsert. These easy-to-use kits are designed to repair damaged threads in straight-through holes and blind holes. Both are available as kits which can handle a variety of sizes and thread patterns. Drill the hole, then tap it with the special included tap. Install the Heli-Coil and the hole is back to its original diameter and thread pitch.*

Regardless of which method you use, be sure to proceed calmly and carefully. A little impatience or carelessness during one of these relatively simple procedures can ruin your whole day's work and cost you a bundle if you wreck an expensive part.

Working facilities

Not to be overlooked when discussing tools is the workshop. If anything more than routine maintenance is to be carried out, some sort of suitable work area is essential.

It is understood, and appreciated, that many home mechanics do not have a good workshop or garage available, and end up removing an engine or doing major repairs outside. It is recommended, however, that the overhaul or repair be completed under the cover of a roof.

A clean, flat workbench or table of comfortable working height is an absolute necessity. The workbench should be equipped with a vise that has a jaw opening of at least four inches.

As mentioned previously, some clean, dry storage space is also required for tools, as well as the lubricants, fluids, cleaning solvents, etc. which soon become necessary.

Sometimes waste oil and fluids, drained from the engine or cooling system during normal maintenance or repairs, present a disposal problem. To avoid pouring them on the ground or into a sewage system, pour the used fluids into large containers, seal them with caps and take them to an authorized disposal site or recycling center. Plastic jugs, such as old antifreeze containers, are ideal for this purpose.

Always keep a supply of old newspapers and clean rags available. Old towels are excellent for mopping up spills. Many mechanics use rolls of paper towels for most work because they are readily available and disposable. To help keep the area under the vehicle clean, a large cardboard box can be cut open and flattened to protect the garage or shop floor.

Whenever working over a painted surface, such as when leaning over a fender to service something under the hood, always cover it with an old blanket or bedspread to protect the finish. Vinyl covered pads, made especially for this purpose, are available at auto parts stores.

Booster battery (jump) starting

Caution: *It is not recommend to jump start an AGM battery system. If it is the only possible method to get the vehicle operational again due to location or availability of proper charging equipment, DO NOT hook the jumper cable directly to the IBS or the clamp, but attach the jumper cable to the negative battery post. Do not remove the IBS for charging purposes, it needs to remain connected at all times.*

Observe these precautions when using a booster battery to start a vehicle:

a) *Before connecting the booster battery, make sure the ignition switch is in the Off position.*

b) *Turn off the lights, heater and other electrical loads.*

c) *Your eyes should be shielded. Safety goggles are a good idea.*

d) *Make sure the booster battery is the same voltage as the dead one in the vehicle.*

e) *The two vehicles MUST NOT TOUCH each other!*

f) *Make sure the transaxle is in Neutral (manual) or Park (automatic).*

g) *If the booster battery is not a maintenance-free type, remove the vent caps and lay a cloth over the vent holes.*

Connect one jumper lead between the positive (+) terminals of the two batteries **(see illustration)**.

Connect the other jumper lead first to the negative (-) terminal of the booster battery, then to a good engine ground on the vehicle to be started.

Start the engine using the booster battery, then, with the engine running at idle speed, disconnect the jumper cables in the reverse order of connection.

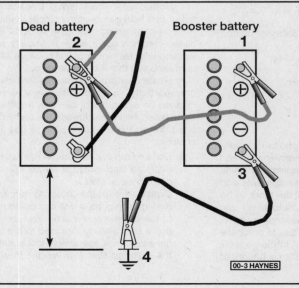

Dead battery
Booster battery

Make the booster battery cable connections in the numerical order shown (note that the negative cable of the booster battery is NOT attached to the negative terminal of the dead battery)

00-3 HAYNES

Jacking and towing

Jacking

Caution: *The jack supplied with the vehicle should only be used for changing a tire or placing jackstands under the frame. Never work under the vehicle or start the engine while this jack is being used as the only means of support.*

The jack supplied with the vehicle should only be used for raising the vehicle for changing a tire or placing jackstands under the frame.

Warning: *Never crawl under the vehicle or start the engine when the jack is being used as the only means of support.*

Note: *Not all models are equipped with a jack and spare tire. Instead, some are equipped with a tire sealant and inflator (compressor) kit.*

Vehicles are supplied with a scissors-type jack or tire inflator kit **(see illustration)**. When jacking the vehicle, it should be engaged with the relief area in the rocker panel flange **(see illustrations)**.

The vehicle should be on level ground with the wheels blocked and the transmission in Park. Pry off the hub cap (if equipped) using the tapered end of the lug wrench. Loosen the wheel bolts one-half turn and leave them in place until the wheel is raised off the ground.

Place the jack under the side of the vehicle in the indicated position. Use the supplied wrench to turn the jackscrew clockwise until the wheel is raised off the ground. Remove the lug nuts, pull off the wheel and install the spare.

Install the wheel bolts and tighten them until snug. Lower the vehicle by turning the jackscrew counterclockwise. Remove the jack and tighten the bolts in a diagonal pattern to the torque listed in the Chapter 1 Specifications. If a torque wrench is not available, have the torque checked by a service station as soon as possible. Install the hubcap by placing it in position and using the heel of your hand or a rubber mallet to seat it.

Towing

Front-wheel drive models

As a general rule, the vehicle should be towed with the front (drive) wheels off the ground or, preferably, on a flat bed car carrier. If the front wheels can't be raised or a carrier isn't available, place them on a dolly. The ignition key must be in the ACC position, since the steering lock mechanism isn't strong enough to hold the front wheels straight while towing.

Towing equipment specifically designed for this purpose should be used and should be attached to the main structural members of the vehicle, not the bumper or brackets.

Safety is a major consideration when towing and all applicable state and local laws must be obeyed. A safety chain system must be used for all towing.

While towing, the parking brake must be released and the transmission must be in Neutral. The steering must be unlocked (ignition switch in the Off position). Remember that power steering and power brakes will not work with the engine off.

Models with CVT transaxles and All-Wheel Drive

A flatbed car carrier must be used to transport these vehicles.

The tire inflator (compressor) kit is located where a spare tire would normally be.

Front of vehicle jacking points. The scissor jack or jackstand fits over the front rocker panel flange (A) - floor jack with jackstand installation point shown (there are two jacking points on each side of the vehicle)

A Front rocker panel flange   B Floor jack lifting point

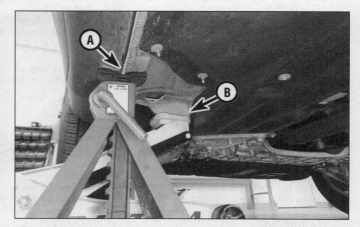

Rear of vehicle jacking points. The scissor jack or jackstand fits over the front rocker panel flange (A) - floor jack and with jackstand installation point shown (there are two jacking points on each side of the vehicle)

A Rear rocker panel flange   B Floor jack lifting point

Conversion factors

Length (distance)
Inches (in)	X	25.4	= Millimeters (mm)	X 0.0394	= Inches (in)
Feet (ft)	X	0.305	= Meters (m)	X 3.281	= Feet (ft)
Miles	X	1.609	= Kilometers (km)	X 0.621	= Miles

Volume (capacity)
Cubic inches (cu in; in^3)	X	16.387	= Cubic centimeters (cc; cm^3)	X 0.061	= Cubic inches (cu in; in^3)
Imperial pints (Imp pt)	X	0.568	= Liters (l)	X 1.76	= Imperial pints (Imp pt)
Imperial quarts (Imp qt)	X	1.137	= Liters (l)	X 0.88	= Imperial quarts (Imp qt)
Imperial quarts (Imp qt)	X	1.201	= US quarts (US qt)	X 0.833	= Imperial quarts (Imp qt)
US quarts (US qt)	X	0.946	= Liters (l)	X 1.057	= US quarts (US qt)
Imperial gallons (Imp gal)	X	4.546	= Liters (l)	X 0.22	= Imperial gallons (Imp gal)
Imperial gallons (Imp gal)	X	1.201	= US gallons (US gal)	X 0.833	= Imperial gallons (Imp gal)
US gallons (US gal)	X	3.785	= Liters (l)	X 0.264	= US gallons (US gal)

Mass (weight)
Ounces (oz)	X	28.35	= Grams (g)	X 0.035	= Ounces (oz)
Pounds (lb)	X	0.454	= Kilograms (kg)	X 2.205	= Pounds (lb)

Force
Ounces-force (ozf; oz)	X	0.278	= Newtons (N)	X 3.6	= Ounces-force (ozf; oz)
Pounds-force (lbf; lb)	X	4.448	= Newtons (N)	X 0.225	= Pounds-force (lbf; lb)
Newtons (N)	X	0.1	= Kilograms-force (kgf; kg)	X 9.81	= Newtons (N)

Pressure
Pounds-force per square inch (psi; lbf/in^2; lb/in^2)	X	0.070	= Kilograms-force per square centimeter (kgf/cm^2; kg/cm^2)	X 14.223	= Pounds-force per square inch (psi; lbf/in^2; lb/in^2)
Pounds-force per square inch (psi; lbf/in^2; lb/in^2)	X	0.068	= Atmospheres (atm)	X 14.696	= Pounds-force per square inch (psi; lbf/in^2; lb/in^2)
Pounds-force per square inch (psi; lbf/in^2; lb/in^2)	X	0.069	= Bars	X 14.5	= Pounds-force per square inch (psi; lbf/in^2; lb/in^2)
Pounds-force per square inch (psi; lbf/in^2; lb/in^2)	X	6.895	= Kilopascals (kPa)	X 0.145	= Pounds-force per square inch (psi; lbf/in^2; lb/in^2)
Kilopascals (kPa)	X	0.01	= Kilograms-force per square centimeter (kgf/cm^2; kg/cm^2)	X 98.1	= Kilopascals (kPa)

Torque (moment of force)
Pounds-force inches (lbf in; lb in)	X	1.152	= Kilograms-force centimeter (kgf cm; kg cm)	X 0.868	= Pounds-force inches (lbf in; lb in)
Pounds-force inches (lbf in; lb in)	X	0.113	= Newton meters (Nm)	X 8.85	= Pounds-force inches (lbf in; lb in)
Pounds-force inches (lbf in; lb in)	X	0.083	= Pounds-force feet (lbf ft; lb ft)	X 12	= Pounds-force inches (lbf in; lb in)
Pounds-force feet (lbf ft; lb ft)	X	0.138	= Kilograms-force meters (kgf m; kg m)	X 7.233	= Pounds-force feet (lbf ft; lb ft)
Pounds-force feet (lbf ft; lb ft)	X	1.356	= Newton meters (Nm)	X 0.738	= Pounds-force feet (lbf ft; lb ft)
Newton meters (Nm)	X	0.102	= Kilograms-force meters (kgf m; kg m)	X 9.804	= Newton meters (Nm)

Vacuum
Inches mercury (in. Hg)	X	3.377	= Kilopascals (kPa)	X 0.2961	= Inches mercury
Inches mercury (in. Hg)	X	25.4	= Millimeters mercury (mm Hg)	X 0.0394	= Inches mercury

Power
Horsepower (hp)	X	745.7	= Watts (W)	X 0.0013	= Horsepower (hp)

Velocity (speed)
Miles per hour (miles/hr; mph)	X	1.609	= Kilometers per hour (km/hr; kph)	X 0.621	= Miles per hour (miles/hr; mph)

Fuel consumption*
Miles per gallon, Imperial (mpg)	X	0.354	= Kilometers per liter (km/l)	X 2.825	= Miles per gallon, Imperial (mpg)
Miles per gallon, US (mpg)	X	0.425	= Kilometers per liter (km/l)	X 2.352	= Miles per gallon, US (mpg)

Temperature
Degrees Fahrenheit = (°C x 1.8) + 32

Degrees Celsius (Degrees Centigrade; °C) = (°F - 32) x 0.56

*It is common practice to convert from miles per gallon (mpg) to liters/100 kilometers (l/100km), where mpg (Imperial) x l/100 km = 282 and mpg (US) x l/100 km = 235

DECIMALS to MILLIMETERS

Decimal	mm	Decimal	mm
0.001	0.0254	0.500	12.7000
0.002	0.0508	0.510	12.9540
0.003	0.0762	0.520	13.2080
0.004	0.1016	0.530	13.4620
0.005	0.1270	0.540	13.7160
0.006	0.1524	0.550	13.9700
0.007	0.1778	0.560	14.2240
0.008	0.2032	0.570	14.4780
0.009	0.2286	0.580	14.7320
		0.590	14.9860
0.010	0.2540		
0.020	0.5080		
0.030	0.7620		
0.040	1.0160	0.600	15.2400
0.050	1.2700	0.610	15.4940
0.060	1.5240	0.620	15.7480
0.070	1.7780	0.630	16.0020
0.080	2.0320	0.640	16.2560
0.090	2.2860	0.650	16.5100
		0.660	16.7640
0.100	2.5400	0.670	17.0180
0.110	2.7940	0.680	17.2720
0.120	3.0480	0.690	17.5260
0.130	3.3020		
0.140	3.5560		
0.150	3.8100		
0.160	4.0640	0.700	17.7800
0.170	4.3180	0.710	18.0340
0.180	4.5720	0.720	18.2880
0.190	4.8260	0.730	18.5420
		0.740	18.7960
0.200	5.0800	0.750	19.0500
0.210	5.3340	0.760	19.3040
0.220	5.5880	0.770	19.5580
0.230	5.8420	0.780	19.8120
0.240	6.0960	0.790	20.0660
0.250	6.3500		
0.260	6.6040		
0.270	6.8580	0.800	20.3200
0.280	7.1120	0.810	20.5740
0.290	7.3660	0.820	20.8280
		0.830	21.0820
0.300	7.6200	0.840	21.3360
0.310	7.8740	0.850	21.5900
0.320	8.1280	0.860	21.8440
0.330	8.3820	0.870	22.0980
0.340	8.6360	0.880	22.3520
0.350	8.8900	0.890	22.6060
0.360	9.1440		
0.370	9.3980		
0.380	9.6520		
0.390	9.9060	0.900	22.8600
0.400	10.1600	0.910	23.1140
0.410	10.4140	0.920	23.3680
0.420	10.6680	0.930	23.6220
0.430	10.9220	0.940	23.8760
0.440	11.1760	0.950	24.1300
0.450	11.4300	0.960	24.3840
0.460	11.6840	0.970	24.6380
0.470	11.9380	0.980	24.8920
0.480	12.1920	0.990	25.1460
0.490	12.4460	1.000	25.4000

FRACTIONS to DECIMALS to MILLIMETERS

Fraction	Decimal	mm	Fraction	Decimal	mm
1/64	0.0156	0.3969	33/64	0.5156	13.0969
1/32	0.0312	0.7938	17/32	0.5312	13.4938
3/64	0.0469	1.1906	35/64	0.5469	13.8906
1/16	0.0625	1.5875	9/16	0.5625	14.2875
5/64	0.0781	1.9844	37/64	0.5781	14.6844
3/32	0.0938	2.3812	19/32	0.5938	15.0812
7/64	0.1094	2.7781	39/64	0.6094	15.4781
1/8	0.1250	3.1750	5/8	0.6250	15.8750
9/64	0.1406	3.5719	41/64	0.6406	16.2719
5/32	0.1562	3.9688	21/32	0.6562	16.6688
11/64	0.1719	4.3656	43/64	0.6719	17.0656
3/16	0.1875	4.7625	11/16	0.6875	17.4625
13/64	0.2031	5.1594	45/64	0.7031	17.8594
7/32	0.2188	5.5562	23/32	0.7188	18.2562
15/64	0.2344	5.9531	47/64	0.7344	18.6531
1/4	0.2500	6.3500	3/4	0.7500	19.0500
17/64	0.2656	6.7469	49/64	0.7656	19.4469
9/32	0.2812	7.1438	25/32	0.7812	19.8438
19/64	0.2969	7.5406	51/64	0.7969	20.2406
5/16	0.3125	7.9375	13/16	0.8125	20.6375
21/64	0.3281	8.3344	53/64	0.8281	21.0344
11/32	0.3438	8.7312	27/32	0.8438	21.4312
23/64	0.3594	9.1281	55/64	0.8594	21.8281
3/8	0.3750	9.5250	7/8	0.8750	22.2250
25/64	0.3906	9.9219	57/64	0.8906	22.6219
13/32	0.4062	10.3188	29/32	0.9062	23.0188
27/64	0.4219	10.7156	59/64	0.9219	23.4156
7/16	0.4375	11.1125	15/16	0.9375	23.8125
29/64	0.4531	11.5094	61/64	0.9531	24.2094
15/32	0.4688	11.9062	31/32	0.9688	24.6062
31/64	0.4844	12.3031	63/64	0.9844	25.0031
1/2	0.5000	12.7000	1	1.0000	25.4000

Automotive chemicals and lubricants

A number of automotive chemicals and lubricants are available for use during vehicle maintenance and repair. They include a wide variety of products ranging from cleaning solvents and degreasers to lubricants and protective sprays for rubber, plastic and vinyl.

Cleaners

Carburetor cleaner and choke cleaner is a strong solvent for gum, varnish and carbon. Most carburetor cleaners leave a dry-type lubricant film which will not harden or gum up. Because of this film it is not recommended for use on electrical components.

Brake system cleaner is used to remove brake dust, grease and brake fluid from the brake system, where clean surfaces are absolutely necessary. It leaves no residue and often eliminates brake squeal caused by contaminants.

Electrical cleaner removes oxidation, corrosion and carbon deposits from electrical contacts, restoring full current flow. It can also be used to clean spark plugs, carburetor jets, voltage regulators and other parts where an oil-free surface is desired.

Demoisturants remove water and moisture from electrical components such as alternators, voltage regulators, electrical connectors and fuse blocks. They are non-conductive and non-corrosive.

Degreasers are heavy-duty solvents used to remove grease from the outside of the engine and from chassis components. They can be sprayed or brushed on and, depending on the type, are rinsed off either with water or solvent.

Lubricants

Motor oil is the lubricant formulated for use in engines. It normally contains a wide variety of additives to prevent corrosion and reduce foaming and wear. Motor oil comes in various weights (viscosity ratings) from 0 to 50. The recommended weight of the oil depends on the season, temperature and the demands on the engine. Light oil is used in cold climates and under light load conditions. Heavy oil is used in hot climates and where high loads are encountered. Multi-viscosity oils are designed to have characteristics of both light and heavy oils and are available in a number of weights from 0W-20 to 20W-50.

Gear oil is designed to be used in differentials, manual transmissions and other areas where high-temperature lubrication is required.

Chassis and wheel bearing grease is a heavy grease used where increased loads and friction are encountered, such as for wheel bearings, balljoints, tie-rod ends and universal joints.

High-temperature wheel bearing grease is designed to withstand the extreme temperatures encountered by wheel bearings in disc brake equipped vehicles. It usually contains molybdenum disulfide (moly), which is a dry-type lubricant.

White grease is a heavy grease for metal-to-metal applications where water is a problem. White grease stays soft under both low and high temperatures (usually from -100 to +190-degrees F), and will not wash off or dilute in the presence of water.

Assembly lube is a special extreme pressure lubricant, usually containing moly, used to lubricate high-load parts (such as main and rod bearings and cam lobes) for initial start-up of a new engine. The assembly lube lubricates the parts without being squeezed out or washed away until the engine oiling system begins to function.

Silicone lubricants are used to protect rubber, plastic, vinyl and nylon parts.

Graphite lubricants are used where oils cannot be used due to contamination problems, such as in locks. The dry graphite will lubricate metal parts while remaining uncontaminated by dirt, water, oil or acids. It is electrically conductive and will not foul electrical contacts in locks such as the ignition switch.

Moly penetrants loosen and lubricate frozen, rusted and corroded fasteners and prevent future rusting or freezing.

Heat-sink grease is a special electrically non-conductive grease that is used for mounting electronic ignition modules where it is essential that heat is transferred away from the module.

Sealants

RTV sealant is one of the most widely used gasket compounds. Made from silicone, RTV is air curing, it seals, bonds, waterproofs, fills surface irregularities, remains flexible, doesn't shrink, is relatively easy to remove, and is used as a supplementary sealer with almost all low and medium temperature gaskets.

Anaerobic sealant is much like RTV in that it can be used either to seal gaskets or to form gaskets by itself. It remains flexible, is solvent resistant and fills surface imperfections. The difference between an anaerobic sealant and an RTV-type sealant is in the curing. RTV cures when exposed to air, while an anaerobic sealant cures only in the absence of air. This means that an anaerobic sealant cures only after the assembly of parts, sealing them together.

Thread and pipe sealant is used for sealing hydraulic and pneumatic fittings and vacuum lines. It is usually made from a Teflon compound, and comes in a spray, a paint-on liquid and as a wrap-around tape.

Chemicals

Anti-seize compound prevents seizing, galling, cold welding, rust and corrosion in fasteners. High-temperature anti-seize, usually made with copper and graphite lubricants, is used for exhaust system and exhaust manifold bolts.

Anaerobic locking compounds are used to keep fasteners from vibrating or working loose and cure only after installation, in the absence of air. Medium strength locking compound is used for small nuts, bolts and screws that may be removed later. High-strength locking compound is for large nuts, bolts and studs which aren't removed on a regular basis.

Oil additives range from viscosity index improvers to chemical treatments that claim to reduce internal engine friction. It should be noted that most oil manufacturers caution against using additives with their oils.

Gas additives perform several functions, depending on their chemical makeup. They usually contain solvents that help dissolve gum and varnish that build up on carburetor, fuel injection and intake parts. They also serve to break down carbon deposits that form on the inside surfaces of the combustion chambers. Some additives contain upper cylinder lubricants for valves and piston rings, and others contain chemicals to remove condensation from the gas tank.

Miscellaneous

Brake fluid is specially formulated hydraulic fluid that can withstand the heat and pressure encountered in brake systems. Care must be taken so this fluid does not come in contact with painted surfaces or plastics. An opened container should always be resealed to prevent contamination by water or dirt.

Weatherstrip adhesive is used to bond weatherstripping around doors, windows and trunk lids. It is sometimes used to attach trim pieces.

Undercoating is a petroleum-based, tar-like substance that is designed to protect metal surfaces on the underside of the vehicle from corrosion. It also acts as a sound-deadening agent by insulating the bottom of the vehicle.

Waxes and polishes are used to help protect painted and plated surfaces from the weather. Different types of paint may require the use of different types of wax and polish. Some polishes utilize a chemical or abrasive cleaner to help remove the top layer of oxidized (dull) paint on older vehicles. In recent years many non-wax polishes that contain a wide variety of chemicals such as polymers and silicones have been introduced. These non-wax polishes are usually easier to apply and last longer than conventional waxes and polishes.

Safety first!

Regardless of how enthusiastic you may be about getting on with the job at hand, take the time to ensure that your safety is not jeopardized. A moment's lack of attention can result in an accident, as can failure to observe certain simple safety precautions. The possibility of an accident will always exist, and the following points should not be considered a comprehensive list of all dangers. Rather, they are intended to make you aware of the risks and to encourage a safety conscious approach to all work you carry out on your vehicle.

Essential DOs and DON'Ts

DON'T rely on a jack when working under the vehicle. Always use approved jackstands to support the weight of the vehicle and place them under the recommended lift or support points.

DON'T attempt to loosen extremely tight fasteners (i.e. wheel lug nuts) while the vehicle is on a jack - it may fall.

DON'T start the engine without first making sure that the transmission is in Neutral (or Park where applicable) and the parking brake is set.

DON'T remove the radiator cap from a hot cooling system - let it cool or cover it with a cloth and release the pressure gradually.

DON'T attempt to drain the engine oil until you are sure it has cooled to the point that it will not burn you.

DON'T touch any part of the engine or exhaust system until it has cooled sufficiently to avoid burns.

DON'T siphon toxic liquids such as gasoline, antifreeze and brake fluid by mouth, or allow them to remain on your skin.

DON'T inhale brake lining dust - it is potentially hazardous (see *Asbestos* below).

DON'T allow spilled oil or grease to remain on the floor - wipe it up before someone slips on it.

DON'T use loose fitting wrenches or other tools which may slip and cause injury.

DON'T push on wrenches when loosening or tightening nuts or bolts. Always try to pull the wrench toward you. If the situation calls for pushing the wrench away, push with an open hand to avoid scraped knuckles if the wrench should slip.

DON'T attempt to lift a heavy component alone - get someone to help you.

DON'T rush or take unsafe shortcuts to finish a job.

DON'T allow children or animals in or around the vehicle while you are working on it.

DO wear eye protection when using power tools such as a drill, sander, bench grinder, etc. and when working under a vehicle.

DO keep loose clothing and long hair well out of the way of moving parts.

DO make sure that any hoist used has a safe working load rating adequate for the job.

DO get someone to check on you periodically when working alone on a vehicle.

DO carry out work in a logical sequence and make sure that everything is correctly assembled and tightened.

DO keep chemicals and fluids tightly capped and out of the reach of children and pets.

DO remember that your vehicle's safety affects that of yourself and others. If in doubt on any point, get professional advice.

Steering, suspension and brakes

These systems are essential to driving safety, so make sure you have a qualified shop or individual check your work. Also, compressed suspension springs can cause injury if released suddenly - be sure to use a spring compressor.

Airbags

Airbags are explosive devices that can **CAUSE** injury if they deploy while you're working on the vehicle. Follow the manufacturer's instructions to disable the airbag whenever you're working in the vicinity of airbag components.

Asbestos

Certain friction, insulating, sealing, and other products - such as brake linings, brake bands, clutch linings, torque converters, gaskets, etc. - may contain asbestos or other hazardous friction material. Extreme care must be taken to avoid inhalation of dust from such products, since it is hazardous to health. If in doubt, assume that they do contain asbestos.

Fire

Remember at all times that gasoline is highly flammable. Never smoke or have any kind of open flame around when working on a vehicle. But the risk does not end there. A spark caused by an electrical short circuit, by two metal surfaces contacting each other, or even by static electricity built up in your body under certain conditions, can ignite gasoline vapors, which in a confined space are highly explosive. Do not, under any circumstances, use gasoline for cleaning parts. Use an approved safety solvent.

Always disconnect the battery ground (-) cable at the battery before working on any part of the fuel system or electrical system. Never risk spilling fuel on a hot engine or exhaust component. It is strongly recommended that a fire extinguisher suitable for use on fuel and electrical fires be kept handy in the garage or workshop at all times. Never try to extinguish a fuel or electrical fire with water.

Fumes

Certain fumes are highly toxic and can quickly cause unconsciousness and even death if inhaled to any extent. Gasoline vapor falls into this category, as do the vapors from some cleaning solvents. Any draining or pouring of such volatile fluids should be done in a well ventilated area.

When using cleaning fluids and solvents, read the instructions on the container carefully. Never use materials from unmarked containers.

Never run the engine in an enclosed space, such as a garage. Exhaust fumes contain carbon monoxide, which is extremely poisonous. If you need to run the engine, always do so in the open air, or at least have the rear of the vehicle outside the work area.

The battery

Never create a spark or allow a bare light bulb near a battery. They normally give off a certain amount of hydrogen gas, which is highly explosive.

Always disconnect the battery ground (-) cable at the battery before working on the fuel or electrical systems.

If possible, loosen the filler caps or cover when charging the battery from an external source (this does not apply to sealed or maintenance-free batteries). Do not charge at an excessive rate or the battery may burst.

Take care when adding water to a non maintenance-free battery and when carrying a battery. The electrolyte, even when diluted, is very corrosive and should not be allowed to contact clothing or skin.

Always wear eye protection when cleaning the battery to prevent the caustic deposits from entering your eyes.

Household current

When using an electric power tool, inspection light, etc., which operates on household current, always make sure that the tool is correctly connected to its plug and that, where necessary, it is properly grounded. Do not use such items in damp conditions and, again, do not create a spark or apply excessive heat in the vicinity of fuel or fuel vapor.

Secondary ignition system voltage

A severe electric shock can result from touching certain parts of the ignition system (such as the spark plug wires) when the engine is running or being cranked, particularly if components are damp or the insulation is defective. In the case of an electronic ignition system, the secondary system voltage is much higher and could prove fatal.

Hydrofluoric acid

This extremely corrosive acid is formed when certain types of synthetic rubber, found in some O-rings, oil seals, fuel hoses, etc. are exposed to temperatures above 750-degrees F (400-degrees C). The rubber changes into a charred or sticky substance containing the acid. *Once formed, the acid remains dangerous for years. If it gets onto the skin, it may be necessary to amputate the limb concerned.*

When dealing with a vehicle which has suffered a fire, or with components salvaged from such a vehicle, wear protective gloves and discard them after use.

Troubleshooting

Contents

1   This section provides an easy reference guide to the more common problems which may occur during the operation of your vehicle. Various symptoms and their possible causes are grouped under headings denoting components or systems, such as Engine, Cooling system, etc. They also refer to the Chapter and/or Section that deals with the problem.

2   Remember that successful troubleshooting isn't a mysterious art practiced only by professional mechanics. It's simply the result of knowledge combined with an intelligent, systematic approach to a problem. Always use a process of elimination, starting with the simplest solution and working through to the most complex - and never overlook the obvious. Anyone can run the gas tank dry or leave the lights on overnight, so don't assume that you're exempt from such oversights.

3   Finally, always establish a clear idea why a problem has occurred and take steps to ensure that it doesn't happen again. If the electrical system fails because of a poor connection, check all other connections in the system to make sure they don't fail as well. If a particular fuse continues to blow, find out why - don't just go on replacing fuses.

Remember, failure of a small component can often be indicative of potential failure or incorrect functioning of a more important component or system.

4   Owner forums: Information from online forums can be anything from first-rate to entirely wrong. The quality of information is not always obvious. Get involved with forums before you need help so you will know who you can trust. Search for confirmed fixes - If someone trustworthy shared the solution to a problem similar to yours, it might be your solution too.

Engine and performance

1   Engine will not rotate when attempting to start

1   Battery terminal connections loose or corroded (Chapter 1).
2   Battery discharged or faulty (Chapter 1).
3   Automatic transaxle not completely engaged in Park (Chapter 7A).
4   Broken, loose or disconnected wiring in the starting circuit (Chapters 5 and 12).
5   Starter motor pinion jammed in flywheel ring gear (Chapter 5).
6   Starter solenoid faulty (Chapter 5).
7   Starter motor faulty (Chapter 5).
8   Ignition switch faulty (Chapter 12).
9   Transmission Range (TR) sensor faulty (Chapter 6).
10   Starter pinion or driveplate teeth worn or broken (Chapter 5).

2   Engine rotates but will not start

1   Fuel tank empty.
2   Battery discharged (engine rotates slowly) (Chapter 5).
3   Battery terminal connections loose or corroded (Chapter 1).
4   Leaking fuel injector(s), fuel pump, pressure regulator, etc. (Chapter 4).
5   Fuel not reaching fuel injection system (Chapter 4).
6   Broken timing belt or chain (Chapter 2A).
7   Ignition system problem (Chapter 5).
8   Defective crankshaft sensor or camshaft sensor (Chapter 6).

3   Engine hard to start when cold

1   Battery discharged or low (Chapter 1).
2   Fuel system malfunctioning (Chapter 4).
3   Emissions or engine control system malfunctioning (Chapter 6).

4   Engine hard to start when hot

1   Air filter clogged (Chapter 1).

2   Fuel not reaching the fuel injection system (Chapter 4).
3   Corroded battery connections, especially ground (Chapter 1).
4   Emissions or engine control system malfunctioning (Chapter 6).

5   Starter motor noisy or excessively rough in engagement

1   Pinion or driveplate gear teeth worn or broken (Chapter 5).
2   Starter motor mounting bolts loose or missing (Chapter 5).

6   Engine starts but stops immediately

1   Insufficient fuel reaching the fuel injectors (Chapter 4).
2   Vacuum leak at the gasket between the intake manifold/plenum and throttle body (Chapters 1 and 4).
3   Restricted exhaust system (most likely the catalytic converter) (Chapters 4 and 6).

7   Oil puddle under engine

1   Oil pan gasket and/or oil pan drain bolt seal leaking (Chapters 1 or 2A).
2   Oil pressure sending unit leaking (Chapter 2C).
3   Valve cover gaskets leaking (Chapter 2A or Chapter 2B)
4   Engine oil seals leaking (Chapter 2A or Chapter 2B)

8   Engine lopes while idling or idles erratically

1   Vacuum leakage (Chapter 4).
2   Leaking EGR valve or plugged PCV valve (Chapter 6).
3   Air filter clogged (Chapter 1).
4   Fuel pump not delivering sufficient fuel to the fuel injection system (Chapter 4).
5   Leaking head gasket (Chapter 2A or Chapter 2B).

6   Camshaft lobes worn (Chapter 2A or Chapter 2B).

9   Engine misses at idle speed

1   Spark plugs worn or not gapped properly (Chapter 1).
2   Faulty coil(s) (Chapter 5).
3   Vacuum leaks (Chapters 1 and 4).
4   Uneven or low compression (Chapter 2C).

10   Engine misses throughout driving speed range

1   Fuel filter clogged and/or impurities in the fuel system (Chapter 4).
2   Low fuel pressure (Chapter 4).
3   Faulty or incorrectly gapped spark plugs (Chapter 1).
4   Faulty emission system components (Chapter 6).
5   Low or uneven cylinder compression pressures (Chapter 2C).
6   Weak or faulty ignition system (Chapter 5).
7   Vacuum leak.

11   Engine stumbles on acceleration

1   Spark plugs fouled (Chapter 1).
2   Fuel injection system problem (Chapter 4).
3   Fuel filter clogged (Chapter 4).
4   Intake manifold air leak (Chapter 4).
5   Problem with emissions/engine control system (Chapter 6).

12   Engine surges while holding accelerator steady

1   Intake air leak (Chapter 4).
2   Fuel pump faulty (Chapter 4).
3   Problem with the fuel injection system (Chapter 4).
4   Problem with the emission or engine control system (Chapter 6).

13 Engine stalls

1   Fuel filter clogged and/or water and impurities in the fuel system (Chapter 4).
2   Faulty emissions or engine control system components (Chapter 6).
3   Faulty or incorrectly gapped spark plugs (Chapter 1).
4   Vacuum leak.

14 Engine lacks power

1   Faulty or incorrectly gapped spark plugs (Chapter 1).
2   Restricted exhaust system (most likely the catalytic converter) (Chapters 4 and 6).
3   Fuel injection system malfunctioning (Chapter 4).
4   Faulty coil(s) (Chapter 5).
5   Brakes binding (Chapter 9).
6   Automatic transaxle fluid level incorrect (Chapter 1).
7   Fuel filter clogged and/or impurities in the fuel system (Chapter 1).
8   Emission control system not functioning properly (Chapter 6).
9   Low or uneven cylinder compression pressures (Chapter 2C).

15 Engine backfires

1   Emissions system not functioning properly (Chapter 6).
2   Fuel injection system malfunctioning (Chapter 4).
3   Vacuum leak at fuel injectors, intake manifold or vacuum hoses (Chapter 4).
4   Valves sticking (Chapter 2A or Chapter 2B).
5   Timing chain worn (Chapter 2A or Chapter 2B).

16 Pinging or knocking engine sounds during acceleration or uphill

1   Incorrect grade of fuel.
2   Fuel injection system malfunctioning (Chapter 4).
3   Improper or damaged spark plugs (Chapter 1).
4   Worn or damaged ignition components (Chapter 5).
5   Faulty emissions or engine control system (Chapter 6).
6   Vacuum leak.

17 Engine runs with oil pressure light on

1   Low oil level (Chapter 1).
2   Short in wiring circuit (Chapter 12).

3   Faulty oil pressure sender (Chapter 2C).
4   Oil viscosity too low or oil diluted.
5   Worn engine bearings and/or oil pump (Chapter 2A, Chapter 2B or Chapter 2C).

18 Engine continues to run after switching off

1   Excessive engine operating temperature (Chapter 3).
2   Excessive carbon deposits on valves and pistons.
3   Leaking fuel injector(s) (Chapter 4).
4   Faulty ignition switch (Chapter 12).

Engine electrical system

19 Battery will not hold a charge

1   Drivebelt or tensioner defective (Chapter 1).
2   Battery terminals loose or corroded (Chapter 1).
3   Alternator not charging properly (Chapter 5).
4   Loose, broken or faulty wiring in the charging circuit (Chapter 5).
5   Internally defective battery (Chapters 1 and 5).

20 Voltage warning light fails to go out

1   Faulty alternator or charging circuit (Chapter 5).
2   Drivebelt or tensioner defective (Chapter 1).
3   Alternator voltage regulator inoperative (Chapter 5).

21 Voltage warning light fails to come on when key is turned on

1   Warning light bulb defective (Chapter 12).
2   Fault in the printed circuit, dash wiring or bulb holder (Chapter 12).

Fuel system

22 Excessive fuel consumption

1   Dirty or clogged air filter element (Chapter 1).
2   Emissions or engine control system not functioning properly (Chapter 6).
3   Fuel injection system malfunctioning (Chapter 4).

4   Low tire pressure or incorrect tire size (Chapter 1).

23 Fuel leakage and/or fuel odor

1   Leak in a fuel feed or vent line (Chapter 4).
2   Tank overfilled.
3   Evaporative emissions control canister defective (Chapter 6).
4   Fuel injector seals faulty (Chapter 4).

Cooling system

24 Overheating

1   Insufficient coolant in system (Chapter 1).
2   Drivebelt or tensioner defective (Chapter 1).
3   Radiator core blocked or grille restricted (Chapter 3).
4   Thermostat faulty (Chapter 3).
5   Electric cooling fan blades broken or cracked (Chapter 3).
6   Radiator cap not maintaining proper pressure (Chapter 3).
7   Faulty water pump (Chapter 3).

25 Overcooling

Incorrect (opening temperature too low) or faulty thermostat (Chapter 3).

26 External coolant leakage

1   Deteriorated/damaged hoses or loose clamps (Chapters 1 and 3).
2   Water pump seal defective (Chapter 3).
3   Leakage from radiator core (Chapter 3).
4   Engine drain or water jacket core plugs leaking.

27 Internal coolant leakage

1   Leaking cylinder head gasket (Chapter 2A or Chapter 2B).
2   Cracked cylinder bore or cylinder head (Chapter 2A, Chapter 2B or Chapter 2C).

28 Coolant loss

1   Too much coolant in system (Chapter 1).
2   Coolant boiling away because of overheating (Chapter 3).
3   Internal or external leakage (Chapter 3).
4   Faulty radiator cap (Chapter 3).

29　Poor coolant circulation

1　Inoperative water pump (Chapter 3).
2　Restriction in cooling system (Chapters 1 and 3).
3　Drivebelt or tensioner defective or out of adjustment (Chapter 1).
4　Thermostat sticking (Chapter 3).

Automatic transaxle

30　Fluid leakage

1　Automatic transmission fluid on these vehicles is clear when new. Fluid leaks should not be confused with engine oil, which can easily be blown by airflow to the transaxle.
2　To pinpoint a leak, first remove all built-up dirt and grime from the transaxle housing with degreasing agents and/or steam cleaning. Drive the vehicle at low speeds so air flow will not blow the leak far from its source. Raise the vehicle and determine where the leak is coming from. Common areas of leakage are:
a)　*Fluid cooler lines*
b)　*Vehicle Speed Sensor (Chapter 6)*

31　Transaxle fluid brown or has a burned smell

Transaxle overheated. Change fluid (Chapter 1).

32　General shift mechanism problems

1　Chapter 7A deals with checking and adjusting the shift cable on automatic transaxles. Common problems which may be attributed to a poorly adjusted cable are:
a)　*Engine starting in gears other than Park or Neutral.*
b)　*Indicator on shifter pointing to a gear other than the one actually being used.*
c)　*Vehicle moves when in Park.*

33　Engine will start in gears other than Park or Neutral

Transmission Range (TR) sensor malfunctioning (Chapter 6).

34　Transaxle slips, shifts roughly, is noisy or has no drive in forward or reverse gears

1　There are many probable causes for the above problems, but the home mechanic should be concerned with only one possibility - fluid level. Before taking the vehicle to a repair shop, check the level and condition of the fluid as described in Chapter 1.
2　Correct the fluid level as necessary or change the fluid and filter if needed. If the problem persists, have a professional diagnose the probable cause.

Driveaxles

35　Clicking noise in turns

Worn or damaged outer CV joint. Check for cut or damaged boots (Chapter 1). Repair as necessary (Chapter 8).

36　Knock or clunk when accelerating after coasting

Worn or damaged CV joint. Check for cut or damaged boots (Chapter 1). Repair as necessary (Chapter 8).

37　Shudder or vibration during acceleration

1　Worn or damaged CV joints. Repair or replace as necessary (Chapter 8).
2　Sticking inner joint assembly. Correct or replace as necessary (Chapter 8).

Brakes

38　Vehicle pulls to one side during braking

1　Incorrect tire pressures (Chapter 1).
2　Front end out of alignment (have the front end aligned).
3　Unmatched tires on same axle.
4　Restricted brake lines or hoses (Chapter 9).
5　Sticking caliper or wheel cylinder piston (Chapter 9).
6　Loose suspension parts (Chapter 10).
7　Contaminated brake pad material (Chapter 9).

39　Noise (grinding or high-pitched squeal) when the brakes are applied

Disc brake pads worn out. Replace pads with new ones immediately (Chapter 9).

40　Brake roughness or chatter (pedal pulsates)

1　Excessive brake disc lateral runout.
2　Parallelism of disc not within specifications (Chapter 9).
3　Defective brake disc (Chapter 9).

41　Excessive pedal effort required to stop vehicle

1　Malfunctioning power brake booster (Chapter 9).
2　Partial system failure (Chapter 9).
3　Excessively worn pads (Chapter 9).
4　One or more caliper or wheel cylinder pistons seized or sticking (Chapter 9).
5　Brake pads contaminated with oil or grease (Chapter 9).
6　New pads or shoes installed and not yet seated. It will take a while for the new material to seat.

42　Excessive brake pedal travel

1　Partial brake system failure (Chapter 9).
2　Insufficient fluid in master cylinder (Chapters 1 and 9).
3　Air trapped in system (Chapter 9).
4　Faulty master cylinder (Chapter 9).

43　Dragging brakes

1　Master cylinder pistons not returning correctly (Chapter 9).
2　Restricted brake lines or hoses (Chapters 1 and 9).
3　Incorrect parking brake adjustment (Chapter 9).
4　Defective brake calipers (Chapter 9).

44　Grabbing or uneven braking action

Contaminated brake pads (Chapter 9).

45　Brake pedal feels spongy when depressed

1　Air in hydraulic lines (Chapter 9).
2　Master cylinder mounting bolts loose (Chapter 9).
3　Master cylinder defective (Chapter 9).

46 Brake pedal travels to the floor with little resistance

Little or no fluid in the master cylinder reservoir caused by leaking caliper, or loose, damaged or disconnected brake lines (Chapter 9).

47 Parking brake does not hold

Parking brake cables improperly adjusted (Chapter 9).

Suspension and steering systems

48 Vehicle pulls to one side

1 Mismatched or uneven tires (Chapter 10).
2 Broken or sagging coil springs (Chapter 10).
3 Wheel alignment incorrect.
4 Front brakes dragging (Chapter 9).

49 Abnormal or excessive tire wear

1 Front wheel alignment incorrect.
2 Sagging or broken springs (Chapter 10).
3 Tire out-of-balance.
4 Worn strut or shock absorber (Chapter 10).
5 Overloaded vehicle.
6 Tires not rotated regularly.

50 Wheel makes a thumping noise

1 Blister or bump on tire (Chapter 1).
2 Improper strut or shock absorber action (Chapter 10).

51 Shimmy, shake or vibration

1 Tire or wheel out-of-balance or out-of-round.
2 Worn wheel bearings (Chapter 10).
3 Worn tie-rod ends (Chapter 10).
4 Worn balljoints (Chapter 10).
5 Excessive wheel runout.
6 Blister or bump on tire (Chapter 1).

52 Hard steering

1 Balljoints, tie-rod ends or steering gear worn (Chapter 10).
2 Front wheel alignment incorrect.
3 Low tire pressure (Chapter 1).

53 Steering wheel does not return to center position correctly

1 Balljoints or tie-rod ends worn (Chapters 1).
2 Defective steering gear (Chapter 10).
3 Front wheel alignment problem.

54 Abnormal noise at the front end

1 Balljoints or tie-rod ends worn (Chapter 1).
2 Loose upper strut mount (Chapter 10).
3 Worn tie-rod ends (Chapter 10).
4 Loose stabilizer bar (Chapter 10).
5 Loose wheel bolts (Chapter 1).
6 Loose suspension bolts (Chapter 10).

55 Wander or poor steering stability

1 Mismatched or uneven tires.
2 Balljoints or tie-rod ends worn (Chapters 1).
3 Worn struts or shock absorbers (Chapter 10).
4 Broken or sagging springs (Chapter 10).
5 Front wheel alignment incorrect.

56 Erratic steering when braking

1 Wheel bearings worn (Chapter 10).
2 Broken or sagging springs (Chapter 10).
3 Leaking caliper (Chapter 9).
4 Warped brake discs (Chapter 9).
5 Wheel alignment incorrect.

57 Excessive pitching and/or rolling around corners or during braking

1 Loose stabilizer bar (Chapter 10).
2 Worn struts/shock absorbers or mounts (Chapter 10).
3 Broken or sagging coil springs (Chapter 10).
4 Overloaded vehicle.

58 Suspension bottoms

1 Overloaded vehicle.
2 Worn struts or shock absorbers (Chapter 10).
3 Incorrect, broken or sagging springs (Chapter 10).

59 Cupped tires

1 Front wheel alignment incorrect.
2 Worn struts or shock absorbers (Chapter 10).

3 Wheel bearings worn (Chapter 10).
4 Excessive tire or wheel runout.
5 Worn balljoints (Chapter 10).

60 Excessive tire wear on outside edge

1 Inflation pressures incorrect (Chapter 1).
2 Excessive speed in turns.
3 Wheel alignment incorrect (excessive toe-in or positive camber). Have professionally aligned.
4 Suspension arm bent (Chapter 10).

61 Excessive tire wear on inside edge

1 Inflation pressures incorrect (Chapter 1).
2 Wheel alignment incorrect (toe-out or excessive negative camber). Have professionally aligned.
3 Loose or damaged steering components (Chapter 10).

62 Tire tread worn in one place

1 Tires out-of-balance.
2 Damaged wheel.
3 Defective tire (Chapter 1).

63 Excessive play or looseness in steering system

1 Wheel bearings worn (Chapter 10).
2 Tie-rod end loose or worn (Chapter 10).
3 Steering gear loose (Chapter 10).

64 Rattling or clicking noise in steering gear

1 Steering gear mounting bolts loose (Chapter 10).
2 Steering gear defective (Chapter 10).

Chapter 1
Tune-up and routine maintenance

Contents

Specifications

Recommended lubricants and fluids

Engine oil
  Type
    2.0L engines .... API SN PLUS "Certified for gasoline engines"
    2.4L and 3.2L engines .... API "Certified for gasoline engines"
  Viscosity
    2.0L engines .... SAE 5W/30 (Full Synthetic)
    2.4L enignes .... SAE 0W-20
    3.2L engines .... SAE 5W-20
Automatic transaxle fluid .... MOPAR® ZF 8&9 Speed ATF Automatic Transmission Fluid, or equivalent
Rear differential .... MOPAR® SAE 70W-80 API GL 5 Gear and Axle Lubricant or equivalent (non-synthetic).
Transfer case (PTU) .... MOPAR® SAE 75W-90 API GL 5 Gear and Axle Lubricant or equivalent (non-synthetic).
Brake fluid .... DOT 3 brake fluid that meets the J1703 specifications from MOPAR (it will be listed on the bottle)
Engine coolant .... 50/50 mixture of MOPAR® 10 year/150,000 mile, antifreeze/coolant with OAT (Organic Additive Technology) and water
Door and liftgate latches .... Multi-purpose grease
Fuel filler door remote control latch mechanism .... Multi-purpose grease
Hood, door and liftgate hinge lubricant .... Engine oil
Key lock cylinder lubricant .... Graphite spray
Parking brake mechanism grease .... MOPAR Spray White Lube or equivalent

Capacities*

Engine oil (including filter)	
2.0L engines	5.0 quarts
2.4L engines	5.5 quarts
3.2L engines	6.0 quarts
948TE Automatic transaxle (dry)**	Up to 6.35 quarts
Transfer case/power Transfer Unit (PTU)	
One-speed PTU	0.75 quart
Two-speed PTU	1.06 quarts
Rear differential	1.3 quarts
Cooling system***	
2.0L engines	9.0 quarts
2.4L engines	7.2 quarts
3.2L engines	10.0 quarts

*All capacities approximate. Add as necessary to bring to appropriate level.
**The best way to determine the amount of fluid to add during a routine fluid change is
to measure the amount drained. It's important to not overfill the transaxle.
***Includes heater and coolant reservoir.

Cylinder location diagram (2.0L and
2.4L four-cylinder engines)

Brakes

Disc brake pad wear limit (minimum)	1/16 inch

Ignition system

Spark plug type and gap	
Type	
2.0L models	Mopar - SPLZFR5C-11
2.4L and 3.2L models	NGK - ZFR5F-11
Gap	
2.0L engines	0.025 inch
2.4L engines	0.047 inch
3.2L engines	0.043 inch
Firing order	1-3-4-2

Cylinder location diagram
(V6 engines)

Torque specifications

Ft-lbs (unless otherwise indicated)

Note: One foot-pound (ft-lb) of torque is equivalent to 12 inch-pounds (in-lbs) of torque. Torque values below approximately 15 ft-lbs are expressed in inch-pounds, since most foot-pound torque wrenches are not accurate at these smaller values.

Automatic transaxle fluid fill plug	17
Automatic transaxle fluid drain plug	26
Transfer case/Power Transfer Unit drain and check/fill plugs	30
Drivebelt tensioner mounting bolt	
2.0L engines	37
2.4L engines	19
3.2L engines	37
Engine oil drain plug	
2.0L and 2.4L engines	20
3.2L engines	30
Spark plugs	
2.0L engines	156 in-lbs
2.4L and 3.2L engines	20
Wheel bolts	100

2.2a Typical engine compartment layout – 2.4L engine shown, other models similar

1	Brake fluid reservoir	4	Windshield washer fluid reservoir	7	Coolant expansion tank
2	Underhood fuse/relay block	5	Air filter housing	8	Engine oil filler cap
3	Battery	6	Engine oil dipstick	9	Cooling system pressure cap

2.2b Typical engine compartment underside components - 2.4L 2WD model shown, other models similar

1	Engine oil drain plug	3	Automatic transaxle fluid drain plug (6-speed transaxle)
2	Oil filter	4	Outer driveaxle boots
		5	Brake calipers
		6	Drivebelt

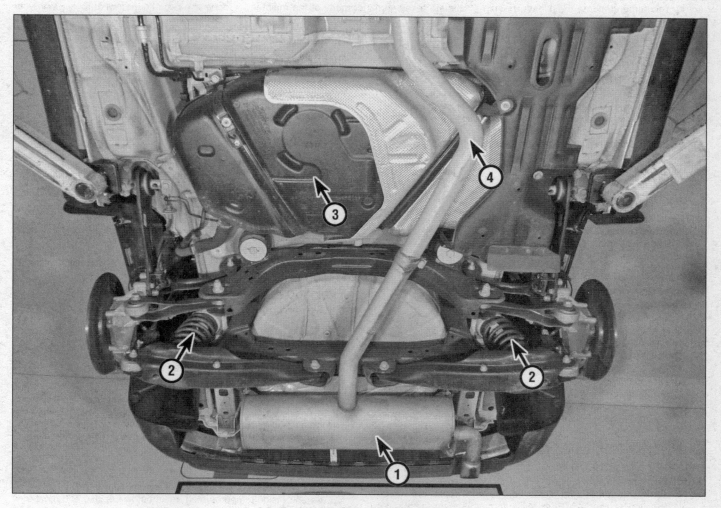

2.2c Typical rear underside components

1   Muffler
2   Rear shock absorber/coil
   spring assemblies
3   Fuel tank
4   Exhaust pipe

1 Maintenance schedule

1   The following maintenance intervals are based on the assumption that the vehicle owner will be doing the maintenance or service work, as opposed to having a dealer service department do the work. Although the time/mileage intervals are loosely based on factory recommendations, most have been shortened to ensure, for example, that such items as lubricants and fluids are checked/changed at intervals that promote maximum engine/driveline service life. Also, subject to the preference of the individual owner interested in keeping his or her vehicle in peak condition at all times, and with the vehicle's ultimate resale in mind, many of the maintenance procedures may be performed more often than recommended in the following schedule. We encourage such owner initiative.

2   When the vehicle is new it should be serviced initially by a factory authorized dealer service department to protect the factory warranty. In many cases the initial maintenance check is done at no cost to the owner (check with your dealer service department for more information).

Every 250 miles or weekly, whichever comes first

Check the engine oil level (Section 4)
Check the engine coolant level (Section 4)
Check the windshield washer fluid level (Section 4)
Check the brake fluid level (Section 4)
Check the tires and tire pressures (Section 5)
Check the operation of all lights
Check the horn operation

Every 3,000 miles or 3 months, whichever comes first

Note: All items listed above, plus:
Change the engine oil and filter (Section 6)

Every 6,000 miles or 6 months, whichever comes first

Note: All items listed above, plus:
Check the wiper blade condition (Section 7)
Check and clean the battery and terminals (Section 8)
Rotate the tires (Section 9)
Check the seatbelts (Section 10)
Check the condition of all underhood hoses and connections (Section 11)
Check the cooling system hoses and connections for leaks and damage (Section 12)
Check and replace, if necessary, the air filter element (Section 13)

Every 12,000 miles or 12 months, whichever comes first

Note: All items listed above, plus:
Check the automatic transaxle fluid level, if leaks are noticed (Section 4) The 948TE/9HP48 automatic transmission is considered by the manufacturer a sealed-for-life design and does not require periodic service, although routine fluid changes may prolong its service life.
Check the brake system (Section 14)
Check the suspension components and driveaxle boots (Section 17)
Check the exhaust pipes and hangers (Section 18)
Check the fuel system hoses and connections for leaks and damage (Section 19)
Replace the cabin air filter (Section 20)

Every 30,000 miles or 30 months, whichever comes first

Note: All items listed above, plus:
Check the drivebelt (Section 21)
Replace the air filter element (Section 13)*
Replace the brake fluid (Section 22)

Every 50,000 miles

Replace the transfer case lubricant (AWD models) (Section 27)
Replace the rear differential lubricant (AWD models) (Section 28)

Every 60,000 miles or 60 months, whichever comes first

Note: All items listed above, plus:
Check and replace, if necessary, the PCV valve (Section 24)*

Every 60 months (regardless of mileage)

Service the cooling system (drain, flush and refill) (Section 25)

Every 100,000 miles

Replace the spark plugs (Section 23)
Change the automatic transaxle fluid (Section 26)*

*This item is affected by severe operating conditions as described below. If the vehicle in question is operated under severe conditions, perform all maintenance procedures marked with an asterisk (*) at the intervals specified by the mileage headings below. Consider the conditions severe if most driving is done. . .
In dusty areas
Towing a trailer
Idling for extended periods and/or low-speed operation
When outside temperatures remain below freezing and most trips are less than four miles
In heavy city traffic where outside temperatures regularly reach 90-degrees F or higher

Every 3,000 miles

Check and replace, if necessary, the air filter element (Section 13)

Every 60,000 miles

Check and replace, if necessary, the PCV valve (Section 24)
Change the automatic transaxle fluid (Section 26)

2   Introduction

1   This Chapter is designed to help the home mechanic maintain the Jeep Cherokee with the goals of maximum performance, economy, safety and reliability in mind.

2   Included is a master maintenance schedule, followed by procedures dealing specifically with each item on the schedule. Visual checks, adjustments, component replacement and other helpful items are included. Refer to the **accompanying illustrations** of the engine compartment and the underside of the vehicle for the locations of various components.

3   Adhering to the mileage/time maintenance schedule and following the step-by-step procedures, which is simply a preventive maintenance program, will result in maximum reliability and vehicle service life. Keep in mind that it's not possible for this comprehensive program to produce the same results if you maintain some items at the specified intervals but not others.

4   As you service the vehicle, you'll discover that many of the procedures can - and should - be grouped together because of the nature of the particular procedure you're performing or because of the close proximity of two otherwise unrelated components to one another.

5   For example, if the vehicle is raised, you should inspect the exhaust, suspension, steering and fuel systems while you're under the vehicle. When you're rotating the tires, it makes good sense to check the brakes, since the wheels are already removed. Finally, let's suppose you have to borrow or rent a torque wrench. Even if you only need it to tighten the spark plugs, you might as well check the torque of as many critical fasteners as time allows.

6   The first step in this maintenance program is to prepare before the actual work begins. Read through all the procedures you're planning, then gather together all the parts and tools needed. If it looks like you might run into problems during a particular job, seek advice from a mechanic or an experienced do-it-yourselfer.

Owner's manual and VECI label information

7   Your vehicle owner's manual was written for your year and model and contains very specific information on component locations, specifications, fuse ratings, part numbers, etc. The owner's manual is an important resource for the do-it-yourselfer to have; if one was not supplied with your vehicle, it can generally be ordered from a dealer parts department.

8   Among other important information, the Vehicle Emissions Control Information (VECI) label contains specifications and procedures for applicable tune-up adjustments and, in some instances, spark plugs (see Chapter 6 for more information on the VECI label). The information on this label is the exact maintenance data recommended by the manufacturer. This data often varies by intended operating altitude, local emissions regulations, month of manufacture, etc.

9   This Chapter contains procedural details, safety information and more ambitious maintenance intervals than you might find in manufacturer's literature. However, you may also find procedures or specifications in your owner's manual or VECI label that differ with what's printed here. In these cases, the owner's manual or VECI label can be considered correct, since it is specific to your particular vehicle.

3   Tune-up general information

1   The term tune-up is used in this manual to represent a combination of individual operations rather than one specific procedure.

2   The engine will be kept in relatively good running condition and the need for additional work will be minimized if the routine maintenance schedule is followed closely and frequent checks are made of fluid levels and high wear items, as suggested throughout this manual from the time the vehicle is new.

3   More likely than not, however, there will be times when the engine is running poorly due to lack of regular maintenance. This is even more likely if a used vehicle, which hasn't received regular and frequent maintenance checks, is purchased. In such cases, an engine tune-up will be needed outside of the regular routine maintenance intervals.

4   The first step in any tune-up or diagnostic procedure to help correct a poor running engine is a cylinder compression check. A compression check (see Chapter 2C) will help determine the condition of internal engine components and should be used as a guide for tune-up and repair procedures. For instance, if a compression check indicates serious internal engine wear, a conventional tune-up will not improve the performance of the engine and would be a waste of time and money. Because of its importance, someone with the right equipment and the knowledge to use it properly should do the compression check.

5   The following procedures are those most often needed to bring a generally poor running engine back into a proper state of tune:

Minor tune-up

Check all engine related fluids
  (see Section 4)
Clean and inspect the battery
  (see Section 8)
Check all underhood hoses
  (see Section 11)
Check and adjust the drivebelts
  (see Section 21)
Check the air filter (see Section 13)
Check the PCV valve (see Section 24)

Major tune-up

Note: *All items listed under Minor tune-up plus…*
  Check the fuel system (see Section 19)
  Replace the air filter (see Section 13)
  Replace the drivebelt (see Section 21)
  Check the charging system (see Chapter 5)
  Replace the spark plugs (see Section)
  Service the cooling system (see Section 25)

4   Fluid level checks (see Maintenance Schedule for service intervals)

Note: *The following are fluid level checks to be done on a 250 mile or weekly basis. Additional fluid level checks can be found in specific maintenance procedures that follow. Regardless of the intervals, develop the habit of checking under the vehicle periodically for evidence of fluid leaks.*

1   Fluids are an essential part of the lubrication, cooling, brake and window washer systems. Because the fluids gradually become depleted and/or contaminated during normal operation of the vehicle, they must be replenished periodically. See *Recommended lubricants and fluids* in this Chapter's Specifications before adding fluid to any of the following components.

Note: *The vehicle must be on level ground when fluid levels are checked.*

Engine oil

2   Engine oil level is checked with a dipstick that is located on the side of the engine facing the front of the vehicle **(see illustration)**. The dipstick extends through a tube and into the oil pan at the bottom of the engine.

3   The oil level should be checked before the vehicle has been driven, or about five minutes after the engine has been shut off. If the oil is checked immediately after driving the vehicle, some of the oil will remain in the upper engine components, resulting in an inaccurate reading on the dipstick.

4.2 The engine oil dipstick is located at the front of the engine and is clearly marked

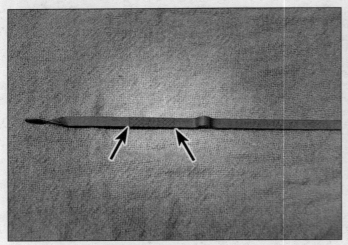

4.4 The oil level should be between the MIN and MAX marks, near the top of the cross-hatched area on the dipstick - if it isn't, add enough oil to bring the level up to or near the upper mark (do not overfill)

4.5 Turn the oil filler cap counterclockwise to remove it

4   Pull the dipstick out of the tube and wipe all the oil off the end with a clean rag or paper towel. Insert the clean dipstick all the way back into the tube, then pull it out again. Note the oil level at the end of the dipstick. Add oil as necessary to bring the oil level to the top of the cross-hatched area, or MAX mark (**see illustration**).

5   Oil is added to the engine after removing a cap located on the valve cover (**see illustration**). Use a funnel to prevent spills as the oil is added.

6   Don't allow the level to drop below the MIN mark on the dipstick or engine damage may occur. On the other hand, don't overfill the engine by adding too much oil - it may result in oil aeration and loss of oil pressure and also could result in oil fouled spark plugs, oil leaks or seal failures.

7   Checking the oil level is an important preventive maintenance step. A consistently low oil level indicates oil leakage through damaged seals, defective gaskets or past worn rings or valve guides. If the oil looks milky in color or has water droplets in it, the block or head may be cracked and leaking coolant is entering the crankcase. The engine should be checked immediately. The condition of the oil should also be checked. Each time you check the oil level, slide your thumb and index finger up the dipstick before wiping off the oil. If you see small dirt or metal particles clinging to the dipstick, the oil should be changed (see Section 6).

Engine coolant

Warning: *Do not allow antifreeze to come in contact with your skin or painted surfaces of the vehicle. Flush contaminated areas immediately with plenty of water. Don't store new coolant or leave old coolant lying around where it's accessible to children or pets –* they're attracted by its sweet smell. Ingestion of even a small amount of coolant can be fatal! Wipe up garage floor and drip pan spills immediately. Keep antifreeze containers covered and repair cooling system leaks as soon as they're noticed.

8   All vehicles covered by this manual are equipped with a pressurized coolant expansion tank, located at the right side of the engine compartment, and connected by hoses to the cooling system.

Warning: *Do not remove the cooling system pressure cap to check the coolant level when the engine is warm!*

9   The coolant level in the tank should be checked regularly. The level in the tank varies with the temperature of the engine. When the engine is cold, the coolant level should be mid-way between the MIN and MAX marks on the reservoir. Once the engine has warmed up, the level should be at or near the MAX

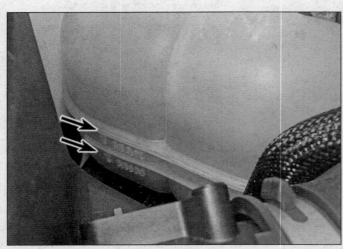

4.9 Maintain the coolant level between the ADD and FULL HOT marks on the reservoir

4.14 The windshield washer fluid reservoir is located in the left (driver's) side of the engine compartment

4.17 Brake fluid level, indicated on the translucent white plastic brake fluid reservoir, should be kept between the lower ADD and upper (MAX) mark

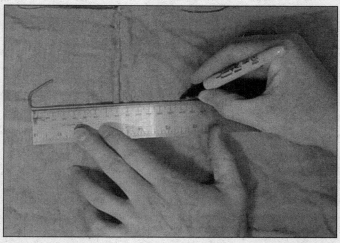

4.24 The dipstick must measure 140 mm from the bend where it will rest on top of the check plug opening. Cut the coat hanger at this point

mark. If it isn't, allow the engine to cool, then remove the cap from the tank and add the specified coolant **(see illustration)**.

10   Drive the vehicle and recheck the coolant level. If only a small amount of coolant is required to bring the system up to the proper level, water can be used. However, repeated additions of water will dilute the antifreeze and water solution. In order to maintain the proper ratio of antifreeze and water, always top up the coolant level with the correct mixture. Don't use rust inhibitors or additives. An empty plastic milk jug or bleach bottle makes an excellent container for mixing coolant.

11   If the coolant level drops consistently, there may be a leak in the system. Inspect the radiator, hoses, filler cap, drain plugs, thermostat housing and water pump (see Section 12). If no leaks are noted, have the pressure cap pressure tested by a service station.

12   If you have to remove the pressure cap, wait until the engine has cooled completely, then wrap a thick cloth around the cap and slowly unscrew it. If coolant or steam escapes, or if you hear a hissing noise, let the engine cool down longer, then remove the cap.

13   Check the condition of the coolant as well. It should be relatively clear. If it's brown or rust colored, the system should be drained, flushed and refilled. Even if the coolant appears to be normal, the corrosion inhibitors wear out, so it must be replaced at the specified intervals.

Windshield and rear window washer fluid

14   The fluid for the windshield and rear window washer system is stored in a plastic reservoir located at the left front corner of the engine compartment **(see illustration)**. The reservoir level should be maintained about one inch (25 mm) below the filler cap.

15   In milder climates, plain water can be used in the reservoir, but it should be kept no

more than two-thirds full to allow for expansion if the water freezes. In colder climates, use windshield washer system antifreeze, available at any auto parts store, to lower the freezing point of the fluid. Mix the antifreeze with water in accordance with the manufacturer's directions on the container. **Caution:** *DO NOT use cooling system antifreeze - it will damage the vehicle's paint. To help prevent icing in cold weather, warm the windshield with the defroster before using the washer.*

Brake fluid

16   The brake fluid reservoir is located on top of the brake master cylinder on the driver's side of the engine compartment near the firewall.

17   The fluid level should be maintained between the lower ADD mark and the upper (FULL or MAX) mark on reservoir **(see illustration)**.

18   If additional fluid is necessary to bring the level up, use a rag to clean all dirt off the top of the reservoir to prevent contamination of the system. Also, make sure all painted surfaces around the reservoir are covered, since brake fluid will ruin paint. Carefully pour new, clean brake fluid obtained from a sealed container into the reservoir. Be sure the specified fluid is used; mixing different types of brake fluid can cause damage to the system. See *Recommended lubricants and fluids* in this Chapter's Specifications or your owner's manual.

19   At this time the fluid and the master cylinder should be inspected for contamination. Normally the brake hydraulic system won't need periodic draining and refilling, but if rust deposits, dirt particles or water droplets are observed in the fluid, the system should be dismantled, cleaned and refilled with fresh fluid. Over time brake fluid will absorb moisture from the air. Moisture in the fluid lowers the fluid boiling point; if the fluid boils, the

brakes will become ineffective. Normal brake fluid is clear in color. If the brake fluid is dark brown in color, it's a good idea to replace it (see Chapter 9).

20   Reinstall the fluid reservoir cap.

21   The brake fluid in the master cylinder will drop slightly as the brake lining material at each wheel wears down during normal operation. If the master cylinder requires repeated replenishing to maintain the correct level, there is a leak in the brake system that should be corrected immediately. Check all brake lines and connections, along with the calipers and power brake booster (see Section 14 and Chapter 9 for more information).

22   If you discover that the reservoir is empty or nearly empty, the system should be thoroughly inspected, refilled and then bled (see Chapter 9 for brake system bleeding).

Automatic transaxle

Note: *The 948TE/9HP48 automatic transmission is considered by the manufacturer to be a sealed-for-life design. There is no service interval recommended for this transaxle when it is operated under normal conditions. These transaxles come pre-filled from the factory, and do not require fluid checking unless there has been a fluid change, shifting problems, a repair or a leak.*

Note: *These transaxles requires the use of a special dipstick tool #10323A (or a homemade equivalent) to measure the fluid level.*

23   Loosen the left-front wheel bolts. Raise the front and rear of the vehicle and support it securely on jackstands in level position, then remove the left front wheel and turn the steering all the way to the left.

Note: *The transaxle fluid must be between 122 and 194-degrees F for this check. Transaxle fluid temperature can be monitored on the instrument cluster display.*

24   If you do not have access to the special tool, fabricate a dipstick from a coat hanger **(see illustration)**.

4.26 The transaxle fluid check plug is located on the rear of the transaxle case, near the rear transaxle mount

4.27 The transaxle fluid temperature can be displayed on the instrument panel

4.30 Transaxle fluid level chart

Fluid temperature (degrees Fahrenheit)	Minimum level (mm)	Desired level (mm)	Maximum level (mm)
122	13	16	19
140	17	20	23
158	18	23	24
176	21	25	27
194	23	27	30
212	27	31	34

25　Apply the parking brake, start the engine and allow it to idle for a minute, then move the shift lever through each gear position, ending in Park. Pause for two seconds in each position.

26　Remove the fluid level check plug (see illustration) from the check port - it is located on the rear of the transaxle.

27　Using the display panel, access the transaxle fluid temperature (see illustration).

a) Press the OK button on the left side of the steering wheel. When the "Chero-

kee" type is displayed, wait about five seconds until "Vehicle Info" appears.

b) Use the left or right arrow to select "Trans. Temp."

28　Insert special dipstick tool no. 10323A or homemade equivalent into the fluid level check port and allow the handle of the tool to rest on the flat surface of the transaxle. It may be necessary to repeat this several times to get an accurate reading.

Note: Be careful not to burn yourself on the hot exhaust manifold.

29　Compare the reading on the dipstick tool with the transaxle fluid temperature reading on the instrument panel.

30　Match the two readings with the transaxle fluid level chart (see illustration) to make sure the transaxle oil level is correct.

31　Add or remove transaxle fluid as necessary, through the check plug hole, then recheck the fluid level and install the check plug, tightening it to the torque listed in this Chapter's Specifications. If too much fluid is added, loosen the drain plug and allow some fluid to drain until the level is correct, or remove it through the check/fill plug hole with a suction gun.

5　Tire and tire pressure checks (every 250 miles or weekly)

1　Periodic inspection of the tires may spare you the inconvenience of being stranded with a flat tire. It can also provide you with vital information regarding possible problems in the steering and suspension systems before major damage occurs.

2　The original tires on this vehicle are equipped with 1/2-inch wide bands that will appear when tread depth reaches 1/16-inch, at which point they can be considered worn out. Tread wear can be monitored with a simple, inexpensive device known as a tread depth indicator (see illustration).

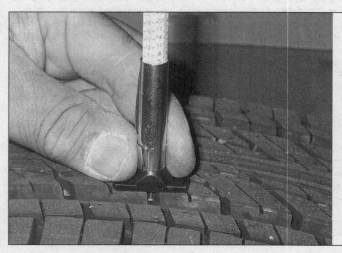

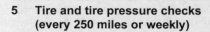

5.2 A tire tread depth indicator should be used to monitor tire wear - they are available at auto parts stores and service stations and cost very little

UNDERINFLATION

CUPPING

Cupping may be caused by:
- Underinflation and/or mechanical irregularities such as out-of-balance condition of wheel and/or tire, and bent or damaged wheel.
- Loose or worn steering tie-rod or steering idler arm.
- Loose, damaged or worn front suspension parts.

OVERINFLATION

INCORRECT TOE-IN OR EXTREME CAMBER

FEATHERING DUE TO MISALIGNMENT

5.3 This chart will help you determine the condition of your tires, the probable cause(s) of abnormal wear and the corrective action necessary

3   Note any abnormal tread wear **(see illustration)**. Tread pattern irregularities such as cupping, flat spots and more wear on one side than the other are indications of front end alignment and/or balance problems. If any of these conditions are noted, take the vehicle to a tire shop or service station to correct the problem.

4   Look closely for cuts, punctures and embedded nails or tacks. Sometimes a tire will hold air pressure for a short time or leak down very slowly after a nail has embedded itself in the tread. If a slow leak persists, check the valve stem core to make sure it is tight **(see illustration)**. Examine the tread for an object that may have embedded itself in the tire or for a plug that may have begun to leak (radial tire punctures are repaired with a plug that is installed in a puncture). If a puncture is suspected, it can be easily verified by

spraying a solution of soapy water onto the puncture area **(see illustration)**. The soapy solution will bubble if there is a leak. Unless the puncture is unusually large, a tire shop or service station can usually repair the tire.

5   Carefully inspect the inner sidewall of each tire for evidence of brake fluid leakage. If you see any, inspect the brakes immediately.

6   Correct air pressure adds miles to the life span of the tires, improves mileage and enhances overall ride quality. Tire pressure cannot be accurately estimated by looking at a tire, especially if it's a radial. A tire pressure gauge is essential. Keep an accurate gauge in the glove compartment. The pressure gauges attached to the nozzles of air hoses at gas stations are often inaccurate.

7   Always check tire pressure when the tires are cold. Cold, in this case, means the

vehicle has not been driven over a mile in the three hours preceding a tire pressure check. A pressure rise of four to eight pounds is not uncommon once the tires are warm.

8   Unscrew the valve cap protruding from the wheel or hubcap and push the gauge firmly onto the valve stem **(see illustration)**. Note the reading on the gauge and compare the figure to the recommended tire pressure shown on the tire placard on the driver's side door. Be sure to reinstall the valve cap to keep dirt and moisture out of the valve stem mechanism. Check all four tires and, if necessary, add enough air to bring them up to the recommended pressure.

9   Don't forget to keep the spare tire (if equipped) inflated to the specified pressure (refer to the pressure molded into the tire sidewall).

5.4a If a tire loses air on a steady basis, check the valve core first to make sure it's snug (special inexpensive wrenches are commonly available at auto parts stores)

5.4b If the valve core is tight, raise the corner of the vehicle with the low tire and spray a soapy water solution onto the tread as the tire is turned slowly - slow leaks will cause small bubbles to appear

5.8 To extend the life of your tires, check the air pressure at least once a week with an accurate gauge (don't forget the spare!)

6   Engine oil and filter change (every 3000 miles or 3 months)

Note: *Some models are equipped with an oil life indicator system that illuminates a light or message on the instrument panel when the system deems it necessary to change the oil. A number of factors are taken into consideration to determine when the oil should be considered worn out. Generally, this system will allow the vehicle to accumulate more miles between oil changes than the traditional 3000-mile interval, but we believe that frequent oil changes is cheap insurance and will prolong engine life. If you do decide not to change your oil every 3000 miles and rely on the oil life indicator instead, make sure you don't exceed 10,000 miles before the oil is changed, regardless of what the oil life indicator shows.*

1   Frequent oil changes are the best preventive maintenance the home mechanic can give the engine, because aging oil becomes diluted and contaminated, which leads to premature engine wear.

2   Make sure you have all the necessary tools before you begin this procedure **(see illustration)**. You should also have plenty of rags or newspapers handy for mopping up any spills.

3   Raise the front of the vehicle and support it securely on jackstands.
Warning: *Do not work under a vehicle which is supported only by a bumper, hydraulic or scissors-type jack.*

4   If this is your first oil change, get under the vehicle and familiarize yourself with the locations of the oil drain plug and the oil filter. The engine and exhaust components will be warm during the actual work, so try to anticipate any potential problems before the engine and accessories are hot.

5   Park the vehicle on a level spot. Start the engine and allow it to reach its normal operating temperature. Warm oil and sludge will flow out more easily. Turn off the engine when it's warmed up. Remove the filler cap from the valve cover.

6   Raise the vehicle and support it securely on jackstands.
Warning: *Never get beneath the vehicle when it is supported only by a jack. The jack provided with your vehicle is designed solely for raising the vehicle to remove and replace the wheels. Always use jackstands to support the vehicle when it becomes necessary to place your body underneath the vehicle.*

7   Locate the oil filter and oil drain access panels **(see illustration)** on the engine splash shield, then rotate the locks with a blade screwdriver and remove the panels.

8   Being careful not to touch the hot exhaust components, place the drain pan under the drain plug in the bottom of the pan and remove the plug **(see illustration)**. You may want to wear gloves while unscrewing the plug the final few turns if the engine is hot.

9   Allow the old oil to drain into the pan. It may be necessary to move the pan farther under the engine as the oil flow slows to a trickle. Inspect the old oil for the presence of metal shavings and chips.

10   After all the oil has drained, wipe off the drain plug with a clean rag. Even minute metal particles clinging to the plug would immediately contaminate the new oil.

11   Clean the area around the drain plug opening, reinstall the plug and tighten it to the torque listed in this Chapter's Specifications.

12   Move the drain pan into position under the oil filter.

13   Loosen the oil filter by turning it counterclockwise with an oil filter wrench **(see illustration)**. Once the filter is loose, use your hands to unscrew it from the block. Keep the open end pointing up to prevent the oil inside the filter from spilling out.
Warning: *The exhaust system may still be hot, so be careful.*

14   With a clean rag, wipe off the mounting surface on the block. If a residue of old oil is allowed to remain, it will smoke when the block is heated up. Also make sure that none of the old gasket remains stuck to the mounting surface. It can be removed with a scraper if necessary.

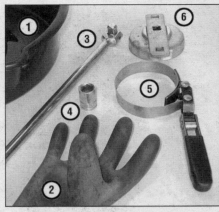

6.2 These tools are required when changing the engine oil and filter

1   **Drain pan** - *It should be fairly shallow in depth, but wide to prevent spills*
2   **Rubber gloves** - *When removing the drain plug and filter, you will get oil on your hands (the gloves will prevent burns)*
3   **Breaker bar** - *Sometimes the oil drain plug is tight, and a long breaker bar is needed to loosen it*
4   **Socket** – *To be used with the breaker bar or a ratchet (must be the correct size to fit the drain plug - six-point preferred)*
5   **Filter wrench** - *This is a metal band-type wrench, which requires clearance around the filter to be effective*
6   **Filter wrench** - *This type fits on the bottom of the filter and can be turned with a ratchet or breaker bar (different-size wrenches are available for different types of filters)*

15   Compare the old filter with the new one to make sure they are the same type. Smear some clean engine oil on the rubber gasket of the new filter **(see illustration)**.

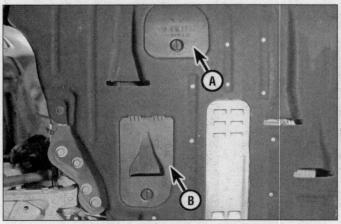

6.7 Locate the oil filter access panel (A) and the oil drain access panel (B)

6.8 Use a proper size box-end wrench or socket to remove the oil drain plug and avoid rounding it off

6.13 Use an oil filter wrench to remove the filter

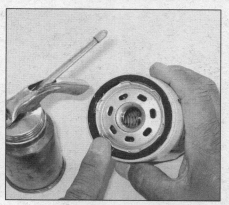

6.15 Lubricate the oil filter gasket with clean engine oil before installing the filter on the engine

the reset procedure must be done again.
Note: *If the message is not reset, it will continue to show up each time you turn the ignition switch On or start the vehicle. It is possible to temporarily turn off the message by pressing and releasing the "Menu" button.*
23 Turn the ignition key to the On position but DO NOT start the engine.
24 Slowly depress the accelerator pedal all the way to the floor, three times within 10 seconds.
25 Turn the ignition key to the Off or Lock position, then start the vehicle.

7 Wiper blade inspection and replacement (every 6,000 miles or 6 months)

16 Attach the new filter to the engine, following the tightening directions printed on the filter canister or packing box. Most filter manufacturers recommend against using a filter wrench due to the possibility of overtightening and damaging the seal.
17 Remove all tools, rags, etc., from under the vehicle, being careful not to spill the oil in the drain pan, then lower the vehicle.
18 Add new oil to the engine through the oil filler cap in the valve cover. Use a funnel, if necessary, to prevent oil from spilling onto the top of the engine. Pour four quarts of fresh oil into the engine. Wait a few minutes to allow the oil to drain into the pan, then check the level on the oil dipstick (see Section 4). If the oil level is at or near the FULL mark on the dipstick, install the filler cap, start the engine and allow the new oil to circulate.
19 Allow the engine to run for about a minute. While the engine is running, look under the vehicle and check for leaks at the oil pan drain plug and around the oil filter. If either is leaking, stop the engine and tighten the plug or filter.
20 Wait a few minutes to allow the oil to trickle down into the pan, recheck the level on

the dipstick and, if necessary, add enough oil to bring the level to the FULL mark.
21 During the first few trips after an oil change, make it a point to check frequently for leaks and proper oil level.
22 The old oil drained from the engine cannot be reused in its present state and should be disposed of. Check with your local auto parts store, disposal facility or environmental agency to see if they will accept the oil for recycling. After the oil has cooled it can be drained into a container (capped plastic jugs, topped bottles, milk cartons, etc.) for transport to one of these disposal sites. Don't dispose of the oil by pouring it on the ground or down a drain!

Oil change indicator resetting
Note: *It is possible that, driving under the best possible conditions, the oil life monitoring system may not indicate the oil needs to be changed. The manufacturer states that the oil and filter must be changed at least once every year and the oil life monitor reset.*
Note: *If the "Oil Change Required" message comes on when the vehicle is immediately restarted, the oil life monitor was not reset and*

1 The wiper and blade assemblies should be inspected periodically for damage, loose components and cracked or worn blade elements.
2 Road film can build up on the wiper blades and affect their efficiency, so they should be washed regularly with a mild detergent solution.
3 The action of the wiping mechanism can loosen bolts, nuts and fasteners, so they should be checked and tightened, as necessary, at the same time the wiper blades are checked.
4 If the wiper blade elements are cracked, worn or warped, or no longer clean adequately, they should be replaced with new ones.

Windshield wiper blades
5 Lift the arm assembly away from the windshield for clearance. Use a small screwdriver to pop the cover open, then slide the wiper blade assembly out of the hook at the end of the arm **(see illustrations)**.
Caution: *Do not allow the wiper arm to snap back against the windshield without the wiper blade installed or the arm could damage the window.*

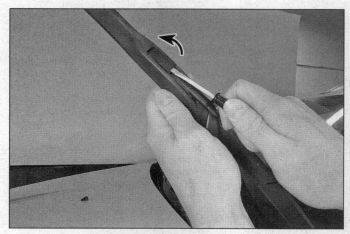

7.5a Use a screwdriver to open the lock on the pivot block . . .

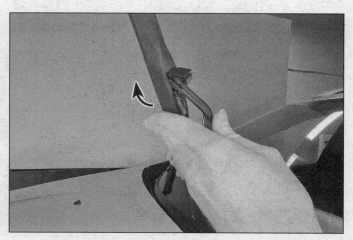

7.5b . . . then rotate the wiper blade off the hook and slide it from the arm

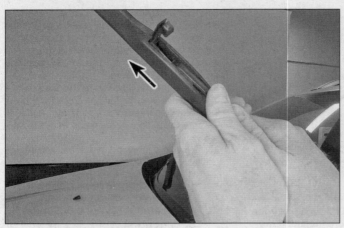

7.6a Attach the new wiper over the hook then slide the wiper up the arm until it clicks into place . . .

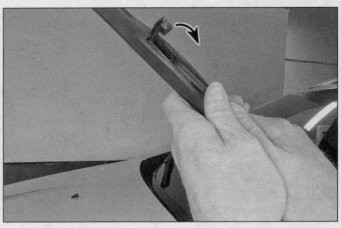

7.6b . . . then snap the lock tab down into the locked position.

6   Attach the new wiper to the arm **(see illustrations)**, then press the release tab down. The connection can be confirmed by an audible click.

Rear wiper blade

7   Pry up the wiper arm pivot cover at the base of the arm **(see illustration)** then lift the arm away from the glass for clearance.

Rotate the blade out from under the arm and past the stop, until it "unsnaps" and slide the wiper blade assembly out of the hook at the end of the arm **(see illustrations)**.
Caution: *Do not allow the wiper arm to snap back against the glass without the wiper blade installed or the arm could damage the window.*
8   Attach the new wiper to the arm; the connection can be confirmed by an audible

click; then lower the arm and snap the pivot cover into place.

8   Battery check, maintenance and charging (every 6,000 miles or 6 months)

Note: *The battery on these vehicles is located at the left front corner of the vehicle, behind the radiator. Refer to Chapter 5 for the removal procedure.*
Warning: *Certain precautions must be followed when checking and servicing the battery. Hydrogen gas, which is highly flammable, is always present in the battery cells, so keep lighted tobacco and all other open flames and sparks away from the battery. The electrolyte inside the battery is actually diluted sulfuric acid, which will cause injury if splashed on your skin or in your eyes. It will also ruin clothes and painted surfaces. When removing the battery cables, always detach the negative cable first and hook it up last!*
Caution: *Some newer vehicles will be equipped from the factory with an AGM (Absorbent Glass Mat) battery. These type of batteries have a different charging and energy absorption rate than the older (standard) type of liquid acid filled (referred to as "flooded") batteries. The typical trickle charger that can be purchased at most parts stores may not be able to adequately recharge an AGM battery unless it specifically state that it is compatible to use with an AGM battery. To recharge an AGM battery, use a battery charger specifically designed to recharge an AGM battery, not one designed for a flooded type battery.*
1   A routine preventive maintenance program for the battery in your vehicle is the only way to ensure quick and reliable starts. But before performing any battery maintenance, make sure that you have the proper equipment necessary to work safely around the battery **(see illustration)**.
2   There are also several precautions that should be taken whenever battery

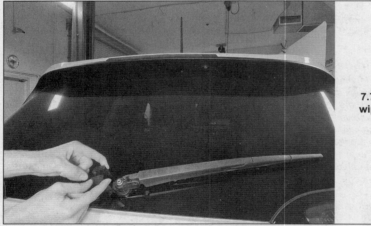

7.7a Pry up the wiper arm pivot cover . . .

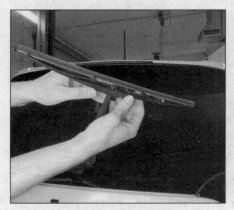

7.7b Rotate the wiper blade past its pivot point . . .

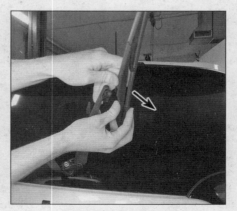

7.7c . . . then slide the wiper blade from the arm

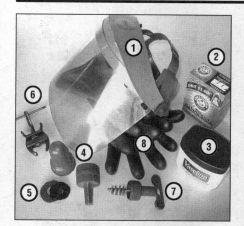

8.1 Tools and materials required for battery maintenance

1   **Face shield/safety goggles** - *When removing corrosion with a brush, the acidic particles can easily fly up into your eyes*

2   **Baking soda** - *A solution of baking soda and water can be used to neutralize corrosion*

3   **Petroleum jelly** - *A layer of this on the battery posts will help prevent corrosion*

4   **Battery post/cable cleaner** - *This wire brush cleaning tool will remove all traces of corrosion from the battery posts and cable clamps*

5   **Treated felt washers** - *Placing one of these on each post, directly under the cable clamps, will help prevent corrosion*

6   **Puller** - *Sometimes the cable clamps are very difficult to pull off the posts, even after the nut/bolt has been completely loosened. This tool pulls the clamp straight up and off the post without damage*

7   **Battery post/cable cleaner** - *Here is another cleaning tool which is a slightly different version of Number 4 above, but it does the same thing*

8   **Rubber gloves** - *Another safety item to consider when servicing the battery; remember that's acid inside the battery!*

8.6a Battery terminal corrosion usually appears as light, fluffy powder

8.7a When cleaning the cable clamps, all corrosion must be removed

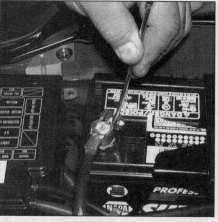

8.6b Removing a cable from the battery post with a wrench - sometimes a pair of special battery pliers are required for this procedure if corrosion has caused deterioration of the nut hex (always remove the ground (-) cable first and hook it up last!)

8.7b Regardless of the type of tool used to clean the battery posts, a clean, shiny surface should be the result

maintenance is performed. Before servicing the battery, always turn the engine and all accessories off and disconnect the cable from the negative terminal of the battery (see Chapter 5).

3   The battery produces hydrogen gas, which is both flammable and explosive. Never create a spark, smoke or light a match around the battery. Always charge the battery in a ventilated area.

4   Electrolyte contains poisonous and corrosive sulfuric acid. Do not allow it to get in your eyes, on your skin on your clothes. Never ingest it. Wear protective safety glasses when working near the battery. Keep children away from the battery.

5   Note the external condition of the battery. If the positive terminal and cable clamp on your vehicle's battery is equipped with a rubber protector, make sure that it's not torn or damaged. It should completely cover the terminal. Look for any corroded or loose connections, cracks in the case or cover or loose hold-down clamps. Also check the entire length of each cable for cracks and frayed conductors.

6   If corrosion, which looks like white, fluffy deposits (see illustration) is evident, particularly around the terminals, the battery should be removed for cleaning. Loosen the cable clamp bolts with a wrench, being careful to remove the ground cable first, and slide them off the terminals (see illustration). Then disconnect the hold-down clamp bolt and nut, remove the clamp and lift the battery from the engine compartment.

7   Clean the cable clamps thoroughly with a battery brush or a terminal cleaner and a solution of warm water and baking soda (see illustration). Wash the terminals and the top of the battery case with the same solution but make sure that the solution doesn't get into the battery. When cleaning the cables, terminals and battery top, wear safety goggles and rubber gloves to prevent any solution from coming in contact with your eyes or hands. Wear old clothes too - even diluted, sulfuric acid splashed onto clothes will burn holes in them. If the terminals have been extensively corroded, clean them up with a terminal cleaner (see illustration). Thoroughly wash all cleaned areas with plain water.

8   Make sure that the battery tray is in good condition and the hold-down clamp fasteners are tight. If the battery is removed from the tray, make sure no parts remain in the bottom of the tray when the battery is reinstalled. When reinstalling the hold-down clamp bolts, do not overtighten them.

9   Information on removing and installing

the battery can be found in Chapter 5. If you disconnected the cable(s) from the negative and/or positive battery terminals, see Chapter 5. Information on jump starting can be found at the front of this manual. For more detailed battery checking procedures, refer to the *Haynes Automotive Electrical Manual.*

Cleaning

10   Corrosion on the hold-down components, battery case and surrounding areas can be removed with a solution of water and baking soda. Thoroughly rinse all cleaned areas with plain water.

11   Any metal parts of the vehicle damaged by corrosion should be covered with a zinc-based primer, then painted.

Charging

Warning: *When batteries are being charged, hydrogen gas, which is very explosive and flammable, is produced. Do not smoke or allow open flames near a charging or a recently charged battery. Wear eye protection when near the battery during charging. Also, make sure the charger is unplugged before connecting or disconnecting the battery from the charger.*

Warning: *A battery that shows signs that it has frozen, shows leakage anywhere on the case or near the posts, or if any terminal is loose, do not recharge, jump, or consider it suitable for testing. Take the battery to a recycle center for disposal.*

Caution: *Battery electrolyte tends to bubble when a battery is being charged. However, if the electrolyte is spilling out of the battery and/or the electrolyte is bubbling like boiling water, the battery is being OVERCHARGED. Immediately disconnect the charging unit from the battery and allow the battery enough time to dissipate the overcharge (15 to 30 minutes). Overcharging a battery can damage the internal plates of the battery.*

12   Slow-rate charging is the best way to restore a battery that's discharged to the point where it will not start the engine. It's also a good way to maintain the battery charge in a vehicle that's only driven a few miles between starts. Maintaining the battery charge is particularly important in the winter when the battery must work harder to start the engine and electrical accessories that drain the battery are in greater use.

13   It's best to use a one or two-amp battery charger (sometimes called a trickle charger). They are the safest and put the least strain on the battery. They are also the least expensive. For a faster charge, you can use a higher amperage charger, but don't use one rated more than 1/10th the amp/hour rating of the battery. Rapid boost charges that claim to restore the power of the battery in one to two hours are hardest on the battery and can damage batteries not in good condition. This type of charging should only be used in emergency situations.

14   The average time necessary to charge a battery should be listed in the instructions that

come with the charger. As a general rule, a trickle charger will charge a battery in 12 to 16 hours.

9   Tire rotation (every 6,000 miles or 6 months)

Caution: *Some models may have high-performance tires, which have a directional tread pattern installed on them. These tires must be installed on the same sides so that they rotate in the correct direction. This is indicated by arrows located on the tire sidewalls.*

1   The tires should be rotated at the specified intervals and whenever uneven wear is noticed.

2   Refer to the **accompanying illustration** for the preferred tire rotation pattern.

3   Refer to the information in Chapter 0, Section 8 for the proper procedures to follow when raising the vehicle and changing a tire. If the brakes are to be checked, don't apply the parking brake as stated. Make sure the tires are blocked to prevent the vehicle from rolling as it's raised.

4   Preferably, the entire vehicle should be raised at the same time. This can be done on a hoist or by jacking up each corner and then lowering the vehicle onto jackstands placed under the frame rails. Always use four jackstands and make sure the vehicle is safely supported.

5   After rotation, check and adjust the tire pressures as necessary. Tighten the wheel bolts to the torque listed in this Chapter's Specifications.

10   Seat belt check (every 6,000 miles or 6 months)

1   Check the seat belts, buckles, latch plates and guide loops for obvious damage and signs of wear.

2   Where the seat belt receptacle bolts to the floor of the vehicle, check that the bolts are secure.

3   See if the seat belt reminder light comes on when the key is turned to the Run or Start position.

11   Underhood hose check and replacement (every 6,000 miles or 6 months)

General

Caution: *Never remove air conditioning components or hoses until the system has been depressurized by a licensed air conditioning technician.*

1   High temperatures in the engine compartment can cause the deterioration of the rubber and plastic hoses used for engine, accessory and emission systems operation. Periodic inspection should be made for cracks, loose clamps, material hardening and

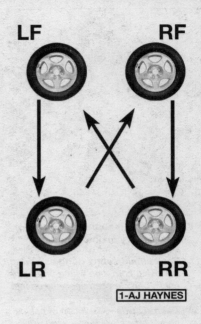

9.2 The recommended four-tire rotation pattern

leaks. Information specific to the cooling system hoses can be found in Section 12.

2   Some, but not all, hoses are secured to their fittings with clamps. Where clamps are used, check to be sure they haven't lost their tension, allowing the hose to leak. If clamps aren't used, make sure the hose has not expanded and/or hardened where it slips over the fitting, allowing it to leak.

Vacuum hoses

3   It's quite common for vacuum hoses, especially those in the emissions system, to be color-coded or identified by colored stripes molded into them. Various systems require hoses with different wall thickness, collapse resistance and temperature resistance. When replacing hoses, be sure the new ones are made of the same material.

4   Often the only effective way to check a hose is to remove it completely from the vehicle. If more than one hose is removed, be sure to label the hoses and fittings to ensure correct installation.

5   When checking vacuum hoses, be sure to include any plastic T-fittings in the check. Inspect the fittings for cracks and the hose where it fits over the fitting for distortion, which could cause leakage.

6   A small piece of vacuum hose (1/4-inch inside diameter) can be used as a stethoscope to detect vacuum leaks. Hold one end of the hose to your ear and probe around vacuum hoses and fittings, listening for the hissing sound characteristic of a vacuum leak.

Warning: *When probing with the vacuum hose stethoscope, be very careful not to come into contact with moving engine components such as the drivebelt, cooling fan, etc.*

Check for a chafed area that could fail prematurely.

Check for a soft area indicating the hose has deteriorated inside.

Overtightening the clamp on a hardened hose will damage the hose and cause a leak.

Check each hose for swelling and oil-soaked ends. Cracks and breaks can be located by squeezing the hose.

12.4 Hoses, like drivebelts, have a habit of failing at the worst possible time - to prevent the inconvenience of a blown radiator or heater hose, inspect them carefully as shown here

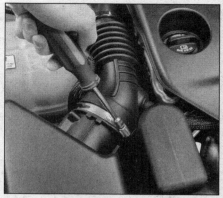

13.3 Disconnect the air filter housing outlet hose clamp and hose - 2.4L models

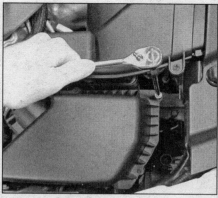

13.4 Loosen the filter cover screws around the edge of the filter housing

Fuel hose

Warning: *There are certain precautions that must be taken when inspecting or servicing fuel system components. Work in a well-ventilated area and do not allow open flames (cigarettes, appliances, etc.) or bare light bulbs near the work area. Mop up any spills immediately and do not store fuel soaked rags where they could ignite. The fuel system is under high pressure, so if any fuel lines are to be disconnected, the pressure in the system must be relieved first (see Chapter 4 for more information).*

7   Check all rubber fuel lines for deterioration and chafing. Check especially for cracks in areas where the hose bends and just before fittings, such as where a hose attaches to the fuel filter.
8   High quality fuel line, made specifically for high-pressure fuel injection systems, must be used for fuel line replacement. Never,

under any circumstances, use unreinforced vacuum line, clear plastic tubing or water hose for fuel lines.
9   Spring-type clamps are commonly used on fuel lines. These clamps often lose their tension over a period of time, and can be "sprung" during removal. Replace all spring-type clamps with screw clamps whenever a hose is replaced.

Metal lines

10   Sections of metal line are routed along the frame, between the fuel tank and the engine. Check carefully to be sure the line has not been bent or crimped and that cracks have not been started in the line.
11   If a section of metal fuel line must be replaced, only seamless steel tubing should be used, since copper and aluminum tubing don't have the strength necessary to withstand normal engine vibration.
12   Check the metal brake lines where they enter the master cylinder and brake proportioning unit for cracks in the lines or loose fittings. Any sign of brake fluid leakage calls for an immediate and thorough inspection of the brake system.

12   Cooling system check (every 6,000 miles or 6 months)

1   Many major engine failures can be attributed to a faulty cooling system. Since the vehicle is equipped with an automatic transaxle, the cooling system also cools the transaxle fluid and thus plays an important role in prolonging transaxle life.
2   The cooling system should be checked with the engine cold. Do this before the vehicle is driven for the day or after it has been shut off for at least three hours.
3   Remove the cooling system pressure cap and thoroughly clean the cap, inside and out, with clean water. Also clean the filler neck. All traces of corrosion should be removed. The coolant in the system should be relatively transparent. If it is rust-colored, the system should be drained, flushed and refilled

(see Section 25). If the coolant level is not up to the top, add additional antifreeze/coolant mixture (see Section 4).
4   Carefully check the large upper and lower radiator hoses along with the smaller diameter heater hoses that run from the engine to the firewall. Inspect each hose along its entire length, replacing any hose that is cracked, swollen or shows signs of deterioration. Cracks may become more apparent if the hose is squeezed (see illustration). Regardless of condition, it's a good idea to replace hoses with new ones every two years.
5   Make sure all hose connections are tight. A leak in the cooling system will usually show up as white or rust-colored deposits on the areas adjoining the leak. If wire-type clamps are used at the ends of the hoses, it may be a good idea to replace them with more secure screw-type clamps.
6   Use compressed air or a soft brush to remove bugs, leaves, etc., from the front of the radiator or air conditioning condenser. Be careful not to damage the delicate cooling fins or cut yourself on them.
7   Every other inspection, or at the first indication of cooling system problems, have the cap and system pressure tested. If you don't have a pressure tester, most repair shops will do this for a minimal charge.

13   Air filter check and replacement (every 6,000 miles or 6 months)

1   The air filter is located inside a housing at the right (passengers's) side of the engine compartment.
2   On 2.0L engines, disconnect the quick-connect fittings for the boost purge hose and the vapor purge hose.
3   On 2.4L and 3.2L models, disconnect the air filter housing outlet hose clamp and hose (see illustration), then remove the fresh air inlet duct from the air filter housing
4   Loosen the cover-to-air filter housing screws around the edge of the housing (see illustration). Do not try to completely remove them; they are captured screws.

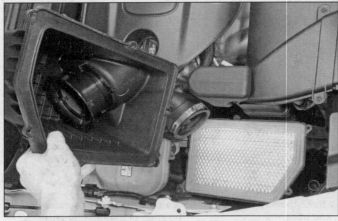

13.5a Once the screws have been removed lift the cover up . . .

13.5b . . . then remove the air filter element

5   To remove the air filter, separate the cover halves and remove the air filter element **(see illustrations)**.

6   Inspect the outer surface of the filter element. If it is dirty, replace it. If it is only moderately dusty, it can be reused by blowing it clean from the back to the front surface with compressed air. Because it is a pleated paper type filter, it cannot be washed or oiled. If it cannot be cleaned satisfactorily with compressed air, discard and replace it. While the cover is off, be careful not to drop anything down into the housing.

7   Wipe out the inside of the air filter housing.

8   Place the new filter into the air filter housing, making sure it seats properly.

9   Reinstall the cover, making sure the cover fasteners are tightened securely.

**14   Brake system check
       (every 12,000 miles or 12 months)**

Warning: *The dust created by the brake system is harmful to your health. Never blow it out with compressed air and don't inhale any of it. An approved filtering mask should be worn*

when working on the brakes. Do not, under any circumstances, use petroleum-based solvents to clean brake parts. Use brake system cleaner only!

Note: *For detailed photographs of the brake system, refer to Chapter 9.*

1   In addition to the specified intervals, the brakes should be inspected every time the wheels are removed or whenever a defect is suspected.

2   Any of the following symptoms could indicate a potential brake system defect: The vehicle pulls to one side when the brake pedal is depressed; the brakes make squealing or dragging noises when applied; brake pedal travel is excessive; the pedal pulsates; or brake fluid leaks, usually onto the inside of the tire or wheel.

3   Disc brakes can be visually checked without removing any parts except the wheels. To check drum brakes, the rear wheels and brake drums will have to be removed. Remove the hub caps (if applicable) and loosen the wheel lug nuts a quarter turn each.

4   Loosen the wheel bolts, then raise the vehicle and support it securely on jackstands. **Warning:** *Never work under a vehicle that is supported only by a jack!*

Disc brakes

5   Remove the wheels. Now visible is the disc brake caliper which contains the pads. There is an outer brake pad and an inner pad. Both must be checked for wear.

6   Measure the thickness of the pads through the inspection hole in the caliper body **(see illustration)**. Compare the measurement with the limit given in this Chapter's Specifications ; if any brake pad thickness is less than specified, then all brake pads must be replaced (see Chapter 9).

7   If you're in doubt as to the exact pad thickness or quality, remove them for measurement and further inspection (see Chapter 9).

8   Check the disc for score marks, wear and burned spots. If any of these conditions exist, the disc should be removed for servicing or replacement (see Chapter 9).

9   Before installing the wheels, check all the brake lines and hoses for damage, wear, deformation, cracks, corrosion, leakage, bends and twists, particularly in the vicinity of the rubber hoses and calipers.

10   Install the wheels, lower the vehicle and tighten the wheel lug nuts to the torque given in this Chapter's Specifications.

Brake booster check

11   Sit in the driver's seat and perform the following sequence of tests.

12   With the brake fully depressed, start the engine - the pedal should move down a little when the engine starts.

13   With the engine running, depress the brake pedal several times - the travel distance should not change.

14   Depress the brake, stop the engine and hold the pedal in for about 30 seconds - the pedal should neither sink nor rise.

15   Restart the engine, run it for about a minute and turn it off. Then firmly depress the brake several times - the pedal travel should decrease with each application.

16   If your brakes do not operate as described, the brake booster has failed. Refer to Chapter 9 for the replacement procedure.

14.6 With the wheel off, check the thickness of the pads through the inspection hole - front brake shown, rear brake similar

17.4 Check the struts and shocks for leakage at the indicated area

17.10a To check the balljoint for wear, try to pry the control arm up . . .

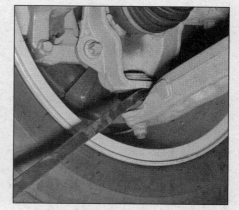

17.10b . . . and down to make sure there is no play in the balljoint (if there is, replace it)

15 Transfer case/Power Transfer Unit (PTU) lubricant level check (AWD/4WD models) (every 12,000 miles or 12 months)

Note: *Make sure the vehicle is on level ground for the check.*

1 The lubricant level is checked by removing a plug from the side of the case. If the vehicle is raised to gain access to the plug, be sure to support it safely on jackstands - DO NOT crawl under the vehicle when it's supported only by a jack!

2 Remove the skid plate, if equipped.

3 Remove the heat shield mounting bolts and heat shield.

4 With the engine and transfer case cold, insert a 3/8 inch breaker bar or ratchet into the square hole in the check/fill plug and remove the plug. If lubricant immediately starts leaking out, thread the plug back into the case - the level is correct. If it doesn't, completely remove the plug and reach inside the hole with your finger. The level should be even with the bottom of the plug hole.

5 If more lubricant is needed, use a syringe or small pump to add it through the opening.

6 Thread the plug back into the case and tighten it securely. Drive the vehicle, then check for leaks around the plug.

16 Differential lubricant level check (AWD/4WD models)

Note: *The differential is considered by the manufacturer to be a sealed-for-life design. There is no service interval recommended for this differential when it is operated under normal conditions. These differentials come pre-filled from the factory, and do not require fluid checking unless there has been a fluid change, repair or a leak.*

Note: *Make sure the vehicle is on level ground for the check.*

1 The differential has a check/fill plug

which must be removed to check the lubricant level. If the vehicle is raised to gain access to the plug, be sure to support it safely on jackstands - DO NOT crawl under the vehicle when it's supported only by the jack!

2 Remove the check/fill plug from the side of the differential and allow a couple of minutes for the fluid to equalize before checking it.

3 Use your finger as a dipstick to make sure the lubricant level is even with the bottom of the plug hole. If not, use a syringe to add the recommended lubricant until it just starts to run out of the opening.

4 Install the plug and tighten it securely.

17 Steering, suspension and driveaxle boot check (every 12,000 miles or 12 months)

Note: *For detailed illustrations of the steering and suspension components, refer to Chapter 10.*

With the wheels on the ground

1 With the vehicle stopped and the front wheels pointed straight ahead, rock the steering wheel gently back and forth. If freeplay is excessive, a front wheel bearing, steering shaft universal joint, lower arm balljoint or steering gear is worn. Refer to Chapter 10 for the appropriate repair procedure.

2 Other symptoms, such as excessive vehicle body movement over rough roads, swaying (leaning) around corners and binding as the steering wheel is turned, may indicate faulty steering and/or suspension components.

3 Check the struts/shock absorbers by pushing down and releasing the vehicle several times at each corner. If the vehicle does not come back to a level position within one or two bounces, the shocks/struts are worn and must be replaced. When bouncing the vehicle up and down, listen for squeaks and noises

from the suspension components.

4 Check the struts and shock absorbers for evidence of fluid leakage **(see illustration)**. A light film of fluid is no cause for concern. Make sure that any fluid noted is from the struts/shocks and not from some other source. If leakage is noted, replace the struts/shocks as a set.

5 Check the struts and shocks to be sure they are securely mounted and undamaged. Check the upper mounts for damage and wear. If damage or wear is noted, replace the shocks as a set (front and rear).

6 If the struts or shocks must be replaced, refer to Chapter 10 for the procedure.

Under the vehicle

7 Raise the vehicle and support it securely on jackstands.

8 Check the tires for irregular wear patterns and proper inflation. See Section 5 in this Chapter for information regarding tire wear and Chapter 10 for information on wheel bearing replacement.

9 Inspect the universal joint between the steering shaft and the steering gear housing. Check the steering gear housing for lubricant leakage. Make sure that the dust seals and boots are not damaged and that the boot clamps are not loose. Check the steering linkage for looseness or damage. Check the tie-rod ends for excessive play. Look for loose bolts, broken or disconnected parts and deteriorated rubber bushings on all suspension and steering components. While an assistant turns the steering wheel from side to side, check the steering components for free movement, chafing and binding. If the steering components do not seem to be reacting with the movement of the steering wheel, try to determine where the slack is located.

10 Check the balljoints for wear by trying to move each control arm up and down with a prybar **(see illustrations)** to ensure that its balljoint has no play. If any balljoint does have play, replace it. See Chapter 10 for the balljoint replacement procedure.

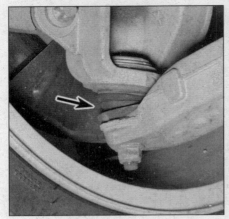

17.11 Check the balljoint boots for damage

17.14 Flex the driveaxle boots by hand to check for cracks and leaking grease

18.2 Check the exhaust system for rust, damage, or broken rubber hangers

19.6 Check the fuel system hoses and clamps for damage and deterioration

11   Inspect the balljoint boots for damage and leaking grease **(see illustration)**. Replace the control arm(s) with new ones if the balljoints are worn (see Chapter 10).

12   At the rear of the vehicle, inspect the suspension arm bushings for deterioration. Additional information on suspension components can be found in Chapter 10.

Driveaxle boot check

13   The driveaxle boots are very important because they prevent dirt, water and foreign material from entering and damaging the constant velocity (CV) joints. Oil and grease can cause the boot material to deteriorate prematurely, so it's a good idea to wash the boots with soap and water. Because it constantly pivots back-and-forth following the steering action of the front hub, the outer CV boot wears out sooner and should be inspected regularly.

14   Inspect the boots for tears and cracks as well as loose clamps **(see illustration)**. If there is any evidence of cracks or leaking lubricant, they must be replaced as described in Chapter 8.

18   Exhaust system check (every 12,000 miles or 12 months)

1   With the engine cold (at least three hours after the vehicle has been driven), check the complete exhaust system from the engine to the end of the tailpipe. Ideally, the inspection should be done with the vehicle on a hoist to permit unrestricted access. If a hoist isn't available, raise the vehicle and support it securely on jackstands.

2   Check the exhaust pipes and connections for evidence of leaks, severe corrosion and damage. Make sure that all brackets and hangers are in good condition and tight **(see illustration)**.

3   At the same time, inspect the underside of the body for holes, corrosion, open seams, etc., which may allow exhaust gases to enter the passenger compartment. Seal all body openings with silicone or body putty.

4   Rattles and other noises can often be traced to the exhaust system, especially the mounts and hangers. Try to move the pipes, muffler and catalytic converter. If the components can come in contact with the body or

suspension parts, secure the exhaust system with new mounts.

5   Check the running condition of the engine by inspecting inside the end of the tailpipe. The exhaust deposits here are an indication of engine state-of-tune. If the pipe is black and sooty or coated with white deposits, the engine may need a tune-up, including a thorough fuel system inspection and adjustment.

19   Fuel system check (every 12,000 miles or 12 months)

Warning: *Gasoline is flammable, so take extra precautions when you work on any part of the fuel system. Don't smoke or allow open flames or bare light bulbs near the work area, and don't work in a garage where a gas-type appliance (such as a water heater or clothes dryer) is present. Since fuel is carcinogenic, wear fuel-resistant gloves when there's a possibility of being exposed to fuel, and, if you spill any fuel on your skin, rinse it off immediately with soap and water. Mop up any spills immediately and do not store fuel-soaked rags where they could ignite. When you perform any kind of work on the fuel system, wear safety glasses and have a Class B type fire extinguisher on hand. The fuel system is under constant pressure, so, before any lines are disconnected, the fuel system pressure must be relieved (see Chapter 4).*

1   If you smell gasoline while driving or after the vehicle has been sitting in the sun, inspect the fuel system immediately.

2   Remove the fuel filler cap and inspect it for damage and corrosion. The gasket should have an unbroken sealing imprint. If the gasket is damaged or corroded, install a new cap.

3   Inspect the fuel feed line for cracks. Make sure that the connections between the fuel lines and the fuel injection system are tight.

Warning: *Your vehicle is fuel injected, so you must relieve the fuel system pressure before servicing fuel system components.*

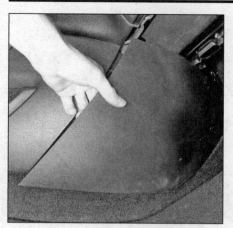

20.1 Remove the passenger's side console front panel

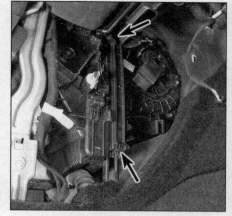

20.2 Press the tabs toward each other to disengage the clips

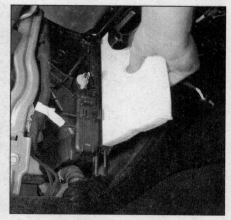

20.3 Remove the filter from the housing, noting the position of the filter as it is removed

The fuel system pressure relief procedure is outlined in Chapter 4.

4   Since some components of the fuel system - the fuel tank and the fuel lines, for example - are underneath the vehicle, they can be inspected more easily with the vehicle raised on a hoist. If that's not possible, raise the vehicle and support it on jackstands.

5   With the vehicle raised and safely supported, inspect the gas tank and filler neck for punctures, cracks and other damage. The connection between the filler neck and the tank is particularly critical. Sometimes a rubber filler neck will leak because of loose clamps or deteriorated rubber. Inspect all fuel tank mounting brackets and straps to be sure that the tank is securely attached to the vehicle.

Warning: *Do not, under any circumstances, try to repair a fuel tank (except rubber components).*

6   Carefully check all hoses and lines leading away from the fuel tank. Check for loose connections, deteriorated hoses, crimped lines and other damage **(see illustration)**. Repair or replace damaged sections as necessary (see Chapter 4).

ACCEPTABLE

Cracks Running Across "V" Portions of Belt

1/2"

Missing Two or More Adjacent Ribs 1/2" or longer

UNACCEPTABLE

Cracks Running Parallel to "V" Portions of Belt

21.3 Here are some of the more common problems associated with drivebelts (check the belts very carefully to prevent an untimely breakdown)

20   Cabin air filter replacement (every 12,000 miles or 12 months)

Warning: *The models covered by this manual are equipped with a Supplemental Restraint System (SRS), more commonly known as airbags. Always disable the airbag system before working in the vicinity of any airbag system component to avoid the possibility of accidental deployment of the airbag, which could cause personal injury (see Chapter 12).*

1   Use a trim tool and carfully pry out the passenger's side console front panel **(see illustration)**.

2   Disengage the two clips at the ends of the cover **(see illustration)** and remove the cover.

3   Remove the filter from the housing **(see illustration)**.

4   Install the filter, making sure the arrow on the filter is pointing toward the floor.

Note: *The cabin air filter is labeled with an arrow and the word "Airflow" on it.*

5   Installation is the reverse of removal.

21   Drivebelt check and replacement/ tensioner replacement (every 30,000 miles or 30 months)

1   The drivebelt is located at the right end of the engine and plays an important role in the operation of the vehicle and its components. Due to its function and material makeup, the belt is prone to failure after a period of time, and should be inspected and adjusted periodically to prevent major damage.

2   All models covered in this manual use

a single serpentine belt to drive all the components.

Check

3   With the engine off, open the hood and use your fingers (and a flashlight, if necessary) to move along the belt checking for cracks and separation of the belt plies. Also check for fraying and glazing, which gives the belt a shiny appearance. Also check the ribs on the underside of the belt. They should all be the same depth, with none of the surface uneven **(see illustration)**.

4   The serpentine belt tension is adjusted by an automatic tensioner.

Replacement

Warning: *On 3.2L engines, wait until the engine is completely cool before performing this procedure.*

21.10 Place a wrench on the tensioner pulley center bolt and rotate it - 2.4L engine shown

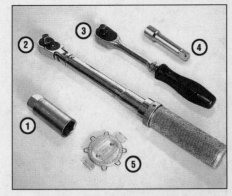

23.2 Tools required for changing spark plugs

1   *Spark plug socket* - This will have special padding inside to protect the spark plug's porcelain insulator
2   *Torque wrench* - Although not mandatory, using this tool is the best way to ensure the plugs are tightened properly
3   *Ratchet* - Standard hand tool to fit the spark plug socket
4   *Extension* - Depending on model and accessories, you may need special extensions and universal joints to reach one or more of the plugs
5   *Spark plug gap gauge* - This gauge for checking the gap comes in a variety of styles. Make sure the gap for your engine is included

5   Remove the air filter housing (see Chapter 4) and the air inlet tube.
6   On 3.2L engines, drain the cooling system (see Section 25), then disconnect the lower radiator hose and heater hose from the water pump.
7   On 2.4L and 3.2L models, apply the parking brake, loosen the right-front wheel bolts, then raise the front of the vehicle and support it securely on jackstands. Remove the wheel, then pull the front fender splash shield back to access the belt.
8   On all models, the automatic tensioner must be released to allow drivebelt replacement.
9   On 2.0L models, place a 3/8-inch drive ratchet or breaker bar into the square hole on the tensioner arm then rotate it until the belt can be removed. Remove the belt and slowly release the tensioner.
10   On 2.4L and 3.2L engines, place a wrench on the tensioner pulley center bolt and rotate it until the belt can be removed **(see illustration)**. Remove the belt and slowly release the tensioner.
Warning: *Damage to the tensioner or possible injury can occur if the tensioner snaps or springs back without the belt in place.*
11   Installation is the reverse of removal. When installing the belt, make sure the belt is centered on the pulleys.
12   On 3.2L engines, install the hoses and refill the cooling system (see Section 25).
13   Install the drivebelt splash shield and wheel. Lower the vehicle and tighten the wheel bolts to the torque listed in this Chapter's Specifications.

Automatic tensioner replacement

14   Remove the wheel, then remove the drivebelt splash shield.
15   Remove the drivebelt (see Step 9 or 10).
16   On 2.0L and 3.2L engines, unscrew the tensioner mounting bolt from the front side of the tensioner and on 2.4L engines from

the rear side and remove the tensioner.
17   Installation is the reverse of removal. Tighten the mounting bolt to the torque listed in this Chapter's Specifications. Lower the vehicle and tighten the wheel bolts to the torque listed in this Chapter's Specifications.

22   Brake fluid change (every 30,000 miles or 30 months)

Warning: *Brake fluid can harm your eyes and damage painted surfaces, so use extreme caution when handling or pouring it. Do not use brake fluid that has been standing open or is more than one year old. Brake fluid absorbs moisture from the air. Excess moisture can cause a dangerous loss of braking effectiveness.*
1   At the specified intervals, the brake fluid should be drained and replaced. Since the brake fluid may drip or splash when pouring it, place plenty of rags around the master cylinder to protect any surrounding painted surfaces.
2   Before beginning work, purchase the specified brake fluid (see *Recommended lubricants and fluids* in this Chapter's Specifications).
3   Remove the cap from the master cylinder reservoir.
4   Using a hand suction pump or similar device, withdraw the fluid from the master cylinder reservoir.
5   Add new fluid to the master cylinder until it rises to the base of the filler neck.
6   Bleed the brake system at all four brakes until new and uncontaminated fluid is expelled from the bleeder screw (see Chapter 9). Be sure to maintain the fluid level in the master cylinder as you perform the bleeding process. If you allow the master cylinder to run dry, air will enter the system.
7   Refill the master cylinder with fluid and check the operation of the brakes. The pedal

should feel solid when depressed, with no sponginess.
Warning: *Do not operate the vehicle if you are in doubt about the effectiveness of the brake system.*

23   Spark plug check and replacement (every 100,000 miles)

1   The spark plugs are located in the center of the valve cover(s).
2   In most cases the tools necessary for spark plug replacement include a spark plug socket which fits onto a ratchet (this special socket is padded inside to protect the porcelain insulators on the new plugs and hold them in place), various extensions and a feeler gauge to check and adjust the spark plug gap **(see illustration)**. Since these engines are equipped with aluminum cylinder heads, a torque wrench should be used when tightening the spark plugs.
3   The best approach when replacing the spark plugs is to purchase the new spark plugs beforehand, adjust them to the proper gap and then replace each plug one at a time. When buying the new spark plugs, be sure

23.5 Spark plug manufacturers recommend using a wire-type gauge when checking the gap - the wire should slide between the electrodes with a slight drag

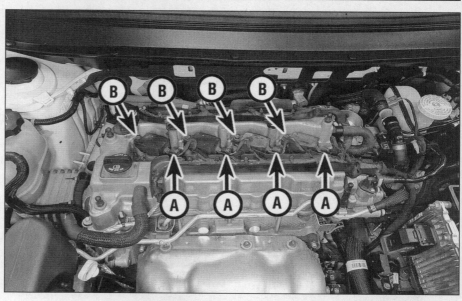

23.7a To remove an ignition coil(s), slide the red lock back and depress the tab (A), disconnect the electrical connector and remove the coil retaining bolt (B) . . .

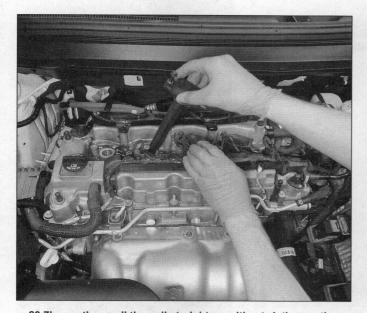

23.7b . . . then pull the coil straight up with a twisting motion

23.9 Use a ratchet, socket and long extension to remove the spark plugs

to obtain the correct plug for your specific engine. This information can be found in this Chapter's Specifications or in your owner's manual.

4   Allow the engine to cool completely before attempting to remove any of the plugs. During this cooling-off time, each of the new spark plugs can be inspected for defects and the gaps can be checked.

5   The gap is checked by inserting the proper thickness gauge between the electrodes at the tip of the plug (see illustration). The gap between the electrodes should be as listed in this Chapter's Specifi-

cations or in your owner's manual. The wire should touch each of the electrodes. Also, at this time check for cracks in the spark plug body (if any are found, the plug must not be used).

Caution: *The manufacturer recommends against checking the gap on platinum-tipped spark plugs; the platinum coating could be scraped off.*

6   Cover the fender to prevent damage to the paint. Fender covers are available from auto parts stores but an old blanket will work just fine.

7   Pull the engine cover upward to disen-

gage the cover from the ballstuds and remove the cover to gain access to the ignition coils (see illustrations).

Note: *On 3.2L models, to access the front cylinder spark plugs the upper intake manifold must be removed (see Chapter 2B).*

8   If compressed air is available, use it to blow any dirt or foreign material away from the spark plug area.

Warning: *Wear eye protection!*

9   Place the spark plug socket over the plug and remove it from the engine by turning it in a counterclockwise direction (see illustration).

A normally worn spark plug should have light tan or gray deposits on the firing tip.

A carbon fouled plug, identified by soft, sooty, black deposits, may indicate an improperly tuned vehicle. Check the air cleaner, ignition components and engine control system.

An oil fouled spark plug indicates an engine with worn piston rings and/or bad valve seals allowing excessive oil to enter the chamber.

This spark plug has been left in the engine too long, as evidenced by the extreme gap- Plugs with such an extreme gap can cause misfiring and stumbling accompanied by a noticeable lack of power.

A physically damaged spark plug may be evidence of severe detonation in that cylinder. Watch that cylinder carefully between services, as a continued detonation will not only damage the plug, but could also damage the engine.

A bridged or almost bridged spark plug, identified by a build-up between the electrodes caused by excessive carbon or oil build-up on the plug.

23.10 Common spark plug conditions

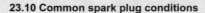

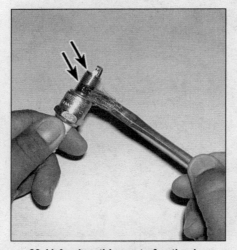

23.11 Apply a thin coat of anti-seize compound to the spark plug threads, but be careful not to get any of it near the electrodes

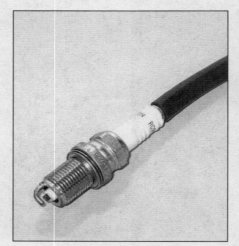

23.12 A length of snug-fitting rubber hose will save time and prevent damaged threads when installing the spark plugs

24.6a Pull the hose off the PCV valve . . .

10   Compare the spark plug with the chart **(see illustration)** to get an indication of the overall running condition of the engine.
11   It's a good idea to lightly coat the threads of the spark plugs with an anti-seize compound **(see illustration)** to insure that the spark plugs do not seize in the aluminum cylinder head.
12   It's often difficult to insert spark plugs into their holes without cross-threading them. To avoid this possibility, fit a piece of rubber hose over the end of the spark plug **(see**

illustration). The flexible hose acts as a universal joint to help align the plug with the plug hole. Should the plug begin to cross-thread, the hose will slip on the spark plug, preventing thread damage. Install the spark plug and tighten it to the torque listed in this Chapter's Specifications.
13   Using a slight twisting motion, install the ignition coils.
14   Follow the above procedure for the remaining spark plugs, replacing them one at a time.

24   Positive Crankcase Ventilation (PCV) valve check and replacement (every 60,000 miles or 60 months)

Warning: *Do not attempt to clean the PCV valve.*
1   Lift the engine cover up and off of the ballstuds and remove the cover.

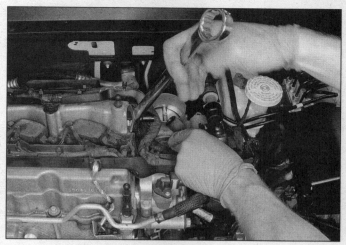

24.6b. . . then use a wrench to unscrew the PCV valve from the valve cover

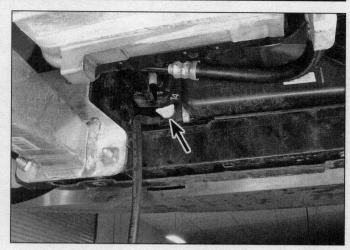

25.6 The drain fitting is located at the left end of the radiator

25.7 This block drain plug is located on the rear side of the cylinder block, below the exhaust manifold - 2.4L engines shown other similar

2.0L engines

2   Disconnect the PCV hose quick-connect fitting and remove the hose from the PCV valve.
3   Rotate the valve counterclockwise and pull the valve out of the valve cover.
4   Inspect the O-ring, install the valve and rotate the valve clockwise until the lock engages, an audible click should be heard.
5   Reconnect the PCV hose quick-connector.

2.4L engines

6   Detach the PCV hose and remove the valve **(see illustrations)**.
7   Install the PCV valve and tighten the valve securely.
8   Shake the valve. The valve should rattle freely - if it doesn't, replace it.
9   Installation is the reverse of removal.

3.2L engines

10 Locate the PCV valve on the end of the valve cover then disconnect the hose from the valve.
11 Remove the two fasteners and remove the valve from the valve cover.

12 Replace the PCV valve with the correct one for your specific vehicle and engine size and tighten the fasteners securely.
13 Installation is the reverse of removal.

25 Cooling system servicing (draining, flushing and refilling) (every 60 months)

Warning: *Do not allow antifreeze to come in contact with your skin or painted surfaces of the vehicle. Flush contaminated areas immediately with plenty of water. Do not store new coolant or leave old coolant lying around where it's accessible to children or pets - they're attracted by its sweet smell. Ingestion of even a small amount of coolant can be fatal! Wipe up garage floor and drip pan spills immediately. Keep antifreeze containers covered and repair cooling system leaks as soon as they're noticed. Check with local authorities about the disposal of used antifreeze. Many communities have collection centers which will see that antifreeze is disposed of properly.*
Warning: *The electric cooling fan(s) on these*

models can activate at any time when the ignition switch is in the ON position. Make sure the ignition is OFF when working in the vicinity of the fan(s). As an added precaution, disconnect the negative battery cable from the remote ground terminal (see Chapter 5).
Note: *These vehicles are originally filled with Mopar 5 year/100,000 mile coolant that shouldn't be mixed with other coolants. Always refill with the correct coolant.*
1   Periodically, the cooling system should be drained, flushed and refilled to replenish the antifreeze mixture and prevent formation of rust and corrosion, which can impair the performance of the cooling system and cause engine damage.
2   At the same time the cooling system is serviced, all hoses and the expansion tank pressure cap should be inspected, tested and replaced if faulty (see Section 12).

Draining

Warning: *Wait until the engine is completely cool before beginning this procedure.*
3   With the engine cold, remove the cooling system pressure cap and set the heater control to maximum heat.
4   Loosen the right-front wheel bolts, then raise the vehicle and support it securely on jackstands.
5   Move a large container under the radiator drain fitting to catch the coolant as it's drained.
6   Connect a piece of hose to the end of the drain fitting, then open the radiator drain fitting by turning it counterclockwise **(see illustration)** and allow the coolant to completely drain out.
7   After the coolant stops flowing out of the radiator, move the container under the engine block drain plugs and allow the coolant in the block to drain **(see illustration)**.
8   While the coolant is draining, check the condition of the radiator hoses, heater hoses and clamps. Replace any damaged clamps or hoses (see Section 12).

26.3 Transaxle drain plug location

26.5 Insert the tube from a hand pump into the check/fill plug opening

Flushing

9   Close the radiator and engine block drain plugs. Fill the cooling system with clean water, following the *Refilling* procedure (see Step 16).

10   Start the engine and allow it to reach normal operating temperature, then rev up the engine a few times.

11   Turn the engine off and allow it to cool completely, then drain the system as described earlier.

12   Repeat Steps 9 through 11 until the water being drained is free of contaminants.

13   Severe cases of radiator contamination or clogging will require removing the radiator (see Chapter 3) and reverse flushing it. This involves inserting a hose in the bottom radiator outlet to allow the clean water to run against the normal flow, draining out through the top. A radiator repair shop should be consulted if further cleaning or repair is necessary.

14   When the coolant is regularly drained and the system refilled with the correct coolant mixture, there should be no need to employ chemical cleaners or descalers.

15   Disconnect the coolant reservoir hose, remove the reservoir from the vehicle and flush it with clean water (see Chapter 3). Inspect it for damage and replace if necessary.

Refilling

16   Install the coolant reservoir, reconnect the hose and close the radiator drain fitting.

17   Remove the cooling system pressure cap. Add the correct mixture of the proper type of antifreeze/coolant and water, in the ratio specified on the antifreeze container or in this Chapter's Specifications, through the filler neck until it reaches the radiator cap seat.

18   Add the same coolant mixture to the reservoir until the level is between the FULL HOT and ADD marks. Install the radiator cap.

19   Run the engine until normal operating temperature is reached (the fans will cycle on,

then off), then allow the engine to cool. With the engine cold, add coolant as necessary to bring it up to the correct level.

20   Keep a close watch on the coolant level and the various cooling system hoses during the first few miles of driving and check for any coolant leaks. Tighten the hose clamps and add more coolant mixture as necessary.

26   Automatic transaxle fluid replacement (every 100,000 miles)

Note: *The 948TE/9HP48 automatic transmission considered by the manufacturer to be a sealed-for-life design. There is no service interval recommended for this transaxle when it is operated under normal conditions. These transaxles come pre-filled from the factory, and do not require fluid checking unless there has been a fluid change, repair or a leak.*

1   Apply the parking brake. Loosen the left-front wheel bolts, then raise the vehicle and support it securely on jackstands.

2   Remove the under-vehicle splash shield.
Note: *These transaxles require the use of a special tool #10323A (or a homemade equivalent) to measure the fluid level (see Section 4).*
Note: *To replace the fluid filter, the transaxle must be removed and disassembled.*

3   Place a container under the transaxle and remove the drain plug **(see illustration)**. Allow the fluid to drain into the container. Measure the amount of fluid drained - that will be the amount of new fluid to add as your starting point.

4   Once the fluid is done draining, install the drain plug and tighten it to torque listed in this Chapter's Specifications.

5   Remove the check/fill plug from the rear of the transaxle case **(see illustration 4.26)** and insert a hand pump tube into the opening **(see illustration)**.

6   Using a hand pump from the left wheel well opening, pump the new fluid (equal to the amount drained) into the transaxle **(see illustration)**.

7   Install the check/fill plug and tighten it securely.

8   Start the engine and allow it to idle for a minute, then slowly shift through each gear

26.6 Add fluid to the transaxle through the check/fill plug hole

position, pausing for a couple seconds in each range, ending in the Park position. Do this two times.

9   Check the fluid level as described in Section 4, adding or removing fluid as necessary.

10   Once the fluid level is correct, turn off the engine and install the front wheel and tighten the wheel bolts to the torque listed in this Chapter's Specifications. Install the check plug and tighten it to the torque listed in this Chapter's Specifications.

---

27   Transfer case/Power Transfer Unit (PTU) lubricant change (AWD/4WD models) (every 50,000 miles)

1   Drive the vehicle for at least 15 minutes to warm the lubricant in the case. Perform this warm-up procedure with 4WD engaged, if possible.

2   Raise the vehicle and support it securely on jackstands.

3   Remove the skid plate, if equipped, then remove the heat shield bolts and lower the heat shield from the PTU.

4   Remove the filler plug from the side of the case.

Note: *Some models are not equipped with a drain plug; on those models remove the check/ fill plug and use a suction gun to remove the fluid through the check/fill plug hole.*

5   Remove the drain plug from the lower part of the case and allow the old lubricant to drain completely.

6   After the lubricant has drained completely, clean the plug and the plug opening, apply thread sealant to the plug, then reinstall the plug and tighten it securely.

7   Fill the case with the specified lubricant until it is level with the lower edge of the filler hole.

8   Clean the filler plug and the plug opening, apply thread sealant to the plug, then reinstall the plug and tighten it securely.

9   Drive the vehicle for a short distance, then check the drain and fill plugs for leakage.

---

28   Differential lubricant and hydraulic fluid change (every 50,000 miles)

Note: *The differential is a sealed for life design. There is no service interval recommended for this differential when it is operated under normal conditions. These differentials come pre-filled from the factory, and do not require fluid checking unless there has been a fluid change, repair or a leak.*

1   This procedure should be performed after the vehicle has been driven so the lubricant will be warm and therefore flow out of the differential more easily.

2   Raise the vehicle and support it securely on jackstands.

Differential lubricant

3   Remove the check/fill plug from the side of the differential; it's a few inches above the drain plug.

4   Using a suction gun or hand pump, insert the hose into the check/fill hole as far as possible then suck the fluid out of the differential.

5   Fill the differential with the specified lubricant until it is level with the lower edge of the check/plug hole.

6   Clean the check/fill plug and the plug opening, apply thread sealant to the plug, then reinstall the plug and tighten it securely.

Hydraulic fluid

Note: *The following procedure checks the hydraulic fluid level in the rear differential. This is different than the differential lubricant level.*

7   Following the Chapter 8, Section 7 procedure, support the rear differential on a jack and remove the following components:

 a) *Muffler*
 b) *Driveshaft rear flange bolts*
 c) *Differential rear support bolt*
 d) *Differential front support bracket*

8   Carefully lower the differential approximately 4" (10cm).

9   Place a drain pan under the differential below the fluid cover and remove the fluid cover bolts.

10   Remove the cover and the gasket.

11   Fill the reservoir with hydraulic fluid until it reaches the full mark on the side of the reservoir (about half-way up the side).

12   Using a scan tool, perform the RDM Bleed procedure. Recheck the fluid level and top off as necessary.

13   Using a new gasket, install the cover and tighten the bolts to the torque listed in this Chapter's Specifications.

14   Raise the rear differential into position and install the removed components.

Notes

Chapter 2 Part A
2.0L and 2.4L four-cylinder engines

Contents

Specifications

General

Bore
- 2.0L engine .... 3.307 inches
- 2.4L engine .... 3.465 inches

Stroke
- 2.0L engine .... 3.54 inches
- 2.4L engine .... 3.819 inches

Compression ratio
- 2.0L engine 10: 1
- 2.4L engine 10.5:1

Displacement
- 2.0L engine .... 122 cubic inches
- 2.4L engine .... 146.5 cubic inches

Firing order 1-3-4-2

Camshaft

Bearing bore
2.4L engine
- Front journal (no.1) .... 1.4181 to 1.4189 inches
- Remaining journals (2 through 6) .... 1.0039 to 1.0047 inches

Camshaft journal diameter
2.0L engine
- No.1 journal .... 1.3773 to 1.3780 inches
- Remaining journals .... 1.1793 to 1.1819 inches
2.4L engine
- Front journal (no.1) .... 1.4162 to 1.4169 inches
- Remaining journals (2 through 6) .... 1.0021 to 1.0028 inches

Bearing clearance
2.0L engines
- No.1 journal .... 0.0005 inch
- Remaining journals .... 0.0012 to 0.0026 inch
2.4L engines .... 0.0008 to 0.0026 inch

Endplay .... 0.006 to 0.010 inch

Lobe lift
2.0L engines .... N/A
2.4L engines
- Intake @ 0.007 inch lash .... 0.203 inch
- Exhaust @ 0.011 inch lash .... 0.210 inch

Cylinder head

Head gasket surface warpage limit	0.004 inch maximum
Exhaust manifold mounting surface warpage limit	0.006 inch maximum

Intake and exhaust manifolds

Warpage limit	0.006 inch maximum

Torque specifications   Ft-lbs (unless otherwise indicated)

Note: *One foot-pound (ft-lb) of torque is equivalent to 12 inch-pounds (in-lbs) of torque. Torque values below approximately 15 ft-lbs are expressed in inch-pounds, because most foot-pound torque wrenches are not accurate at these smaller values.*

Idler pulley bolt	
2.0L engines	18
2.4L engines	21
Camshaft bearing cap bolts	
2.0L engines (in sequence - **see illustration 10.26**)	89
2.4L engines (in sequence - **see illustration 10.31**)	
Step 1	44 in-lbs
Step 2	89 in-lbs
Camshaft phaser-sprocket/oil control valve (2.0L engines)	110
Camshaft sprocket bolt (2.4L engines)	
Step 1	89 in-lbs
Step 2	Tighten an additional 65-degrees
Crankshaft pulley bolt*	
Step 1	37
Step 2	Tighten an additional 68-degrees
Cylinder head bolts	
2.0L engines (in sequence - **see illustration 11.32a**)	
Step 1, M11 inner bolts	41
Step 2, M11 inner bolts	Tighten an additional 180-degrees
Step 3, Side M8 bolts	21
2.4L engines (in sequence - **see illustration 11.32b**)	
Step 1	84 in-lbs
Step 2	144 in-lbs
Step 3	26
Step 4	Tighten an additional 160-degrees
Driveplate-to-crankshaft bolts	
2.0L engine*	81
2.4L engine	
Step 1	22
Step 2	Tighten an additional 51-degrees
Engine (and transaxle) mounts	
Rear mount (torque strut)	
2.0L engines	
Mount bracket-to-transaxle M14 bolts	120
Mount insulator-to-mount bracket through (M14) bolt and nut	81
Mount insulator-to-subframe through bolt (M14)	125
2.4L engines	
Mount insulator-to-subframe through bolt/nut	81
Mount-to-transaxle bracket through bolt/nut	85
Mount bracket-to-subframe bolts	46
Left (transaxle) mount)	
2.0L engines	
Mount bracket-to-transaxle M12 bolts	74
Mount insulator-to-mount bracket M14 bolts	87
Mount-to-frame rail M12 bolts	74
Mount-to-strut tower M10 bolt	47
Mount-to-frame rail bolts	77
Mount-to-strut tower bolt	48
Mount-to-adapter bracket bolt	116

Right (Front) mount
    Mount-to-engine mount bracket bolt.................................... 83
    Mount-to-frame rail M12 bolts
        2.0L engines................................. 48
        2.4L engines................................. 52
    Mount support bracket bolts................................ 120 in-lbs
    Mount-to-strut tower bolt.................................... 48
    Mount-to-timing chain cover bolts
        2.0L engines................................. 37
        2.4L engines................................. 58
Exhaust manifold-to-cylinder head bolts - 2.4L engines........................ 25
Exhaust manifold-to-exhaust pipe bolts - 2.4L engines.......................... 21
Intake manifold bolts
    2.0L engines................................. 102 in-lbs
    2.4L engines................................. 108 in-lbs
Intake manifold support bracket bolts.......................... 81 in-lbs
Driveaxle intermediate shaft bracket-to-engine block bolts.................... 41
Oil pan bolts
    2.0L engines
        Upper oil pan bolts
            M6 .... 89 in-lbs
            M8 18
            M10 37
        Acoustic cover .... 80 in-lbs
        Lower oil pan M6 bolts.................................. 80 in-lbs
    2.4L engines
        M6 bolts.................................. 89 in-lbs
        M8 bolts.................................. 17
Oil pump bolts - 2.0L engines.................................. 80 in-lbs
Oil pump pick-up tube bolts - 2.0L engines .... 80 in-lbs
Oil pump drive chain tensioner bolts - 2.0L engines.................................. 80 in-lbs
Oil pump drive chain guide bolts - 2.0L engines.................................. 89 in-lbs
Oil pump sprocket bolt - 2.0L engines 24
Oil pump displacement control solenoid stud/bolt .... 71 in-lbs
Balance shaft retaining bolt - 2.0L engines .... 89 in-lbs
Intake balance shaft sprocket bolt - 2.0L engines 23
Balance shaft module - 2.4L engines
    New bolts - 180 mm
        Step 1 .... 132 in-lbs
        Step 2 22
        Step 3 .... Tighten an additional 1/4-turn (90-degrees)
    New bolts - 185 mm
        Step 1 .... 132 in-lbs
        Step 2 22
        Step 3 .... Tighten an additional 1/4-turn (90-degrees)
Timing chain cover bolts
    M6 bolts.................................. 80 in-lbs
    M8 bolts and studbolt.................................. 19
    M10 bolts.................................. 48
Timing chain tensioner assembly bolts
    2.0L engines
        M6 bolts.................................. 80 in-lbs
        M8 bolts.................................. 21
    2.4L engines.................................. 80 in-lbs
Timing chain guide bolts
    2.0L engines
        M6 bolts.................................. 89 in-lbs
        M8 bolts.................................. 17
    2.4L engines.................................. 106 in-lbs
Vacuum pump 17
Valve cover bolts
    2.0L engines.................................. 97 in-lbs
    2.4L engines
        Step 1 .... 44 in-lbs
        Step 2 .... 90 in-lbs

1 General information

1   This Part of Chapter 2 is devoted to in-vehicle engine repair procedures. Information concerning engine removal and installation can be found in Chapter 2C.

2   These engines utilize an aluminum in-line four cylinder block. The aluminum cylinder head is heat treated and equipped with replaceable valve guides, seats, mechanical lifters and four valves per cylinder.

3   The turbocharged 2.0L engines utilize a double over head camshaft (DOHC) design with four valves per cylinder. On 2.4L engines, the cylinder head utilizes a single overhead camshaft (SOHC) and a Variable Valve Actuator Assembly (VVAA) system that replaces the traditional intake camshaft. The intake valves are actuated by hydraulic pumping elements via solenoid-operated hydraulic ports, controlled by the Powertrain Control Module (PCM). Both engines are NOT free-wheeling; meaning that the pistons will contact the valves in the event of a timing chain failure.

4   On 2.0L engines, two balance shafts located in the engine block are used. 2.4L engines use an externally mounted balance shaft module/oil pump. On 2.0L engines, a complex variable displacement oil pump is used, controlled by a heat exchanger in the engine oil cooler. On 2.4L engines, the oil pump is integrated into the module and is serviced as a unit with the balance shaft that is installed below the crankshaft.

5   The following repair procedures are based on the assumption that the engine is installed in the vehicle. If the engine has been removed from the vehicle and mounted on a stand, many of the steps outlined in this Part of Chapter 2 will not apply.

6   The Specifications included in this Part of Chapter 2 apply only to the procedures contained in this Part.

2 Repair operations possible with the engine in the vehicle

1   Many major repair operations can be accomplished without removing the engine from the vehicle.

2   Clean the engine compartment and the exterior of the engine with some type of degreaser before any work is done. It will make the job easier and help keep dirt out of the internal areas of the engine.

3   Depending on the components involved, it may be helpful to remove the hood to improve access to the engine as repairs are performed (refer to Chapter 11 if necessary). Cover the fenders to prevent damage to the paint. Special pads are available, but an old bedspread or blanket will also work.

4   If vacuum, exhaust, oil or coolant leaks develop, indicating a need for gasket or seal replacement, the repairs can generally be made with the engine in the vehicle. The intake and exhaust manifold gaskets, oil pan gasket, camshaft and crankshaft oil seals and cylinder head gasket are all accessible with the engine in place.

5   Exterior engine components, such as the intake and exhaust manifolds, the oil pan, the oil pump, the water pump, the starter motor, the alternator, the distributor and the fuel system components can be removed for repair with the engine in place.

6   Since the camshaft and cylinder head can be removed without pulling the engine, valve component servicing can also be accomplished with the engine in the vehicle. Replacement of the timing belt and sprockets is also possible with the engine in the vehicle.

7   In extreme cases caused by a lack of necessary equipment, repair or replacement of piston rings, pistons, connecting rods and rod bearings is possible with the engine in the vehicle. However, this practice is not recommended because of the cleaning and preparation work that must be done to the components involved.

3 Top Dead Center (TDC) for number one piston - locating

1   Top Dead Center (TDC) is the highest point in the cylinder that each piston reaches as it travels up-and-down when the crankshaft turns. Each piston reaches TDC on the compression stroke and again on the exhaust stroke, but TDC generally refers to piston position on the compression stroke. When the notched timing mark on the crankshaft pulley is aligned with the "I" mark of the indicator on the timing chain cover, number one piston is at TDC (see illustration 3.7).

2   Positioning a specific piston at TDC is an essential part of certain procedures such as camshaft(s) removal, and timing chain and sprocket replacement.

3   Remove all of the spark plugs, as this will make it easier to rotate the engine by hand (see Chapter 1).

4   Insert a compression gauge (screw-in type with a hose) in the number 1 spark plug hole. Place the gauge dial where you can see it while turning the crankshaft pulley bolt.

Note: *The number one cylinder is located at the front (timing chain end) of the engine.*

3.7 The notched timing mark on the crankshaft pulley (A) aligns with the "I" mark of the indicator on the timing cover (B) when TDC for number one piston is reached - 2.4L engine shown

the "I" mark on the timing chain cover indicator (see illustration). This is TDC compression for cylinder number one.

8   After the number one piston has been positioned at TDC on the compression stroke, TDC for any of the remaining cylinders can be located by turning the crankshaft 180-degrees (1/2-turn) at a time and following the firing order (see this Chapter's Specifications).

4 Valve cover - removal and installation

Removal

1   Disconnect the cable from the negative terminal of the battery (see Chapter 5).

2   Remove the engine cover by pulling it up and off of the ballstuds.

3   Remove the plastic push-pins that hold the ignition coil wiring in place then remove the ignition coils (see Chapter 5).

4   Clearly label and disconnect any wiring harnesses which connect to, or cross over, the valve cover (see illustration).

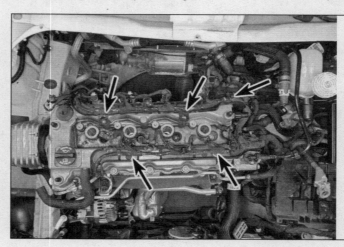

4.4 Disconnect the wiring harness retainers then reposition the wiring harnesses (2.4L model shown)

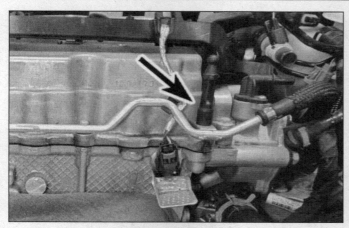

4.12 Remove the engine cover ballstud

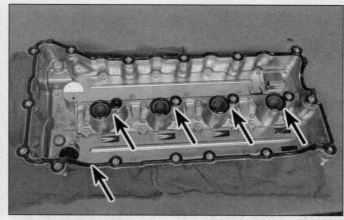

4.15 Install new inner and outer gaskets on the valve cover

2.0L engines

5   Remove the fuel rail and injectors (see Chapter 4).
6   Disconnect the Variable Valve Timing (VVT) solenoids wire harness connectors then remove the solenoids from the front of the valve cover (see Chapter 6).
Note: *It may be necessary to remove the right engine mount bracket bolt to access the VVT solenoid lower mounting bolt.*
7   Remove the Exhaust Gas Recirculation (EGR) valve (see Chapter 6).
8   Disconnect the PCV valve hose (rear) and breather hose from the valve cover.
9   Disconnect the PCV valve hose (front) and breather hose from the valve cover.
10 Remove the upstream oxygen sensor connector bracket and the ignition capacitor bracket.

2.4L engines

11 Disconnect the PCV valve hose and breather hose from the valve cover.
12 Remove the engine cover ballstud (see illustration), then move the cooling tube out of the way.

All models

13 Remove the valve cover bolts in the reverse order of the tightening sequence (see illustration 4.17a or 4.17b), clean any debris from the cover, then lift off the cover. If the cover sticks to the cylinder head, tap on it with a soft-faced hammer or place a wood block against the cover and tap on the wood with a hammer.
Caution: *If you have to pry between the valve cover and the cylinder head, be extremely careful not to gouge or nick the gasket surfaces of either part. A leak could develop after reassembly.*
14 Remove the valve cover perimeter rubber seal and spark plug tube seal. Thoroughly clean the valve cover and cylinder head mating surfaces. After cleaning the surfaces, degrease them with a rag soaked in brake system cleaner.

Installation

15 Install new gaskets into the channels on the cover (see illustration). Place the cover on the engine and install the cover bolts.
16 Clean the surfaces of the cylinder head

sealing surfaces then apply a small amount of RTV at all the joint locations.
17 Tighten the bolts, in the proper sequence (see illustrations), to the torque listed in this Chapter's Specifications.
18 The remainder of installation is the reverse of removal. Run the engine and check for oil leaks.

5   Intake manifold - removal and installation

Removal

1   Relieve the fuel system pressure (see Chapter 4), then disconnect the cable from the negative terminal of the battery (see Chapter 5).
2   Remove the engine cover by pulling it up and off of the ballstuds.
3   Remove the cowl panel (see Chapter 11).
4   Remove the fresh air inlet duct and the air intake duct between the air filter housing and the throttle body (see Chapter 4).

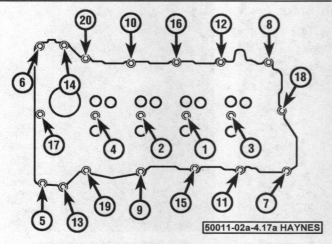

4.17a Valve cover bolt tightening sequence - 2.0L engines

4.17b Valve cover bolt tightening sequence - 2.4L engines

5.21 Remove the intake manifold support bracket nuts and bolts

5.25 Move the right side of the engine forward approximately 3 inches

2.0L engines

5   Remove the turbocharger outlet pipe (see Chapter 4).

6   Disconnect the EVAP purge solenoid hose and move it out of the way, then remove the EVAP purge solenoid and vent valve (see Chapter 6).

7   Remove the EGR valve, Temperature and Manifold Air Pressure (TMAP) sensor and the intake Camshaft Position (CMP) sensor (see Chapter 6).

8   Disconnect the quick-connect fittings from the charge air cooler and reposition the coolant supply hoses, then remove the charge air cooler Y-pipe.

9   Disconnect the wire harness connectors from the throttle body, the charge air cooler coolant temperature sensor and fuel pressure sensor (see Chapter 6).

10   Remove the two bolts securing the lower part of the intake manifold to the bottom of the cylinder head.

11   Support the engine with a floor jack and wooden block placed between the jack and the engine.

12   Remove the right engine mount (see Section 17), then carefully move the right end of the engine towards the front of the vehicle and slightly down.

13   Remove the five bolts securing the upper portion of the intake manifold to the cylinder head.

14   Pull the intake manifold away from the engine until the hose clamp can be loosened and the hose removed from the turbocharger coolant supply pipe and remove the intake manifold.

15   Remove and replace the intake gasket seals.

16   If your're replacing the intake manifold, remove the throttle body (see Chapter 4).

2.4L engines

17   Disconnect the MAP sensor electri-cal connector (see Chapter 6), then unclip the wiring harness from the eyelets on the manifold.

18   Raise the vehicle up and place it securely on jackstands, then remove the engine lower splash shield.

19   Remove the skid plates, if equipped.

20   Remove the exhaust pipe flange nuts, support bolt and lower the exhaust.

21   From under the vehicle, remove the intake manifold support bracket nuts and bolts, then remove the support bracket **(see illustration)**.

22   Disconnect the electrical connector from the throttle body. Remove the fasteners from the transaxle-to-throttle body support bracket at the throttle body end of the bracket and the throttle body (see Chapter 4).

23   Remove the air filter housing bracket nuts and remove the bracket from the right side of the frame.

24   Remove the coolant expansion tank fas-

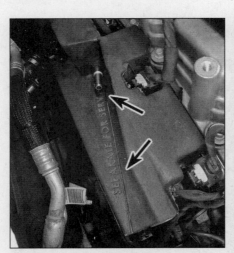

5.26 Injector manifold silencer cover "service access line"

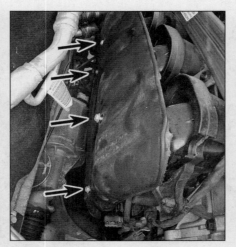

5.28 Remove the manifold silencer cover fasteners and cover

5.29 Disconnect the fuel injector electrical connectors

5.31a Careully remove the intake manifold gasket from the engine

5.31b Remove the intake manifold gasket from the manifold

teners and move the tank out of the way.
25 Support the engine from below with a floor jack and block of wood and remove the right engine mount **(see illustration)**, then use a large prybar and move the right side of the engine forward approximately 3 inches.
26 Disconnect the hoses from the canister purge valve (see Chapter 6) and the fuel rail (see Chapter 4), then remove the injector silencer pad by cutting a diagonal line across the back side of the pad so it can be removed around the fuel rail **(see illustration)**.
27 Unplug the electrical connectors from the fuel injectors (see Chapter 4), the Variable Valve Timing (VVT) solenoid and the intake Camshaft Position (CMP) sensor (see Chapter 6), and move the electrical harness out of the way.
28 Remove the cover from the side of the intake manifold **(see illustration)**.
29 Remove the injector electrical connectors from the injectors **(see illustration)** and

move the harness out of the way.
30 Label, then disconnect the vacuum line(s) from the manifold.
31 Remove the intake manifold fasteners, then remove the intake manifold and the manifold gasket seals from the intake manifold **(see illustrations)**.

Inspection
32 Using a straightedge and feeler gauge, check the intake manifold mating surface for warpage. Check the intake manifold surface on the cylinder head also. If the warpage on either surface exceeds the limit listed in this Chapter's Specifications, the intake manifold and/or the cylinder head must be resurfaced at an automotive machine shop or, if the warpage is too excessive for resurfacing, replaced.

Installation
33 Clean the mating surfaces of the manifold and cylinder head. Using a new manifold

gasket, install the intake manifold onto the manifold studs.
34 Tighten the intake manifold fasteners gradually and evenly, in the indicated sequence **(see illustrations)**, to the torque listed in this Chapter's Specifications.
35 The remainder of installation is the reverse of removal.

---

6 Exhaust manifold (2.4L engines) - removal, inspection and installation

---

Warning: *Allow the engine to cool completely before beginning this procedure.*
Note: *The exhaust manifold and catalytic converter have been integrated and is also called a maniverter.*
Note: *2.0L engines do not use a exhaust manifold - the manifold has been incorporated into the turbocharger assembly (see Chapter 4).*

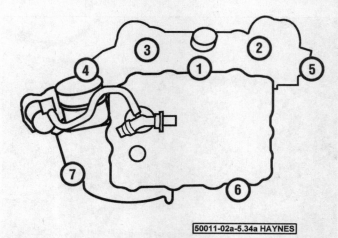

50011-02a-5.34a HAYNES

5.34a Intake manifold fastener tightening sequence - 2.0L engines

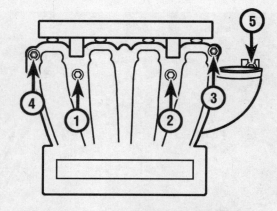

50011-02a-5.34b HAYNES

5.34b Intake manifold fastener tightening sequence - 2.4L engines

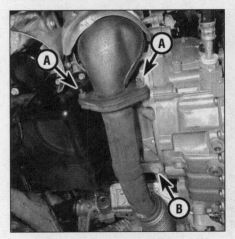

6.4 Remove the crossunder pipe-to-maniverter mounting nuts (A) and pipe support bracket bolt (B)

6.5 Remove the maniverter lower support bracket bolts

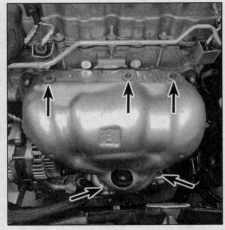

6.6 Exhaust manifold heat shield fasteners

Removal

1   Raise the vehicle and support it securely on jackstands.
2   Remove the engine lower splash shield from the bottom of the vehicle.
3   Remove the cross-under pipe support bracket mounting bolt.
4   Remove the crossunder pipe nuts and disconnect the exhaust crossunder pipe from the maniverter outlet flange, then support the exhaust crossunder pipe to prevent possible damage to the flex joint **(see illustration)**.
5   Remove the maniverter lower support bracket **(see illustration)**.
6   Remove the exhaust manifold heat shield **(see illustration)**.
7   Unplug the electrical connector for the oxygen sensors. It's not necessary to remove the oxygen sensors unless the manifold is going to be replaced (see Chapter 6).
8   Unscrew the mounting bolts **(see illustration)** and remove the exhaust manifold and the old manifold gasket.

Inspection

9   Inspect the exhaust manifold for cracks and any other obvious damage. If the manifold is cracked or damaged in any way, replace it.
10   Using a wire brush, clean up the threads of the exhaust manifold bolts and inspect the threads for damage. Replace any bolts that have thread damage.
11   Using a scraper, remove all traces of gasket material from the mating surfaces and inspect them for wear and cracks.
Caution: *When removing gasket material from any surface, especially aluminum, be very careful not to scratch or gouge the gasket surface. Any damage to the surface may result in a leak after reassembly. Gasket removal solvents are available from auto parts stores and may prove helpful.*
12   Using a straightedge and feeler gauge, inspect the exhaust manifold mating surface for warpage. Check the exhaust manifold surface on the cylinder head also. If the warpage

on any surface exceeds the limits listed in this Chapter's Specifications, the exhaust manifold and/or cylinder head must be replaced or resurfaced at an automotive machine shop.

Installation

13   Using a new exhaust manifold gasket (and NO sealant), install the exhaust manifold and tighten the mounting bolts, a little at a time and working from the center outward, to the torque listed in this Chapter's Specifications.
14   The remainder of installation is the reverse of removal.

---

7   Crankshaft pulley - removal and installation

Removal

1   Disconnect the cable from the negative terminal of the battery (see Chapter 5).

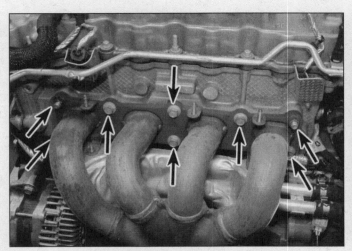

6.8 Exhaust manifold fasteners

7.5 Use a special holding tool to prevent the crankshaft from turning while loosening the bolt

7.6 Slide the pulley from the end of the crankshaft; a puller shouldn't be required

8.2 Use a hook tool and pry the seal from the timing cover

8.3 Another way of removing an oil seal is to screw a self-tapping screw partially into the seal, then use pliers as a lever to pull it from the engine - typical engine shown

2   Loosen the right-front wheel lug nuts, then raise the vehicle and support it securely on jackstands.
3   Remove the right-front wheel and splash shield (see Chapter 11, Section 11).
4   Remove the drivebelt (see Chapter 1).
5   The crankshaft pulley bolt is very tight; using a breaker bar, socket and special tool #9707 or equivalent **(see illustration)**, hold the pulley from turning while loosening the bolt.
6   Pull the crankshaft pulley off the crankshaft **(see illustration)**.
Caution: *On 2.0L engines, a friction shim is attached to the front and rear of the crankshaft sprocket. Verify that the friction shim is still in place on the front of the crankshaft sprocket once the pulley is removed.*

Installation

7   Apply clean engine oil or multi-purpose grease to the seal contact surface of the pulley hub (if it isn't lubricated, the seal lip could be damaged and oil leakage would result).
8   Install the crankshaft pulley, aligning the keyway on the crankshaft with the slot in the

pulley hub. Install a new washer and bolt then tighten it by hand.
9   Prevent the engine from rotating (see Step 5), then tighten the bolt to the torque listed in this Chapter's Specifications.
10   The remainder of installation is the reverse of removal.

8   Crankshaft front oil seal - replacement

1   Remove the crankshaft pulley (see Section 7).
2   Use a screwdriver or hook tool to carefully pry out the seal **(see illustration)**.
Note: *Be careful not to damage the oil pump cover bore where the seal is seated or the nose and sealing surface of the crankshaft.*
3   Another procedure for removing the seal is to drill a small hole on each side of the seal and place a self-tapping screw in each hole **(see illustration)**. Use these screws as a means of pulling the seal out without having to pry on it.

4   If the seal is being replaced when the timing chain cover is removed, support the cover on top of two blocks of wood and drive the seal out from the backside with a hammer and punch.
Caution: *Be careful not to scratch, gouge or distort the area that the seal fits into or a leak will develop.*
5   Apply clean engine oil or multi-purpose grease to the outer edge of the new seal, then install it in the cover with the lip (spring side) facing IN. Drive the seal into place with a seal driver or large socket and a hammer **(see illustration)**. Make sure the seal enters the bore squarely and stop when the front face is at the proper depth.
6   Check the surface on the crankshaft pulley hub that the oil seal rides on. If the surface has been grooved from long-time contact with the seal, the pulley will have to be replaced.
7   Lubricate the pulley hub with clean engine oil, then install the crankshaft pulley (see Section 7).
8   The remainder of installation is the reverse of removal.

9   Timing chain cover, chain, balance shafts and sprockets - removal, inspection and installation

Warning: *Wait until the engine is completely cool before beginning this procedure.*
Caution: *The timing system is complex, and severe engine damage will occur if you make any mistakes. Do not attempt this procedure unless you are highly experienced with this type of repair. If you are at all unsure of your abilities, be sure to consult an expert. Double-check all your work and be sure everything is correct before you attempt to start the engine.*
Caution: *Do not rotate the crankshaft or camshaft separately during this procedure (with the timing chains removed), as damage to the valves may occur.*

8.5 Drive the seal squarely into the cover using a seal driver or socket and hammer

Removal
Timing chain cover

1   Relieve the fuel system pressure (see Chapter 4), then disconnect the cable from the negative terminal of the battery (see Chapter 4).
2   Remove the engine cover by pulling the cover up and off of the ballstuds.
3   Loosen the right-front wheel lug nuts, then raise the front of the vehicle and support it securely on jackstands.
4   Drain the engine coolant (see Chapter 1).
5   Drain the engine oil (see Chapter 1).
6   Remove the right-front wheel and drive-belt splash shield (see Chapter 1).
7   Remove the intake tube and air filter housing (see Chapter 4), then remove and position aside the coolant expansion tank (see Chapter 3).
8   Remove the drivebelt, drivebelt tensioner and idler pulley (see Chapter 1).
9   Remove the ignition coils (see Chapter 5).
10   Remove the valve cover (see Section 4).
11   Remove the water pump pulley bolts and pulley (see Chapter 3).
12   Position the number one piston at Top Dead Center on the compression stroke (see Section 3).

2.0L models

13   Remove the oil pan, then temporarily reinstall the oil pan and hand-tighten the bolts.
14   Support the engine with a floor jack and block of wood, slightly raise the engine, then remove the right-side engine mount (see Section 17).
15   Remove the drivebelt idler pulley.
16   Continue turning the crankshaft until the notch in the crankshaft pulley is aligned with the "l" mark on the timing chain cover indicator **(see illustration 3.7)**.
17   Remove the crankshaft pulley (see Section 7).
18   Remove the timing chain cover bolts, then carefully separate the cover from the block. Use a putty knife or gasket scraper to loosen the seal around the front cover at the prying points ONLY.
19   Remove the timing chain cover, replace the crankshaft front oil seal if necessary (see Section 8).
20   Once the cover is removed, RTV gasket material must be thoroughly cleaned from the cylinder head, engine block and back side of the timing chain cover.

2.4L models

21   Remove all of the oil pan bolts except for the bolts at the opposite end of the timing chain cover, which should only be loosened a few turns. Once the bolts are removed/loosened, the pan must be briefly tilted from the rear and separated off the timing chain cover to fully break the oil pan-to-timing chain cover seal. Once the seal is broken, reinstall the pan bolts except the pan-to-cover bolts.
22   Remove the crankshaft pulley (see Section 7).

23   Support the engine with a floor jack and wooden block placed on the jack head. Slightly raise the engine, then remove the right engine mount (see Section 17).
24   Remove the right-side engine mount bracket bolts and bracket from the timing chain cover (see Section 17).
25   Remove the oil pan-to-timing chain cover bolts from the bottom of the timing chain cover.
26   Remove the timing chain cover mounting bolts, noting the locations of the mounting bolts. There are several different types of bolts used that must be installed in their original locations. There are four indented prying points, one upper and one lower on the right side, and one upper and one lower on the left side. Carefully pry the cover free of the engine block and cylinder head and remove the cover from the bottom of the vehicle. If it still sticks, slip a putty knife between the engine block and cover to break the bond (but be careful not to scratch the surfaces).
27   Once the cover is removed, RTV gasket material must be thoroughly cleaned from the cylinder head, engine block and back side of the timing chain cover.

Timing chain

Caution: *When the timing chains are removed, do not rotate the camshafts or crankshaft; the valves and pistons can be damaged if contact is made.*

2.0L models

28   Verify that the crankshaft sprocket timing mark is just past the 6 o'clock position and the mark is in the middle of the two camshaft timing chain colored timing links. If the colored links are hard to see, make sure you make your own marks if you're reusing the chain.
29   The arrow marks on camshaft phaser sprockets should be pointing upwards (intake sprocket mark at approximately 12 o'clock and the exhaust sprocket mark at 1 o'clock), and the marks aligned with the single colored links. If the colored links are hard to see make sure you mark them if you're reusing the chain.
30   Remove the top chain guide retaining bolt and guide from the camshaft bearing cap.
31   Using the camshaft chain tensioner arm, push the tensioner piston in and insert special tensioner pin tool no. 8514 (or equivalent) to hold the tensioner piston in the compressed position, then remove the tensioner mounting bolts and tensioner.
Caution: *If the tensioner pin can't be inserted, the tensioner will have to be reset off of the engine. When the tensioner is removed without the pin tool the piston can shoot out from the tensioner body under extremely high force.*
Note: *A drill bit can be used if the special tool is not available.*
32   Allow the chain guide/tenioner arm to move away from the chain, then lift the chain off of the camshaft phaser sprockets and lower it down and remove it from the crankshaft sprocket.

33   If you're removing the crankshaft sprocket, remove the oil pump drive chain (see Section 14).
34   Remove the crankshaft sprocket and rear friction shim on the ends of the gear, if necessary.
Note: *There are two friction shims attached to the front and rear of the crankshaft gear, verify that both shims have been removed. It is possible that the outer shim will stay with the crankshaft pulley.*
35   Check that the two woodruff keys are on the end of the crankshaft.
36   Place a wrench on the flat spots just behind the camshaft front bearing cap, then loosen the intake and exhaust oil control valves. Unscrew the oil control valve(s) from the camshaft phaser sprocket(s) and carefully remove the sprocket from the end of the camshaft(s).

2.4L models

37   If the engine has moved from TDC, temporarily install the crankshaft pulley bolt. Turn the crankshaft with the bolt to TDC number 1 to align the timing marks on the crankshaft and camshaft sprockets. Rotate the engine clockwise only, until the crankshaft keyway aligns with the line made where the engine block and ladder frame meet **(see illustration)**.
Note: *The sprocket timing mark is closer to the 3 o'clock position and the crankshaft keyway is aligned at the 9 o'clock position, pointing to the line made where the engine block and ladder frame meet.*
Note: *If the timing chain plated links are faded or can no longer be seen, mark the links to the corresponding timing marks before removing the chain (if you plan to reuse the old chain).*
38   The camshaft dowel at the hub of the sprocket should be facing 90-degrees upwards from the horizontal cylinder head surface.
Note: *Use paint or a permanent marker to mark the direction of rotation on all chains before removing them so they can be installed in the same direction.*
39   Remove the timing chain tensioner mounting bolts and remove the tensioner and guide from the left side of the timing chain; the tensioner will not come apart when it is removed.
40   Remove the timing chain from the camshaft sprocket and crankshaft sprocket.
41   If necessary, remove the oil pump/balance shaft chain (see Section 14), then remove the crankshaft sprocket (see Section 8).
42   If necessary, remove the chain guide bolts and guide.

Inspection

43   Inspect the timing chain dampeners (guide) for cracks and wear and replace it, if necessary.
44   Clean the timing chain and sprockets with solvent and dry them with compressed air (if available).
Warning: *Wear eye protection when using compressed air.*

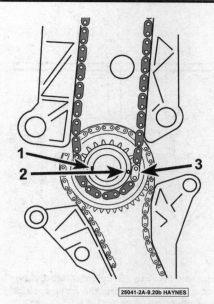

9.37 Align the keyway of the crankshaft to the 9 o'clock position; at this position, the keyway will be pointing to the line made where the engine block and ladder frame meet

1   Crankshaft keyway at the 9 o'clock position
2   Timing mark
3   Timing chain plated link

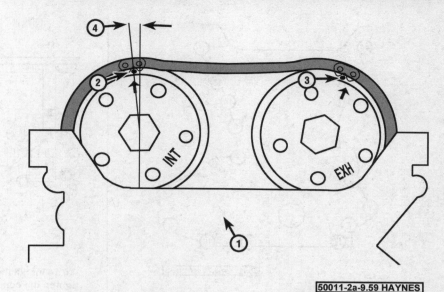

9.59 Camshaft phaser/sprocket timing mark alignment - 2.0L engines

1   Timing chain cover
2   Intake phaser timing alignment mark
3   Exhaust camshaft phaser/sprocket timing mark - there should be 22 chain pins between the two camshaft phaser marks
4   Verify that the intake phaser timing alignment mark is positioned 7 degrees to the left of a vertical line

45   Inspect the components for wear and damage. Look for teeth that are deformed, chipped, pitted, and cracked.

46   The timing chain and sprockets should be replaced with new ones if the engine has high mileage or the chain has visible damage. Failure to replace a worn timing chain and sprockets may result in erratic engine performance, loss of power, and decreased fuel mileage. Loose chains can jump timing. In the worst case, chain jumping or breakage will result in severe engine damage.

Installation

Caution: *Before starting the engine, carefully rotate the crankshaft by hand through at least two full revolutions (use a socket and breaker bar on the crankshaft pulley center bolt). If you feel any resistance, STOP! There is something wrong - most likely, valves are contacting the pistons. You must find the problem before proceeding.*

47   Use a plastic gasket scraper to remove all traces of old gasket material and sealant from the cover, engine block and cylinder heads. The components are all made of aluminum, so be careful not to nick or gouge them. Only clean the gasket sealing surfaces with rubbing alcohol (isopropyl) or brake system cleaner.

Timing chain

2.0L engine

48   If removed, install the crankshaft gear with the friction shims on each end of the

crankshaft gear. Install the oil pump drive chain (see Section 14).

49   If removed, verify the notch on the camshafts are at the 12 o'clock position then install the camshaft phaser/sprockets. Hold the camshaft(s) with a wrench on the flat spots on the camshaft(s) then install the oil control solenoid in the middle of the camshaft phaser/sprocket(s) and tighten the oil control solenoid(s) to the torque listed in this Chapter's Specifications.

50   Install the timing chain guides and tighten the bolts to the torque listed in this Chapter's Specifications.

51   Make sure the keyway is installed on the crankshaft and is at TDC, with the keyway pointing toward the 9 o'clock position in line with the line made where the engine block and bearing cap meet.

52   Place the timing chain around the bottom of the crankshaft sprocket with two links on both sides of the timing mark of the sprocket.

53   Route the chain up to the camshaft phaser/sprockets, looping the chain over the exhaust phaser/sprocket and the intake phaser/sprocket. The arrow marks on camshaft phaser sprockets should be pointing upwards with the intake sprocket mark at approximately 12 o'clock and the exhaust sprocket mark at 1 o'clock, placing the single colored links on the marks.

54   If the timing chain tensioner must be reset before installing it, follow these procedures:

a)   *Insert the timing chain tensioner into a soft jawed vise and slowly apply a small amount of force against the piston.*

b)   *Working from the backside of the tensioner, spread the ratchet clip apart using snap-ring pliers and hold the clip apart. Slowly compress the tensioner in the vise until special pin tool no. 8541 or a drill bit can be inserted into the hole in the body locking the piston in the compressed position.*

55   Install the timing chain tensioner and tighten the mounting bolts to the torque listed in this Chapter's Specifications.

56   Place the tensioner arm/guide against the chain tensioner and remove the pin.

57   Install the top camshaft chain guide and tighten the mounting bolt to the torque listed in this Chapter's Specifications.

58   Temporarily install the timing chain cover and crankshaft pulley.

59   Rotate the crankshaft two compete revolutions and verify that the timing marks are all aligned **(see illustration)**.

Caution: *If you feel any resistance, STOP! There is something wrong - most likely, valves are contacting the pistons. You must find the problem before proceeding.*

2.4L engine

60   If removed, install the crankshaft sprocket and oil pump/balance shaft module chain (see Section 14).

61   If removed, install the right side chain guide and tighten the mounting bolts to the torque listed in this Chapter's Specifications.

62   Make sure the keyway is installed on the crankshaft and is at TDC, with the keyway pointing toward the 9 o'clock position in line

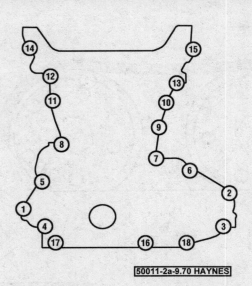

9.70 Timing chain cover tightening sequence - 2.0L engines

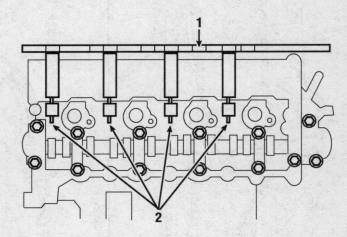

10.14 Install the special tool (1) onto the cylinder head, then tighten the compressor assemblies (2) until the valve springs are fully compressed

with the line made where the engine block and ladder frame meet and the crankshaft gear timing mark is at the 3 o'clock position.

63   Verify the camshaft sprocket is at TDC; the camshaft dowel at the hub of the sprocket should be facing 90-degrees upwards from the horizontal cylinder head surface.

64   Using clean engine oil, coat the sprocket and chain. Place the chain on the crankshaft sprockets, with the plated links aligned with the machined dots on the camshaft sprocket.

65   Pre-align the chain with the corresponding mark on the camshaft sprocket, then lower the chain and sprocket and loop the chain around the crankshaft sprocket. Be sure the crankshaft sprocket marks and plated link are aligned properly (3 o'clock position). Install the camshaft sprocket (with the chain in place) onto the camshaft. Make sure the dowel, sprocket and plate link marks are aligned. While holding the camshaft with a wrench on the flats, tighten the camshaft sprocket bolt to the torque listed this Chapter's Specifications

66   While holding the timing chain tensioner with light pressure against the plunger, use a pick to lift up on the plunger ratchet through the front hole until the plunger can be pressed in and 1/8-inch drill bit can be inserted through the rear hole of the tensioner body, holding the plunger in the compressed position.

67   Install the chain guide and tensioner, then tighten the fasteners to the torque listed in this Chapter's Specifications. Remove the special tool from the tensioner plunger.

68   Temporarily reinstall the crankshaft pulley and rotate the engine two complete turns, with the line made where the engine block and ladder frame meet as the reference point. Verify all the marks line up; if the marks are off, rotate the engine two more complete turns and check again.

Caution: *If you feel any resistance, STOP! There is something wrong - most likely, valves*

are contacting the pistons. You must find the problem before proceeding.

Timing chain cover

69   Once the timing marks are correct, apply a continuous bead of RTV sealant along the left and right-side timing chain cover sealing surfaces. Also apply sealant around the bolt contact surfaces that are located inside of the cover.

Note: *On 2.0L engines, there are six locations that must have a bead of RTV around the hole openings.*

70   Install the timing chain cover bolts in their original locations. On 2.0L engines tighten the bolts in sequence **(see illustration)**, and on 2.4L enignes tighten them in a criss-cross pattern, in three steps, to the torque listed in this Chapter's Specifications.

71   Remove the oil pan, then reinstall it using RTV sealant (see Section 13) after the timing chain cover has been installed.

72   The remainder of installation is the reverse of removal.

73   Add oil and coolant (see Chapter 1), start the engine and check for leaks.

---

10   Camshaft(s) – removal, inspection and installation

Warning: *Wait until the engine is completely cool before beginning this procedure.*

Caution: *On 2.4L engines, this procedure requires the use of MOPAR special tool #10259A/B - attempting to perform this procedure without the use of this special tool will cause damage to the valves, cylinder head or the VVAA system.*

Caution: *The timing system is complex, and severe engine damage will occur if you make any mistakes. Do not attempt this procedure unless you are highly experienced with this type of repair. If you are at all unsure of your*

abilities, be sure to consult an expert. Double-check all your work and be sure everything is correct before you attempt to start the engine.

Removal

1   Remove the engine cover by pulling the cover up and off of the ballstuds.

2   Disconnect the cable from the negative terminal of the battery (see Chapter 5).

3   Loosen the right-front wheel bolts, then raise the front of the vehicle and support it securely on jackstands. Remove the right front wheel and the drivebelt splash shield.

4   Drain the engine oil and coolant, then remove the drivebelt (see Chapter 1).

5   Remove the ignition coils (see Chapter 5) and the spark plugs (see Chapter 1).

6   Remove the brake vacuum pump (see Chapter 9).

7   Remove the valve cover (see Section 4).

8   Rotate the crankshaft clockwise and place the no. 1 piston at TDC on the compression stroke (see Section 3).

9   Remove the timing chain cover and camshaft sprocket/phasers and timing chain(s) (see Section 9).

2.0L models

10   Remove the camshaft bearing caps, loosening the bolts a little at a time, in the reverse order of the tightening sequence **(see illustration 10.25)**.

11   Remove the camshafts from the cylinder head.

2.4L models

12   Prepare the special valve spring compressor tool 10259A/B - pre-position the compressor assemblies and stops at the 2.4L markings on the bracket.

13   Remove the first four outer VVAA bolts **(see illustration 12.4)**.

14   Install the special tool onto the cylinder head, adjusting the compressor assemblies to

10.19 Use a micrometer to measure cam lobe height

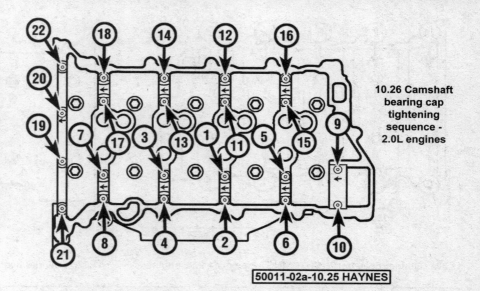

10.26 Camshaft bearing cap tightening sequence - 2.0L engines

50011-02a-10.25 HAYNES

align over the valve springs. Tighten the compressor assemblies until all the valve springs are fully compressed (see illustration).

15 You must place match marks on the camshaft bearing caps to identify them properly for location and direction when installing.

16 Remove the camshaft bearing caps, loosening the bolts a little at a time, in the reverse order of the tightening sequence (see illustration 10.30).

17 Carefully remove the camshaft from the engine.

Inspection

18 Check the camshaft bearing surfaces for pitting, score marks, galling, and abnormal wear. If the bearing surfaces are damaged, the cylinder head will have to be replaced.

19 Compare the camshaft lobe height by measuring each lobe with a micrometer (see illustration). Measure each of the intake lobes and record the measurements and relative positions. Then measure each of the exhaust lobes and record the measurements and relative positions also. This will let you compare all of the intake lobes to one another and all of the exhaust lobes to one another. If the difference between the lobes exceeds 0.005 inch, the camshaft should be replaced. Do not compare intake lobe heights to exhaust lobe heights as lobe lift may be different. Only compare intake lobes to intake lobes and exhaust lobes to exhaust lobes for this comparison.

20 Check the lifters for abnormal wear, pits, galling, score marks, and rough spots. Replace defective parts.

Installation

Caution: *Before starting the engine, carefully rotate the crankshaft by hand through at least two full revolutions (use a socket and breaker bar on the crankshaft pulley center bolt). If you feel any resistance, STOP! There is something wrong - most likely, valves are contacting the pistons. You must find the problem before proceeding.*

2.0L models

21 If removed, have a machine shop press new roller camshaft bearings onto the camshafts.

22 Clean, then coat the camshaft bearing surfaces, camshaft caps, and camshaft with clean engine oil.

23 Carefully install the camshafts onto the bearing surfaces - the dowel pin for the sprocket ends of the camshafts should be pointing straight up.

24 Lubricate the camshaft bearing journals with clean engine oil, then install them in their correct locations on the camshaft - noting their match marks made prior to removal.

25 Install the camshaft bearing cap bolts, partially tighten each cam cap bolt, one turn at a time, to seat the camshafts to the head.

26 Tighten the camshaft bearing cap bolts, a little at a time, in sequence (see illustration), to the torque settings listed in this Chapter's Specifications.

Caution: *Do not torque to specification until the cam bearing caps are in full contact with the cylinder head.*

2.4L models

27 With special tool 10259A still in position, coat the camshaft bearing surfaces, camshaft caps, and camshaft with clean engine oil.

28 Carefully install the camshaft onto the bearing surface - the dowel pin for the sprocket should be pointing straight up.

Note: *If you cannot lay the camshaft easily onto the bearing surfaces because the lifters are contacting it, you must adjust/ compress the lifters further inward with the special tool.*

29 With the rearmost camshaft cap mating surfaces clean and dry, apply RTV sealant to the cap end where it mates with the cylinder head surface.

30 Lubricate the camshaft bearing journals with clean engine oil, then install them in their correct locations on the camshaft - noting their match marks made prior to removal.

31 Tighten the camshaft bearing cap bolts, a little at a time, in sequence (see illustration), to the torque settings listed in this Chapter's Specifications.

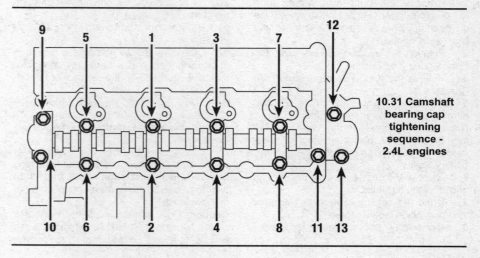

10.31 Camshaft bearing cap tightening sequence - 2.4L engines

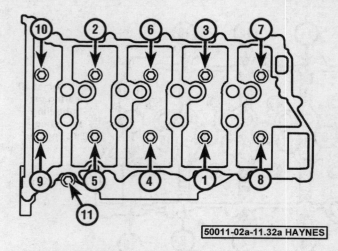

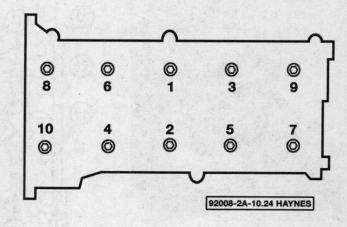

11.32a Cylinder head bolt TIGHTENING sequence - 2.0L engines   **11.32b Cylinder head bolt TIGHTENING sequence - 2.4L engines**

---

32   Loosen the special tool's valve spring compressor assemblies completely, then remove the special tool from the cylinder head.

All models
33   Install the timing chain and sprocket(s) (see Section 9).
34   The remainder of installation is the reverse of removal. Fill the engine with oil (see Chapter 1).

11   Cylinder head - removal and installation

Warning: *Allow the engine to cool completely before beginning this procedure.*
Caution: *It is recommended that new cylinder head bolts be installed upon reassembly.*

Removal
1   Loosen the right-front wheel bolts, then raise the front of the vehicle and support it securely on jackstands.
2   Remove the right-front wheel, then remove the under-vehicle splash shield, the drivebelt splash shield and the inner fender liner (see Chapter 11).
3   Position the number one piston at Top Dead Center (see Section 3).
4   Relieve the fuel system pressure (see Chapter 4).
5   Disconnect the cable from the negative terminal of the battery (see Chapter 5).
Caution: *If equipped with an Intelligent Battery Sensor (IBS), disconnect the IBS connector first before disconnecting the negative battery cable.*
6   Remove the engine cover by pulling it up and off of the ballstuds.
7   Drain the cooling system and remove the spark plugs (see Chapter 1).
8   Remove the air filter housing (see Chapter 4).

9   Remove the coolant reservoir (see Chapter 3).
10   Remove the drivebelt (see Chapter 1).
11   On 2.0L models, remove the turbocharger oil supply, oil return and coolant return lines.
12   On 2.0L models, remove the oil pan (see Section 13) and dipstick tube fastener and remove the tube.
13   Remove the thermostat (see Chapter 3), and on 2.0L models the coolant manifold. On 2.4L models, remove the vacuum pump (see Chapter 9).
14   Remove the intake manifold (see Section 5). Cover the intake ports with duct tape to keep out debris.
15   On 2.4L models, remove the exhaust manifold (see Section 6).
16   On 2.4L models, remove the VVAA assembly (see Section 12).
17   On 2.0L models, remove the high-pressure fuel pump (see Chapter 4).
18   Remove the valve cover (see Section 4).
19   On 2.4L models, remove the water pump pulley, the air conditioning compressor and its bracket (see Chapter 3).
20   Remove the timing chain cover and timing chain (see Section 9).
21   Remove the camshaft(s) (see Section 10).
22   Disengage the wiring harness retainers, then disconnect and remove any connector that may interfere with the removal of the cylinder head.
Note: *On 2.0L models, leave the turbocharger attached to the cylinder head, then once it's out from the vehicle, remove it from the cylinder head.*
23   Loosen the cylinder head bolts, 1/4-turn at a time, in the reverse of the tightening sequence (**see illustration 11.32a or 11.32b**) until they can be removed by hand from the cylinder head.
Caution: *On 2.0L engines, there is one bolt on the left side that must be removed, along with all eight head bolts located on the outside*

of the cylinder head inline with the no. 2 camshaft bearing cap.
Note: *The cylinder head bolt washers are "captured washers," meaning they will stay on the bolts after the bolts have been removed, except for the two nearest the timing chain end of the head. The first two bolts have removable washers; one side is flat and the other side is beveled.*
24   Carefully lift the cylinder head straight up and place the head on wood blocks to prevent damage to the sealing surfaces. If the head sticks to the engine block, dislodge it by placing a wood block against the head casting and tapping the wood with a hammer, or by prying the head with a prybar placed carefully on a casting protrusion.
Caution: *The cylinder head is aluminum, so you must be very careful not to gouge the sealing surfaces.*
Note: *It's a good idea to have the head checked for warpage, even if you're just replacing the gasket.*
25   Once the cylinder head is removed, use a pair of needle-nose pliers to remove the VVT filter from the engine block.
Note: *On 2.0L models the VVT filter is located at the left rear front corner and on 2.4L models, the VVT filter is located at the right front corner of the cylinder head.*
26   Remove all traces of old gasket material from the block and head. Special gasket removal solvents that soften gaskets and make removal much easier are available at auto parts stores. Do not allow anything to fall into the engine. Clean and inspect all threaded fasteners and be sure the threaded holes in the block are clean and dry.

Installation
27   Install a new VVT filter into the hole in the the left rear front corner on 2.0L models or the right front corner of the cylinder block on 2.4L models.
28   Apply clean engine oil to the cylinder head bolt threads prior to installation.

12.4 Remove the first four outer bolts counting from the timing chain end of the engine

12.20 VVAA mounting bolt tightening sequence

29   Place the washers, beveled side up, on the first two head bolts.

30   Apply two small beads of RTV sealant at the timing chain end of the cylinder block face.

Note: *The cylinder head must be installed within 10 minutes after the sealant has been applied.*

31   Place a new gasket and the cylinder head in position on the engine block.

32   Install the head bolts and tighten them in several stages, in the recommended sequence **(see illustrations)**, to the torque listed in this Chapter's Specifications.

Note: *The final step in the tightening procedure requires you to tighten the bolts a specific number of degrees. An angle-torque gauge is available at most auto parts stores and is highly recommended for this procedure. If the tool is not available, paint marks on the bolt heads and tighten them in sequence until the mark is the specified number of degrees from the starting point.*

33   Reinstall the timing chain and cover (see Section 9).

34   The remainder of installation is the reverse of removal.

35   Refill the cooling system and change the engine oil and filter (see Chapter 1). Rotate the crankshaft clockwise slowly by hand through six complete revolutions. Recheck the camshaft timing marks (see Section 9).

36   Start the engine and run it until normal operating temperature is reached. Check for leaks and proper operation.

12   Variable Valve Actuation Assembly (VVAA) - removal and installation (2.4L engines only)

Caution: *This procedure requires the use of MOPAR special tool #10259A/B along with alignment pins #2025300090 - attempting to*

perform this procedure without the use of this special tool will cause damage to the valves, cylinder head or VVAA system.

Note: *The VVAA is made up of a series of complex, non-serviceable parts. It also houses the hydraulic lifters, rocker arms, and oil temperature sensor, which are serviceable. If any further components of the VVAA assembly are malfunctioning, it must be replaced with an entire new assembly.*

1   Remove the valve cover (see Section 4).

2   Disconnect the oil temperature sensor harness connector (near the end of the fuel rail).

3   Disconnect the VVAA electrical connectors (they are adjacent to the fuel injector connectors and have yellow locking tabs).

4   Remove the first four **(see illustration)** outer VVAA bolts (counting from the timing chain end of the engine) before installing the special tool (when the tool is installed you won't be able to access these bolts).

5   Prepare and install the special tool 10259A/B onto the VVAA assembly **(see illustration 10.14)**.

6   Tighten the special tool to compress the valve springs completely off of the camshaft (see Section 10).

7   Once compressed, remove the remaining four bolts from the camshaft side of the VVAA assembly.

8   Install the special dowel pins #2025300090 in place of the bolts that were removed at each end, diagonally from each other.

9   Carefully lift the VVAA assembly up to break the seal, but be careful to avoid gouging the mating surfaces. Remove the VVAA assembly together with the special tool installed. Discard the old gasket.

Caution: *While the VVAA assembly is removed, keep it level and don't tilt it - oil displacement inside the assembly must be kept at a minimal level.*

10   Loosen the compressor assemblies and remove the special tool from the VVAA assembly.

11   Set the VVAA across two blocks of wood while removed from the engine.

12   If desired, the rocker arms can now be replaced.

13   Clean the mating surfaces of the cylinder head and VVAA assembly of all old gasket material.

14   Install the tool onto the VVAA, then compress the valve springs fully. Ensure that the locating pins are still installed in the VVAA.

15   With three of the special alignment pins #2025300090 in place on the cylinder head, using a new gasket, install the VVAA assembly onto the pins. The pins MUST be installed to ensure centering of the VVAA over the valve stems. The VVAA should also be seated evenly over the cylinder head with only a minimal amount of clearance between the two.

16   By visually inspecting through the openings on the camshaft side, make sure that the VVAA plungers are contacting the valve stems evenly before installing the VVAA mounting bolts.

17   Install the four camshaft-side VVAA mounting bolts hand-tight.

18   Remove the special tool then remove the special alignment pins.

19   Install the remaining VVAA mounting bolts hand-tight.

20   Tighten the VVAA mounting bolts, in sequence **(see illustration)**, to the torque settings listed in this Chapter's Specifications.

21   Connect the electrical connectors for the VVAA assembly and oil temperature sensor.

Note: *Be careful not to mix-up the electrical connectors for the oil temperature sensor and any of the VVAA connectors.*

22   Install the valve cover (see Section 4).

23   Remaining installation is the reverse of removal.

13.16 Remove the compressor and mounting bracket bolts

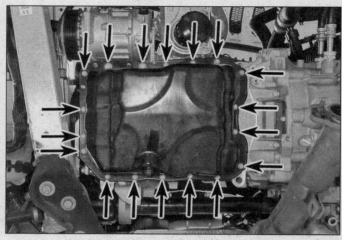

13.17 Oil pan bolt locations

13   Oil pan - removal and installation

Removal

1   Disconnect the cable from the negative terminal of the battery (see Chapter 5).
2   Raise the vehicle and support it securely on jackstands.
3   Drain the engine oil (see Chapter 1).
4   Remove the drivebelt splash shield.
5   Remove the skid plate, if equipped.

2.0L engines

Oil pan (non-Trailhawk) and lower oil pan (Trailhawk)

Note: *On Trailhawk models, it is not necessary to remove the lower oil pan to remove the upper oil pan.*
6   Remove the cross-under pipe (see Chapter 4).
7   Remove the acoustic sound shield fasteners and shield from the oil pan, if equipped.
8   On Trailhawk models, remove the oil dipstick tube fastener and remove the tube.
9   Remove the electric vacuum pump bracket fasteners and move the vacuum pump away from the transfer case (see Chapter 9).
10   Remove the transfer case support bracket bolts and bracket.
11   Remove the four screw covers from the oil pan at the transaxle then remove the four vertical bolts now visible.
12   Remove the oil pan bolts, then carefully separate the oil pan from the block. Use a putty knife or gasket scraper to loosen the seal around the pan at the prying point ONLY, but don't pry between the block and the pan or damage to the sealing surfaces could occur and oil leaks may develop.

Lower oil pan (Trailhawk models)

13   Remove the oil filter (see Chapter 1).
14   Remove the oil pan bolts, then carefully separate the lower oil pan-to-upper oil pan. Use a putty knife or gasket scraper to loosen the seal around the pan.

15   Thoroughly clean the lower oil pan and sealing surfaces on the upper oil pan. Use a scraper to remove all traces of old gasket material. Check the oil pan sealing surface for distortion. Straighten or replace as necessary, then wipe the gasket surfaces of the pan and upper oil pan with a rag soaked in brake system cleaner.

2.4L engines

16   Remove the air conditioning compressor and the lower mounting bracket (**see illustration**).
Warning: *Do not disconnect the refrigerant lines. Support the compressor with a length of wire.*
17   Remove the oil pan bolts (**see illustration**), then carefully separate the oil pan from the block. Use a putty knife or gasket scraper to loosen the seal around the pan, but don't pry between the block and the pan or damage to the sealing surfaces could occur and oil leaks may develop.
18   Thoroughly clean the oil pan and sealing surfaces on the block and pan. Use a scraper to remove all traces of old gasket material. Gasket removal solvents are available at auto parts stores and may prove helpful. Check the oil pan sealing surface for distortion. Straighten or replace as necessary, then wipe the gasket surfaces of the pan and block with a rag soaked in brake system cleaner.

Installation

19   Apply a 1/8-inch bead of RTV sealant at the cylinder block-to-front cover joint at the oil pan flange.
20   Apply a 1/8-inch wide by 1/16-inch high bead of RTV sealant to the sealing surface of the pan. Install the pan and the bolts, then tighten the bolts finger-tight.
Note: *The oil pan must be installed and tightened within 10 minutes of applying the RTV sealant.*
21   Working side-to-side from the center out, tighten the oil pan bolts to the torque listed in this Chapter's Specifications.
22   The remainder of installation is the reverse of removal.

23   Refill the crankcase with the correct quantity and grade of oil, then run the engine and check for leaks.

14   Oil pump and Balance Shaft Module (BSM) and chain - removal, inspection and installation

Note: *On 2.0L engines there are two balance shafts used on each side of the crankshaft. The oil pump is mounted to the front of the left balance shaft.*
Note: *On 2.4L engines the oil pump is an integral component of the balance shaft module and can't be removed or disassembled from the module. If there is a problem with the oil pump or the oil pump drive gear bolt is removed, the balance shaft module must be replaced*

2.0L engines

Removal

Oil pump drive chain

1   Remove the timing chain cover and camshaft timing chain (see Section 9).
2   Verify that the crankshaft sprocket timing mark is at the 6 o'clock position and the mark is in the middle of the two oil pump drive chain colored timing links. If the colored links are hard to see, make sure you mark them if you're reusing the chain.
3   Verify that the oil pump sprocket gear timing mark is just past the 2 o'clock position and is aligned with the single chain colored timing link. If the colored link is hard to see make sure you mark it if you're reusing the chain.
4   Verify that the balance shaft sprocket timing mark is at approximately the 11 o'clock position and is aligned with the single chain colored timing link. If the colored link is hard to see make sure you mark it if you're reusing the chain.
5   Press the oil pump drive chain tensioner guide/shoe inwards then insert tensioner pin

tool no. 8514 to hold the tensioner in the compressed position.

Note: *A drill bit can be used if the special tool is not available.*

6 Remove the oil pump drive chain tensioner bolts and remove the tensioner with the pin tool in place.

7 Remove the two oil pump drive chain guide plates fasteners then remove both chain guides.

8 Lift the chain off of the oil pump drive sprocket and balance shaft, then the crankshaft sprocket, and remove the chain guide next to the oil pump drive sprocket.

9 Remove the timing chain guide mounting bolts and the guide from the front of the engine.

Oil pump

Note: *Several special tools are needed to replace the oil pump. It is not possible to preload and time the oil pump to the balance shaft without special tool kit no. 202710090.*

10 Remove the oil pump drive chain (see Steps 1 through 9).

11 Hold the oil pump sprocket from turning using a two pin spanner type wrench and remove the mounting bolt. Note which side of the gear is facing outwards; the timing mark is only on one side but the sprocket can be installed on either side.

12 Remove the oil pump sprocket friction shim from the end of the oil pump driveshaft.

13 Support the engine above, then remove the oil pan, if not already done.

14 Disconnect the oil pump displacement control solenoid electrical connector from the backside of the pump.

15 Remove the oil pump mounting bolts from the front of the pump and withdraw the pump from the cavity on the side of the engine block.

16 Remove and replace the two seals on the back of the oil pump.

Left balance shaft

17 Remove the oil pump (see Steps 10 through 15).

18 Remove the balance shaft mounting bolt and withdraw the left balance shaft from the engine block.

19 Once the balance shaft is removed, unclip the needle bearing shaft retainers and replace both balance shaft needle bearings from the ends of the balance shaft.

Right balance shaft

20 Remove the engine oil pump drive chain (see Steps 1 through 9).

21 Remove the balance shaft mounting bolt and withdraw the left balance shaft from the engine block.

22 Once the balance shaft is removed, unclip the needle bearing shaft retainers and replace both balance shaft needle bearings from the ends of the balance shaft.

Installation

Right balance shaft

23 Apply clean engine oil to the new needle bearings and cage.

24 Install the bearings and cage onto the balance shaft and snap the cage into the locked position.

25 Insert the balance shaft into the cylinder block, then tighten the mounting bolt to the torque listed in this Chapter's Specifications.

26 Install the oil pump drive chain (see Steps 46 through 51).

Left balance shaft

27 Apply clean engine oil to the new bearing shaft needle bearings and cage.

28 Install the bearings and cage onto the balance shaft and snap the cage into the locked position.

29 Insert the balance shaft into the cylinder block then tighten the mounting bolt to the torque listed in this Chapter's Specifications.

30 Install the oil pump (see Steps 31 through 45).

Oil pump

31 Install new O-ring type gaskets to the oil pump.

32 Position one oil pump wrench no. 2027103090 on the outer gear resting against the engine oil pump displacement control solenoid and the second oil pump wrench no. 2027103090 on the engine oil pump drive shaft.

33 Rotate the engine oil pump drive shaft to align the two gears and install the oil pump gear teeth holder no. 2027104090 to lock the gears in this preload position.

Note: *When the gears are properly aligned, the inner tab is positioned in the left half of the slot and the holder is positioned between the gear clip alignment marks.*

34 Once the preload is set and the gears are locked into position, remove the wrenches used for preloading, then attach the cable portion of the gear tooth holder to the holder so it can be removed once the pump is installed.

35 Install the oil pump shaft alignment tool no. 202710590 onto the end of the oil pump shaft.

36 Insert the two long special alignment pins no. 2027101090 through the case and the oil pump mounting holes.

37 Feed the cable end of the gear teeth holder through the openings at the front of the engine then around and back, out through the opening at the front of the engine above the crankshaft, then slide the oil pump onto the alignment pins.

38 As the oil pump is installed, the oil pump alignment shaft tool will rotate clockwise until it comes in contact with the lower boss on the pump. Once the alignment tool makes contact and the pump is seated, the pump and balance shaft gear are meshed properly. If the alignment tool hits the boss before the pump is seated or the pump is seated and the alignment tool is not against the boss, the pump is not correctly timed and must be removed.

39 Once the pump is properly aligned and seated, hold the pump against the engine and install three mounting bolts hand-tight.

40 Pull the cable and tooth holder off and out through the openings in the engine.

41 Remove the alignment pins, install the remaining mounting bolts and tighten the bolts in a star pattern to the torque listed in this Chapter's Specifications.

42 Temporarily install the oil pump drive gear on the oil pump drive shaft then insert the longer of the two alignment pins no. 2027101090 through the balance shaft alignment hole. Verify that the oil pump reference mark on the body of the pump and the mark on the oil pump drive gear mark are aligned. If the oil pump and balance shaft timing is not correct, repeat Steps 32 through 40.

43 Connect the electrical connector to the oil pump displacement control solenoid.

44 Install the oil pump sprocket and tighten the bolt to the torque listed in this Chapter's Specifications.

45 Install the oil pump drive chain (see Steps 46 through 51).

Oil pump drive chain

46 Verify the oil pump drive chain mark on the crankshaft sprocket is at the 6 o'clock position.

47 Install the drive chain guide and loosely install the fasteners.

48 Install the chain starting at the crankshaft, align the two colored links, one on each side of the crankshaft timing mark, then loop the chain over the oil pump drive sprocket and match the mark on the sprocket with the single plated link on the chain at approximately the 2 o'clock position. Place the chain over the right balance shaft sprocket, aligning the single colored link and the timing mark at approximately the 2 o'clock position.

49 Once all of the timing marks and colored links on the chain are aligned, tighten the chain guides to the torque listed in this Chapter's Specifications.

50 Install the oil pump drive chain tensioner and tighten the bolts to the torque listed in this Chapter's Specifications, then remove the tensioner retaining pin and release the piston.

51 Remaining installation is the reverse of removal (see Steps 79 though 85).

2.4L engines

Removal

52 Relieve the fuel pressure (see Chapter 4), then disconnect the cable from the negative terminal of the battery (see Chapter 5).

53 Rotate the engine to Top Dead Center (TDC) for #1 cylinder on the compression stroke (see Section 3).

54 Loosen the right-front wheel lug nuts, then raise the front of the vehicle and support it securely on jackstands.

55 Remove the right-front wheel, then remove the splash shield and inner fender splash shield (see Chapter 11).

56 Remove the valve cover (see Section 4).

57 Remove the oil pan (see Section 13).

58 Remove the timing chain cover, timing chain and crankshaft sprocket (see Section 9).

59 If the engine has moved from TDC, temporarily install the crankshaft pulley bolt. Turn the crankshaft with the bolt to TDC number 1 to align the timing marks on the crankshaft and camshaft sprockets. Rotate the engine clockwise only, until the crankshaft keyway aligns with the line made where the engine block and ladder frame meet.

Note: *The sprocket timing mark is closer to the 3 o'clock position and the crankshaft keyway is aligned at the 9 o'clock position, pointing to the line made where the engine block and ladder frame meet.*

Note: *If the timing chain plated links are faded or can no longer be seen, mark the links to the corresponding timing marks before removing the chain (if you plan to reuse the old chain).*

60   The camshaft dowel at the hub of the sprocket should be facing 90-degrees upwards from the horizontal cylinder head surface.

Note: *Use paint or a permanent marker to mark the direction of rotation on all chains before removing them so they can be installed in the same position.*

61   Remove the timing chain tensioner mounting bolts and remove the tensioner and guide from the left side of the timing chain; the tensioner will not come apart when it is removed.

62   Remove the timing chain from the camshaft sprocket and crankshaft sprocket.

63   If necessary, remove the oil pump/ balance shaft chain (see Section 14), then remove the crankshaft sprocket (see Section 8).

64   If necessary, remove the chain guide fasteners and guide.

65   Remove the oil splash shield fasteners and splash shield covering the balance shaft/ oil pump drive sprocket.

66   Align the drive chain plated links with the timing marks on the crankshaft sprocket (approximately 12 o'clock position) and the Balance Shaft Module (BCM) drive gear (approximately 7 o'clock position). The drive gear mark should be aligned with the mark on the oil pump/balance shaft module body.

Note: *If the marks or plated links can't be found, mark the oil pump/Balance Shaft Module (BSM) drive chain to the BSM drive sprocket, the crankshaft sprocket and the oil pump/ balance shaft module body, so the chain can be installed in the same position. The mark on the oil pump drive gear must align with the mark on the oil pump/balance shaft module.*

67   Press the oil pump/BSM tensioner piston back into the tensioner body. While holding the piston in, insert special tool #9703 or a 3 mm drill bit into the hole in the side of the tensioner to retain the piston in the locked position.

Caution: *Do not remove the oil pump/BSM drive sprocket.*

68   Remove the BSM mounting bolts, in the reverse of the tightening sequence **(see illustration 14.77).** There are two different length bolts that are used.

69   Lower the rear of the balance shaft module, remove the timing chain from the sprocket, then remove the BSM.

70   Remove the chain from the crankshaft sprocket.

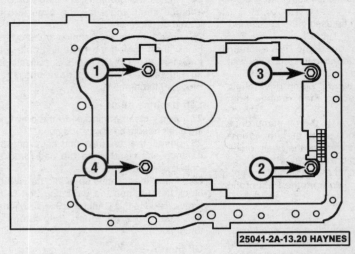

14.77 Balance Shaft Module (BSM) bolt **TIGHTENING** sequence

25041-2A-13.20 HAYNES

Inspection

71   Two different lengths of mounting bolts can be used on the BSM: 180 mm and 185 mm length bolts. The 180 mm bolts must be discarded and replaced with new bolts. Measure the BSM mounting bolts and replace the bolts as needed.

72   Place a straightedge or ruler against the threads of each 185 mm mounting bolt; if there is a gap or space between the edges of the threads and the straightedge, the mounting bolt(s) must be replaced. Apply clean engine oil to the mounting bolt threads prior to installation.

Installation

73   Clean the bolt holes for the BSM mounting bolts.

74   Place the timing chain over the crankshaft sprocket and align the plated link with the timing mark on the sprocket, or marks made prior to removal.

75   Lift up the BSM and place the drive sprocket into the timing chain, aligning the plated link with the timing mark on the drive gear, or marks made prior to removal and the BSM drive gear mark with the mark on the body of the BSM. Pivot the BSM up into place against the ladder frame on the engine block.

76   While holding the BSM in place, insert the mounting bolts and tighten by hand in several even stages.

77   Tighten the bolts in several stages, in the recommended sequence **(see illustration),** to the torque listed in this Chapter's Specifications.

Note: *The final step in the tightening procedure requires you to tighten the bolts a specific number of degrees. An angle-torque gauge is available at most auto parts stores and is highly recommended for this procedure. If the tool is not available, paint marks on the bolt heads and tighten them in sequence until the mark is the specified number of degrees from the starting point.*

78   Remove the pin from the tensioner and

release the piston, then verify that the timing marks are aligned.

79   Install the timing chain and timing cover (see Section 9).

80   Install the oil pan (see Section 13).

81   Install the valve cover (see Section 4).

82   The remainder of installation is the reverse of removal.

83   Install a new oil filter and engine oil (see Chapter 1).

84   Start the engine and check for oil pressure and leaks.

85   Recheck the engine oil level.

---

15   Driveplate - removal and installation

Removal

1   Remove the transaxle (see Chapter 7A).

2   To ensure correct alignment during reinstallation, mark the position of the driveplate to the crankshaft before removal **(see illustration).**

3   Remove the bolts that secure the driveplate to the crankshaft **(see illustration).** A tool is available at most auto parts stores to hold the driveplate while loosening the bolts. If the tool is not available, wedge a screwdriver in the ring gear teeth to jam the driveplate.

Caution: *Do not use an impact socket or thick walled socket to remove the driveplate, possible damage to the crankshaft, internal engine or transmission may happen.*

Caution: *The manufacturer recommends replacing the driveplate mounting bolts.*

4   Remove the large washer and the driveplate from the crankshaft.

Note: *On 2.0L models the large washer is permanently attached to the driveplate and can't be removed separately.*

5   Clean and inspect the mating surfaces of the driveplate and the crankshaft. If the crankshaft rear main seal is leaking, replace it before reinstalling the driveplate (see Section 16).

15.2 Mark the relative position of the driveplate to the crankshaft...

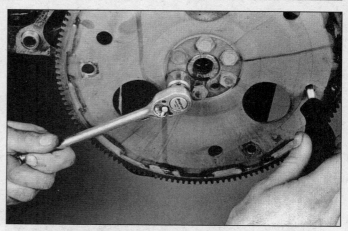

15.3 ... and, using an appropriate tool to hold the driveplate, remove the bolts

Installation

6   Position the driveplate against the crankshaft. Align the previously applied match marks. Before installing the bolts, apply thread locking compound to the threads.

7   Hold the driveplate with the holding tool, or wedge a screwdriver in the ring gear teeth to keep the driveplate from turning as you tighten the bolts to the torque listed in this Chapter's Specifications.

Caution: *Do not use an impact socket or thick walled socket to install the driveplate, to avoid possible damage to the crankshaft.*

8   The remainder of installation is the reverse of removal.

16   Rear main oil seal - replacement

1   Remove the driveplate (see Section 15).

2   Use a screwdriver wrapped with tape to pry out the seal, being careful not to gouge or nick the crankshaft or housings.

3   Lubricate the crankshaft seal journal and the lip of the new seal with multi-purpose grease.

4   Install the seal with the seal lip toward the engine and the dust seal toward the transaxle.

5   Tap the seal into place using a seal driver to make sure that it doesn't become tilted.

6   Install the seal so that its rear edge is flush with the face of the engine block, or up to 0.020 inch recessed.

7   The remainder of installation is the reverse of removal.

17   Engine mounts - check and replacement

Check

1   During the check, the engine must be raised slightly to remove the weight from the mounts.

2   Raise the vehicle and support it securely on jackstands. Remove the front wheels and tires. Position two jacks, one under the crankshaft pulley and the other under the transaxle bellhousing. Place a block of wood between a floor jack head and the crankshaft pulley or bellhousing, then carefully raise the engine/transaxle just enough to take the weight off the mounts.

Warning: *DO NOT place any part of your body under the engine when it's supported only by a jack!*

3   Check the mounts to see if the rubber is cracked, hardened or separated from the metal sleeve in the center of the mount.

4   Check for relative movement between the mount bracket and the engine, subframe or chassis (use a large screwdriver or pry-bar to attempt to move the mounts). If movement is noted, lower the engine and tighten the mount fasteners.

Replacement

5   Remove the engine cover.

6   Disconnect the cable from the negative terminal of the battery (see Chapter 5), then raise the vehicle and support it securely on jackstands.

7   Remove the engine splash shield from under the vehicle.

Left mount

8   Remove the battery and battery tray (see Chapter 5).

9   Remove the cover of the underhood relay center and remove the mounting bolts. Unclip the main wiring harness retainers, then move the harness and relay center out of the way.

10   Support the transaxle with a floor jack and wooden block placed between the jack and the transaxle.

11   Raise the transaxle enough to take the weight off of the mount.

12   Remove the mount-to-frame rail bolts **(see illustration)**.

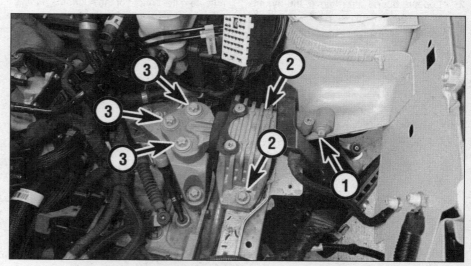

17.12 Left mount details - 2.4L engine shown

1 *Mount-to-strut tower bolt*
2 *Mount-to-frame rail bolts*
3 *Mount-to-transaxle bolts*

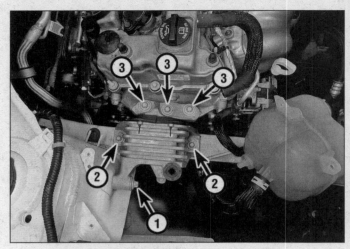

17.19 Right mount details - 2.4L engine shown

1 Mount-to-strut tower bolt   3 Mount-to-transaxle bolts
2 Mount-to-frame rail bolts

17.28 Rear mount (Torque strut) details - 2.4L engine shown

1 Rear mount nuts   3 Rear mount through bolt
2 Rear mount bracket bolts   and nut

13   Remove the mount-to-transaxle bolts.
14   Loosen, but do not remove the tranaxle mount-to-strut tower bolt and remove the mount.
15   Installation is the reverse of removal. Tighten the fasteners to the torque values listed in this Chapter's Specifications.

Right mount

16   Remove the coolant expansion tank (see Chapter 3).
17   Remove the air cleaner assembly (see Chapter 4).
18   Support the engine with a floor jack and wooden block placed between the jack and the engine.
19   Remove the mount-to-timing chain cover bracket bolts **(see illustration)**.
20   Remove the mount-to-frame bolts.
21   Loosen, but do not remove, the mount-to-strut tower bolt, then remove the mount.

22   Installation is the reverse of removal. Tighten the mounting bolts to the torque listed in this Chapter's Specifications, in the following order:

   a) mount-to-strut tower bolt
   b) mount-to-frame bolts
   c) mount-to-timing chain cover bolts

23   The remainder of installation is the reverse of removal.

Rear mount (Torque strut)

24   Remove the left side wheel well splash shield (see Chapter 11).
25   Disconnect the negative battery cable from the transaxle.
26   Remove the downstream oxygen sensor (see Chapter 6).
27   Remove the skid plate, if equipped.
28   Remove the rear mount (torque strut) nuts from the bottom of the subframe and discard the nuts **(see illustration)**.

29   Remove the rear mount center bolt.
30   Support the engine with a floor jack and wooden block placed between the jack and the engine and slightly raise the transaxle.
31   Remove the rear mount-to-transaxle bracket through-bolt.
32   Using a large prybar, move the engine forward until the rear mount (torque strut) can be removed from the rear mount bracket.
33   Install the new mount into the bracket, then install the through-bolt and new nut, but don't tighten it yet.
34   Align the rear mount end to the transaxle, then install and tighten the bolt/nut to the torque listed in this Chapter's Specifications.
35   Tighten the through-bolt to the torque listed in this Chapter's Specifications.
36   The remainder of installation is the reverse of removal.

Chapter 2 Part B
3.2L V6 engine

Contents

Specifications

General

Displacement	195 cubic inches
Bore	3.583 inches
Stroke	3.268 inches
Compression ratio	10.7: 1
Cylinder numbers (drivebelt end-to-transaxle end)	
Rear bank	1-3-5
Front bank	2-4-6
Firing order	1-2-3-4-5-6
Oil pressure	
At idle speed	5 psi (minimum)
At 1,200 to 3,000 rpm	30 to 139 psi

Front of Vehicle

$\begin{array}{ccc} 1 & 3 & 5 \\ 2 & 4 & 6 \end{array}$

30013-1-specs HAYNES

Cylinder and coil terminal locations

Camshaft

Bore diameter	
Cam tower 1	1.2606 to 1.2615 inches
Cam tower 2, 3, and 4	0.9457 to 0.9465 inch
Bearing journal diameter	
No. 1	1.2589 to 1.2596 inches
No. 2, 3, and 4	0.9440 to 0.9447 inch
Bearing clearance	
No. 1	0.0001 to 0.0026 inch
No. 2, 3, and 4	0.0009 to 0.0025 inch
End play	0.003 to 0.010 inch

Cylinder head

Gasket thickness (compressed)	0.019 to 0.024 inch
Warpage limit	0.0035 inch

Torque specifications

Note: One foot-pound (ft-lb) of torque is equivalent to 12 inch-pounds (in-lbs) of torque. Torque values below approximately 15 ft-lbs are expressed in inch-pounds, since most foot-pound torque wrenches are not accurate at these smaller values.

Ft-lbs (unless otherwise indicated)

Crankshaft pulley bolt (M16 bolt)	
Step 1	30
Step 2	Tighten an additional 105-degrees
Cylinder head bolts* (in sequence - **see illustrations 10.29a and 10.29b**)	
Note: *When using a new block follow steps 1 through 9. If using a used block follow Steps 6 through 9.*	
Step 1	22
Step 2	33
Step 3	33
Step 4***	Tighten an additional 125-degrees
Step 5	Loosen all in reverse of tightening sequence
Step 6	22
Step 7	33
Step 8	Tighten an additional 40-degrees
Step 9	Tighten an additional 90-degrees
Drivebelt idler sprocket bolt	18
Driveplate-to-crankshaft bolts*	70
Catalytic converter to cylinder head fasteners	27
Exhaust crossover bolts	21
Intake manifold (upper) bracket M6 bolts	80 in-lbs
Intake manifold (upper) bracket M8 bolts	177 in-lbs
Intake manifold (upper) retaining M6 bolts**	89 in-lbs
Intake manifold (lower)-to-block M6 bolts	106 in-lbs
Oil cooler	
Bolts	35 in-lbs
Screws	106 in-lbs
Oil pan drain plug	20
Oil pan	
Lower pan-to-upper pan nut/bolts	80 in-lbs
Upper pan-to-cylinder block (M8 bolts)	17
Upper pan-to-transaxle bolts	37
Rear main oil seal-to-retainer bolts	106 in-lbs
Oil pump pick-up tube mounting bolts	106 in-lbs
Oil pump cover (plate) screws	105 in-lbs
Oil pump-to-engine block fasteners	106 in-lbs
Rear main oil seal retainer bolts	105 in-lbs
Timing chain cover bolts	
M6 bolts	106 in-lbs
M8 bolts	18
M10 bolts	41
Timing chain tensioner bolts	106 in-lbs
Timing chain guide bolts	106 in-lbs
Timing sprocket splash shield bolts	35 in-lbs
Camshaft oil control valves - Cam phaser (sprocket)	111
Oil pump timing chain sprocket (T45)	18
Valve cover-to-cylinder head M6 bolts	106 in-lbs
Water pump bolts	See Chapter 3

* Use new bolts.
** Apply a non-hardening thread-locking compound to the bolt threads before installation.
*** If the torque can't be completed in one rotation, you can break Step 4 into two steps. Tighten the bolts
    an additional 35-degrees then tighten the bolts an additional 90-degrees.

1 General information

1   This Part of Chapter 2 is devoted to in-vehicle repair procedures for the 3.2L V6 engines.

2   The 3.2 liter (195.3 CID) flexible fuel V-6 engine features Variable Valve Timing (VVT), Dual Overhead Camshafts (DOHC) and a high-pressure die-cast aluminum cylinder block with steel liners in a 60-degree configuration. The 3.2 liter engine has a chain driven variable discharge oil pump with a two-stage pressure regulator for improved fuel economy. The exhaust manifolds are integrated into the cylinder heads for reduced weight.

Caution: *This engine is not of a freewheeling design and severe engine damage will occur if the timing chain breaks.*

3   The cylinders are numbered from front to rear. The rear bank is numbered 1, 3, 5 and the front bank is numbered 2, 4, 6. The firing order is 1–2–3–4–5–6.

4   Information concerning engine removal and installation can be found in Chapter 2C. The following repair procedures are based on the assumption that the engine is installed in the vehicle. If the engine has been removed from the vehicle and mounted on a stand, many of the steps outlined in this Part of Chapter 2 do not apply.

2 Repair operations possible with the engine in the vehicle

1   Many major repair operations can be done without removing the engine from the vehicle.

2   Clean the engine compartment and the exterior of the engine with degreaser before any work is done. It'll make the job easier and help keep dirt out of internal parts of the engine.

3   It may be helpful to remove the hood to improve engine access when repairs are performed (see Chapter 11). Cover the fenders to prevent damage to the paint. Special pads are available, but an old bedspread or blanket will also work.

4   If vacuum, exhaust, oil, or coolant leaks develop, indicating a need for gasket or seal replacement, the repairs can generally be done with the engine in the vehicle. The intake and exhaust manifold gaskets, timing chain cover gasket, oil pan gasket, crankshaft oil seals, and cylinder head gaskets are all accessible with the engine in the vehicle.

5   Exterior engine components, such as the intake and exhaust manifolds, the oil pan, the oil pump, the timing chain cover, the water pump, the starter motor, the alternator, and fuel system components can be removed for repair with the engine in the vehicle.

6   Cylinder heads can be removed without pulling the engine. Valve component servicing can also be done with the engine in the vehicle. Replacement of the timing chain and sprockets is also possible with the engine

4.4 Lift the insulator up and off of the retaining posts, then remove it from the front valve cover

in the vehicle, as is camshaft and valvetrain removal and installation.

7   Repair or replacement of piston rings, pistons, connecting rods, and rod bearings is possible with the engine in the vehicle, however, this practice is not recommended because of the cleaning and preparation work that must be done to the components.

3 Top Dead Center (TDC) for number one piston - locating

1   Top Dead Center (TDC) is the highest point in the cylinder that each piston reaches as it travels up the cylinder bore. Each piston reaches TDC on the compression stroke and again on the exhaust stroke, but TDC generally refers to piston position on the compression stroke.

2   Positioning the piston(s) at TDC is an essential part of certain procedures such as camshaft and timing chain/sprocket removal.

3   Before beginning this procedure, be sure to place the transaxle in Neutral and apply the parking brake or block the rear wheels. Disconnect the cable from the negative terminal of the battery (see Chapter 5). Remove the ignition coils (see Chapter 5) and the spark plugs (see Chapter 1).

4   Install a compression pressure gauge in the number one spark plug hole (see Chapter 2C). It should be a gauge with a screw-in fitting and a hose at least six inches long.

5   Rotate the crankshaft using a socket and breaker bar on the crankshaft pulley bolt while observing for pressure on the compression gauge. The moment the gauge shows pressure, indicates that the number one cylinder has begun the compression stroke.

6   Once the compression stroke has begun, TDC for the compression stroke is reached by bringing the piston to the top of the cylinder.

Note: *If a compression gauge is not available, you can simply place a blunt object over the spark plug hole and listen for compression as the engine is rotated. Once compression at the No.1 spark plug hole is noted, the remainder of the Step is the same.*

7   This engine is not equipped with external components (crankshaft pulley, flywheel, timing hole, etc.) that are marked to identify the position of number 1 TDC. Therefore, the only method to double-check the location of TDC number 1 is to remove the valve cover to access the camshaft sprockets and alignment marks (see Section 8).

8   After the number one piston has been positioned at TDC on the compression stroke, TDC for any of the remaining cylinders can be located by turning the crankshaft 120-degrees and following the firing order (refer to this Chapter's Specifications). For example, rotating the engine 120-degrees past TDC number 1 will put the engine at TDC compression for cylinder number 2.

4 Valve covers - removal and installation

Removal

1   Disconnect the cable from the negative terminal of the battery (see Chapter 5).

2   Remove the engine cover.

3   Remove the upper intake manifold (see Section 5).

Note: *Cover open ports on the intake to prevent debris from entering the engine.*

Caution: *Once the valve covers are removed, the magnetic timing wheels are exposed(see illustration 9.9). The magnetic timing wheels on the camshafts must not come in contact with any type of magnet or magnetic field. If contact is made, the timing wheels will need to be replaced.*

4   Remove insulator from the front valve cover **(see illustration)**.

5   Before removing the variable valve timing solenoids from the front of each valve cover, mark them appropriately so they can be reinstalled in their original locations, then remove them (see Chapter 6).

6   Disconnect the wiring harness retainers from the valve cover and move the harnesses out of the way.

7   Remove the ignition coils on both sides of the engine (see Chapter 5).

4.10 Front valve cover mounting bolts

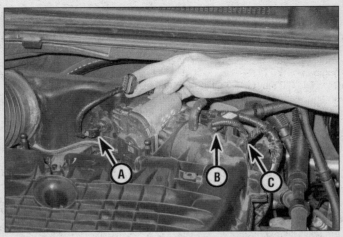

5.6 Disconnect the ETC connectors (A), the MAP sensor (B) and the electrical harness (C) retainer

8   Mark the Camshaft Position (CMP) sensors to each valve cover so they can be reinstalled in their original locations, then remove the sensor(s) (see Chapter 6).
9   Remove the PCV valve from the rear cover (see Chapter 1).
10   Remove the valve cover fasteners **(see illustration)** and remove the cover(s).
Caution: *If the cover is stuck to the cylinder head, tap one end with a block of wood and a hammer to jar it loose. If that doesn't work, slip a flexible putty knife between the cylinder head and cover to break the gasket seal. Don't pry at the cover-to-cylinder head joint or damage to the sealing surfaces may occur (leading to future oil leaks).*
11   Remove the valve cover gasket, then remove the spark plug tube seals.
Note: *The cover gaskets can be reused if they are not damaged.*

Installation

12   The mating surfaces of each cylinder head and valve cover must be perfectly clean when the covers are installed. Use a gasket scraper to remove all traces of sealant and old gasket material, then clean the mating surfaces with brake system cleaner. If there's sealant or oil on the mating surfaces when the cover is installed, oil leaks may develop.
13   Inspect the spark plug tube seals; if damaged, carefully remove the seals using an appropriate pry tool. Position the new seal with the part number facing the valve cover, then use a socket that contacts the outer edge to drive the seal in place.
14   Apply a dab of RTV sealant at the joints where the engine front cover meets the cylinder head.
15   Install the valve cover and bolts, then tighten the bolts to the torque listed in this Chapter's Specifications.
16   The remainder of installation is the reverse of removal.

5   Intake manifolds - removal and installation

Warning: *Wait until the engine is completely cool before beginning this procedure.*

Removal

1   If you will be removing the lower intake manifold, relieve the fuel system pressure (see Chapter 4).
2   Disconnect the cable from the negative terminal of the battery (see Chapter 5).
3   Remove the engine cover.

Upper intake manifold

4   Remove the upper radiator hose retainer from the upper intake manifold.
5   Remove the intake resonator (see Chapter 4).
6   Disconnect the wiring harness from the MAP sensor and the Electronic Throttle Control (ETC) **(see illustration)** and secure the harnesses out of the way.
7   Disconnect the PCV valve hose (see Chapter 1), vapor purge hose and brake booster hoses.
8   Disconnect the wiring harness retainers from the upper intake support bracket and the retainer from the stud bolt **(see illustration)**.
9   Remove the nuts and stud bolt, then remove the upper intake manifold bracket **(see illustration)**.

5.8 Pry the wiring harness retainer off of the bracket stud

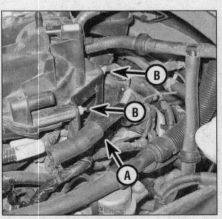

5.9 Remove the stud bolt (A) and bracket nuts (B), and remove the bracket

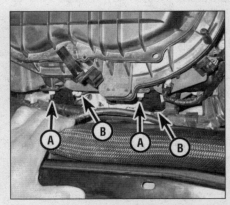

5.11 Pull the upper radiator hose back, remove the support bracket upper nuts (A), loosen the lower nuts (B) and remove the brackets from the upper intake manifold

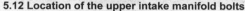

5.12 Location of the upper intake manifold bolts

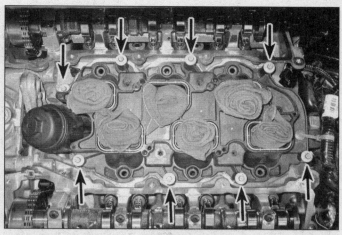

5.19 Lower intake manifold bolt locations

10   Remove the nut from the bracket on the heater core return tube.

11   Remove the support bracket-to-upper manifold nuts (see illustration).

12   Loosen, but do not remove, the bolts on the manifold, and remove the upper intake manifold (see illustration).

13   Discard the six upper-to-lower intake manifold seals, and cover the open intake ports to prevent debris from entering the engine.

14   If required, remove the insulator from the front valve cover (see illustration 4.4).

Lower intake manifold

15   Remove the upper intake manifold (see Steps 4 through 14).

16   Disconnect the fuel line at the fuel rail (see Chapter 4).

17   Remove the fuel rail and fuel injectors (see Chapter 4).

Note: *If desired, the lower intake manifold can be removed with the injectors and fuel rail in place. Be careful not to damage the fuel injectors once the manifold is removed.*

18   Pry the wiring harness retainer from the end of the manifold and move the harness out

of the way.

19   Remove the lower intake manifold bolts (see illustration), and remove the manifold from the cylinder heads.

20   Discard the six manifold-to-cylinder head seals.

Installation
Lower intake manifold

Note: *The mating surfaces of the cylinder heads, cylinder block, and the intake manifold must be perfectly clean when the lower intake manifold is installed. Gasket removal solvents are available at most auto parts stores and may be helpful when removing old gasket material that's stuck to the cylinder heads, cylinder block and lower intake manifold (the lower intake manifold is made of aluminum - aggressive scraping can cause damage). Be sure to follow the instructions printed on the solvent container.*

21   Use a gasket scraper to remove all traces of sealant and old gasket material, then clean the mating surfaces with lacquer thinner or acetone. If there's old sealant or oil on the mating surfaces when the lower intake

manifold is installed, oil or vacuum leaks may develop. Use a vacuum cleaner to remove gasket material that falls into the intake ports or the lifter valley.

22   If removed, install the fuel injectors and the fuel rail (see Chapter 4).

23   Install new intake manifold seals to the manifold.

Note: *Remove any rags or towels used in the manifold ports.*

24   Carefully lower the lower intake manifold into place (see illustration) and install the mounting bolts finger-tight.

25   Tighten the mounting bolts in steps, following the tightening sequence (see illustration), to the torque listed in this Chapter's Specifications.

26   Install the upper intake manifold. The remainder of installation is the reverse of removal.

Upper intake manifold

27   Check the condition of the rubber seals that are installed into each intake runner on the upper intake manifold. If they are damaged, replace the seals in the upper intake manifold.

5.24 Install the manifold making sure the new intake seals do not fall out of the manifold

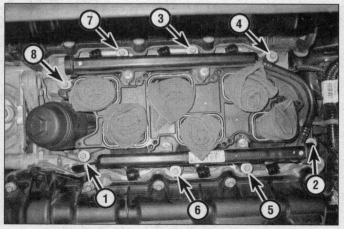

5.25 Lower intake manifold tightening sequence

5.30 Upper intake manifold bolt tightening sequence

6.5 Using a special holding tool to prevent the crankshaft from turning, loosen, then remove the bolt

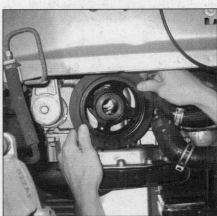

6.6 Slide the pulley from the end of the crankshaft; a puller shouldn't be required

7.2 Use a hook tool to pry the seal from the timing chain cover

7.3 Another way of removing an old oil seal is to screw a self-tapping screw partially into the seal, then use pliers as a lever to pull it from the engine

28   Place the insulator on the mounting pins, if removed.

29   Install the upper intake manifold onto the lower intake manifold while pulling the bolts up.

Note: *The bolts are specially made for the composite material and should be turned slowly to prevent damage to the upper intake manifold.*

30   Tighten the mounting bolts in sequence **(see illustration)** to the torque listed in this Chapter's Specifications.

31   The remainder of installation is the reverse of removal.

6   Crankshaft pulley - removal and installation

Removal

1   Disconnect the cable from the negative terminal of the battery (see Chapter 1).

Caution: *If equipped with an Intelligent Battery Sensor (IBS), disconnect the IBS con-* nector first before disconnecting the negative battery cable.

2   Loosen the wheel bolts on the right front wheel, then raise the vehicle and support it securely on jackstands.

3   Remove the right front wheel.

4   Remove the drivebelt (see Chapter 1).

5   The crankshaft pulley bolt is very tight; using a breaker bar, socket and special tool #10198 or equivalent **(see illustration)**, hold the pulley from turning while loosening the bolt.

6   Pull the crankshaft pulley off the crankshaft **(see illustration)**.

Installation

7   Apply clean engine oil or multi-purpose grease to the seal contact surface of the balancer hub (if it isn't lubricated, the seal lip could be damaged and oil leakage would result).

8   Install the crankshaft pulley, aligning the keyway on the crankshaft with the slot in the pulley hub. Install the bolt and tighten it by hand.

9   Prevent the engine from rotating (see Step 5) then tighten the bolt to the torque listed in this Chapter's Specifications.

10   The remainder of installation is the reverse of removal.

7   Crankshaft front oil seal - replacement

1   Remove the crankshaft pulley (see Section 6).

2   Use a screwdriver or hook tool to carefully pry out the seal **(see illustration)**.

Note: *Be careful not to damage the seal bore or the nose and sealing surface of the crankshaft.*

3   Another method for removing the seal is to drill a small hole on each side of the seal and place a self-tapping screw in each hole **(see illustration)**. Use these screws as a means of pulling the seal out without having to pry on it.

7.5 Drive the seal squarely into the cover using a socket and hammer

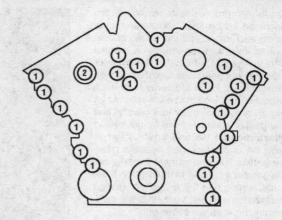

8.12 Timing chain cover bolt size and locations:
1 M6 bolt locations   2 M8 bolt location

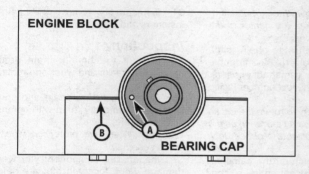

8.14 Align the dimple (A) on the crankshaft with the line (B) made where the engine block and bearing cap meet

4 If the seal is being replaced when the timing chain cover is removed, support the cover on top of two blocks of wood and drive the seal out from the backside with a hammer and punch.
Caution: *Be careful not to scratch, gouge or distort the area that the seal fits into or a leak will develop.*
5 Apply clean engine oil or multi-purpose grease to the outer edge of the new seal, then install it in the cover with the lip (spring side) facing IN. Drive the seal into place with a large socket and a hammer **(see illustration)**. Make sure the seal enters the bore squarely and stop when the front face is at the proper depth.
Note: *If a large socket isn't available, a piece of pipe will also work.*
6 Check the surface on the balancer hub that the oil seal rides on. If the surface has been grooved from long-time contact with the seal, the balancer will need to be replaced.
7 Lubricate the balancer hub with clean engine oil and install the crankshaft pulley (see Section 6).
8 The remainder of installation is the reverse of the removal.

8 Timing chain cover, chain and sprockets - removal, inspection and installation

Warning: *Wait until the engine is completely cool before beginning this procedure.*

Caution: *The timing system is complex, and severe engine damage will occur if you make any mistakes. Do not attempt this procedure unless you are highly experienced with this type of repair. If you are at all unsure of your abilities, be sure to consult an expert. Double-check all your work and be sure everything is correct before you attempt to start the engine.*
Caution: *Do not rotate the crankshaft or camshafts separately during this procedure (with the timing chains removed), as damage to the valves may occur.*
Note: *Several special tools are required to complete these procedures, so read through the entire Section and obtain the special tools before beginning work.*

Removal
Timing chain cover
1 Disconnect the cable from the negative terminal of the battery (see Chapter 5).
2 Drain the engine coolant (see Chapter 1).
3 Loosen the right-front wheel bolts. Raise the vehicle and support it securely on jackstands. Drain the engine oil (see Chapter 1).
4 Remove the right-front wheel and drive-belt splash shield (see Chapter 1).
5 Remove the drivebelt, drivebelt tensioner and idler pulley (see Chapter 1).
6 Remove the thermostat housing and upper radiator hose, and disconnect the heater hose from the water pump (see Chapter 3).

7 Remove the heater core supply pipe fasteners from the rear cylinder head and move the pipe out of the way.
8 Remove the crankshaft pulley (see Section 6).
9 Remove the valve covers (see Section 4).
Caution: *Once the valve covers are removed, the magnetic timing wheels are exposed (see illustration 9.9). The magnetic timing wheels on the camshafts must not come in contact with any type of magnet or magnetic field. If contact is made, the timing wheels will need to be replaced.*
10 Remove the upper and lower oil pans (see Section 11).
11 Once the oil pans are removed, temporarily install the engine mount crossmember and mount through-bolts. Place a floor jack under the engine (with a block of wood between the jack head and engine) and raise the engine slightly. Remove the right engine mount and bracket (see Section 16).
12 Remove the timing chain cover mounting bolts **(see illustration)**. There are seven indented prying points, one on top and three on each side; carefully pry the cover free of the engine block and cylinder heads. If it still sticks, slip a putty knife between the engine block and cover to break the bond (but be careful not to scratch the surfaces).
13 Remove and discard the coolant housing and water pump gaskets from the back side of the timing chain cover.

Timing chain
Caution: *When the timing chains are removed, do not rotate the camshafts or crankshaft; the valves and pistons can be damaged if contact is made.*
14 Temporarily install the crankshaft pulley bolt. Turn the crankshaft with the bolt to TDC number 1, on the *exhaust* stroke to align the timing marks on the crankshaft and camshaft sprockets. Rotate the engine clockwise only, until the mark on the crankshaft aligns with the line where the engine block and bearing cap meet **(see illustration)**.

15 On the left (front) side camshaft phaser, the machined scribe lines should be facing away from each other, and the arrows should be pointing towards each other in a parallel line with the gasket surface of the cylinder head. On the right (rear) side camshaft phaser, the arrows should be facing away from each other and the machined scribe lines should be pointing towards each other in a parallel line with the gasket surface of the cylinder head (see illustrations 9.10a and 9.10b). If, when you align the crankshaft mark with the bearing cap parting line, the camshaft marks are not in alignment as shown in illustration 8.58, rotate the engine one full revolution, realign the crankshaft mark, and verify that the camshaft marks are in proper alignment.

16 Verify the phaser marks are aligned with the plated links; if the plated links cannot be distinguished, make sure there are 12 pins between the two marks (see illustration).

Note: *Use paint or a permanent marker to mark the direction of rotation on all chains before removing them so they can be installed in the same direction.*

17 Starting with the right side chain tensioner, press the tensioner plunger in until special tool #8514 or a 3 mm Allen wrench can be inserted through both small holes in the top and bottom of the tensioner body, holding the plunger in the compressed position.

18 Working on the left side chain tensioner, locate the access hole on the side of the tensioner. Working through the hole, lift and hold the pawl off of the rack of the plunger in the tensioner. Press the plunger in until special tool #8514 or a 3 mm Allen wrench can be inserted through both small holes in the top and bottom of the tensioner body, holding the plunger in the compressed position.

19 Remove the timing gear splash shield fasteners, then remove the shield from the oil pump housing.

20 Remove the oil pump tensioner and sprocket (see Section 12), then remove the oil pump chain from the crankshaft sprocket.

Note: *The oil pump chain and sprocket do not have to be timed, but the chain should be marked to make sure it is installed in the same direction of rotation.*

21 Starting with the right side chain, slide camshaft phaser lock tool #10202-1 from the front, between the two camshaft phasers, towards the chain (with the tool number facing up).

Note: *It may be necessary to rotate the intake camshaft a few degrees using a wrench on the camshaft flat when installing the phaser lock tool.*

22 Using a large wrench on the camshaft flats and a socket and ratchet on the oil control valves, loosen, but do not remove, the oil control valves.

23 Remove the right side camshaft phaser lock tool, then unscrew the intake camshaft oil control valve from the center of the phaser.

24 Slide the intake camshaft phaser off of the end of the camshaft, then remove the right side timing chain.

8.16 Verify that there are 12 pins between the mark on each phaser

Note: *If necessary, remove the exhaust camshaft oil control valve from the center of the phaser and remove the phaser.*

25 Working on the left side chain, slide camshaft phaser lock tool #10202-2 from the front, between the two camshaft phasers, towards the chain (with the tool number facing up).

Note: *It may be necessary to rotate the intake camshaft a few degrees using a wrench on the camshaft flat when installing the phaser lock tool.*

26 Using a large wrench on the camshaft flats and a socket and ratchet on the oil control valves, loosen, but do not remove, the oil control valves

27 Remove the left side camshaft phaser lock tool, then unscrew the exhaust camshaft oil control valve from the center of the phaser.

28 Slide the exhaust camshaft phaser off of the end of the camshaft, then remove the left side timing chain.

Note: *If necessary, remove the intake camshaft oil control valve from the center of the phaser and remove the phaser.*

29 Locate the primary chain tensioner to the side of the crankshaft chain and press the tensioner plunger in until special tool #8514 or a 3 mm Allen wrench can be inserted through the small hole in the side of the tensioner body, holding the plunger in the compressed position.

30 With the tensioner in the compressed position, remove the Torx (T30) mounting fasteners and the tensioner.

31 Remove the primary chain guide Torx (T30) mounting fasteners and the guide.

32 Remove the idler sprocket Torx (T45) mounting fastener and washer, then remove the idler sprocket, primary chain and crankshaft sprocket.

Note: *The chain should be marked to make sure it is installed in the same direction of rotation.*

33 If necessary, remove the chain tensioner (T30) fasteners and remove the tensioner(s), keeping the tensioners in the compressed position.

34 If necessary, remove the chain guide fasteners and guides for both chains.

Inspection

35 Inspect the timing chain dampener (guide) for cracks and wear and replace it, if necessary.

36 Clean the timing chain and sprockets with solvent and dry them with compressed air (if available).

Warning: *Wear eye protection when using compressed air.*

37 Inspect the components for wear and damage. Look for teeth that are deformed, chipped, pitted, and cracked.

38 The timing chain and sprockets should be replaced with new ones if the engine has high mileage, the chain has visible damage, or total freeplay midway between the sprockets exceeds one inch. Failure to replace a worn timing chain and sprockets may result in erratic engine performance, loss of power, and decreased fuel mileage. Loose chains can jump timing. In the worst case, chain jumping or breakage will result in severe engine damage.

Installation

Caution: *Before starting the engine, carefully rotate the crankshaft by hand through at least two full revolutions (use a socket and breaker bar on the crankshaft pulley center bolt). If you feel any resistance, STOP! There is something wrong - most likely, valves are contacting the pistons. You must find the problem before proceeding. Check your work and see if any updated repair information is available.*

39 Use a plastic gasket scraper to remove all traces of old gasket material and sealant from the cover, engine block and cylinder heads. The cover is made of aluminum, so be careful not to nick or gouge it. Only clean the gasket sealing surfaces with rubbing alcohol (isopropyl) - do not use any oil based fluids.

40 If removed, install the chain guides and tensioners (still in the compressed position).

41 Make sure the keyway is installed on the crankshaft and the dimple on the crank-

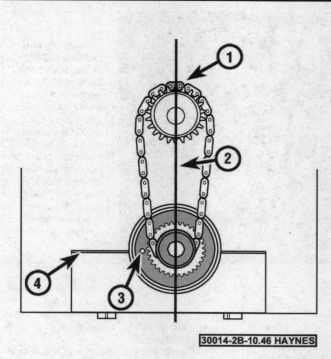

30014-2B-10.46 HAYNES

8.45 Primary chain alignment details

1   *Primary chain plated link*
2   *12 o'clock position*
3   *Crankshaft dimple*
4   *Line formed where engine block and bearing cap meet*

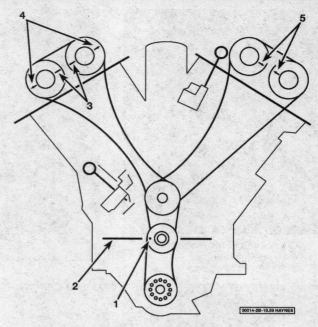

30014-2B-10.59 HAYNES

8.58 Timing mark alignment details

1   *Dimple on crankshaft*
2   *Junction of main bearing cap and cylinder block*
3   *Lines on rear bank cam phasers - must be pointing toward each other and parallel with cylinder head*
4   *Arrows on rear bank cam phasers - must be pointing away from each other*
5   *Arrows on front bank cam phasers - must be pointing toward each other*

shaft is aligned with the line made where the engine block and bearing cap meet (**see illustration 8.14**).

42   Verify the camshafts are at TDC, with the alignment holes pointing up (**see illustration 9.29**).

43   Place the primary chain on the crankshaft sprocket, with the plated link of the primary chain aligned with the arrow on the bottom of the sprocket. Insert the idler sprocket into the chain, aligning the other plated link with the machined mark on the idler sprocket.

44   Using clean engine oil, coat the sprockets and chain. Install the assembly while keeping the marks aligned, then install the idler sprocket mounting fastener finger-tight.

45   Check the alignment of the marks; the plated link on the idler sprocket should be on top (12 o'clock) and the machined mark on the crankshaft should be aligned with the line where the engine block and bearing cap meet (**see illustration**). If the marks are all aligned, tighten the idler sprocket fastener to the torque listed in this Chapter's Specifications.

46   Install the primary chain guide and tensioner, then tighten the fasteners to the torque listed in this Chapter's Specifications. Remove the special tool from the tensioner plunger.

47   Starting with the front bank chain, install the intake camshaft phaser and oil control valve, then tighten the valve finger-tight.

48   Place the left side chain over the intake phaser and around the inside cogs of the idler sprocket so that the plate link of the chain is aligned with the machined arrow on the sprocket.

49   With the chain aligned at the idler sprocket, install the exhaust camshaft phaser so that the arrows are pointing towards each other and in a parallel line with the cylinder head gasket surface (**see illustration 9.10a**), then install the oil control valve finger-tight.

50   Slide camshaft phaser lock tool #10202-2 from the front, between the two camshaft phasers towards the chain with the tool number facing up.

51   Using a large wrench on the camshaft flats and a socket and ratchet on the oil control valves, tighten both valves to the torque listed in this Chapter's Specifications.

52   Working on the rear bank chain, install the exhaust camshaft phaser and oil control valve, tightening the valve finger-tight.

53   Place the rear bank chain over the intake phaser and around the outside cogs of the idler sprocket so that the plated link of the chain is aligned with the machined circle on the sprocket.

54   With the chain aligned at the idler sprocket, install the intake camshaft phaser so that the machined lines are pointing towards each other and in a parallel line with the gasket surface of the cylinder head (**see**

illustration 9.10b), then install the oil control valve finger-tight.

55   Slide camshaft phaser lock tool #10202-1 from the front, between the two camshaft phasers, towards the chain (with the tool number facing up).

56   Using a large wrench on the camshaft flats to hold them stationary, tighten both oil control valve bolts to the torque listed in this Chapter's Specifications.

57   Install the oil pump chain, tensioner, sprocket and splash shield (see Section 12).
Note: *There are no timing marks on the oil pump chain or sprocket.*

58   Verify all the marks are aligned (**see illustration**), then remove the special tool or Allen wrenches from the primary and secondary tensioners. Also remove the camshaft phaser lock tools.

59   Rotate the engine two complete turns using the machined mark on the crankshaft with the line made where the engine block and bearing caps meet as the reference. Verify all the marks are aligned and there are 12 pins between the phaser marks (**see illustration 8.16**); if the marks are off, rotate the engine two more complete turns and check again.

60   Once the timing marks are correct, install the new coolant housing and water pump housing gaskets into the grooves on the back side of the timing cover.

9.9 Location of the magnetic timing wheels

9.10a With the engine at TDC #1, the front bank camshaft phaser scribe marks (A) should be pointing away from each other; the arrow marks (B) should be pointing towards each other in a straight line and that line should be parallel with the cylinder head surface

9.10b The rear bank phaser scribe marks should be pointing towards each other in a straight line (and that line should be parallel with the cylinder head surface)

61 Apply a 1/8-inch wide by 1/16-inch high, bead of RTV sealant to the sealing surface of the cover, then install the cover on the alignment dowels.

62 Install the cover bolts **(see illustration 8.12)** and tighten them a little at a time, in a criss-cross pattern, to the torque listed in this Chapter's Specifications.

63 The remainder of installation is the reverse of removal.

64 Add oil and coolant (see Chapter 1), then start the engine and check for leaks.

---

9   Camshaft(s) – removal, inspection and installation

Warning: *Wait until the engine is completely cool before beginning this procedure.*
Caution: *The timing system is complex, and severe engine damage will occur if you make any mistakes. Do not attempt this procedure unless you are highly experienced with this type of repair. If you are at all unsure of your abilities, be sure to consult an expert. Double-check all your work and be sure everything is*

correct before you attempt to start the engine.
Caution: *Once the valve covers are removed, the magnetic timing wheels are exposed. The magnetic timing wheels on the camshafts must not come in contact with any type of magnet or magnetic field. If contact is made, the timing wheels will need to be replaced.*
Note: *The timing chain for each camshaft can be removed from the camshafts individually, without removing all the timing chains, using the tools outlined in this Section. If the tools are not available, the timing chain cover and all chains will have to be removed before the camshafts can be removed (see Section 8).*

Removal

1 Disconnect the cable from the negative terminal of the battery (see Chapter 5).

2 Loosen the wheel bolts on the right front wheel, then raise the front of the vehicle and support it securely on jackstands. Remove the right front wheel and the drivebelt splash shield.

3 Drain the engine oil and coolant, then remove the drivebelt (see Chapter 1).

4 Remove the air filter housing (see Chapter 4) and resonator **(see illustration 5.5)**.

5 Remove the intake manifolds (see Section 5).

6 Disconnect all wires and vacuum hoses that are in the way. Label them to simplify reinstallation.

7 Disconnect the ignition coils and remove the spark plugs (see Chapter 1). Label the ignition coils to simplify reinstallation.

8 Remove the valve covers (see Section 4).

9 Once the valve covers are removed, the magnetic timing wheels are exposed **(see illustration)**. The magnetic timing wheels on the camshafts must not come in contact with any type of magnet or magnetic field. If contact is made, the timing wheels will have to be replaced.

10 Rotate the crankshaft clockwise and place the #1 piston at TDC on the exhaust stroke. On the front bank camshaft phasers, the machined scribe lines should be facing away from each other, and the arrows should be pointing towards each other in a parallel line with the gasket surface of the cylinder head. On the right bank camshaft phasers, the arrows should be facing away from each other, and the machined scribe lines should be pointing towards each other in a parallel line with the gasket's surface of the cylinder head **(see illustrations)**.

11 Using a permanent marker or paint, mark the camshaft phasers to the timing chains for reinstallation.

12 Working from the top of the timing chain cover, insert special tool #10200-3 down the side of the tensioner to the access hole on the side of the tensioner. Working through the small hole in the side of the tensioner, lift and hold the pawl off of the rack of the plunger in the tensioner. Slide chain holding tool #10200-1 between the cylinder head and the back side of the chain against the chain guide, forcing the rack and plunger back into the tensioner body.
Caution: *The chain holding tool must remain in place while the phasers are removed or the timing chain will fall off into the timing chain cover.*

9.22 Use a micrometer to measure cam lobe height

9.28 Camshaft bearing cap tightening sequence – left (front) side shown, right side is identical

13 Slide camshaft phaser lock tool #10202-1 (right side) or 10202-2 (left side), from the front, between the two camshaft phasers, towards the chain.
Note: *It may be necessary to rotate the intake camshaft a few degrees using a wrench on the camshaft flat when installing the phaser lock tool.*
14 Using a large wrench on the camshaft flats and a socket and ratchet on the oil control valves, loosen, then remove each of the oil control valves from the phaser end of the camshaft.
15 At the same time, carefully slide both the intake and exhaust phaser (with the phaser lock securely between them) forward until they are off the end of the camshafts.
Caution: *Do not remove the phaser lock or try to disassemble the phasers.*
16 Using the alignment holes in the camshaft as a reference point, slowly rotate both camshafts counterclockwise approximately 30-degrees Before Top Dead Center (BTDC). In this position, the camshafts are in a neutral or no load position.
Note: *The camshaft bearing caps are marked with a number and letter code; " 1I " is for the number one Intake camshaft bearing cap. The notch on the caps should always be installed towards the front.*
17 Loosen the camshaft bearing cap bolts in the reverse of the tightening sequence **(see illustration 9.28)**.
18 Remove the camshaft bearing caps and carefully lift the camshafts from the cylinder head.
19 Mark the rocker arms so they can be installed in their original locations, then remove them.
20 Mark the hydraulic lash adjusters so they can be installed in their original locations, then remove them from the cylinder head.

Inspection

21 Check the camshaft bearing surfaces for pitting, score marks, galling, and abnormal wear. If the bearing surfaces are damaged, the cylinder head will have to be replaced.
22 Compare the camshaft lobe height by

9.29 Locate the alignment holes on the camshafts and make sure they are in the neutral position (pointing straight up) – right (rear) side shown, left side is identical

measuring each lobe with a micrometer **(see illustration)**. Measure each of the intake lobes and record the measurements and relative positions. Then measure each of the exhaust lobes and record the measurements and relative positions also. This will let you compare all of the intake lobes to one another and all of the exhaust lobes to one another. If the difference between the lobes exceeds 0.005 inch, the camshaft should be replaced. Do not compare intake lobe heights to exhaust lobe heights as lobe lift may be different. Only compare intake lobes to intake lobes and exhaust lobes to exhaust lobes for this comparison.
23 Check the rocker arms and shafts for abnormal wear, pits, galling, score marks, and rough spots. Don't attempt to restore rocker arms by grinding the pad surfaces. Replace defective parts.

Installation

Caution: *Before starting the engine, carefully rotate the crankshaft by hand through at least two full revolutions (use a socket and breaker bar on the crankshaft pulley center bolt). If you feel any resistance, STOP! There is something wrong - most likely, valves are contacting the pistons. You must find the problem before*

proceeding. Check your work and see if any updated repair information is available.
24 Dip the hydraulic lash adjusters in clean engine oil and install them into their original locations.
25 Apply moly-base grease or engine assembly lube to the rocker arm contact points and rollers and install them into their original locations.
26 Lubricate the camshaft bearing journals and lobes with moly-base grease or engine assembly lube, then install them carefully in the cylinder head about 30-degrees before (counterclockwise of) TDC. Don't scratch the bearing surfaces with the cam lobes!
Caution: *Do not rotate the camshafts more than a few degrees to prevent the valves from contacting the pistons.*
27 Install the camshaft bearing caps, then install the mounting bolts and finger tighten them.
28 Tighten the bearing caps in sequence **(see illustration)** to the torque listed in this Chapter's Specifications.
29 Rotate the camshafts clockwise 30-degrees, and verify the alignment holes in the camshafts are in the 12 o'clock (pointing straight up) or neutral position **(see illustration)**.

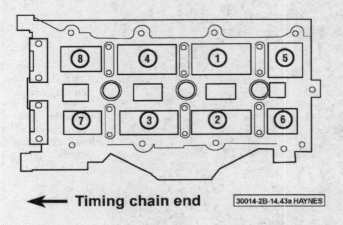

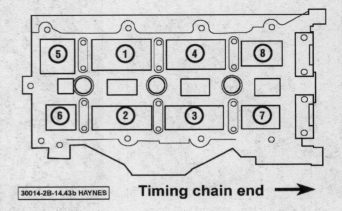

10.29a Left (front) side cylinder head bolt TIGHTENING sequence   **10.29b Right (rear) side cylinder head bolt TIGHTENING sequence**

30   Carefully slide both the intake and exhaust phaser (with the phaser lock tool securely between them) onto the camshafts and verify the marks are aligned.

31   Install the oil control valves onto the camshaft phasers and install the bolts, then tighten the bolts to the torque listed in this Chapter's Specifications. Remove the chain holding tool and release the tensioner plunger.

Caution: *Make sure to prevent the camshafts from turning by holding the camshaft with a large wrench on the camshaft flats.*

32   Slowly rotate the engine two complete turns (720-degrees) and verify the alignment marks are correct **(see illustrations 9.10a and 9.10b).**

33   The remainder of installation is the reverse of removal.

10   Cylinder heads - removal and installation

Warning: *Wait until the engine is completely cool before beginning this procedure.*

Removal

1   Disconnect the cable from the negative terminal of the battery (see Chapter 1).

2   Loosen the wheel bolts on the right front wheel, then raise the front of the vehicle and support it securely on jackstands. Remove the right front wheel and the drivebelt splash shield.

3   Drain the engine oil and coolant, then remove the drivebelt (see Chapter 1).

4   Remove the air filter housing and resonator (see Chapter 4).

5   Remove the intake manifolds (see Section 5).

6   Disconnect all wires and vacuum hoses that may be in the way. Label them to simplify reinstallation.

7   Disconnect the ignition coils and remove the spark plugs (see Chapter 1).

8   Remove the catalytic converter(s) (see Chapter 6).

9   Remove the valve covers (see Section 4).

10   Remove the crankshaft pulley (see Section 6).

11   Remove the oil pans (see Section 11).

12   If you're working on the front cylinder head:

   a) *Remove the alternator (see Chapter 5).*

   b) *Remove the oil dipstick tube fastener and remove the tube from the oil pan.*

   c) *Remove the air conditioning compressor (see Chapter 3).*

   d) *Disconnect the main engine harness connectors at the rear of the cylinder and move the harness and retainers out of the way.*

13   If you're working on the rear cylinder head, remove the heater core tube fasteners and move the tube away from the cylinder head.

14   Remove the timing chain cover (see Section 8).

15   Rotate the crankshaft clockwise and place the #1 piston at TDC on the *exhaust* stroke. When the crankshaft is at TDC, the dimple on the crankshaft will be in line with the line made where the bearing cap meets the engine block. The front cylinder bank cam phaser arrows should be pointing toward each other and be parallel with where the cylinder head and valve cover meets. The rear side cam phaser arrows should point away from each other and the lines on the phasers should be pointing towards each other **(see illustration 8.58).**

16   Remove the timing chain for the cylinder head or, if both cylinder heads are being removed, remove both chains (see Section 8).

17   Remove the oil control valves from the cam phasers (sprockets) (see Section 9).

18   Remove the timing chain tensioner and chain guides (see Section 8).

19   Remove the camshafts, rocker arms and lash adjusters (see Section 9).

Caution: *Once the valve covers are removed the magnetic timing wheels are exposed. The*

magnetic timing wheels on the camshafts must not come in contact with any type of magnet or magnetic field. If contact is made the timing wheels will need to be replaced (see Section 9).

Note: *Keep the rocker arms and lash adjusters in order so that they can be installed in their original locations.*

20   Loosen the cylinder head bolts in the reverse of the tightening sequence **(see illustrations 10.29a and 10.29b).**

21   Lift the cylinder head off the block. If resistance is felt, dislodge the cylinder head by striking it with a wood block and hammer. If prying is required, pry only on a casting protrusion - be very careful not to damage the cylinder head or block!

Caution: *Do not set the cylinder head on its gasket side; the sealing surface can be easily damaged.*

22   Have the cylinder head inspected and serviced by a qualified automotive machine shop.

Installation

23   The mating surfaces of each cylinder head and the engine block must be perfectly clean when the cylinder head is installed.

24   Carefully use a gasket scraper to remove all traces of carbon and old gasket material, then clean the mating surfaces with brake system cleaner. If there's oil on the mating surfaces when the cylinder head is installed, the gasket may not seal correctly and leaks may develop.

25   When working on the engine block, it's a good idea to cover the lifter valley with shop rags to keep debris out of the engine. Use a shop rag or vacuum cleaner to remove any debris that falls into the cylinders.

26   Check the engine block and cylinder head mating surfaces for nicks, deep scratches, and other damage. If damage is slight, it can be removed with a file; if it's excessive, machining may be the only alternative.

11.5 Typical lower oil pan fastener locations

27 Position the new gasket over the dowel pins in the engine block. Some gaskets are marked TOP or FRONT to ensure correct installation.

28 Carefully position the cylinder head on the engine block without disturbing the gasket.

29 Install NEW cylinder head bolts and tighten them in the recommended sequence **(see illustrations)** to the torque steps listed in this Chapter's Specifications. **Caution:** *Do not use a torque wrench for steps requiring additional rotation or turns; apply a paint mark to the bolt head or use a torque-angle gauge (available at most automotive parts stores) and a socket and breaker bar.*

30 The remainder of installation is the reverse of removal.

31 Change the engine oil and filter (see Chapter 1).

32 Refill the cooling system (see Chapter 1). Start the engine and check for leaks and proper operation.

11 Oil pans - removal and installation

Removal

1 Disconnect the cable from the negative terminal of the battery (see Chapter 5).

2 Raise the front of the vehicle and support it securely on jackstands. Apply the parking brake and block the rear wheels to keep it from rolling off the stands.

3 Drain the engine oil (see Chapter 1).

4 Remove the lower splash shield fasteners and remove the splash shield.

Lower oil pan

5 Remove the bolts and nuts, then carefully separate the lower oil pan from the upper oil pan **(see illustration)**. Don't pry between the upper pan and the lower pan or damage to the sealing surfaces could occur and oil leaks may develop. Tap the pan with a soft-faced hammer to break the gasket seal.

If it still sticks, slip a putty knife between the upper pan and lower pan to break the bond (but be careful not to scratch the surfaces).

Upper oil pan

6 Remove the dipstick tube bracket mounting bolt. Using a twisting motion, pull the dipstick tube out of the upper oil pan.

7 Remove the right-side driveaxle (see Chapter 8).

8 Remove the lower oil pan (see Step 5).

9 Disconnect the exhaust crossunder pipe flange fasteners and remove the crossunder pipe.

10 Remove the engine mount crossmember (see Chapter 10).

11 Remove the coolant tube-to-upper pan fastener and move the tube back.

12 Remove the five upper oil pan-to-transaxle mounting bolts.

13 Remove the torque converter access plate, and the rubber plugs just below the plate.

14 Remove the two upper pan-to-rear main seal housing bolts (M6 size). **Caution:** *The oil pan-to-rear main seal bolts are hard to see and can easily be missed. If they are not removed, the rear main seal housing will be severely damaged when the pan is lowered.*

15 Remove the nineteen upper oil pan bolts (M8 size) around the perimeter of the pan, then carefully separate the oil pan from the engine block. Use the two indented prying points on each side of the oil pan to carefully pry the pan free of the engine block. If it still sticks, slip a putty knife between the engine block and oil pan to break the bond (but be careful not to scratch the surfaces).

Installation

16 Clean the pan(s) with solvent and remove all old sealant and gasket material from the engine block and pan mating surfaces. Clean the mating surfaces with brake system cleaner and make sure the bolt holes in the engine block are clear. Check the oil

pan flange(s) for distortion, particularly around the bolt holes. If necessary, place the pan(s) on a wood block and use a hammer to flatten and restore the gasket surface.

Upper oil pan

17 Apply a 1/8-inch wide by 1/16-inch diameter bead of RTV sealant to the sealing surface of the pan. Install the upper pan and the bolts, then tighten the bolts finger-tight.

18 Tighten the upper pan-to-transaxle bolts to the torque listed in this Chapter's Specifications.

19 Tighten the remaining bolts in a circular pattern, starting from the middle and working your way outwards, to the torque listed in this Chapter's Specifications.

20 The remainder of installation is the reverse of removal.

21 Refill the engine with oil (see Chapter 1) if the lower pan is attached. Start and run the engine until normal operating temperature is reached, then check for leaks.

Lower oil pan

22 Apply a 1/8-inch wide by 1/16-inch high bead of RTV sealant to the sealing surface of the pan. Install the lower pan and the bolts.

23 Tighten the bolts in a circular pattern, starting from the middle and working your way outwards, to the torque listed in this Chapter's Specifications.

24 The remainder of installation is the reverse of removal.

25 Refill the engine with oil (see Chapter 1). Start and run the engine until normal operating temperature is reached, then check for leaks.

12 Oil pump - removal, inspection and installation

Removal

1 Disconnect the cable from the negative terminal of the battery (see Chapter 1).

2 Raise the front of the vehicle and support it securely on jackstands. Apply the parking brake and block the rear wheels to keep it from rolling off the stands.

3 Drain the engine oil (see Chapter 1).

4 Remove the lower splash shield fasteners and remove the splash shield.

5 Remove the lower and upper oil pans (see Section 11).

6 Remove the oil pump pick-up tube fastener, and remove the tube from the pump. Discard the pick-up tube O-ring.

7 Disconnect the oil pump solenoid electrical connector from the side of the engine, then slide the locking clip towards the rear of the vehicle until it can be removed.

8 Working from the side of the block, depress the oil pump solenoid electrical connector locking tab and push the connector into the block. **Note:** *The connector will have to be maneuvered around the tensioner mounting bolt.*

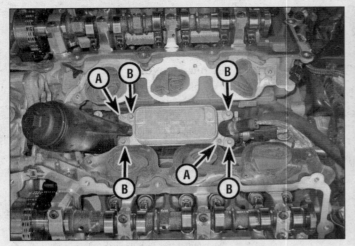

13.4 Remove the oil cooler mounting screws (A) and mounting bolts (B)

14.4 Mark the relative position of the driveplate to the crankshaft and, using an appropriate tool to hold the driveplate, remove the bolts

9   Remove the oil pump timing gear splash shield bolts and remove the splash shield.
10   Press the oil pump chain tensioner away from the chain until a 3 mm Allen wrench can be inserted into the housing to hold the tensioner back.
11   Using a permanent marker or paint, make reference marks on the chain and oil pump sprocket.
12   Hold the oil pump gear from moving, then remove the T45 Torx mounting bolt and the oil pump sprocket.
13   Hold the tensioner and remove the Allen wrench, allowing the tensioner to release. Remove the spring from the dowel pin and slide the tensioner from the oil pump.
14   Remove the oil pump mounting bolts and remove the pump.

Inspection
15   The oil pump is not serviceable; if there is a problem or the solenoid is bad, the pump assembly must be replaced.

Installation
16   Place the oil pump onto the engine block using the aligning dowels. Install the mounting bolts and tighten them to the torque listed in this Chapter's Specifications.
17   Slide the oil pump chain tensioner onto the pivot, then push the tensioner back against the spring. Insert a 3 mm Allen wrench into the tensioner to hold it in place.
18   Place the oil pump timing chain sprocket into the chain, center it onto the oil pump shaft and install the T45 mounting bolt. Tighten the bolt to the torque listed in this Chapter's Specifications.
Note: Make sure the sprocket is facing the same way as when it was removed (see Step 11). There are no timing marks on the pump sprocket or chain, and no timing is necessary.
19   Maneuver the oil pump solenoid into position and insert it through the block opening until it snaps in place.

20   Install the timing sprocket splash shield and bolts, then tighten the bolts to the torque listed in this Chapter's Specifications.
21   The remainder of installation is the reverse of removal.
22   Refill the engine with oil and change the oil filter (see Chapter 1).

13   Oil cooler - removal and installation

Warning: *Wait until the engine is completely cool before beginning this procedure.*

Removal
1   Disconnect the cable from the negative terminal of the battery (see Chapter 1).
2   Drain the engine coolant (see Chapter 1).
3   Remove the lower intake manifold (see Section 5).
4   Remove the oil cooler mounting fasteners **(see illustration)**.
5   Remove the oil cooler and discard the seals.
Note: *The oil cooler cannot be cleaned out. If the engine requires rebuilding or replacement due to engine failure, replace the oil cooler.*

Installation
6   Install new seals to the oil cooler.
7   Place the oil cooler onto the block and install the two mounting screws **(see illustration 13.4)**.
8   Install the mounting bolts and tighten the fasteners to the torque listed in this Chapter's Specifications.
9   The remainder of installation is the reverse of removal.
10   Refill the cooling system and add oil, as necessary (see Chapter 1). Run the engine until normal operating temperature is reached, and check for leaks.

14   Driveplate - removal and installation

Removal
1   Raise the vehicle and support it securely on jackstands.
2   Remove the transaxle (see Chapter 7A).
3   To ensure correct alignment during reinstallation, match-mark the driveplate and backing plate to the crankshaft so they can be reassembled in the same position.
4   Remove the bolts that hold the driveplate to the crankshaft **(see illustration)**. A special tool is available at most auto parts stores to hold the driveplate while loosening the bolts. If the tool is not available, wedge a screwdriver in the starter ring gear teeth to jam the driveplate.
5   Remove the driveplate from the crankshaft. The driveplate is fairly heavy; be sure to support it while removing the last bolt.
6   Clean the driveplate to remove grease and oil. Inspect the driveplate for damage or other defects.
7   Clean and inspect the mating surfaces of the driveplate and the crankshaft.
8   If the crankshaft rear main seal is leaking, replace it before reinstalling the driveplate (see Section 15).

Installation
9   Position the driveplate and backing plate against the crankshaft. Align the previously applied match marks. Before installing the bolts, apply thread-locking compound to the threads.
10   Hold the driveplate with the holding tool, or wedge a screwdriver in the starter ring gear teeth to keep the driveplate from turning. Tighten the bolts to the torque listed in this Chapter's Specifications.
11   The remainder of installation is the reverse of removal.

15 Rear main oil seal - replacement

1   Remove the oil pans (see Section 11).
2   Remove the driveplate (see Section 14).
3   Unbolt the seal retainer from the engine block and slide the retainer and seal off the end of the crankshaft.
Note: *The rear main oil seal has been incorporated into the seal retainer and must be replaced as a unit.*
4   Clean the engine block, oil pan and crankshaft.
5   The new seal and retainer assembly comes with a plastic installation sleeve; make sure it's in place.
6   Apply a 1/4-inch bead of RTV sealant where the lower corners of the seal retainer meet the oil pan.
7   Place the assembly over the crankshaft and push it squarely into place, making sure the dowels in the seal retainer engage the locating holes in the engine block.
8   Install, but don't fully tighten, the seal retainer bolts.
9   Remove the plastic installation sleeve, then tighten the bolts, using an alternating pattern, to the torque listed in this Chapter's Specifications.
10   The remainder of installation is the reverse of removal.

16 Engine mounts - check and replacement

1   The engine mounting system on these models consists of four molded mounts. The right and left mounts support the engine/transaxle assembly while the front and rear mounts restrict torquing action of the powertrain.
2   Engine mounts seldom require attention, but broken or deteriorated mounts should be replaced immediately, or the added strain placed on driveline components may cause damage or accelerated wear.

Check

3   During the check, the engine must be raised slightly to remove the weight from the mounts.
4   Raise the vehicle and support it securely on jackstands, then position a jack under the engine oil pan. Place a large wood block between the jack head and the oil pan to prevent oil pan damage, then carefully raise the engine just enough to take the weight off the mounts.
Warning: *DO NOT place any part of your body under the engine when it's supported only by a jack!*
5   Check the mounts to see if the rubber is cracked, hardened or separated from the metal backing. Sometimes the rubber will split right down the center.
6   Check for relative movement between the mount plates and the engine or frame (use a large screwdriver or pry bar to attempt to move the mounts). If movement is noted, lower the engine and tighten the mount fasteners.
7   Rubber preservative may be applied to the mounts to slow deterioration.

Replacement

Right mount

8   Disconnect the cable from the negative terminal of the battery (see Chapter 5).
9   Remove the air filter housing (see Chapter 4).
10   Raise the front of the vehicle and support it securely on jackstands.
11   Place a floor jack under the engine (with a wood block between the jack head and oil pan) and raise the engine slightly to relieve the weight from the mounts.
12   Remove the two right engine mount insulator vertical fasteners from the frame rail and loosen the one horizontal fastener to the strut tower.
13   Remove the mount-to-engine bracket center bolt.

14   Remove the mount-to-engine bracket outer bolts and remove the mount.
15   Install the new mount and tighten the bolts securely.

Left mount

16   Raise the front of the vehicle and support it securely on jackstands. Remove the lower splash shield fasteners and remove the splash shield.
17   Remove the battery (see Chapter 5).
18   Power Distribution Center (PDC) cover, then remove the three mounting bolts and secure the PDC out of the way.
19   Place a floor jack under the transaxle (with a wood block between the jack head and transaxle) and raise the tranaxle slightly to relieve the weight from the mounts.
20   Unclip the wiring harness retainers and move the harness away from the mount.
21   Remove the two transaxle mount-to-frame vertical fasteners from the frame rail and loosen the one horizontal fastener.
22   Remove the three bolts from the transaxle mount insulator-to-transaxle bracket, then remove the mount.
23   Install the new mount and tighten the bolts securely.

Rear mount

24   Raise the front of the vehicle and support it securely on jackstands.
25   Place a floor jack under the engine (with a wood block between the jack head and oil pan) and raise the engine slightly to relieve the weight from the mounts.
26   Remove the exhaust cross-under pipe (see Chapter 4).
27   Remove the transmission torque strut-to-pivot bracket through bolt and nut.
28   Remove the transmission torque strut-to-crossmember bolt and remove the mount.
Note: *If the transaxle rear mount bracket has to be removed, it requires a reverse six-point socket.*
29   Install the new mount and tighten the bolts securely.

Notes

Chapter 2 Part C
General engine overhaul procedures

Contents

Specifications

General

Displacement
2.0L engine	122 cubic inches
2.4L engine	146.5 cubic inches
3.2L engine	195 cubic inches

Bore
2.0L engine	3.307 inches
2.4L engine	3.465 inches
3.2L engine	3.583 inches

Stroke
2.0L engine	3.540 inches
2.4L engine	3.819 inches
3.2L engine	3.268 inches

Compression ratio
2.0L engine	10.0: 1
2.4L engine	10.5: 1
3.2L engine	10.7: 1

Compression pressure .... 100 psi minimum and no more than 25-percent variance between cylinders

Oil pressure*
  At idle speed
2.0L engine	Not available
2.4L engine	4 psi (minimum)
3.2L engine	5 psi (minimum)

  At 3000 rpm
2.0L engine	Not available
2.4L engine	25 to 80 psi
3.2L engine	30 psi (warm)

*If the idle oil pressure test result was zero, don't perform the 3000 rpm or higher test.

Torque specifications

Note: *One foot-pound (ft-lb) of torque is equivalent to 12 inch-pounds (in-lbs) of torque. Torque values below approximately 15 ft-lbs are expressed in inch-pounds, since most foot-pound torque wrenches are not accurate at these smaller values.*

Ft-lbs (unless otherwise indicated)

Connecting rod bearing cap bolts*
  2.0L engine
    Step 1 15
    Step 2 .... Tighten an additional 100-degrees
  2.4L engine
    Step 1 15
    Step 2 .... Tighten an additional 92-degrees
  3.2L engine
    Step 1 15
    Step 2 .... Tighten an additional 90-degrees
Crankshaft target wheel bolts*
  2.0L engine .... 120 in-lbs
  3.2L engine .... 97 in-lbs
Driveplate-to-crankshaft bolts*
  2.0L engine 81
  2.4L engine
    Step 1 21
    Step 2 .... Tighten an additional 51-degrees
  3.2L engine 70
Main bearing cap bolts*
  2.0L engine (in sequence - **see illustration 10.33e**)
    Step 1 .... 120 in-lbs
    Step 2 30
    Step 3 .... Tighten an additional 90-degrees
    Windage tray bolts .... 89 in-lbs
  2.4L engine (in sequence, **see illustration 10.33a**)
    Step 1 .... 132 in-lbs
    Step 2 33
    Step 3 .... Tighten an additional 45-degrees
  3.2L engine (in sequence, **see illustrations 10.33b, 10.33c and 10.33d**)
    Inner M11 bolts
      Step 1 15
      Step 2 .... Tighten an additional 90-degrees
    Outer bolts and windage tray M8 bolts
      Step 1 16
      Step 2 .... Tighten an additional 90-degrees
    Side bolts (tie bolts)
      2.0L engine 17
      3.2L engine 22

*Use new bolts

1.9a An engine block being bored. An engine rebuilder will use special machinery to recondition the cylinder bores

1.9b If the cylinders are bored, the machine shop will normally hone the engine on a machine like this

1   General information - engine overhaul

1   Included in this Part of Chapter 2 are general information and diagnostic testing procedures for determining the overall mechanical condition of your engine.
2   The information ranges from advice concerning preparation for an overhaul and the purchase of replacement parts and/or components to detailed, step-by-step procedures covering removal and installation.
3   The following Sections have been written to help you determine whether your engine needs to be overhauled and how to remove and install it once you've determined it needs to be rebuilt. For information concerning in-vehicle engine repair, see Chapter 2A or Chapter 2B.
4   It's not always easy to determine when, or if, an engine should be completely overhauled, because a number of factors must be considered.
5   High mileage is not necessarily an indication that an overhaul is needed, while low mileage doesn't preclude the need for an overhaul. Frequency of servicing is probably the most important consideration. An engine that's had regular and frequent oil and filter changes, as well as other required maintenance, will most likely give many thousands of miles of reliable service. Conversely, a neglected engine may require an overhaul very early in its service life.
6   Excessive oil consumption is an indication that piston rings, valve seals and/or valve guides are in need of attention. Make sure that oil leaks aren't responsible before deciding that the rings and/or guides are bad. Perform a cylinder compression check to determine the extent of the work required (see Section 3). Also check the vacuum readings under various conditions (see Section 4).
7   Check the oil pressure with a gauge installed in place of the oil pressure sending unit and compare it to this Chapter's Specifications (see Section 2). If it's extremely low,

the bearings and/or oil pump are probably worn out.
8   Loss of power, rough running, knocking or metallic engine noises, excessive valve train noise and high fuel consumption rates may also point to the need for an overhaul, especially if they're all present at the same time. If a complete tune-up doesn't remedy the situation, major mechanical work is the only solution.
9   An engine overhaul involves restoring the internal parts to the specifications of a new engine. During an overhaul, the piston rings are replaced and the cylinder walls are reconditioned (rebored and/or honed) **(see illustrations)**. If a rebore is done by an automotive machine shop, new oversize pistons will also be installed. The main bearings, connecting rod bearings and camshaft bearings are generally replaced with new ones and, if necessary, the crankshaft may be reground to restore the journals **(see illustration)**. Generally, the valves are serviced as well, since they're usually in less-than-perfect condition at this point. While the engine is being overhauled, other components, such as the starter and alternator, can be rebuilt as well. The end

result should be similar to a new engine that will give many trouble free miles.
Note: *Critical cooling system components such as the hoses, drivebelts, thermostat and water pump should be replaced with new parts when an engine is overhauled. The radiator should be checked carefully to ensure that it isn't clogged or leaking (see Chapter 3). If you purchase a rebuilt engine or short block, some rebuilders will not warranty their engines unless the radiator has been professionally flushed. Also, we don't recommend overhauling the oil pump - always install a new one when an engine is rebuilt.*
10   Overhauling the internal components on today's engines is a difficult and time-consuming task which requires a significant amount of specialty tools and is best left to a professional engine rebuilder **(see illustrations)**. A competent engine rebuilder will handle the inspection of your old parts and offer advice concerning the reconditioning or replacement of the original engine. Never purchase parts or have machine work done on other components until the block has been thoroughly inspected by a professional machine shop. As a general rule, time is the primary cost of an overhaul,

1.9c A crankshaft having a main bearing journal ground

1.10a A machinist checks for a bent connecting rod, using specialized equipment

1.10b A bore gauge being used to check a cylinder bore

1.10c Uneven piston wear like this indicates a bent connecting rod

2.2 The oil pressure sensor located just below the water pump on the front side of the engine - 2.4L engine shown

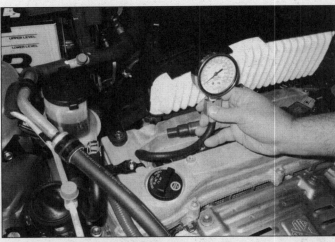

3.5 A compression gauge with a threaded fitting for the spark plug hole is preferred over the type that requires hand pressure to maintain the seal

4.4 A simple vacuum gauge can be handy in diagnosing engine condition and performance

especially since the vehicle may be tied up for a minimum of two weeks or more. Be aware that some engine builders only have the capability to rebuild the engine you bring them while other rebuilders have a large inventory of rebuilt exchange engines in stock. Also be aware that many machine shops could take as much as two weeks time to completely rebuild your engine depending on shop workload. Sometimes it makes more sense to simply exchange your engine for another engine that's already rebuilt to save time.

2   Oil pressure check

1   Low engine oil pressure can be a sign of an engine in need of rebuilding. A low oil pressure indicator (often called an idiot light) is not a test of the oiling system. Such indicators only come on when the oil pressure is dangerously low. Even a factory oil pressure gauge in the instrument panel is only a relative indication, although much better for driver

information than a warning light. A better test is with a mechanical (not electrical) oil pressure gauge.
2   On four-cylinder engines, unscrew and remove the oil pressure sensor **(see illustration)** and screw in the hose for your oil pressure gauge. If necessary, install an adapter fitting. Use Teflon tape or thread sealant on the threads of the adapter and/or the fitting on the end of your gauge's hose.
3   On 3.2L engines, the oil pressure is taken using a special filter cap #2021500090. Remove the oil filter cap and filter (see Chapter 1), then transfer the oil filter to the special filter cap and install the test cap and filter. Tighten the test filter cap securely, then screw in the hose for your oil pressure gauge.
4   Check the oil pressure with the engine running (normal operating temperature) at the specified engine speed, and compare it to this Chapter's Specifications. If it's extremely low, the bearings and/or oil pump are probably worn out. If the pressure is within specifications the oil pressure sensor may be at fault.

5   On 3.2L engine models, once the test is complete reinstall the original filter cap and filter (see Chapter 1).

3   Cylinder compression check

1   A compression check will tell you what mechanical condition the upper end of your engine (pistons, rings, valves, head gaskets) is in. Specifically, it can tell you if the compression is down due to leakage caused by worn piston rings, defective valves and seats or a blown head gasket.
Note: *The engine must be at normal operating temperature and the battery must be fully charged for this check.*
2   Begin by cleaning the area around the ignition coils before you remove them (compressed air should be used, if available). The idea is to prevent dirt from getting into the cylinders as the compression check is being done.

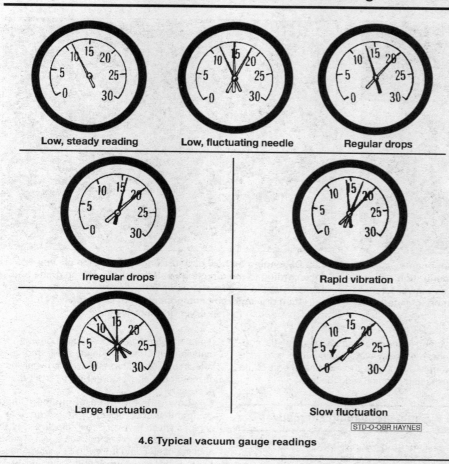

Low, steady reading

Low, fluctuating needle

Regular drops

Irregular drops

Rapid vibration

Large fluctuation

Slow fluctuation

STD-O-OBR HAYNES

4.6 Typical vacuum gauge readings

manifold gaskets, restricted exhaust, stuck or burned valves, weak valve springs, improper ignition or valve timing and ignition problems.

2   Unfortunately, vacuum gauge readings are easy to misinterpret, so they should be used in conjunction with other tests to confirm the diagnosis.

3   Both the absolute readings and the rate of needle movement are important for accurate interpretation. Most gauges measure vacuum in inches of mercury (in-Hg). The following references to vacuum assume the diagnosis is being performed at sea level. As elevation increases (or atmospheric pressure decreases), the reading will decrease. For every 1,000 foot increase in elevation above approximately 2,000 feet, the gauge readings will decrease about one inch of mercury.

4   Connect the vacuum gauge directly to the intake manifold vacuum, not to ported (throttle body) vacuum **(see illustration)**. Be sure no hoses are left disconnected during the test or false readings will result.

5   Before you begin the test, allow the engine to warm up completely. Block the wheels and set the parking brake. With the transaxle in Park, start the engine and allow it to run at normal idle speed.

Warning: *Keep your hands and the vacuum gauge clear of the fans.*

6   Read the vacuum gauge; an average, healthy engine should normally produce about 17 to 22 in-Hg with a fairly steady needle **(see illustration)**. Refer to the following vacuum gauge readings and what they indicate about the engine's condition:

7   A low, steady reading usually indicates a leaking gasket between the intake manifold and cylinder head(s) or throttle body, a leaky vacuum hose, late ignition timing or incorrect camshaft timing. Check ignition timing with a timing light and eliminate all other possible causes, utilizing the tests provided in this Chapter before you remove the timing chain cover to check the timing marks.

8   If the reading is three to eight inches below normal and it fluctuates at that low reading, suspect an intake manifold gasket leak at an intake port or a faulty fuel injector.

9   If the needle has regular drops of about two-to-four inches at a steady rate, the valves are probably leaking. Perform a compression check or leak-down test to confirm this.

10   An irregular drop or down-flick of the needle can be caused by a sticking valve or an ignition misfire. Perform a compression check or leak-down test and read the spark plugs.

11   A rapid vibration of about four in-Hg vibration at idle combined with exhaust smoke indicates worn valve guides. Perform a leak-down test to confirm this. If the rapid vibration occurs with an increase in engine speed, check for a leaking intake manifold gasket or head gasket, weak valve springs, burned valves or ignition misfire.

12   A slight fluctuation, say one inch up and down, may mean ignition problems. Check all the usual tune-up items and, if necessary, run the engine on an ignition analyzer.

3   Remove all of the spark plugs from the engine (see Chapter 1).

4   Remove the rear seat cushion and disable the fuel system by unplugging the fuel pump module electrical connector (see Chapter 4).

5   Install a compression gauge in the spark plug hole **(see illustration)**.

6   Have an assistant depress the accelerator pedal and crank the engine over at least seven compression strokes while you watch the gauge. The compression should build up quickly in a healthy engine. Low compression on the first stroke, followed by gradually increasing pressure on successive strokes, indicates worn piston rings. A low compression reading on the first stroke, which doesn't build up during successive strokes, indicates leaking valves or a blown head gasket (a cracked head could also be the cause). Deposits on the undersides of the valve heads can also cause low compression. Record the highest gauge reading obtained.

7   Repeat the procedure for the remaining cylinders and compare the results to this Chapter's Specifications.

8   Add some engine oil (about three squirts from a plunger-type oil can) to each cylinder, through the spark plug hole, and repeat the test.

9   If the compression increases after the oil is added, the piston rings are definitely worn. If the compression doesn't increase signifi-

cantly, the leakage is occurring at the valves or head gasket. Leakage past the valves may be caused by burned valve seats and/or faces or warped, cracked or bent valves.

10   If two adjacent cylinders have equally low compression, there's a strong possibility that the head gasket between them is blown. The appearance of coolant in the combustion chambers or the crankcase would verify this condition.

11   If one cylinder is slightly lower than the others, and the engine has a slightly rough idle, a worn lobe on the camshaft could be the cause.

12   If the compression is unusually high, the combustion chambers are probably coated with carbon deposits. If that's the case, the cylinder head(s) should be removed and decarbonized.

13   If compression is way down or varies greatly between cylinders, it would be a good idea to have a leak-down test performed by an automotive repair shop. This test will pinpoint exactly where the leakage is occurring and how severe it is.

4   Vacuum gauge diagnostic checks

1   A vacuum gauge provides inexpensive but valuable information about what is going on in the engine. You can check for worn rings or cylinder walls, leaking head or intake

6.3a After tightly wrapping water-vulnerable components, use a spray cleaner on everything, with particular concentration on the greasiest areas, usually around the valve cover and lower edges of the block. If one section dries out, apply more cleaner

6.3b Depending on how dirty the engine is, let the cleaner soak in according to the directions and then hose off the grime and cleaner. Get the rinse water down into every area you can get at, then dry important components with compressed air, a hair dryer or paper towels

6.6 Get an engine stand sturdy enough to firmly support the engine while you're working on it. Stay away from three-wheeled models; they have a tendency to tip over more easily, so get a four-wheeled unit

13   If there is a large fluctuation, perform a compression or leak-down test to look for a weak or dead cylinder or a blown head gasket.

14   If the needle moves slowly through a wide range, check for a clogged PCV system, incorrect idle fuel mixture, throttle body or intake manifold gasket leaks.

15   Check for a slow return after revving the engine by quickly snapping the throttle open until the engine reaches about 2,500 rpm and let it shut. Normally the reading should drop to near zero, rise above normal idle reading (about 5 in-Hg over) and then return to the previous idle reading. If the vacuum returns slowly and doesn't peak when the throttle is snapped shut, the rings may be worn. If there is a long delay, look for a restricted exhaust

system (often the muffler or catalytic converter). An easy way to check this is to temporarily disconnect the exhaust ahead of the suspected part and redo the test.

5   Engine rebuilding alternatives

1   The do-it-yourselfer is faced with a number of options when purchasing a rebuilt engine. The major considerations are cost, warranty, parts availability and the time required for the rebuilder to complete the project. The decision to replace the engine block, piston/connecting rod assemblies and crankshaft depends on the final inspection results of your engine. Only then can you make a cost effective decision whether to have your engine overhauled or simply purchase an exchange engine for your vehicle.

2   Some of the rebuilding alternatives include:

3   **Individual parts** - If the inspection procedures reveal that the engine block and most engine components are in reusable condition, purchasing individual parts and having a rebuilder rebuild your engine may be the most economical alternative. The block, crankshaft and piston/connecting rod assemblies should all be inspected carefully by a machine shop first.

4   **Short block** - A short block consists of an engine block with a crankshaft and piston/connecting rod assemblies already installed. All new bearings are incorporated and all clearances will be correct. The existing camshafts, valve train components, cylinder head and external parts can be bolted to the short block with little or no machine shop work necessary.

5   **Long block** - A long block consists of a short block plus an oil pump, oil pan, cylinder head, valve cover, camshaft and valve train components, timing sprockets and chain or

gears and timing cover. All components are installed with new bearings, seals and gaskets incorporated throughout. The installation of manifolds and external parts is all that's necessary.

6   **Low mileage used engines** - Some companies now offer low mileage used engines which is a very cost effective way to get your vehicle up and running again. These engines often come from vehicles which have been in totaled in accidents or come from other countries which have a higher vehicle turnover rate. A low mileage used engine also usually has a similar warranty like the newly remanufactured engines.

7   Give careful thought to which alternative is best for you and discuss the situation with local automotive machine shops, auto parts dealers and experienced rebuilders before ordering or purchasing replacement parts.

6   Engine removal - methods and precautions

1   If you've decided that an engine must be removed for overhaul or major repair work, several preliminary steps should be taken. Read all removal and installation procedures carefully prior to committing to this job.

2   Locating a suitable place to work is extremely important. Adequate work space, along with storage space for the vehicle, will be needed. If a shop or garage isn't available, at the very least a flat, level, clean work surface made of concrete or asphalt is required.

3   Cleaning the engine compartment and engine before beginning the removal procedure will help keep tools clean and organized (**see illustrations**).

4   An engine hoist will also be necessary. Make sure the hoist is rated in excess of the combined weight of the engine and transaxle. Safety is of primary importance, considering

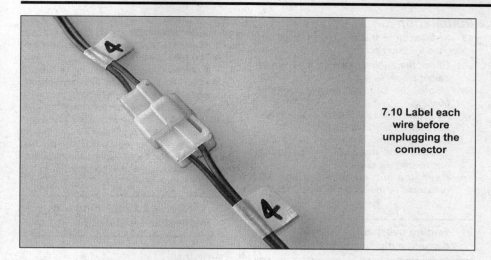

7.10 Label each wire before unplugging the connector

the potential hazards involved in removing the engine from the vehicle.

5   If you're a novice at engine removal, get at least one helper. One person cannot easily do all the things you need to do to remove a big heavy engine and transaxle assembly from the engine compartment. Also helpful is to seek advice and assistance from someone who's experienced in engine removal.

6   Plan the operation ahead of time. Arrange for or obtain all of the tools and equipment you'll need prior to beginning the job **(see illustration)**. Some of the equipment necessary to perform engine removal and installation safely and with relative ease are (in addition to a vehicle hoist and an engine hoist) a heavy duty floor jack (preferably fitted with a transmission jack head adapter), complete sets of wrenches and sockets as described in the front of this manual, wooden blocks, plenty of rags and cleaning solvent for mopping up spilled oil, coolant and gasoline.

7   Plan for the vehicle to be out of use for quite a while. A machine shop can do the work that is beyond the scope of the home mechanic. Machine shops often have a busy schedule, so before removing the engine, consult the shop for an estimate of how long it will take to rebuild or repair the components that may need work.

7   Engine - removal and installation

Warning: *Gasoline is extremely flammable, so take extra precautions when you work on any part of the fuel system. Don't smoke or allow open flames or bare light bulbs near the work area, and don't work in a garage where a gas-type appliance (such as a water heater or clothes dryer) is present. Since gasoline is carcinogenic, wear fuel-resistant gloves when there's a possibility of being exposed to fuel, and, if you spill any fuel on your skin, rinse it off immediately with soap and water. Mop up any spills immediately and do not store fuel-soaked rags where they could ignite. The fuel system is under constant pressure, so, if*

any fuel lines are to be disconnected, the fuel pressure in the system must be relieved first (see Chapter 4 for more information). When you perform any kind of work on the fuel system, wear safety glasses and have a Class B type fire extinguisher on hand.
Warning: *The engine must be completely cool before beginning this procedure.*
Warning: *The air conditioning system is under high pressure. Do not loosen any hose fittings or remove any components until after the system has been discharged. Air conditioning refrigerant must be properly discharged into an EPA-approved recovery/recycling unit at a dealer service department or an automotive air conditioning repair facility. Always wear eye protection when disconnecting air conditioning system fittings.*
Caution: *Engine removal on these models is a difficult job, especially for the do-it-yourself mechanic working at home. Because of the vehicle's design, the manufacturer states that the engine and transmission have to be removed as a unit from the bottom of the vehicle, not the top. With a floor jack and jackstands, the vehicle can't be raised high enough and supported safely enough for the suspension, engine/transmission assembly to slide out from underneath. The manufacturer recommends that removal of the engine/transmission assembly only be performed on a vehicle hoist.*
Caution: *If the engine has sustained severe engine damage, such as broken pistons, valves or block, the intake manifold must be replaced with a new one.*
Note: *Read through the entire Section before beginning this procedure.*

Removal

1   On 3.2L engines, have the air conditioning system discharged by an automotive air conditioning technician.
2   Park the vehicle on a frame-contact type vehicle hoist, with the front wheels pointing straight ahead. The pads of the hoist arms must contact the body welt along each side of the vehicle.
3   Remove the engine cover (see Chapter 1).

4   Relieve the fuel system pressure (see Chapter 4), then remove the battery (see Chapter 5).
5   Place protective covers on the fenders and cowl and remove the hood (see Chapter 11).
6   Remove the Powertrain Control Module (PCM) and its bracket (see Chapter 6).
7   Remove the air filter housing (see Chapter 4) and, on 3.2L engines, remove the resonator.
8   Remove the Power Distribution Center (PDC) mounting bolts and retainers in the engine compartment (see Chapter 12). Once the main engine harness connectors have been disconnected, secure the engine harness and power distribution center out of the way.
9   Secure the steering wheel from rotating. Working inside the vehicle, remove the steering intermediate shaft coupler bolt and separate the coupler from the steering gear (see Chapter 10, Section 20).
10   Clearly label and disconnect all vacuum lines, emissions hoses, wiring harness connectors, ground straps and fuel lines. Once all of the harness connectors have been disconnected, move the engine harness out of the way. Masking tape and/or a touch up paint applicator work well for marking items **(see illustration)**. Take instant photos or sketch the locations of components and brackets.
11   Loosen the front wheel bolts, then remove the front wheels and the under-vehicle splash shields (and skid plates, if equipped). Remove the wheels and both inner fenderwell splash shields (see Chapter 11).
12   Unstake and remove the driveaxle/hub nuts (see Chapter 8).
13   Drain the cooling system and engine oil and remove the drivebelt (see Chapter 1).
14   Remove the coolant expansion tank (see Chapter 3), then remove the return hose bolts and remove the hose assembly.
15   Remove both driveaxles (see Chapter 8), then remove the intermediate shaft and bracket.
16   Remove the radiator support panel, then remove the front bumper cover (see Chapter 11).
17   Disconnect the fuel lines (see Chapter 4) and canister purge lines (see Chapter 6).
18   Detach the heater hoses at the firewall.
19   Detach the radiator hoses, coolant hoses and heater hoses from the thermostat housing and oil cooler (see Chapter 3).
20   Remove the bolt securing the heater core supply tube to the left engine bracket.
21   Disconnect the wiring harness retainer on the bottom of the battery tray and remove the windshield wiper reservoir bolt, then the battery tray (see Chapter 5).
22   Remove the starter motor (see Chapter 5).
Note: *On 2.4L engines, the upper starter mounting bolt will not back out completely because of the lack of clearance. Leave the bolt in the transmission housing at this time.*
23   On 3.2L engines, remove the electric vacuum pump and bracket (see Chapter 9).
24   Disconnect and plug the transmission cooler lines (see Chapter 7A).

25   Disconnect the main harness wiring retainers along the transmission.

26   Remove the air conditioning compressor (see Chapter 3).

Note: *On 2.4L models, unbolt the air compressor without disconnecting the refrigerant lines and secure the compressor out of the way.*

27   On 3.2L engines, remove the nut and separate the air conditioning liquid and suction manifold connection from the internal heater exchanger (IHX) located at the front of the engine compartment, then cap all the openings to prevent contamination.

28   Remove the alternator (see Chapter 5).

29   Remove the load beam extensions and load beams (see Chapter 10, Section 5).

30   Disconnect the shift cables from the transaxle (see Chapter 7A). Also disconnect the ground cable from the transaxle.

31   On AWD models, remove the driveshaft (see Chapter 8) and the transfer case (see Chapter 7B).

32   Detach the exhaust pipe from the exhaust manifold(s) and remove the crossunder pipe, then remove the exhaust manifold on 2.4L engines (see Chapter 2A) or the rearbank exhaust manifold on 3.2L engines (see Chapter 2B).

33   On 2.4L engines, remove the rear engine mount insulator (see Chapter 2A).

Note: *On 2.4L models, the exhaust manifold and catalytic converters are combined and are referred to as a "maniverter."*

34   Remove the torque converter inspection cover and remove the torque converter bolts (see Chapter 7A).

35   Remove the front suspension crossmember (see Chapter 10).

36   Place four jackstands on the outer four points of the engine and transaxle assembly, make sure they are secure and the load is evenly placed. Lower the vehicle enough to support the full weight of the engine and transaxle assembly, then secure the jackstands to the assembly with wire or tiedowns to prevent the jackstands from moving. Also support the transaxle with a floor jack.

Note: *There are four points or locating holes, two on the engine block and two on the oil pan rail.*

37   With the engine securely attached and supported, slowly remove the left engine mounting bolts and remove the engine mount.

38   Slowly remove the right engine mounting bolts and remove the engine mount and bracket.

39   Slowly raise the vehicle, making sure there is nothing attached.

40   With the transaxle supported with the floor jack, remove the transaxle-to-engine mounting bolts.

41   Carefully separate the transaxle from the engine and remove the transaxle.

42   Connect an engine hoist and chain to the engine, then slightly lift the engine enough to remove the jacks and roll the engine out from under the vehicle. Place the engine on an engine stand and disconnect the hoist and chain.

Installation

43   Installation is the reverse of removal, noting the following points:

a) *Check the engine mount. If it's worn or damaged, replace it.*

b) *Inspect the torque converter seal and bushing.*

c) *Add coolant, oil and transmission fluids as needed (see Chapter 1).*

d) *Run the engine and check for proper operation and leaks. Shut off the engine and recheck fluid levels.*

e) *Have the air conditioning system recharged by the shop that discharged it.*

8   Engine overhaul - disassembly sequence

1   It's much easier to remove the external components if it's mounted on a portable engine stand. A stand can often be rented quite cheaply from an equipment rental yard. Before the engine is mounted on a stand, the driveplate should be removed from the engine.

2   If a stand isn't available, it's possible to remove the external engine components with it blocked up on the floor. Be extra careful not to tip or drop the engine when working without a stand.

3   If you're going to obtain a rebuilt engine, all external components must come off first, to be transferred to the replacement engine. These components include:

    Driveplate
    Ignition system components
    Emissions-related components
    Engine mounts and mount brackets
    Engine rear cover (spacer plate between
      driveplate and engine block)
    Intake/exhaust manifolds
    Fuel injection components
    Oil filter
    Thermostat and housing assembly
    Water pump

Note: *When removing the external components from the engine, pay close attention to details that may be helpful or important during installation. Note the installed position of gaskets, seals, spacers, pins, brackets, washers, bolts and other small items.*

4   If you're going to obtain a short block (assembled engine block, crankshaft, pistons and connecting rods), then remove the timing belt/timing chain, cylinder head, oil pan, oil pump pick-up tube, oil pump and water pump from your engine so that you can turn in your old short block to the rebuilder as a core. See Section 5 for additional information regarding the different possibilities to be considered.

9   Pistons and connecting rods - removal and installation

Removal

Note: *On 2.4L models, prior to removing the piston/connecting rod assemblies, remove the cylinder head, oil pan, balance shaft assembly, timing chain cover (see Chapter 2A), the alternator bracket bolts, intermediate shaft bearing bolts and the oil dipstick tube. On 3.2L models, remove the cylinder heads, oil pan, timing chain cover and oil pump (see Chapter 2B).*

1   Use your fingernail to feel if a ridge has formed at the upper limit of ring travel (about 1/4-inch down from the top of each cylinder). If carbon deposits or cylinder wear have produced ridges, they must be completely removed with a special tool **(see illustration)**. Follow the manufacturer's instructions provided with the tool. Failure to remove the ridges before attempting to remove the piston/connecting rod assemblies may result in piston breakage.

2   After the cylinder ridges have been removed, turn the engine so the crankshaft is facing up. On 2.0L engines remove the oil pump pick up tube, then remove the windage tray (see Section 10). On 2.4L engines remove the balance shaft/oil pump assembly (see Chapter 2A), then remove the ladder frame and the bearing beam (see Section 10). On 3.2L engines, remove the oil

9.1 Before you try to remove the pistons, use a ridge reamer to remove the raised material (ridge) from the top of the cylinders

9.3 Checking the connecting rod endplay (side clearance)

9.4 If the connecting rods or caps are not marked, use permanent ink or paint to mark the caps to the rods by cylinder number (for example, this would be number 4 cylinder connecting rod)

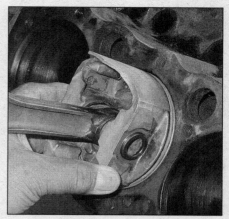

9.13 Install the piston ring into the cylinder, then push it down into position using a piston so the ring will be square in the cylinder

pump (see Chapter 2B), then remove the outer crankshaft main bearing cap bolts and the windage tray (see Section 10).

3   Before the main bearing caps and connecting rods are removed, check the connecting rod endplay with feeler gauges. Slide them between the first connecting rod and the crankshaft throw until the play is removed (see illustration). Repeat this procedure for each connecting rod. The endplay is equal to the thickness of the feeler gauge(s). Check with an automotive machine shop for the endplay service limit (a typical end play limit should measure between 0.005 to 0.015 inch [0.127 to 0.396 mm]). If the play exceeds the service limit, new connecting rods will be required. If new rods (or a new crankshaft) are installed, the endplay may fall under the minimum allowable. If it does, the rods will have to be machined to restore it. If necessary, consult an automotive machine shop for advice.

4   Check the connecting rods and caps for identification marks. If they aren't plainly

marked, use paint or marker to clearly identify each rod and cap (1, 2, 3, etc., depending on the cylinder they're associated with) (see illustration).
Caution: Do not use a punch and hammer to mark the connecting rods or they may be damaged.

5   Loosen each of the connecting rod cap bolts 1/2-turn at a time until they can be removed by hand.
Note: New connecting rod cap bolts must be used when reassembling the engine, but save the old bolts for use when checking the connecting rod bearing oil clearance.

6   Remove the number one connecting rod cap and bearing insert. Don't drop the bearing insert out of the cap.

7   Remove the bearing insert and push the connecting rod/piston assembly out through the top of the engine. Use a wooden or plastic hammer handle to push on the upper bearing surface in the connecting rod. If resistance is felt, double-check to make sure that all of the ridge was removed from the cylinder.

8   Repeat the procedure for the remaining cylinders.

9   After removal, reassemble the connecting rod caps and bearing inserts in their respective connecting rods and install the cap bolts finger-tight. Leaving the old bearing inserts in place until reassembly will help prevent the connecting rod bearing surfaces from being accidentally nicked or gouged.

10   The pistons and connecting rods are now ready for inspection and overhaul at an automotive machine shop.

Piston ring installation

11   Before installing the new piston rings, the ring end gaps must be checked. It's assumed that the piston ring side clearance has been checked and verified correct.

12   Lay out the piston/connecting rod assemblies and the new ring sets so the ring sets will be matched with the same piston and cylinder during the end gap measurement and engine assembly.

13   Insert the top (number one) ring into the first cylinder and square it up with the cylinder walls by pushing it in with the top of the piston (see illustration). The ring should be near the bottom of the cylinder, at the lower limit of ring travel.

14   To measure the end gap, slip feeler gauges between the ends of the ring until a gauge equal to the gap width is found (see illustration). The feeler gauge should slide between the ring ends with a slight amount of drag. A typical ring gap should fall between 0.010 and 0.020 inch [0.25 to 0.50 mm] for compression rings and up to 0.030 inch [0.76 mm] for the oil ring steel rails. If the gap is larger or smaller than specified, double-check to make sure you have the correct rings before proceeding.

15   If the gap is too small, it must be enlarged or the ring ends may come in contact with each other during engine opera-

9.14 With the ring square in the cylinder, measure the ring end gap with a feeler gauge

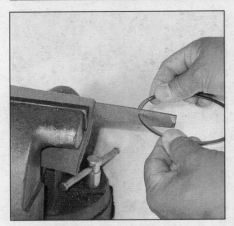

9.15 If the ring end gap is too small, clamp a file in a vise as shown and file the piston ring ends - be sure to remove all raised material

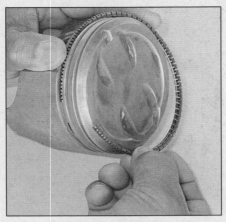

9.19a Installing the spacer/expander in the oil ring groove

9.19b DO NOT use a piston ring installation tool when installing the oil control side rails

tion, which can cause serious damage to the engine. If necessary, increase the end gaps by filing the ring ends very carefully with a fine file. Mount the file in a vise equipped with soft jaws, slip the ring over the file with the ends contacting the file face and slowly move the ring to remove material from the ends. When performing this operation, file only by pushing the ring from the outside end of the file towards the vise **(see illustration)**.

16   Excess end gap isn't critical unless it's greater than 0.040 inch (1.01 mm). Again, double-check to make sure you have the correct ring type.

17   Repeat the procedure for each ring that will be installed in the first cylinder and for each ring in the remaining cylinders. Remember to keep rings, pistons and cylinders matched up.

18   Once the ring end gaps have been checked/corrected, the rings can be installed on the pistons.

19   The oil control ring (lowest one on the piston) is usually installed first. It's composed of three separate components. Slip the spacer/expander into the groove **(see illustration)**. If an anti-rotation tang is used, make sure it's inserted into the drilled hole in the ring groove. Next, install the upper side rail in the same manner **(see illustration)**. Don't use a piston ring installation tool on the oil ring side rails, as they may be damaged. Instead, place one end of the side rail into the groove between the spacer/expander and the ring land, hold it firmly in place and slide a finger around the piston while pushing the rail into the groove. Finally, install the lower side rail.

20   After the three oil ring components have been installed, check to make sure that both the upper and lower side rails can be rotated smoothly inside the ring grooves.

21   The number two (middle) ring is installed next. It's usually stamped with a mark which must face up, toward the top of the piston. Do not mix up the top and middle rings, as they have different cross-sections.

Note: *Always follow the instructions printed on the ring package or box - different manufacturers may require different approaches.*

22   Use a piston ring installation tool and make sure the identification mark is facing the top of the piston, then slip the ring into the middle groove on the piston **(see illustration)**. Don't expand the ring any more than necessary to slide it over the piston.

23   Install the number one (top) ring in the same manner. Make sure the mark is facing up. Be careful not to confuse the number one and number two rings.

24   Repeat the procedure for the remaining pistons and rings.

Installation

25   Before installing the piston/connecting rod assemblies, the cylinder walls must be perfectly clean, the top edge of each cylinder bore must be chamfered, and the crankshaft must be in place.

26   Remove the cap from the end of the number one connecting rod (refer to the marks made during removal). Remove the original bearing inserts and wipe the bearing surfaces of the connecting rod and cap with a clean, lint-free cloth. They must be kept spotlessly clean.

Connecting rod bearing oil clearance check

27   Clean the back side of the new upper bearing insert, then lay it in place in the connecting rod.

28   Make sure the tab on the bearing fits into the recess in the rod. Don't hammer the bearing insert into place and be very careful not to nick or gouge the bearing face. Don't lubricate the bearing at this time.

29   Clean the back side of the other bearing insert and install it in the rod cap. Again, make sure the tab on the bearing fits into the recess in the cap, and don't apply any lubricant. It's critically important that the mating surfaces of the bearing and connecting rod are perfectly clean and oil free when they're assembled.

30   Position the piston ring gaps at 90-degree

intervals around the piston as shown **(see illustration)**.

31   Lubricate the piston and rings with clean engine oil and attach a piston ring compressor to the piston. Leave the skirt protruding about 1/4-inch to guide the piston into the cylinder. The rings must be compressed until they're flush with the piston.

32   Rotate the crankshaft until the number one connecting rod journal is at BDC (bottom dead center) and apply a liberal coat of engine oil to the cylinder walls.

33   With the directional stamp (arrow) on top of the piston facing the front (timing belt/ timing chain end) of the engine, gently insert the piston/connecting rod assembly into the number one cylinder bore and rest the bottom edge of the ring compressor on the engine block. Install the pistons with the (arrow) mark facing toward the timing belt/timing chain end.

34   Tap the top edge of the ring compressor to make sure it's contacting the block around its entire circumference.

35   Gently tap on the top of the piston with the end of a wooden or plastic hammer handle **(see illustration)** while guiding the end of the connecting rod into place on the crankshaft journal. The piston rings may try to pop out of the ring compressor just before entering the cylinder bore, so keep some downward pressure on the ring compressor. Work slowly, and if any resistance is felt as the piston enters the cylinder, stop immediately. Find out what's hanging up and fix it before proceeding. Do not force the piston into the cylinder - you might break a ring and/or the piston.

36   Once the piston/connecting rod assembly is installed, the connecting rod bearing oil clearance must be checked before the rod cap is permanently installed.

37   Cut a piece of the appropriate size Plastigage slightly shorter than the width of the connecting rod bearing and lay it in place on the number one connecting rod journal, parallel with the journal axis **(see illustration)**.

38   Clean the connecting rod cap bearing face and install the rod cap. Make sure the mating mark on the cap is on the same

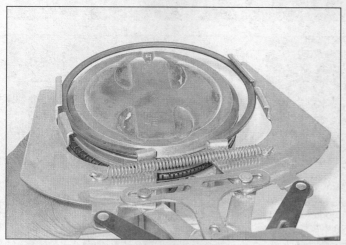

9.22 Use a piston ring installation tool to install the number 2 and the number 1 (top) rings - be sure the directional mark on the piston ring(s) is facing toward the top of the piston

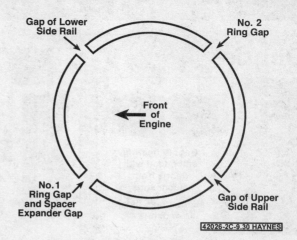

9.30 Position the piston ring end gaps as shown here before installing the piston/connecting rod assemblies into the engine

A Top compression ring gap
B Second compression ring and oil ring spacer gap
C Upper oil ring gap
D Lower oil ring gap

9.35 Use a plastic or wooden hammer handle to push the piston into the cylinder

9.37 Place Plastigage on each connecting rod bearing journal parallel to the crankshaft centerline

9.41 Use the scale on the Plastigage package to determine the bearing oil clearance - be sure to measure the widest part of the Plastigage and use the correct scale; it comes with both standard and metric scales

side as the mark on the connecting rod (see illustration 9.4).

39 Install the old rod bolts at this time, and tighten them to the torque listed in this Chapter's Specifications.

Note: *Use a thin-wall socket to avoid erroneous torque readings that can result if the socket is wedged between the rod cap and the bolt. If the socket tends to wedge itself between the bolt and the cap, lift up on it slightly until it no longer contacts the cap. DO NOT rotate the crankshaft at any time during this operation.*

40 Remove the bolts and detach the rod cap, being very careful not to disturb the Plastigage. Discard the cap bolts at this time as they cannot be reused.

Note: *You MUST use new connecting rod bolts.*

41 Compare the width of the crushed Plastigage to the scale printed on the Plastigage envelope to obtain the oil clearance (see illustration). The connecting rod oil clear-

ance is usually about 0.001 to 0.002 inch. Consult an automotive machine shop for the clearance specified for the rod bearings on your engine.

42 If the clearance is not as specified, the bearing inserts may be the wrong size (which means different ones will be required). Before deciding that different inserts are needed, make sure that no dirt or oil was between the bearing inserts and the connecting rod or cap when the clearance was measured. Also, recheck the journal diameter. If the Plastigage was wider at one end than the other, the journal may be tapered. If the clearance still exceeds the limit specified, the bearing will have to be replaced with an undersize bearing.

Caution: *When installing a new crankshaft, always use a standard size bearing.*

Final installation

43 Carefully scrape all traces of the Plastigage material off the rod journal and/or bear-

ing face. Be very careful not to scratch the bearing - use your fingernail or the edge of a plastic card.

44 Make sure the bearing faces are perfectly clean, then apply a uniform layer of clean moly-base grease or engine assembly lube to both of them. You'll have to push the piston into the cylinder to expose the face of the bearing insert in the connecting rod.

Caution: *Install new connecting rod cap bolts. Do NOT reuse old bolts - they have stretched and cannot be reused.*

45 Slide the connecting rod back into place on the journal, install the rod cap, install the NEW bolts and tighten them to the torque listed in this Chapter's Specifications.

46 Repeat the entire procedure for the remaining pistons/connecting rods.

ENGINE BEARING ANALYSIS

Debris

Babbitt bearing embedded with debris from machinings

Microscopic detail of debris

Microscopic detail of gouges

Overplated copper alloy bearing gouged by cast iron debris

Aluminum bearing embedded with glass beads

Microscopic detail of glass beads

Damaged lining caused by dirt left on the bearing back

Misassembly

Result of a lower half assembled as an upper - blocking the oil flow

Excessive oil clearance is indicated by a short contact arc

Polished and oil-stained backs are a result of a poor fit in the housing bore

Result of a wrong, reversed, or shifted cap

Overloading

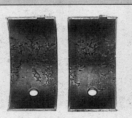

Damage from excessive idling which resulted in an oil film unable to support the load imposed

Damaged upper connecting rod bearings caused by engine lugging; the lower main bearings (not shown) were similarly affected

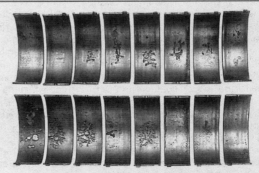

The damage shown in these upper and lower connecting rod bearings was caused by engine operation at a higher-than-rated speed under load

Misalignment

A warped crankshaft caused this pattern of severe wear in the center, diminishing toward the ends

A poorly finished crankshaft caused the equally spaced scoring shown

A tapered housing bore caused the damage along one edge of this pair

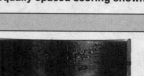

A bent connecting rod led to the damage in the "V" pattern

Lubrication

Result of dry start: The bearings on the left, farthest from the oil pump, show more damage

Result of a low oil supply or oil starvation

Severe wear as a result of inadequate oil clearance

Corrosion

Microscopic detail of corrosion

Corrosion is an acid attack on the bearing lining generally caused by inadequate maintenance, extremely hot or cold operation, or inferior oils or fuels

Microscopic detail of cavitation

Example of cavitation - a surface erosion caused by pressure changes in the oil film

Damage from excessive thrust or insufficient axial clearance

Bearing affected by oil dilution caused by excessive blow-by or a rich mixture

© 1986 Federal-Mogul Corporation
Copy and photographs courtesy of Federal Mogul Corporation

10.1 Checking crankshaft endplay with a dial indicator

10.3 Checking crankshaft endplay with feeler gauges at the thrust bearing journal

47 The important points to remember are:

a) *Keep the back sides of the bearing inserts and the insides of the connecting rods and caps perfectly clean when assembling them.*

b) *Make sure you have the correct piston/ rod assembly for each cylinder.*

c) *The mark on the piston must face the front (timing belt end or timing chain of the engine).*

d) *Lubricate the cylinder walls liberally with clean oil.*

e) *Lubricate the bearing faces when installing the rod caps after the oil clearance has been checked.*

48 After all the piston/connecting rod assemblies have been correctly installed, rotate the crankshaft a number of times by hand to check for any obvious binding.

49 As a final step, check the connecting rod endplay again.

50 Compare the measured endplay to the tolerance listed in this Chapter's Specifications to make sure it's acceptable. If it was correct before disassembly and the original crankshaft and rods were reinstalled, it should still be correct. If new rods or a new crankshaft were installed, the endplay may be inadequate. If so, the rods will have to be removed and taken to an automotive machine shop for resizing.

51 On 2.4L engines, apply a bead of Mopar engine sealant RTV along the sealing surface of the cylinder block, then install the bearing beam and tighten the bolts in sequence (see Section 10) to the torque listed in this Chapter's Specifications. **Caution:** *Once the RTV is applied, the bearing beam must be installed within 10 minutes and the bolts torqued to specifications within the next 10 minutes or it may leak oil.*

10 Crankshaft - removal and installation

Removal

Note: *The crankshaft can be removed only after the engine has been removed from the vehicle. It's assumed that the driveplate, crankshaft pulley, timing belt/timing chain, timing sprockets, oil pan, oil pump body, oil filter, oil pump pick-up tube, windage tray and piston/connecting rod assemblies have already been removed. On 2.4L engines, the oil pump/ balance shaft module and the rear main oil seal must be removed (see Chapter 2A) and on 3.2L engines, the rear main oil seal retainer must be unbolted and separated from the block before proceeding with crankshaft removal.*

1 Before the crankshaft is removed, measure the endplay. Mount a dial indicator with the indicator in line with the crankshaft and just touching the end of the crankshaft as shown **(see illustration)**.

2 Pry the crankshaft all the way to the rear and zero the dial indicator. Next, pry the crankshaft to the front as far as possible and check the reading on the dial indicator. The distance traveled is the endplay. A typical crankshaft endplay will fall between 0.003 to 0.010 inch (0.076 to 0.254 mm). If it is greater than that, check the crankshaft thrust surfaces for wear after it's removed. If no wear is evident, new main bearings should correct the endplay.

3 If a dial indicator isn't available, feeler gauges can be used. Gently pry the crankshaft all the way to the front of the engine. Slip feeler gauges between the crankshaft and the front face of the thrust bearing or washer to determine the clearance **(see illustration)**.

4 On 2.0L engines, remove the windage tray bolts **(see illustration 10.33f)** and windage tray.

5 On 2.4L engines, remove the alternator mounting bracket, intake manifold support bracket and the driveaxle intermediate bearing housing, then remove the ladder frame mounting bolts **(see illustration 10.37)** and carefully separate the ladder frame from the block using the pry points (cast into the block) at the rear and right side of the engine block.

6 On 3.2L engines, remove the outer crankshaft main bearing cap and the windage tray bolts, then remove the windage tray **(see illustration 10.33c)**.

7 Loosen the main bearing cap bolts 1/4-turn at a time each, until they can be removed by hand. On 3.2L and 2.0L engine models, also remove the main bearing cross bolts (tie bolts) first, in reverse order of the installation tightening sequence **(see illustration 10.33d or 10.33e)**.

Note: *On 2.4L models, the center three bearing caps are one piece, called a bearing beam, and must be removed and installed before the outer two remaining bearing caps (see illustration 10.33a).*

8 Gently tap the main bearing cap with a soft-faced hammer around the perimeter of the assembly. Pull the main bearing cap straight up and off the cylinder block. Try not to drop the bearing inserts if they come out with the assembly.

Note: *New main bearing cap bolts must be used when reassembling the engine, but save the old bolts for use when checking the main bearing oil clearance.*

9 Carefully lift the crankshaft out of the engine. It may be a good idea to have an assistant available, since the crankshaft is quite heavy and awkward to handle. With the bearing inserts in place inside the engine block and main bearing caps, reinstall the bedplate/main bearing caps onto the engine block and tighten the bolts finger-tight. Make sure you install the bedplate/main bearing caps with the arrow facing the front end of the engine.

10.20 Place the Plastigage onto the crankshaft bearing journal as shown

10.24 Use the scale on the Plastigage package to determine the bearing oil clearance - be sure to measure the widest part of the Plastigage and use the correct scale; it comes with both standard and metric scales

Installation

10   Crankshaft installation is the first step in engine reassembly. It's assumed at this point that the engine block and crankshaft have been cleaned, inspected and repaired or reconditioned. Install the target wheel to the crankshaft and tighten the new bolts to the torque listed in this Chapter's Specifications, if removed.
11   Position the engine block with the bottom facing up then remove the mounting bolts and lift off the main bearing caps.
12   If they're still in place, remove the original bearing inserts from the block main bearing caps. Wipe the bearing surfaces of the block and caps/bearing beam with a clean, lint-free cloth. They must be kept spotlessly clean. This is critical for determining the correct bearing oil clearance.

Main bearing oil clearance check

13   Without mixing them up, clean the back sides of the new upper main bearing inserts (with grooves and oil holes) and lay one in each main bearing saddle in the block. Each upper bearing has an oil groove and oil hole in it.
Caution: *The oil holes in the block must line up with the oil holes in the upper bearing inserts.*
14   The thrust washer or thrust bearing insert must be installed in the number 2 crankshaft journal with the notches facing the crankshaft. Clean the back sides of the lower main bearing inserts and lay them in the corresponding location in the main bearing caps. Make sure the tab on the bearing insert fits into the recess in the block or bedplate or main bearing caps. The upper bearings with the oil holes are installed into the engine block, while the lower bearings without the oil holes are installed in the main bearing caps.
Caution: *Do not hammer the bearing insert into place and don't nick or gouge the bearing faces. DO NOT apply any lubrication at this time.*
15   Clean the faces of the bearing inserts in the block and the crankshaft main bearing journals with a clean, lint-free cloth.

16   Check or clean the oil holes in the crankshaft, as any dirt here can go only one way - straight through the new bearings.
17   Once you're certain the crankshaft is clean, carefully lay it in position in the cylinder block.
18   Before the crankshaft can be permanently installed, the main bearing oil clearance must be checked.
19   Cut several strips of the appropriate size of Plastigage. They must be slightly shorter than the width of the main bearing journal.
20   Place one piece on each crankshaft main bearing journal, parallel with the journal axis as shown **(see illustration)**.
21   Clean the faces of the bearing inserts in the main bearing caps. Hold the bearing inserts in place and install the assembly onto the crankshaft and cylinder block. DO NOT disturb the Plastigage. Make sure you install the main bearing caps with the arrow facing the front (timing belt/timing chain end) of the engine.
Caution: *The number 2 main bearing cap must be centered over the inner bolt holes of the block. If the bearing cap is not centered, the crankshaft counterweights can contact the main bearing cap and cause severe engine damage.*
22   Apply clean engine oil to all bolt threads prior to installation, then install the old bolts finger-tight; do not install the side bolts at this time, if equipped. Tighten all the bolts in the sequences shown **(see illustrations 10.33a, 10.33b or 10.33e)** to the torque listed in this Chapter's Specifications. On 3.2L engines only install and tighten the inner bolts. It is not necessary to install the main bearing cap outer bolts or side bolts at this time. On 2.0L engines, its not necessary to instal the side (tie) bolts at this time.
23   Remove the bolts in the reverse order of the tightening sequence and carefully lift the caps straight up and off the block. Do not disturb the Plastigage or rotate the crankshaft. If the cap(s) is difficult to remove, tap it gently from side-to-side with a soft-faced hammer to loosen it.

24   Compare the width of the crushed Plastigage on each journal to the scale printed on the Plastigage envelope to determine the main bearing oil clearance **(see illustration)**. Check with an automotive machine shop for the crankshaft main bearing oil clearance limits.
25   If the clearance is not as specified, the bearing inserts may be the wrong size (which means different ones will be required). Before deciding if different inserts are needed, make sure that no dirt or oil was between the bearing inserts and the cap assembly or block when the clearance was measured. If the Plastigage was wider at one end than the other, the crankshaft journal may be tapered. If the clearance still exceeds the limit specified, the bearing insert(s) will have to be replaced with an undersize bearing insert(s).
Caution: *When installing a new crankshaft, always install a standard bearing insert set.*
26   Carefully scrape all traces of the Plastigage material off the main bearing journals and/or the bearing insert faces. Be sure to remove all residue from the oil holes. Use your fingernail or the edge of a plastic card - don't nick or scratch the bearing faces.

Final installation

27   Carefully lift the crankshaft out of the cylinder block.
28   Clean the bearing insert faces in the cylinder block, then apply a thin, uniform layer of moly-base grease or engine assembly lube to each of the bearing surfaces. Coat the thrust faces as well as the journal face of the thrust bearing.
29   Make sure the crankshaft journals are clean, then lay the crankshaft back in place in the cylinder block.
30   Clean the bearing insert faces and then apply the same lubricant to them.
31   Install the main bearing caps onto the designated journals.
32   Prior to installation, apply clean engine oil to the **NEW** bolt threads, wiping off any excess, then install all bolts finger-tight.

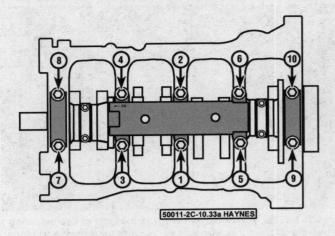

10.33a Main bearing cap bolt and bearing beam bolt tightening sequence - 2.4L engines

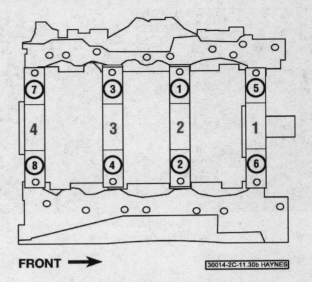

FRONT ➤

10.33b Main bearing cap inner bolt tightening sequence - 3.2L engines

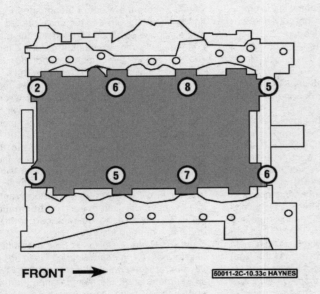

FRONT ➤

10.33c Main bearing cap outer bolt and windage tray tightening sequence - 3.2L engines

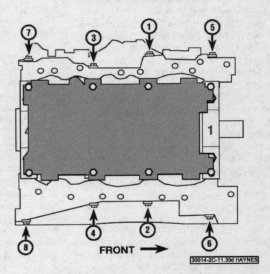

FRONT ➤

10.33d Main bearing cap side bolt tightening sequence - 3.2L engines

---

33   Tighten the cap bolts, in sequence **(see illustrations)**, to the torque listed in this Chapter's Specifications.

34   Recheck crankshaft endplay with a feeler gauge or a dial indicator. The endplay should be correct if the crankshaft thrust faces aren't worn or damaged and if new bearings have been installed.

35   Rotate the crankshaft a number of times by hand to check for any obvious binding. It should rotate with a running torque of 50 in-lbs or less. If the running torque is too high, correct the problem at this time.

36   On 2.4L engines, clean the ladder frame and block sealing surfaces with brake cleaner or isopropyl alcohol, then apply a 2 mm bead of Mopar engine RTV sealant along the sealing surfaces of the block **(see illustration)**.

37   Once the RTV sealant is applied, install

the ladder frame and bolts, then tighten the bolts in sequence **(see illustration)** to the torque listed this Chapter's Specifications. **Caution:** *The ladder frame must be installed within 10 minutes and fully tightened within the next 10 minutes. If it's not done within this timeframe, oil leaks may occur.*

38   Install the new rear main oil seal (see Chapter 2A or 2B).

---

11   Engine overhaul - reassembly sequence

---

1   Before beginning engine reassembly, make sure you have all the necessary new parts, gaskets and seals as well as the following items on hand:

Common hand tools
A 1/2-inch drive torque wrench
New engine oil
Gasket sealant
Thread locking compound

2   If you obtained a short block, it will be necessary to install the cylinder head, the oil pump and pick-up tube, the oil pan, the water pump, the timing belt/timing chain and timing cover, and the valve cover (see Chapter 2A) and balance shaft module on 2.4L models (see Chapter 2A). In order to save time and avoid problems, the external components must be installed in the following general order:

Thermostat and housing cover
Water pump
Intake and exhaust manifolds
Fuel injection components
Emissions control components

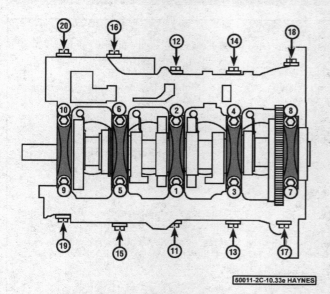

10.33e Main bearing cap bolts and outer (tie) bolt tightening sequence - 2.0L engines

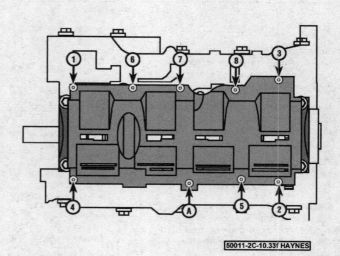

10.33f Windage tray tightening sequence - 2.0L engines. Bolt "A" is used on non-Trailhawk engines

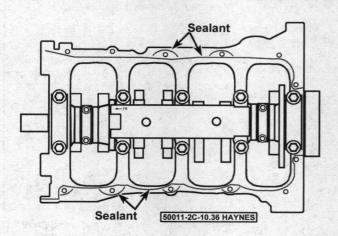

10.36 Apply a bead of sealant along the block - 2.4L engine shown

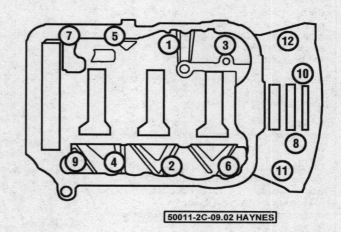

10.37 Ladder frame bolt tightening sequence - 2.4L engines

Spark plug wires and spark plugs
Ignition coils
Oil filter
Engine mounts and mount brackets
Driveplate

12 Initial start-up and break-in after overhaul

Warning: *Have a fire extinguisher handy when starting the engine for the first time.*

1   Once the engine has been installed in the vehicle, double-check the engine oil and coolant levels.

2   With the spark plugs out of the engine and the fuel pump disabled (see Section 3,

Step 5), crank the engine until oil pressure registers on the gauge or the light goes out.

3   Install the spark plugs, install the coils, and reconnect the electrical connector to the fuel pump module.

4   Start the engine. It may take a few moments for the fuel system to build up pressure, but the engine should start without a great deal of effort.

5   After the engine starts, it should be allowed to warm up to normal operating temperature. While the engine is warming up, make a thorough check for fuel, oil and coolant leaks.

6   Shut the engine off and recheck the engine oil and coolant levels.

7   Drive the vehicle to an area with minimum traffic, accelerate from 30 to 50 mph,

then allow the vehicle to slow to 30 mph with the throttle closed. Repeat the procedure 10 or 12 times. This will load the piston rings and cause them to seat properly against the cylinder walls. Check again for oil and coolant leaks.

8   Drive the vehicle gently for the first 500 miles (no sustained high speeds) and keep a constant check on the oil level. It is not unusual for an engine to use oil during the break-in period.

9   At approximately 500 to 600 miles, change the oil and filter.

10   For the next few hundred miles, drive the vehicle normally. Do not pamper it or abuse it.

11   After 2000 miles, change the oil and filter again and consider the engine broken in.

COMMON ENGINE OVERHAUL TERMS

B

Backlash - The amount of play between two parts. Usually refers to how much one gear can be moved back and forth without moving gear with which it's meshed.

Bearing Caps - The caps held in place by nuts or bolts which, in turn, hold the bearing surface. This space is for lubricating oil to enter.

Bearing clearance - The amount of space left between shaft and bearing surface. This space is for lubricating oil to enter.

Bearing crush - The additional height which is purposely manufactured into each bearing half to ensure complete contact of the bearing back with the housing bore when the engine is assembled.

Bearing knock - The noise created by movement of a part in a loose or worn bearing.

Blueprinting - Dismantling an engine and reassembling it to EXACT specifications.

Bore - An engine cylinder, or any cylindrical hole; also used to describe the process of enlarging or accurately refinishing a hole with a cutting tool, as to bore an engine cylinder. The bore size is the diameter of the hole.

Boring - Renewing the cylinders by cutting them out to a specified size. A boring bar is used to make the cut.

Bottom end - A term which refers collectively to the engine block, crankshaft, main bearings and the big ends of the connecting rods.

Break-in - The period of operation between installation of new or rebuilt parts and time in which parts are worn to the correct fit. Driving at reduced and varying speed for a specified mileage to permit parts to wear to the correct fit.

Bushing - A one-piece sleeve placed in a bore to serve as a bearing surface for shaft, piston pin, etc. Usually replaceable.

C

Camshaft - The shaft in the engine, on which a series of lobes are located for operating the valve mechanisms. The camshaft is driven by gears or sprockets and a timing chain. Usually referred to simply as the cam.

Carbon - Hard, or soft, black deposits found in combustion chamber, on plugs, under rings, on and under valve heads.

Cast iron - An alloy of iron and more than two percent carbon, used for engine blocks and heads because it's relatively inexpensive and easy to mold into complex shapes.

Chamfer - To bevel across (or a bevel on) the sharp edge of an object.

Chase - To repair damaged threads with a tap or die.

Combustion chamber - The space between the piston and the cylinder head, with the piston at top dead center, in which air-fuel mixture is burned.

Compression ratio - The relationship between cylinder volume (clearance volume) when the piston is at top dead center and cylinder volume when the piston is at bottom dead center.

Connecting rod - The rod that connects the crank on the crankshaft with the piston. Sometimes called a con rod.

Connecting rod cap - The part of the connecting rod assembly that attaches the rod to the crankpin.

Core plug - Soft metal plug used to plug the casting holes for the coolant passages in the block.

Crankcase - The lower part of the engine in which the crankshaft rotates; includes the lower section of the cylinder block and the oil pan.

Crank kit - A reground or reconditioned crankshaft and new main and connecting rod bearings.

Crankpin - The part of a crankshaft to which a connecting rod is attached.

Crankshaft - The main rotating member, or shaft, running the length of the crankcase, with offset throws to which the connecting rods are attached; changes the reciprocating motion of the pistons into rotating motion.

Cylinder sleeve - A replaceable sleeve, or liner, pressed into the cylinder block to form the cylinder bore.

D

Deburring - Removing the burrs (rough edges or areas) from a bearing.

Deglazer - A tool, rotated by an electric motor, used to remove glaze from cylinder walls so a new set of rings will seat.

E

Endplay - The amount of lengthwise movement between two parts. As applied to a crankshaft, the distance that the crankshaft can move forward and back in the cylinder block.

F

Face - A machinist's term that refers to removing metal from the end of a shaft or the face of a larger part, such as a flywheel.

Fatigue - A breakdown of material through a large number of loading and unloading cycles. The first signs are cracks followed shortly by breaks.

Feeler gauge - A thin strip of hardened steel, ground to an exact thickness, used to check clearances between parts.

Free height - The unloaded length or height of a spring.

Freeplay - The looseness in a linkage, or an assembly of parts, between the initial application of force and actual movement. Usually perceived as slop or slight delay.

Freeze plug - See Core plug.

G

Gallery - A large passage in the block that forms a reservoir for engine oil pressure.

Glaze - The very smooth, glassy finish that develops on cylinder walls while an engine is in service.

H

Heli-Coil - A rethreading device used when threads are worn or damaged. The device is installed in a retapped hole to reduce the thread size to the original size.

I

Installed height - The spring's measured length or height, as installed on the cylinder head. Installed height is measured from the spring seat to the underside of the spring retainer.

J

Journal - The surface of a rotating shaft which turns in a bearing.

K

Keeper - The split lock that holds the valve spring retainer in position on the valve stem.

Key - A small piece of metal inserted into matching grooves machined into two parts fitted together - such as a gear pressed onto a shaft - which prevents slippage between the two parts.

Knock - The heavy metallic engine sound, produced in the combustion chamber as a result of abnormal combustion - usually detonation. Knock is usually caused by a loose or worn bearing. Also referred to as detonation, pinging and spark knock. Connecting rod or main bearing knocks are created by too much oil clearance or insufficient lubrication.

L

Lands - The portions of metal between the piston ring grooves.

Lapping the valves - Grinding a valve face and its seat together with lapping compound.

Lash - The amount of free motion in a gear train, between gears, or in a mechanical assembly, that occurs before movement can begin. Usually refers to the lash in a valve train.

Lifter - The part that rides against the cam to transfer motion to the rest of the valve train.

M

Machining - The process of using a machine to remove metal from a metal part.

Main bearings - The plain, or babbit, bearings that support the crankshaft.

Main bearing caps - The cast iron caps, bolted to the bottom of the block, that support the main bearings.

O

O.D. - Outside diameter.

Oil gallery - A pipe or drilled passageway in the engine used to carry engine oil from one area to another.

Oil ring - The lower ring, or rings, of a piston; designed to prevent excessive amounts of oil from working up the cylinder walls and into the combustion chamber. Also called an oil-control ring.

Oil seal - A seal which keeps oil from leaking out of a compartment. Usually refers to a dynamic seal around a rotating shaft or other moving part.

O-ring - A type of sealing ring made of a special rubberlike material; in use, the O-ring is compressed into a groove to provide the sealing action.

Overhaul - To completely disassemble a unit, clean and inspect all parts, reassemble it with the original or new parts and make all adjustments necessary for proper operation.

P

Pilot bearing - A small bearing installed in the center of the flywheel (or the rear end of the crankshaft) to support the front end of the input shaft of the transmission.

Pip mark - A little dot or indentation which indicates the top side of a compression ring.

Piston - The cylindrical part, attached to the connecting rod, that moves up and down in the cylinder as the crankshaft rotates. When the fuel charge is fired, the piston transfers the force of the explosion to the connecting rod, then to the crankshaft.

Piston pin (or wrist pin) - The cylindrical and usually hollow steel pin that passes through the piston. The piston pin fastens the piston to the upper end of the connecting rod.

Piston ring - The split ring fitted to the groove in a piston. The ring contacts the sides of the ring groove and also rubs against the cylinder wall, thus sealing space between piston and wall. There are two types of rings: Compression rings seal the compression pressure in the combustion chamber; oil rings scrape excessive oil off the cylinder wall.

Piston ring groove - The slots or grooves cut in piston heads to hold piston rings in position.

Piston skirt - The portion of the piston below the rings and the piston pin hole.

Plastigage - A thin strip of plastic thread, available in different sizes, used for measuring clearances. For example, a strip of plastigage is laid across a bearing journal and mashed as parts are assembled. Then parts are disassembled and the width of the strip is measured to determine clearance between journal and bearing. Commonly used to measure crankshaft main-bearing and connecting rod bearing clearances.

Press-fit - A tight fit between two parts that requires pressure to force the parts together. Also referred to as drive, or force, fit.

Prussian blue - A blue pigment; in solution, useful in determining the area of contact between two surfaces. Prussian blue is commonly used to determine the width and location of the contact area between the valve face and the valve seat.

R

Race (bearing) - The inner or outer ring that provides a contact surface for balls or rollers in bearing.

Ream - To size, enlarge or smooth a hole by using a round cutting tool with fluted edges.

Ring job - The process of reconditioning the cylinders and installing new rings.

Runout - Wobble. The amount a shaft rotates out-of-true.

S

Saddle - The upper main bearing seat.

Scored - Scratched or grooved, as a cylinder wall may be scored by abrasive particles moved up and down by the piston rings.

Scuffing - A type of wear in which there's a transfer of material between parts moving against each other; shows up as pits or grooves in the mating surfaces.

Seat - The surface upon which another part rests or seats. For example, the valve seat is the matched surface upon which the valve face rests. Also used to refer to wearing into a good fit; for example, piston rings seat after a few miles of driving.

Short block - An engine block complete with crankshaft and piston and, usually, camshaft assemblies.

Static balance - The balance of an object while it's stationary.

Step - The wear on the lower portion of a ring land caused by excessive side and back-clearance. The height of the step indicates the ring's extra side clearance and the length of the step projecting from the back wall of the groove represents the ring's back clearance.

Stroke - The distance the piston moves when traveling from top dead center to bottom dead center, or from bottom dead center to top dead center.

Stud - A metal rod with threads on both ends.

T

Tang - A lip on the end of a plain bearing used to align the bearing during assembly.

Tap - To cut threads in a hole. Also refers to the fluted tool used to cut threads.

Taper - A gradual reduction in the width of a shaft or hole; in an engine cylinder, taper usually takes the form of uneven wear, more pronounced at the top than at the bottom.

Throws - The offset portions of the crankshaft to which the connecting rods are affixed.

Thrust bearing - The main bearing that has thrust faces to prevent excessive endplay, or forward and backward movement of the crankshaft.

Thrust washer - A bronze or hardened steel washer placed between two moving parts. The washer prevents longitudinal movement and provides a bearing surface for thrust surfaces of parts.

Tolerance - The amount of variation permitted from an exact size of measurement. Actual amount from smallest acceptable dimension to largest acceptable dimension.

U

Umbrella - An oil deflector placed near the valve tip to throw oil from the valve stem area.

Undercut - A machined groove below the normal surface.

Undersize bearings - Smaller diameter bearings used with re-ground crankshaft journals.

V

Valve grinding - Refacing a valve in a valve-refacing machine.

Valve train - The valve-operating mechanism of an engine; includes all components from the camshaft to the valve.

Vibration damper - A cylindrical weight attached to the front of the crankshaft to minimize torsional vibration (the twist-untwist actions of the crankshaft caused by the cylinder firing impulses). Also called a harmonic balancer.

W

Water jacket - The spaces around the cylinders, between the inner and outer shells of the cylinder block or head, through which coolant circulates.

Web - A supporting structure across a cavity.

Woodruff key - A key with a radiused backside (viewed from the side).

Notes

Chapter 3
Cooling, heating and air conditioning systems

Contents

Specifications

General

Refrigerant type..	R-134a or R-1234yf; refer to the underhood HVAC label
Radiator cap pressure rating	21 psi
Thermostat rating (opening temperature).................................	190-degrees F
Cooling system capacity...	See Chapter 1
Refrigerant capacity*	
R-134a	1.19 lbs
R-1234yf..	1.06 lbs

* Check the refrigerant capacity listed on the underhood HVAC label; if the charge capacity listed on the label differs from that shown here, assume the label is correct.

Torque specifications
Note: One foot-pound (ft-lb) of torque is equivalent to 12 inch-pounds (in-lbs) of torque. Torque values below approximately 15 ft-lbs are expressed in inch-pounds, since most foot-pound torque wrenches are not accurate at these smaller values.

Ft-lbs (unless otherwise indicated)

Thermostat housing bolts	
2.0L and 2.4L engines..	89 in-lbs
3.2L engines..	108 in-lbs
2.0L engines	
Thermostat manifold bolts...	108 in-lbs
Water pump bolts (M8)..	18
Water pump inlet tube bolt (M5)...	71 in-lbs
2.4L engines	
Coolant return tube-to-water pump inlet pipe.....................	33
Coolant return tube-to-oil filter housing.............................	30
Coolant supply tube-to-oil filter housing............................	80 in-lbs
Coolant supply tube-to-thermostat housing........................	80 in-lbs
Water pump bolts/nut..	89 in-lbs
Water pump inlet tube...	80 in-lbs
Water inlet pipe support bracket	89 in-lbs
Water pump pulley bolts...	80 in-lbs
3.2L engines	
Water pump bolts M6	108 in-lbs
Water pump bolts M8	17
Air conditioning compressor mounting bolts.............................	21
Refrigerant line-to-compressor nut...	15
Refrigerant line-to-condenser nut...	18
All other refrigerant line-to-connection nuts.............................	15

1   General information

Warning: *Do not allow antifreeze to come in contact with your skin or painted surfaces of the vehicle. Rinse off spills immediately with plenty of water. Antifreeze is highly toxic if ingested. Never leave antifreeze lying around in an open container or in puddles on the floor; children and pets are attracted by its sweet smell and may drink it. Check with local authorities about disposing of used antifreeze. Many communities have collection centers which will see that antifreeze is disposed of safely. Never dump used antifreeze on the ground or pour it into drains.*

Engine cooling system

1   All modern vehicles employ a pressurized engine cooling system with thermostatically controlled coolant circulation. The cooling system consists of a radiator, an expansion tank, a pressure cap (located on the expansion tank, a thermostat, a cooling fan, and a water pump.

2   The water pump circulates coolant through the engine. The coolant flows around each cylinder and around the intake and exhaust ports, near the spark plug areas and in close proximity to the exhaust valve guides.

3   A thermostat controls engine coolant temperature. During warm up, the closed thermostat prevents coolant from circulating through the radiator. As the engine nears normal operating temperature, the thermostat opens and allows hot coolant to travel through the radiator, where it's cooled before returning to the engine.

Heating system

4   The heating system consists of a blower fan and heater core located in a housing under the dash, the hoses connecting the heater core to the engine cooling system and the heater/air conditioning control head on the dashboard. Hot engine coolant is circulated through the heater core. When the heater mode is activated, a flap door in the housing opens to expose the heater core to the passenger compartment through air ducts. A fan switch on the control head activates the blower motor, which forces air through the core, heating the air.

Air conditioning system

5   The air conditioning system consists of a condenser mounted in front of the radiator, an evaporator mounted adjacent to the heater core, a compressor mounted on the engine, a receiver-drier or accumulator and the plumbing connecting all of the above components.

6   A blower fan forces the warmer air of the passenger compartment through the evaporator core (sort of a radiator-in-reverse), transferring the heat from the air to the refrigerant. The liquid refrigerant boils off into low pressure vapor, taking the heat with it when it leaves the evaporator.

2   Troubleshooting

Coolant leaks

1   A coolant leak can develop anywhere in the cooling system, but the most common causes are:

a) A loose or weak hose clamp
b) A defective hose
c) A faulty pressure cap
d) A damaged radiator
e) A bad heater core
f) A faulty water pump
g) A leaking gasket at any joint that carries coolant

2   Coolant leaks aren't always easy to find. Sometimes they can only be detected when the cooling system is under pressure. Here's where a cooling system pressure tester comes in handy. After the engine has cooled completely, the tester is attached in place of the pressure cap, then pumped up to the pressure value equal to that of the pressure cap rating **(see illustration)**. Now, leaks that only exist when the engine is fully warmed up will become apparent. The tester can be left connected to locate a nagging slow leak.

Coolant level drops, but no external leaks

3   If you find it necessary to keep adding coolant, but there are no external leaks, the probable causes include:

a) A blown head gasket
b) A leaking intake manifold gasket (only on engines that have coolant passages in the manifold), or a cracked cylinder head or cylinder block

4   Any of the above problems will also usually result in contamination of the engine oil, which will cause it to take on a milkshake-like appearance. A bad head gasket or cracked head or block can also result in engine oil contaminating the cooling system.

2.2 The cooling system pressure tester is connected in place of the pressure cap, then pumped up to pressurize the system

5   Combustion leak detectors (also known as block testers) are available at most auto parts stores. These work by detecting exhaust gases in the cooling system, which indicates a compression leak from a cylinder into the coolant. The tester consists of a large bulb-type syringe and bottle of test fluid **(see illustration)**. A measured amount of the fluid is added to the syringe. The syringe is placed over the cooling system filler neck and, with the engine running, the bulb is squeezed and a sample of the gases present in the cooling system are drawn up through the test fluid **(see illustration)**. If any combustion gases are present in the sample taken, the test fluid will change color.

6   If the test indicates combustion gas is present in the cooling system, you can be sure that the engine has a blown head gasket or a crack in the cylinder head or block, and will require disassembly to repair.

2.5a The combustion leak detector consists of a bulb, syringe and test fluid

2.5b Place the tester over the cooling system filler neck and use the bulb to draw a sample into the tester

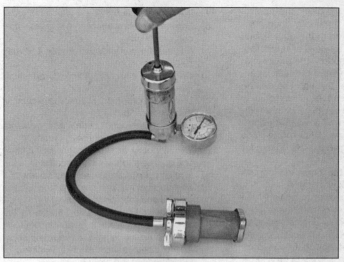

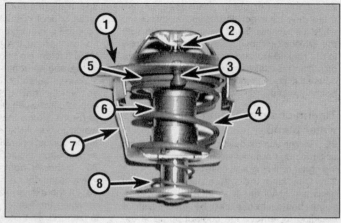

2.8 Checking the cooling system pressure cap with a cooling system pressure tester

2.10 Typical thermostat:

1	Flange	5	Valve seat
2	Piston	6	Valve
3	Jiggle valve	7	Frame
4	Main coil spring	8	Secondary coil spring

Pressure cap

Warning: *Wait until the engine is completely cool before beginning this check.*

7 The cooling system is sealed by a spring-loaded cap, which raises the boiling point of the coolant. If the cap's seal or spring are worn out, the coolant can boil and escape past the cap. With the engine completely cool, remove the cap and check the seal; if it's cracked, hardened or deteriorated in any way, replace it with a new one.

8 Even if the seal is good, the spring might not be; this can be checked with a cooling system pressure tester **(see illustration)**. If the cap can't hold a pressure within approximately 1-1/2 lbs of its rated pressure (which is marked on the cap), replace it with a new one.

9 The cap is also equipped with a vacuum relief spring. When the engine cools off, a vacuum is created in the cooling system. The vacuum relief spring allows air back into the system, which will equalize the pressure and prevent damage to the radiator (the radiator tanks could collapse if the vacuum is great enough). If, after turning the engine off and allowing it to cool down you notice any of the cooling system hoses collapsing, replace the pressure cap with a new one.

Thermostat

10 Before assuming the thermostat **(see illustration)** is responsible for a cooling system problem, check the coolant level (see Chapter 1), drivebelt tension (see Chapter 1) and temperature gauge (or light) operation.

11 If the engine takes a long time to warm up (as indicated by the temperature gauge or heater operation), the thermostat is probably stuck open. Replace the thermostat with a new one.

12 If the engine runs hot or overheats, a thorough test of the thermostat should be performed.

13 Definitive testing of the thermostat can only be made when it is removed from the

vehicle. If the thermostat is stuck in the open position at room temperature, it is faulty and must be replaced.

Caution: *Do not drive the vehicle without a thermostat. The computer may stay in open loop and emissions and fuel economy will suffer.*

14 To test a thermostat, suspend the (closed) thermostat on a length of string or wire in a pot of cold water.

15 Heat the water on a stove while observing the thermostat. The thermostat should fully open before the water boils.

16 If the thermostat doesn't open and close as specified, or sticks in any position, replace it.

Caution: *The thermostat and the housing must be replaced as an assembly, if you try and remove the thermostat from the housing, the thermostat can be damaged.*

Cooling fan

17 If the engine is overheating and the cooling fan is not coming on when the engine temperature rises to an excessive level, unplug the fan motor wiring plug(s) and connect the motor directly to the battery with fused jumper wires. If the fan motor doesn't come on, replace the motor.

18 If the radiator fan motor is okay, but it isn't coming on when the engine gets hot, the fan relay might be defective. A relay is used to control a circuit by turning it on and off in response to a control decision by the engine management Electronic Control Module (ECM). These control circuits are fairly complex, and checking them should be left to a qualified automotive technician. Sometimes, the control system can be fixed by simply identifying and replacing a faulty relay.

19 Locate the fan relays in the engine compartment fuse/relay box.

20 Test the relay (see Chapter 12).

21 If the relay is okay, check all wiring and connections to the fan motor. Refer to the

wiring diagrams in Chapter 12. If no obvious problems are found, the problem could be the Engine Coolant Temperature (ECT) sensor or the engine management Electronic Control Module (ECM). Have the cooling fan system and circuit diagnosed by a dealer service department or suitably equipped repairer.

Water pump

22 A failure in the water pump can cause serious engine damage due to overheating.

Drivebelt-driven water pump

23 There are two ways to check the operation of the water pump while it's installed on the engine. If the pump is found to be defective, it should be replaced with a new or rebuilt unit.

24 Coolant pumps are normally equipped with weep (or vent) holes **(see illustration)**. If a failure occurs in the pump seal, coolant will leak from the hole.

2.24 The water pump weep hole is generally located on the underside of the pump

25 If the water pump shaft bearings fail, there may be a howling sound at the pump while it's running. Shaft wear can be felt with the drivebelt removed if the water pump pulley is rocked up and down (with the engine off). Don't mistake drivebelt slippage, which causes a squealing sound, for water pump bearing failure.

Timing chain or timing belt-driven water pump

26 Water pumps driven by the timing chain or timing belt are located underneath the timing chain or timing belt cover.

27 Checking the water pump is limited because of where it is located. However, some basic checks can be made before deciding to remove the coolant pump. If the pump is found to be defective, it should be replaced with a new or rebuilt unit.

28 One sign that the water pump may be failing is that the heater (climate control) may not work well. Warm the engine to normal operating temperature, confirm that the coolant level is correct, then run the heater and check for hot air coming from the ducts.

29 Check for noises coming from the water pump area. If the coolant pump impeller shaft or bearings are failing, there may be a howling sound at the pump while the engine is running.

Note: *Be careful not to mistake drivebelt noise (squealing) for water pump bearing or shaft failure.*

30 It you suspect water pump failure due to noise, wear can be confirmed by feeling for play at the pump shaft. This can be done by rocking the drive sprocket on the pump shaft up and down. To do this you will need to remove the tension on the timing chain or belt as well as access the water pump.

All water pumps

31 In rare cases or on high-mileage vehicles, another sign of water pump failure may be the presence of coolant in the engine oil. This condition will adversely affect the engine in varying degrees.

Note: *Finding coolant in the engine oil could indicate other serious issues besides a failed water pump, such as a leaking head gasket or a cracked cylinder head or block.*

32 Even a pump that exhibits no outward signs of a problem, such as noise or leakage, can still be due for replacement. Removal for close examination is the only sure way to tell. Sometimes the fins on the back of the impeller can corrode to the point that cooling efficiency is diminished significantly.

Heater system

33 If the fan motor will run at all speeds, the electrical part of the system is okay. The three basic heater problems fall into the following general categories:

a) *Not enough heat*
b) *Heat all the time*
c) *No heat*

34 If there's not enough heat, the control valve or door is stuck in a partially open position, the coolant coming from the engine isn't hot enough, or the heater core is restricted. If the coolant isn't hot enough, the thermostat in the engine cooling system is stuck open, allowing coolant to pass through the engine so rapidly that it doesn't heat up quickly enough. If the vehicle is equipped with a temperature gauge instead of a warning light, watch to see if the engine temperature rises to the normal operating range after driving for a reasonable distance.

35 If there's heat all the time, the control valve or the door is stuck wide open.

36 If there's no heat, coolant is probably not reaching the heater core, or the heater core is plugged. The likely cause is a collapsed or blocked hose, core, or a seized heater control valve. If the heater is the type that flows coolant all the time, the cause is likely to be a stuck door or a broken or kinked control cable.

Air conditioning system

37 If the cool air output is inadequate:

a) *Inspect the condenser coils and fins to make sure they're clear*
b) *Check the compressor clutch for slippage*
c) *Check the blower motor for proper operation*
d) *Inspect the blower discharge passage for obstructions*
e) *Check the system air intake filter for clogging*

38 If the system provides intermittent cooling air:

a) *Check the fuse, blower switch and blower motor for a malfunction*
b) *Make sure the compressor clutch isn't slipping*
c) *Inspect the plenum door to make sure it's operating properly*
d) *Inspect the evaporator to make sure it isn't blocked*

39 If the system provides no cooling air:

a) *Inspect the compressor drivebelt; make sure it isn't loose or broken*
b) *Make sure the compressor clutch c) engages; if it doesn't, check for a blown fuse*
d) *Inspect the wire harness for broken or disconnected wires*
e) *If the compressor clutch doesn't engage, bridge the terminals of the AC pressure switch(es) with a jumper wire; if the clutch now engages, and the system is properly charged, the pressure switch is faulty*
f) *Make sure the blower motor is not disconnected or burned out*
g) *Make sure the compressor isn't partially or completely seized*
h) *Inspect the refrigerant pipes for leaks*
i) *Check the components for leaks*
j) *Inspect the receiver-drier/accumulator or expansion valve/tube for blocked filters*

40 If the system is noisy:

a) *Look for loose panels in the passenger compartment*
b) *Inspect the compressor drivebelt; it may be loose or worn*
c) *Check the security of the compressor mounting bolts*
d) *Listen carefully to the compressor; it may be worn out*
e) *Listen to the idler pulley and bearing, and the clutch; either may be bad*
f) *The winding in the compressor clutch coil or solenoid may be defective*
g) *The compressor oil level may be low*
h) *The blower motor fan bushing or the motor itself may be worn out*
i) *If there is an excessive charge in the system, you'll hear a rumbling noise in the high pressure pipe, a thumping noise in the compressor, or see bubbles or cloudiness in the sight glass*
j) *If there is a low charge in the system, you might hear hissing in the evaporator case at the expansion valve, or see bubbles or cloudiness in the sight glass*

---

3   Air conditioning and heating system - check and maintenance

Air conditioning system

Warning: *The air conditioning system is under high pressure. Do not loosen any hose fittings or remove any components until after the system has been discharged. Air conditioning refrigerant should be properly discharged into an EPA-approved recovery/recycling unit at a dealer service department or an automotive air conditioning repair facility. Always wear eye protection when disconnecting air conditioning system fittings.*

Caution: *All models covered by this manual use environmentally friendly R-134a or R-1234yf. These refrigerants (and their appropriate refrigerant oils) are not compatible with R-12 refrigerant system components and must never be mixed or the components will be damaged.*

Caution: *When replacing entire components, additional refrigerant oil should be added equal to the amount that is removed with the component being replaced. Be sure to read the can before adding any oil to the system, to make sure it is compatible with the R-134a system.*

1 The following maintenance checks should be performed on a regular basis to ensure that the air conditioning continues to operate at peak efficiency.

a) *Inspect the condition of the drivebelt. If it is worn or deteriorated, replace it (see Chapter 1).*
b) *Check the drivebelt tension (see Chapter 1).*
c) *Inspect the system hoses. Look for cracks, bubbles, hardening and deterioration. Inspect the hoses and all fittings*

for oil bubbles or seepage. If there is any
evidence of wear, damage, or leakage,
replace the hose(s).
d) Inspect the condenser fins for leaves,
bugs and any other foreign material that
may have embedded itself in the fins.
Use a fin comb or compressed air to
remove debris from the condenser.
e) Make sure the system has the correct
refrigerant charge.
f) If you hear water sloshing around in the
dash area or have water dripping on the
carpet, check the evaporator housing
drain tube, and insert a piece of wire into
the opening to check for blockage.
Note: *The evaporator housing drain tube exits
the floorpan through a grommet in the driver's
side footwell.*

2   It's a good idea to operate the system
for about ten minutes at least once a month.
This is particularly important during the winter months because long term non-use can
cause hardening, and subsequent failure, of
the seals. Note that using the Defrost function
operates the compressor.
3   If the air conditioning system is not working properly, proceed to Step 6 and perform
the general checks outlined below.
4   Because of the complexity of the air conditioning system and the special equipment
necessary to service it, in-depth troubleshooting and repairs beyond checking the refrigerant charge and the compressor clutch operation are not included in this manual. However,
simple checks and component replacement
procedures are provided in this Chapter. For
more complete information on the air conditioning system, refer to the *Haynes Automotive Heating and Air Conditioning Manual.*
5   The most common cause of poor cooling
is simply a low system refrigerant charge. If a
noticeable drop in system cooling ability occurs,
one of the following quick checks will help you
determine if the refrigerant level is low.

Checking the refrigerant charge

6   Warm the engine up to normal operating
temperature.
7   Place the air conditioning temperature
selector at the coldest setting and put the
blower at the highest setting.
8   After the system reaches operating temperature, feel the larger pipe exiting the evaporator at the firewall. The outlet pipe should
be cold (the tubing that leads back to the
compressor). If the evaporator outlet pipe is
warm, the system probably needs a charge.
9   Insert a thermometer in the center air
distribution duct **(see illustration)** while
operating the air conditioning system at its
maximum setting - the temperature of the
output air should be 35 to 40 degrees F
below the ambient air temperature (down to
approximately 40 degrees F). If the ambient (outside) air temperature is very high,
say 110 degrees F, the duct air temperature
may be as high as 60 degrees F, but generally the air conditioning is 35 to 40 degrees F
cooler than the ambient air.

**3.9 Insert a thermometer in the center
vent, turn on the air conditioning system
and wait for it to cool down; depending on
the humidity, the output air should be
35 to 40 degrees cooler than the
ambient air temperature**

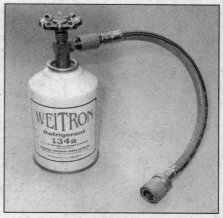

**3.11 Typical automotive air conditioning
charging kit**

**3.13 Low-side
charging port (A)
and high-side
charging port
(B, DON'T use)
locations**

10   Further inspection or testing of the system requires special tools and techniques and
is beyond the scope of the home mechanic.

Adding refrigerant

Caution: *Make sure any refrigerant, refrigerant oil or replacement component you
purchase is designated as compatible with
R-134a systems.*
11   Purchase an R-134a or R-1234yf automotive charging kit (as applicable) at an auto
parts store **(see illustration)**. A charging kit
includes a can of refrigerant, a tap valve and
a short section of hose that can be attached
between the tap valve and the system low
side service valve.
Caution: *Never add more than one can of refrigerant to the system. If more refrigerant than
that is required, the system should be evacuated and leak tested.*
12   Back off the valve handle on the charging kit and screw the kit onto the refrigerant
can, making sure first that the O-ring or rubber seal inside the threaded portion of the kit
is in place.

Warning: *Wear protective eyewear when
dealing with pressurized refrigerant cans.*
13   Remove the dust cap from the low-side
charging port and attach the hose's quick-
connect fitting to the port **(see illustration)**.
Warning: *DO NOT attempt to hook the charging kit hose to the system high side! The fittings on the charging kit are designed to fit
only on the low side of the system.*
14   Warm up the engine and turn the air conditioning on. Keep the charging kit hose away
from the fan and other moving parts.
Note: *The charging process requires the
compressor to be running. If the clutch cycles
off, you can put the air conditioning switch on
High and leave the car doors open to keep
the clutch on and compressor working. The
compressor can be kept on during the charging by removing the connector from the pressure switch and bridging it with a paper clip or
jumper wire during the procedure.*
15   Turn the valve handle on the kit until the
stem pierces the can, then back the handle out
to release the refrigerant. You should be able
to hear the rush of gas. Keep the can upright at

3.24 Remove the cowl panel and insert the nozzle into the cowl plenum

4.10 Disengage the hose clamps and remove the upper radiator hose and heater hose from the thermostat housing

all times, but shake it occasionally. Allow stabilization time between each addition.

Note: *The charging process will go faster if you wrap the can with a hot-water-soaked rag to keep the can from freezing up.*

16   If you have an accurate thermometer, you can place it in the center air conditioning duct inside the vehicle and keep track of the output air temperature. A charged system that is working properly should cool down to approximately 40 degrees F. If the ambient (outside) air temperature is very high, say 110 degrees F, the duct air temperature may be as high as 60 degrees F, but generally the air conditioning is 35 to 40 degrees F cooler than the ambient air.

17   When the can is empty, turn the valve handle to the closed position and release the connection from the low-side port. Reinstall the dust cap.

18   Remove the charging kit from the can and store the kit for future use with the piercing valve in the UP position, to prevent inadvertently piercing the can on the next use.

Heating systems

19   If the carpet under the heater core is damp, or if antifreeze vapor or steam is coming through the vents, the heater core is leaking. Remove it (see Section 10) and install a new unit (most radiator shops will not repair a leaking heater core).

20   If the air coming out of the heater vents isn't hot, the problem could stem from any of the following causes:

a) *The thermostat is stuck open, preventing the engine coolant from warming up enough to carry heat to the heater core. Replace the thermostat (see Section 4).*

b) *There is a blockage in the system, preventing the flow of coolant through the heater core. Feel both heater hoses at the firewall. They should be hot. If one of them is cold, there is an obstruction in one of the hoses or in the heater core, or the heater control valve is shut. Detach the hoses and back flush the heater core with a water hose. If*

the heater core is clear but circulation is impeded, remove the two hoses and flush them out with a water hose.

c) *If flushing fails to remove the blockage from the heater core, the core must be replaced (see Section 10).*

Eliminating air conditioning odors

21   Unpleasant odors that often develop in air conditioning systems are caused by the growth of a fungus, usually on the surface of the evaporator core. The warm, humid environment there is a perfect breeding ground for mildew to develop.

22   The evaporator core on most vehicles is difficult to access, and factory dealerships have a lengthy, expensive process for eliminating the fungus by opening up the evaporator case and using a powerful disinfectant and rinse on the core until the fungus is gone. You can service your own system at home, but it takes something much stronger than basic household germ-killers or deodorizers.

23   Aerosol disinfectants for automotive air conditioning systems are available in most auto parts stores, but remember when shopping for them that the most effective treatments are also the most expensive. The basic procedure for using these sprays is to start by running the system in the RECIRC mode for ten minutes with the blower on its highest speed. Use the highest heat mode to dry out the system and keep the compressor from engaging by disconnecting the wiring connector at the compressor.

24   The disinfectant can usually comes with a long spray hose. Remove the cowl panel (see Chapter 11) and insert the nozzle into an air conditioning fresh air intake in the cowl plenum **(see illustration)**, and spray according to the manufacturer's recommendations. Try to cover the whole surface of the evaporator core, by aiming the spray up, down and sideways. Follow the manufacturer's recommendations for the length of spray and waiting time between applications.

25   Once the evaporator has been cleaned, the best way to prevent the mildew from coming back again is to make sure your evaporator housing drain tube is clear.

Automatic heating and air conditioning systems

26   Some vehicles are equipped with an optional automatic climate control system. This system has its own computer that receives inputs from various sensors in the heating and air conditioning system. This computer, like the PCM, has self-diagnostic capabilities to help pinpoint problems or faults within the system. Vehicles equipped with automatic heating and air conditioning systems are very complex and considered beyond the scope of the home mechanic. Vehicles equipped with automatic heating and air conditioning systems should be taken to a dealer service department or other qualified facility for repair.

---

4   Thermostat - replacement

Warning: *Wait until the engine is completely cool before beginning this procedure.*
Note: *On all models the thermostat and housing are replaced as an assembly.*

Removal

1   Disconnect the cable from the negative terminal of the battery (see Chapter 5).
2   Remove the engine cover.
3   Drain the cooling system (see Chapter 1). If the coolant is relatively new or in good condition, save it and reuse it. Read the **Warning** in Section 2.

2.0L engines

4   Using hose clamp pliers, release the spring hose clamps then detach the upper radiator hose and coolant hose from the thermostat housing. If it's stuck, grasp it near the engine end with a pair of adjustable pliers and twist it to

4.13 Disconnect the coolant temperature sensor electrical connector (A) then disconnect the coolant reservoir hose (B) quick-connect fitting

4.14 Remove the intake manifold upper support bracket bolts and nuts

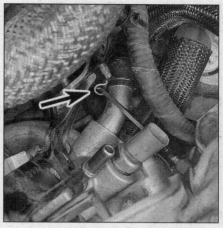

4.15 Pry the retaining clip out using a small screwdriver

4.16a Remove the bolts from the left side of the housing . . .

4.16b . . . then the lower bolt from the rear. The upper rear bolt has already been removed with the support bracket

4.17 Use a screwdriver to bend the tube bracket down enough to allow the housing to be removed

break the seal, then pull it off. If the hose is old or deteriorated, cut it off and install a new one.

5   Remove the Torx head fasteners and remove the thermostat housing from the coolant manifold.

2.4L engines

Note: *The thermostat is located on the end of the cylinder head, below the vacuum pump.*

6   Remove the battery and battery tray (see Chapter 5).

7   Remove the under-hood power distribution center three mounting bolts and move the assembly out of the way.

8   Remove the intake manifold (see Chapter 2A).

9   Disengage the wiring harness retainer attached to the upper radiator hose, if equipped.

10   Disengage the hose clamps from the radiator hose and coolant hose **(see illustration)** using pliers.

11   Remove the engine vacuum pump (see Chapter 2A).

12   Remove the shift cable (see Chapter 7A).

13   Disconnect the coolant temperature sensor electrical connector, then disconnect the coolant reservoir hose **(see illustration)**.

14   Remove the intake manifold upper support bracket bolts and nuts, then remove the bracket **(see illustration)**.

Note: *Depending on the tool combination you're using, it can actually be easier to remove the intake manifold to access the thermostat housing bolts (see Chapter 2A).*

15   Pry out the hose retaining clip **(see illustration)** then disconnect the hose from the thermostat housing.

16   Remove the thermostat housing bolts **(see illustrations)**.

17   Carefully bend the tube bracket back **(see illustration)** away from the thermostat housing.

18   Remove the thermostat housing and discard the O-ring gasket from the groove in the housing.

3.2L engines

Note: *Some models use a special type hose clamp called CLIC E and special pliers no. 10288 must be used to disengage the clamps.*

19   Remove the air filter housing (see Chapter 4).

20   Disconnect the radiator hoses and heater hoses from the coolant adapter/thermostat housing.

21   Disconnect the electrical connector at the top of the housing.

22   Unscrew the two mounting bolts and remove the housing from the cylinder head.

23   Remove the O-ring from the thermostat housing.

Installation

Note: *It is standard practice to use a thin layer of RTV sealant when installing flat replacement gaskets. However, if the gasket is designed with a raised crushable sealing surface (not flat), or if it is an O-ring, no RTV sealant is necessary.*

4.25 Install the O-ring into the groove, making sure it's seated into the groove - 2.4L engine shown

5.4 Remove the air intake fasteners then unclip the intake from the air deflector

5.6 Ambient air temperature sensor connector location

24   On 2.0L engines, install the thermostat housing assembly and tighten the Torx fasteners to the torque listed in this Chapter's Specifications.

25   On 2.4L and 3.2L engines, install the new O-ring gasket into the groove on the thermostat housing **(see illustration)**.

26   The remainder of installation is the reverse of removal. Make sure that the replacement thermostat is installed in the same direction and position as the one removed. Tighten the fasteners to the torque listed in this Chapter's Specifications.

27   Reattach the hose(s) to the housing cover and fitting(s), then tighten the hose clamp(s) securely.

28   Reconnect the battery (see Chapter 5).

29   Refill the cooling system (see Chapter 1).

30   Start the engine and allow it to reach normal operating temperature, then check for leaks and proper thermostat operation (as described in Section 2).

5   Engine cooling fans - removal and installation

Warning: *To avoid possible injury or damage, DO NOT operate the engine with a damaged fan. Do not attempt to repair fan blades - replace a damaged fan with a new one.*

Warning: *The electric fans can start at any time; keep hands, clothes and tools away from the fan until the battery is disconnected to avoid possible injury or damage.*

Warning: *Wait until the engine is completely cool before beginning this procedure.*

1   Disconnect the cable from the negative terminal of the battery (see Chapter 5).

2   Set the parking brake, raise the front of the vehicle and support it securely on jackstands.

3   Remove the engine lower splash shield and drain the cooling system to a level that is just below the upper radiator hose (see Chapter 1).

4   Remove the air intake duct (see Chapter 4), then remove the air intake fasteners and intake from the air deflector **(see illustration)**.

5   Remove the close-out panel between the grille and the radiator support (see Chapter 11, Section 10).

6   Disconnect the electrical connector to the ambient air temperature sensor **(see illustration)**.

7   Remove the transmission cooler line support bracket bolt **(see illustration)**.

8   Remove the transmission cooler mounting bolts **(see illustration)** and the cooler from the condenser, then secure it out of the way without disconnecting the lines.

9   Remove the horn bracket and horns, then disengage the harness retainers (see Chapter 12).

10   Remove the hood release cable and wiring harness from the air deflector **(see illustration)** and, on 2019 models, remove the hood latch (see Chapter 11).

5.7 Transmission cooler line support bracket bolt location

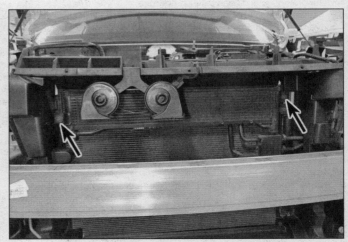

5.8 Transmission cooler-to-condenser bolt locations

5.10 Disengage the retainers for the hood release cable (A) and the wiring harness (B) along the air deflector

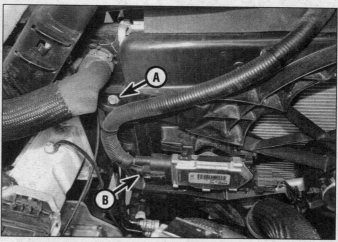

5.11 Remove the fan shroud left mounting bolt (A) then disconnect the electrical connector (B) to the cooling fan module

11 Remove the fan shroud left mounting bolt and disconnect the electrical connector from the cooling fan module, then disengage the harness retainers and move the harness out of the way **(see illustration)**.

12 Disconnect the electrical connector from the air conditioning pressure switch, disengage the harness retainers, remove the bracket fastener, then move the harness and bracket out of the way **(see illustration)**.

13 Working under the front of the vehicle, remove the push-pins that secure the side close-out air deflector to the lower deflector.

14 Disconnect the upper radiator hose from the thermostat and secure the hose out of the way.

15 Remove the air deflector fasteners and remove the deflector and side baffles as a unit **(see illustrations)**.

5.12 Disconnect the electrical connector to the air conditioning pressure switch (A), then disengage the wiring harness retainer (B) and remove the bracket nut (C)

5.15a Remove the air deflector fasteners . . .

5.15b . . . then lift the deflector and and side baffles off the radiator support

5.16a Remove the radiator mount rear fastener (left-side shown) . . .

5.16b . . . then remove the fasteners from the front side and remove the mount

16   On 2018 and earlier models, remove the radiator upper mount fasteners then slide the radiator forward until the mounts can be

5.18 Remove the fan shroud right side fastener

removed **(see illustrations)** and on 2019 models remove the radiator support bolts and support.

17   Remove the locking clip **(see illustration 7.7)** and disconnect the lower radiator hose.

18   Remove the fan shroud right-side mounting bolt **(see illustration)**.

19   Remove the cooling fan assembly by pulling it straight up until the shroud mount contacts the upper hose, then tilt it down until it can clear the upper hose and out of the engine compartment **(see illustration)**.

Note: *It's a good idea to place a piece of cardboard between the radiator cooling fins and the shroud to prevent any damage to the radiator when the shroud is installed.*

20   Installation is the reverse of removal. Place the fan assembly back into the retaining clips for the side and bottom.

21   Refill the cooling system (see Chapter 1).

6   Coolant reservoir - removal and installation

Warning: *Wait until the engine is completely cool before beginning this procedure.*

1   Drain the cooling system (see Chapter 1).

2   On 2018 and earlier models, remove the air filter housing (see Chapter 4).

3   On 2019 models, remove the radiator support panel plastic push-pin fasteners and remove the panel.

4   On 2.4L and 3.2L engines, pull the harness retainer off the reservoir stud mounting bolt.

5   Loosen the clamps, then disconnect the hoses from the top and bottom of the reservoir.

6   Remove the coolant reservoir mounting bolts and the reservoir **(see installation)**.

7   While the reservoir is off the vehicle, it should be cleaned with soapy water and a

5.19 Carefully lift the cooling fan shroud straight up

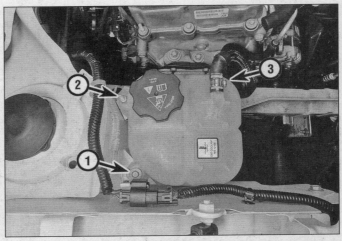

6.6 2018 and earlier coolant reservoir details

1   Reservoir mounting bolt   3   Coolant hose (top)
2   Reservoir mounting stud-bolt

7.7 Use a small screwdriver or pick and pull the locking clip upwards to release the connector

7.8 Remove the air conditioning junction block nut, then separate the block

7.11 Remove the radiator mounting brackets from each side of the radiator

brush to remove any deposits inside. Inspect it for damage and replace it if necessary.
8   Installation is the reverse of removal. Fill the reservoir with the proper type and amount of coolant (see Chapter 1).

7   Radiator - removal and installation

Warning: *The air conditioning system is under high pressure. DO NOT loosen any fittings or remove any components until after the system has been discharged. Air conditioning refrigerant must be properly discharged into an EPA-approved container at a dealer service department or an automotive air conditioning repair facility. Always wear eye protection when disconnecting air conditioning system fittings.*
Warning: *Wait until the engine is completely cool before beginning this procedure.*

Removal
2018 and earlier models
1   Have the air conditioning system discharged and the refrigerant recovered by an air conditioning technician.
2   Disconnect the cable from the negative terminal of the battery (see Chapter 5).
3   Set the parking brake, raise the front of the vehicle and support it securely on jackstands.
4   Drain the cooling system (see Chapter 1).
5   Remove the engine splash shields and skid plate, if equipped.
6   Remove the engine cooling fans (see Section 5).
7   Disconnect the lower radiator hose from the radiator **(see illustration)**.
8   Remove the air conditioning refrigerant line junction block nut **(see illustration)** then separate the junction block. Replace the O-ring seals and cover the lines and block to prevent moisture and debris from entering the openings.

9   Remove the condenser-to-radiator fasteners and move the condenser slightly forward (see Section 14).
10   Remove the radiator upper radiator mounting bracket bolts **(see illustrations 5.16a and 5.16b)**.
11   Pull the radiator forward until the upper mounting brackets can be removed **(see illustration)**.
12   Disengage the air conditioning line junction block from the molded bracket on the left side of the radiator.
13   Lift the radiator out of the vehicle.
14   Bugs and dirt can be removed from the radiator by spraying it from the back side with a garden hose. The radiator should be flushed out with a garden hose before reinstallation.
15   Check the radiator rubber mounts for deterioration and replace them if necessary.

2019 models
16   Disconnect the cable from the negative terminal of the battery (see Chapter 5).
17   Drain the cooling system (see Chapter 1).
18   Remove the cooling fan shroud assembly (see Section 5).
19   On 2.4L models, remove the lower radiator hose retainer bolts, then lift the hose quick-connector clip up and separate the hose from the radiator.
20   Disconnect the ambient air temperature sensor wire harness connector and remove the sensor.
21   Remove the transmission cooler mounting bolts and secure the cooler out of the way without disconnecting the lines.
22   Remove the side air deflector push-pins, retainers and deflectors.
23   Disconnect the air conditioning pressure switch electrical connector then remove the condenser tube bracket bolt at the top.
24   Remove the junction block bracket retaining nut and move the bracket off of the stud.
25   Remove the condenser mounting bolts and move the condenser back from the radiator.

26   Remove the radiator bracket mounting bolts from each end of the radiator.
27   Pull the radiator forward to release the mounts and lift the radiator up and out of the vehicle.

Installation
28   Installation is the reverse of removal. Make sure the air conditioning condenser is properly attached to the radiator before seating the radiator into the lower rubber mounts.
Note: *Be sure that the flexible air seals on each side of the radiator are in the correct position while installing the radiator.*
29   After installation, fill the cooling system with the proper mixture of antifreeze and water (see Chapter 1).
30   Start the engine and check for leaks. Allow the engine to reach normal operating temperature, indicated by the upper radiator hose becoming hot. Recheck the coolant level and add more if required.

8   Water pump - replacement

Warning: *Wait until the engine is completely cool before beginning this procedure.*
1   Disconnect the cable from the negative terminal of the battery (see Chapter 5).
2   Loosen the right-front wheel lug nuts. Set the parking brake, then raise the front of the vehicle and support it securely on jackstands. Remove the wheel.
3   Drain the cooling system (see Chapter 1).
4   Remove the drivebelt splash shield and the inner fender splash shield (see Chapter 11).

2.0L and 2.4L engines
5   On 2.0L models, remove the air conditioning compressor (see Section 12) and secure it out of the way without disconnecting the lines.

8.6 On 2.4L engines, loosen the water pump pulley bolts before removing the drivebelt

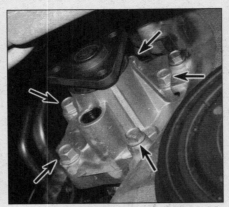

8.11 Water pump mounting bolts - 2.4L engines

8.12 Carefully pry the pump to separate it from the housing - 2.4L engines

6   Loosen the water pump pulley bolts (the drivebelt will prevent the pulley from turning) **(see illustration)**.
7   Remove the drivebelt (see Chapter 1).
8   On 2.4L engines, remove the water pump pulley bolts and separate the pulley from the pump.
9   On 2.0L engines, disconnect the lower radiator hose, EGR hose and oil cooler hose from the back of the water pump.
10   On 2.0L engines, disconnect the wiring harness retainers and move the harness from the water pump.
11   Remove the water pump mounting bolts **(see illustration)**.
Note: *On 2.0L models, the water pump and pump housing are one piece, bolted to the side of the engine. On 2.4L engines, the water pump is bolted to the water pump housing, which is mounted to the side of the engine block. If the pump housing is damaged it should be removed and replaced along with the pump.*
12   Use a small prybar to free the pump from the housing **(see illustration)**.
13   Remove all traces of old gasket material from the water pump housing. Clean the mating surface with brake system cleaner.

3.2L engines

14   Remove the air filter housing (see Chapter 4).

15   Remove the coolant reservoir (see Section 6).
16   Place a large wood block between the jack head and the oil pan to prevent oil pan damage, then carefully raise the engine just enough to take the weight off the right engine mount. Remove the mount and mounting bracket from the timing chain cover (see Chapter 2B).
17   Remove the upper idler pulley mounting bolt and idler pulley.
18   Remove the lower heater hose and the lower radiator hose from the water pump.
19   Remove the water pump mounting bolts, taking note of each bolt and its original location. The bolts are different sizes and lengths and must be reinstalled into their original locations.
20   Remove the water pump and gasket from the timing chain cover.
Caution: *Do not pry against the timing chain cover to remove the pump, the timing chain cover is easily damaged.*

All models

21   Install a new gasket on the back of the water pump **(see illustration)**, then carefully mate the pump to the engine.
Note: *It's a good idea to use gasket cement on the pump surface to prevent the gasket from shifting as the pump is guided into place.*
22   Install the water pump mounting bolts and tighten them in an alternating pattern to the

torque listed in this Chapter's Specifications.
Note: *On 3.2L engines, tighten the M6 bolts first then the M8 bolts.*
23   The remainder of installation is the reverse of removal. Refill and bleed the cooling system (see Chapter 1). Run the engine and check for leaks and proper operation.

---

9   Blower motor resistor/power module and blower motor assembly - replacement

---

Warning: *The models covered by this manual are equipped with a Supplemental Restraint System (SRS), more commonly known as airbags. Always disable the airbag system before working in the vicinity of any airbag system component to avoid the possibility of accidental deployment of the airbag, which could cause personal injury (see Chapter 12).*
1   Disconnect the cable from the negative terminal of the battery (see Chapter 5).
2   Remove the insulation panel plastic push pins and the panel from underneath the glove box (see Chapter 11).

Blower motor power module

3   Disconnect the electrical connectors for the blower motor power module and the blower motor **(see illustration 9.8)**.
4   Remove the screws and detach the power module from the blower housing **(see illustration 9.8)**.
5   Installation is the reverse of removal.

Blower motor assembly

Note: *The blower motor and blower wheel are balanced to each other at the factory and can only be replaced as an assembly.*
6   Remove the blower motor power module (see Steps 3 through 5).
7   Disconnect the electrical connector from the blower motor.
8   Remove the three screws holding the blower motor **(see illustration)**. Remove the blower motor from the housing.
9   Installation is the reverse of removal.

8.21 Install a new gasket to the pump, making sure all the bolt holes are aligned - 2.4L engines

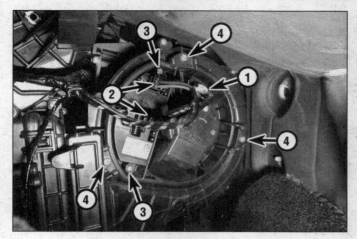

9.8 Blower motor and power module details

1   *Blower motor electrical connector*
2   *Blower motor power module electrical connectors*
3   *Blower motor power module mounting fasteners*
4   *Blower motor fasteners*

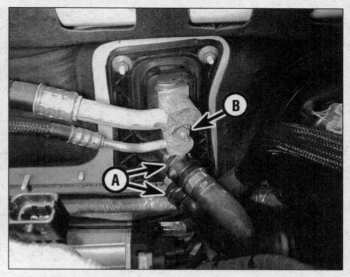

**10.5 Detach the heater hoses from the heater core tubes (A)
and the refrigerant lines at the evaporator (B)**

**10.11 Disconnect the distribution air
ducts from the heating/air
conditioning housing**

**10.12 Remove the nut holding the
heating/air conditioning housing to the
passenger's side of the firewall**

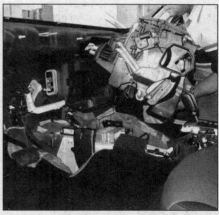

**10.13 Remove the heating/air conditioner
housing through the passenger's
side of the vehicle**

10   Heater core - replacement

Warning: *The air conditioning system is
under high pressure. DO NOT loosen any
fittings or remove any components until after the system has been discharged. Air
conditioning refrigerant must be properly
discharged into an EPA-approved container
at a dealer service department or an automotive air conditioning repair facility. Always
wear eye protection when disconnecting air
conditioning system fittings.*
Warning: *Wait until the engine is completely
cool before beginning this procedure.*
Warning: *The models covered by this manual
are equipped with a Supplemental Restraint
System (SRS), more commonly known as
airbags. Always disable the airbag system
before working in the vicinity of any airbag
system component to avoid the possibility of*
*accidental deployment of the airbag, which
could cause personal injury (see Chapter 12).*
1   Have the air conditioning system discharged and the refrigerant recovered by an
air conditioning technician.
2   Disconnect the cable from the negative
terminal of the battery (see Chapter 5).
3   Drain the cooling system (see Chapter 1).
4   Remove the instrument panel (see
Chapter 11).
5   Detach the hoses from the heater core
tubes at the firewall **(see illustration)**.
6   Remove the bolt securing the refrigerant
lines to the air conditioning evaporator. Disconnect the lines and remove the seals.
Note: *To prevent the entry of moisture or debris, place plugs in the lines, or use tape to
cover the openings.*
7   Remove the front sill trim on both the
passenger's and driver's sides. Remove the
front seats (see Chapter 11).
8   Pull back the carpet to expose the rear
seat ducts.
9   Remove the screws holding the left front
floor duct to the heating/air conditioning housing and remove the duct.
10   Remove the air conditioner condensation tube.
11   Remove the fasteners holding the left
and right rear distribution ducts. Disconnect
the ducts from the heating and air conditioning housing **(see illustration)**.
12   Remove the nut holding the heater/air
conditioner housing to the passenger's side of
the firewall **(see illustration)**.
13   Pull the heater/air conditioning unit rearward. Remove the heating/air conditioning
housing through the passenger compartment
(see illustration).
Note: *During removal of the heating/air conditioning housing, ensure that the interior of
the car is properly covered with towels to*

10.14 Place the heating/air conditioner housing on a work bench

10.16 Unclip the fastener and remove the flange from the heating/air conditioning housing

10.18 Pull the heater core from the heater/ air conditioning housing

catch any fluids that may come off the housing components.

14   Place the heater/air conditioning housing on a clean working surface **(see illustration)**.

15   Remove the foam seal from the connection tube flange holding the heater core outlets.

16   Unclip the fasteners securing the flange and remove the flange from the heating/air conditioning housing **(see illustration)**.

17   Remove the heater core tube cover fasteners and cover.

18   Remove the heater core from the heater/ air conditioning housing **(see illustration)**.

19   Installation is the reverse of removal. Use new seals for the heater core fittings and refill the cooling system (see Chapter 1).

Note: *If a new heater core is being installed, the cooling system must be flushed (see Chapter 1).*

20   Have the air conditioning system evacuated, recharged and leak tested by the shop that discharged it.

11 Heater/air conditioner control assembly - removal and installation

Warning: *The models covered by this manual are equipped with a Supplemental Restraint System (SRS), more commonly known as airbags. Always disable the airbag system before working in the vicinity of any airbag system component to avoid the possibility of accidental deployment of the airbag, which could cause personal injury (see Chapter 12).*

Note: *The heater/air conditioner control assembly are part of the Integrated Center Stack (ICS) and trim panel and cannot be disassembled.*

1   Disconnect the cable from the negative terminal of the battery (see Chapter 5).

2   Carefully pry the heater/air conditioning control assembly from the instrument panel **(see illustration)**.

3   Disconnect all electrical connectors from

the back of the heater/air conditioning control assembly **(see illustration)** and remove the control assembly.

4   Installation is the reverse of removal. If the heater/air conditioning control assembly is being replaced, calibration/diagnostic tests will be necessary. This will require a specialized scan tool; take the vehicle to a dealer service department or other qualified repair shop to have this service performed.

12 Air conditioning compressor - removal and installation

Warning: *The air conditioning system is under high pressure. DO NOT loosen any fittings or remove any components until after the system has been discharged. Air conditioning refrigerant must be properly discharged into an EPA-approved container at a dealer service department or an automotive air conditioning repair facility. Always wear eye protection when dis-*

11.2 Pry the control panel from the instrument panel

11.3 Disconnect all electrical connectors from the back of the heating/air conditioning control assembly - automatic heating/air conditioning model shown

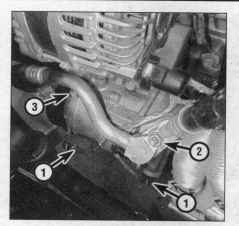

12.5 Air conditioning compressor details

1   Air conditioning compressor
    electrical connectors
2   Refrigerant manifold fastener
3   Compressor mounting bolt -
    one of three shown

connecting air conditioning system fittings.
Caution: *When replacing entire components, additional refrigerant oil must be added equal to the amount that is removed with the component being replaced. Read the label on the oil container to verify that it is compatible with the R-134a or R-1234yf system before adding any of it to the system.*
Note: *The receiver-drier should always be replaced when the compressor is replaced (see Section 13).*

Removal

1   Have the system discharged and the refrigerant recovered by an air conditioning technician.
2   Disconnect the cable from the negative terminal of the battery (see Chapter 5).
3   Remove the radiator close-out panel pushpins (see Chapter 11, Section 9).
4   Remove the drivebelt (see Chapter 1).
5   Disconnect the wire harness connected to the air conditioning compressor **(see illustration)**.
6   Remove the fasteners securing the refrigerant lines to the compressor and detach the refrigerant lines. Plug all open fittings to prevent entry of dirt and moisture.
7   Remove the compressor mounting fasteners and lower the compressor from the vehicle.
8   If a new compressor is being installed, remove the drain plug and drain 1.0 ounce (30 ml) of oil into a graduated container. Also follow any directions included with the new compressor.

Installation

Caution: *On clutch-type compressors, ensure the clutch coil wiring is not damaged during installation. Be careful not to damage the contact surface of the pulley.*
9   Installation is the reverse of removal. Install new O-rings onto the line fittings and

lightly coat them with the correct refrigerant oil.
Note: *Only use O-rings that are designed specifically for A/C system applications.*
10   Have the air conditioning system evacuated, recharged and leak tested by the shop that discharged it.

13   Air conditioning receiver-drier - replacement

Warning: *The air conditioning system is under high pressure. DO NOT loosen any fittings or remove any components until after the system has been discharged. Air conditioning refrigerant must be properly discharged into an EPA-approved container at a dealer service department or an automotive air conditioning repair facility. Always wear eye protection when disconnecting air conditioning system fittings.*
Caution: *When replacing entire components, additional refrigerant oil must be added equal to the amount that is removed with the component being replaced. Read the label on the oil container to verify that it is compatible with the R-134a or Rf-1234yf system before adding any of it to the system.*
Note: *The receiver-drier housing is not separately serviceable from the condenser. If there is a problem with the receiver-drier housing the condenser must be replaced.*

Removal

1   Have the system discharged and the refrigerant recovered by an air conditioning technician.
2   On 2018 and earlier models, remove the condenser (see Section 14) and place the condenser on a clean work bench.
3   Raise the front of the vehicle and support it securely on jackstands.
4   Remove the front bumper cover (see Chapter 11) and lower radiator splash shield plastic fasteners to access to the receiver-drier.
5   Remove the plug from the tube on the condenser then remove the receiver/drier filter from the tube.
Note: *Plug all openings immediately to prevent contamination.*

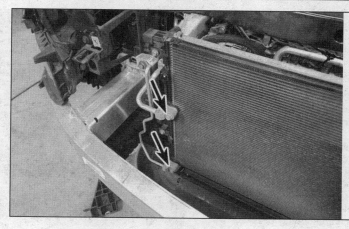

14.5 Disconnect the refrigerant lines to the condenser

Installation

6   Install the new receiver/drier filter into the condenser tube and tighten the plug securely. Install new O-rings onto the line fittings and lightly coat them with the correct refrigerant oil.
Note: *Only use O-rings that are designed specifically for A/C system applications.*
7   If you are replacing the receiver-drier with a new unit, add 1.0-ounce (30 ml) of refrigerant oil to the system.
8   Have the system evacuated, recharged and leak tested by the shop that discharged it.

14   Air conditioning condenser - removal and installation

Warning: *The air conditioning system is under high pressure. DO NOT loosen any fittings or remove any components until after the system has been discharged. Air conditioning refrigerant must be properly discharged into an EPA-approved container at a dealer service department or an automotive air conditioning repair facility. Always wear eye protection when disconnecting air conditioning system fittings.*
Caution: *When replacing entire components, additional refrigerant oil must be added equal to the amount that is removed with the component being replaced. Read the label on the oil container to verify that it is compatible with the R-134a system before adding any of it to the system.*

Removal

1   Have the system discharged and the refrigerant recovered by an air conditioning technician.
2   Disconnect the cable from the negative terminal of the battery (see Chapter 5).

2018 and earlier models

3   Remove the air deflector (see Section 5, Steps 2 through 15).
4   Remove the engine splash shields and skid plate, if equipped.
5   Remove the retaining bolts and disconnect the refrigerant lines **(see illustration)**. Plug all open fittings to prevent entry of dirt and moisture.

6   Remove the condenser upper mounting brackets **(see illustration)**.

7   Carefully pull straight up to release the condenser from the lower clips, then remove the condenser from the vehicle.

2019 models

8   Drain the cooling system (see Chapter 1).

9   Remove the radiator close-out panel fasteners and panel.

10   Remove the transmission cooler mounting bolts and secure the cooler out of the way without disconnecting the lines.

11   On 2.0L engines, release the clips and disconnect the two low temperature radiator (LTR) hoses from the condenser assembly.

12   Disconnect the air conditioning pressure switch electrical connector, then remove the top bolt that condenser tube to the radiator without disconnecting the air conditioning line.

13   Locate the junction block for the air conditioning lines on the right-side of the condenser and remove the mounting nut that secures the block to the condenser.

14   Remove the condenser mounting bolts and carefully remove the condenser.

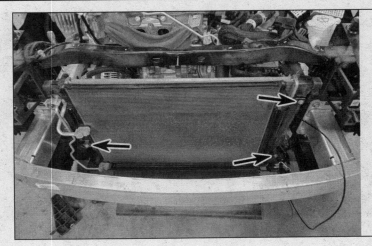

14.6 Condenser upper mounting bolt locations

Installation

15   If you are replacing the condenser with a new unit, add 0.7-ounce (20 ml) of refrigerant oil to the replacement.

16   Installation is the reverse of removal. Make certain to fully seat the condenser into the mounting clips and retainers. Install new O-rings onto the line fittings and lightly coat them with the proper refrigerant oil.

Note: *Only use O-rings that are designed specifically for A/C system applications.*

17   Have the system evacuated, recharged and leak tested by the shop that discharged it.

Chapter 4
Fuel and exhaust systems

Contents

Specifications

Fuel system

Fuel system pressure (all models)............ 58 psi +/- 5 psi (400 kpa +/- 34 kpa)

Torque specifications   Ft-lbs (unless otherwise indicated)

Note: *One foot-pound (ft-lb) of torque is equivalent to 12 inch-pounds (in-lbs) of torque. Torque values below approximately 15 ft-lbs are expressed in inch-pounds, since most foot-pound torque wrenches are not accurate at these smaller values.*

Fuel pressure sensor	24	33
Fuel rail bolts		
2.0L engines	17	23
2.4L and 3.2L engines	62 in-lbs	7
High-pressure fuel pump bolts	97 in-lbs	11
High-pressure fuel pipe fittings	24	32
Throttle body mounting bolts/nuts	71 in-lbs	8
Turbocharger-to-head nuts*	18	25
Turbocharger oil supply/coolant return pipe bolts	97 in-lbs	11
Turbocharger oil return pipe bolts	102 in-lbs	12
Turbocharger coolant supply pipe bolts	84 in-lbs	10

* Use new fasteners

1   General information and precautions

Fuel system warnings

Note: *Gasoline is extremely flammable and repairing fuel system components can be dangerous. Consider your automotive repair knowledge and experience before attempting repairs which may be better suited for a professional mechanic.*

a) *Don't smoke or allow open flames or bare light bulbs near the work area*
b) *Don't work in a garage with a gas-type appliance (water heater, clothes dryer)*
c) *Use fuel-resistant gloves. If any fuel spills on your skin, wash it off immediately with soap and water*
d) *Clean up spills immediately*
e) *Do not store fuel-soaked rags where they could ignite*
f) *Prior to disconnecting any fuel line, you must relieve the fuel pressure (see Section 3)*
g) *Wear safety glasses*
h) *Have a proper fire extinguisher on hand*
i) *The high pressure fuel system on 2.0L engines is under high pressure and can be dangerous (up to 3000 psi). Always relieve the fuel pressure before working on the fuel system, particularly the high pressure fuel system*

Fuel system

1   On 2.0L engines, the fuel system consists of the fuel tank, electric fuel pump/fuel level sending unit (located in the fuel tank), mechanical high pressure fuel pump, fuel rail and fuel injectors. The fuel injection system is a direct injection system; direct injection uses timed impulses to inject high-pressure fuel directly into the cylinder. The Powertrain Control Module (PCM) controls the injectors. The PCM monitors various engine parameters and delivers the exact amount of fuel required into the cylinders.

2   On 2.4L and 3.2L engines, the fuel system consists of the fuel tank, electric fuel pump/fuel level sending unit (located in the fuel tank), fuel rail and fuel injectors. The fuel injection system is a multi-port system; multi-port fuel injection uses timed impulses to inject the fuel directly into the intake port of each cylinder. The Powertrain Control Module (PCM) controls the injectors. The PCM monitors various engine parameters and delivers the exact amount of fuel required into the intake ports.

3   On all models, fuel is circulated from the fuel pump to the fuel rail through fuel lines running along the underside of the vehicle. Various sections of the fuel line are either rigid metal or nylon, or flexible fuel hose. The various sections of the fuel hose are connected either by quick-connect fittings or threaded metal fittings. On 2.0L direct injection models, high-pressure fuel pipes are used between the high-pressure fuel pump and fuel rail. The fuel pipe must be replaced whenever removed.

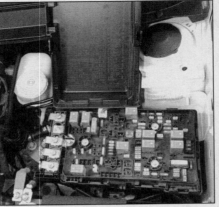

2.2 The underhood fuse block is located at the left side of the engine compartment

Exhaust system

4   The exhaust system consists of the exhaust manifold(s), catalytic converter(s), muffler(s), tailpipe and all connecting pipes, flanges and clamps. The catalytic converters are an emission control device added to the exhaust system to reduce pollutants.

Turbocharger system

5   2.0L engines have a turbocharger system that uses exhaust gas to compress and pressurize the incoming air to the engine to allow more fuel to be added, creating more power. The turbocharger system consists on the turbocharger, intercooler, blow-off valve, boost pressure sensor, turbocharger piping, oil supply and return lines, and coolant lines. The intercooler (charge air cooler) is located inside of the intake manifold. It can be serviced by removing the manifold, however, the procedure was not available from the manufacturer at time of publication.

2   Troubleshooting

Fuel pump

1   The fuel pump is located inside the fuel tank. Sit inside the vehicle with the windows closed, turn the ignition key to On (not Start) and listen for the sound of the fuel pump as it's briefly activated. You will only hear the sound for a second or two, but that sound tells you that the pump is working. Alternatively, have an assistant listen at the fuel filler cap.

2   If the pump does not come on, check all of the fuses in the underhood fuse block **(see illustration)**.

Note: *There is no replaceable fuel pump relay; it is actually just a circuit incorporated into the Totally Integrated Power Module, which is part of the underhood fuse/relay block.*

3   If the fuses are okay, check the wiring back to the fuel pump. If the wiring is okay, the fuel pump module or Totally Integrated Power Module is probably defective. If the pump runs continuously with the ignition key in the On

2.10 An automotive stethoscope is used to listen to the fuel injectors in operation

position, the Totally Integrated Power Module or Powertrain Control Module (PCM) is probably defective. Have the circuit checked by a professional mechanic.

Fuel injection system

Note: *The following procedure is based on the assumption that the fuel pump is working and the fuel pressure is adequate (see Section 4).*

4   Check all electrical connectors that are related to the system. Check the ground wire connections for tightness.

5   Verify that the battery is fully charged (see Chapter 5).

6   Inspect the air filter element (see Chapter 1).

7   Check all fuses related to the fuel system (see Chapter 12).

8   Check the air induction system between the throttle body and the intake manifold for air leaks. Also inspect the condition of all vacuum hoses connected to the intake manifold and to the throttle body.

9   Remove the air intake duct from the throttle body and look for dirt, carbon, varnish, or other residue in the throttle body, particularly around the throttle plate. If it's dirty, clean it with carb cleaner, a toothbrush and a clean shop towel.

10   With the engine running, place an automotive stethoscope against each injector, one at a time, and listen for a clicking sound that indicates operation **(see illustration)**.

Warning: *Stay clear of the drivebelt and any rotating or hot components.*

11   If you can hear the injectors operating, but the engine is misfiring, the electrical circuits are functioning correctly, but the injectors might be dirty or clogged. Try a commercial injector cleaning product (available at auto parts stores). If cleaning the injectors doesn't help, replace the injectors.

12   If an injector is not operating (it makes no sound), disconnect the injector electrical connector and measure the resistance across the injector terminals with an ohmmeter. Compare this measurement to the other injectors. If the resistance of the non-operational injec-

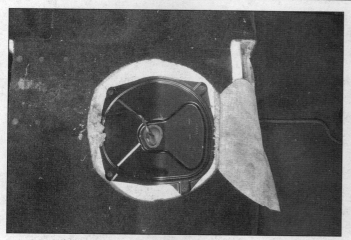

3.4 Cut the floor covering to access the fuel pump module

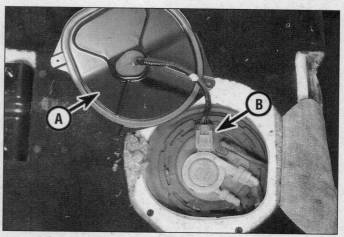

3.5 Remove the cover (A) and disable the electric fuel pump by unplugging the electrical connector (B)

tor is quite different from the other injectors, replace it.

13   If the injector is not operating, but the resistance reading is within the range of resistance of the other injectors, the PCM or the circuit between the PCM and the injector might be faulty.

3   Fuel pressure relief procedure

Warning: *Gasoline is extremely flammable. See* Fuel system warnings *in Section 1.*
1   Remove the fuel filler cap to relieve any pressure built up in the fuel tank.

2.0L models
2   Remove the fuel pump fuse from the underhood Power Distribution Center (PDC).

2.4L and 3.2L models
3   On 2.4L and 3.2L models, remove the lower rear seat cushion.
4   Cut the floor covering along the perforations to access the fuel pump module cover(s) **(see illustration)**.
5   Remove the fuel pump module cover **(see illustration)**.
6   Unplug the electrical connector from the fuel pump module **(see illustration 3.5)**.

All models
7   Start the engine; it should run momentarily then stall. Crank the engine several more times to ensure the fuel system has been completely relieved. Disconnect the cable from the negative terminal of the battery (see Chapter 5) before working on the fuel system.
Warning: *On 2.0L models, wait at least two hours before performing any work on the high-pressure side of the fuel system.*
8   It's a good idea to cover any fuel connection to be disassembled with rags to absorb the residual fuel that may leak out. Properly dispose of the rags.

9   After servicing the fuel system, diagnostic trouble codes may have been stored in the PCM's memory due to disconnecting the fuel pump circuit (see Chapter 6).

4   Fuel pressure - check

Warning: *Gasoline is extremely flammable. See* Fuel system warnings *in Section 1.*
Note: *The following procedure assumes that the fuel pump is receiving voltage and runs.*
Warning: *The following procedure applies to all 2.4L and 3.2L engines, and to the low-pressure side of the system (ONLY) on 2.0L engines. Never attempt to check the pressure on the high side of the system on 2.0L models.*
1   Relieve the fuel system pressure (see Section 3).
2   In addition to a fuel pressure gauge capable of reading fuel pressure up to 70 psi, you'll need a hose and an adapter suitable for tee-ing into the fuel system at the quick-connect fitting between the fuel delivery hose and the fuel rail **(see illustration)**.
3   Disconnect the quick-connect fitting at the connection between the fuel feed line and

the fuel rail (if you're unfamiliar with quick-connect fittings, refer to Section 5).
4   Tee-in the fuel pressure gauge between the fuel delivery hose and the fuel rail.
5   Start the engine and allow it to idle. Note the gauge reading as soon as the pressure stabilizes, and compare it with the pressure listed in this Chapter's Specifications.
6   If the fuel pressure is not within specifications, check the following:

a) If the pressure is lower than specified, check for a restriction in the fuel system (kinked fuel line, plugged fuel pump inlet strainer or clogged fuel filter). If no restrictions are found, replace the fuel pump module (see Section 8).

b) If the fuel pressure is higher than specified, replace the fuel pump module (see Section 8).

7   Turn off the engine. Fuel pressure should not fall more than 8 psi over five minutes. If it does, the problem could be a leaky fuel injector, fuel line leak, or faulty fuel pump module.
8   Relieve the fuel system pressure, then disconnect the fuel pressure gauge. Reconnect the fuel line and wipe up any spilled gasoline.

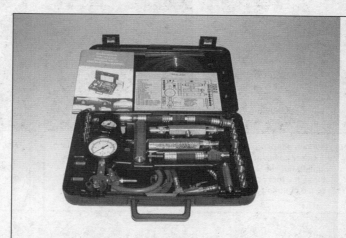

4.2 This typical fuel pressure testing kit contains all the necessary fittings and adapters, along with the fuel pressure gauge, to test most automotive fuel systems

Disconnecting Fuel Line Fittings

Two-tab type fitting; depress both tabs with your fingers, then pull the fuel line and the fitting apart

On this type of fitting, depress the two buttons on opposite sides of the fitting, then pull it off the fuel line

Threaded fuel line fitting; hold the stationary portion of the line or component (A) while loosening the tube nut (B) with a flare-nut wrench

Plastic collar-type fitting; rotate the outer part of the fitting

Metal collar quick-connect fitting; pull the end of the retainer off the fuel line and disengage the other end from the female side of the fitting . . .

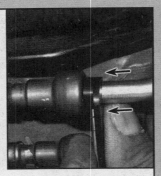

. . . insert a fuel line separator tool into the female side of the fitting, push it into the fitting and pull the fuel line off the pipe

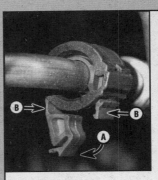

Some fittings are secured by lock tabs. Release the lock tab (A) and rotate it to the fully-opened position, squeeze the two smaller lock tabs (B) . . .

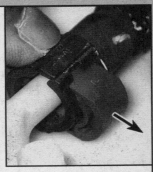

. . . then push the retainer out and pull the fuel line off the pipe

Spring-lock coupling; remove the safety cover, install a coupling release tool and close the tool around the coupling . . .

. . . push the tool into the fitting, then pull the two lines apart

Hairpin clip type fitting: push the legs of the retainer clip together, then push the clip down all the way until it stops and pull the fuel line off the pipe

5 Fuel lines and fittings - general information and disconnection

Warning: *Gasoline is extremely flammable. See* Fuel system warnings *in Section 1.*

1   Relieve the fuel pressure before servicing fuel lines or fittings (see Section 3), then disconnect the cable from the negative battery terminal (see Chapter 5) before proceeding.

2   The fuel supply line connects the fuel pump in the fuel tank to the fuel rail on the engine. The Evaporative Emission (EVAP) system lines connect the fuel tank to the EVAP canister and connect the canister to the intake manifold.

3   Whenever you're working under the vehicle, be sure to inspect all fuel and evaporative emission lines for leaks, kinks, dents and other damage. Always replace a damaged fuel or EVAP line immediately.

4   If you find signs of dirt in the lines during disassembly, disconnect all lines and blow them out with compressed air. Inspect the fuel strainer on the fuel pump pick-up unit for damage and deterioration.

Steel tubing

5   It is critical that the fuel lines be replaced with lines of equivalent type and specification.

6   Some steel fuel lines have threaded fittings. When loosening these fittings, hold the stationary fitting with a wrench while turning the tube nut.

Plastic tubing

Warning: *When removing or installing plastic fuel line tubing, be careful not to bend or twist it too much, which can damage it. Also, plastic fuel tubing is NOT heat resistant, so keep it away from excessive heat.*

7   When replacing fuel system plastic tubing, use only original equipment replacement plastic tubing.

Flexible hoses

8   When replacing fuel system flexible hoses, use only original equipment replacements.

9   Don't route fuel hoses (or metal lines) within four inches of the exhaust system or within ten inches of the catalytic converter. Make sure that no rubber hoses are installed directly against the vehicle, particularly in places where there is any vibration. If allowed to touch some vibrating part of the vehicle, a hose can easily become chafed and it might start leaking. A good rule of thumb is to maintain a minimum of 1/4-inch clearance around a hose (or metal line) to prevent contact with the vehicle underbody.

6 Exhaust system servicing - general information

Warning: *Allow exhaust system components to cool before inspection or repair. Also, when working under the vehicle, make sure it is securely supported on jackstands.*

6.1 Inspect the exhaust system rubber hangers for damage. This is a typical exhaust hanger for the intermediate exhaust pipe and muffler.

1   The exhaust system consists of the exhaust manifolds, catalytic converter, muffler, tailpipe and all connecting pipes, flanges and clamps. The exhaust system is isolated from the vehicle body and from chassis components by a series of rubber hangers. Periodically inspect these hangers for cracks or other signs of deterioration, replacing them as necessary **(see illustration)**.

2   Conduct regular inspections of the exhaust system to keep it safe and quiet. Look for any damaged or bent parts, open seams, holes, loose connections, excessive corrosion or other defects which could allow exhaust fumes to enter the vehicle. Do not repair deteriorated exhaust system components; replace them with new parts.

3   If the exhaust system components are extremely corroded, or rusted together, a cutting torch is the most convenient tool for removal. Consult a properly-equipped repair shop. If a cutting torch is not available, you can use a hacksaw, or if you have compressed air, there are special pneumatic cutting chisels that can also be used. Wear safety goggles to protect your eyes from metal chips and wear work gloves to protect your hands.

4   Here are some simple guidelines to follow when repairing the exhaust system:

a) *Work from the back to the front when removing exhaust system components.*

b) *Apply penetrating oil to the exhaust system component fasteners to make them easier to remove.*

c) *Use new gaskets, hangers and clamps.*

d) *Apply anti-seize compound to the threads of all exhaust system fasteners during reassembly.*

e) *Be sure to allow sufficient clearance between newly installed parts and all points on the underbody to avoid overheating the floor pan and possibly damaging the interior carpet and insulation. Pay particularly close attention to the catalytic converter and heat shield.*

7 Fuel tank - removal and installation

Warning: *Gasoline is extremely flammable. See* Fuel system warnings *in Section 1.*

Note: *The following procedure is much easier to perform if the fuel tank is empty. If the fuel tank isn't empty or nearly empty, you can siphon fuel from the tank with a siphon kit, available at most auto parts stores.*

Warning: *NEVER start the siphoning action with your mouth!*

1   Relieve the fuel system pressure (see Section 3).

2   Disconnect the cable from the negative terminal of the battery (see Chapter 5).

3   Raise the rear of the vehicle and support it securely on jackstands.

4   Disconnect the primary fuel pump module and, on AWD models, the secondary module (see Section 8).

5   Remove the exhaust pipe and muffler from below the fuel tank.

6   On AWD models, remove the driveshaft (see Chapter 8, Section 3).

7   Loosen the hose clamp and disconnect the fuel filler hose from the fuel tank **(see illustration)**.

7.7 Loosen the clamp and detach the filler hose from the fuel tank

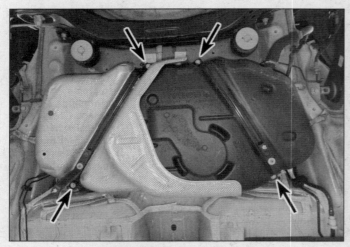

7.10 Fuel tank strap bolts

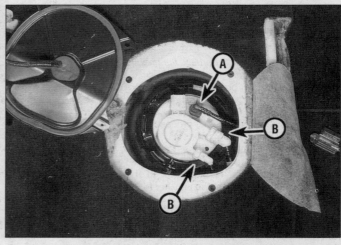

**8.5 Fuel pump module fuel (A) and EVAP (B) line
quick-connect fittings**

8   Remove the fuel tank skid plate(s), if equipped.

9   Support the fuel tank with a transmission jack or with a floor jack. If you're using a floor jack, put a piece of plywood between the jack head and the tank to protect the tank.

10   Remove the fuel tank support strap bolts and carefully lower the fuel tank from the vehicle, making sure no hoses or wiring harnesses are still attached **(see illustration)**.

11   Installation is the reverse of removal. Tighten the fuel tank strap bolts securely.

12   Start the engine and check for leaks at any fuel line connectors that were disconnected.

8   Fuel pump module - removal and installation

Warning: *Gasoline is extremely flammable. See* Fuel system warnings *in Section 1.*

Note: *All Wheel Drive (AWD) models have a saddle-type fuel tank configuration with a primary and secondary fuel pump module. Each module has a sending unit. Front Wheel Drive (FWD) models do not have a saddle tank and are only equipped with a primary fuel pump module. The primary fuel pump module has an electric fuel pump, venturi jet pump, fuel pump reservoir, strainer, fuel pressure regulator, fuel sending unit and fuel filter. The secondary fuel pump module contains the fuel pick-up line connection and fuel level sending unit. If there is a problem with any of the components the module(s) must be replaced.*

Note: *On AWD models, the primary fuel pump module is located on the right side of the tank and the secondary fuel pump module is located on the left side. The secondary fuel pump module may also be referred to as the auxiliary fuel pump module.*

Removal

1   Relieve the fuel system pressure (see Section 3).

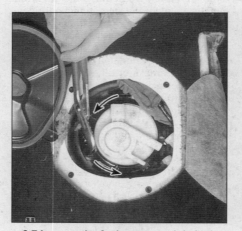

8.7 Loosen the fuel pump module lock ring using a large pair of pliers - the ring must be turned counterclockwise

2   Disconnect the cable from the negative terminal of the battery (see Chapter 5).

3   With the rear seat cushion removed, cut the floor covering along the perforations to access the fuel pump module cover(s) **(see illustration 3.4)**.

4   Remove the screws and lift the fuel pump module cover up enough to disconnect the connector(s) at the module **(see illustration 3.4)**.

5   Disconnect the fuel delivery and EVAP line quick-connect fittings from the primary fuel pump module (see Section 5) **(see illustration)**. Cap the primary module fuel line fittings.

6   Before removing the primary or secondary module, make alignment marks on the assembly and the fuel tank (if marks don't already exist), to ensure the assembly will be correctly realigned when it's installed again.

7   Using large water pump pliers or equivalent, loosen the lock ring that secures the fuel pump module. Alternatively, use a brass drift

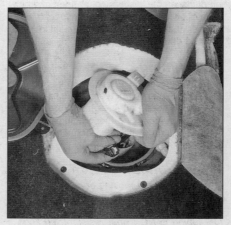

8.9 The fuel pump module is a tight fit and must be removed carefully to avoid damaging the sending unit float arm.

to carefully tap the locking ring counterclockwise until it is free **(see illustration)**.

Warning: *Don't use a steel punch - it could produce sparks.*

8   On vehicles equipped with both a primary and secondary fuel pump module, raise each module up enough to disconnect the internal fuel line at the bottom of the module.

9   Carefully lift the module from the fuel tank **(see illustration)**. Angle the module so that you don't bend the float arm of the fuel level sending unit or damage the fuel pump inlet strainer.

Caution: *When you're removing the primary fuel pump module, the reservoir does not empty out when the tank is drained. The fuel in the reservoir will spill out when the module is removed. Have a small container and lots of rags ready to catch any fuel once the module is pulled up from the tank.*

10   While the module is removed, inspect the inlet strainer. Make sure that it's not clogged or damaged. If the inlet strainer is dirty, try washing it in clean solvent.

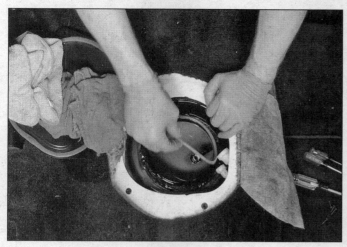

8.11 Remove and inspect the O-ring and replace as necessary

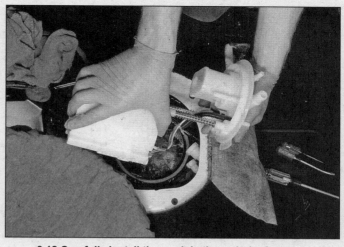

8.12 Carefully install the module through the fuel tank opening to prevent damage

Installation

11   Clean out the groove for the rubber O-ring. Check the O-ring for cuts or damage and replace it as necessary, then install the O-ring into the groove on the tank **(see illustration)**.

12   Carefully install the module into the tank, using care not to damage the float arm **(see illustration)**.

13   On vehicles equipped with both a primary and secondary fuel pump module, connect the internal fuel line to the bottom of the module.

14   Make sure the module is in the proper position on the tank with the locating lug seated.

15   Line up the marks, and tighten the fuel pump module lock ring securely.

16   Reconnect the fuel and EVAP lines and electrical connector.

17   Turn the ignition on and check for leaks before installing the fuel pump module cover(s) and seat.

18   The remainder of the procedure is reverse of removal.

9   High-pressure fuel pump - removal and installation

Warning: *Gasoline is extremely flammable. See* Fuel system warnings *in Section 1.*

Note: *2.0L engines are equipped with direct injection and are equipped with a high-pressure fuel pump mounted to the cylinder head of the engine. This fuel pump is in addition to the in-tank fuel pump and module.*

Removal

1   Relieve the fuel system pressure (see Section 3).

2   Disconnect the cable from the negative terminal of the battery (see Chapter 5, Section 3).

3   Remove the engine cover.

4   Remove the Powertrain Control Module (PCM) (see Chapter 6, Section 17).

Note: *The following step releases the mechanical pressure on the fuel pump.*

5   While looking at the crankshaft pulley/balancer, rotate the engine until the notch in the balancer aligns with the mark in the timing chain cover. Rotate the engine an additional 90 degrees clockwise.

6   Remove the bolt securing the coolant pipe to the cylinder head above the transaxle bell housing.

7   Disconnect the high-pressure fuel pump electrical connector.

8   Remove the high-pressure fuel pipe from the fuel pump fitting. It may be necessary to loosen the fitting at the fuel rail to be able to detach the pipe from the pump.

9   Disconnect the fuel supply line quick connect fitting from the high pressure fuel pump.

10   Remove the foam insulation cover from the fuel pump.

11   Loosen the fuel pump nuts a little at a time so the fuel pump is released from the cylinder head evenly.

Note: *When removing the fuel pump after the nuts are removed, note that an additional component is installed in the cylinder head above the fuel pump. Use care not to drop or damage when removing the high-pressure fuel pump.*

12   Remove the fuel pump and roller tappet from the cylinder head.

13   Discard the gasket and O-ring from the pump.

Installation

14   Lubricate the roller tappet and the bore in the cylinder head and install the roller tappet using the groove to position correctly.

15   Using a new gasket and O-ring, install the fuel pump into the cylinder head. Install the nuts by hand and tighten each nut a few turns at a time so the pump is installed evenly. Tighten the nuts to the torque listed in this Chapter's Specifications.

16   Install the foam insulation cover onto the fuel pump. Attach the high pressure fuel pipe to the fuel pump and tighten both ends to the torque listed in this Chapter's Specifications.

17   The remainder of the installation is reverse of removal.

18   Turn the ignition on and check for fuel leaks before starting the engine.

10   Fuel Pump Control Module (FPCM) - removal and installation

Note: *2019 and later models are equipped with an FPCM. The FPCM is located in the passenger's rear corner of the vehicle under the quarter panel trim.*

1   Disconnect the cable from the negative terminal of the battery (see Chapter 5).

2   Remove the passenger's rear quarter trim panel (see Chapter 11).

3   Locate the FPCM and disconnect the electrical connector.

4   Remove the nuts and remove the FPCM from the vehicle.

5   Installation is reverse of removal.

11   Fuel pressure sensors - replacement

Warning: *Gasoline is extremely flammable. See* Fuel system warnings *in Section 1.*

Note: *2.0L models with direct injection are equipped with fuel pressure sensors.*

1   Relieve the fuel system pressure (see Section 3).

2   Disconnect the negative battery cable (see Chapter 5, Section 3).

3   Remove the engine cover.

Fuel Pressure Sensor (FPS)

Note: *The fuel pressure sensor is part of the fuel supply line attached to the high-pressure fuel pump.*

4   Disconnect the FPS electrical connector at the end of the fuel supply line near the high-pressure fuel pump.

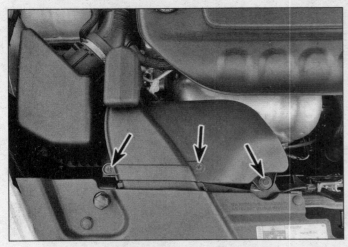

12.1 Remove the fasteners and pull the air inlet duct from the air filter housing

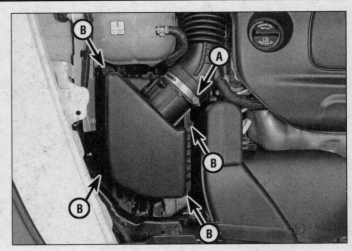

12.2 Loosen the clamp (A) and screws (B) to remove the air filter lid

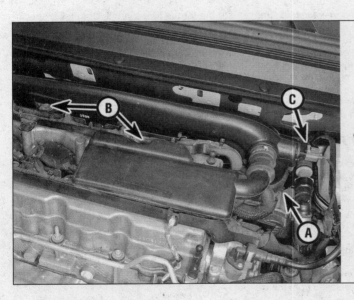

12.10 Loosen the clamp at the throttle body (A), remove the bolts (B) and disconnect the IAT sensor (C)

5   Disconnect the fuel supply line quick connect fitting from the high-pressure fuel pump and hard line.

6   Installation is reverse of removal.

7   Turn the ignition on and check for fuel leaks before starting the engine.

Fuel Rail Pressure Sensor (FRPS)

Note: *The fuel rail pressure sensor is attached to the fuel rail.*

8   Disconnect the electrical connector from the sensor.

9   Unscrew the sensor from the fuel rail to remove.

10   Installation is reverse of removal. Lubricate the threads of the sensor with hydraulic oil before installing and tighten it to the torque listed in this Chapter's Specifications.

11   Turn the ignition on and check for fuel leaks before starting the engine.

12   Air filter housing - removal and installation

1   Remove the retainers for the fresh air inlet duct, then remove the fresh air inlet duct from the air filter housing **(see illustration)**.

Air filter lid

2   Loosen the intake air duct clamp and disconnect the duct from the lid **(see illustration)**.

3   Loosen the screws and remove the lid from the vehicle.

4   The air filter can be serviced with the lid removed.

5   Installation is reverse of removal.

Air intake duct

Note: *The following procedures apply to 2.4L and 3.2L engines. For 2.0L engines see Section 15.*

2.4L engines

6   Disconnect the negative battery cable (see Chapter 5, Section 3).

7   Remove the engine cover.

8   Disconnect the quick connect fitting in the duct near the air filter lid, and remove the hose.

9   Disconnect the IAT sensor connector.

10   Loosen the band clamps at the air filter lid and throttle body end **(see illustration)**.

11   Remove the two retainers attaching the duct to the valve cover.

12   Lift the duct up enough to disconnect the Intake Air Temperature (IAT) sensor connector on the duct.

13   Remove the duct from the vehicle.

14   Installation is the reverse of removal.

3.2L engines

15   Remove the engine cover.

16   Disconnect the quick connect fitting from the duct and remove the hose.

17   Loosen the band clamp from both ends of the duct and remove the duct from the engine.

18   Installation is reverse of removal.

Resonator

Note: *The following procedure applies to 3.2L engines.*

19   Remove the engine cover.

20   Disconnect the negative battery cable (see Chapter 5, Section 3).

21   Remove the air intake duct.

22   Disconnect the Intake Air Temperature (IAT) sensor electrical connector (see Chapter 6, Section 10).

23   Disconnect the hose from the retainer on the resonator.

24   Remove the three retainers securing the resonator to the intake manifold.

25   Pull the resonator straight up and off of the locating pins and throttle body.

Note: *Keep track of the rubber grommets, some may stay with the engine, some with the resonator.*

26   Installation is reverse of removal.

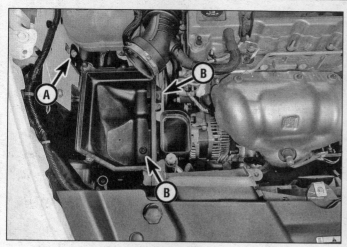

12.33 Remove the bolt (A) and pull up to disengage the pins from the grommets (B)

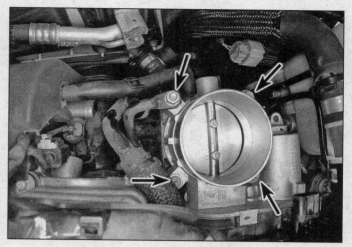

13.8 Remove the throttle body fasteners and bracket

Air filter housing

27 Disconnect the cable from the negative terminal of the battery (see Chapter 5).
28 Disconnect the quick connect fittings on the lid/air intake duct.
29 On 2.0L engines, disconnect the MAF/IAT electrical connector.
30 On 2.4L engines, remove the bolt and screws and remove the intake resonator.
31 On 2.0L and 2.4L models, loosen the intake air duct clamp and disconnect from the lid. On 3.2L models, remove the duct.
32 On all models, detach the harness from the retainers on the air filter housing.
33 Remove the bolt attaching the housing bracket to the vehicle **(see illustration)**.
34 Pull the housing upwards to disengage the pins from the grommets.
35 Inspect the rubber mounting grommets on the underside of the air filter housing. If the grommets are cracked, dried out, torn or otherwise damaged, replace them.
36 Installation is the reverse of removal.

13 Throttle body - removal and installation

Warning: *Wait until the engine is completely cool before beginning this procedure.*
Note: *On 2.0L engines, the manufacturer states to remove the intake manifold first, then remove the throttle body from the intake. The throttle body may be able to be removed with the intake installed.*

1 Disconnect the cable from the negative terminal of the battery (see Chapter 5). Remove the engine cover.
2 Remove the engine cover.
3 On 2.0L engines, remove the turbocharger pipe between the turbo and throttle body (see Section 15).
4 Disconnect the coolant hoses from the throttle body.

13.9 Throttle body gasket location

5 On 2.4L engines, detach the air intake duct from the throttle body (see Section 12).
6 On 3.2L engines, remove the resonator (see Section 12).
7 On all models, disconnect the throttle body electrical connector.
8 Remove the throttle body mounting fasteners and bracket and remove the throttle body from the intake manifold **(see illustration)**.
9 Remove the throttle body gasket **(see illustration)** and inspect it for cracks, tears and deterioration. If it isn't in perfect condition, replace it.
10 Make sure that the gasket mating surfaces of the throttle body and the intake manifold are clean.
11 Installation is the reverse of removal. Tighten the throttle body bolts a little at a time to the torque listed in this Chapter's Specifications.
Caution: *Do not overtighten the bolts - it can cause damage to the throttle body, the gasket, the bolts and/or the intake manifold.*

14 Fuel rail and injectors - removal and installation

Warning: *Gasoline is extremely flammable. See* Fuel system warnings *in Section 1.*

Removal
Warning: *Wait until the engine is completely cool before beginning this procedure.*
1 Remove the engine cover.
2 Relieve the fuel system pressure (see Section 3).
3 Disconnect the cable from the negative terminal of the battery (see Chapter 5, Section 3).

2.0L engines
4 Remove the air outlet pipe (see Section 15).
5 Remove the ignition coils (see Chapter 5, Section 9).
6 Remove the sound dampening material from the valve cover.

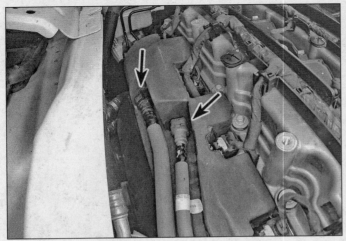

14.13 Disconnect the fuel line fittings

14.14 Separate the insulation as instructed to remove
from the intake manifold

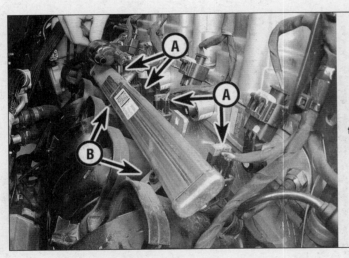

14.15 Slide the
connector lock up
and disconnect the
electrical connector
from the fuel injector
(A) and remove the
fuel rail mounting
bolts (B)

7   Disconnect the fuel rail pressure sensor connector.

8   Loosen the fittings at the high pressure fuel pump and fuel rail and remove the high pressure fuel pipe.

9   Remove the fuel rail bolts and remove the fuel rail and injectors from the cylinder head.

Note: *A special tool (Remover, Fuel Rail 2044500140) to remove the injectors may be required if an injector is stuck in the cylinder head.*

2.4L and 3.2L engines

10   On 2.4L engines, remove the bolt and screws and remove the intake resonator.

11   Remove the EVAP purge control valve (see Chapter 6, Section 20).

12   On 3.2L engines, remove the upper intake manifold and insulator from the front valve cover (see Chapter 2B, Section 5).

13   On all engines, disconnect the fuel delivery line quick-connect fittings from the fuel rail **(see illustration)** (if you're unfamiliar with quick-connect fittings, see Section 5).

14   Carefully cut the sound insulation at the line shown and remove from the intake manifold **(see illustration)**.

15   Disconnect the fuel injector electrical connectors **(see illustration)**. Detach the injector wiring harness clips from the fuel rail (if equipped) and set the harness aside.

16   Disconnect any harness retainers from the fuel rail.

17   Remove the fuel rail mounting bolts.

Note: *During the next step, on 3.2L engines, some of the injectors may remain in the lower intake manifold. This is OK as they are not attached to the fuel rail with clips like 2.4L engines.*

18   Carefully pull up on the fuel rail to disengage the injectors from their respective bores in the intake manifold, then remove the fuel rail and injectors as a single assembly. The injectors might initially stick in their bores, but they'll pull free when sufficient force is applied.

19   On 2.4L engines, remove the fuel injector retaining clips and remove the injectors **(see illustrations)**.

Injector service

2.0L engines

20   To remove the injectors from the fuel rail, remove the pin retaining clips from the fuel rail and remove the two pins securing the injector to the fuel rail.

21   Pill the injector(s) out of the fuel rail.

22   Remove the old combustion chamber Teflon sealing ring and the upper O-ring and support ring from each injector **(see illustration)**.

Caution: *Be extremely careful not to damage the groove for the seal or the rib in the floor of the groove. If you damage the groove or the rib, you must replace the injector.*

23   Before installing the new Teflon seal on each injector, thoroughly clean the groove for the seal and the injector shaft. Remove all combustion residue and varnish with a clean shop rag.

24   Teflon seal installation requires a couple of special tools, available at most auto parts stores or automotive tool suppliers; a seal installation cone and a seal sizing sleeve **(see illustration)**. Install the installation cone onto the injector and place the Teflon seal onto the cone. Use the special sleeve to push the Seal onto the injector and into its groove.

Caution: *Do not use any lubricants to do this.*

25   Pushing the Teflon seal into place in its groove expands it slightly. The use of the sizing sleeve is used to install the seals and then to shrink the seals after they've been installed. Using a clockwise rotating motion of about 180 degrees, install the sleeve onto the injector and over the Teflon seal until the sleeve hits its stop, then carefully turn the sleeve counterclockwise 180 degrees as you pull it off the injector **(see illustration)**.

26   At the top of the injector at the fuel rail end, remove the O-ring and support ring from each injector and discard them. Install new O-rings and support rings and coat them with some clean engine oil to facilitate installation of the injectors **(see illustration)**.

14.19a Using a screwdriver or pliers, remove the injector retaining clip. . .

14.19b . . . and withdraw the injector from the fuel rail (2.4L engines)

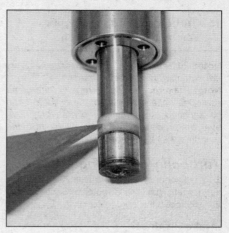

14.22 To remove the Teflon sealing ring from the injector, cut it off with a hobby knife (be careful not to scratch the injector groove)

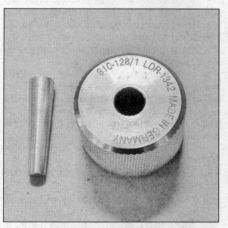

14.24 The special tools recommended for installing and sizing the Teflon seals (typical)

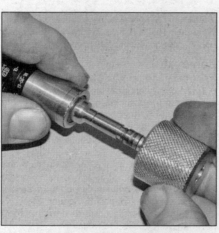

14.25 Slide the seal onto the injector with a rotary motion

14.26 Note that the upper O-ring (1) is installed above the support ring (2)

2.4L and 3.2L engines

27   Remove the O-rings from each injector **(see illustration)** and discard them. Install new O-rings and coat them with some clean engine oil to facilitate installation of the injectors.

28   Make sure that the injector is square to the bore of the mounting pipe and push it down into the mounting pipe until it's fully seated **(see illustration)**.

Installation

29   Installation is the reverse of removal. Tighten the fuel rail retaining bolts (and high pressure fuel pipe on 2.0L) to the torque listed in this Chapter's Specifications.

30   Start the engine and check for leaks at the quick-connect fitting that connects the fuel supply hose to the fuel rail. Also look for leaks at the upper end of each injector, where it's installed into the fuel rail.

14.27 Carefully remove the O-rings from the injectors

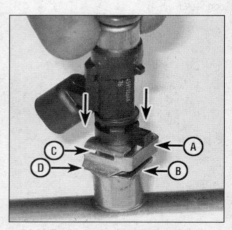

14.28 Fuel injector installation details: align the flat on the retainer (A) with the flat on the flange (B), and engage the slots in the retainer (C) with the semi-circular flanges (D) when the injector is pushed into fuel rail pipe

15   Turbocharger components - removal and installation

Note: *2019 and later 2.0L gasoline engines are equipped with a turbocharger.*
Note: *The turbocharger intercooler (charge air cooler) is bolted to the intake manifold. It can be serviced by removing the manifold, however, the procedure was not available from the manufacturer at time of publication.*

Turbocharger piping

1   Disconnect the cable from the negative battery terminal (see Chapter 5, Section 3).
2   Remove the engine cover.

Intake air duct

Note: *The intake air duct is located between the air filer lid and turbocharger inlet.*
3   Disconnect the blow-off valve hose from the turbocharger and position it to the side.
4   Disconnect the quick-connect fitting and the small hose from the Crankcase Vent (CCV) heater assembly on the intake air duct.
5   Disconnect the CCV electrical connector.
6   Loosen the band clamps at the air filter lid and turbocharger and remove the duct from the vehicle.
7   Installation is the reverse of removal.

Air outlet pipe

Note: *The air outlet pipe is the duct between the turbocharger and the throttle body.*
8   Disconnect the blow-off valve hose from the valve and position it to the side.
9   Disconnect the PCV quick-connect fitting from the pipe.
10   Disconnect the quick-connect fittings and retainer and remove the crankcase vent hose from the engine.
11   Disconnect the boost and IAT sensor connectors located on the pipe near the throttle body.
12   Disconnect the blow-off valve electrical connector.

13   Remove the bolt attaching the pipe to the valve cover.
14   Loosen the band clamps at the turbocharger and the throttle body.
15   Remove the air outlet pipe from the vehicle.
16   Installation is reverse of removal.

Blow-off valve

Note: *The blow-off valve may also be referred to as the surge valve.*
17   Disconnect the negative battery cable (see Chapter 5, Section 3).
18   Remove the engine cover.
19   Disconnect the blow-off valve hose from the valve and position it to the side.
20   Disconnect the blow-off valve electrical connector.
21   Remove the bolts and remove the valve from the air outlet pipe.
22   Installation is reverse of removal. Use a new gasket during installation.

Turbocharger

Warning: *Wait until the engine is completely cool before beginning this procedure.*

Removal

23   Raise the front of the vehicle and support it securely on jackstands.
24   Disconnect the negative battery cable (see Chapter 5, Section 3).
25   Remove the engine cover.
26   Drain the engine coolant (see Chapter 1, Section 25).
27   Remove the intake air duct from the vehicle.
28   Remove the crankcase pressure sensor and bracket (see Chapter 6, Section 21).
29   Remove the clips and the engine compartment trim above the radiator.
30   Disconnect the hoses, remove the bolts and the coolant expansion tank from the vehicle.
31   Disconnect the upper and lower O2 sensor connectors.

32   Remove the bolts and the catalytic converter heat shield.
33   Remove the EGR pipe (see Chapter 6, Section 19).
34   Remove the bolts attaching the catalytic converter to the turbo, bracket and rear exhaust pipe and remove from the vehicle.
35   Remove the two bolts at the engine block and one bolt at the turbocharger and remove the oil return pipe. Discard the O-rings.
36   Remove the one bolt at the engine block, one bolt at the turbocharger, and one bolt for the bracket and remove the oil supply pipe. Discard the O-rings.
37   Remove the one bolt at the turbocharger and one bolt at the bracket and disconnect the coolant supply pipe at the turbocharger. Discard the O-rings. Secure out of the way.
38   Remove the one bolt at the turbocharger and disconnect the coolant return pipe at the turbocharger. Discard the O-rings. Secure out of the way.
39   Remove the two nuts and two bolts and remove the turbocharger heat shield.
40   Disconnect the blow-off valve hose from the turbo and position it to the side.
41   Disconnect the wastegate actuator electrical connector at the turbo.
42   Loosen the band clamp and disconnect the air outlet pipe from the turbocharger.
43   Remove the three remaining nuts attaching the turbocharger to the cylinder head.
w45   Remove the gasket from the cylinder head and discard.

Installation

46   Installation is the reverse of removal noting the following items:

a)   *Use NEW O-rings on the oil and coolant pipes.*
b)   *Use a new gasket for the turbocharger at the cylinder head.*
c)   *Tighten all fasteners to the torque listed in this Chapter's Specifications.*
d)   *Refill the cooling system and change the engine oil and filter (see Chapter 1).*

Chapter 5
Engine electrical systems

Contents

Specifications

Charging system
Charging voltage .... 13.5 to 14.5 volts

Torque specifications
Ft-lbs   **Nm**

Note: One foot-pound (ft-lb) of torque is equivalent to 12 inch-pounds (in-lbs) of torque. Torque values below approximately 15 ft-lbs are expressed in inch-pounds, since most foot-pound torque wrenches are not accurate at these smaller values.

Alternator mounting bolts
2.0L	35	48
2.4L / 3.2L	18	25

Starter mounting bolts
2.0L
Starter-to-motor	19	26
Starter-to-transaxle	35	48

2.4L
2018 and earlier models	40	54

2019 and later models
Starter-to-motor	41	56
Starter-to-transaxle	40	54

3.2L
2018 and earlier models	40	54
2019 and later models	41	56

Torque reaction bracket bolts
Start/stop	40	54

Non-start/stop
Upper bolt	35	47
Lower bolt	40	54

1 General information and precautions

General information

Battery system

1   The battery system consists of the battery, battery cables, the Intelligent Battery Sensor (IBS), and the Voltage Stability Module (VSM). The IBS monitors battery current, voltage and temperature to assist the PCM in controlling alternator output for proper charging of the battery. On models with the Engine Start Stop (ESS) system, the Voltage Stability Modules (VSM) power the exterior lights, radio, gauges/display, AC, factory equipped trailer tow module and the Parktronic (PTS) system when the engine is stopped such as at a stop light.

Ignition system

2   The electronic ignition system consists of the Crankshaft Position (CKP) sensor, the Camshaft Position (CMP) sensor, the Knock Sensor (KS), the Powertrain Control Module (PCM), the ignition switch, the battery, the individual ignition coils, and the spark plugs. For more information on the CKP, CMP and KS sensors, as well as the PCM, refer to Chapter 6.

Charging system

3   The charging system includes the alternator, the Powertrain Control Module (PCM), which incorporates the Electronic Voltage Regulator (EVR), the Body Control Module (BCM), a charge indicator light on the dash, voltage gauge (if equipped), the battery, a fuse or fusible link and the wiring connecting all of these components. The charging system supplies electrical power for the ignition system, the lights, the radio, etc. The alternator is driven by the drivebelt.

Starting system

4   The starting system consists of the battery, the ignition switch, the starter relay, the Powertrain Control Module (PCM), the Body Control Module (BCM), the clutch start switch (manual transaxle models), the Transmission Range (TR) switch, Neutral position sensor (on manual transaxle models with start/stop system), the starter motor and solenoid assembly, and the wiring connecting all of the components.

Engine Stop Start (ESS) system

5   The ESS system consists of the PCM, alternator, IBS, battery, starter, starter relay, in-rush current reduction relay, instrument cluster, start/stop off switch, radio frequency hub, BCM, VSMs, and transmission neutral sensor (manual transaxle models). When enabled and the vehicle comes to a stop (such as at a stop light) and the proper conditions are met, the engine stops running to conserve fuel. When stopped, the instrument cluster ESS light illuminates and displays an ESS message and the VSM provides steady voltage to the vehicle systems. The engine then starts again

when the brake is released to take off from the stopped position. The engine may start while the vehicle is stopped if the battery voltage is low, brake booster vacuum is low, the climate control system is working harder than normal (such as a cold or hot day), the steering wheel is turned while stopped, or the transmission is shifted to another position. The engine will also start when stopped if the start/stop off switch is pressed, cancelling the feature. The ESS will not restart the engine when stopped if the hood is opened, the vehicle senses the driver has exited the vehicle or the shift lever is placed in a selection that is deemed unsafe for auto start.

Precautions

6   Always observe the following precautions when working on the electrical system:
a) Be extremely careful when servicing engine electrical components. They are easily damaged if checked, connected or handled improperly.
b) Never leave the ignition switched on for long periods of time when the engine is not running.
c) Never disconnect the battery cables while the engine is running.
d) Maintain correct polarity when connecting battery cables from another vehicle during jump starting - see Booster battery (jump) starting at the front of this manual.
e) Always disconnect the cable from the negative battery terminal before working on the electrical system, but read the battery disconnection procedure first (see Section 3).

7   It's also a good idea to review the safety-related information regarding the engine electrical systems located in the front of this manual before beginning any operation included in this Chapter.

2 Troubleshooting

Ignition system

1   If a malfunction occurs in the ignition system, do not immediately assume that any particular part is causing the problem. First,

check the following items:
a) Make sure that the cable clamps at the battery terminals are clean and tight.
b) Test the condition of the battery (see Steps 14 through 18). If it doesn't pass all the tests, replace it.
c) Check the ignition coil or coil pack connections.
d) Check any relevant fuses in the engine compartment fuse and relay box (see Chapter 12). If they're burned, determine the cause and repair the circuit.

Check

Warning: Because of the high voltage generated by the ignition system, use extreme care when performing a procedure involving ignition components.
Note: The ignition system components on these vehicles are difficult to diagnose. In the event of ignition system failure that you can't diagnose, have the vehicle tested at a dealer service department or other qualified auto repair facility.
Note: You'll need a spark tester for the following test. Spark testers are available at most auto supply stores.
2   If the engine turns over but won't start, verify that there is sufficient ignition voltage to fire the spark plugs as follows.
3   On models with a coil-over-plug type ignition system, remove a coil and install the tester between the boot at the lower end of the coil and the spark plug **(see illustration)**.
4   Crank the engine and note whether or not the tester flashes.
Caution: Do NOT crank the engine or allow it to run for more than five seconds; running the engine for more than five seconds may set a Diagnostic Trouble Code (DTC) for a cylinder misfire.
5   If the tester flashes during cranking, the coil is delivering sufficient voltage to the spark plug to fire it. Repeat this test for each cylinder to verify that the other coils are OK.
6   If the tester doesn't flash, remove a coil from another cylinder and swap it for the one being tested. If the tester now flashes, you know that the original coil is bad. If the tester still doesn't flash, the PCM or wiring harness is probably defective. Have the PCM checked out by a dealer service department or other

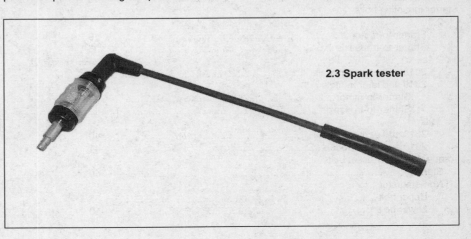

2.3 Spark tester

2.15 To test the open circuit voltage of the battery, connect the black probe of the voltmeter to the negative terminal and the red probe to the positive terminal of the battery; a fully charged battery should be at least 12.6 volts

2.17 Connect a battery load tester to the battery and check the battery condition under load following the tool manufacturer's instructions

qualified repair shop (testing the PCM is beyond the scope of the do-it-yourselfer because it requires expensive special tools).

7   If the tester flashes during cranking but a misfire code (related to the cylinder being tested) has been stored, the spark plug could be fouled or defective.

Charging system

8   If a malfunction occurs in the charging system, do not automatically assume the alternator is causing the problem. First check the following items:

a) Check the drivebelt tension and condition, as described in Chapter 1. Replace it if it's worn or deteriorated.
b) Make sure the alternator mounting bolts are tight.
c) Inspect the alternator wiring harness and the connectors at the alternator and voltage regulator. They must be in good condition, tight and have no corrosion.
d) Check the fusible link (if equipped) or main fuse in the underhood fuse/relay box. If it is burned, determine the cause, repair the circuit and replace the link or fuse (the vehicle will not start and/or the accessories will not work if the fusible link or main fuse is blown).
e) Start the engine and check the alternator for abnormal noises (a shrieking or squealing sound indicates a bad bearing).
f) Check the battery. Make sure it's fully charged and in good condition (one bad cell in a battery can cause overcharging by the alternator).
g) Disconnect the battery cables (negative first, then positive). Inspect the battery posts and the cable clamps for corrosion. Clean them thoroughly if necessary (see Chapter 1). Reconnect the cables (positive first, negative last).

Alternator - check

9   Use a voltmeter to check the battery voltage with the engine off. It should be at least 12.6 volts (see illustration 2.15).
10   Start the engine and check the battery voltage again. It should now be approximately 13.5 to 15 volts.
11   If the voltage reading is more or less than the specified charging voltage, the alternator might be defective, the Electronic Voltage Regulator (EVR) within the Powertrain Control Module (PCM) might be defective, or there might be a problem in the circuitry between the alternator, PCM or battery. Check for the presence of trouble codes related to the system (see Chapter 6). If no codes are found, remove the alternator and have it bench tested (most auto parts stores will do this for you); if it checks out ok, inspect all connectors and wiring in the circuit. If no problems are found, have the PCM checked by a dealer service department or other qualified repair shop.
12   The charging system (battery) light on the instrument cluster lights up when the ignition key is turned to On, but it should go out when the engine starts.
13   If the charging system light stays on after the engine has been started, there is a problem with the charging system.

Battery - check

14   Check the battery state of charge. Visually inspect the indicator eye on the top of the battery (if equipped with one); if the indicator eye is black in color, charge the battery as described in Chapter 1. Next perform an open circuit voltage test using a digital voltmeter.
Note: *The battery's surface charge must be removed before accurate voltage measurements can be made. Turn on the high beams for ten seconds, then turn them off and let the vehicle stand for two minutes.*

15   With the engine and all accessories Off, touch the negative probe of the voltmeter to the negative terminal of the battery and the positive probe to the positive terminal of the battery (see illustration). The battery voltage should be 12.6 volts or slightly above. If the battery is less than the specified voltage, charge the battery before proceeding to the next test. Do not proceed with the battery load test unless the battery charge is correct.
16   Disconnect the negative battery cable, then the positive cable from the battery.
17   Perform a battery load test. An accurate check of the battery condition can only be performed with a load tester (see illustration). This test evaluates the ability of the battery to operate the starter and other accessories during periods of high current draw. Connect the load tester to the battery terminals. Load test the battery according to the tool manufacturer's instructions. This tool increases the load demand (current draw) on the battery.
18   Maintain the load on the battery for 15 seconds and observe that the battery voltage does not drop below 9.6 volts. If the battery condition is weak or defective, the tool will indicate this condition immediately.
Note: *Cold temperatures will cause the minimum voltage reading to drop slightly. Follow the chart given in the manufacturer's instructions to compensate for cold climates. Minimum load voltage for freezing temperatures (32 degrees F) should be approximately 9.1 volts.*

Starting system

The starter rotates, but the engine doesn't

19   Remove the starter (see Section 12). Check the overrunning clutch and bench test the starter to make sure the drive mechanism extends fully for proper engagement with the flywheel ring gear. If it doesn't, replace the starter.

20   Check the flywheel ring gear for missing teeth and other damage. With the ignition turned off, rotate the flywheel so you can check the entire ring gear.

The starter is noisy

21   If the solenoid is making a chattering noise, first check the battery (see Steps 14 through 18). If the battery is okay, check the cables and connections.

22   If you hear a grinding, crashing metallic sound when you turn the key to Start, check for loose starter mounting bolts. If they're tight, remove the starter and inspect the teeth on the starter pinion gear and flywheel ring gear. Look for missing or damaged teeth.

23   If the starter sounds fine when you first turn the key to Start, but then stops rotating the engine and emits a zinging sound, the problem is probably a defective starter drive that's not staying engaged with the ring gear. Replace the starter.

The starter rotates slowly

24   Check the battery (see Steps 14 through 18).

25   If the battery is okay, verify all connections (at the battery, the starter solenoid and motor) are clean, corrosion-free and tight. Make sure the cables aren't frayed or damaged.

26   Check that the starter mounting bolts are tight so it grounds properly. Also check the pinion gear and flywheel ring gear for evidence of a mechanical bind (galling, deformed gear teeth or other damage).

The starter does not rotate at all

27   Check the battery (see Steps 14 through 18).

28   If the battery is okay, verify all connections (at the battery, the starter solenoid and motor) are clean, corrosion-free and tight. Make sure the cables aren't frayed or damaged.

29   Check all of the fuses in the underhood fuse/relay box.

30   Check that the starter mounting bolts are tight so it grounds properly.

31   Check for voltage at the starter solenoid "S" terminal when the ignition key is turned to the start position. If voltage is present, replace the starter/solenoid assembly. If no voltage is present, the problem could be the starter relay, the Transmission Range (TR) switch (see Chapter 6), or with an electrical connector somewhere in the circuit (see the wiring diagrams at the end of this manual). Also, on many modern vehicles, the Powertrain Control Module (PCM) and the Body Control Module (BCM) control the voltage signal to the starter solenoid; on such vehicles a special scan tool is required for diagnosis.

3   Battery - disconnection

Warning: *Always disconnect the cable from the negative battery terminal FIRST and hook*

it up LAST or the battery may be shorted by the tool being used to loosen the cable clamps. **Warning:** *Hydrogen gas is produced by the battery, so keep open flames and lighted cigarettes away from it at all times. Always wear eye protection when working around the battery. Rinse off spilled electrolyte immediately with large amounts of water.*

1   Some systems on the vehicle require battery power to be available at all times, either to maintain continuous operation (alarm system, power door locks, etc.), or to maintain control unit memory (radio station presets, Powertrain Control Module and other control units). When the battery is disconnected, the power that maintains these systems is cut. So, before you disconnect the battery, please note that on a vehicle with power door locks, it's a wise precaution to remove the key from the ignition and to keep it with you, so that it does not get locked inside if the power door locks should engage accidentally when the battery is reconnected!

2   Devices known as "memory-savers" can be used to avoid some of these problems. Precise details vary according to the device used. The typical memory saver is plugged into the cigarette lighter and is connected to a spare battery. Then the vehicle battery can be disconnected from the electrical system. The memory saver will provide sufficient current to maintain audio unit security codes, PCM memory, etc., and will provide power to always hot circuits such as the clock and radio memory circuits.

Warning: *Some memory savers deliver a considerable amount of current in order to keep vehicle systems operational after the main battery is disconnected. If you're using a memory saver, make sure that the circuit concerned is actually open before servicing it.*

Warning: *If you're going to work near any of the airbag system components, the battery MUST be disconnected and a memory saver must NOT be used. If a memory saver is used, power will be supplied to the airbag, which means that it could accidentally deploy and cause serious personal injury.*

Caution: *If the vehicle is equipped with an Intelligent Battery Sensor (IBS), disconnect*

the IBS electrical connector BEFORE disconnecting the negative battery terminal from the battery.

3   The Intelligent Battery Sensor (IBS), used on models with the start/stop feature, measures the current, voltage, and temperature for the power management system. It will calculate the state of charge, health, and function qualities of the battery. The IBS creates an electrical connection between the body and the negative battery terminal where it can take the various measurements for the power management system (BCM and the PCM). The IBS is part of the precise charging control for the AGM battery vehicles. *Whenever the IBS is disconnected from the battery it will lose its stored 'learned' values and will go into a relearn mode when it is reconnected. While the IBS is in the 'relearn' status the START/STOP operation will not function. The start/stop operation may take several hours to several days to reactivate depending on the IBS relearn time. (Anytime the start/stop is not operational a message will be displayed stating the start/stop status.)*

4   To disconnect the battery for service procedures requiring power to be cut from the vehicle, loosen the cable clamp nut and disconnect the cable from the negative battery terminal (see Section 4). Isolate the cable end to prevent it from coming into accidental contact with the battery terminal.

4   Battery and battery tray - removal and installation

Battery

1   Install a memory saver device to avoid having to reprogram several of the vehicle's systems (see Section 3).

Caution: *If the vehicle is equipped with an Intelligent Battery Sensor (IBS), disconnect the IBS electrical connector BEFORE disconnecting the cable from the negative terminal of the battery.*

2   Disconnect the negative battery cable, then the positive battery cable, from the battery **(see illustration)**.

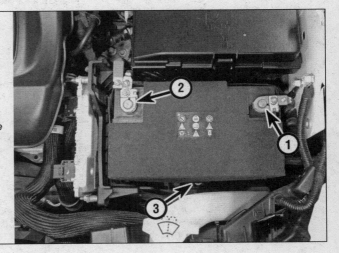

4.2 Battery details

1 Negative battery cable
2 Positive battery cable
3 Hold-down clamp

4.9 Remove the upper fasteners

4.12 Remove the washer reservoir bolt (A) and the frame rail bolt (B)

Warning: *Always disconnect the negative cable first and hook it up last or the battery may be shorted by the tool being used to loosen the cable clamps.*

3   Pull the battery insulator up and off of the battery.

4   Unscrew the bolt and remove the hold-down clamp from the bottom edge of the battery.

5   Lift out the battery. Special battery removal and installation tools are available at auto parts stores; lifting and moving the battery is much easier if you use one.

6   Installation is the reverse of removal. If equipped, and if you're replacing the battery, transfer the battery insulator to the new battery. Connect the positive cable first, then the negative cable.

Battery tray

7   Remove the battery (see Steps 1 through 5).

8   Detach the PCM from the PCM mount. See Chapter 6, Section 17. If replacing the tray, remove the PCM mount to allow removal of the battery tray.

9   Remove the two upper battery tray fasteners (**see illustration**).

10   Raise and support the vehicle and remove the under-vehicle splash shield.

11   Remove the front fasteners for the inner fender liner and pull back to expose the two lower battery tray fasteners.

12   Remove the fastener attaching the washer reservoir to the tray, then remove the battery tray-to-frame fastener (**see illustration**).

13   Detach the hood cable from the battery tray.

14   Remove the two bolts attaching the battery tray to the frame rail (**see illustration**).

15   Installation is the reverse of removal.

5   Battery cables - replacement

1   When removing the cables, always disconnect the cable from the battery negative terminal first and hook it up last, or you might accidentally short out the battery with the tool you're using to loosen the cable clamps. Even if you're only replacing the cable for the positive terminal, aways disconnect the negative cable from the battery first.

2   On models equipped with an Intelligent Battery Sensor (IBS), the negative battery cable is disconnected from the IBS. The IBS is separate from the cable.

Caution: *Always disconnect the electrical connector from the IBS before disconnecting the cable from the negative terminal of the battery.*

3   Disconnect the old cables from the battery, then trace each of them to their opposite ends and disconnect them. Be sure to note the routing of each cable before disconnecting it to ensure correct installation.

4   If you are replacing any of the old cables, take them with you when buying new cables. It is vitally important that you replace the cables with identical parts.

5   Clean the threads of the solenoid or ground connection with a wire brush to remove rust and corrosion. Apply a light coat of battery terminal corrosion inhibitor or petroleum jelly to the threads to prevent future corrosion.

6   Attach the cable to the solenoid or ground connection and tighten the mounting nut/bolt securely.

7   Before connecting a new cable to the battery, make sure that it reaches the battery post without having to be stretched.

8   Connect the cable to the positive battery terminal first, *then* connect the ground cable to the negative battery terminal.

6   Intelligent Battery Sensor (IBS) - removal and installation

Note: *The IBS is part of the negative battery terminal and replaced as one unit.*

Caution: *Always disconnect the IBS electrical connector BEFORE disconnecting the negative battery terminal from the battery.*

Removal

1   Disconnect the IBS electrical connector.

2   Remove the nut attaching the negative battery cable to the battery terminal and disconnect the cable.

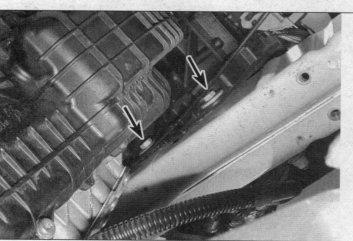

4.14 Remove the two bolts at the frame rail

3   Loosen the negative battery terminal and remove the IBS from the battery.

Installation

4   During installation, connect the negative battery cable to the negative battery terminal BEFORE connecting the terminal to the negative battery post.
5   Attach the negative terminal to the battery.
6   Connect the IBS electrical connector.

7   Voltage Stability Module (VSM) - replacement

Note: *Only models with the start/stop feature are equipped with a VSM. This model is equipped with two VSM, one located near the body control module and a second one is located behind the glove box.*
Caution: *If the vehicle is equipped with an Intelligent Battery Sensor (IBS), disconnect the IBS electrical connector BEFORE disconnecting the negative battery terminal from the battery.*
1   Disconnect the cable from the negative terminal of the battery (see Section 3).
2   For the left (driver's) side VSM, remove the driver's side knee bolster (see Chapter 11, Section 21).
3   Disconnect the upper BCM connector.
4   For the right (passenger's) side VSM, remove the glove box (see Chapter 11, Section 21).
5   For either side, disconnect the VSM connector.
6   Remove the bolts securing the VSM and bracket to the support.
7   Remove the VSM from the vehicle.
8   If the VSM is to be replaced remove the VSM from the bracket.
9   Installation is reverse of removal.
Caution: *When the VSM is being replaced, a scan tool is required to determine if alignment of PROXI configuration data into the new VSM*

9.5a Ignition coil electrical connectors (A) and coil retaining bolts (B)

is needed. A qualified technician or repair facility should preform this procedure.

8   In-rush current reduction relay - replacement

Note: *Only models with the start/stop feature are equipped with an In-rush Current Reduction (ICR) relay. The relay is attached to a bracket on top of the starter.*
Caution: *If the vehicle is equipped with an Intelligent Battery Sensor (IBS), disconnect the IBS electrical connector BEFORE disconnecting the negative battery terminal from the battery.*
1   Disconnect the cable from the negative terminal of the battery (see Section 3).
2   Locate the ICR relay near the starter and disconnect the electrical connector.
3   Remove the nuts and disconnect the cables from the ICR.
4   Remove the bolts attaching the ICR to the bracket and remove the relay.
5   Installation is reverse of removal.

9   Ignition coils - removal and installation

1   If available, spray compressed air around the tops of the coils to ensure debris will not fall into the spark plug tube upon removal.
Warning: *Wear eye protection when using compressed air.*
2   Remove the engine cover by pulling it straight up.
3   Disconnect the cable from the negative terminal of the battery (see Section 3).
4   On 3.2L engines, to access the front coils (cylinders 2, 4 and 6), remove the intake duct from the radiator core support. To access the rear coils (cylinders 1, 3 and 5), remove the upper intake manifold (see Chapter 2B, Section 5).
5   On all engines, disconnect the electrical connector from the ignition coil **(see illustrations)**.
6   Remove the bolt attaching the ignition coil to the valve cover.

9.5b To disconnect an electrical connector from a coil, slide the red lock outward, then depress the lock and pull the connector off

9.7 Pull the coil(s) off the spark plug using a twisting motion

**10.2 Ignition capacitor location -
2.4L engine**

**11.14 Remove the front bolts (A) and
loosen the rear AC compressor bolt (B)**

**11.15 Position the front of the compressor
downwards to gain access to the
alternator for service**

7   Grasp the ignition coil firmly and pull it off the spark plug using a twisting motion **(see illustration)**.
8   Installation is the reverse of removal.

10 Ignition capacitor - replacement

Note: *On 2.0L engines, the capacitor is located at the left (driver's side) rear corner of the cylinder head. On 2.4L engines, the capacitor is bolted to the right front end of the cylinder head. On 3.2L engines, a capacitor is bolted to the rear of each cylinder head.*
Caution: *If the vehicle is equipped with an Intelligent Battery Sensor (IBS), disconnect the IBS electrical connector BEFORE disconnecting the negative battery terminal from the battery.*
1   Disconnect the cable from the negative terminal of the battery (see Section 3). Remove the engine cover.
2   Locate the capacitor on the cylinder head **(see illustration)**.
3   On 2.4L engines, remove the nut and heat shield from the capacitor.
4   On all engines, disconnect the capacitor electrical connector.

5   Remove the bolt/stud and remove the capacitor from the engine.
6   Installation is reverse of removal.

11 Alternator - removal and installation

Caution: *If the vehicle is equipped with an Intelligent Battery Sensor (IBS), disconnect the IBS electrical connector BEFORE disconnecting the negative battery terminal from the battery.*
1   Disconnect the negative battery cable (see Section 3).
Note: *If you're working on a 3.2L engine, relieve the fuel system pressure before disconnecting the battery.*

2.0L engines
Note: *On 2.0L Turbocharged engines, the alternator is on the back side of the engine.*
2   Raise and support the front of the vehicle on jackstands.
3   Remove the under-vehicle splash shield.
4   Remove the drivebelt (see Chapter 1, Section 21).
5   On AWD models, remove the transfer case (see Chapter 7B).

6   On all models, unplug the field connector from the alternator, then remove the nut that secures the B+ wire terminal to the stud on the back of the alternator.
7   Remove the alternator bolts and remove the alternator from the vehicle.
8   Installation is reverse of removal. Tighten all fasteners to the torque listed in this Chapter's Specifications.

2.4L engines
Note: *On 2.4L engines, the alternator is on the front side of the engine.*
9   Remove the engine cover.
10   Loosen the right front wheel lug nuts, then raise the front of the vehicle and support it securely on jackstands. Remove the wheel.
11   Remove the fasteners at the front of the inner fender splash shield and pull back the shield to access the resonator.
12   Remove the nut and remove the resonator from the vehicle.
13   Remove the drivebelt (see Chapter 1, Section 21).
14   Remove the two front air conditioning compressor mounting bolts and loosen the rear bolt **(see illustration)**.
15   Pivot the compressor downwards at the front to allow access to the alternator bolts **(see illustration)**.
16   Unplug the field connector from the alternator, then remove the nut that secures the B+ wire terminal to the stud on the back of the alternator **(see illustration)**.
17   Remove the alternator bolts and remove the alternator from the vehicle **(see illustration)**.
18   Installation is reverse of removal. Tighten all fasteners to the specifications in this Chapter's Specifications.

3.2L engines
Warning: *Gasoline is extremely flammable. See the Warnings in Chapter 4, Section 1.*
19   Perform the fuel pressure release procedure prior to disconnecting the negative battery cable. See Chapter 4, Section 3.
20   Remove the air filter housing assembly (see Chapter 4, Section 12).

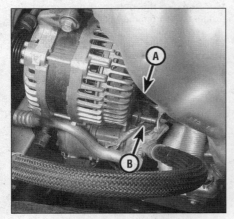

**11.16 Unplug connector (A), then remove
the nut and the B+ terminal (B)
from the alternator**

**11.17 Remove the alternator bolts
and alternator**

12.8 Starter upper mounting bolt - 2.4L engine

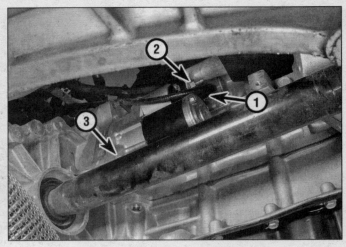

12.10 Starter lower mounting details

1   Solenoid electrical connector   3   Lower mounting bolt
2   B+ cable nut

21   Loosen the right-front wheel lug nuts, then raise the front of the vehicle and support it securely on jackstands. Remove the wheel.
22   Remove the drivebelt (see Chapter 1, Section 21).
23   Remove the fasteners at the front of the inner fender splash shield and pull back the shield to access the duct and resonator.
24   Remove the fasteners and the intake air duct and resonator from before the air filter housing assembly.
25   Remove the under-vehicle splash shield.
26   Remove the right (passenger's side) tow hook (if equipped).
27   Remove the air conditioning compressor bolts and position the compressor to the side to allow access to the alternator bolts.
Warning: *Do not disconnect the refrigerant lines.*
28   Unplug the field connector from the alternator, then remove the nut that secures the B+ wire terminal to the stud on the back of the alternator.
29   Support the engine by the oil pan using a floor jack and block of wood.
30   Remove the three bolts attaching the front engine mount to the bracket on the engine.
31   Disconnect the fuel feed line quick-connect fitting at the fuel rail.
32   Lower the engine as needed to access and remove the alternator.
33   Remove the shield (drip tray) attached to the alternator (if equipped).
34   Remove the alternator bolts.
35   Carefully remove the alternator through the upper and lower frame rail opening.
36   Installation is reverse of removal. Tighten all fasteners to torque listed in this Chapter's Specifications.
37   Cycle the ignition to turn the fuel pump

on and check for fuel leaks. Repair leaks as necessary prior to starting the vehicle.

12   Starter motor - removal and installation

Caution: *If the vehicle is equipped with an Intelligent Battery Sensor (IBS), disconnect the IBS electrical connector BEFORE disconnecting the negative battery terminal from the battery.*
1   Disconnect the cable from the negative terminal of the battery (see Section 3).

2.0L engines
2   Raise the front of the vehicle and support it securely on jackstands. Remove the under-vehicle splash shield.
3   On AWD models, remove the transfer case to access the starter (see Chapter 7B, Section 7)
4   Disconnect the starter electrical connector and remove the nut and battery terminal connector.
5   Remove the starter bolts and remove the starter from the vehicle.
6   Installation is reverse of removal. Tighten the mounting bolts to the torque listed in this Chapter's Specifications.

2.4L engines
Note: *Removing the intake manifold makes access to the starter upper mounting bolt easier on FWD models, and is necessary on AWD models. See Chapter 2A for the intake manifold removal procedure.*
7   Remove the engine cover by pulling the corners straight up.
8   Loosen the starter upper mounting bolt

(see illustration). This starter bolt cannot be removed all the way.
Note: *The upper mounting bolt has a 15 mm head.*
9   On AWD models, remove the intake manifold assembly (see Chapter 2A, Section 5).
10   On all models, disconnect the starter electrical connector and remove the nut and battery terminal connector **(see illustration).**
11   Remove the starter lower mounting bolt and remove the starter from the vehicle.
Note: *The lower mounting bolt has a 14 mm head.*
12   Installation is reverse of removal. Tighten the mounting bolts to the torque listed in this Chapter's Specifications.

3.2L engines
13   Raise the front of the vehicle and support it securely on jackstands.
14   Remove the under-vehicle splash shield.
15   Locate and disconnect the upstream and downstream O2 sensor connectors for the front catalytic converter.
16   Remove the nuts and disconnect the exhaust pipe from the bottom of the front catalytic converter.
17   Remove the bolt securing the converter support bracket to the bracket on the engine.
18   Remove the bolts attaching the converter assembly to the cylinder head and remove the converter from the vehicle.
19   Disconnect the starter electrical connector and remove the nut and battery terminal connector.
20   Remove the starter bolts and remove the starter from the vehicle.
21   Installation is reverse of removal. Tighten the starter mounting bolts to the torque listed in this Chapter's Specifications.

Chapter 6
Emissions and engine control systems

Contents

Specifications

Torque specifications

Ft-lbs (unless otherwise indicated)

Note: *One foot-pound (ft-lb) of torque is equivalent to 12 inch-pounds (in-lbs) of torque. Torque values below approximately 15 ft-lbs are expressed in inch-pounds, since most foot-pound torque wrenches are not accurate at these smaller values.*

Accelerator Pedal Position (APP) sensor	53 in-lbs
Camshaft/Crankshaft Position (CMP/CKP) sensor mounting bolt	80 in-lbs
Engine Coolant Temperature sensor	
2.4L engines	15
2.0L and 3.2L engines	22
EGR Cooler Bolts	18
EGR Valve Torx Screws	96 in-lbs
EGR Temperature Sensor	27
Oil temperature/pressure sensor	
2.0L engines	31
2.4L engines	35
3.2L engines	
Oil pressure	17
Oil temperature	22
Oxygen sensors	37
Knock sensor bolt*	
2.0L turbocharged engines	21
2.4L, 3.2L engines	15
VVT Solenoid Bolts (2.0L and 3.2L engines)	35 in-lbs
VVAA assembly bolts (2.4L engines)	
Step 1	89 in-lbs
Step 2	16
Step 3	16

* DO NOT apply sealant or thread lock to knock sensor bolt threads.

1   General Information

1   To prevent pollution of the atmosphere from incompletely burned and evaporating gases, and to maintain good driveability and fuel economy, a number of emission control systems are incorporated. They include the:

Catalytic converter

2   A catalytic converter is an emission control device in the exhaust system that reduces certain pollutants in the exhaust gas stream. There are two types of converters: oxidation converters and reduction converters.

3   Oxidation converters contain a monolithic substrate (a ceramic honeycomb) coated with the semi-precious metals platinum and palladium. An oxidation catalyst reduces unburned hydrocarbons (HC) and carbon monoxide (CO) by adding oxygen to the exhaust stream as it passes through the substrate, which, in the presence of high temperature and the catalyst materials, converts the HC and CO to water vapor (H_2O) and carbon dioxide (CO_2).

4   Reduction converters contain a monolithic substrate coated with platinum and rhodium. A reduction catalyst reduces oxides of nitrogen (NOx) by removing oxygen, which in the presence of high temperature and the catalyst material produces nitrogen (N) and carbon dioxide (CO_2).

5   Catalytic converters that combine both types of catalysts in one assembly are known as "three-way catalysts" or TWCs. A TWC can reduce all three pollutants.

Evaporative Emissions Control (EVAP) system

6   The Evaporative Emissions Control (EVAP) system prevents fuel system vapors (which contain unburned hydrocarbons) from escaping into the atmosphere. On warm days, vapors trapped inside the fuel tank expand until the pressure reaches a certain threshold. Then the fuel vapors are routed from the fuel tank through the fuel vapor vent valve and the fuel vapor control valve to the EVAP canister, where they're stored temporarily until the next time the vehicle is operated. When the conditions are right (engine warmed up, vehicle up to speed, moderate or heavy load on the engine, etc.) the PCM opens the canister purge valve, which allows fuel vapors to be drawn from the canister into the intake manifold. Once in the intake manifold, the fuel vapors mix with incoming air before being drawn through the intake ports into the combustion chambers where they're burned up with the rest of the air/fuel mixture. The EVAP system is complex and virtually impossible to troubleshoot without the right tools and training.

Exhaust Gas Recirculation (EGR) system

7   The EGR system reduces oxides of nitrogen by recirculating exhaust gases from the exhaust manifold, through the EGR valve and intake manifold, then back to the combustion chambers, where it mixes with the incoming air/fuel mixture before being consumed. These recirculated exhaust gases dilute the incoming air/fuel mixture, which cools the combustion chambers, thereby reducing NOx emissions.

8   The EGR system consists of the Powertrain Control Module (PCM), the EGR valve, the EGR valve position sensor and various other information sensors that the PCM uses to determine when to open the EGR valve. The degree to which the EGR valve is opened is referred to as "EGR valve lift." The PCM is programmed to produce the ideal EGR valve lift for varying operating conditions. The EGR valve position sensor, which is an integral part of the EGR valve, detects the amount of EGR valve lift and sends this information to the PCM. The PCM then compares it with the appropriate EGR valve lift for the operating conditions. The PCM increases current flow to the EGR valve to increase valve lift and reduces the current to reduce the amount of lift. If EGR flow is inappropriate to the operating conditions (idle, cold engine, etc.) the PCM simply cuts the current to the EGR valve and the valve closes.

Powertrain Control Module (PCM)

9   The Powertrain Control Module (PCM) is the brain of the engine management system. It also controls a wide variety of other vehicle systems. In order to program the new PCM, the dealer needs the vehicle as well as the new PCM. If you're planning to replace the PCM with a new one, there is no point in trying to do so at home because you won't be able to program it yourself.

Positive Crankcase Ventilation (PCV) system

10   The Positive Crankcase Ventilation (PCV) system reduces hydrocarbon emissions by scavenging crankcase vapors, which are rich in unburned hydrocarbons. A PCV valve or orifice regulates the flow of gases into the intake manifold in proportion to the amount of intake vacuum available.

11   The PCV system generally consists of the fresh air inlet hose, the PCV valve or orifice and the crankcase ventilation hose (or PCV hose). The fresh air inlet hose connects the air intake duct to a pipe on the valve cover. The crankcase ventilation hose (or PCV hose) connects the PCV valve or orifice in the valve cover to the intake manifold.

Variable Valve Timing (VVT)

2.0L turbocharged and 3.2L engines

12   The Variable Valve Timing (VVT) system adjusts the timing of the camshafts using solenoids and Oil Control Valve (OCV) to direct oil pressure to the camshaft phasers. The phasers are located on the front of the camshafts, inside of the timing chain cover.

2.4L engines

13   2.4L engines are equipped with a Variable Valve Actuator Assembly (VVAA). The variable valve actuation module is located on the top of the head above the intake valves, next to the camshaft. The camshaft intake lobes operate hydraulic actuators instead of directly opening the intake valves. The actuators sit directly on top of the intake valves. The actuators use high-pressure oil to open the valves. The timing between the camshaft lobe and the intake valves is controlled by the solenoid operated hydraulic port. By controlling solenoid operation, the Powertrain Control Module (PCM) is able to control the intake valve lift and duration.

Vehicle Emission Control Information (VECI) label

14   This label (see illustration) , located on the underside of the hood, indicates what emission control systems the vehicle is equipped with and for what market the vehicle is certified (California, Federal, etc.), as well as any tune-up specifications and adjustments that may be needed.

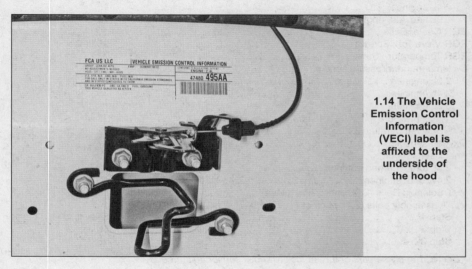

1.14 The Vehicle Emission Control Information (VECI) label is affixed to the underside of the hood

Information Sensors

Accelerator Pedal Position (APP) sensor - as you press the accelerator pedal, the APP sensor alters its voltage signal to the PCM in proportion to the angle of the pedal, and the PCM commands a motor inside the throttle body to open or close the throttle plate accordingly

Camshaft Position (CMP) sensor - produces a signal that the PCM uses to identify the number 1 cylinder and to time the firing sequence of the fuel injectors

Crankshaft Position (CKP) sensor - produces a signal that the PCM uses to calculate engine speed and crankshaft position, which enables it to synchronize ignition timing with fuel injector timing, and to detect misfires

Engine Coolant Temperature (ECT) sensor - a thermistor (temperature-sensitive variable resistor) that sends a voltage signal to the PCM, which uses this data to determine the temperature of the engine coolant

Fuel tank pressure sensor - measures the fuel tank pressure and controls fuel tank pressure by signaling the EVAP system to purge the fuel tank vapors when the pressure becomes excessive

Intake Air Temperature (IAT) sensor - monitors the temperature of the air entering the engine and sends a signal to the PCM to determine injector pulse-width (the duration of each injector's on-time) and to adjust spark timing (to prevent spark knock)

Knock sensor - a piezoelectric crystal that oscillates in proportion to engine vibration which produces a voltage output that is monitored by the PCM. This retards the ignition timing when the oscillation exceeds a certain threshold

Manifold Absolute Pressure (MAP) sensor - monitors the pressure or vacuum inside the intake manifold. The PCM uses this data to determine engine load so that it can alter the ignition advance and fuel enrichment

Mass Air Flow (MAF) sensor - measures the amount of intake air drawn into the engine. It uses a hot-wire sensing element to measure the amount of air entering the engine

Oxygen sensors - generates a small variable voltage signal in proportion to the difference between the oxygen content in the exhaust stream and the oxygen content in the ambient air. The PCM uses this information to maintain the proper air/fuel ratio. A second oxygen sensor monitors the efficiency of the catalytic converter

Throttle Position (TP) sensor - a potentiometer that generates a voltage signal that varies in relation to the opening angle of the throttle plate inside the throttle body. Works with the PCM and other sensors to calculate injector pulse width (the duration of each injector's on-time)

Photos courtesy of Wells Manufacturing, except APP and MAF sensors.

2   On Board Diagnosis (OBD) system

General description

1   All models are equipped with the second generation OBD-II system. This system consists of an on-board computer known as the Powertrain Control Module (PCM), and information sensors, which monitor various functions of the engine and send data to the PCM. This system incorporates a series of diagnostic monitors that detect and identify fuel injection and emissions control system faults and store the information in the computer memory. This system also tests sensors and output actuators, diagnoses drive cycles, freezes data and clears codes.

2   The PCM is the brain of the electronically controlled fuel and emissions system. It receives data from a number of sensors and other electronic components (switches, relays, etc.). Based on the information it receives, the PCM generates output signals to control various relays, solenoids (fuel injectors) and other actuators. The PCM is specifically calibrated to optimize the emissions, fuel economy and driveability of the vehicle.

2.4a   Simple code readers are an economical way to extract trouble codes when the CHECK ENGINE light comes on

3   It isn't a good idea to attempt diagnosis or replacement of the PCM or emission control components at home while the vehicle is under warranty. Because of a federally-mandated warranty which covers the emissions system components and because any owner-induced damage to the PCM, the sensors and/or the control devices may void this warranty, take the vehicle to a dealer service department if the PCM or a system component malfunctions.

Scan tool information

4   Because extracting the Diagnostic Trouble Codes (DTCs) from an engine management system is now the first step in troubleshooting many computer-controlled systems and components, a code reader, at the very least, will be required **(see illustration)**. More powerful scan tools can also perform many of the diagnostics once associated with expensive factory scan tools **(see illustration)**. If you're planning to obtain a generic scan tool for your vehicle, make sure that it's compatible with OBD-II systems. If you don't plan to purchase a code reader or scan tool and don't have access to one, you can have the codes extracted by a dealer service department or an independent repair shop.

Note: *Some auto parts stores even provide this service.*

3   Obtaining and clearing Diagnostic Trouble Codes (DTCs)

1   All models covered by this manual are equipped with on-board diagnostics. When the PCM recognizes a malfunction in a monitored emission or engine control system, component or circuit, it turns on the Malfunction Indicator Light (MIL) on the dash. The PCM will continue to display the MIL until the problem is fixed and the Diagnostic Trouble Code (DTC) is cleared from the PCM's memory. You'll need a scan tool to access any DTCs stored in the PCM.

2   Before outputting any DTCs stored in the PCM, thoroughly inspect ALL electrical connectors and hoses. Make sure that all electrical connections are tight, clean and free of corrosion. And make sure that all hoses are correctly connected, fit tightly and are in good condition (no cracks or tears).

Accessing the DTCs

3   The Diagnostic Trouble Codes (DTCs) can only be accessed with a code reader or scan tool. Professional scan tools are expensive, but relatively inexpensive generic code readers or scan tools **(see illustrations 2.4a and 2.4b)** are available at most auto parts stores. Simply plug the connector of the scan tool into the diagnostic connector **(see illustration)**. Then follow the instructions included with the scan tool to extract the DTCs.

4   Once you have outputted all of the stored DTCs, look them up on the accompanying DTC chart.

5   After troubleshooting the source of each DTC, make any necessary repairs or replace the defective component(s).

Clearing the DTCs

6   Clear the DTCs with the code reader or scan tool in accordance with the instructions provided by the tool's manufacturer.

Diagnostic Trouble Codes

7   The accompanying tables are a list of the Diagnostic Trouble Codes (DTCs) that can be accessed by a do-it-yourselfer working at home (there are many, many more DTCs available to professional mechanics with proprietary scan tools and software, but those codes cannot be accessed by a generic scan tool). If, after you have checked and repaired the connectors, wire harness and vacuum hoses (if applicable) for an emission-related system, component or circuit, the problem persists, have the vehicle checked by a dealer service department or other qualified repair shop.

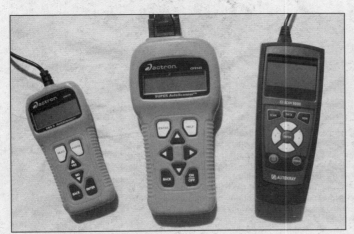

2.4b   Hand-held scan tools like these can extract computer codes and also perform diagnostics

3.3 The 16-pin Data Link Connector (DLC) is located under the left side of the dash, next to the hood release lever

OBD-II Diagnostic Trouble Codes (DTCs) (includes transmission codes)

Note: *Not all trouble codes apply to all models.*

Code	Probable cause
P000A	Camshaft 1 position, (bank no.1), slow response
P000B	Camshaft 2 position, (bank no.1), slow response
P0010	Camshaft 1 position, (bank no.1), actuator circuit open
P0013	Camshaft 2 position, (bank no.1), actuator circuit open
P0016	Crankshaft/camshaft timing (bank no.1. sensor no.1) misalignment
P0017	Crankshaft/camshaft timing (bank no.1. sensor no.2) misalignment
P0031	Upstream oxygen sensor (cylinder bank no. 1), heater circuit low voltage
P0032	Upstream oxygen sensor heater (cylinder bank no. 1), heater circuit high voltage
P0037	Downstream oxygen sensor (cylinder bank no. 1), heater circuit low voltage
P0038	Downstream oxygen sensor (cylinder bank no. 1), heater circuit high voltage
P0068	Manifold pressure/throttle position correlation - high-flow/vacuum leak
P0070	Ambient temperature sensor stuck
P0071	Ambient temperature sensor performance
P0072	Ambient temperature sensor, low voltage
P0073	Ambient temperature sensor, high voltage
P0107	Manifold Absolute Pressure (MAP) sensor, low voltage
P0108	Manifold Absolute Pressure (MAP) sensor, high voltage
P0110	Intake Air Temperature (IAT) sensor, stuck
P0111	Intake Air Temperature (IAT) sensor performance
P0112	Intake Air Temperature (IAT) sensor, low voltage
P0113	Intake Air Temperature (IAT) sensor, high voltage
P0116	Engine Coolant Temperature (ECT) sensor performance
P0117	Engine Coolant Temperature (ECT) sensor, low voltage
P0118	Engine Coolant Temperature (ECT) sensor, high voltage
P0121	Throttle Position (TP) sensor performance
P0122	Throttle Position (TP) sensor, low voltage
P0123	Throttle Position (TP) sensor, high voltage
P0125	Insufficient coolant temperature for closed-loop control; closed-loop temperature not reached
P0128	Thermostat rationality

OBD-II Diagnostic Trouble Codes (DTCs) (includes transmission codes)

Note: *Not all trouble codes apply to all models.*

Code	Probable cause
P0129	Barometric pressure out-of-range (low)
P0131	Upstream oxygen sensor (cylinder bank no. 1), low voltage or shorted to ground
P0132	Upstream oxygen sensor (cylinder bank no. 1), high voltage or shorted to voltage
P0133	Upstream oxygen sensor (cylinder bank no. 1), slow response
P0134	Upstream oxygen sensor (cylinder bank no. 1), sensor remains at center (not switching)
P0135	Upstream oxygen sensor (cylinder bank no. 1), heater failure
P0137	Downstream oxygen sensor (cylinder bank no. 1), low voltage or shorted to ground
P0138	Downstream oxygen sensor (cylinder bank no. 1), high voltage or shorted to voltage
P0139	Downstream oxygen sensor (cylinder bank no. 1), slow response
P0140	Downstream oxygen sensor (cylinder bank no. 1), sensor remains at center (not switching)
P0141	Downstream oxygen sensor (cylinder bank no. 1), heater failure
P0171	Fuel control system too lean (cylinder bank no. 1)
P0172	Fuel control system too rich (cylinder bank no. 1)
P0201	Injector circuit malfunction - cylinder no. 1
P0202	Injector circuit malfunction - cylinder no. 2
P0203	Injector circuit malfunction - cylinder no. 3
P0204	Injector circuit malfunction - cylinder no. 4
P0300	Multiple cylinder misfire detected
P0301	Cylinder no. 1 misfire detected
P0302	Cylinder no. 2 misfire detected
P0303	Cylinder no. 3 misfire detected
P0304	Cylinder no. 4 misfire detected
P0315	No crank sensor learned
P0320	No crankshaft reference signal at Powertrain Control Module (PCM)
P0325	Knock sensor circuit malfunction
P0335	Crankshaft Position (CKP) sensor circuit
P0339	Crankshaft Position (CKP) sensor intermittent
P0340	Camshaft Position (CMP) sensor circuit
P0344	Camshaft Position (CMP) sensor intermittent

Code	Probable cause
P0351	Ignition coil no. 1, primary circuit
P0352	Ignition coil no. 2, primary circuit
P0353	Ignition coil no. 3, primary circuit
P0354	Ignition coil no. 4, primary circuit
P0365	Camshaft Position (CMP) sensor circuit (bank no.1. sensor no.2)
P0369	Camshaft Position (CMP) sensor intermittent (bank no.1. sensor no.2)
P0440	General Evaporative Emission Control (EVAP) system failure
P0441	Evaporative Emission Control (EVAP) system, incorrect purge flow
P0442	Evaporative Emission Control (EVAP) system, medium leak (0.040-inch) detected
P0443	Evaporative Emission Control (EVAP) system, purge solenoid circuit malfunction
P0452	Natural Vacuum Leak Detector (NVLD) pressure sensor circuit, low voltage
P0453	Natural Vacuum Leak Detector (NVLD) pressure sensor circuit, high input
P0455	Evaporative Emission Control (EVAP) system, large leak detected
P0456	Evaporative Emission Control (EVAP) system, small leak (0.020-inch) detected
P0460	Fuel level sending unit, no change as vehicle is operated
P0461	Fuel level sensor circuit, range or performance problem
P0462	Fuel level sending unit or sensor circuit, low voltage
P0463	Fuel level sending unit or sensor circuit, high voltage
P0480	Low-speed fan control relay circuit malfunction
P0498	Natural Vacuum Leak Detector (NVLD) canister vent valve solenoid circuit, low voltage
P0499	Natural Vacuum Leak Detector (NVLD) canister vent valve solenoid circuit, high voltage
P0500	No vehicle speed signal (four-speed automatic transaxles)
P0501	Vehicle speed sensor, range or performance problem
P0503	Vehicle speed sensor 1, erratic
P0506	Idle speed control system, rpm lower than expected
P0507	Idle speed control system, rpm higher than expected
P0508	Idle Air Control (IAC) valve circuit, low voltage
P0509	Idle Air Control (IAC) valve circuit, high voltage
P0513	Invalid SKIM key (engine immobilizer problem)
P0516	Battery temperature sensor, low voltage
P0517	Battery temperature sensor, high voltage

OBD-II Diagnostic Trouble Codes (DTCs) (includes transmission codes)

Note: *Not all trouble codes apply to all models.*

Code	Probable cause
P0519	Idle speed performance
P0522	Engine oil pressure sensor/switch circuit, low voltage
P0532	Air conditioning refrigerant pressure sensor, low voltage
P0533	Air conditioning refrigerant pressure sensor, high voltage
P0551	Power Steering Pressure (PSP) switch circuit, range or performance problem
P0562	Battery voltage low
P0563	Battery voltage high
P0579	Speed control switch circuit, range or performance problem
P0580	Speed control switch circuit, low voltage
P0581	Speed control switch circuit, high voltage
P0582	Speed control vacuum solenoid circuit
P0858	Speed control switch 1/2 correlation
P0586	Speed control vent solenoid circuit
P0591	Speed control switch 2 circuit, performance problem
P0592	Speed control switch 2 circuit, low voltage
P0593	Speed control switch circuit 2, high voltage
P0594	Speed control servo power circuit
P0600	Serial communication link malfunction
P0601	Powertrain Control Module (PCM), internal controller failure
P0622	Alternator field control circuit malfunction or field not switching correctly
P0627	Fuel pump relay circuit
P0630	Vehicle Identification Number (VIN) not programmed in Powertrain Control Module (PCM)
P0632	Odometer not programmed in Powertrain Control Module (PCM)
P0633	SKIM key not programmed in Powertrain Control Module (PCM)
P0642	Sensor reference voltage 2 circuit, low voltage
P0643	Sensor reference voltage 2 circuit, high voltage
P0645	Air conditioning clutch relay circuit
P0685	Automatic Shutdown (ASD) relay control circuit
P0688	Automatic Shutdown (ASD) relay sense circuit, low voltage

Code	Probable cause
P0700	Electronic Automatic Transaxle (EATX) control system malfunction or DTC present
P0703	Brake switch circuit malfunction
P0833	Clutch released switch circuit
P0850	Park/Neutral switch malfunction
P0856	Traction control torque request circuit

4   Accelerator Pedal Position (APP) sensor - replacement

1   Disconnect the cable from the negative terminal of the battery (see Chapter 5).
2   Disconnect the electrical connector from the upper end of the APP sensor **(see illustration)**.
3   Remove the accelerator pedal/APP sensor assembly mounting nuts and remove the assembly.
4   Installation is the reverse of removal. Tighten the mounting fasteners to the torque listed in this Chapter's Specifications.

5   Boost pressure sensor - replacement

Note: *2019 and later 2.0L gasoline engines are equipped with a turbocharger. The sensor is located in the turbocharger piping on top of the engine above the throttle body.*
1   Disconnect the negative battery cable cable from the negative terminal of the battery (see Chapter 5).
2   Remove the engine cover.
3   Locate and disconnect the boost pressure sensor electrical connector.
4   Remove the bolt and pull the sensor out of the turbocharger piping.
5   Inspect the O-ring and replace if damaged.
6   Installation is reverse of removal.

6   Camshaft Position (CMP) sensor - replacement

Warning: *Wait until the engine is completely cool before beginning this procedure.*
Caution: *After the sensor has been removed, do not insert any magnetic tools into the hole in the valve cover. Doing so could*

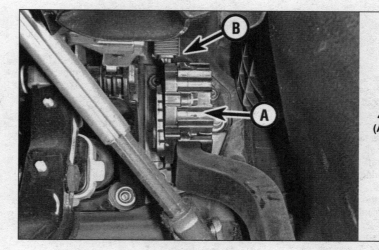

4.2 APP sensor (A) and electrical connector (B)

damage the magnetic timing wheels on the ends of the camshafts.
Note: *On 2.0L turbocharged and 3.2L V6 engines there are two CMP sensors. On 2.0L engines they are located at the left end of the cylinder head, at the front (intake) and rear (exhaust), just below the valve cover. On 3.2L engines, they are located at the front, on top of each valve cover. 2.4L engines are equipped with a single CMP sensor located at the left end of the cylinder head, at the front, just below the valve cover.*
1   Remove the engine cover.
2   Disconnect the cable from the negative terminal of the battery (see Chapter 5).

2.0L turbocharged engines
Sensor 1 - Exhaust
Warning: *Wait until the engine is completely cool before beginning this procedure.*
Note: *Sensor 1 is located on the front of the engine. Access to the CMP sensor requires removal of the engine coolant manifold that runs along the front of the valve cover.*
3   Drain the cooling system (see Chapter 1, Section 25).

4   Disconnect the oxygen sensor connectors.
5   Remove the right-side turbocharger heat shield bolts and the heat shield.
6   Disconnect the electrical connectors and radiator and coolant hoses attached to the coolant manifold.
7   Remove the left side turbocharger heat shield bolts and the heat shield.
8   Remove the lower Torx bolt attaching the coolant manifold to the cylinder head near the thermostat housing.
9   Remove the remaining bolts from the coolant manifold and remove it from the vehicle.
10   Remove the nut attaching the CMP heat shield to the cylinder head.
11   Unlock the connector lock and disconnect the electrical connector from the sensor.
12   Remove the bolt/stud and pull the sensor from the cylinder head.
13   Inspect the O-ring and replace if damaged.
14   Installation is reverse of removal. Apply clean engine oil to the O-ring when installing.
15   Tighten the sensor bolt/stud to the torque listed in this Chapter's Specifications.
16   Refill the cooling system (see Chapter 1).

6.23 Remove the heat shield to access the CMP sensor connector and bolt (2.4L engines)

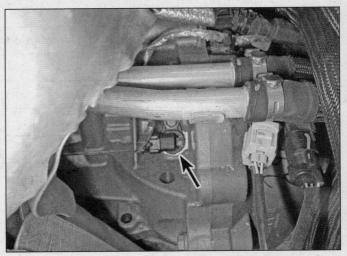

7.6 Location of the CKP sensor (2.4L model shown)

Sensor 2 - Intake

Note: *Sensor 2 is located on the rear of the engine*

17   Remove the air charge pipe to the throttle body. See Chapter 4, Section 12.

18   Locate the CMP sensor above the throttle body and disconnect the electrical connector.

Caution: *Use care not to drop the CMP sensor bolt into the throttle body opening.*

19   Remove the bolt and pull the sensor from the cylinder head.

20   Inspect the O-ring and replace if damaged.

21   Installation is the reverse of removal. Apply clean engine oil to the O-ring when installing.

22   Tighten the sensor bolt/stud to the torque listed in this Chapter's Specifications.

2.4L engines

23   Remove the nut attaching the CMP heat shield to the cylinder head **(see illustration)**.

24   Disconnect the electrical connector from the sensor.

25   Remove the bolt/stud and pull the sensor from the cylinder head.

26   Inspect the O-ring and replace if damaged.

27   Installation is reverse of removal. Apply clean engine oil to the O-ring when installing.

28   Tighten the sensor bolt/stud to the torque listed in this Chapter's Specifications.

3.2L engines

29   If you're removing the bank 1 (rear) CMP sensor, remove the upper intake manifold (see Chapter 2B, Section 5).

30   Disconnect the electrical connector from the sensor.

31   Unscrew the sensor mounting bolt and pull the sensor from the valve cover.

32   If you're going to reinstall the same sensor, check the O-ring for damage. If it's OK, it can be reused.

33   Apply a film of clean engine oil to the O-ring, then insert the sensor into the valve cover and install the mounting bolt, tightening it securely.

34   Installation is the reverse of removal.

7   Crankshaft Position (CKP) sensor - replacement

Note: *The CKP sensor is located at the left end of the cylinder block, near the transmission. On 2.0L and 3.2L engines it's on the rear side of the block. On 2.4L engines it's on the front side of the block.*

1   Disconnect the cable from the negative terminal of the battery (see Chapter 5).

2   Raise the vehicle and support it securely on jackstands.

3   On 2.0L turbocharged engines, remove the starter (see Chapter 5, Section 12).

4   On 3.2L engines with all-wheel drive, remove the transfer case (see Chapter 7B, Section 7).

5   On all models, remove the heat shield (if equipped) from over the sensor.

6   Disconnect the electrical connector from the sensor **(see illustration)**.

7   Remove the sensor mounting bolt and pull the sensor from the engine block.

8   If you're going to reinstall the same sensor, check the O-ring for damage.

9   Apply a film of clean engine oil to the O-ring and insert the sensor into the cylinder block.

10   Install the mounting bolt and tighten it to the torque listed in this Chapter's Specifications.

8   Variable valve timing solenoids - removal and installation

Note: *On 2.0L turbocharged and 3.2L engines, the variable valve timing solenoids*

are located at the front of the engine, in the valve cover. On 2.4L engines, the solenoids are parts of the Variable Valve Actuation Module (VVAA) assembly located under the valve cover.

1   Disconnect the cable from the negative terminal of the battery (see Chapter 5).

2   Remove the engine cover.

2.0L turbocharged engines

3   Remove the air inlet duct to the engine (see Chapter 4, Section 15).

4   Locate the VVT solenoids and disconnect the electrical connectors.

5   Remove the three bolts attaching the solenoids to the valve cover.

Note: *One of the engine mount bolts may have to be removed to the access the lower bolt for the intake VVT solenoid.*

6   Remove the solenoid from the engine. Inspect the rubber gasket and replace if necessary.

2.4L engines

Note: *See Chapter 2A, Section 12 for this procedure.*

3.2L engines

7   If removing the solenoids on the rear bank cylinder head, have the air conditioning system discharged by a licensed HVAC technician, then remove the upper refrigerant lines between the evaporator and condenser to access the VVT solenoids.

8   On either cylinder head, mark the solenoids prior to removal so they can be reinstalled in the correct location.

9   Disconnect the electrical connector for the solenoid.

10   Remove the three bolts attaching the solenoid to the valve cover.

11   Remove the solenoid from the engine. Inspect the rubber gasket and replace if necessary.

Chapter 6 Emissions and engine control systems

9.6 Locating ECT sensor (2.4L engines)

10.10 Location of IAT sensor (2.4L models)

11.10 The knock sensor is located on the side of the cylinder block behind the exhaust manifold (2.4L engine)

9   Engine Coolant Temperature (ECT) sensor - replacement

Warning: *Wait until the engine has cooled completely before beginning this procedure.*
Caution: *Handle the Engine Coolant Temperature (ECT) sensor with care. Damage to the ECT sensor will affect the operation of the entire fuel injection system.*
Note: *On 2.0L Turbocharged and 2.4L engines, the ECT sensor is located at the left end of the engine on the coolant adapter housing. On 3.2L engines, the ECT sensor is located at the rear of the left cylinder head.*

1   Remove the engine cover.
2   Disconnect the cable from the negative terminal of the battery (see Chapter 5).
3   Drain the engine coolant to a point lower than that of the sensor (see Chapter 1).
4   On 2.4L models, remove the battery (see Chapter 5, Section 4).
5   On 2.4L models, remove the PCM and bracket. See Section 17.
6   On all models, locate the ECT and disconnect the electrical connector **(see illustration)**.
7   Unscrew the ECT sensor from the engine.
8   Installation is the reverse of removal.
9   Refill the cooling system (see Chapter 1).

10   Intake Air Temperature (IAT) sensor - replacement

Caution: *The IAT sensor must be installed with the correct orientation to the air duct in order to function properly.*
Note: *The IAT sensor is located on the air inlet ducting. 2.0L turbocharged engines are quipped with two sensors.*

2.0L turbocharged engines
Air Intake Sensor
Note: *This sensor measures the temperature of the ambient air from the air filter housing.*
1   Locate the air intake temperature sensor near the air filter housing.
2   Disconnect the sensor electrical connector.
3   Press the locking tab and rotate the sensor 1/4-turn counterclockwise and pull it from the air filter housing.
4   Inspect the O-ring and replace if damaged.
5   Installation is the reverse of removal. Rotate clockwise until the locking tab engages.

Air Inlet Sensor
Note: *This sensor measures the temperature of the compressed air from the turbocharger that is entering the engine.*
6   Remove the engine cover.
7   Locate the inlet sensor on the intake air duct near the throttle body.
8   Disconnect the electrical connector.
9   Unscrew and remove the inlet air temperature sensor. Installation is the reverse of removal.

2.4L engines
10   Locate the IAT sensor and disconnect the electrical connector (see illustration).
11   Rotate the sensor 1/4-turn counterclockwise and pull it from the ducting.
12   Inspect the O-ring and replace if damaged.
13   Installation is reverse of removal.

3.2L engines
14   Remove the air intake resonator (see Chapter 4, Section 12).
15   Rotate the sensor 1/4-turn counterclockwise and pull it from the ducting.

16   Inspect the O-ring and replace if damaged.
17   Installation is reverse of removal.

11   Knock sensor - replacement

Warning: *Wait for the engine to cool completely before performing this procedure.*
Note: *On 2.0 turbocharged engines, the two knock sensors are located on the front and rear of the engine block, behind the alternator (front) and under the intake manifold (rear). On 2.4L engines, the single knock sensor is located on the side of the engine block, under the exhaust manifold. On 3.2L engines, the two knock sensors are located in the valley below the intake manifold.*
1   Disconnect the cable from the negative terminal of the battery (see Chapter 5).
2   Remove the engine cover.

2.0L turbocharged engines
3   To service the front knock sensor, remove the alternator (see Chapter 5, Section 11).
4   To service the rear knock sensor, remove the intake manifold (see Chapter 2A, Section 5).
5   Disconnect the knock sensor electrical connector.
6   Remove the knock sensor mounting bolt and remove the sensor.
7   Installation is the reverse of removal.
8   Tighten the knock sensor bolt to the torque listed in this Chapter's Specifications.

2.4L engines
9   Remove the exhaust manifold (see Chapter 2A, Section 6).
10   Disconnect the electrical connector from the knock sensor **(see illustration)**.
11   Remove the mounting bolt and detach the sensor from the engine block.

12.4 On 2.4L models, the MAP sensor is located on the passenger's end of the intake manifold

13.5 Locating the upstream (A) and downstream (B) O2 sensors (2.4L engines)

12   Installation is the reverse of removal. Tighten the knock sensor bolt to the torque listed in this Chapter's Specifications.

3.2L engines

Note: *Knock sensor 1 is the one nearest the front of the engine. Knock sensor 2 is the one closer to the transaxle end of the engine.*
13   Remove the lower intake manifold and oil filter housing (see Chapter 2B, Section 5).
14   Disconnect the knock sensor electrical connector.
15   Remove the mounting bolt and detach the sensor from the engine block.
16   Installation is the reverse of removal. Tighten the knock sensor bolt to the torque listed in this Chapter's Specifications.

12   Manifold Absolute Pressure (MAP) sensor - replacement

Note: *2.0L turbocharged engines are equipped with a TMAP which includes a temperature and pressure sensor.*
Note: *On 2.0L turbocharged models, the TMAP sensor is located below the EVAP vent valve on the intake manifold. On 2.4L engines, the MAP sensor is located on the passenger's end of the intake manifold. On 3.2L models, the MAP sensor is located on top of the intake manifold.*
1   Remove the engine cover.
2   On 2.0L turbocharged models, remove the EVAP vent valve (see Section 20).
3   On 2.4L models, raise and support the vehicle on jackstands and remove the under-vehicle splash shield.
4   On all models, locate and disconnect the electrical connector from the MAP sensor **(see illustration)**.
5   On 2.0L turbocharged models, remove the screw(s) and pull the sensor from the manifold. On 2.4L and 3.2L models, rotate the sensor 1/4- turn counterclockwise to remove.

6   Inspect the MAP sensor O-ring for cracks, tears and deterioration; if it's damaged, replace it.
7   Installation is the reverse of removal.

13   Oxygen sensors - general information and replacement

1   Be particularly careful when servicing an oxygen sensor:
a) Oxygen sensors have a permanently attached pigtail and an electrical connector that cannot be removed. Damaging or removing the pigtail or electrical connector will render the sensor useless.
b) Keep grease, dirt and other contaminants away from the electrical connector and the louvered end of the sensor.
c) Do not use cleaning solvents of any kind on an oxygen sensor.
d) Oxygen sensors are extremely delicate. Do not drop a sensor or handle it roughly.
e) Make sure that the silicone boot on the sensor is installed in the correct position. Otherwise, the boot might melt and it might prevent the sensor from operating correctly.
Note: *Because it is installed in the exhaust manifold, catalytic converter or pipe, all of which contract when cool, an oxygen sensor might be very difficult to loosen when the engine is cold. Rather than risk damage to the sensor, start and run the engine for a minute or two, then shut it off. Be careful not to burn yourself during the following procedure.*
Note: *Use an oxygen sensor socket, if available, for removal and installation of oxygen sensors.*
Note: *The downstream sensor is located on the side of each catalytic converter.*
2   Disconnect the cable from the negative terminal of the battery (see Chapter 5).

Upstream oxygen sensor

Note: *The upstream sensor is located in the exhaust manifold.*
Note: *On 4-cylinder engines, the upstream O2 sensor is referred to as Bank 1/Sensor 1. On V6 engines, the upstream O2 sensor on the rear cylinder head is referred to as Bank 1/Sensor 1, on the front cylinder head, Bank 2/Sensor 1.*
3   Remove the engine cover.
4   Disconnect the oxygen sensor wire harness mounting clips from the engine or body, if equipped.
5   Disconnect the oxygen sensor connector from the engine wiring harness **(see illustration)**.
6   Remove the oxygen sensor from the exhaust manifold.
7   Installation is otherwise the reverse of removal.

Downstream oxygen sensor

Note: *The downstream sensor is located on the side of each catalytic converter.*
Note: *On 4-cylinder engines, the downstream O2 sensor is referred to as Bank 1/Sensor 2. On V6 engines, the downstream O2 sensor on the rear cylinder head is referred to as Bank 1/Sensor 2, on the front cylinder head, Bank 2/Sensor 2.*
8   Disconnect the oxygen sensor connector mounting clips from the engine or body, if equipped.
9   Raise the vehicle and support it securely on jackstands.
10   On 3.2L models, remove the under-vehicle splash shield to access the connector for the front (bank 1/sensor 2) O2 sensor.
11   On all models, disconnect the oxygen sensor connector from the engine wiring harness.
12   Remove the oxygen sensor from the catalytic converter.
13   Installation is the reverse of removal.

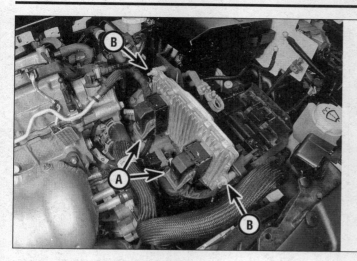

17.2 PCM mounting details

A Connector latches (flip up to release connectors)
B Mounting nuts (two are shown, there are three total)

14 Throttle Position (TP) sensor - replacement

1   The TP sensor is an integral component of the electronic throttle body, and is not separately serviceable. If you need to replace the TP sensor, you must replace the throttle body (see Chapter 4).

15 Transmission Range (TR) and transmission temperature sensors - replacement

1   The TR sensor and transmission temperature sensor (which is an integral part of the TR sensor) are located on the automatic transaxle valve body. In order to replace the TR sensor/transmission temperature sensor, you must remove the valve body.

16 Transaxle speed sensors - replacement

1   Transaxle speed sensors are located in the valve body and/or below the valve body internally in the transaxle. In order to replace the speed sensors, you must remove the valve body.

17 Powertrain Control Module (PCM) - replacement

Caution: To avoid electrostatic discharge damage to the PCM, handle the PCM only by its case. Do not touch the electrical terminals during removal and installation. If available, ground yourself to the vehicle with an anti-static ground strap, available at computer supply stores.
Note: This procedure applies only to disconnecting, removing and installing the PCM that is already installed in your vehicle. If, however, you need to replace the PCM, it must be pro-

grammed with new software and calibrations, and information from the old PCM must be transferred to the new one. This will require the use of a special scan tool, so you will not be able to replace the PCM at home.
Note: The PCM is located next to the battery.
1   Disconnect the cable from the negative terminal of the battery (see Chapter 5).
2   Unlock the electrical connectors and disconnect them from the PCM **(see illustration)**.
3   Remove the mounting nuts and remove the PCM.
4   Installation is the reverse of removal.

18 Catalytic converter - replacement

Warning: Wait until the engine has cooled completely before beginning this procedure.
1   Raise the vehicle and place it securely on jackstands.
Note: Before trying to loosen the nuts and bolts at the flange(s) and the clamp bolt and nut behind the converter (on models so equipped), spray them with penetrating oil and wait the specified amount of time (see the instructions on the can) for the penetrant to loosen things up.

2.0L turbocharged and 3.2L engines

2   Remove the oxygen sensor from the converter (see Section 13).
3   Remove the rear portion of the exhaust system.
4   Remove the exhaust manifold heat shields.
5   On 2.0L models, remove the flange nuts at the exhaust manifold and detach the converter from the exhaust manifold.
6   On 3.2L models, for the rear converter, remove the converter bracket. On FWD models, remove the intermediate shaft and support bracket (see Chapter 8, Section 2).
7   If equipped with AWD, remove the transfer case (see Chapter 7B, Section 7).
8   Remove the flange bolts and detach the converter from the cylinder head.

9   On all models, before installing the converter, coat the threads of the exhaust manifold flange nuts and bolts, and the clamp bolt with anti-seize compound. Tighten the fasteners securely.
10   Installation is otherwise the reverse of removal.

2.4L engines

11   The catalytic converter is part of the exhaust manifold and is replaced as an assembly (see Chapter 2A, Section 6).

19 Exhaust Gas Recirculation (EGR) - component replacement

Note: 2.0L turbocharged engines are equipped with EGR.
Note: Before trying to loosen the nuts and bolts at the flange(s) and the clamp bolt and nut behind the converter (on models so equipped), spray them with penetrating oil and wait the specified amount of time (see the instructions on the can) for the penetrant to loosen things up.

EGR valve

1   Disconnect the cable from the negative terminal of the battery (see Chapter 5).
2   Remove the air outlet pipe (see Chapter 4, Section 15).
3   Disconnect the EGR valve electrical connector.
4   Disconnect the hose from the EGR valve.
5   Remove the four Torx screws attaching the EGR valve to the intake manifold.
6   Installation is the reverse of removal. Use a NEW O-ring when installing.
7   Tighten the EGR screws to the torque listed in this Chapter's Specifications.

EGR temperature sensor

Note: The EGR temperature sensor is located on the cylinder head, near the turbocharger inlet.
8   Disconnect the cable from the negative terminal of the battery (see Chapter 5).
9   Remove the air duct between the air cleaner assembly and the turbocharger.
10   Disconnect the EGR temp sensor electrical connector.
11   Unscrew the sensor from the engine.
12   Installation is reverse of removal.

EGR tube

Note: The EGR tube runs between the turbocharger exhaust outlet and the EGR cooler.
13   Raise and support the vehicle on jackstands.
14   Remove the vehicle under cover.
15   Remove the upstream oxygen sensor (see Section 13).
16   Remove the bolts and the heat shields for the turbocharger and converter.
17   Remove the two nuts for the EGR tube at the exhaust outlet.

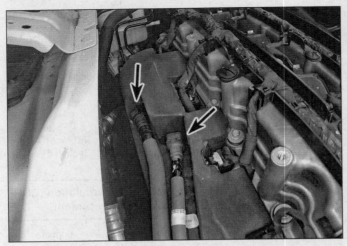

20.3 Disconnect the fuel supply line and EVAP solenoid quick connect fittings

20.4 Cut the insulation along the line to remove

18   Remove the two bolts attaching the EGR tube to the EGR cooler.

19   Remove the tube from the vehicle.

20   Installation is the reverse of removal. Use NEW gaskets when installing the EGR tube.

EGR cooler

Warning: *Wait until the engine is completely cool before beginning this procedure.*

Note: *The EGR cooler is attached to the front of the engine block behind the catalytic converter.*

21   Raise and support the vehicle on jackstands and remove the vehicle under cover.

22   Drain the engine cooling system (see Chapter 1, Section 25).

23   Remove the EGR tube as described earlier.

24   Remove the catalytic converter (see Section 18).

25   Disconnect the hose from the EGR cooler.

26   Remove the turbocharger oil return pipe from the block and the turbocharger.

27   Remove the four bolts attaching the EGR cooler to the engine block.

28   Installation is the reverse of removal. Use NEW gaskets when installing the EGR cooler.

29   Tighten the bolts to the torque listed in this Chapter's Specifications.

---

20   Evaporative Emissions Control (EVAP) system - component replacement

---

EVAP canister purge solenoid

Note: *The EVAP canister purge solenoid is located on the left side of the firewall, below the power brake booster.*

2.4L engines

1   Remove the engine cover.

2   Remove the air intake duct (see Chapter 4, Section 12).

3   Disconnect the fuel supply line and EVAP purge solenoid quick-connect fittings **(see illustration)**.

4   Cut along the line shown and remove the fuel rail insulation **(see illustration)**.

5   Slide out the red lock and disconnect the EVAP purge solenoid electrical connector; remove the vapor hose **(see illustration)**.

6   Depress the retaining tab and detach the purge solenoid from the mounting bracket.

7   Installation is the reverse of removal.

EVAP canister

Note: *The EVAP canister is located behind the left rear wheel opening.*

Note: *The Leak Detection Pump (LDP) is part of the canister and is not serviceable.*

8   Loosen the right rear wheel lug nuts,

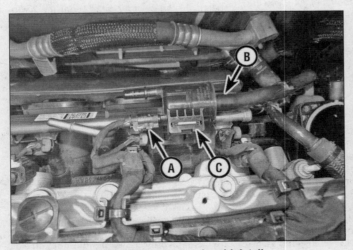

20.5 Canister purge solenoid details

A   *Electrical connector*
B   *Fuel tank vapor hose*
C   *Mounting bracket*

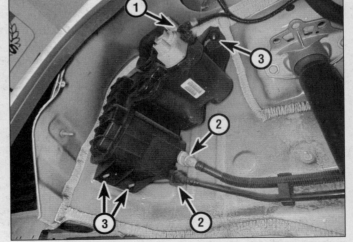

20.11 Disconnect the electrical connector (1) and disconnect all of the hoses (2), then remove the nuts (3) to remove the EVAP canister

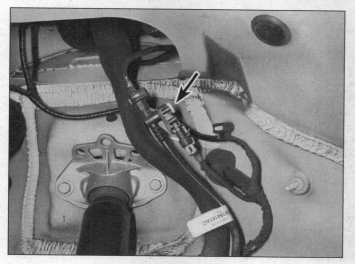

20.18 Identifying the FTPS

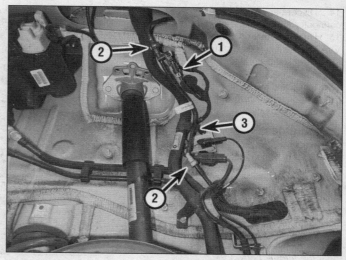

20.19 Disconnect the electrical connector (1), the quick-connect fittings (2) and the mounting clip (3) to remove the FTPS

then raise the vehicle and support it securely on jackstands.

9   Remove the right rear wheel.

10   Remove the inner fender splash shield to expose the EVAP components.

11   Disconnect the electrical connector from the EVAP canister (see illustration).

12   Disconnect the hoses from the EVAP canister.

13   Remove the mounting fasteners from the mounting bracket and remove the EVAP canister assembly.

14   Installation is the reverse of removal.

Fuel Tank Pressure Sensor (FTPS)

Note: *The FTPS is located behind the left rear wheel opening.*

15   Loosen the left rear wheel lug nuts, then raise the vehicle and support it securely on jackstands.

16   Remove the left rear wheel.

17   Remove the inner fender splash shield.

18   The Fuel Tank Pressure Sensor is part of a tube assembly and is not serviceable separately (see illustration).

19   Disconnect the FTPS electrical connector (see illustration).

20   Disconnect the quick-connect fittings.

21   Detach the tube assembly from the bracket.

22   Installation is the reverse of removal.

21   Positive Crankcase Ventilation (PCV) system

1   The Positive Crankcase Ventilation (PCV) system reduces hydrocarbon emissions by scavenging crankcase vapors. It does this by circulating fresh air from the air filter housing through the crankcase, where it mixes with blow-by gases, before being drawn through a PCV valve into the intake manifold.

2   The PCV system consists of the PCV valve and two hoses. The fresh air inlet hose connects the air filter housing to the valve cover. The crankcase ventilation hose (or PCV hose) connects the valve cover to the intake manifold. The PCV valve is located at the right front corner of the valve cover.

3   To maintain idle quality, the PCV valve restricts the flow when the intake manifold vacuum is high. If abnormal operating conditions (such as piston ring problems) arise, the system is designed to allow excessive amounts of blow-by gases to flow back through the crankcase vent tube into the air cleaner to be consumed by normal combustion.

4   Checking and replacement of the PCV valve is covered in Chapter 1.

Crankcase pressure sensor - replacement

Note: *2.0L turbocharged models are equipped with crankcase pressure sensor.*

5   Disconnect the cable from the negative terminal of the battery (see Chapter 5).

6   Locate the sensor near the dipstick. Disconnect the electrical connector.

7   Disconnect the pressure hose from the sensor.

8   Remove the mounting bracket bolt and remove the sensor.

9   Installation is the reverse of removal.

22   Oil pressure/temperature sensor - replacement

Oil pressure sensor

Four-cylinder engines

Note: *2.0L turbocharged engines have a combination pressure and temperature sensor. 2.4L engines have separate pressure and temperature sensors.*

Note: *The oil temperature/pressure sensor is located on the rear of engine block. On 2.0L engines, it is behind the alternator.*

1   Raise and support the vehicle on jackstands.

2   Remove the vehicle under cover.

3   On 2.0L turbocharged models, remove the alternator bolts and position to the side (see Chapter 5, Section 11).

4   On all models, depress the tab and disconnect the electrical connector from the sensor.

5   Unscrew the sensor from the engine block.

6   Before installing the new sensor, wrap the threads with Teflon sealing tape or coat the threads with thread sealant.

7   Thread the sensor into the cylinder head, then tighten it to the torque listed in this Chapter's Specifications. Reconnect the electrical connector.

V6 engines

Note: *On 3.2L engines, the oil pressure and temperature sensors are located under the lower intake manifold.*

8   Remove the lower intake manifold (see Chapter 2B, Section 5).

9   Locate the oil temperature sensor (upper sensor) or oil pressure sensor (lower senor) and disconnect the electrical connector.

10   Unscrew the oil temperature or pressure sensor from the oil filter housing.

11   Installation is reverse of removal.

12   Tighten the sensor to the torque listed in this Chapter's Specifications.

Oil Temperature sensor

2.4L engines

Note: *The oil temperature sensor is located on the rear of the cylinder head on the passenger's end.*

13   Locate the oil temperature sensor on the VVAA assembly (see illustration 8.8).

14   Disconnect the oil temp sensor electrical connector and bracket **(see illustration)**.
15   Unscrew the oil temp sensor from the VVAA assembly **(see illustration)**.
16   Check the condition of the sensor gasket. If damaged, replace.
17   Installation is reverse of removal. Tighten the sensor to the torque listed in this Chapter's Specifications.

3.2L engines
18   Refer to the procedure for replacement of the oil pressure sensor.

23   Turbocharger Boost Pressure Sensor - replacement

Note: *The boost pressure sensor is located next to the MAP sensor in the intake air duct near the throttle body.*
1   Disconnect the cable from the negative terminal of the battery (see Chapter 5).
2   Remove the engine cover.
3   Locate and disconnect the boost pressure sensor electrical connector.
4   Remove the bolt and pull the sensor from the duct.
5   Inspect the O-ring and replace if damaged.
6   Installation is the reverse of removal.

22.14 Disconnect oil temp sensor connector (A), the connector from the bracket (B) and remove the oil temp sensor (C) (2.4L engines)

24   Turbocharger Surge Valve - replacement

Note: *The surge valve is located in the intake air duct. The surge valve may also be called the blow-off valve.*
1   Disconnect the cable from the negative terminal of the battery (see Chapter 5).
2   Remove the engine cover.
3   Disconnect the bypass hose from the valve.
4   Disconnect the surge valve electrical connector.
5   Remove the three bolts attaching the valve to the duct and remove the valve.
6   Inspect the O-ring and replace it if damaged.
7   Installation is the reverse of removal.

Chapter 7 Part A
Automatic transaxle

Contents

Specifications

General

Lubricant type and capacity .... See Chapter 1

Torque specifications   Ft-lbs (unless otherwise indicated)

Note: *One foot-pound (ft-lb) of torque is equivalent to 12 inch-pounds (in-lbs) of torque. Torque values below approximately 15 ft-lbs are expressed in inch-pounds, since most foot-pound torque wrenches are not accurate at these smaller values.*

Drain plug	26
Oil cooler-to-transaxle bolts	18
Oil cooler line fitting bolt	22
Shift cable adjustment lever bolt	71 in-lbs
Transaxle bellhousing-to-transaxle case bolts	18
Torque converter-to-driveplate bolts	30
Engine-to-transaxle bolts	
M12	69
M10	37
Transaxle-to-engine bolts	
M12 x 1.25 x 97.1	46
M12 x 1.25 x 50.00	85
Oil pan-to-transaxle	47
Torque strut bracket bolts	120
Transaxle bracket-to-transaxle bolts	
M6	88 in-lbs
M12 (driver's side)	77

1   General information

1　These models are equipped with the 948TE (9-speed) automatic transaxle or the 9HP48 (9-speed) automatic transaxle. The automatic transaxle and the differential are housed in a compact, lightweight, two-piece aluminum alloy housing.

2　These models are equipped with a Transmission Control Module (TCM) which is the brain of the transaxle. The TCM monitors engine and transaxle operating parameters through numerous sensors, then generates output signals to various relays and solenoids to regulate hydraulic pressures, optimize drivability, provide efficient torque management and maintain maximum fuel economy. All models incorporate the TCM into the PCM. The TCM is part of the On-Board Diagnostic system (OBD-II). For more information, see Chapter 6.

3　Because of the complexity of the automatic transaxles and the specialized equipment necessary to perform most service operations, this Chapter contains only those procedures related to general diagnosis, adjustment and removal and installation procedures.

4　If the transaxle requires major repair work, it should be left to a dealer service department or an automotive or transmission repair shop. Once properly diagnosed you can, however, remove and install the transaxle yourself and save the expense, even if the repair work is done by a transmission shop.

2   Diagnosis - general

1　Automatic transaxle malfunctions may be caused by five general conditions:

　　a) *Poor engine performance*
　　b) *Improper adjustment*
　　c) *Hydraulic malfunctions*
　　d) *Mechanical malfunctions*
　　e) *Malfunctions in the computer or its signal network*

2　Diagnosis of these problems should always begin with a check of the easily repaired items: fluid level and condition (see Chapter 1), shift cable adjustment and shift lever installation. Next, perform a road test to determine if the problem has been corrected or if more diagnosis is necessary. If the problem persists after the preliminary tests and corrections are completed, additional diagnosis should be performed by a dealer service department or other qualified transmission repair shop. Refer to *Troubleshooting* at the front of this manual for information on symptoms of transaxle problems.

Preliminary checks

3　Drive the vehicle to warm the transaxle to normal operating temperature.

4　Check the fluid level as described in Chapter 1 :

　　a) *If the fluid level is unusually low, add enough fluid to bring the level within the designated area of the dipstick, then check for external leaks.*
　　b) *If the fluid level is abnormally high, drain off the excess, then check the drained fluid for contamination by coolant. The presence of engine coolant in the automatic transaxle fluid indicates that a failure has occurred in the internal radiator oil cooler walls that separate the coolant from the transaxle fluid (see Chapter 3).*
　　c) *If the fluid is foaming, drain it and refill the transaxle, then check for coolant in the fluid, or a high fluid level.*

5　Check the engine idle speed.
Note: *If the engine is malfunctioning, do not proceed with the preliminary checks until it has been repaired and runs normally.*
6　Check and adjust the shift cable, if necessary (see Section 4).
7　If hard shifting is experienced, inspect the shift cable under the center console and at the manual lever on the transaxle (see Section 4).

Fluid leak diagnosis

8　Most fluid leaks are easy to locate visually. Repair usually consists of replacing a seal or gasket. If a leak is difficult to find, the following procedure may help.
9　Identify the fluid. Make sure it's transaxle fluid and not engine oil or brake fluid.
10　Try to pinpoint the source of the leak. Drive the vehicle several miles, then park it over a large sheet of cardboard. After a minute or two, you should be able to locate the leak by determining the source of the fluid dripping onto the cardboard.
11　Make a careful visual inspection of the suspected component and the area immediately around it. Pay particular attention to gasket mating surfaces. A mirror is often helpful for finding leaks in areas that are hard to see.
12　If the leak still cannot be found, clean the suspected area thoroughly with a degreaser or solvent, then dry it thoroughly.
13　Drive the vehicle for several miles at normal operating temperature and varying speeds. After driving the vehicle, visually inspect the suspected component again.
14　Once the leak has been located, the cause must be determined before it can be properly repaired. If a gasket is replaced but the sealing flange is bent, the new gasket will not stop the leak. The bent flange must be straightened.
15　Before attempting to repair a leak, check to make sure that the following conditions are corrected or they may cause another leak.
Note: *Some of the following conditions cannot be fixed without highly specialized tools and expertise. Such problems must be referred to a qualified transmission shop or a dealer service department.*

Gasket leaks

16　Check the pan periodically. Make sure the bolts are tight, no bolts are missing, the gasket is in good condition and the pan is flat (dents in the pan may indicate damage to the valve body inside).
17　If the pan gasket is leaking, the fluid level or the fluid pressure may be too high, the vent may be plugged, the pan bolts may be too tight, the pan sealing flange may be warped, the sealing surface of the transaxle housing may be damaged, the gasket may be damaged or the transaxle casting may be cracked or porous. If sealant instead of gasket material has been used to form a seal between the pan and the transaxle housing, it may be the wrong type of sealant.

Seal leaks

18　If a transaxle seal is leaking, the fluid level may be too high, the vent may be plugged, the seal bore may be damaged, the seal itself may be damaged or improperly installed, the surface of the shaft protruding through the seal may be damaged or a loose bearing may be causing excessive shaft movement.
19　Make sure the dipstick tube seal is in good condition and the tube is properly seated. Periodically check the area around the sensors for leakage. If transaxle fluid is evident, check the seals for damage.

Case leaks

20　If the case itself appears to be leaking, the casting is porous and will have to be repaired or replaced.
21　Make sure the oil cooler hose fittings are tight and in good condition.

Fluid comes out vent pipe or fill tube

22　If this condition occurs, the possible causes are: the transaxle is overfilled; there is coolant in the fluid; the dipstick is incorrect; the vent is plugged or the drain-back holes are plugged.

3   Driveaxle oil seals - replacement

Note: *On AWD models, the right-side driveaxle oil seal replacement procedure is covered in Chapter 7B.*
1　The driveaxle oil seals are located on the sides of the transaxle, where the inner ends of the driveaxles are splined into the differential side gears. If you suspect that a driveaxle oil seal is leaking, raise the vehicle and support it securely on jackstands. If the seal is leaking, you'll see lubricant on the side of the transaxle, below the seal.
2　Remove the driveaxle (see Chapter 8).
3　Drill or use a pick to put a small hole into the metal part of the seal. Thread a screw into the hole and use a small slide hammer or similar tool to remove the seal.
4　Using a seal installer, install the new oil seal **(see illustration)**. Drive it into the bore squarely until it bottoms.
5　Install the driveaxle or intermediate shaft/driveaxle (see Chapter 8).
6　Check the fluid level (see Chapter 1) and adjust as necessary.

3.4 Using a seal installer, large section of pipe or a large deep socket as a drift, drive the new seal squarely into the bore and make sure that it's completely seated; lubricate the lip of the new seal with multi-purpose grease

4.4 Pry the shift cable from the manual lever using a trim panel tool or flat-bladed screwdriver

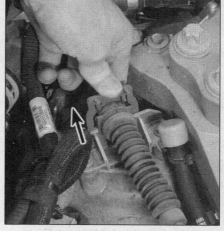

4.5 Squeeze the retaining clip, then pull the shift cable up off the bracket on the transaxle

4   Shift cable - removal, installation and adjustment

Warning: *The models covered by this manual are equipped with a Supplemental Restraint System (SRS), more commonly known as airbags. Always disarm the airbag system before working in the vicinity of any airbag system component to avoid the possibility of accidental deployment of the airbag, which could cause personal injury (see Chapter 12). Do not use a memory saving device to preserve the PCM's memory when working on or near airbag system components.*

Warning: *Do not attempt this procedure until the vehicle has cooled completely. The exhaust system components must be cold to avoid physical harm.*

Removal and installation

1   Shift the vehicle into Park.
2   Remove the battery and battery tray (see Chapter 5).
3   Remove the air filter housing (see Chapter 4).
4   Disconnect the shift cable from the shift lever **(see illustration)**.
5   Disconnect the shift cable from the bracket **(see illustration)**.
6   Remove the center console (see Chapter 11).
7   Disconnect the shift cable from the shifter assembly **(see illustration)**.
8   Disconnect the shift cable from the shift lever bracket **(see illustration)**.
9   Raise the vehicle and support it securely on jackstands.
10   Working under the vehicle, remove the exhaust heat shield fasteners and heat shield.
11   Disconnect the cable from the bracket and remove the grommet from the floorpan and pull shift cable out of opening.

12   Carefully unfasten the cable from the retainers under the vehicle.
13   Disconnect the stabilizer bar links to allow the bar to be rotated for shift cable removal.
14   Remove the cable from the vehicle.
15   Installation is the reverse of removal. Feed the shift cable into the passenger compartment and ensure the grommet is installed properly. Lubricate the grommet if necessary to ensure proper installation.

Adjustment

16   Park the vehicle on a flat surface and set the parking brake.
17   Place the shift lever in the Park position. Remove the key from the ignition.
18   Remove the center console to access the adjustment on the cable at the shift lever (see Chapter 11, Section 24).
19   Loosen the shift cable adjustment bolt at the shift lever **(see illustration)**.
20   Make sure the shift lever at the transaxle

4.7 Pry the shift cable from the shifter lever using a trim panel tool or flat-bladed screwdriver

4.8 Squeeze the retaining clip, then pull the shift cable up off the bracket on the shift lever

4.19 Loosen the shift cable adjustment bolt (A) and slide the cable (B) to adjust

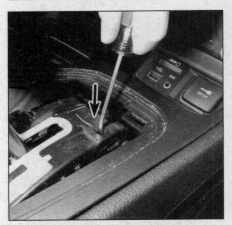

5.12 Move the BTSI solenoid bypass lever forward as you shift the gear select lever out of Park

6.4 Use a trim tool or similar to pry the shift boot away from the center console.

7.3 Disconnect the shift lever electrical connector

is in the Park position by pulling it forward all the way. The parking pawl must be engaged when adjusting the cable. If applied, release the parking brake, then rock the vehicle back and forth to ensure that the parking pawl is fully engaged.

21 Tighten the shift cable adjustment bolt to the torque listed in this Chapter's Specifications.

22 Check the shift lever for proper operation. It should operate smoothly without binding. The engine should start only in the Park or Neutral positions.

23 Shift the transaxle into all gear positions to make sure the cable is functioning properly. Readjust if necessary.

5 Brake Transmission Shift Interlock (BTSI) system - description, check, replacement and adjustment

Description

1 The Brake Transmission Shift Interlock (BTSI) system prevents the shift lever from being moved out of Park unless the brake pedal is depressed. The BTSI system also prevents the ignition key from being turned to the Lock or Accessory position unless the shift lever is fully locked into the Park position.

2 The components of the BTSI system are integrated into the ignition switch (node) and the Electronic Shift Module (ESM) in the shift lever assembly. There are no serviceable components for the BTSI system.

Check

3 With the ignition key in the Acc position and the brake pedal depressed, the shifter CAN be shifted out of Park.

4 With the ignition key in the On position, and the brake pedal NOT depressed, the shifter CANNOT be shifted out of Park.

5 With the ignition key in the On position,

and the brake pedal depressed, the shifter CAN be shifted out of Park.

6 With the shifter in any gear except Park, the ignition key CANNOT be rotated to the Lock position.

7 With the shifter in Park, the ignition key CAN be removed (after rotating to the Lock position).

8 With the ignition key removed, and the brake depressed, the shifter CANNOT be shifted out of Park.

9 If the BTSI system doesn't operate as described, the cable requires service. The BTSI is part of the shift lever assembly and is not serviceable. First, attempt to adjust the shift cable.

Bypassing the BTSI solenoid

Note: *In the event that the vehicle needs to be placed into Neutral and moved while deep into a repair, and the transaxle won't come out of gear, there is a simple work-around for this without the need to install the battery. Make sure the vehicle is on level ground and/or can be safely stopped when doing this.*

Note: *This also serves as a temporary fix if the BTSI components aren't functioning properly and the transaxle needs to be placed in whichever gear necessary to drive the vehicle. Make absolutely sure that the transaxle can be shifted safely while the vehicle is driven, and diagnose and fix the problems related to the BTSI components as soon as possible (see previous Steps).*

10 Set the parking brake.

11 Use a trim tool to carefully pry the shift boot away from the center console **(see illustration 6.4)**.

12 After detaching the shift boot, locate the shift lever override access hole at the front right corner. While pressing the brake pedal, use a small screwdriver to push down on the lever in the hole to allow the transmission shift select lever to be placed into Neutral **(see illustration)**.

13 If necessary, the vehicle can be started in the Neutral position.

6 Shift knob and boot - replacement

1 Pull the shift boot down and away from the base of the shift knob.

2 Remove the screws on the sides of the shift knob.

3 Pull the shift knob up to remove.

4 Use a trim tool to detach the shift boot from the center console trim **(see illustration)**.

5 Disconnect the shift indicator electrical connector.

6 Remove the shift boot.

7 Installation is reverse of removal. Pull the shift boot upwards towards the shift knob until it is properly seated.

7 Shift lever - removal and installation

Caution: *The Electronic Shift Module (ESM) is part of the shift lever assembly and is not serviceable separately. If the shifter is being replaced with a new unit, a scan tool MUST be used to determine if PROXI configuration data must be input into the new ESM. If needed, follow the scan tool instructions for the PROXI Configuration Alignment procedure.*

1 Disconnect the battery negative cable (see Chapter 5).

2 Remove the center floor console (see Chapter 11).

3 Disconnect the electrical connector and harness from the shift lever housing **(see illustration)**.

4 Pry the shift cable end from the lever and detach the cable housing from the shift lever base (see Section 4).

5 Disconnect any harness clips from the shift lever assembly.

6 Remove the shifter assembly mounting nuts and detach the shifter from the floor.

7 Installation is the reverse of removal.

8 Adjust the shift cable (see Section 4).

8.4 Remove the lower PCM bolts through the wheel well opening

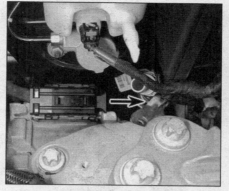

8.5a Locate the TCM connector lock . . .

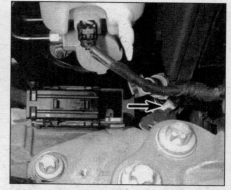

8.5b . . . and slide it away from the connector to unlock and disconnect the TCM connector.

8   Transmission Control Module (TCM) - replacement

Caution: *When the TCM is being replaced, a scan tool is required to program it. If the TCM is not programmed, the check engine light may come on. A qualified technician or repair facility should perform this procedure.*

1   Disconnect the negative battery cable (see Chapter 5, Section 3).
2   Loosen the left front wheel lug nuts, then raise and support the front of the vehicle on jackstands.
3   Remove the wheel and the inner fender splash shield.
4   Remove the TCM lower bolts below the brake booster **(see illustration)**.
5   Working in the engine compartment, remove the engine cover and locate the TCM. Disengage the connector locks and remove the connector from the TCM **(see illustrations)**.
6   Remove the bolts attaching the TCM to the transaxle and remove the TCM from the vehicle.
7   Have a qualified technician or repair facility program the TCM.

9   Transaxle oil cooler - removal and installation

Warning: *Wait until the engine is completely cool before beginning this procedure.*
Note: *The transaxle oil cooler is located behind the front bumper and in front of the condenser. The cooler is equipped with a thermal bypass valve that is not serviceable.*

1   Raise and support the front of the vehicle on jackstands.
2   Remove the vehicle under cover and any additional components to gain access to the cooler.
3   Place a drain pan under the fittings and disconnect and cap the coolant lines to the cooler, then remove the transaxle cooler lines and cap all the ends.
4   Disconnect and cap the transaxle cooler lines and ends of the cooler.

5   Remove the transaxle cooler mounting bolts and remove the cooler.
6   Install a new O-rings onto the cooler.
7   Installation is the reverse of removal. Tighten fasteners to the torque listed in this Chapter's Specifications.
8   Check the transaxle fluid level (see Chapter 1).

10   Automatic transaxle - removal and installation

Warning: *Wait until the engine is completely cool before beginning this procedure.*

Removal

1   Disconnect the negative battery cable from the battery (see Chapter 5, Section 3).
2   Remove the engine cover.
3   Remove the battery and battery tray (see Chapter 5, Section 4).
4   Loosen the front wheel lug nuts and the driveaxle/hub nuts.
Note: *Depending on the type of wheels installed on the vehicle and the thickness of the socket you are using, you may have to loosen the driveaxle/hub nuts after the wheels have been removed (see Chapter 8).*
5   Loosen the front wheel lug nuts, then raise and support the vehicle on a lift or jackstands and remove the front wheels.

6   Remove the Powertrain Control Module (PCM) (see Chapter 6, Section 17).
7   Remove the Power Distribution Center (PDC) (see Chapter 12).
8   On 2.4L models, remove the front driveaxles (see Chapter 8, Section 2).
9   On 3.2L models, disconnect the vacuum pump vacuum lines and disconnect the pump electrical connector. The vacuum pump is located above the transaxle bellhousing at the rear of the engine.
10   Remove the vacuum pump bolts and remove the bracket and pump from the engine.
11   On all models, remove the fasteners and clips and remove the driver's and passenger's inner fender liners.
12   Remove the vehicle under cover.
13   On 2019 and later 2.0L and all 2.4L models equipped with an auxiliary coolant pump, drain the engine coolant (see Chapter 1, Section 25).
14   Disconnect the hoses from the coolant pipe that runs along the side and bottom of the radiator.
15   Remove the nuts and bolts attaching the coolant pipe and remove the coolant pipe from the vehicle.
16   On all models, disengage the connector locks and remove the connector from the TCM (see Section 8).
17   Remove the bolts attaching the wiring harness bracket and ground cable to the top of the transaxle **(see illustration)**.

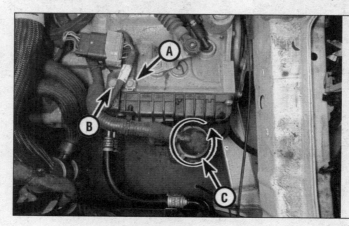

10.17 Remove the ground cable (A) and harness bracket (B) bolts to the top of the transaxle, and rotate the transaxle connector (C) counterclockwise and disconnect

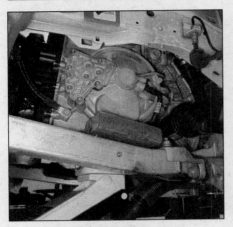

**10.22 Support the transaxle
with a floor jack**

**10.23 Remove the transaxle upper mount
bolts and mount through-bolt (not shown)**

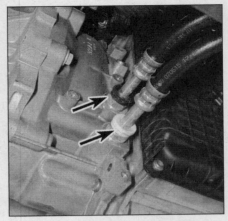

**10.31 Disconnect the transaxle cooler
lines by removing the plastic dust cap and
using a special tool to depress the clips
and disconnect the lines**

18 Disconnect the shift cable from the shift lever and the bracket (see Section 4).
19 Rotate the connector lock counterclockwise to unlock and unplug the electrical connector from the transaxle.
20 On 3.2L models, remove the front driveaxles (see Chapter 8, Section 2).
21 On AWD models, remove the transfer case. See Chapter 7B, Section 7. After removal, reinstall the passenger's side engine mount bolts into the frame rail through the mount.
22 On all models, place a floor jack under the transaxle for support, then slightly lift the transaxle to take the weight off of the mount **(see illustration)**.
23 Remove the transmission mount upper bolts. Then remove the lower bolts attaching the mount bracket to the transaxle **(see illustration)**.
24 Place a block of wood between the driver's side cross member and transaxle and lower the transaxle onto the wood block **(see illustration 10.22)**. Remove the floor jack.
25 Remove the transaxle mount spacer.

26 Remove the upper transaxle bolt that secures the harness bracket and position to the side.
27 Remove the starter (see Chapter 5, Section 12).
28 Detach the harness clips from the transmission bell housing and secure the harness to the side.
29 Remove the upper transaxle bolts.
30 Remove the bolt at the bottom of the transaxle attaching the ground cable.
31 Place a drain pan under the transaxle cooler lines where they attach to the transaxle. Disconnect the cooler line quick connect fittings at the transaxle **(see illustration)**.
32 On 2.4L FWD only models, remove the bolts and the exhaust pipe from under the engine **(see illustration)**.
33 On all models, remove the inspection cover from the transaxle bellhousing or oil pan **(see illustration)**. 2018 and earlier 2.4L models are attached with a bolt.
34 Mark the relationship of the torque converter to the driveplate (if possible) so they

can be installed in the same position.
35 Wedge a screwdriver between the teeth on the driveplate and the opening to prevent the engine from rotating, then remove the torque converter-to-driveplate bolts **(see illustration)**. Rotate the crankshaft with a socket and breaker bar on the crankshaft pulley bolt to bring the bolts into view.
36 After all the bolts are removed, push the torque converter into the bellhousing so it doesn't stay with the engine when the transaxle is removed.
37 Support the engine from above with a hoist, or place a floor jack under the oil pan. Place a wood block on the jack head to spread the load on the oil pan.
38 Support the transaxle with a transmission jack, if available, or use a floor jack. Secure the transaxle to the jack using straps or chains so it doesn't fall off during removal.
39 Lift the transaxle enough to remove the wooden support block.
40 Remove the bolts attaching the rear

**10.32 Disconnect and remove the lower
exhaust pipe on 2.4L FWD models**

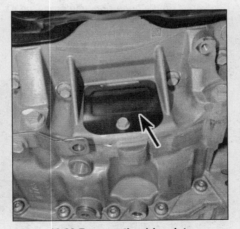

**10.33 Remove the driveplate
inspection cover**

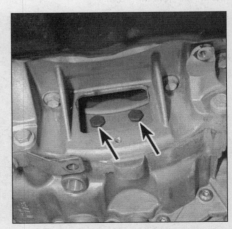

**10.35 Remove the torque converter-to-
driveplate bolts**

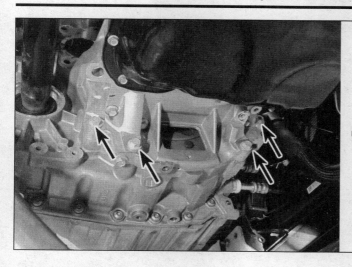

10.42 Remove the remaining bolts from the bottom of the transaxle

engine mount support and mount to the engine and the transaxle and remove the mount.

41 Remove the left load beam (see Chapter 10, Section 5).

42 Remove the remaining transaxle-to-engine bolts at the side and bottom of the transaxle bell housing **(see illustration).**

43 Separate the transaxle from the engine. Ensure the torque converter remains in the transaxle during removal.

44 Make a final check that all connectors, harnesses and hoses have been disconnected from the transaxle, then move the transaxle jack toward the side of the vehicle until the transaxle is clear of the engine locating dowels. Make sure you keep the transaxle level as you do this.

Installation

45 Installation is the reverse of removal, noting the following points:

Note: *Wedge a screwdriver between the teeth*

on the driveplate and the opening to prevent the engine from rotating while tightening the torque converter bolts.

a) *As the torque converter is reinstalled, ensure that the drive tangs at the center of the torque converter hub engage with the recesses in the automatic transaxle fluid pump inner gear. This can be confirmed by turning the torque converter while pushing it toward the transaxle. If it isn't fully engaged, it will clunk into place.*

b) *When installing the transaxle, make sure the match marks you made on the torque converter and driveplate line up.*

c) *Install all of the driveplate-to-torque converter bolts before tightening any of them.*

d) *Tighten the driveplate-to-converter bolts to the torque listed in this Chapter's Specifications.*

e) *Tighten the transaxle mounting bolts to the torque listed in this Chapter's Specifications.*

f) *Tighten the driveaxle/hub nuts to the torque listed in the Chapter 8 Specifications.*

g) *Tighten the wheel lug nuts to the torque listed in the Chapter 1 Specifications.*

h) *Fill the transaxle with the correct type and amount of fluid (see Chapter 1).*

i) *Refill the cooling system, if drained (see Chapter 1).*

j) *Adjust the shift cable (see Section 4).*

11 Transaxle mounts - check and replacement

1 Refer to Chapter 2A, Section 17 or Chapter 2B, Section 16 for the mount check and replacement procedure.

12 Automatic transaxle overhaul - general information

1 In the event of a problem occurring, it will be necessary to establish whether the fault is electrical, mechanical or hydraulic in nature, before repair work can be contemplated. Diagnosis requires detailed knowledge of the transaxle's operation and construction, as well as access to specialized test equipment, and so is deemed to be beyond the scope of this manual. It is therefore essential that problems with the automatic transaxle are referred to a dealer service department or other qualified repair facility for assessment.

2 Note that a faulty transaxle should not be removed before the vehicle has been diagnosed by a knowledgeable technician equipped with the proper tools, as troubleshooting must be performed with the transaxle installed in the vehicle.

Notes

Chapter 7 Part B
Transfer case

Contents

Specifications

Fluid Type

Transfer case fluid type	See Chapter 1

Torque specifications*   Ft-lbs (unless otherwise indicated)

Note: *One foot-pound (ft-lb) of torque is equivalent to 12 inch-pounds (in-lbs) of torque. Torque values below approximately 15 ft-lbs are expressed in inch-pounds, because most foot-pound torque wrenches are not accurate at these smaller values.*

Drain/fill plugs	30
Transfer case bracket bolts	16
Transfer case bracket-to-engine bolts	32
Transfer case bracket-to-intake manifold bolts	108 in-lbs
Transfer case-to-transaxle bolts	35

* When reusing fasteners, use a thread locker when installing.

1   General information

1   There are three different transfer cases available. There are three different one-speed transfer case models - one for automatic transaxle models, and one for manual transaxle models, and a two-speed transfer case.

2   Due to the complexity of the transfer case covered in this manual and the need for specialized equipment to perform most service operations, this Chapter contains only removal and installation procedures.

3   If the transfer case requires major repair work, it should be taken to a dealer service department or an automotive or transmission repair shop. You can, however, remove and install the transfer case yourself and save the expense of that labor, even if the repair work is done by a transmission shop.

2   Shift actuator - replacement

Caution: *On models with a 2-speed transfer case, if the transfer case actuator works fine but is being removed to fix a fluid leak, the transfer case should be placed in the 2WD mode before removing the actuator. If the actuator is removed and the transfer case is not in the 2WD mode, it will be difficult to install the shift forks onto the shift sleeves in the transfer case. The shift forks can be aligned by placing a large zip tie between the shift fork and the actuator housing to position the shift fork closer to the center of the actuator. Do not try to wrap and connect the ends of the zip tie around the shift mechanism. The zip tie acts as a shim and can be pulled out after the actuator is properly positioned in the transfer case.*

1   Remove the transfer case (see Section 7).

2   Remove the shift actuator fasteners.

3   Pull the shift actuator away from the transaxle. A shift fork attached to the actuator is engaged with the transfer case internals. Use care when removing.

4   Replace the shift actuator gasket before installation.

Note: *If a new shift actuator is installed, remove any locating dowels that remained in the transfer case when the actuator was removed, as the new actuator has dowels of its own.*

5   Installation is reverse of removal.

3 4x4 switch - replacement

Note: *The 4x4 switch is also referred to as the terrain select switch or Terrain Switch Bank Module (TSBM).*

1   Disconnect the cable from the negative terminal of the battery (see Chapter 5, Section 3).

2   Remove the shift lever bezel (see Chapter 11, Section 24).

3   Using a trim stick, work around the edges of the center console trim bezel to detach the clips. Disconnect the electrical connectors and remove the trim bezel and switches.

4   Release the clips and remove the 4x4 switch from the trim bezel.

5   Installation is reverse of removal.

4 Output shaft seal - replacement

1   Raise the vehicle and support it securely on jackstands.

2   Remove the driveshaft (see Chapter 8).

3   Carefully remove the circlip from the end of the output shaft.

4   Remove the O-ring from the output shaft near the seal. Discard the O-ring.

5   Pry the dust cover from the transfer case housing to expose the seal.

6   Use a seal remover to pull the seal straight out. It may be difficult to use a screwdriver or similar type of seal remover that pries the seal out. Use care not to damage the sealing surfaces inside the transfer case.

7   Inspect the output shaft and case sealing surface and remove any imperfections before installing the new seal.

8   Lubricate the lip of the new seal with multi-purpose grease.

9   Using a seal installer or a large deep socket as a drift, install the new oil seal. Drive it into the bore squarely and make sure it's completely seated.

10 Install the dust cover securely and use a NEW O-ring on the output shaft.

11 Installation is the reverse of removal. Check the transfer case and transaxle fluid levels and fill as necessary (see Chapter 1).

5 Driveaxle oil seal (right side) - replacement

1   Loosen the right front wheel driveaxle/hub nut and wheel bolts. Raise the vehicle and support it securely on jackstands. Remove the wheel.

2   Remove the right-side driveaxle and intermediate shaft (see Chapter 8, Section 2).

3   Carefully pry out the driveaxle oil seal with a seal removal tool or a large screwdriver. Be careful not to damage or scratch the seal bore.

4   Using a seal installer or a large deep socket as a drift, install the new oil seal. Drive it into the bore squarely and make sure it's completely seated.

5   Lubricate the lip of the new seal with multi-purpose grease.

6   Install the right side driveaxle and intermediate shaft.

7   Check the transfer case fluid level and add some if necessary, to bring it to the appropriate level (see Chapter 1).

6 Extension housing dust shield - replacement

1   Loosen the right front wheel driveaxle/hub nut and the wheel bolts. Raise the vehicle and support it securely on jackstands. Remove the wheels.

2   Remove the driveshaft (see Chapter 8).

3   Remove the extension housing bolts then pull the extension housing off and inspect the housing O-ring. If the O-ring has not been damaged it can be reused.

4   Drill holes in the seal and use screws and a slide hammer to remove the seal. Use care not to get metal shavings inside the transfer case.

5   Place the extension housing in a vise, then use a hammer and chisel to drive the dust shield off the end of the housing.

6   Lightly lubricate the new dust shield, then center the shield on the end of the extension housing.

7   Place a block of wood against the end of the dust shield and use a hammer to install the dust shield onto the extension housing. Drive it onto the housing squarely and make sure it's completely seated.

8   The remainder of installation is the reverse of removal.

7 Transfer case - removal and installation

Removal

1   Disconnect the cable from the negative terminal of the battery (see Chapter 5).

2   Remove the engine undercover, if equipped.

3   Remove the right driveaxle (see Chapter 8, Section 2).

4   On 2.4L models, remove the intake manifold (see Chapter 2A, Section 5).

5   On all models, remove the driveshaft (see Chapter 8, Section 3).

Caution: *DO NOT allow the driveshaft to hang from the front, rear or center support bearing - always support the driveshaft. Damage to the joints, boots and or center support bearing may occur, resulting in vibration.*

6   On 3.2L models, disconnect the O2 sensor connectors for the rear catalytic converter. Remove the upper support bracket bolt.

7   Remove the intermediate shaft support bracket.

8   Remove the bolts for the rear catalytic converter and position upwards and to the right. Secure the converter in place using a bungee cord, bailing wire, or equivalent.

9   On all models, remove the exhaust pipe from under the engine.

10 Remove the bolts and heat shield from the transfer case.

11 Remove the transfer case-to-support bracket bolts.

12 Remove the engine-to-support bracket bolts and remove the transfer case support bracket.

13 Disconnect the shift actuator electrical connector.

14 Remove the transfer case-to-transaxle bolts and separate the transfer case from the transaxle.

15 Slide the transfer case away from the transaxle and tilt the transaxle end of the transfer case downwards to remove it from the vehicle.

Installation

16 Installation is the reverse of removal, noting the following points:

a) *Install a new O-ring seal between the transfer case and transaxle.*

b) *Tighten the exhaust system fasteners to the torque listed in this Chapter's Specifications.*

c) *Tighten the driveshaft fasteners to the torque listed in the Chapter 8 Specifications.*

d) *Tighten the transfer case mounting bolts to the torque listed in this Chapter's Specifications.*

e) *Refill the transfer case and transaxle with the proper type and amount of lubricant (see Chapter 1, Section 15).*

f) *Tighten the driveaxle/hub nut to the torque listed in the Chapter 8 Specifications.*

g) *Tighten the wheel bolts to the torque listed in the Chapter 1 Specifications.*

Chapter 8
Driveline

Contents

Specifications

Fluid type

Rear differential fluid*	70W-80 Gear lube
Rear differential hydraulic fluid	Synthetic hydraulic control fluid (must meet MS-2155 specifications)

The fluid contains a special additive for the wet clutch. Use of fluid not meeting manufacturer specifications will cause damage to the wet clutch and rear differential assembly.

Torque specifications

Note: *One foot-pound (ft-lb) of torque is equivalent to 12 inch-pounds (in-lbs) of torque. Torque values below approximately 15 ft-lbs are expressed in inch-pounds, because most foot-pound torque wrenches are not accurate at these smaller values.*

	Ft-lbs (unless otherwise indicated)	Nm
Driveaxles		
Driveaxle/hub nut*		
Front	148	200
Rear	129	175
Intermediate shaft bearing bracket fasteners	48	65
Wheel lug nuts	See Chapter 1	
Driveshaft (AWD models)		
Center support bearing mounting nuts	17	23
Driveshaft-to-rear differential bolts*	15	21
Rear differential assembly (AWD models)		
Differential-to-crossmember front bolts	41	55
Differential-to-crossmember rear bolt	89	120
Hydraulic fluid cover bolts	53 in-lbs	6
Pressure sensor	15	20
Pinion flange nut*	Matches measured torque specification recorded during removal +3 to +5 in-lbs	

Fastener(s) must be replaced

1   General information

1   The information in this Chapter deals with the components from the rear of the engine to the wheels, except for the transaxle, which is dealt with in Chapter 7A and the transfer case on AWD models, which is covered in Chapter 7B.
2   Vehicles with AWD can be equipped with either a single or a two-speed rear differential.
3   Since nearly all the procedures covered in this Chapter involve working under the vehicle, make sure it's securely supported on sturdy jackstands or a hoist where the vehicle can be easily raised and lowered.

2   Driveaxle - removal and installation

Front

Removal

1   Set the parking brake. Loosen the wheel bolts, then raise the vehicle and support it securely on jackstands. Remove the wheel.
2   Unstake the driveaxle/hub nut **(see illustration)**. Prevent the brake disc from turning by applying the brakes or by inserting a long punch into a disc cooling vane and letting it come to rest against the caliper mounting bracket, or have an assistant apply the brake and remove the driveaxle/hub nut, then the washer **(see illustration)**.
Caution: *Discard the driveaxle/hub nut and obtain a new one for reassembly.*
3   Remove the under-vehicle splash shield.
4   Separate the control arm from the steering knuckle (see Chapter 10, Section 5).
5   While pulling the steering knuckle out and away from the vehicle, remove the outer CV joint stub axle shaft of the driveaxle **(see illustrations)** from the hub. Strike the end of the stub shaft with a soft-faced hammer to separate the splines from the hub and bearing assembly, if necessary.
Note: *If the driveaxle is stuck in the hub, push it out with a puller.*

6   On models with a passenger's side intermediate shaft as part of the driveaxle, remove the intermediate shaft support bracket bolts **(see illustration)**.
7   If removing the left-side driveaxle, insert a prybar between the inner CV joint and the transaxle case **(see illustration)**. Pry out sharply to disengage the inner CV joint from the transaxle.
8   Carefully withdraw the inner CV joint or intermediate shaft from the transaxle. Do not let the splines or the circlip drag across the sealing lip of the driveaxle oil seal.
9   Inspect the circlip and replace as necessary **(see illustration)**.

Installation

10   Installation is the reverse of removal, noting the following additional points:

a) *Thoroughly clean the splines and bearing shield on the outer CV joint. This is very important, as the bearing shield protects the wheel bearings from water and contamination. Also clean the wheel bearing area of the steering knuckle. Don't forget to install the washer on the stub shaft.*

2.2a Use a small chisel to unstake the driveaxle/hub nut

2.2b Prevent the brake disc from turning by applying the brakes or inserting a long punch into a disc cooling vane, then loosen and remove the driveaxle/hub nut

b) *Thoroughly clean the splines and oil seal sealing surface on the inner CV joint. Apply an even bead of multi-purpose grease around the oil seal sealing surface of the inner CV joint.*
c) *When installing the driveaxle, push it in sharply to seat the snap-ring on the inner CV joint stub shaft into its groove in the differential gears inside the transaxle. Pull out on the inner CV joint housing to ensure it's seated.*
d) *On models equipped with a passenger's side intermediate shaft, insert the splined shaft assembly into the splined differential gears inside the transaxle, then install the support bearing mounting bolts and tighten the bolts to the torque listed in this Chapter's Specifications.*
e) *Reconnect the control arm to the steering knuckle (see Chapter 10).*
f) *Tighten the NEW driveaxle/hub nut to the torque listed in this Chapter's Specifications.*
g) *Stake the axle nut (see illustration).*
h) *Tighten the wheel bolts to the torque listed in the Chapter 1 Specifications.*

2.5a Use a soft-faced hammer to push the axle out of the hub . . .

2.5b . . . and pull the steering knuckle away from the outer CV joint

2.6 Intermediate shaft support bracket mounting bolts

2.7 From under the transaxle, pry the inner CV joint out sharply to disengage the circlip from the differential side gear

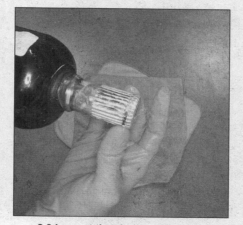

2.9 Inspect the circlip on the axle

2.10a Stake the axle nut using a punch

Rear

Removal

11 Block the front wheels, loosen the rear wheel lug nuts, then raise the rear of the vehicle and support it securely on jackstands. Remove the wheel.

12 Unstake and remove the driveaxle/hub nut.

13 Remove the rear suspension knuckle. See Chapter 10, Section 17.

14 Support the outer end of the driveaxle and insert a prybar between the inner CV joint and the differential case. Pry out sharply to disengage the inner CV joint from the differential.

15 Carefully withdraw the inner CV joint from the differential. Do not let the splines or the circlip drag across the sealing lip of the driveaxle oil seal.

Note: *Note any driveaxle shims (if installed) for installation.*

Installation

16 Installation is the reverse of removal, noting the following additional points:

a) *Thoroughly clean the splines and bearing shield on the outer CV joint.*

b) *This is very important, as the bearing shield protects the wheel bearings from water and contamination. Also clean the wheel bearing area of the steering knuckle.*

c) *Thoroughly clean the splines and oil seal sealing surface on the inner CV joint. Apply an even bead of multi-purpose grease around the oil seal sealing surface of the inner CV joint.*

d) *When installing the driveaxle, push it in sharply to seat the circlip on the inner CV joint stub shaft into its groove in the rear differential gears. Pull out on the inner CV joint housing to ensure it's seated.*

e) *Tighten the driveaxle/hub nut to the torque listed in this Chapter's Specifications.*

f) *Tighten the lug nuts to the torque listed in the Chapter 1 Specifications.*

3 Driveshaft (AWD models) - removal and installation

Caution: *DO NOT allow the driveshaft to hang from the front, rear or center support bearing - always suppport the driveshaft. Damage to the U-joints, boots and/or center support bearing may occur, resulting in vibration.*
Note: *The manufacturer recommends replacing driveshaft fasteners and transfer case output shaft circlip with new ones when installing the driveshaft.*

1 Place the shift selector lever in Neutral.

2 Raise the vehicle and support it securely on jackstands.

3 Use chalk or a scribe to index the relationship of the driveshaft to the differential pinion flange.

4 Remove the fasteners and disconnect the rear driveshaft from the rear axle flange. Support the rear of the driveshaft.

5 Remove the center support heat shield and remove the bolts attaching the driveshaft center support to the vehicle. Support the center of the driveshaft.

6 With the help of an assistant, if needed, support the entire driveshaft and slide the end of the driveshaft out from the transfer case. The force of the circlip retaining the yoke to the output shaft needs to be overcome when removing.

7 Remove the driveshaft from the vehicle.

8 Installation is the reverse of removal, noting the following points:

a) *Make sure the marks you made previously are aligned.*

b) *Apply a light coating of grease to the splines of the driveshaft yoke at the transfer case before installing.*

c) *Push the driveshaft into the transfer case until the circlip locks the yoke in. Confirm by pulling and pushing on the driveshaft.*

d) *Tighten the fasteners to the torques listed in this Chapter's Specifications. The driveshaft rear flange bolts can only be torqued once.*

4 Driveshaft center support bearing (AWD models) - replacement

1 The center support bearing is not replaceable separately; if it is in need of replacement, the entire driveshaft must be replaced.

5 Rear differential driveaxle oil seals (AWD models) - replacement

Caution: *If the vehicle is equipped with an Intelligent Battery Sensor (IBS), disconnect the IBS electrical connector BEFORE disconnecting the negative battery terminal from the battery.*

1 Disconnect the cable from the negative terminal of the battery (see Chapter 5).

2 Raise the vehicle and support it securely on jackstands. Place the transaxle in Neutral with the parking brake off.

3 Remove the driveaxles (see Section 2).

4 On both sides of single-speed rear differentials or driver's side of two-speed rear differentials, use a slide-hammer and attachment to remove the output shaft(s).

5 For the passenger's side of two-speed rear differentials, use a slide-hammer and attachment to remove the dust deflector (locker style) or output shaft (non-locker).

6 On all models, a seal remover that pulls the seal straight out may be required as it may be difficult to use a screwdriver or similar type of seal remover that pries the seal out. Carefully remove the driveaxle oil seal. Be careful not to damage or scratch the seal bore.

7 Using a seal installer or a large deep socket as a drift, install the new oil seal. Drive it into the bore squarely and make sure it's completely seated.

8 Lubricate the lip of the new seals with multi-purpose grease.

9 The manufacturer recommends a new circlip on the output shaft. Lightly coat the splines on both ends of the driveaxle with grease prior to installation.

10 Check the differential lubricant level and add some, if necessary, to bring it to the appropriate level.

---

6   Rear differential pinion seal (AWD models) - replacement

1 Raise the vehicle and support it securely on jackstands.
2 Use chalk or a scribe to index the relationship of the driveshaft to the differential pinion yoke.
Caution: *DO NOT allow the driveshaft to hang from the front, rear or center support bearing - always support the driveshaft. Damage to the joints, boots and or center support bearing may occur, resulting in vibration.*
3 Remove the fasteners and disconnect the rear driveshaft from the differential pinion yoke. Support the rear of the driveshaft to the side.
4 Rotate the pinion a few times by hand. Use a beam-type or dial-type inch-pound torque wrench to check the torque required to rotate the pinion shaft. Record it for use later.
5 Unstake the pinion nut.
6 Unstake the pinion nut. Hold the pinion flange with a suitable tool to prevent rotating, then unscrew the nut.
7 Use a puller to remove the flange from the differential.
8 Use a seal remover that pulls the seal straight out as it may be difficult to use a screwdriver or similar type of seal remover that pries the seal out. Carefully remove the driveaxle oil seal. Be careful not to damage or scratch the seal bore.
9 Using a seal installer or a large deep socket as a drift, install the new oil seal. Drive it into the bore squarely and make sure it's completely seated.
10 Lubricate the lip of the new seal with multi-purpose grease.
11 Installation is the reverse of removal, noting the following points:
a) *Measure the torque required to rotate the pinion and tighten the nut in small increments (no more than 5 ft-lbs) until it matches the figure recorded in Step 4. To compensate for the drag of the new oil seal, the nut should be tightened a little more until the rotational torque of the pinion exceeds the earlier recording by 5 in-lbs.*
b) *Tighten the driveshaft fasteners to the torque listed in this Chapter's Specifications.*
c) *Check the differential lubricant level and add some, if necessary, to bring it to the appropriate level.*

---

7   Rear differential assembly (AWD models) - removal and installation

Caution: *If the vehicle is equipped with an Intelligent Battery Sensor (IBS), disconnect the IBS electrical connector BEFORE disconnecting the negative battery terminal from the battery.*
1 Disconnect the cable from the negative terminal of the battery (see Chapter 5).
2 Raise the vehicle and support it securely on jackstands.
3 Remove the band clamp and exhaust hanger bolts and remove the muffler.
4 Disconnect the following electrical connectors:
a) *Differential pressure sensor*
b) *Differential pump motor*
c) *Differential actuator*
5 Disconnect the differential vent hose.
6 Make the driveshaft in relation to the pinion flange, remove the bolts and disconnect and support the rear of the driveshaft.
7 Remove the left rear driveaxle (see Section 2).
8 Remove the driveaxle/hub nut for the passenger's (right) rear driveaxle. Drive the passenger's driveaxle from the hub so it is free.
9 Support the rear differential with a suitable jack. Secure it to the jack using chains or a strap.
10 Remove the rear stabilizer bar (see Chapter 10).
11 Remove the rear differential mount bolt.
12 Remove the front differential mount-to-vehicle bolts.
13 Remove the bolts and slide the differential bracket as far forward as possible.
14 Lower the rear differential partially with the passenger's driveshaft connected. Remove the passenger's driveaxle from the hub.
15 Carefully lower and remove the differential from the vehicle.
16 Remove the passenger's drive axle from the differential.
17 Installation is the reverse of removal, noting the following points:
a) *Don't tighten any of the mounting fasteners until all of them have been installed.*
b) *Tighten all fasteners to the torque listed in this Chapter's Specifications.*

---

8   Rear differential actuator (AWD models) - replacement

Note: *Only two-speed rear differentials are equipped with an actuator. The actuator switches between the two speeds. A scan tool is required to perform this procedure by placing the differential into the 4-HI position. A qualified technician or repair facility should perform this procedure.*
1 Using a scan tool, place the rear differential into 4-HI position.
2 Remove the rear differential from the vehicle to service the actuator (see Section 7).
3 Remove the actuator fasteners and remove the actuator from the differential.

4 Installation is reverse of removal, noting the following items:
a) *Replace the gasket as necessary.*
b) *Line up the shift fork on the actuator with the sliding collar grooves in the differential.*
c) *Ensure the locating pins are not stuck in the differential housing. A new actuator comes with locating pins installed in the actuator itself, old pins must be removed if present.*
d) *Top off the differential fluid as necessary after installation of the rear differential.*

---

9   Rear differential pump motor (AWD models) - removal and installation

Note: *A scan tool is required to perform this procedure by placing the Rear Driveline Module (RDM) into the Park position. A qualified technician or repair facility should perform this procedure.*
1 Raise the rear of the vehicle and support it securely on jackstands.
2 Using a scan tool, perform the RDM Bleed procedure. This places the RDM in the Park position.
3 Turn the ignition off.
4 Disconnect the motor electrical connector.
5 Place a drain pan under the differential below the motor and remove the pump-to-differential bolts (not the motor-to-pump bolts).
6 Remove the motor and pump assembly from the vehicle. The motor and the pump are replaced as one unit.
7 Installation is the reverse of removal, noting the following points:
a) *Replace the O-rings on the pump.*
b) *Top off the hydraulic fluid (see Chapter 1, Section 16).*
c) *Tighten all fasteners to the torque listed in this Chapter's Specifications.*

---

10   Rear differential pressure sensor (AWD models) - replacement

1 Raise the rear of the vehicle and support it securely on jackstands.
2 Locate the pressure sensor above the motor and pump. Disconnect the electrical connector.
3 Place a drain pan under the differential below the pressure sensor.
4 Unscrew the pressure sensor from the rear differential case.
5 To install, screw the sensor into the case and tighten to the torque listed in this Chapter's Specifications.
6 If any fluid drains out, check the rear differential hydraulic fluid level (see Chapter 1).

Chapter 9
Brakes

Contents

Specifications

General

Brake fluid type	See Chapter 1

Disc brakes

Brake pad minimum thickness	See Chapter 1
Disc lateral run-out limit	0.0008 inch
Disc minimum thickness	Cast into disc
Thickness variation (parallelism)	
Front	0.0003 inch
Rear	0.0004 inch

Torque specifications — Ft-lbs (unless otherwise indicated)

Note: *One foot-pound (ft-lb) of torque is equivalent to 12 inch-pounds (in-lbs) of torque. Torque values below approximately 15 ft-lbs are expressed in inch-pounds, since most foot-pound torque wrenches are not accurate at these smaller values.*

Brake booster mounting nuts	15
Brake hose banjo bolt to caliper	159 in lbs
Caliper mounting bolts	32
Caliper mounting bracket bolts	
Front	129
Rear	89
Master cylinder-to-brake booster mounting nuts	18
Wheel speed sensor mounting bolt	
Front	106 in lbs
Rear	106 in lbs
Disc-to-hub bolt	177 in-lbs
Disc splash shield bolts	71 in-lbs
Brake booster mounting nuts	15
ABS controller - mounting fasteners	
Mounting bolt to bracket	71 in lbs
Mounting screws to frame	221 in lbs
Wheel lug bolts	See Chapter 1

1   General Information

1   The vehicles covered by this manual are equipped with hydraulically operated front and rear brake systems. The front and rear brakes are disc type. Both the front and rear brakes are self adjusting. The disc brakes automatically compensate for pad wear.

Hydraulic system

2   The basic hydraulic system consists of two separate hydraulic circuits which make up the front and rear brake systems. The master cylinder has separate reservoirs for the two circuits, and, in the event of a leak or failure in one hydraulic circuit, the other circuit will remain operative. These vehicles also incorporate an Anti-lock Braking System (ABS) that is an integral part of the basic hydraulic system (see Section 3 for details).

EVBP - Electronic Valve Brake Proportioning

3   The amount of brake fluid utilized to the rear braking system is proportionally controlled electronically through the HCU (Hydraulic Control Unit) and the LPA (Low Pressure Accumulator). In order to reduce the hydraulic brake pressure to the rear brakes, the fluid is pulsed to the rear which in turn reduces the amount of actual fluid allowed to the rear brakes. This is required during heavy braking conditions, and to help the driver maintain vehicle control by balancing the hydraulic pressure for the rear brakes to keep the vehicle veering or pitching (nose diving) during heavy braking. Even though the EVBP is essential part of the ABS system, at any time the ABS warning lights are on the EVBP will, in many instances, remain active even without a working ABS system.

Power brake booster

4   The power brake booster, utilizing engine manifold vacuum and atmospheric pressure to provide assistance to the hydraulically operated brakes, is mounted on the firewall in the engine compartment.

Parking brake

5   The parking brake system is a fully electric bi-directional 12 volt motor system that is controlled by a processor through the Electric Parking Brake module. The parking brake actuators are attached directly to the rear calipers and operate the rear brake pads by applying force to the rear calipers when supplied with voltage, and release the pads in the same manner. The parking brake will remain engaged even when the vehicle is off (unless otherwise requested).

Service

6   After completing any operation involving disassembly of any part of the brake system, always test drive the vehicle to check for proper braking performance before resuming normal driving. When testing the brakes, perform the tests on a clean, dry, flat surface. Conditions other than these can lead to inaccurate test results.

7   Test the brakes at various speeds with both light and heavy pedal pressure. The vehicle should stop evenly without pulling to one side or the other.

8   Tires, vehicle load and wheel alignment are factors which also affect braking performance.

Precautions

8   There are some general cautions and warnings involving the brake system on this vehicle:

a) *Use only brake fluid conforming to DOT 3 specifications.*

b) *The brake pads and linings contain fibers that are hazardous to your health if inhaled. Whenever you work on brake system components, clean all parts with brake system cleaner. Do not allow the fine dust to become airborne. Also, wear an approved filtering mask.*

c) *Safety should be paramount whenever any servicing of the brake components is performed. Do not use parts or fasteners that are not in perfect condition, and be sure that all clearances and torque specifications are adhered to. If you are at all unsure about a certain procedure, seek professional advice. Upon completion of any brake system work, test the brakes carefully in a controlled area before putting the vehicle into normal service. If a problem is suspected in the brake system, don't drive the vehicle until it's fixed.*

d) *Used brake fluid is considered a hazardous waste and it must be disposed of in accordance with federal, state and local laws. DO NOT pour it down the sink, into septic tanks or storm drains, or on the ground. Clean up any spilled brake fluid immediately and then wash the area with large amounts of water. This is especially true for any finished or painted surfaces.*

2   Troubleshooting

PROBABLE CAUSE	CORRECTIVE ACTION
No brakes - pedal travels to floor	
1 Low fluid level 2 Air in system	1 and 2 Low fluid level and air in the system are symptoms of another problem a leak somewhere in the hydraulic system. Locate and repair the leak
3 Defective seals in master cylinder	3 Replace master cylinder
4 Fluid overheated and vaporized due to heavy braking	4 Bleed hydraulic system (temporary fix). Replace brake fluid (proper fix)
Brake pedal slowly travels to floor under braking or at a stop	
1 Defective seals in master cylinder	1 Replace master cylinder
2 Leak in a hose, line, caliper or wheel cylinder	2 Locate and repair leak
3 Air in hydraulic system	3 Bleed the system, inspect system for a leak
Brake pedal feels spongy when depressed	
1 Air in hydraulic system	1 Bleed the system, inspect system for a leak
2 Master cylinder or power booster loose	2 Tighten fasteners
3 Brake fluid overheated (beginning to boil)	3 Bleed the system (temporary fix). Replace the brake fluid (proper fix)
4 Deteriorated brake hoses (ballooning under pressure)	4 Inspect hoses, replace as necessary (it's a good idea to replace all of them if one hose shows signs of deterioration)

PROBABLE CAUSE   **CORRECTIVE ACTION**

Brake pedal feels hard when depressed and/or excessive effort required to stop vehicle

1 Power booster faulty	1 Replace booster
2 Engine not producing sufficient vacuum, or hose to booster clogged, collapsed or cracked	2 Check vacuum to booster with a vacuum gauge. Replace hose if cracked or clogged, repair engine if vacuum is extremely low
3 Brake linings contaminated by grease or brake fluid	3 Locate and repair source of contamination, replace brake pads or shoes
4 Brake linings glazed	4 Replace brake pads or shoes, check discs and drums for glazing, service as necessary
5 Caliper piston(s) or wheel cylinder(s) binding or frozen	5 Replace calipers or wheel cylinders
6 Brakes wet	6 Apply pedal to boil-off water (this should only be a momentary problem)
7 Kinked, clogged or internally split brake hose or line	7 Inspect lines and hoses, replace as necessary

Excessive brake pedal travel (but will pump up)

1 Drum brakes out of adjustment	1 Adjust brakes
2 Air in hydraulic system	2 Bleed system, inspect system for a leak

Excessive brake pedal travel (but will not pump up)

1 Master cylinder pushrod misadjusted	1 Adjust pushrod
2 Master cylinder seals defective	2 Replace master cylinder
3 Brake linings worn out	3 Inspect brakes, replace pads and/or shoes
4 Hydraulic system leak	4 Locate and repair leak

Brake pedal doesn't return

1 Brake pedal binding	1 Inspect pivot bushing and pushrod, repair or lubricate
2 Defective master cylinder	2 Replace master cylinder

Brake pedal pulsates during brake application

1 Brake drums out-of-round	1 Have drums machined by an automotive machine shop
2 Excessive brake disc runout or disc surfaces out-of-parallel	2 Have discs machined by an automotive machine shop
3 Loose or worn wheel bearings	3 Adjust or replace wheel bearings
4 Loose lug nuts	4 Tighten lug nuts

Brakes slow to release

1 Malfunctioning power booster	1 Replace booster
2 Pedal linkage binding	2 Inspect pedal pivot bushing and pushrod, repair/lubricate
3 Malfunctioning proportioning valve	3 Replace proportioning valve
4 Sticking caliper or wheel cylinder	4 Repair or replace calipers or wheel cylinders
5 Kinked or internally split brake hose	5 Locate and replace faulty brake hose

Brakes grab (one or more wheels)

1 Grease or brake fluid on brake lining	1 Locate and repair cause of contamination, replace lining
2 Brake lining glazed	2 Replace lining, deglaze disc or drum

Troubleshooting (continued)

PROBABLE CAUSE	CORRECTIVE ACTION

Vehicle pulls to one side during braking

PROBABLE CAUSE	CORRECTIVE ACTION
1 Grease or brake fluid on brake lining	1 Locate and repair cause of contamination, replace lining
2 Brake lining glazed	2 Deglaze or replace lining, deglaze disc or drum
3 Restricted brake line or hose	3 Repair line or replace hose
4 Tire pressures incorrect	4 Adjust tire pressures
5 Caliper or wheel cylinder sticking	5 Repair or replace calipers or wheel cylinders
6 Wheels out of alignment	6 Have wheels aligned
7 Weak suspension spring	7 Replace springs
8 Weak or broken shock absorber	8 Replace shock absorbers

Brakes drag (indicated by sluggish engine performance or wheels being very hot after driving)

PROBABLE CAUSE	CORRECTIVE ACTION
1 Brake pedal pushrod incorrectly adjusted	1 Adjust pushrod
2 Master cylinder pushrod (between booster and master cylinder)	2 Adjust pushrod incorrectly adjusted
3 Obstructed compensating port in master cylinder	3 Replace master cylinder
4 Master cylinder piston seized in bore	4 Replace master cylinder
5 Contaminated fluid causing swollen seals throughout system	5 Flush system, replace all hydraulic components
6 Clogged brake lines or internally split brake hose(s)	6 Flush hydraulic system, replace defective hose(s)
7 Sticking caliper(s) or wheel cylinder(s)	7 Replace calipers or wheel cylinders
8 Parking brake not releasing	8 Inspect parking brake linkage and parking brake mechanism, repair as required
9 Improper shoe-to-drum clearance	9 Adjust brake shoes
10 Faulty proportioning valve	10 Replace proportioning valve

Brakes fade (due to excessive heat)

PROBABLE CAUSE	CORRECTIVE ACTION
1 Brake linings excessively worn or glazed	1 Deglaze or replace brake pads and/or shoes
2 Excessive use of brakes	2 Downshift into a lower gear, maintain a constant slower speed (going down hills)
3 Vehicle overloaded	3 Reduce load
4 Brake drums or discs worn too thin	4 Measure drum diameter and disc thickness, replace drums or discs as required
5 Contaminated brake fluid	5 Flush system, replace fluid
6 Brakes drag	6 Repair cause of dragging brakes
7 Driver resting left foot on brake pedal	7 Don't ride the brakes

Brakes noisy (high-pitched squeal)

PROBABLE CAUSE	CORRECTIVE ACTION
1 Glazed lining	1 Deglaze or replace lining
2 Contaminated lining (brake fluid, grease, etc.)	2 Repair source of contamination, replace linings
3 Weak or broken brake shoe hold-down or return spring	3 Replace springs
4 Rivets securing lining to shoe or backing plate loose	4 Replace shoes or pads
5 Excessive dust buildup on brake linings	5 Wash brakes off with brake system cleaner
6 Brake drums worn too thin	6 Measure diameter of drums, replace if necessary
7 Wear indicator on disc brake pads contacting disc	7 Replace brake pads
8 Anti-squeal shims missing or installed improperly	8 Install shims correctly

PROBABLE CAUSE	CORRECTIVE ACTION

Brakes noisy (scraping sound)

1 Brake pads or shoes worn out; rivets, backing plate or brake	1 Replace linings, have discs and/or drums machined (or replace) shoe metal contacting disc or drum

Brakes chatter

1 Worn brake lining	1 Inspect brakes, replace shoes or pads as necessary
2 Glazed or scored discs or drums	2 Deglaze discs or drums with sandpaper (if glazing is severe, machining will be required)
3 Drums or discs heat checked	3 Check discs and/or drums for hard spots, heat checking, etc. Have discs/drums machined or replace them
4 Disc runout or drum out-of-round excessive	4 Measure disc runout and/or drum out-of-round, have discs or drums machined or replace them
5 Loose or worn wheel bearings	5 Adjust or replace wheel bearings
6 Loose or bent brake backing plate (drum brakes)	6 Tighten or replace backing plate
7 Grooves worn in discs or drums	7 Have discs or drums machined, if within limits (if not, replace them)
8 Brake linings contaminated (brake fluid, grease, etc.)	8 Locate and repair source of contamination, replace pads or shoes
9 Excessive dust buildup on linings	9 Wash brakes with brake system cleaner
10 Surface finish on discs or drums too rough after machining	10 Have discs or drums properly machined (especially on vehicles with sliding calipers)
11 Brake pads or shoes glazed	11 Deglaze or replace brake pads or shoes

Brake pads or shoes click

1 Shoe support pads on brake backing plate grooved or excessively worn	1 Replace brake backing plate
2 Brake pads loose in caliper	2 Loose pad retainers or anti-rattle clips
3 Also see items listed under Brakes chatter	

Brakes make groaning noise at end of stop

1 Brake pads and/or shoes worn out	1 Replace pads and/or shoes
2 Brake linings contaminated (brake fluid, grease, etc.)	2 Locate and repair cause of contamination, replace brake pads or shoes
3 Brake linings glazed	3 Deglaze or replace brake pads or shoes
4 Excessive dust buildup on linings	4 Wash brakes with brake system cleaner
5 Scored or heat-checked discs or drums	5 Inspect discs/drums, have machined if within limits (if not, replace discs or drums)
6 Broken or missing brake shoe attaching hardware	6 Inspect drum brakes, replace missing hardware

Rear brakes lock up under light brake application

1 Tire pressures too high	1 Adjust tire pressures
2 Tires excessively worn	2 Replace tires
3 Defective proportioning valve	3 Replace proportioning valve

Brake warning light on instrument panel comes on (or stays on)

1 Low fluid level in master cylinder reservoir (reservoirs with fluid level sensor)	1 Add fluid, inspect system for leak, check the thickness of the brake pads and shoes
2 Failure in one half of the hydraulic system	2 Inspect hydraulic system for a leak
3 Piston in pressure differential warning valve not centered	3 Center piston by bleeding one circuit or the other (close bleeder valve as soon as the light goes out)

Troubleshooting (continued)

PROBABLE CAUSE	CORRECTIVE ACTION

Brake warning light on instrument panel comes on (or stays on) (continued)

4 Defective pressure differential valve or warning switch	4 Replace valve or switch
5 Air in the hydraulic system	5 Bleed the system, check for leaks
6 Brake pads worn out (vehicles with electric wear sensors - small probes that fit into the brake pads and ground out on the disc when the pads get thin)	6 Replace brake pads (and sensors)

Brakes do not self adjust

Disc brakes

1 Defective caliper piston seals	1 Replace calipers. Also, possible contaminated fluid causing soft or swollen seals (flush system and fill with new fluid if in doubt)
2 Corroded caliper piston(s)	2 Same as above

Drum brakes

1 Adjuster screw frozen	1 Remove adjuster, disassemble, clean and lubricate with high-temperature grease
2 Adjuster lever does not contact star wheel or is binding	2 Inspect drum brakes, assemble correctly or clean or replace parts as required
3 Adjusters mixed up (installed on wrong wheels after brake job)	3 Reassemble correctly
4 Adjuster cable broken or installed incorrectly (cable-type adjusters)	4 Install new cable or assemble correctly

Rapid brake lining wear

1 Driver resting left foot on brake pedal	1 Don't ride the brakes
2 Surface finish on discs or drums too rough	2 Have discs or drums properly machined
3 Also see Brakes drag	

3   Anti-lock Brake System (ABS) - general information

General information

1   The Anti-lock Brake System is designed to maintain vehicle steerability, directional stability and optimum deceleration under severe braking conditions on most road surfaces. It does so by monitoring the rotational speed of each wheel and controlling the brake line pressure to each wheel during braking. This prevents the wheels from locking up.

2   The basic ABS system has three main components: the wheel speed sensors, an electronic control unit and a hydraulic unit. The four wheel speed sensors - one at each wheel - send a variable voltage signal to the control unit, which monitors these signals, compares them to its program and determines whether a wheel is traveling at the same speed as the other wheels. When a wheel is about to lock up, the control unit signals the hydraulic unit to reduce the hydraulic pressure (or not increase the braking pressure any further) at that wheel's brake caliper. Pressure modulation is handled by electrically operated solenoid valves within the hydraulic control unit (**see illustration**).

3   Today's ABS systems incorporate the same functions of the basic ABS, but now have a larger capacity to adapt to the ever changing road conditions with the ICU (Integrated Control Unit), the HCU (Hydraulic Control Unit), and the ABM (AntiLock Brake Module). The ABS uses the four wheel speed sensors mounted at each wheel to determine the speed of each individual wheel by calculating the tire circumference based on the input data. A steering angle sensor, which is mounted on the steering column, works with the EPS (Electronic Power Steering module - part of the steering gear assembly) to inform the ABS system of the position of the steered wheels. A DSM (Dynamic Sensor Module), a yaw rate, longitudinal and lateral acceleration sensors located in the ORC (Occupants Restraint Controller) are used to verify the pitch and tilt of the vehicle and the exact forward momentum. Not only is information received, but is also sent from the ICU to other modules such as the PCM, to dictate the correct throttle angle and response, transmission control, and engine rpm for a given situation. This information is passed on to operate and control the ESC (Electronic Stability Control) system and the TCS (Traction Control System). This is all accomplished on a high-speed data line that is interconnected to each module located in the vehicle.

4   If a problem develops within the system, an ABS warning light will illuminate on the dashboard. Sometimes, a visual inspection of the ABS system can help you locate the problem. Carefully inspect the ABS wiring harness. Pay particularly close attention to the harness and connections near each wheel. Look for signs of chafing and other damage caused by incorrectly routed wires. If a wheel speed sensor harness is damaged, it must be replaced along with the sensor (if they are assembled together). **Warning:** *Do NOT try to repair an ABS wiring harness. The ABS system is sensitive to even the smallest changes in resistance. Repairing the harness could alter resistance values and cause the system to malfunction. If the ABS wiring harness is damaged in any way, it must be replaced.* **Caution:** *Make sure the ignition is turned off before unplugging or reattaching any electrical connections.*

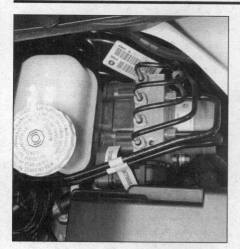

3.2 The integrated electronic and hydraulic control unit is located in the left rear corner of the engine compartment below the master cylinder

3.10a The front wheel speed sensor is mounted to the steering knuckle

3.10b The rear wheel speed sensor is mounted to the top of the rear knuckle

Diagnosis and repair

5   If the ABS warning light comes on and stays on while the vehicle is in operation, the ABS system requires attention. Although special electronic ABS diagnostic testing tools are necessary to properly diagnose the system, you can perform a few preliminary checks before taking the vehicle to a dealer service department.

a) *Check the brake fluid level in the reservoir.*
b) *Verify that the computer electrical connectors are securely connected.*
c) *Check the electrical connectors at the hydraulic control unit.*
d) *Check the fuses.*
e) *Follow the wiring harness to each wheel and verify that all connections are secure and that the wiring is undamaged.*

6   If the above preliminary checks do not solve the problem, the vehicle should be diagnosed by a dealer service department or other qualified repair shop. Due to the complex nature of the ABS system, all actual repair work must be done by a qualified automotive technician.

Wheel speed sensor - removal and installation

7   Loosen the wheel lug bolts, then raise the vehicle and support it securely on jackstands. Remove the wheel.

8   Make sure the ignition key is turned to the Off position.

9   Trace the wiring back from the sensor, detaching all brackets, grommets and clips while noting its correct routing, then disconnect the electrical connector. The front speed sensor electrical connector may be easier to reach on some models from under the hood. To reach the electrical connector for the rear speed sensor(s), remove the cargo floor cover.

10   Remove the mounting fasteners and carefully detach the sensor from the steering knuckle or rear knuckle (**see illustrations**).

Note: *The rear sensor on AWD models is held in place by a spring-loaded retainer.*

11   Installation is the reverse of the removal procedure. Tighten the bolt to the torque listed in this Chapter's Specifications.

12   Install the wheel and lug bolts, then lower the vehicle and tighten the lug bolts to the Chapter 1 Specifications.

4   Disc brake pads - replacement

Warning: *Disc brake pads must be replaced on both front or both rear wheels at the same time; never replace the pads on only one side. Also, the dust created by the brake system is harmful to your health. Never blow it out with compressed air and don't inhale any of it. An approved filtering mask should be worn when working on the brakes. Do not,*

under any circumstances, use petroleum-based solvents to clean brake parts. Use brake system cleaner only!

Caution: *Don't depress the brake pedal with the caliper removed.*

1   Using a syringe or equivalent, remove approximately two-thirds of the fluid from the master cylinder reservoir and discard it.

Caution: *Brake fluid will damage paint. If any fluid is spilled, wash it off immediately with plenty of clean, cold water.*

2   Loosen the wheel bolts, raise the end of the vehicle you will be working on and support it securely on jackstands. Block the wheels that remain on the ground.

3   Remove the wheels. Work on one brake assembly at a time, using the assembled brake for reference if necessary.

Front

4   Position a drain pan under the brake assembly and clean the caliper and surrounding area with brake system cleaner (**see illustration**).

4.4 Spray the disc and brake pads with brake cleaner to remove brake dust; DO NOT blow brake dust off with compressed air - collect the contaminated fluid in a suitable container and dispose of it properly!

5   Push the piston back into its bore using a C-clamp **(see illustration)**. As the piston is depressed to the bottom of the caliper bore, the fluid in the master cylinder will rise as the brake fluid is displaced. Make sure it doesn't overflow. If necessary, remove more of the fluid.

6   To replace the brake pads, follow the accompanying photos, beginning with **illustration 4.6a**. Stay in order and read the caption under each illustration.

7   While the pads are removed, inspect the caliper for brake fluid leaks and ruptures of the piston dust boot. Replace the caliper if necessary (see Section 5). Also inspect the brake disc carefully (see Section 6). If machining is necessary, follow the information in that section to remove the disc. Inspect the brake hoses for damage and replace if necessary (see Section 8).

8   Before installing the caliper, clean and inspect the caliper mounting bolts for corro-sion and damage. If they're significantly cor-roded or damaged, replace them. Also check the guide pin rubber bushings for wear. When installing the caliper, tighten the mounting bolts to the torque listed in this Chapter's Specifications.

9   Repeat the procedure on the opposite wheel, then install the wheels and bolts, lower the vehicle back to the ground and tighten the wheel bolts to the torque listed in the Chapter 1 Specifications.

10   Add the specified type of brake fluid to the reservoir until it's full (see Chapter 1).

11   Pump the brake pedal a few times to bring the pads into contact with the disc. Check the level of the brake fluid, adding some if necessary.

12   Check the operation of the brakes care-fully before placing the vehicle into normal service. Try to avoid heavy brake application until the brakes have been applied several times to seat the pads.

Warning: *The first time you apply the brakes, the pedal will fall a great deal further than you are expecting. Be aware of this before you try to move the vehicle. Pump the brakes until the pedal returns to its normal position. Check for any leaks or misaligned components if the pedal does not return to the normal position.*

Rear

13   Refer to Section 11 and retract the caliper pistons, placing them in the "service mode."

14   Disconnect the cable from the negative terminal of the battery (see Chapter 5, Sec-tion 3).

Caution: *Any time the rear calipers are go-ing to be removed, always have all the battery voltage sources disconnected. Failure to do so could allow the electronic parking brake to operate and screw outward to the point that the caliper will become un-serviceable and will need to be replaced.*

4.5 Use a C-clamp to press the caliper piston into its bore

4.6a Remove the caliper lower mounting bolt . . .

4.6b. . . then rotate the caliper up on the mounting bracket

4.6c Remove the outer brake pad

4.6d Remove the inner brake pad

4.6e Remove the upper brake pad support plate from the caliper bracket

4.6f Remove the lower brake pad support plate from the caliper bracket

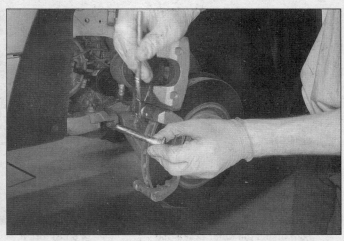

4.6g Pull out the lower guide pin and clean it, then apply a coat of high-temperature grease to the pin and reinstall it in the caliper bracket

4.6h Slide the caliper and upper guide pin from the mounting bracket, then clean and lubricate it, then reinsert it into the mounting bracket

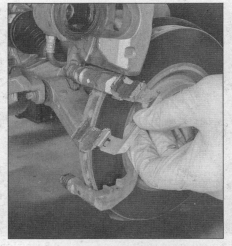

4.6i Clean the support plates and lubricate the pad contact areas with high-temperature brake grease

4.6j Press the lower support plate in firmly by hand . . .

4.6k . . . followed by the upper support plate

4.6l Install the inner brake pad. The inner pad is the one with the wear indicator, which must be positioned at the top

4.6m Install the outer brake pad

4.6n Before lowering the caliper into position, be sure the pads are facing in the right direction and are seated in the caliper bracket and support plates

4.6o Lower the caliper, then install and tighten the caliper mounting bolt to the torque listed in this Chapter's Specifications

4.16a Use an open-end wrench to hold the caliper guide pin while loosening and tightening the mounting bolt

4.16b Swing the caliper up and support it in this position with a length of wire

15   Position a drain pan under the brake assembly and clean the caliper and surrounding area with brake system cleaner (**see illustration 4.4**).

16   Remove the caliper lower mounting bolt, then pivot the caliper up and support it with a length of wire (**see illustrations**), then follow the illustrations for the front brake pads starting with **illustration 4.6c**.

17   While the pads are removed, inspect the caliper for brake fluid leaks and ruptures of the piston dust boot. Replace the caliper if necessary (see Section 5). Also inspect the brake disc carefully (see Section 6). If machining is necessary, follow the information in that Section to remove the disc. Inspect the brake hoses for damage and replace if necessary (see Section 8).

18   Before installing the caliper mounting bolts, clean and inspect them for corrosion and damage. If they're significantly corroded or damaged, replace them. Also check the guide pin rubber bushings for wear. Tighten the bolt to the torque listed in this Chapter's Specifications.

19   Repeat the procedure on the opposite wheel, then install the wheels and wheel bolts, lower the vehicle and tighten the bolts to the torque listed in the Chapter 1 Specifications.

20   Follow the procedure for reactivating the parking brake (see Section 11).

21   Add the specified type of brake fluid to the reservoir until it's up to the appropriate level (see Chapter 1).

22   Pump the brake pedal a few times to bring the pads into contact with the disc. Check the level of the brake fluid, adding some if necessary.

23   Check the operation of the brakes carefully before placing the vehicle into normal service. Try to avoid heavy brake application until the brakes have been applied several times to seat the pads.

Warning: *The first time you apply the brake, the pedal will fall a great deal further than you are expecting. Be aware of this before you try to move the vehicle. Pump the brakes until the pedal returns to its normal position. Check for any leaks or misaligned components if the pedal does not return to the normal position.*

---

5   Disc brake caliper - removal and installation

Warning: *Dust created by the brake system is harmful to your health. Never blow it out with compressed air and don't inhale any of it. An approved filtering mask should be worn when working on the brakes. Do not, under any circumstances, use petroleum-based solvents to clean brake parts. Use brake system cleaner only.*

Note: *If replacement is indicated (usually because of fluid leakage), it is recommended that the calipers be replaced, not overhauled. New and factory rebuilt units are available on an exchange basis. Always replace the calipers in pairs - never replace just one of them.*

Note: *Depressing the brake pedal about one inch and holding it there with a suitable device will minimize fluid leakage when the brake hoses/lines are disconnected.*

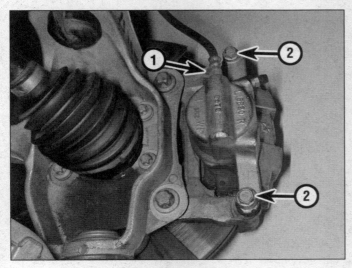

5.2 Front brake caliper mounting details
1 Brake hose fitting   2 Caliper mounting bolts

5.5 Rear brake caliper mounting details

1 Parking brake actuator electrical connector
2 Brake line bracket nut
3 Brake line fitting
4 Caliper mounting bolts
5 Caliper guide pins

Removal

1   Loosen the wheel bolts, then raise the vehicle and support it securely on jackstands. Remove the wheel.

Front

2   Loosen (but do not try to unscrew) the brake hose fitting, then remove the caliper mounting bolts **(see illustration)**. Remove the caliper from the bracket, then unscrew the caliper from the hose. Plug the brake hose to keep contaminants out of the brake system and to prevent losing any more brake fluid than is necessary.

Rear

Caution: *Any time a rear caliper is going to be removed, always have all the battery voltage sources disconnected. Failure to do so could allow the electronic parking brake to operate and screw outward to the point that the caliper will become un-serviceable and will need to be replaced.*

3   Refer to Section 11 and retract the caliper pistons, placing them in the "service mode."
4   Disconnect the cable from the negative terminal of the battery (see Chapter 5, Section 3).
5   Disconnect the electrical connector from the parking brake actuator **(see illustration)**.
6   Unscrew the brake line bracket nut and detach the bracket from the stud on the caliper upper mounting bolt.
7   Unscrew the brake line fitting from the caliper. Plug the brake hose to keep contaminants out of the brake system and to prevent losing any more brake fluid than is necessary.
Note: *If the caliper is being removed for access to other components, don't disconnect the hose.*
8   Remove the caliper mounting bolts, then detach the caliper from the mounting bracket.
Note: *Use an open-end wrench to hold the caliper guide pins while loosening and tightening the mounting bolts (see illustration 4.16a).*

Installation

9   Install the caliper by reversing the removal procedure. On front calipers, thread the caliper onto the brake hose until it is partially tight, then install the caliper to the mounting bracket and tighten the hose fitting securely; make sure the hose isn't twisted. Tighten the caliper mounting bolts to the torque listed in this Chapter's Specifications.
10   On rear calipers, follow the procedure for reactivating the parking brake (see Section 11).
11   Bleed the brake circuit (see Section 9). Make sure there are no leaks from the hose connections.
Warning: *The first time you apply the brake, the pedal will fall a great deal further than you are expecting. Be aware of this before you try to move the vehicle. Pump the brakes until the pedal returns to its normal position. Check for any leaks or misaligned components if the pedal does not return to the normal position.*
12   Test the brakes carefully before returning the vehicle to normal service.

6   Brake disc - inspection, removal and installation

Warning: *Dust created by the brake system is harmful to your health. Never blow it out with compressed air and don't inhale any of it. An approved filtering mask should be worn when working on the brakes. Do not, under any circumstances, use petroleum-based solvents to clean brake parts. Use brake system cleaner only.*
Note: *This procedure applies to both front and rear brake discs.*

Inspection

1   Loosen the wheel lug bolts, raise the vehicle and support it securely on jackstands. Remove the wheel and reinstall the wheel bolts to hold the disc in place (washers may

be required). If the rear brake disc is being worked on, release the parking brake, see Section 11, then disconnect the cable from the negative terminal of the battery (see Chapter 5, Section 3).
2   Remove the brake caliper and pads (see Sections 4 and 5). Don't disconnect the brake hose from the caliper, or you'll have to bleed the brakes when everything is reassembled. After removing the caliper, suspend it out of the way with a piece of wire.
3   Visually inspect the disc surface for score marks and other damage. Light scratches and shallow grooves are normal after use and may not always be detrimental to brake operation, but deep scoring requires disc removal and refinishing by an automotive machine shop. Check both sides of the disc **(see illustration)**. If pulsating has been noticed during application of the brakes, suspect excessive disc runout.

6.3 The brake pads on this vehicle were obviously neglected - they wore down completely and cut deep grooves into the disc (wear this severe means the disc must be replaced)

6.4a Use a dial indicator to measure disc runout - if the reading exceeds the maximum allowable runout limit, the disc will have to be machined or replaced

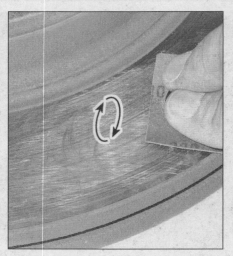

6.4b Using a swirling motion, remove the glaze from the disc surface with sandpaper or emery cloth

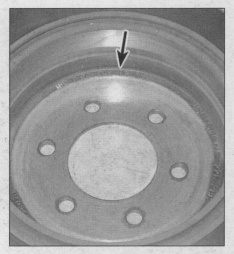

6.5a The minimum wear dimension is cast into the back side of the disc on most vehicles (typical)

6.5b Use a micrometer to measure disc thickness

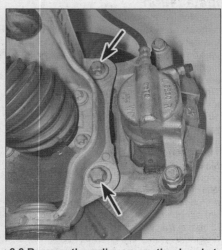

6.6 Remove the caliper mounting bracket bolts and remove the bracket (front caliper shown, rear similar)

6.7 Disc retaining bolt

4   To check disc runout, place a dial indicator at a point about 1/2-inch from the outer edge of the disc **(see illustration)**. Set the indicator to zero and turn the disc. The indicator reading should not exceed the specified allowable runout limit. If it does, the disc should be refinished by an automotive machine shop.

Note: *The discs should be resurfaced regardless of the dial indicator reading, as this will impart a smooth finish and ensure a perfectly flat surface, eliminating any brake pedal pulsation or other undesirable symptoms related to questionable discs. At the very least, if you elect not to have the discs resurfaced, remove the glaze from the surface with emery cloth using a swirling motion (see illustration).*

5   It's absolutely critical that the disc not be machined to a thickness under the specified minimum allowable thickness. The minimum

thickness is cast into the inside of the disc **(see illustration)** or on the perimeter of the disc. The disc thickness can be checked with a micrometer **(see illustration)**.

Removal

6   Remove the caliper mounting bracket bolts **(see illustration)** and remove the bracket from the knuckle.

7   Remove the wheel bolts which were put on to hold the disc in place. Remove the disc retaining bolt **(see illustration)**, then remove the disc from the hub.

Installation

8   Place the disc in position and install the retaining bolt, tightening it to the torque listed in this Chapter's Specifications. Install the mounting bracket, tightening the bolts to the torque listed in this Chapter's Specifications.

9   Install the brake pads and caliper (see Section 4). Tighten the caliper mounting bolts to the torque listed in this Chapter's Specifications.

10   Install the wheel and wheel bolts, then lower the vehicle and tighten the bolts to the torque listed in the Chapter 1 Specifications.

11   Pump the brake pedal a few times to bring the brake pads into contact with the disc. Bleeding won't be necessary unless the brake hose was disconnected from the caliper. Check the operation of the brakes carefully before driving the vehicle.

Warning: *The first time you apply the brake, the pedal will fall a great deal further than you are expecting. Be aware of this before you try to move the vehicle. Pump the brakes until the pedal returns to its normal position. Check for any leaks or misaligned components if the pedal does not return to the normal position.*

6.13 Backing plate bolts

7.7 Unscrew these two fittings from the ABS ICU

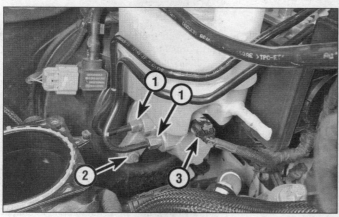

7.8 Master cylinder details:

1 Brake line fittings
2 Mounting nut
   (other nut not visible)
3 Fluid level switch
   electrical connector

7.11 The best way to bleed air from the master cylinder before installing it on the vehicle is with a pair of bleeder tubes that direct brake fluid into the reservoir during bleeding

Backing plate removal

12 Remove the disc.

13 Remove the three retaining bolts from the backing plate (**see illustration**).

14 Installation is the reverse of removal. Tighten all fasteners to the torque values listed in this Chapter's Specifications. Tighten the wheel bolts to the torque listed in the Chapter 1 Specifications.

7 Master cylinder - removal and installation

Caution: *Brake fluid will quickly damage paint. Cover all body parts and be careful not to spill fluid during any of the following procedures. Wipe up any spilled fluid immediately and then flush the area thoroughly with water.*

Removal

Note: *The master cylinder is located in the engine compartment, mounted to the power brake booster.*

1 Disconnect the cable from the negative terminal of the battery (see Chapter 5).

2 Pump the brake pedal several times to relieve the vacuum reserve inside the power brake booster.

Note: *Pumping the brake pedal several times (at least 4 or 5 times) before removing the master cylinder will prevent contaminants from being sucked into the power brake booster when the master cylinder is removed.*

3 Remove the engine cover, if equipped.

4 Remove the Power Distribution Center (PDC).

5 Using a syringe or equivalent, siphon the brake fluid from the master cylinder reservoir and dispose of it properly.

6 Disconnect the brake fluid level switch connector and move the harness out of the way.

7 Place rags under the fluid fittings and prepare caps or plastic bags to cover the ends of the lines once they are disconnected. Unscrew the fittings at the ends of the master cylinder brake lines where they are attached to the ABS Integrated Control Unit (ICU) (**see illustration**). Pull the brake lines slightly away and quickly plug the ends to prevent contamination.

Caution: *To prevent rounding off the corners on these nuts, the use of a flare-nut wrench,*

which wraps around the nut, is preferred.

8 Thoroughly clean the area where the master cylinder mounts to the power booster. Remove the nuts attaching the master cylinder to the power booster. Pull the master cylinder off the studs and out of the engine compartment. Again, be careful not to spill any fluid as this is done (**see illustration**).

Caution: *Be careful not to lose the "O" ring seal between the master cylinder and the booster.*

9 If necessary, disengage the retaining tabs holding the reservoir and transfer the reservoir to the new master cylinder.

Note: *Install new seals between the master cylinder and reservoir.*

Installation

10 Bench bleed the new master cylinder before installing it. Mount the master cylinder in a vise, with the jaws of the vise clamping on the mounting flange.

11 Attach a pair of master cylinder bleeder tubes to the outlet ports of the master cylinder (**see illustration**).

12 Fill the reservoir with brake fluid of the recommended type (see Chapter 1).

13   Slowly push the pistons into the master cylinder (a large Phillips screwdriver can be used for this) - air will be expelled from the pressure chambers and into the reservoir. Because the tubes are submerged in fluid, air can't be drawn back into the master cylinder when you release the pistons.

14   Repeat the procedure until no more air bubbles are present.

15   Remove the bleed tubes, one at a time, and install plugs in the open ports to prevent fluid leakage and air from entering. Install the reservoir cap.

16   Replace the vacuum seal "O" ring between the master cylinder and the power booster.

Warning: *Do not skip this step or a vacuum leak could occur and render the power booster ineffective; this results in greatly increased pedal effort and longer stopping distances.*

Warning: *The manufacturer states that new master cylinder mounting nuts should be used.*

17   Install the master cylinder over the studs on the power brake booster and tighten the attaching nuts only finger-tight at this time.

18   Carefully thread the brake line fittings into the ICU. Since the master cylinder is still a bit loose, it can be moved slightly in order for the fittings to thread in easily. Do not strip the threads as the fittings are tightened.

Warning: *Do not use a wrench on the fittings until you can easily thread them on by hand. Use a flare wrench for final tightening.*

19   Fully tighten the mounting nuts, and then the brake line fittings. Tighten the nuts to the torque listed in this Chapter's Specifications.

20   Fill the master cylinder reservoir with fluid, and if needed, bleed the master cylinder and the brake system (see Section 9). To bleed the cylinder on the vehicle, have an assistant depress the brake pedal and hold the pedal to the floor. Loosen the master cylinder brake line fittings at the ICU, one at a time, to allow air and fluid to escape. Repeat this procedure on both fittings until the fluid is clear of air bubbles.

Caution: *Have plenty of rags on hand to catch the fluid - brake fluid will ruin painted surfaces. After the bleeding procedure is completed, rinse the area under the master cylinder thoroughly with clean water.*

21   Bleed the remainder of the brake system (see Section 9).

22   Install the ICU and the engine cover, then reconnect the battery.

23   Test the operation of the brake system carefully before placing the vehicle into normal service.

Warning: *Do not operate the vehicle if you are in doubt about the effectiveness of the brake system. It is possible for air to become trapped in the anti-lock brake system hydraulic control unit; if the pedal continues to feel spongy after repeated bleedings or the BRAKE or ANTI-LOCK light stays on, have the vehicle towed to a dealer service department or other qualified shop to be bled with the aid of a scan tool.*

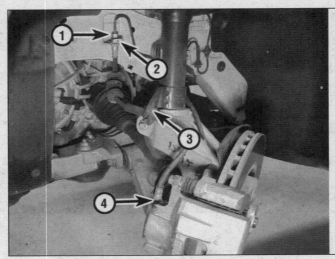

8.3 Front brake hose/ line details

1 Brake line fitting
2 Brake hose retaining clip
3 Brake hose-to-strut bracket
4 Brake hose fitting at caliper

8   Brake hoses and lines - inspection and replacement

Brake hose inspection

1   Whenever the vehicle is raised and supported securely on jackstands, the rubber hoses which connect the steel brake lines with the front and rear brake assemblies should be inspected for cracks, chafing of the outer cover, leaks, blisters and other damage. These are important and vulnerable parts of the brake system and inspection should be thorough. A light and mirror will be helpful for a complete check. If a hose exhibits any of the above conditions, replace it immediately.

Flexible hose replacement

Note: *Depressing the brake pedal about one inch and holding it there with a suitable device will minimize fluid leakage when the brake hoses/lines are disconnected.*

Front

2   Clean all dirt away from the hose and line fittings.

3   Using a flare-nut wrench, disconnect the metal brake line from the hose fitting and immediately plug the metal line to prevent excessive leakage and contamination **(see illustration)**. Be careful not to bend the metal line. If the threaded fitting is corroded, spray it with a penetrating oil and allow it to soak in for about 10 minutes, then try again. If you try to break loose a brake tube nut that's stuck, you will kink the metal line, which will then have to be replaced.

4   Remove the clip retaining the brake hose to the bracket.

5   Detach the hose grommet from the bracket on the strut.

6   Unscrew the hose fitting from the brake caliper.

7   Attach the new brake hose to the caliper.

8   Tighten the hose fitting to the torque listed this Chapter's Specifications.

9   Attach the brake hose bracket to the strut, making sure the hose isn't kinked or twisted. Then connect the hose to the bracket on the chassis and install the retaining clip.

10   Connect the metal line to the hose fitting, tightening the fitting securely.

Rear

11   Clean all dirt away from the hose and line fittings.

12   Using a flare-nut wrench, disconnect the metal brake line from each end of the hose and immediately plug the metal line to prevent excessive leakage and contamination **(see illustration)**. Be careful not to bend the metal line. If the threaded fitting is corroded, spray it with a penetrating oil and allow it to soak in for about 10 minutes, then try again. If you try to break loose a brake tube nut that's stuck, you will kink the metal line, which will then have to be replaced.

13   Remove the clip retaining the brake hose to the bracket.

14   Remove the brake hose bracket nut and detach the bracket from the caliper.

15   Connect the hose bracket to the caliper and install the nut, tightening it securely.

16   Connect the forward end of the hose to the bracket on the knuckle and install the retaining clip.

17   Connect the brake line fittings to the hose and tighten them securely.

Front or rear

18   Carefully check to make sure the suspension or steering components don't make contact with the hose. Have an assistant push down on the vehicle while you watch to see whether the hose interferes with suspension operation. If you're replacing a front hose, have your assistant turn the steering wheel lock-to-lock while you make sure the hose doesn't interfere with the steering linkage or the steering knuckle.

19   After installation, check the master cylinder fluid level and add fluid as necessary. Bleed the brakes (see Section 9). Carefully

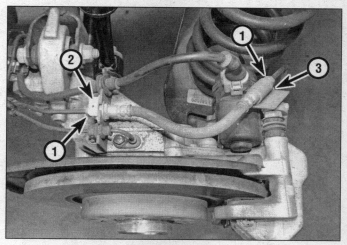

8.12 Rear brake hose/line details (disc brake model)

1   Brake line fitting
2   Brake hose retaining clip
3   Brake hose bracket nut

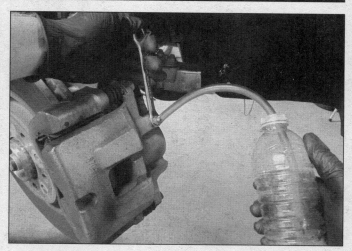

9.8 When bleeding the brakes, a hose is connected to the bleed screw at the caliper or wheel cylinder and then submerged in clean brake fluid - air will be seen as bubbles exiting the tube (all air must be expelled before moving to the next wheel)

test brake operation before resuming normal operation.

Metal brake line replacement

20   When replacing brake lines, be sure to use the correct parts. Do not use copper tubing for any brake system components. Purchase steel brake lines from a dealer parts department or auto parts store.

21   Prefabricated brake lines, with the tube ends already flared and fittings installed, are available at auto parts stores and dealer parts departments. These lines can be bent to the proper shapes using a tubing bender.

22   When installing the new line make sure it's well supported in the brackets and has plenty of clearance between moving or hot components. Make sure you tighten the fittings securely.

23   After installation, check the master cylinder fluid level and add fluid as necessary. Bleed the brakes (see Section 9). Carefully test brake operation before resuming normal operation.

9   Brake system - bleeding

Warning: *The following procedure is a manual bleeding procedure. This is the only bleeding procedure which can be performed at home without special tools. However, if air has found its way into the hydraulic control unit, the entire system must be bled manually, then with a DRB scan tool (or equivalent), then manually a second time. If the brake pedal feels spongy even after bleeding the brakes, or the ABS light on the instrument panel does not go off, or if you have any doubts whatsoever about the effectiveness of the brake system, have the vehicle towed to a dealer service department or other repair shop equipped with the necessary tools for bleeding the system.*

Warning: *Wear eye protection when bleeding the brake system. If the fluid comes in contact with your eyes, immediately rinse them with water and seek medical attention.*

Note: *Bleeding the hydraulic system is necessary to remove any air that manages to find its way into the system when it's been opened during removal and installation of a hydraulic component.*

1   It will be necessary to bleed the complete system if air has entered the system due to low fluid level, or if the brake lines have been disconnected at the master cylinder.

2   If a brake line was disconnected only at a wheel, then only that caliper or wheel cylinder must be bled.

3   If a brake line is disconnected at a fitting located between the master cylinder and any of the brakes, that part of the system served by the disconnected line must be bled. The following procedure describes bleeding the entire system, however.

4   Remove any residual vacuum from the brake power booster by applying the brake several times with the engine off.

5   Remove the cap from the master cylinder reservoir and fill the reservoir with brake fluid. Reinstall the cap.

Note: *Check the fluid level often during the bleeding operation and add fluid as necessary to prevent the fluid level from falling low enough to allow air bubbles into the master cylinder.*

6   Have an assistant on hand, as well as a supply of new brake fluid, a clear container partially filled with clean brake fluid, a length of clear tubing to fit over the bleeder valve and a wrench to open and close the bleeder valve.

7   Begin the bleeding process by bleeding the first wheel in the bleeding sequence, loosen the bleeder valve slightly, then tighten it to a point where it is snug but can still be loosened quickly and easily. The bleeding

sequence is as follows:

a)   Left rear
b)   Right front
c)   Right rear
d)   Left front

8   Place one end of the hose over the bleeder valve and submerge the other end in brake fluid in the container **(see illustration)**.

9   Have the assistant push the brake pedal slowly to the floor, then hold the pedal firmly depressed.

10   While the pedal is held depressed, open the bleeder valve just enough to allow a flow of fluid to leave the valve. Watch for air bubbles to exit the submerged end of the tube. When the fluid flow slows after a couple of seconds, close the valve and have your assistant release the pedal.

11   Repeat Steps 9 and 10 until no more air is seen leaving the tube, then tighten the bleeder valve and proceed to bleed the other calipers/wheel cylinders, in the proper sequence, using the same procedure. Check the fluid in the master cylinder reservoir frequently.

Note: *Be careful not to over-tighten the bleeder valve.*

12   Never use old brake fluid. It contains moisture which can boil, rendering the brakes inoperative.

13   Refill the master cylinder with fluid at the end of the operation.

14   Check the operation of the brakes. The pedal should feel solid when depressed, with no sponginess. If necessary, repeat the entire process.

Warning: *If, after bleeding the system, you do not have a firm brake pedal, if the ABS light on the instrument panel does not go off, or if you have any doubts whatsoever about the effectiveness of the brake system, have it towed to a dealer service department or other repair shop to have the system bled.*

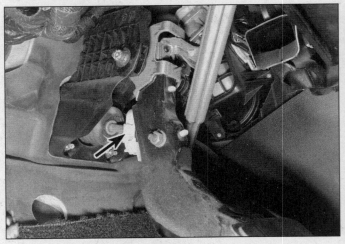

10.11 Booster pushrod keeper retainer clip (left side shown, other side identical)

10.12 Power brake booster mounting nuts

10 Power brake booster - check, removal and installation

Note: *The power brake booster unit requires no special maintenance apart from periodic inspection of the vacuum hoses and the case. The booster should never be disassembled. If a problem develops, it must be replaced with a new one.*

Operating check

1   Depress the pedal and start the engine. If the pedal goes down slightly, operation is normal.

2   Depress the brake pedal several times with the engine running and make sure that there is no change in the pedal reserve distance.

Airtightness check

3   Start the engine and turn it off after one or two minutes. Depress the brake pedal several times slowly. If the pedal goes down farther the first time but gradually rises after the second or third depression, the booster is airtight.

4   Depress the brake pedal while the engine is running, then stop the engine with the pedal depressed. If there is no change in the pedal reserve travel after holding the pedal for 30 seconds, the booster is airtight.

Removal

5   Remove any vacuum from the booster by pumping the pedal several times with the engine off, until the pedal feels hard to push.

6   Remove the Power Distribution Center (PDC, see Chapter 12), and the ABS ICU and its mounting bracket.

7   Clean the area where the master cylinder attaches to the power brake booster.

8   Remove the master cylinder (see Section 7). Also disconnect the brake lines from the junction block below the power brake booster. Plug all open lines.

9   Disconnect the vacuum hose from the check valve that's located on the outside of the brake booster. Also disconnect the electrical connector from the vacuum sensor.
Warning: *Do not remove the check valve from the booster.*

10   Working under the dash, remove the knee bolster (see Chapter 11), then disconnect and remove the brake light switch (see Section 12).

11   Disengage the clips on the pushrod keeper retainer, then slide the retainer upwards and detach the pushrod from the pedal **(see illustration)**. For safety reasons, discard the keeper retainer and buy a new one for reassembly.

12   Remove the nuts attaching the booster to the firewall **(see illustration)**.

13   Remove the nuts attaching the booster to the firewall.
Note: *If necessary for clearance, remove the steering intermediate shaft lower U-joint and disconnect the shaft from the steering gear input shaft.*

14   Working inside the engine compartment, carefully withdraw the brake booster unit from the firewall and out of the engine compartment.

Installation

15   To install the booster, place it into position on the firewall, then tighten the retaining nuts to the torque listed in this Chapter's Specifications. Connect the brake pedal to the brake booster pushrod using a *new* keeper retainer.
Warning: *DO NOT reuse the old booster pushrod keeper retainer.*

16   The remainder of installation is the reverse of removal. Install a new vacuum seal on the master cylinder before reinstalling it to the power brake booster.

17   Bleed the brake system (see Section 9).

18   Carefully test the operation of the brakes before placing the vehicle into normal operation.
Warning: *If, after bleeding the system, you do not have a firm brake pedal, if the ABS light on the instrument panel does not go off, or if you have any doubts whatsoever about the effectiveness of the brake system, have it towed to a dealer service department or other repair shop to have the system bled.*

11 Electric Parking Brake (EPB) - general information and servicing

Warning: *If the Electric Parking Brake (EPB) switch is activated at any time the rear caliper is removed and the battery was not disconnected, the EPB motor will sense this and fully extend the caliper piston outward. This will jam the piston and damage the caliper. The caliper will then have to be replaced.*

1   The EPB system consists of a warning light, switch, electronic controller, and two bi-directional motors attached to the rear calipers. The electromagnetically operated gears provide the clamping power to the rear brake pads.

2   There is no constant power to the bi-directional motors. Once they clamp down onto the pads, the internal motor amperage rise is the indication for the controller to remove the voltage. So any time the caliper has been removed and the battery was not disconnected there is a very likely chance the EPB will extend the caliper even more trying to reach that amperage load it requires to shut off the voltage supply.

Rear caliper piston retracting procedure (Service Mode)

Caution: *The caliper must be fully released in order to do any work on the rear brake pads or calipers.*

Note: *There are two ways to release the caliper. First is with a scanner that has the capabilities to perform such tasks. The other method can be done from the touch screen in the vehicle. If your vehicle is equipped with the*

11.6 Once you've entered the brake's Service Mode, select "Yes" to retract the rear caliper pistons

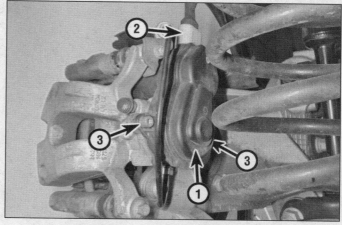

11.16 Parking brake actuator details:

1   Actuator
2   Electrical connector

3   Mounting bolts (forward bolt not visible here)

UConnect display system, follow these steps to complete the task.

Note: *Perform the retract procedure before disconnecting the battery.*

3   Release the parking brake.

4   From the on screen menu, select "Settings" from the bottom of the screen, then select the "Brakes" heading.

5   Select "Service Mode."

6   Select "Yes" to retract the electric parking brake (**see illustration**).

7   You may hear the parking brake motors run as the caliper pistons are retracted. This is perfectly normal.

8   Click the exit "X" to get back to the original screen.

9   Now it is safe to disconnect the IBS (Intelligent Battery Sensor) and then the negative battery terminal from the battery post (see Chapter 5, Section 3).

10   Loosen the wheel bolts on the rear wheels. Raise and support the vehicle on jackstands, then remove the wheels.

11   The rear brake caliper(s) can now be removed without the risk of damage.

12   When service is complete, reconnect the battery and follow the on-screen prompts to reset the rear caliper pistons to their normal operating positions.

Electric Parking Brake actuator

Removal and installation

13   Perform the caliper piston retraction procedure as described above.

14   Disconnect the Intelligent Battery Sensor (IBS), if equipped, then the negative battery cable from the battery. Isolate the cable to prevent it from accidentally coming in contact with the post at any time while you are working on the vehicle.

Caution: *Always disconnect the IBS connection at the battery prior to disconnecting the main battery terminal.*

15   Loosen the rear wheel bolts, then raise the rear of the vehicle and support it securely on jackstands. Remove the rear wheels.

16   Disconnect the EPB actuator wiring harness connector (**see illustration**).

17   Remove the two bolts securing the EPB actuator to the caliper.

18   Maneuver the actuator off of the caliper.

19   Be careful not to lose the O-ring seal between the caliper and the actuator.

20   Before replacing the unit, clean the surface thoroughly and replace the O-ring.

21   Installation is the reverse of removal.

22   Reconnect the cable to the negative terminal of the battery and reconnect the IBS electrical connector, if equipped.

Calibrating and resetting

23   Be sure the battery is fully charged and connected. If equipped with an IBS (Intelligent Battery Sensor), make sure it is connected as well.

24   Depress the brake pedal and hold it there. Using the EPB switch, set the switch to release, then to the applied position. Press the switch to the release position again, then back to the applied position. This will ensure both actuators are in sync and should function as designed.

12   Brake light switch - check, replacement and adjustment

1   The brake light switch is located along the arm of the brake pedal and is attached to a bracket near the power brake booster mount (**see illustration**). When the brake pedal is applied, the pedal arm moves away from the switch and a spring-loaded plunger closes the circuit to the brake lights.

2   Disconnect the cable from the negative terminal of the battery (see Chapter 5).

Check

Note: *Special hooked ohmmeter probes (or bent paperclips) may be necessary to access the terminals of the switch.*

3   Disconnect the electrical connector from the switch.

4   Using an ohmmeter, check for continuity between the outer two terminals of the switch. With the pedal released (at rest), there should be continuity. With the pedal depressed there should be no continuity.

5   With the probes of the ohmmeter on the inner two terminals, there should be no continuity with the pedal released and continuity with the pedal depressed.

Replacement

6   Rotate the brake light switch about 45-degrees in a counterclockwise direction to align the tabs, then remove it from the mounting bracket.

7   Unplug the electrical connector from the switch, remove the switch.

8   Install the switch into the bracket by aligning the slots, inserting the switch and rotating it about 45-degrees clockwise to lock it into place.

9   Plug the electrical connector into the switch.

10   Reconnect the battery and test the brake lights for proper operation.

12.1 Brake light switch location

Notes

Chapter 10
Suspension and steering systems

Contents

Specifications

Torque specifications

Ft-lbs (unless otherwise indicated)

Note: *One foot-pound (ft-lb) of torque is equivalent to 12 inch-pounds (in-lbs) of torque. Torque values below approximately 15 ft-lbs are expressed in inch-pounds, since most foot-pound torque wrenches are not accurate at these smaller values.*

Front suspension

Driveaxle/hub nut	See Chapter 8 Specifications
Control arm front pivot (horizontal) bolt*	
Step 1	35
Step 2	Tighten an additional 300 degrees
Control arm rear pivot (vertical) bolt/nut*	
Step 1	27
Step 2	Tighten an additional 106 degrees
Balljoint-to-control arm nut*	
Step 1	22
Step 2	Tighten an additional 95 degrees
Hub and bearing assembly-to-steering knuckle bolts*	83
Stabilizer bar	
Stabilizer bar link nuts	44
Bushing bolts	
Front	38
Rear	44
Strut-to-steering knuckle bolt/nut	77
Strut rod nut	48
Crossmember-to-front support beam bolts	
2016 and earlier models	70
2017 and later models	66
Crossmember	
M12 mounting bolts	97
M14 mounting bolts	93
Crossmember bolts above the control arms	
2016 and earlier models	89
2017 and later models	74
Load beam bracket bolts	70
Load beam extension bolts	33
Load beam link bolts	20
Wheel bolts	See Chapter 1 Specifications

*Replace with a new fastener(s) whenever removed

Rear suspension

Hub and bearing mounting bolts*	
2018 and earlier models	70
2019 models	82
Driveaxle/hub nut (AWD models)	See Chapter 8 Specifications
Shock absorber	
Shock to knuckle bolt	139
Shock upper mounting nuts	37
Shock rod nut	22
Stabilizer bar	
Link nuts	41
Bracket-to-crossmember bolts	
2018 and earlier models	44
2019 and later models	37
Trailing link-to-body mounting bolts	
2018 and earlier models	79
2019 models	81
Trailing link-to-knuckle bolts	90
Camber link-to-crossmember nut	
Step 1	44
Step 2	Tighten an additional 90 degrees
Camber link-to-knuckle nut	
Step 1	44
Step 2	Tighten an additional 90 degrees
Toe link-to-crossmember nut*	
2018 and earlier models	133
2019 models	96
Toe link-to-knuckle nut*	
2018 and earlier models	116
2019 models	122
Lower control arm-to-crossmember nut*	
2018 and earlier models	113
2019 models	92
Lower control arm-to-knuckle bolt*	
2018 and earlier models	
Step 1	59
Step 2	Tighten an additional 90 degrees
2019 models	85
Rear crossmember-to-body bolts	96
Wheel bolts	See Chapter 1 Specifications

Replace with a new fastener(s) whenever removed

Steering system

Steering wheel nut	37
Steering column mounting fasteners	18
Intermediate shaft bolt*	22
2018 and earlier models	22
2019 models	18
Tie-rod end-to-steering knuckle nut	
Step 1	22
Step 2	Tighten an additional 90 degrees
Steering gear mounting bolts	72

Replace with a new fastener(s) whenever removed

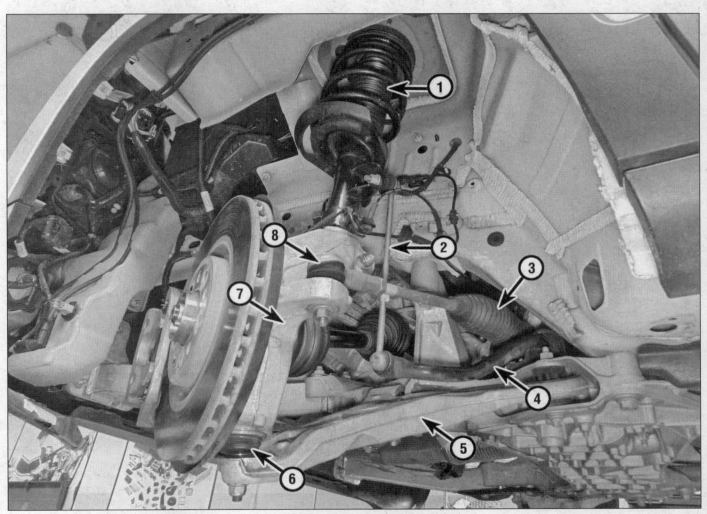

1.1 Front suspension and steering components

1	Strut assembly	4	Stabilizer bar	7	Steering knuckle
2	Stabilizer bar link	5	Control arm	8	Tie-rod end
3	Steering gear boot	6	Balljoint		

1   General information

Front suspension

1   The front suspension on these vehicles is a MacPherson strut design **(see illustration)**. The upper end of each strut is attached to the vehicle's body strut support. The lower end of the strut is connected to the upper end of the steering knuckle. The lower end of the steering knuckle is attached by a balljoint mounted to the outer end of the suspension control arm. The control arm is connected to the front suspension crossmember. A stabilizer bar, mounted to the crossmember and connected to the strut, reduces body roll while cornering.

1.2 Rear suspension components

1	Trailing link	4	Toe link	7	Crossmember
2	Camber link	5	Rear knuckle		
3	Coil spring	6	Lower control arm		

Rear suspension

2   The rear suspension is of a multi-link design, using camber links, toe-links, trailing links, lower control arms, coil springs, shock absorbers, and a stabilizer bar **(see illustration)**.

Steering

3   The Electric Power Steering (EPS) rack-and-pinion steering gear is attached to the front suspension main crossmember. The steering gear actuates the tie-rods, which are attached to the steering knuckles. The steering column is designed to collapse in the event of an accident.

4   The steering system utilizes a Steering Angle Sensor (SAS); this sensor informs various modules of the angle and speed at which the wheel is rotated during every phase of operation. The SAS is only serviced with the steering gear.

Note: *If the steering is replaced, it will require programming by a qualified repair facility using the latest software from the manufacturer.*

Service precautions

5   Frequently, when working on the suspension or steering system components, you may come across fasteners that seem impossible to loosen. These fasteners on the underside of the vehicle are continually subjected to water, road grime, mud, etc., and can become rusted or frozen, making them extremely difficult to remove. In order to unscrew these stubborn fasteners without damaging them (or other components), use lots of penetrating oil and allow it to soak in for a while. Using a wire brush to clean exposed threads will also ease removal of the nut or bolt and prevent damage to the threads. Sometimes a sharp blow with a hammer and punch will break the bond between a nut and bolt threads, but care must be taken to prevent the punch from slipping off the fastener and ruining the threads. Heating the stuck fastener and surrounding area with a torch sometimes helps too, but isn't recommended because of the obvious dangers associated with fire. Long breaker bars and extension, or cheater, pipes will increase leverage, but never use

an extension pipe on a ratchet - the ratcheting mechanism could be damaged. Sometimes tightening the nut or bolt first will help to break it loose. Fasteners that require drastic measures to remove should always be replaced with new ones.

6   Since most of the procedures dealt with in this Chapter involve jacking up the vehicle and working underneath it, a good pair of jackstands will be needed. A hydraulic floor jack is the preferred type of jack to lift the vehicle, and it can also be used to support certain components during various operations.

Warning: *Never, under any circumstances, rely on a jack to support the vehicle while working on it.*

7   Whenever any of the suspension or steering fasteners are loosened or removed they must be inspected and, if necessary, replaced with new ones of the same part number or of original equipment quality and design. Torque specifications must be followed for proper reassembly and component retention. Never attempt to heat or straighten any suspension or steering components. Instead, replace any bent or damaged part with a new one.

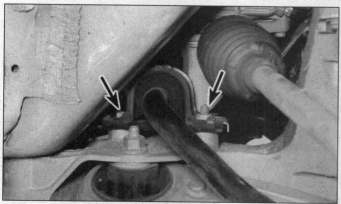

2.3 Stabilizer bar mounting bracket bolts

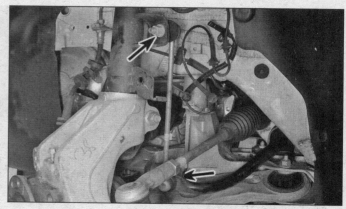

2.7 Stabilizer bar link nuts

2 Stabilizer bar, bushings and links - removal and installation

Stabilizer bar and bushings

1   Loosen the front wheel bolts, then raise the front of the vehicle and support it securely on jackstands. Apply the parking brake and block the rear wheels to keep the vehicle from rolling off the stands. Remove the front wheels.
2   Remove the main crossmember (see Section 22).
3   Remove the four stabilizer bar bracket bolts to detach the stabilizer bar from the crossmember **(see illustration)**.
4   Check the bushings for hardness or deterioration, replacing them if necessary.
Note: *Before removal, note the orientation of the slits in the bushings.*
5   Installation is the reverse of removal. Tighten all fasteners to the torque values listed in this Chapter's Specifications.

Stabilizer bar links

6   Loosen the front wheel bolts, then raise the front of the vehicle and support it securely on jackstands. Apply the parking brake and block the rear wheels to keep the vehicle from rolling off the stands. Remove the front wheels.

7   Remove the upper and lower fasteners that secure the link to the strut and stabilizer bar **(see illustration)**.
Note: *Hold the stud on the link with an Allen wrench so that it does not rotate when removing the nut.*
8   Installation is the reverse of removal. Tighten the nuts to the torque listed in this Chapter's Specifications.

3 Strut assembly (front) - removal, inspection and installation

Removal

Warning: *Always replace the struts and/or coil springs in pairs - never replace just one strut or one coil spring; this could cause dangerous handling peculiarities.*
Note: *If both strut assemblies are going to be removed, mark the assemblies Right and Left so they will be reinstalled on the correct side.*
1   Loosen the wheel bolts, then raise the vehicle and support it securely on jackstands. Remove the wheels.
2   Unstake the driveaxle/hub nut, then have an assistant apply the brake while you loosen the nut (see Chapter 8).
3   Remove the brake disc (see Chapter 9).

4   Disconnect the stabilizer bar link from the strut (see Section 2) and detach the brake hose from its bracket from the strut.
5   Remove the wheel speed sensor from the steering knuckle and detach the harness from its bracket on the strut (see Chapter 9).
6   Detach the tie-rod end from the steering knuckle (see Section 19).
7   Separate the balljoint from the control arm (see Section 6).
8   Separate the driveaxle from the hub by prying down on the control arm as you swing the steering knuckle rearward. Support the driveaxle out of the way with a length of wire - don't let it hang by the inner CV joint.
9   Temporarily slip the balljoint back into the control arm to hold the strut in place while removing the upper strut fastener.
10   With a floor jack positioned under the lower control arm (as near the balljoint area as possible), raise the jack to compress the strut just enough to release the pressure on the upper strut retaining clip **(see illustration)**.
11   Using two screwdrivers, pry the ends of the retaining clip in opposite directions forcing the clip to snap in half **(see illustrations)**.
Warning: *Discard the retaining clip - a new one must be used during reassembly.*
12   Slowly lower the floor jack to reduce the pressure on the spring.

3.10 Lift up on the floor jack to apply pressure to the spring. This will reduce the pressure on the upper strut fastener

3.11a Remove the dust cover from the upper mount

3.11b Use two screwdrivers to remove the upper fastener

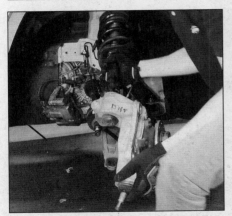

3.13a Remove the strut assembly with the steering knuckle

3.13b Lay the strut assembly on a flat surface and remove the nut and pinch bolt

3.13c Slide the strut from the steering knuckle

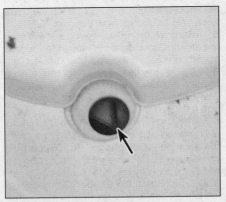

3.18 Make sure the slot on the strut upper mount is aligned with the hole in the strut tower

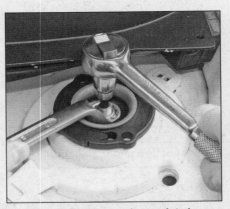

4.2 Use an offset box-end wrench to loosen the strut rod nut while holding the rod from turning with a hex bit or Allen wrench

4.4 Spring compressors are available at most auto parts stores and equipment rental yards

13   Remove the strut and steering knuckle as an assembly, then remove the pinch bolt and separate the steering knuckle from the strut **(see illustrations)**.
Note: *Rust and debris can make removing the strut and steering knuckle difficult. Letting water soak into the joint between the two components is one good method of loosening the strut.*

Inspection

14   Check the strut body for leaking fluid, dents, cracks and other obvious damage which would warrant repair or replacement.
15   Check the coil spring for chips or cracks in the spring coating (this will cause premature spring failure due to corrosion). Inspect the spring seat for cuts, hardness and general deterioration.
16   If any undesirable conditions exist, proceed to the strut disassembly procedure (see Section 4).

Installation

17   Insert the bottom of the strut into the steering knuckle until the hole in the alignment tab is aligned with the pinch bolt hole in the steering knuckle, then install the pinch bolt and nut. Tighten the nut to the torque listed in this Chapter's Specifications.

18   Insert the strut into the strut tower with the slot in the upper strut mount aligned with the forward hole in the body of the strut tower **(see illustration)**.
19   Install the upper strut and each half of the strut retaining clip.
20   Install each half of the new strut retaining clip. Press each clip towards each other and make sure they are fully closed and all the serrations are engaged.
21   The remainder of the installation is the reverse of the removal procedure.
22   Tighten all fasteners to the torque values listed in this Chapter's Specifications.
23   Have the front end alignment checked, and if necessary, adjusted.

---

4   Strut/coil spring - replacement

Warning: *Struts and/or coil springs must be replaced in pairs - never replace just one of them.*
Note: *You'll need a spring compressor for this procedure. Spring compressors are available on a daily rental basis at most auto parts stores or equipment rental yards.*
1   If the struts or coil springs exhibit the telltale signs of wear (leaking fluid, loss of damping capability, chipped, sagging or

cracked coil springs) explore all options before beginning any work. The strut body is not serviceable and must be replaced if a problem develops. However, complete strut assemblies (with springs) may be available on an exchange basis, which eliminates much time and work. Whichever route you choose to take, check on the cost and availability of parts before disassembling your vehicle.
Warning: *Disassembling a strut assembly is potentially dangerous and utmost attention must be directed to the job, or serious injury may result. Use only a high-quality spring compressor and carefully follow the manufacturer's instructions furnished with the tool. After removing the coil spring from the strut, set it aside in a safe, isolated area.*

Disassembly

2   Before removing the strut, remove the cap from the strut upper mount and break loose, but DO NOT remove, the strut rod nut **(see illustration)**.
3   Remove the strut and spring assembly (see Section 3).
4   Following the tool manufacturer's instructions, install the spring compressor on the spring and compress it sufficiently to relieve all pressure from the upper mount

4.6 Remove the upper mount . . .

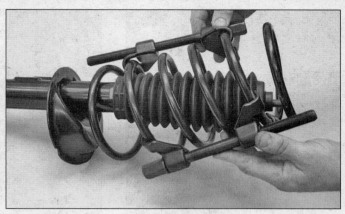

4.7 . . . and the spring

4.8 Slide the dust boot off the strut body

4.9 Remove the bumper from the strut rod

(see illustration). This can be verified by wiggling the spring.

5   While holding the strut rod from turning, unscrew the nut.

6 Remove the nut and upper mount (see illustration). Inspect the pivot bearing for smooth operation. If it doesn't turn smoothly, replace it. Remove the upper spring seat and check the upper spring isolator for cracking and general deterioration. Replace any parts that are damaged or worn.

7   Carefully lift the compressed spring from the assembly (see illustration).

Warning: When removing the compressed spring, lift it off very carefully and set it in a safe place. Keep the ends of the spring away from your body.

8   Remove the dust boot (see illustration).

9   Slide the rubber bumper off the strut rod (see illustration). Check the lower spring isolator for cracking and hardness; replace it if necessary.

Reassembly

10   Install the rubber bumper to the strut rod.

11   Install the dust boot onto the strut rod and strut body.

12   Carefully place the coil spring onto the strut. Align the coil spring on the damper using the reference marks made during disassembly. If a new spring or strut damper unit is

being installed, use the marks on the old component to help you orient the spring properly.

Note: When installing the spring, make sure the end with the ID tag is placed upwards. Be sure to have the bottom of the spring end facing at the 9 o'clock position as viewed looking down from the top with the assembly facing as it would be if it were installed in the car.

13   Install the upper mount to the strut rod, noting its alignment.

14   Install the nut on the strut rod and tighten it to the torque listed in this Chapter's Specifications.

15   Loosen the coil spring compressor until the top coil is properly seated against the upper spring seat and upper mount. Relieve all tension from the spring compressor and remove the tool from the coil spring.

16   Install the strut/spring assembly (see Section 3).

---

5   Control arm - removal, inspection and installation

Removal

1   Loosen the wheel bolts, then raise the front of the vehicle and support it securely on jackstands. Remove the wheel.

2   Loosen (a few turns) the nut that attaches the balljoint to the control arm (see illustration).

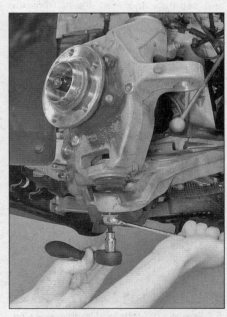

5.2 Balljoint-to-control arm nut. If the ballstud turns, hold it with an Allen wrench

5.3a Balljoint separator tools like this are available at most auto parts stores and, when used properly, won't damage the balljoint boot

5.3b Position the separator tool so that you can easily tighten the tool to separate the balljoint from the control arm

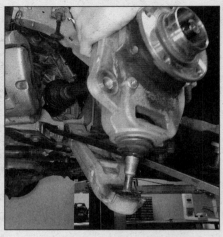

5.4 Position a prybar as shown to separate the control arm from the steering knuckle

3   Release the balljoint from the control arm by using the proper balljoint separation tool **(see illustrations)**.
Note: *Once the balljoint is separated, do not pull outward on the knuckle; this can lead to separation and damage to the driveaxle inner CV joint.*
4   Remove the nut and separate the control arm from the steering knuckle **(see illustration)**.
5   Remove the front bumper cover (see Chapter 11).
6   Remove the lower load beam extension **(see illustration)**.
7   Remove the load beam bracket from the side of the load beam to the chassis.
8   Remove the load beam bracket bolts and separate the load beam from the crossmember and the radiator lower support, then remove the control arm forward

pivot bolt and nut **(see illustration)**.
9   Remove the control arm rear pivot bolt and nut **(see illustration)**, then remove the control arm.

Inspection

10   Make sure the control arm is straight. If it is bent, replace it. Do not attempt to straighten a bent control arm.
11   Inspect all bushings for cracks, distortion, and tears. If a bushing is torn or worn, replace the control arm.

Installation

12   Position the control arm in the subframe and install the NEW front and rear pivot bolts and nuts, but do not tighten the nuts yet.
Note: *Make certain that the rear bushing is positioned correctly in the crossmember.*
13   Reconnect the balljoint to the control

arm and tighten the NEW nut to the torque listed in this Chapter's Specifications.
14   Install the load beam, load beam extension and the bumper cover.
15   Raise the outer end of the control arm with a floor jack to simulate normal ride height, then tighten the pivot bolt nuts to the torque listed in this Chapter's Specifications.
16   Install the wheel and wheel bolts, lower the vehicle and tighten the bolts to the torque listed in the Chapter 1 Specifications.
17   Have the front wheel alignment checked and, if necessary, adjusted.

6   Balljoints - replacement

1   The balljoint is serviced with the steering knuckle; it is not replaceable separately (see Section 8).

5.6 Remove the four load beam extension bolts beneath the bumper beam (fourth bolt not visible)

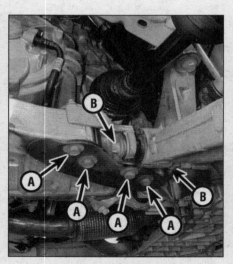

5.8 Load beam bracket-to-beam and crossmember bolts (A) and control arm front pivot bolt and nut (B)

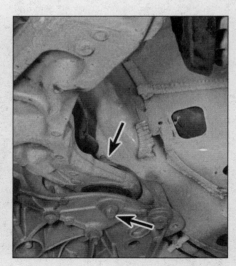

5.9 Control arm rear pivot bolt and nut

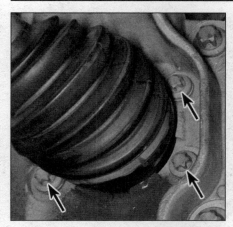

7.4 Remove the bolts and discard them (only two shown). The manufacturer states that new bolts must be used

7 Hub and bearing assembly (front) - removal and installation

Removal

1   Loosen the wheel bolts, raise the vehicle and support it securely on jackstands, then remove the wheel.
2   Unstake the driveaxle/hub nut, then have an assistant apply the brakes as you loosen and remove the nut (see Chapter 8, Section 2).
3   Remove the brake caliper, the caliper mounting bracket, brake disc and the disc splash shield (see Chapter 9).
Note: *Be sure to support the brake caliper as described in Chapter 9.*
4   Remove the hub/bearing assembly mounting bolts from the rear of the steering knuckle **(see illustration)**.
5   Remove the hub/bearing assembly from

the steering knuckle and driveaxle. If the driveaxle splines stick in the hub, use a puller to push it out as the hub and bearing assembly is withdrawn.

Installation

6   Make sure that the mounting surfaces inside the steering knuckle and on the driveaxle splines are smooth and free of rust, burrs and nicks prior to installing the hub/bearing assembly.
7   Assemble the hub and bearing onto the steering knuckle, guiding the driveaxle into the splines of the hub.
8   Install the hub/bearing assembly-to-steering knuckle bolts. Tighten the NEW bolts in a criss-cross pattern until the hub/bearing assembly is seated securely against the steering knuckle. Tighten the bolts to the torque listed in this Chapter's Specifications.
9   Install the brake disc, the caliper mounting bracket and the caliper; tighten the fasteners to the torque values listed in the Chapter 9 Specifications.
10   Install the wheel and wheel bolts. Lower the vehicle and tighten the wheel bolts to the torque listed in the Chapter 1 Specifications.

8 Steering knuckle - removal and installation

Removal

1   Loosen the wheel bolts, then raise the vehicle and support it securely on jackstands. Remove the wheel.
2   Remove the driveaxle/hub nut (see Chapter 8).
3   Remove the brake disc and the ABS wheel speed sensor (see Chapter 9).
4   Remove the hub and bearing assembly (see Section 7).
5   Remove the brake disc dust shield.

6   Separate the control arm from the steering knuckle (see Section 5).
7   Remove the steering knuckle-to-strut pinch bolt and slide the steering knuckle from the strut (see Section 3).

Installation

8   Installation is the reverse of removal. Tighten all suspension fasteners to the torque listed in this Chapter's Specifications.
9   Tighten the driveaxle/hub nut to the torque listed in the Chapter 8 Specifications. Install the wheel, lower the vehicle and tighten the wheel bolts to the torque listed in the Chapter 1 Specifications.
10   Have the front end alignment checked and, if necessary, adjusted.

9 Shock absorber (rear) - removal and installation

Removal

Warning: *Always replace the shock absorbers in pairs - never replace just one shock absorber; this could cause dangerous handling peculiarities.*
1   Loosen the rear wheel bolts. Raise the vehicle and support it securely on jackstands, then remove the rear wheels.
2   Remove the inner fender splash shield (see Chapter 11).
3   Support the rear lower control arm with a floor jack positioned underneath the coil spring.
Warning: *The jack must remain in this position until the new shock absorber is installed.*
4   Remove the shock absorber lower mounting bolt **(see illustration)**.
5   Remove the two shock absorber upper mounting bolts and remove the shock absorber **(see illustration)**.

9.4 Shock absorber lower mounting bolt

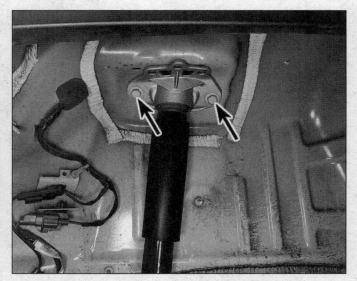

9.5 Sock absorber upper mounting bolts

10.2 Camber link details

1   Camber link   2   Mounting fasteners

11.2 Toe link details

1   Place floor jack here   3   Toe link-to-crossmember bolt/
2   Toe link-to-knuckle bolt   nut (note alignment marks)

Installation

6   Guide the shock absorber into position and align the upper mounting bolt holes. Install the upper mounting bolts and tighten them to the torque listed in this Chapter's Specifications.

7   Install the lower mounting bolt. Raise the control arm with the floor jack to simulate normal ride height, then tighten the lower mounting bolt to the torque listed in this Chapter's Specifications.

8   Install the inner fender splash shield.

9   Install the wheel and wheel bolts. Lower the vehicle and tighten the bolts to the torque listed in the Chapter 1 Specifications.

10   Camber link - removal and installation

1   Loosen the wheel bolts. Raise the rear of the vehicle and support it securely on jackstands. Remove the wheel.

2   Support the lower control arm with a floor jack placed underneath the coil spring. Remove the camber link-to-crossmember nut and bolt **(see illustration)**.

3   Remove the camber link-to-rear knuckle nut and bolt, then remove the camber link.

4   Installation is the reverse of removal.

5   Raise the lower control arm with the jack to simulate normal ride height, then tighten the bolts to the torque listed in this Chapter's Specifications.

11   Toe link - removal and installation

1   Loosen the wheel bolts. Raise the vehicle and support it securely on jackstands. Remove the wheel. Support the lower control arm with a floor jack positioned under the coil spring.

2   Mark the relationship of the alignment cam to the crossmember, then remove and discard the toe link-to-crossmember and knuckle fasteners and remove the toe link **(see illustration)**.
Warning: *Obtain new fasteners for installation.*

3   Installation is the reverse of removal, using NEW fasteners. Align the cam with the previously made match marks. Raise the lower control arm with the floor jack to simulate normal ride height, then tighten the fasteners to the torque listed in this Chapter's Specifications.

4   Install the wheel and wheel bolts, then lower the vehicle and tighten the bolts to the torque listed in the Chapter 1 Specifications.

5   Have the wheel alignment checked and, if necessary, adjusted.

12   Trailing link - removal and installation

1   Loosen the wheel bolts. Raise the vehicle and support it securely on jackstands. Remove the wheel.

2   Detach the parking brake harness grommet from the trailing arm routing clip. Also remove the retainer and detach the brake hose fitting from the routing clip **(see illustration)**.

3   Remove the three bolts attaching the trailing link to the knuckle.

4   Remove the two bolts attaching the trailing link to the body and remove the link.

5   Installation is the reverse of removal. Tighten the fasteners to the torque values listed in this Chapter's Specifications.

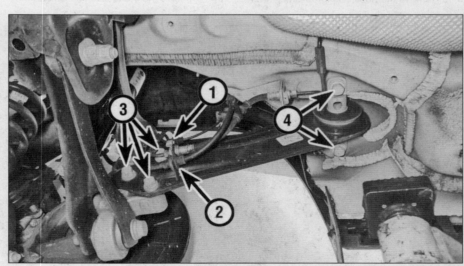

12.2 Trailing link details

1   Brake hose retaining clip   3   Trailing link-to-knuckle bolts
2   Electric Parking Brake (EPB) wiring harness   4   Trailing link-to-body bolts

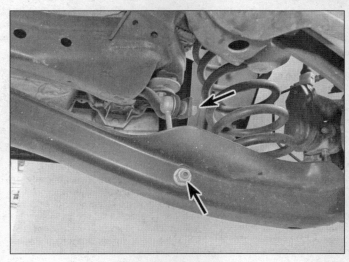

13.2 Stabilizer bar link nuts

13.3 Stabilizer bar bushing bracket bolts

6   Install the wheel and bolts. Lower the vehicle and tighten the bolts to the torque listed in the Chapter 1 Specifications.

13 Stabilizer bar, bushings and links (rear) - removal and installation

Removal

1   Loosen the rear wheel bolts. Raise the rear of the vehicle and support it securely on jackstands. Remove the rear wheels.
2   Remove the upper stud nut from the end link on each side of the stabilizer bar (see illustration). If the ballstud turns, hold it with an Allen wrench.
3   Remove the stabilizer bar bushing bracket bolts (see illustration).
4   Remove the bushing brackets and pull out the stabilizer bar.
5   Check the bushings for hardness or deterioration, replacing them if necessary.
Note: *Before removal, note the orientation of the slits in the bushings.*
6   Installation is the reverse of removal. Tighten all fasteners to the torque values listed in this Chapter's Specifications.

Installation

7   Place the stabilizer bar on the crossmember and install the bolts, tightening them to the torque listed in this Chapter's Specifications.
8   Install the stabilizer bar links and tighten the nuts to the torque listed in this Chapter's Specifications.
9   Install the wheel and wheel bolts. Lower the vehicle and tighten the lug nuts to the torque listed in the Chapter 1 Specifications.

14 Hub and bearing assembly (rear) - removal and installation

Removal

1   Loosen the wheel bolts, raise the rear of the vehicle, support it securely on jackstands and remove the wheel.
2   On AWD models, unstake the driveaxle/hub nut (see Chapter 8). Have an assistant apply the brakes while you unscrew the nut.
3   Remove the ABS wheel speed sensor (see Chapter 9).
4   Remove the brake disc and splash shield (see Chapter 9).

14.5 Rear hub and bearing assembly mounting bolts

5   Remove the bolts retaining the hub and bearing assembly to the knuckle (see illustration).
Warning: *Obtain new bolts for installation.*
6   Remove the hub/bearing assembly. On all wheel drive models, slide the driveaxle out of the hub assembly. If the shaft sticks in the hub, push it out with a two-jaw or flange-type puller.

Installation

7   Installation is the reverse of removal. Tighten the NEW hub and bearing mounting bolts to the torque listed in this Chapter's Specifications. Tighten the caliper mounting bracket bolts to the torque listed in the Chapter 9 Specifications.
8   On AWD models, tighten the driveaxle/hub nut to the torque listed in the Chapter 8 Specifications.
9   Install the wheel and wheel bolts. Lower the vehicle and tighten the bolts to the torque listed in the Chapter 1 Specifications.

15 Coil spring (rear) - removal and installation

Warning: *Coil springs should be replaced in pairs - never replace just one of them.*
1   Loosen the rear wheel bolts, raise the rear of the vehicle and support it securely on jackstands. Block the front wheels. Remove the rear wheels.
2   Detach the stabilizer bar links from the stabilizer bar (see Section 13).
3   Support the lower control arm with a floor jack placed under the coil spring.
4   Remove the lower control arm-to-knuckle pivot bolt and nut (see Section 16).
Warning: *Obtain new fasteners for installation.*
5   Slowly lower the jack until the spring is extended, then remove the coil spring.
6   Remove the spring isolators from each end of the spring. Inspect the isolators for damage, replacing them if necessary.

7   When installing the spring, be sure the lower end of the spring and isolator are positioned correctly; the lower end of the spring must be facing outward and positioned against the protrusion on the lower control arm.

Note: *The label on the spring is always on the top end of the spring.*

8   Raise the floor jack to compress the spring, then install the NEW lower control arm-to-knuckle pivot bolt and nut. Raise the lower control arm to simulate normal ride height, then tighten the nut to the torque listed in this Chapter's Specifications.

9   The remainder of installation is the reverse of removal.

10   Install the wheel and wheel bolts. Lower the vehicle and tighten the bolts to the torque listed in the Chapter 1 Specifications.

16   Lower control arm - removal and installation

1   Loosen the rear wheel bolts, raise the rear of the vehicle, support it securely on jackstands and remove the wheels.

2   Support the lower control arm with a floor jack placed underneath the coil spring.

3   Detach the stabilizer bar link from the lower control arm (see Section 13).

4   Remove and discard the lower control arm-to-knuckle bolt and nut (**see illustration**).

Warning: *Obtain a new bolt and nut for installation.*

5   Slowly lower the floor jack to allow the coil spring to extend fully, then remove the spring.

6   Mark the relationship of the inner pivot bolt alignment cam to the crossmember, then remove the nut and inner pivot bolt (**see illustration**).

Note: *On AWD models the inner control arm bolt can't be removed because there is not enough clearance between the lower control arm and the driveaxle. Slide the bolt out as far as possible, cut the bolt off and pull the remaining portion of the bolt out. (Alternatively, the driveaxle can be removed.)*

7   Remove the lower control arm.

8   Installation is the reverse of removal. See Section 15 for coil spring installation details. Use NEW fasteners and tighten them to the torque listed in this Chapter's Specifications after the control arm has been raised to simulate normal ride height.

Note: *On AWD models, install the inner pivot*

bolt in the opposite direction than it was originally installed.

9   Install the wheel and wheel bolts. Lower the vehicle and tighten the bolts to the torque listed in the Chapter 1 Specifications.

10   Have the wheel alignment checked and, if necessary, adjusted.

17   Rear knuckle - removal and installation

1   Loosen the rear wheel bolts, raise the rear of the vehicle, support it securely on jackstands and remove the wheels.

2   Remove the rear hub and bearing assembly (see Section 14).

3   Remove the coil spring (see Section 15).

4   Remove the shock absorber lower mounting bolt (see Section 9).

5   Remove the trailing link-to-knuckle bolts (see Section 12).

6   Remove the toe link-to-knuckle nut and bolt (see Section 11).

7   Remove the camber link-to-knuckle nut and bolt (see Section 10).

8   Remove the knuckle.

9   Installation is the reverse of removal. Tighten the trailing link-to-knuckle bolts to the torque listed in this Chapter's Specifications.

10   Raise the lower control arm with the floor jack and tighten the NEW suspension arms-to-knuckle fasteners to the torque listed in this Chapter's Specifications.

11   Have the wheel alignment checked and, if necessary, adjusted.

18   Steering wheel - removal and installation

Warning: *These models have airbags. Always disarm the airbag system before working in the vicinity of the impact sensors, steering column, or instrument panel to avoid accidental deployment of the airbag, which could cause personal injury (see Chapter 12).*

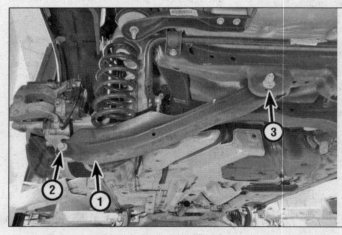

16.4 Lower control arm details

1 *Place floor jack here*
2 *Lower control arm-to- knuckle bolt*
3 *Lower control arm inner pivot bolt*

16.6 Mark the position of the inner pivot bolt cam to the crossmember

18.2 An Allen wrench can be used to release the airbag retaining springs

18.5 Lift the orange safety tabs, then disconnect the yellow connectors

18.7 Mark the relationship of the steering wheel to the shaft, then remove the nut

Warning: *Do not use a memory saving device to preserve the PCM's memory when working on or near airbag system components.*

Removal

1   Park the vehicle with the wheels pointing straight ahead and the steering wheel centered. Disconnect the cable from the negative terminal of the battery (see Chapter 5).
Warning: *Wait at least two minutes before proceeding with the following steps.*
2   Locate the two access holes on the sides of the lower close out trim of the steering wheel. Slide an Allen wrench or small punch (or equivalent tool) into the hole and guide it inward until it comes in airbag retaining spring (**see illustration**).
3   Push inward on the retaining spring until the airbag pops free.
4   Repeat to release the retaining spring on the opposite side access hole.
5   Disconnect the electrical connectors from the airbag module (**see illustration**).
6   Set the module aside in a safe, isolated area, with the airbag side of the module facing UP.
Warning: *When carrying the airbag module, keep the driver's (trim) side facing away from you.*
7   Mark the relationship of the steering wheel to the shaft. While firmly holding the steering wheel in the straight ahead position, loosen and remove the steering wheel retaining nut (**see illustration**).
8   With the retaining nut removed, use the palm of both hands to bump the back side of the steering wheel upwards off of the column shaft. This will free the steering wheel if it is stuck onto the steering shaft.
Caution: *Do not hammer on the steering shaft or the steering wheel in an attempt to free the steering wheel from the shaft. Also, do not use a slide hammer puller to remove the steering wheel.*
Caution: *While the steering wheel is removed, DO NOT turn the steering shaft. If you do so, the airbag clockspring could be damaged when the vehicle is put back in service.*

Installation

Caution: *If the clockspring has become uncentered, the entire Steering Column Control Module (SCCM) must be replaced (see Chapter 12).*
9   Install the wheel on the steering shaft, aligning the wide spline on the shaft with the gap in the steering wheel splines. Push the wheel onto the shaft and ensure the clockspring lines up on the back of the steering wheel.
Note: *Make sure the clockspring wires are routed correctly through the steering wheel.*
10   Install the steering wheel retaining nut and tighten it to the torque listed in this Chapter's Specifications.
11   Reconnect the clockspring connectors to the airbag and press the airbag into place until the retaining springs engage with their posts.
12   Connect the cable to the negative battery terminal (see Chapter 5).
13   Turn the ignition key On and verify that

19.2 Hold the tie-rod end while breaking loose the jam nut

the airbag system is operating properly by watching the airbag warning light in the instrument cluster (see Chapter 12).
Warning: *If the airbag system is not operating properly (as indicated by the airbag warning light), DO NOT drive the vehicle. Have the airbag system repaired at a dealership service department or other qualified repair shop.*

19 Tie-rod ends - removal and installation

Removal

1   Loosen the wheel bolts, raise the front of the vehicle and support it securely on jackstands. Apply the parking brake and block the rear wheels to keep the vehicle from rolling off the jackstands. Remove the wheel.
2   Loosen the tie-rod end jam nut (**see illustration**).

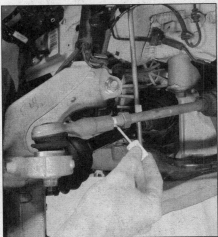
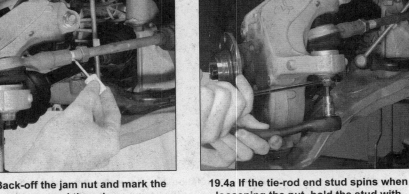

19.3 Back-off the jam nut and mark the exposed threads

19.4a If the tie-rod end stud spins when loosening the nut, hold the stud with a wrench or socket

19.4b Use a puller to break loose the tie-rod end ballstud

3   Mark the relationship of the tie-rod end to the threaded portion of the tie-rod. This will ensure the toe-in setting is restored when reassembled **(see illustration)**.
4   Loosen the nut on the tie-rod end ballstud a few turns **(see illustration)**. Break loose the tie-rod end ballstud from the steering knuckle arm with a puller **(see illustration)**.
Note: *An alternative method to break the tie rod free from the steering knuckle is to use a ball peen hammer and strike the steering knuckle joint parallel to the joint. A few well placed blows will jar the tie rod from the knuckle.*
5   Remove the nut and separate the tie-rod end from the steering knuckle, then unscrew the tie-rod end from the tie-rod.

Installation

6   Thread the tie-rod end onto the tie-rod to the marked position and connect the tie-rod end to the steering knuckle arm. Install

the nut on the ballstud and tighten it to the torque listed in this Chapter's Specifications.
7   Tighten the jam nut securely and install the wheel. Lower the vehicle and tighten the wheel bolts to the torque listed in the Chapter 1 Specifications.
8   Have the front end alignment checked and, if necessary, adjusted.

20   Steering column - removal and installation

Warning: *These models have airbags. Always disarm the airbag system before working in the vicinity of the impact sensors, steering column, or instrument panel to avoid accidental deployment of the airbag, which could cause personal injury (see Chapter 12).*
Warning: *Do not use a memory saving device to preserve the PCM's memory when working on or near airbag system components.*

Removal

1   Park the vehicle with the wheels pointing straight ahead. Disconnect the cable from the negative terminal of the battery.
2   Position the tilt steering wheel in the full down position, then remove the steering column covers (see Chapter 11).
3   Remove the knee bolster (see Chapter 11).
4   Remove the driver's airbag (see Section 18).
5   Disconnect the electrical connectors from the Steering Column Control Module (SCCM) (see Chapter 12).
6   Disconnect the remaining electrical connections attached to the steering column.
7   Remove the intermediate shaft pinch bolt, and separate the intermediate shaft from the steering gear **(see illustration)**. Discard the bolt and obtain a new one for reassembly.
Warning: *Do not rotate the steering shaft after the intermediate shaft has been removed or damage to the clockspring could occur. To ensure this doesn't happen, make sure the steer-*

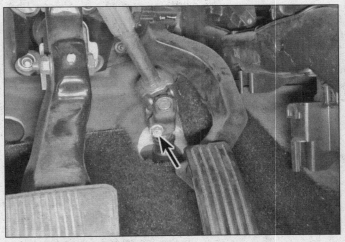
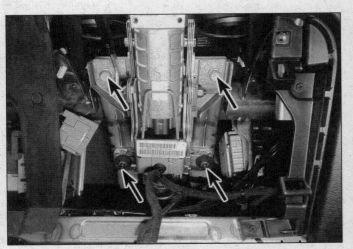

20.7 Mark the intermediate shaft to the steering gear input shaft, then remove the coupler pinch bolt

20.9 Steering column mounting fasteners

21.13 Steering gear electrical connectors

**21.18 Crossmember-to-chassis upper mounting bolt
(left side shown)**

ing column is secured by locking it in place or by manually holding it in position.

8   Remove the steering wheel (see Section 18).

9   Remove the fasteners securing the steering column to the dash (**see illustration**).

10   Carefully guide the steering column out of the car.

Installation

11   Guide the steering column into position, then install the steering column mounting fasteners and tighten them to the torque listed in this Chapter's Specifications.

12   Connect the intermediate shaft and install the NEW pinch bolt, tightening it to the torque listed in this Chapter's Specifications.

13   The remainder of installation is the reverse of removal.

---

21   Steering gear - removal and installation

Warning: *Lock the steering wheel to keep it from moving while the steering shaft is disconnected or damage to the airbag system*

could occur when the vehicle is placed back in service. With the ignition key in the LOCK position, turn the steering wheel just enough to lock it or secure it with the seatbelt.
Warning: *The steering gear is an electrical device that will need to be programmed if replaced.*

Removal

Note: *On AWD models, the power transfer unit will have to be removed before continuing with the following procedures for steering gear removal (see Chapter 8).*

1   Park the vehicle with the wheels pointing straight ahead. Disconnect the cable from the negative terminal of the battery (see Chapter 5).

2   Prevent the steering shaft from turning by ensuring the steering column is locked, or by using a steering wheel holder, or by passing the seat belt through the steering wheel and clipping it into its latch.

3   Disconnect the intermediate shaft pinch bolt and separate the intermediate shaft from the steering gear (see Section 20). Discard the bolt and obtain a new one for reassembly.

4   Loosen the front wheel bolts, then raise the vehicle and support it securely on jackstands. Remove the wheels.

5   Remove the under-vehicle splash shield.

6   Detach the tie-rod ends from the steering knuckles (see Section 19).

7   Detach the stabilizer bar links from the stabilizer bar (see Section 2).

8   Separate the control arms from the steering knuckle balljoints (see Section 5).

9   Remove the four bolts securing the crossmember to the support beam bracket. Remove the bracket.

10   Remove the front bumper cover (see Chapter 11).

11   Remove the load beam extensions and load beams (see Section 5).

12   Disconnect the downstream O2 sensor connections (to gain access) and remove the exhaust pipe extension (see Chapter 4).

13   Disconnect the electrical connectors from the steering gear control module (**see illustration**).

14   Separate the steering gear harness hold-down fasteners from the crossmember and body.

15   Remove the rear engine mount (see Chapter 2A or Chapter 2B).

16   Mark the position and location of the crossmember in reference to the body and subframe area.

17   Support the crossmember with a floor jack so that the crossmember weight is balanced on the jack.

18   Remove the upper mounting bolt to the crossmember from each side (**see illustration**).

19   Remove the four rear mounting bolts that attach the crossmember to the body (**see illustration**).

20   Slowly lower the crossmember (and steering gear) down to clear the vehicle.

21   With the crossmember down and out of the vehicle, remove the bolts and separate the steering gear from the crossmember.

22   Installation is the reverse of removal. Tighten the steering gear mounting bolts to the torque listed in this Chapter's Specifications.

23   Raise the crossmember into position and realign it to the chassis using the marks you made earlier.

21.19 Crossmember-to-chassis rear mounting bolts

24 Install the mounting fasteners and tighten them to the torque listed in this Chapter's Specifications.

25 Have the vehicle towed to a dealer service department or other qualified repair shop to have the steering gear programmed to the vehicle.

26 Have the wheel alignment checked and, if necessary, adjusted.

22 Main crossmember - removal and installation

1 The main crossmember removal is part of the steering gear removal and installation procedure (see Section 21).

23 Wheels and tires - general information

1 All vehicles covered by this manual are equipped with metric-sized fiberglass or steel belted radial tires **(see illustration)**. Use of other size or type of tires may affect the ride and handling of the vehicle. Don't mix different types of tires, such as radials and bias belted, on the same vehicle as handling may be seriously affected. It's recommended that tires be replaced in pairs on the same axle, but if only one tire is being replaced, be sure it's the same size, structure and tread design as the other.

2 Because tire pressure has a substantial effect on handling and wear, the pressure on all tires should be checked at least once a month or before any extended trips (see Chapter 1).

3 Wheels must be replaced if they are bent, dented, leak air, have elongated bolt holes, are heavily rusted, out of vertical symmetry or if the lug bolts won't stay tight. Wheel repairs that use welding or peening are not recommended.

Note: *Always use a torque wrench to properly tighten the wheel bolts to the torque listed in* the Chapter 1 Specifications.

4 Tire and wheel balance is important in the overall handling, braking and performance of the vehicle. Unbalanced wheels can adversely affect handling and ride characteristics as well as tire life. Whenever a tire is installed on a wheel, the tire and wheel should be balanced by a shop with the proper equipment.

24 Wheel alignment - general information

1 A wheel alignment refers to the adjustments made to the wheels so they are in proper angular relationship to the suspension and the ground. Wheels that are out of proper alignment not only affect vehicle control, but also increase tire wear. The front end angles normally measured are camber, caster and toe-in **(see illustration)**. Toe-in is the only routine adjustment made; both front camber and caster are set at the factory and are not considered to be adjustable. However, front camber and caster can be slightly adjusted by shifting the position of the crossmember in relation to the chassis.

2 Getting the proper wheel alignment is a very exacting process, one in which complicated and expensive machines are necessary to perform the job properly. Because of this, you should have a technician with the proper equipment perform these tasks. We will, however, use this space to give you a basic idea of what is involved with a wheel alignment so you can better understand the process and deal intelligently with the shop that does the work.

3 Toe-in is the turning in of the wheels. The purpose of a toe specification is to ensure parallel rolling of the wheels. In a vehicle with zero toe-in, the distance between the front edges of the wheels will be the same as the distance between the rear edges of the wheels. The actual amount of toe-in is normally only a fraction of an inch. On the front end, toe-in is controlled by the tie-rod end position on the tie-rod. On the rear end it is adjusted by repositioning the cam bolts at the inner end of the toe links. Incorrect toe-in will cause the tires to wear improperly by making them scrub against the road surface.

4 Camber is the tilting of the wheels from vertical when viewed from one end of the vehicle. When the wheels tilt out at the top, the camber is said to be positive (+). When the wheels tilt in at the top the camber is negative (-). The amount of tilt is measured in degrees from vertical and this measurement is called the camber angle. This angle affects the amount of tire tread which contacts the road and compensates for changes in the suspension geometry when the vehicle is cornering or traveling over an undulating surface. On the front end it can be slightly adjusted by altering the position of the crossmember. On the rear end it can be adjusted by repositioning the cam bolts at the inner ends of the lower control arm and toe link.

5 Caster is the tilting of the front steering axis from the vertical. A tilt toward the rear is positive caster and a tilt toward the front is negative caster. It can be slightly adjusted by altering the position of the front crossmember on the chassis.

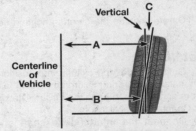

CAMBER ANGLE (FRONT VIEW)

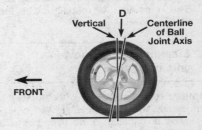

CASTER ANGLE (SIDE VIEW)

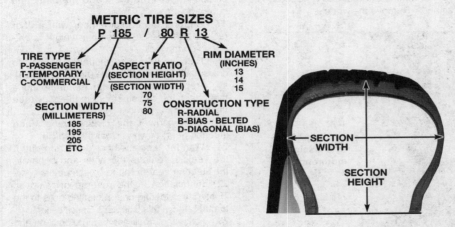

23.1 Metric tire size code

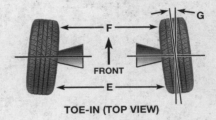

TOE-IN (TOP VIEW)

24.1 Wheel alignment details

A minus B = C (degrees camber)
D = caster (expressed in degrees)
E minus F = toe-in (measured in inches)
G = toe-in (expressed in degrees)

Chapter 11
Body

Contents

Specifications

Torque specifications — Ft-lbs (unless otherwise indicated)

Note: *One foot-pound (ft-lb) of torque is equivalent to 12 inch-pounds (in-lbs) of torque. Torque values below approximately 15 ft-lbs are expressed in inch-pounds, since most foot-pound torque wrenches are not accurate at these smaller values.*

Front seats	
Seat belt anchor to B pillar	43
Seat belt anchor to inner sill	33
Seat belt buckle anchor to seat	33
Seat mounting bolts	30
Rear seats	
Seat belt retractor to shelf panel	33
Seat belt anchor to floor	33
Seat mounting bolts	63
Seat back mounting bolts	18
Knee bolster to dash	80 in-lbs
Passenger's airbag to dash	80 in-lbs
Door	
Door glass to regulator fasteners	10 in-lbs
Door hinge pin bolts*	18
Door check strap bolts	22

*Replace with new bolts

1 General Information

Warning: *The models covered by this manual are equipped with Supplemental Restraint Systems (SRS), more commonly known as airbags. Always disable the airbag system before working in the vicinity of any airbag system components to avoid the possibility of accidental deployment of the airbags, which could cause personal injury (see Chapter 12).*

1 Certain body components are particularly vulnerable to accident damage and can be unbolted and repaired or replaced. Among these parts are the hood, doors, tailgate, liftgate, bumpers and front fenders.

2 Only general body maintenance practices and body panel repair procedures within the scope of the do-it-yourselfer are included in this Chapter.

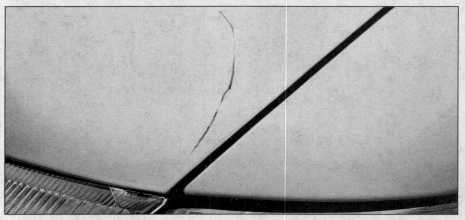

2.1a Make sure the damaged area is perfectly clean and rust free. If the touch-up kit has a wire brush, use it to clean the scratch or chip. Or use fine steel wool wrapped around the end of a pencil. Clean the scratched or chipped surface only, not the good paint surrounding it. Rinse the area with water and allow it to dry thoroughly

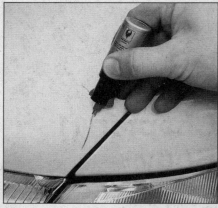

2.1b Thoroughly mix the paint, then apply a small amount with the touch-up kit brush or a very fine artist's brush. Brush in one direction as you fill the scratch area. Do not build up the paint higher than the surrounding paint

2   Repairing minor paint scratches

1   No matter how hard you try to keep your vehicle looking like new, it will inevitably be scratched, chipped or dented at some point. If the metal is actually dented, seek the advice of a professional. But you can fix minor scratches and chips yourself (see illustrations). Buy a touch-up paint kit from a dealer service department or an auto parts store. To ensure that you get the right color, you'll need to have the specific make, model and year of your vehicle and, ideally, the paint code, which is located on a special metal plate under the hood or in the door jamb.

3   Body repair - minor damage

Plastic body panels

1   The following repair procedures are for minor scratches and gouges. Repair of more serious damage should be left to a dealer service department or qualified auto body shop. Below is a list of the equipment and materials necessary to perform the following repair procedures on plastic body panels.

   Wax, grease and silicone removing solvent
   Cloth-backed body tape
   Sanding discs
   Drill motor with three-inch disc holder
   Hand sanding block
   Rubber squeegees
   Sandpaper
   Non-porous mixing palette
   Wood paddle or putty knife
   Wood paddle or putty knife
   Curved-tooth body file
   Flexible parts repair material

Flexible panels (bumper trim)

2   Remove the damaged panel, if necessary or desirable. In most cases, repairs can be carried out with the panel installed.

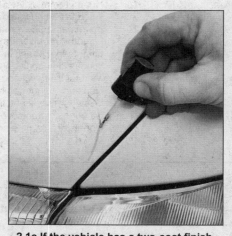

2.1c If the vehicle has a two-coat finish, apply the clear coat after the color coat has dried

3   Clean the area(s) to be repaired with a wax, grease and silicone removing solvent applied with a water-dampened cloth.
4   If the damage is structural, that is, if it extends through the panel, clean the backside of the panel area to be repaired as well. Wipe dry.
5   Sand the rear surface about 1-1/2 inches beyond the break.
6   Cut two pieces of fiberglass cloth large enough to overlap the break by about 1-1/2 inches. Cut only to the required length.
7   Mix the adhesive from the repair kit according to the instructions included with the kit, and apply a layer of the mixture approximately 1/8-inch thick on the backside of the panel. Overlap the break by at least 1-1/2 inches.
8   Apply one piece of fiberglass cloth to the adhesive and cover the cloth with additional adhesive. Apply a second piece of fiberglass cloth to the adhesive and immediately cover the cloth with additional adhesive in sufficient quantity to fill the weave.

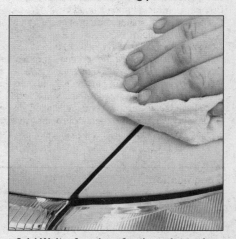

2.1d Wait a few days for the paint to dry thoroughly, then rub out the repainted area with a polishing compound to blend the new paint with the surrounding area. When you're happy with your work, wash and polish the area

9   Allow the repair to cure for 20 to 30 minutes at 60-degrees to 80-degrees F.
10   If necessary, trim the excess repair material at the edge.
11   Remove all of the paint film over and around the area(s) to be repaired. The repair material should not overlap the painted surface.
12   With a drill motor and a sanding disc (or a rotary file), cut a "V" along the break line approximately 1/2-inch wide. Remove all dust and loose particles from the repair area.
13   Mix and apply the repair material. Apply a light coat first over the damaged area; then continue applying material until it reaches a level slightly higher than the surrounding finish.
14   Cure the mixture for 20 to 30 minute at 60-degrees to 80-degrees F.

15 Roughly establish the contour of the area being repaired with a body file. If low areas or pits remain, mix and apply additional adhesive.

16 Block sand the damaged area with sandpaper to establish the actual contour of the surrounding surface.

17 If desired, the repaired area can be temporarily protected with several light coats of primer. Because of the special paints and techniques required for flexible body panels, it is recommended that the vehicle be taken to a paint shop for completion of the body repair.

Steel body panels

Repairing simple dents

18 When repairing dents, the first job is to pull the dent out until the affected area is as close as possible to its original shape. There is no point in trying to restore the original shape completely as the metal in the damaged area will have stretched on impact and cannot be restored to its original contours. It is better to bring the level of the dent up to a point that is about 1/8-inch below the level of the surrounding metal. In cases where the dent is very shallow, it is not worth trying to pull it out at all.

19 If the backside of the dent is accessible, it can be hammered out gently from behind using a soft-face hammer. While doing this, hold a block of wood firmly against the opposite side of the metal to absorb the hammer blows and prevent the metal from being stretched.

20 If the dent is in a section of the body which has double layers, or some other factor makes it inaccessible from behind, a different technique is required. Drill several small holes through the metal inside the damaged area, particularly in the deeper sections. Screw long, self-tapping screws into the holes just enough for them to get a good grip in the metal. Now pulling on the protruding heads of the screws with locking pliers can pull out the dent.

21 The next stage of repair is the removal of paint from the damaged area and from an inch or so of the surrounding metal. This is easily done with a wire brush or sanding disk in a drill motor, although it can be done just as effectively by hand with sandpaper. To complete the preparation for filling, score the surface of the bare metal with a screwdriver or the tang of a file or drill small holes in the affected area. This will provide a good grip for the filler material. To complete the repair, see the Section on filling and painting.

Repair of rust holes or gashes

22 Remove all paint from the affected area and from an inch or so of the surrounding metal using a sanding disk or wire brush mounted in a drill motor. If these are not available, a few sheets of sandpaper will do the job just as effectively.

23 With the paint removed, you will be able to determine the severity of the corrosion and decide whether to replace the whole panel, if possible, or repair the affected area. New body panels are not as expensive as most people think and it is often quicker to install a new panel than to repair large areas of rust.

24 Remove all trim pieces from the affected area except those which will act as a guide to the original shape of the damaged body, such as headlight shells, etc. Using metal snips or a hacksaw blade, remove all loose metal and any other metal that is badly affected by rust. Hammer the edges of the hole in to create a slight depression for the filler material.

25 Wire-brush the affected area to remove the powdery rust from the surface of the metal. If the back of the rusted area is accessible, treat it with rust inhibiting paint.

26 Before filling is done, block the hole in some way. This can be done with sheet metal riveted or screwed into place, or by stuffing the hole with wire mesh.

27 Once the hole is blocked off, the affected area can be filled and painted. See the following subsection on filling and painting.

Filling and painting

28 Many types of body fillers are available, but generally speaking, body repair kits which contain filler paste and a tube of resin hardener are best for this type of repair work. A wide, flexible plastic or nylon applicator will be necessary for imparting a smooth and contoured finish to the surface of the filler material. Mix up a small amount of filler on a clean piece of wood or cardboard (use the hardener sparingly). Follow the manufacturer's instructions on the package, otherwise the filler will set incorrectly.

29 Using the applicator, apply the filler paste to the prepared area. Draw the applicator across the surface of the filler to achieve the desired contour and to level the filler surface. As soon as a contour that approximates the original one is achieved, stop working the paste. If you continue, the paste will begin to stick to the applicator. Continue to add thin layers of paste at 20-minute intervals until the level of the filler is just above the surrounding metal.

30 Once the filler has hardened, the excess can be removed with a body file. From then on, progressively finer grades of sandpaper should be used, starting with a 180-grit paper and finishing with 600-grit wet-or-dry paper. Always wrap the sandpaper around a flat rubber or wooden block, otherwise the surface of the filler will not be completely flat. During the sanding of the filler surface, the wet-or-dry paper should be periodically rinsed in water. This will ensure that a very smooth finish is produced in the final stage.

31 At this point, the repair area should be surrounded by a ring of bare metal, which in turn should be encircled by the finely feathered edge of good paint. Rinse the repair area with clean water until all of the dust produced by the sanding operation is gone.

32 Spray the entire area with a light coat of primer. This will reveal any imperfections in the surface of the filler. Repair the imperfections with fresh filler paste or glaze filler and once more smooth the surface with sandpa-

per. Repeat this spray-and-repair procedure until you are satisfied that the surface of the filler and the feathered edge of the paint are perfect. Rinse the area with clean water and allow it to dry completely.

33 The repair area is now ready for painting. Spray painting must be carried out in a warm, dry, windless and dust free atmosphere. These conditions can be created if you have access to a large indoor work area, but if you are forced to work in the open, you will have to pick the day very carefully. If you are working indoors, dousing the floor in the work area with water will help settle the dust that would otherwise be in the air. If the repair area is confined to one body panel, mask off the surrounding panels. This will help minimize the effects of a slight mismatch in paint color. Trim pieces such as chrome strips, door handles, etc., will also need to be masked off or removed. Use masking tape and several thickness of newspaper for the masking operations.

34 Before spraying, shake the paint can thoroughly, then spray a test area until the spray painting technique is mastered. Cover the repair area with a thick coat of primer. The thickness should be built up using several thin layers of primer rather than one thick one. Using 600-grit wet-or-dry sandpaper, rub down the surface of the primer until it is very smooth. While doing this, the work area should be thoroughly rinsed with water and the wet-or-dry sandpaper periodically rinsed as well. Allow the primer to dry before spraying additional coats.

35 Spray on the top coat, again building up the thickness by using several thin layers of paint. Begin spraying in the center of the repair area and then, using a circular motion, work out until the whole repair area and about two inches of the surrounding original paint is covered. Remove all masking material 10 to 15 minutes after spraying on the final coat of paint. Allow the new paint at least two weeks to harden, then use a very fine rubbing compound to blend the edges of the new paint into the existing paint. Finally, apply a coat of wax

4 Body repair - major damage

1 Major damage must be repaired by an auto body shop specifically equipped to perform body and frame repairs. These shops have the specialized equipment required to do the job properly.

2 If the damage is extensive, the frame must be checked for proper alignment or the vehicle's handling characteristics may be adversely affected and other components may wear at an accelerated rate.

3 Due to the fact that all of the major body components (hood, fenders, etc.) are separate and replaceable units, any seriously damaged components should be replaced rather than repaired. Sometimes the components can be found in a wrecking yard that specializes in used vehicle components, often at considerable savings over the cost of new parts.

These photos illustrate a method of repairing simple dents. They are intended to supplement *Body repair - minor damage* in this Chapter and should not be used as the sole instructions for body repair on these vehicles.

1 If you can't access the backside of the body panel to hammer out the dent, pull it out with a slide-hammer-type dent puller. In the deepest portion of the dent or along the crease line, drill or punch hole(s) at least one inch apart . . .

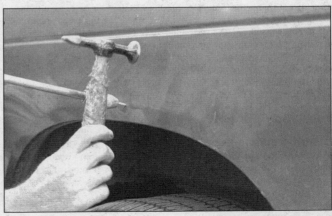

2 . . . then screw the slide-hammer into the hole and operate it. Tap with a hammer near the edge of the dent to help 'pop' the metal back to its original shape. When you're finished, the dent area should be close to its original contour and about 1/8-inch below the surface of the surrounding metal

3 Using coarse-grit sandpaper, remove the paint down to the bare metal. Hand sanding works fine, but the disc sander shown here makes the job faster. Use finer (about 320-grit) sandpaper to feather-edge the paint at least one inch around the dent area

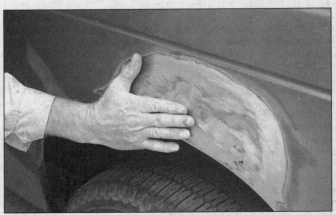

4 When the paint is removed, touch will probably be more helpful than sight for telling if the metal is straight. Hammer down the high spots or raise the low spots as necessary. Clean the repair area with wax/silicone remover

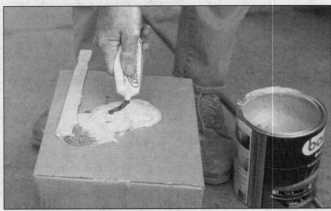

5 Following label instructions, mix up a batch of plastic filler and hardener. The ratio of filler to hardener is critical, and, if you mix it incorrectly, it will either not cure properly or cure too quickly (you won't have time to file and sand it into shape)

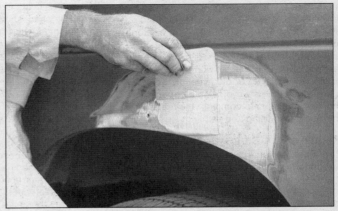

6 Working quickly so the filler doesn't harden, use a plastic applicator to press the body filler firmly into the metal, assuring it bonds completely. Work the filler until it matches the original contour and is slightly above the surrounding metal

7 Let the filler harden until you can just dent it with your fingernail. Use a body file or Surform tool (shown here) to rough-shape the filler

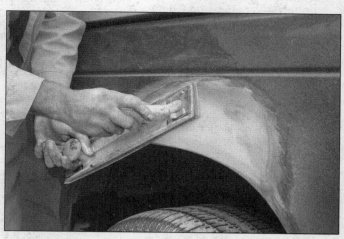

8 Use coarse-grit sandpaper and a sanding board or block to work the filler down until it's smooth and even. Work down to finer grits of sandpaper - always using a board or block - ending up with 360 or 400 grit

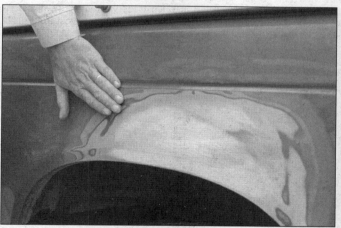

9 You shouldn't be able to feel any ridge at the transition from the filler to the bare metal or from the bare metal to the old paint. As soon as the repair is flat and uniform, remove the dust and mask off the adjacent panels or trim pieces

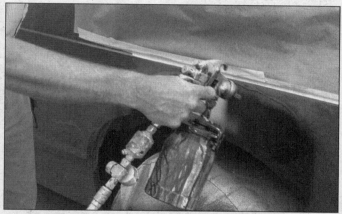

10 Apply several layers of primer to the area. Don't spray the primer on too heavy, so it sags or runs, and make sure each coat is dry before you spray on the next one. A professional-type spray gun is being used here, but aerosol spray primer is available inexpensively from auto parts stores

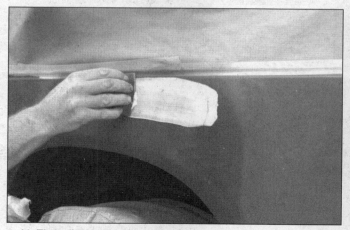

11 The primer will help reveal imperfections or scratches. Fill these with glazing compound. Follow the label instructions and sand it with 360 or 400-grit sandpaper until it's smooth. Repeat the glazing, sanding and respraying until the primer reveals a perfectly smooth surface

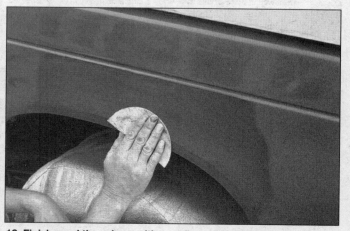

12 Finish sand the primer with very fine sandpaper (400 or 600-grit) to remove the primer overspray. Clean the area with water and allow it to dry. Use a tack rag to remove any dust, then apply the finish coat. Don't attempt to rub out or wax the repair area until the paint has dried completely (at least two weeks)

5   Upholstery, carpets and vinyl trim - maintenance

Upholstery and carpets

1   Every three months remove the floormats and clean the interior of the vehicle (more frequently if necessary). Use a stiff whiskbroom to brush the carpeting and loosen dirt and dust, then vacuum the upholstery and carpets thoroughly, especially along seams and crevices.

2   Dirt and stains can be removed from carpeting with basic household or automotive carpet shampoos available in spray cans. Follow the directions and vacuum again, then use a stiff brush to bring back the "nap" of the carpet.

3   Most interiors have cloth or vinyl upholstery, either of which can be cleaned and maintained with a number of material-specific cleaners or shampoos available in auto supply stores. Follow the directions on the product for usage, and always spot-test any upholstery cleaner on an inconspicuous area (bottom edge of a backseat cushion) to ensure that it

doesn't cause a color shift in the material.

4   After cleaning, vinyl upholstery should be treated with a protectant.

Note: *Make sure the protectant container indicates the product can be used on seats - some products may make a seat too slippery.* **Caution:** *Do not use protectant on vinyl-covered steering wheels.*

5   Leather upholstery requires special care. It should be cleaned regularly with saddlesoap or leather cleaner. Never use alcohol, gasoline, nail polish remover or thinner to clean leather upholstery.

6   After cleaning, regularly treat leather upholstery with a leather conditioner, rubbed in with a soft cotton cloth. Never use car wax on leather upholstery.

7   In areas where the interior of the vehicle is subject to bright sunlight, cover leather seating areas of the seats with a sheet if the vehicle is to be left out for any length of time.

Vinyl trim

8   Don't clean vinyl trim with detergents, caustic soap or petroleum-based cleaners. Plain soap and water works just fine, with a soft brush to clean dirt that may be ingrained. Wash

the vinyl as frequently as the rest of the vehicle.

9   After cleaning, application of a high-quality rubber and vinyl protectant will help prevent oxidation and cracks. The protectant can also be applied to weather-stripping, vacuum lines and rubber hoses, which often fail as a result of chemical degradation, and to the tires.

6   Fastener and trim removal

1   There is a variety of plastic fasteners used to hold trim panels, splash shields and other parts in place in addition to typical screws, nuts and bolts. Once you are familiar with them, they can usually be removed without too much difficulty.

2   The proper tools and approach can prevent added time and expense to a project by minimizing the number of broken fasteners and/or parts.

3   The following illustration shows various types of fasteners that are typically used on most vehicles and how to remove and install them (see illustration). Replacement fasteners are commonly found at most auto parts stores, if necessary.

Fasteners

This tool is designed to remove special fasteners. A small pry tool used for removing nails will also work well in place of this tool

A Phillips head screwdriver can be used to release the center portion, but light pressure must be used because the plastic is easily damaged. Once the center is up, the fastener can easily be pried from its hole

Here is a view with the center portion fully released. Install the fastener as shown, then press the center in to set it

This fastener is used for exterior panels and shields. The center portion must be pried up to release the fastener. Install the fastener with the center up, then press the center in to set it

This type of fastener is used commonly for interior panels. Use a small blunt tool to press the small pin at the center in to release it . . .

. . . the pin will stay with the fastener in the released position

Reset the fastener for installation by moving the pin out. Install the fastener, then press the pin flush with the fastener to set it

This fastener is used for exterior and interior panels. It has no moving parts. Simply pry the fastener from its hole like the claw of a hammer removes a nail. Without a tool that can get under the top of the fastener, it can be very difficult to remove

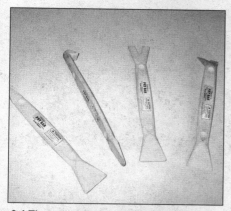

6.4 These small plastic pry tools are ideal for prying off trim panels

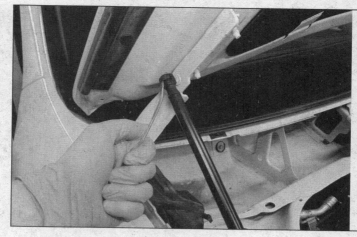

7.2 Be sure to brace the hood before removing the retainer clip from the hood shock

4 Trim panels are typically made of plastic and their flexibility can help during removal. The key to their removal is to use a tool to pry the panel near its retainers to release it without damaging surrounding areas or breaking-off any retainers. The retainers will usually snap out of their designated slot or hole after force is applied to them. Stiff plastic tools designed for prying on trim panels are available at most auto parts stores **(see illustration)**. Tools that are tapered and wrapped in protective tape, such as a screwdriver or small pry tool, are also very effective when used with care.

7 Hood - removal, installation and adjustment

Note: *The hood is heavy and somewhat awkward to remove and install - at least two people should perform this procedure.*

Removal and installation
1 Use blankets or pads to cover the cowl area of the body and the fenders. This will protect the body and paint as the hood is lifted off.
2 Start by removing the hood shocks from the hood. Use a small flat tip screwdriver to pry the retainer clips from the end of the

shock and then remove the shock **(see illustration)**.
3 Scribe alignment marks around the bolt heads and hinge attachment locations to insure proper alignment during installation - a permanent-type felt-tip marker also will work for this **(see illustration)**.
4 Remove the underhood lamp wire connector to the engine compartment wire harness, if so equipped.
5 Disconnect the windshield washer hose from the hood.
6 Remove the top bolts holding the hood to the hinge and loosen the bottom bolts until they can be removed by hand.
7 Have an assistant on the opposite side of the vehicle support the weight of the hood. Simultaneously remove the bottom bolts holding the hood to the hinge and lift off the hood **(see illustration)**.
8 Installation is the reverse of removal.

Adjustment
9 Front-and-back and side-to-side adjustment of the hood is done by moving the hood in relation to the hinge plate after loosening the bolts.
10 Scribe or trace a line around the entire hinge plate so you can judge the amount of movement.

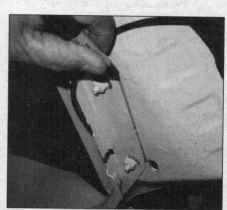

7.3 Before removing the hood, draw a mark around the hinge plates

11 Loosen the bolts or nuts and move the hood into correct alignment. Move it only a little at a time. Tighten the hinge bolts or nuts and carefully lower the hood to check the alignment.
12 Mark the hood latch as a guide for adjustment (or removal and replacement). The hood latch assembly can also be adjusted up-and-down and side-to-side after loosening the bolts **(see illustration)**.

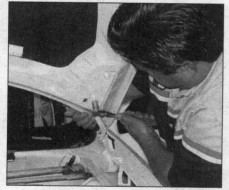

7.7 Support the hood with your shoulder as you remove the bolts securing the hood to the hinge plates

7.12 Mark the position of the hood latch, loosen the bolts and move the latch to adjust the hood in the closed position

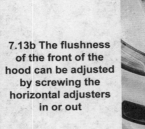

7.13a Adjust the hood height by screwing the hood bumpers in or out

7.13b The flushness of the front of the hood can be adjusted by screwing the horizontal adjusters in or out

13   Adjust the hood bumpers on the radiator support so the hood is flush with the fenders when closed (see illustrations).

14   The hood latch assembly, as well as the hinges, should be periodically lubricated with white lithium-base grease to prevent sticking and wear.

8   Hood latch and cable - removal and installation

Latch

1   Remove the radiator close out panel push pins and remove the close out panel.
2   If applicable, disconnect the hood ajar switch harness.
3   Detach the hood release cable from the latch (see illustrations).
4   Mark the position of the latch to the radiator support, then remove the bolts holding the hood latch to the radiator sup-

port and detach the latch assembly (see illustration 7.12).
5   Installation is the reverse of removal.

Cable

6   Remove the radiator close out pushpins and remove the close out panel.
7   Detach the hood release cable from the hood latch (see illustrations 8.3a and 8.3b).
8   From inside the vehicle, raise the hood release handle as high as it will go, then release the cable end by sliding the cable end sideways in the keyhole slot of the inside hood release handle.
9   From under the driver's side of the dash, follow along the hood release cable and disconnect any cable stays you find. Making sure you are able to spot where they are when reinstalling the new cable.
10   From the engine bay area, continue to follow the hood release cable along the frame rail and disconnect any cable stays along the way.

11   Under the dash, dislodge the cable grommet from the hole in the firewall.
12   Connect a long string or piece of wire to the engine compartment end of the cable, then pull the cable through the firewall and into the passenger compartment.
13   Connect the string or wire to the new cable and pull it back through the firewall into the engine compartment.
14   The remainder of installation is the reverse of removal.

9   Bumper covers - removal and installation

Front

1   Remove the inner fender splash shield by turning the steering wheel in the appropriate direction which will allow access to the splash shield pushpins. Remove the pushpins and leave the front section of the

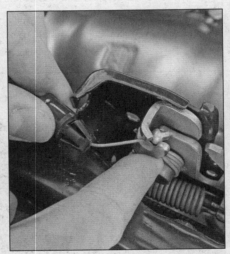

8.3a Squeeze the tangs on the cable retainer and detach the cable from the bracket . . .

8.3b . . . then pass the inner cable out of the slot in the latch

9.2 The outer fender trim is held on with pressure clips

9.3 Hidden bumper cover-to-fender bolt. Inner fender splash shield has been removed already

9.4 Remove the push pins, then remove the close out panel

fenderwell loose for the rest of the procedure (see Section 11).

2   Pull the front portion of the fender outer trim off of the bumper cover just past the fender and cover joining area (see illustration).

3   Remove the hidden 10 mm bolt that secures the bumper cover to the fender (hidden by the inner fender splash shield) (see illustration).

4   Remove the radiator closeout panel pushpins (see illustration).

5   Remove the bolt hidden by the radiator close out panel (see illustration).

6   Raise the front of the vehicle and support it securely on jackstands.

7   There are five quarter-turn type fasteners that are reachable from the underside of the vehicle, one in each fenderwell area and three across the bottom front edge of the

fascia. Turn each one a quarter turn counterclockwise to disengage them.

8   Lower the vehicle and grasp the fender and the front bumper cover joint area. With a firm jerk separate the cover from the fender (see illustrations).

9   Repeat on the other side of the bumper cover.

10   Grasp the radiator area of the cover and pull the pressure clips free.

11   Lift the cover up and away from the car to remove it.

12   Installation is the reverse of removal.

Rear

13   Remove any inner fender trim and fender flare molding pieces that are attached to the cover (see Section 10).

14   Open the liftgate and remove the lower bumper cover fasteners (see illustration).

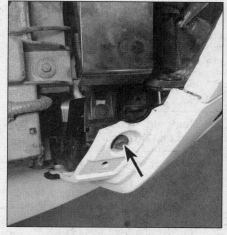

9.5 Bumper cover bolt that was hidden by the close out panel

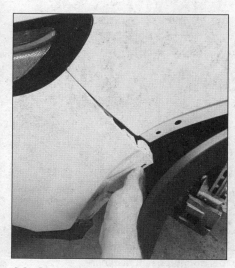

9.8a Start on the outside edge to separate the cover from the fender

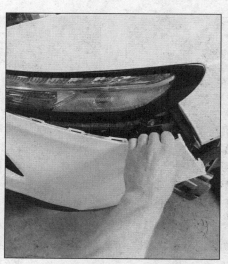

9.8b Work your way around the headlamp assembly until all the fasteners are released

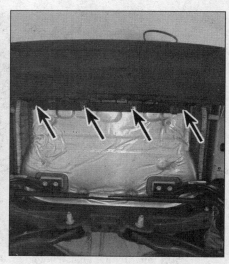

9.14 Remove the lower pushpin fasteners

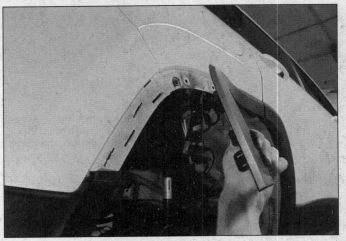

9.15a Pull the fender trim free . . .

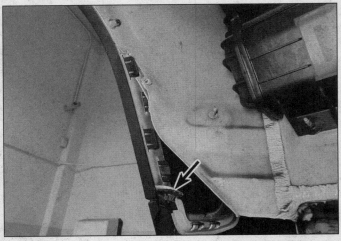

9.15b . . . then remove the retainer holding the bumper cover to the fender

15 Remove the fender trim at the rear section of the fenderwell area **(see illustrations)**.
16 Remove the upper push pin fasteners, then carefully pull the cover free. Slowly remove the cover while checking for any obstructions or fasteners that may have been missed.
17 Installation is the reverse of removal.

10 Bumpers - removal and installation

Front

1 Remove the fasteners securing the inner fender splash shield in place **(see illustration)**.
2 Remove the front bumper cover (see Section 9).
3 Remove the bumper support beam-to-

frame bolts from both sides of the bumper and remove the bumper **(see illustration)**.
4 Installation is the reverse of removal.

Rear

5 Remove inner fender splash shield **(see illustration)**.
6 Open the liftgate and remove the rear bumper cover (see Section 9).
7 Remove the nuts securing the rear bumper to the frame and remove the rear bumper.
8 Installation is the reverse of removal.

11 Front fender - removal and installation

1 Remove the front bumper cover (see Section 9).
2 Remove the headlight housing (see Chapter 12).

3 Remove the inner fender inner splash shield (see Section 9), then remove any foam insulation that may be tucked up inside the fender.
4 Remove the fasteners to the radiator close out panel (mounted on the radiator core support), then position the bracket out of the way to gain access to the fender fasteners.
5 Remove the small trim piece (cowl mucket trim) from the cowling attaching the upper corner of the fender to the cowling area. Under this mucket trim is a single bolt holding the fender in place **(see illustration)**. Remove the bolt.
6 Open the door and remove the fender-to-door pillar mounting fastener **(see illustration)**.
7 Remove the bolt at the bottom of the fender, near the lower forward corner of the front door and the mud guard area **(see illustration)**.
8 Remove the two bolts that were hidden

10.1 Inner fender splash shield fastener locations

10.3 Bumper support beam fasteners

10.5 Inner fender splash shield fastener locations

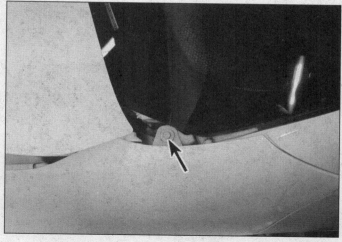

11.5 Upper bolt securing the fender to the cowling, hidden by the mucket trim

by the front bumper cover in the headlight housing area **(see illustration)**.

9   Remove the two inner fender seal bolts that were hidden by the inner fender splash shield. These bolts are located to the rear section inside of the fender.

10   Remove the two bolts across the top edge of the fender.

11   Remove the bolts at the front upper corner of the fender to radiator support area **(see illustration)**.

12   Remove the fender flare from the fender **(see illustration)**.

13   With the remaining fender bolts removed, use a sharpened trim tool (plastic is the best) to release the foamed section to the rear of the inner fender that joins the fender to the door hinge pillar (A pillar).

14   Detach the fender. It's a good idea to have an assistant support the fender while it's being moved away from the vehicle to prevent damage to the surrounding body panels.

15   Installation is the reverse of removal.

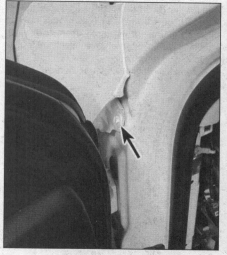

11.6 You can access this bolt with the door open

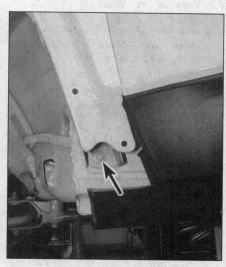

11.7 Remove the lower bolt securing the fender to the door hinge pillar (A pillar)

11.8 With the bumper cover removed, you can gain access to these bolts

11.11 Some bolts will be a Torx type, some will be of various sizes. Reinstall them in their original locations

11.12 Carefully pry the fender flare from the fender

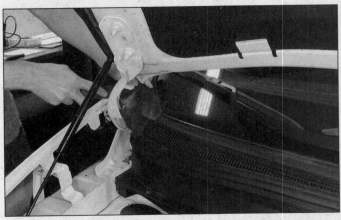

12.3 Lift the foam at both sides to expose the plastic fasteners, then remove the fasteners

12.4 Pull the front of the cowl cover up and away from the windshield, then guide it out from the engine compartment

12 Cowl cover - removal and installation

1   Disconnect the cable from the negative battery terminal (see Chapter 5).
2   Remove the wiper arms (see Chapter 12).

3   Remove the hood seal and corner trim pieces that attach the cowl cover to the body and fender **(see illustration)**.
4   Lift the front of the cowl cover up and disengage the inner hooks from the windshield, then carefully maneuver it out of the vehicle **(see illustration)**.
5   Installation is the reverse of removal.

13 Door trim panel - removal and installation

1   Models covered by this manual are equipped with a Supplemental Restraint System (SRS), more commonly known as airbags. Always disable the airbag system before working in the vicinity of any airbag system component to avoid the possibility of accidental deployment of the airbag, which could cause personal injury (see Chapter 12).

Door trim panel
2   Pry out the trim cover for the inside door release lever, and the trim cover of the inside handle grip and remove the retaining screws **(see illustrations)**.
3   Remove the switch panel by prying it upwards with a flat trim tool and disconnect the electrical connector **(see illustration)**.
4   Working around the perimeter of the door panel, starting in the outside corner, pry the panel edges of the panel free. Then, lift the panel vertically to free the upper retaining clips **(see illustration)**. With panel free, disconnect the remaining electrical connections.

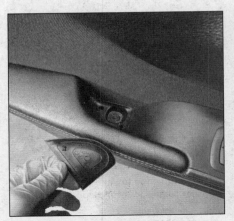

13.2a Remove the cover in the armrest and the screw underneath it

13.2b Pry out the trim piece from the door handle . . .

13.2c . . . then remove the screw underneath

13.3 Use a plastic trim tool to pry the switch panel from the armrest

13.4 Pry the panel retainers out from the door with a plastic trim tool, working around the perimeter

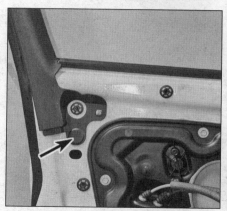

13.8a Pry out the fastener at the rear of the window trim . . .

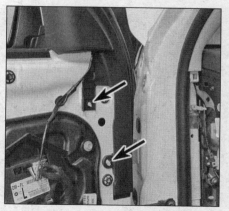

13.8b . . . and the two at the front of the trim . . .

13.8c . . . then remove the trim from the window frame

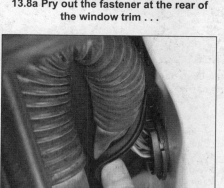

14.1a Pry the rubber boot from the connector

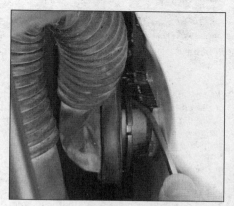

14.1b Release the tabs and pry the plastic connector housing from the door jamb, then pull the connector housing out of the jamb to disconnect the electrical connectors

14.2a Door check strap retaining bolt

14.2b Remove the lower hinge pin bolt . . .

14.2c . . . and the upper hinge pin bolt, then lift the door from the hinge pins

Note: *Once the retainers are free, try putting your knee under the door and lift up on the panel slightly. Then, while using the palm of your hand, bump the upper edge of the trim panel towards the outside of the car. The upward pressure with your knee and the bumping of the panel will release the upper hidden catches holding the door panel to the door.*
5   Installation is the reverse of removal.

Window belt molding and trim

6   Remove the door trim panel as described previously.
7   Pull up on the rubber belt trim (inside window scraper piece) to remove it.
8   The trim around the window frame of the door is held on with three pushpins - one in the rear edge and two in the front edge. Remove the pushpins, then pull the belt trim down to free it from the door **(see illustrations)**.
9   Installation is the reverse of removal.

14 Door - removal and installation

Warning: *Models covered by this manual are equipped with a Supplemental Restraint System (SRS), more commonly known as airbags. Always disable the airbag system*

before working in the vicinity of any airbag system component to avoid the possibility of accidental deployment of the airbag, which could cause personal injury (see Chapter 12).
Note: *Disconnect the cable from the negative battery terminal before beginning the procedure (see Chapter 5).*
1   Disconnect the door harness electrical con-

nector from the body harness **(see illustration)**.
Note: *If a jack is used, place a towel between it and the door to protect the door's painted surfaces.*
2   Unbolt the door check strap from the door opening. Remove the hinge pin bolts and carefully lift off the door up and off the hinge pins **(see illustrations)**.
Caution: *Discard the door hinge pin bolts and obtain new ones for installation.*

15.7 Use a Torx bit to loosen the latch bolts

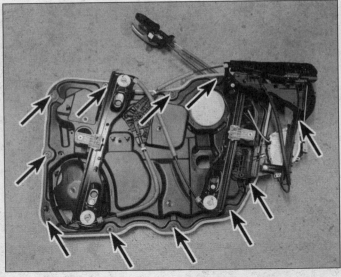

15.9 Carrier plate fastener locations (back side of the carrier plate shown)

3   Installation is the reverse of removal.
4   Following installation of the door, check the alignment and adjust it if necessary as follows:
a) *Up-and-down and in-and-out adjustments are made by loosening the hinge-to-door fasteners and moving the door as necessary.*
b) *Forward-and-backward adjustments are made by loosening the hinge-to-body fasteners and moving the door as necessary.*
c) *The door lock striker can also be adjusted both up-and-down and sideways to provide positive engagement with the lock mechanism. This is done by loosening the mounting screws and moving the striker as necessary.*

15 Door carrier plate, latch, outside handle, and door mechanical lock - removal and installation

Warning: *Models covered by this manual are equipped with a Supplemental Restraint System (SRS), more commonly known as airbags. Always disable the airbag system before working in the vicinity of any airbag system component to avoid the possibility of accidental deployment of the airbag, which could cause personal injury (see Chapter 12).*
1   Disconnect the cable from the negative terminal of the battery (see Chapter 5).

Carrier plate
Note: *Every component that makes up the interior components of the door are mounted onto the carrier plate. By removing the carrier you have essentially removed all the moving parts, including the door speaker, from the interior of the door.*
Note: *Window motor replacement does not require removal of the carrier plate. The win-*

dow motor can be accessed from the outside of the carrier. The serviceable parts from the inside of the door (back side of the carrier) are the door latch assembly, the window cable assembly, and the carrier plate itself.
Note: *Front door shown, but the rear doors are similar in design.*
2   Remove the door trim panel (see Section 13).
3   Separate the main wiring harness leading to the carrier plate.
4   Remove the window glass-to-regulator fasteners, then lift the glass all the way up and secure it to the door window frame with tape (see Section 16).
5   Remove the exterior door handle as described later in this Section.
6   Remove the fastener below the exterior door handle.
7   Remove the three screws securing the door latch to the door **(see illustration)**.
8   Disconnect the electrical connections for the outside mirror.

9   Remove the fasteners from around the carrier plate (eleven total) **(see illustration)**. Leave one fastener in place.
10   With a good grip on the carrier plate to avoid it moving or slipping, take the final fastener out.
11   Check for any electrical connections that need to be disconnected.
12   Remove the entire carrier plate from the door.
13   Installation is the reverse of removal.

Door latch
14   Remove the door trim panel (see Section 13).
15   Remove the plate carrier (see Section 15).
16   Follow along with the accompanying photo sequence for removal of the door latch from the carrier plate **(see illustrations)**.
Note: *In some applications the cables are replaced with the latch assembly*
17   Installation is the reverse of removal.

15.16a Locate the door lock lever arm's plastic fastener

15.16b Lift the plastic fastener and remove the door lock lever arm

15.16c Flip the plate carrier over (outside downward). You'll see the plastic retaining tabs that will have to be disconnected to release the latch assembly from the carrier plate

15.16d With a small flat screwdriver, gently pry the tabs upward to free the latch from the bracket . . .

15.16e . . . then do the same to the other tab

15.16f Release the small tab on the top edge of the latch assembly, pry up and pull the latch assembly away from the carrier plate

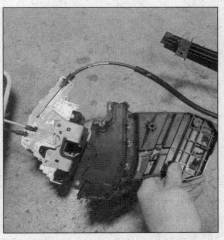

15.16g Remove the latch assembly from the plate carrier

15.16h Gently pry the cover off of the latch assembly

15.16i Remove the cables from the latch assembly housing

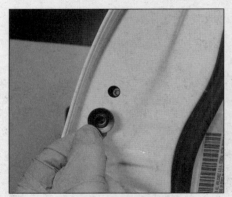

15.18 This cover conceals the Torx bit for removing the outside handle

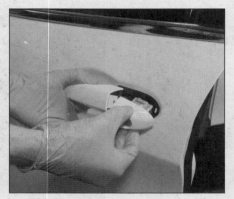

15.21 The door lock and outside handle will separate into two pieces at this point of the removal procedure

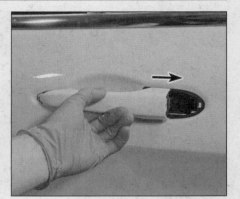

15.23 Slide the handle towards the edge of the door

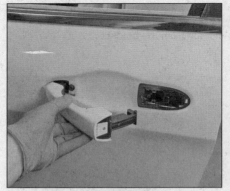

15.24 Rotate the handle outward, then detach it from the door

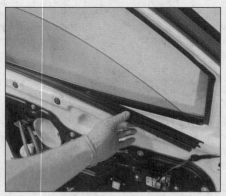

16.2 Pull up on the weatherstrip to remove it

24   Lift the exterior handle outward (**see illustration**).
Note: *If applicable, disconnect the electrical connector from the exterior handle.*
25   Installation is the reverse of removal.

Lock cylinder

26   The front door lock cylinder is removed after removing the outside door handle. With the handle removed, the lock cylinder slides out of the handle.
27   Installation is the reverse of removal.

16   Door window glass and regulator motor - removal and installation

Note: *This procedure applies to front and rear doors.*
1   Remove the door trim panel (see Section 13).
2   Remove the window frame trim (see Section 13). Also remove the inner weatherstrip (**see illustration**).
3   Disconnect the window regulator wire harness.

Outside handle

18   With a small flat-bladed screwdriver, remove the access plug hole trim cover (**see illustration**).
19   Use a T25 Torx bit to turn the screw counterclockwise so the slide moves rearward in the handle bracket.

20   Keep loosening the screw until the door handle cap falls off.
21   Pull lightly on the handle cap and catch it before it falls (**see illustration**).
22   At this point the lock cylinder and cap can be removed.
23   Pull the exterior handle rearward slightly (**see illustration**).

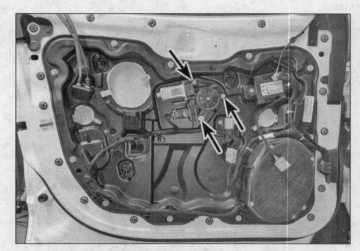

16.4 Window motor fastener locations

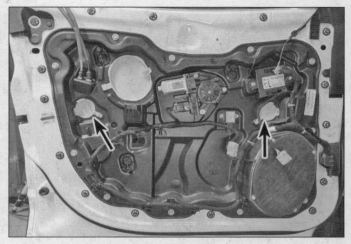

16.6 Window glass fasteners access holes

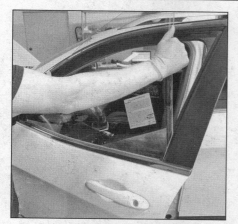

16.9 With the glass disconnected, carefully guide the window glass from the door

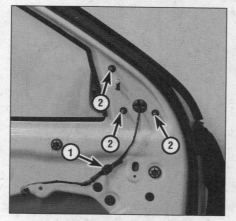

17.2 Disconnect the electrical connector (1) and remove the outside mirror mounting fasteners (2)

17.4 Grasp the mirror firmly and rotate it counterclockwise

4   Remove the three window motor fasteners **(see illustration)**.
5   Remove the window motor from the carrier plate.
6   Remove the glass panel access plugs in the carrier plate **(see illustration)**.
7   Lower the window by hand until the glass fasteners align with the access holes.
8   Remove the fasteners.
9   Lift the rear portion of the glass vertically, then slide the glass out of the door **(see illustration)**.
10   Installation is the reverse of removal.

17   Mirrors - removal and installation

Outside mirrors

1   Remove the door trim panel and window frame trim (see Section 13).
2   Disconnect the electrical connector and

remove the outside mirror mounting fasteners **(see illustration)**, then remove the mirror.
Note: *Hold the mirror as you remove the nuts securing it.*
3   Installation is the reverse of removal.

Inside mirror
Basic mirror

4   Grasp the mirror base and twist it counterclockwise to release it from the adapter mounted on the windshield **(see illustration)**.
5   Installation is the reverse of removal.

Telematics mirror

6   Use a flat trim tool to remove the mirror trim covers.
7   Open the access panel and disconnect the electrical connectors.
8   Remove the pushpin that secures the wiring harness, then move the wiring harness out of the way.
9   Twist the mirror counterclockwise to

release it from the adapter mounted on the windshield.
10   Installation is the reverse of removal.

18   Liftgate trim panel, latch, strut support shocks, lock cylinder, outside handle, and hinges - removal and installation

Trim paneling

Note: *The liftgate trim is divided into three sections. Side trim pieces, a bottom trim piece and upper trim panel over the window.*

Top trim piece

1   Start by removing the upper trim panel above the window glass. Grasp the edge and slide around to the two sides while pulling outward away from the window glass **(see illustrations)**.

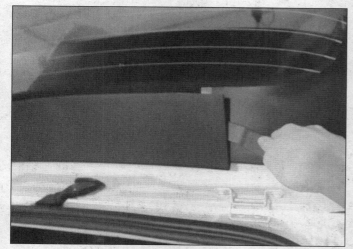

18.1a Start by sliding a trim tool under the trim panel near one of the retaining clips

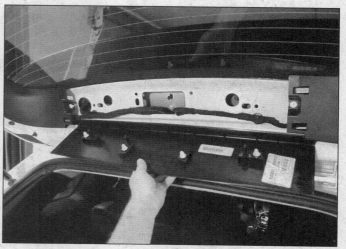

18.1b Applying pressure near the retaining clips will help prevent any damage from occurring to the panel

18.2a Remove the panel by prying with a plastic trim tool . . .

18.2b . . . then do the same to the opposite side

18.3 Remove the two grab handle pull cups by prying them out with a trim tool

Side trim panels

2   Using a flat-bladed trim tool, work your way around the sides of the trim panel until all of the retaining clips have been released **(see illustrations)**. Make sure to pry as close to the clips as possible to prevent breaking the plastic.

Bottom trim panel

3   Remove the two pull cups by prying them out from their edges **(see illustration)**.
4   Pry around the outer edge of the panel with a flat trim tool, releasing each of the retaining clips until all of them have been disengaged **(see illustration)**.

5   Installation is the reverse of removal.

Liftgate latch

6   Remove the liftgate trim panels as described previously in this Section.
7   Disconnect the electrical connectors **(see illustration)**.
8   Remove the three fasteners securing the latch to the door **(see illustration)**.
9   Remove the latch from the door.
10   Installation is the reverse of removal.

Latch - manual override

11   Remove the access panel located in the bottom center of the liftgate **(see illustration)**.
12   Push the manual override lever to unlatch the liftgate **(see illustration)**.

Support struts

13   Open the liftgate and have an assistant or an approved device safely support it as you replace the struts. With a small flat tip screwdriver, pry the retainer outward that secures the strut to the ball socket **(see illustration)**, then disconnect the strut end from the socket. Repeat this for the strut's other end.
14   To install, align the strut to the ball socket and push it firmly onto the socket. Be sure the strut is installed in the correct direction.

18.4 Pry the trim panel off with a flat trim tool

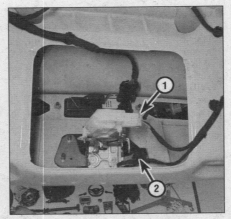

18.7 Liftgate latch electrical connectors

1 Door lock actuator   2 Door ajar indicator

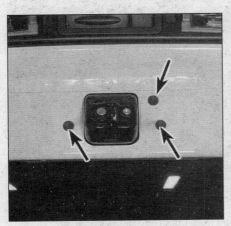

18.8 Liftgate latch screws

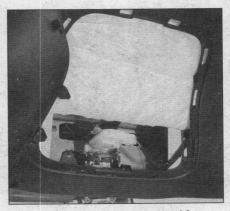

18.11 Remove the access panel from the liftgate trim panel for the liftgate latch mechanism

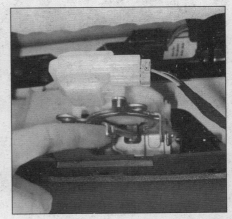

18.12 You can manually open the liftgate by moving this lever

18.13 Pry the retaining clip outward to disengage the strut from the ball socket

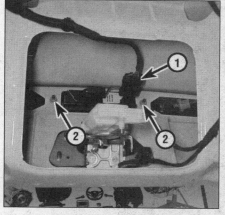

18.16 Disconnect the electrical connector (1) to the outside release handle, then remove the handle mounting nuts (2)

19.2 The rear section of the headliner is held in place with plastic serrated fasteners. Gently pulling down the headliner will release the fasteners

Outside release handle

15   Remove the liftgate trim panels as described earlier.
16   Remove the handle mounting nuts, then disconnect the electrical connection from the handle **(see illustration)** and remove the handle.
17   Installation is the reverse of removal.

19   Liftgate - removal and installation

1   Disconnect the cable from the negative terminal of the battery (see Chapter 5). **Warning:** *Due to its heavy weight, it is recommended that the liftgate removal procedure is performed with the aid of an assistant.*
2   Remove the quarter trim (edge of the headliner trim at the liftgate) and pull down the headliner just far enough to expose the hinges **(see illustration)**.
3   Reaching in between the headliner, disconnect the harness electrical connector and washer fluid line from the liftgate **(see illustrations)**.

4   To ensure correct realignment, mark the locations of the hinge plates in relation to where they are positioned on the liftgate **(see illustration)**.

5   With the help of an assistant or two and/or an approved supporting device, detach the liftgate support struts (see Section 18).

19.3a Disconnect the washer fluid line and the liftgate harness electrical connector by pulling this boot off of the connector, then removing the connector

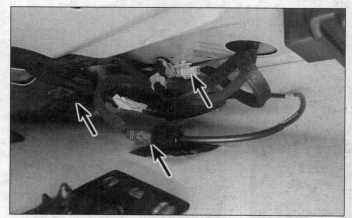

19.3b These are the electrical leads and rear washer hose connections you'll find under the headliner. Disconnect these and pull them through the opening created when you remove the boot and connector

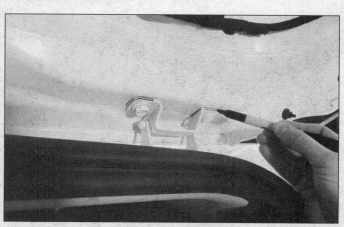

19.4 Mark the hinge plate to liftgate placement for easier realignment

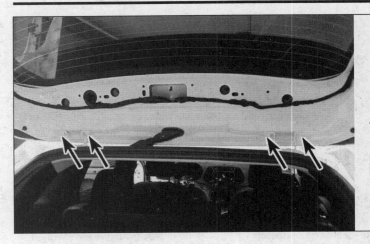

19.6 Remove the bolts carefully to avoid damage to the painted surfaces

20.1 Screw locations (looking up from the underside of the steering column)

6   With the liftgate still safely supported, remove the hinge fasteners and remove the liftgate **(see illustration)**.

7   Check the condition of the liftgate hinges, and replace if necessary (see Section 18).

8   Installation is the reverse of removal.

20   Steering column covers - removal and installation

Warning: *Models covered by this manual are equipped with a Supplemental Restraint System (SRS), more commonly known as airbags. Always disable the airbag system before working in the vicinity of any airbag system component to avoid the possibility of accidental deployment of the airbag, which could cause personal injury (see Chapter 12).*

1   Remove the four screws securing the lower column cover to the steering column **(see illustration)**.

2   Release the clips from the top and bottom covers, and remove the covers from the steering column **(see illustration)**.

3   If equipped, remove the wiring harness hold-down tab to completely remove the steering column cover **(see illustration)**.

4   Installation is the reverse of removal.

21   Dashboard and interior trim panels - removal and installation

Warning: *The models covered by this manual are equipped with a Supplemental Restraint System (SRS), more commonly known as airbags. Always disable the airbag system before working in the vicinity of any airbag system component to avoid the possibility of accidental deployment of the airbag, which could cause personal injury (see Chapter 12). Wait approximately two minutes after disconnecting the negative battery cable before proceeding.*

20.2 Carefully pry the covers apart

21.2 Pry the instrument panel end cap out to disengage the panel mounting clips

20.3 Disconnect this wire harness tab from the steering column lower cover, if equipped.

21.5a Use a flat trim tool or small screwdriver to pry the trim cap off to expose the upper retaining screw

21.5b There is one screw hidden behind the knee bolster trim panel

21.6 Working from the outside edges, gently pry the bezel loose using a flat trim tool

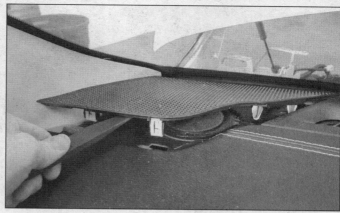

21.9 Use a flat (smooth) trim tool to work the edges of the speaker cover upward to avoid damaging the trim or the dash

1   Disconnect the cable from the negative terminal of the battery (see Chapter 5).

Instrument panel end caps

2   Use a trim tool to pry out and release the clips holding the end cap covers on the left and right sides of the instrument panel **(see illustration)**.

3   Installation is the reverse of removal.

Instrument cluster bezel

4   Remove the driver's side knee bolster trim panel (see Step 25).

5   Remove the trim cap to expose the upper retaining screw, and remove the lower left retaining screw **(see illustrations)**.

6   Using the flat trim tool again, carefully separate the bezel from the dash by working your way around the outside edge **(see illustration)**.

7   With the bezel loose, carefully guide the bezel out of the vehicle.

8   Installation is the reverse of removal.

Speaker covers

9   The dash speaker covers are held in place with retaining clips. Use a flat trim tool

to lift up on the speaker cover, then work your way around until they are all free **(see illustration)**.

10   Now remove the speaker cover.

11   Installation only requires you to align the clips with the proper holes and push down to lock it back into position.

Defroster vent grille

12   Using a flat trim tool, pry up on the defroster grille and release the retaining clips. Do this all the way around the grille to remove it **(see illustration)**.

13   Installation is the reverse of removal.

Center trim panel bezel (radio bezel trim)

14   Using a flat trim tool, work around the outer edges of the bezel (but never at or near the radio screen - always along the outer edge of the bezel). As you work your way around, the retaining clips will release **(see illustration)**.

15   Once the retaining clips have been released, turn the bezel over and disconnect any wire connections.

16   Installation is the reverse of removal.

Glove box

17   Remove the close-out panel below the glove box (see Step 30).

18   Remove the floor duct below the glove box **(see illustration)**.

21.12 Use a plastic trim tool to pry along the defroster trim panel until all the clips have been disengaged

21.14 A smooth plastic trim tool works best to prevent damage to the trim panel and the dash

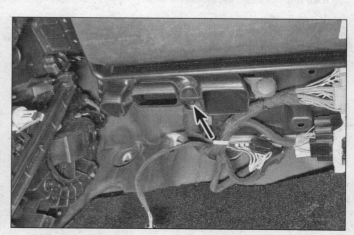

21.18 Remove the push fastener and detach the floor duct

21.19a Push down on this lever to release the glove box door

21.19b Remove the glove box door by pressing down on both of the levers at the same time

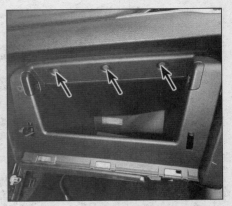

21.20a Remove the screws securing the glove box to the dash panel

21.20b Working under the dash, remove the screw near the passenger's airbag electrical connector . . .

21.20c . . . the screw under the left side of the glove box . . .

21.20d . . . and the screw near the firewall (shown here looking straight up)

19   Open the glove box and remove the door by pressing down on the hinge release arms **(see illustrations)**.

20   Remove the three screws in the front edge of the glove box and the screws below the instrument panel **(see illustrations)**.

21   Disconnect the glove box wiring harness electrical connector **(see illustration)**.

22   Use a flat trim tool to release the retain- ing clips that secure the glove box to the dash panel **(see illustration)**.

23   Slide the glove box out of the dash **(see illustration)**.

24   Installation is the reverse of removal.

Knee bolster trim panel (driver's side)

25   Remove the instrument panel end cap (see Step 2).

26   Remove the lower A-pillar trim (see Step 33).

27   Remove the screws and push pins that are securing the knee bolster to the dash **(see illustration)**.

28   The upper right corner and near the steering column area of the knee bolster trim are held on by retaining clips. Use a flat trim

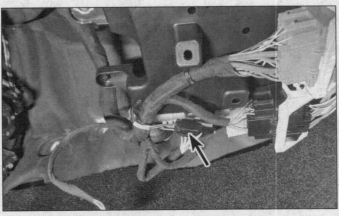

21.21 Unplug the glove box harness connector

21.22 Use a smooth plastic trim tool to release the retaining clips . . .

21.23 . . . then slide the glove box out straight to remove it from the dash

21.27 Location of the screws (1), push pins (2), and retaining clips (3)

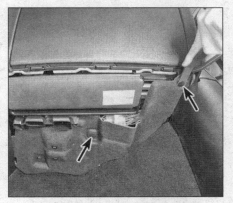

21.30 Remove the push pin clips with a trim tool

21.35 Pry the lower A-pillar trim free with a plastic trim tool

21.36 Pull outwards away from the A pillar area to release the clips

tool to pull the trim panel away from the dash, releasing the clips.

29   Installation is the reverse of removal.

Close-out panel (passenger's side, under glove box)

30   Remove the two push pins securing the close out panel to the dash **(see illustration)**.

31   Lower the close out panel and slide it

out, then disconnect the lighting wire harness connector.

32   Installation is the reverse of removal.

A-pillar trim

Warning: *The A pillar trim is part of the airbag system. Follow all the procedures and safety concerns regarding the airbag system listed (see Chapter 12). When working with*

any components of the airbag system, always reconnect any airbag leads and safety tethers that you previously disconnected.

33   Apply protective tape to the defroster grille and lower section of the A-pillar to prevent any damage while they are being removed.

34   Remove the dash end caps as described previously in this Section.

35   With a flat trim tool, remove the A-pillar lower trim piece next to the dash and door jamb area **(see illustration)**.

36   Starting at the top of the upper A-pillar trim, pry the trim outward and work your way downward **(see illustration)**.

37   The upper A-pillar trim will still be connected by way of a tether clip **(see illustration)**. Use a small flat screwdriver to release the tether clip from the A pillar trim.

Warning: *This tethering clip prevents the A-pillar trim from becoming a projectile in the event of a side airbag deployment. Reconnect this safety feature when reinstalling the A-pillar trim panel.*

38   Pull the A-pillar trim slightly upwards to free it from the dash on the bottom edge.

39   When reinstalling, slide this extended tongue of the A pillar around the headliner **(see illustration)**.

40   Installation is the reverse of removal.

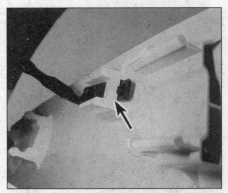

21.37 The tether needs to be disconnected when removing the A pillar. Always reconnect this safety feature when reinstalling the A pillar

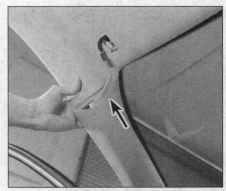

21.39 The edge of the headliner fits into this groove created by the extended tongue of the upper section of the A pillar

21.42a Pry up on the sill plate to release the pressure clips

21.42b Once it is up high enough, you can grab onto the sill plate to release the remaining pressure clips

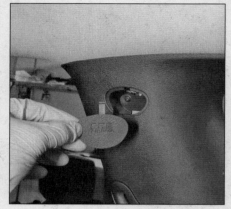

21.53 The trim cover can be removed with a pocket screwdriver, pry the edge up and remove it to gain access to the screw

Door sill plate trim

41   Remove the lower A-pillar trim (see Step 33).
42   The sill plate trim and kick panels are held in place with retaining clips. Gently pry up on the sill plate with a trim tool to release the clips **(see illustrations)**.
43   Installation is the reverse of removal.

B-pillar upper trim panel

44   Remove the screw behind the trim cap on the upper top edge.
45   Remove the trim cover and anchor bolt securing the seat belt to the B-pillar.
46   Pry off the upper end of the lower B-pillar trim, enough to allow the upper B-pillar trim space for removal.
47   Using a firm grip along the edge of the upper B-pillar trim, pull outwards to release the retaining clips, then remove the panel.
48   Installation is the reverse of removal.

Liftgate scuff plate

49   The scuff plate is held in place with retaining clips. Use a flat trim tool to pry an edge of the scuff plate up, then pull the panel upward to remove it.

Rear quarter trim panels

Upper section

50   Disconnect the cable from the negative terminal of the battery (see Chapter 5).
51   Fold down the rear seat back.
52   If equipped with a rear cargo net, remove the cargo net hooks from the quarter panel area.
53   Remove the trim cap at the upper edge of the quarter panel trim, then remove the screw **(see illustration)**.
54   Separate the seat belt anchor **(see illustrations)** and pull the door seals off far enough to expose the edges of the quarter panel.
55   Using a flat trim tool, work the pressure clips loose around the outside edges of the quarter panel **(see illustration)**.
56   With all the clips released, check for any electrical connections or wire harnesses that may be attached to the back side of the quarter panel and remove or detach them.
57   Remove the quarter panel.
58   Installation is the reverse of removal.

Lower section

59   Disconnect the cable from the negative

terminal of the battery (see Chapter 5).
60   Remove the rear door sill trim.
61   Open the liftgate and remove the liftgate upper center trim with a flat trim tool, prying it up to release it from the pressure clips.
62   Remove the spare tire access panels and carpeting.
63   Remove the upper quarter panel trim.
64   Remove the liftgate scuff plate.
65   Pull the liftgate weatherstripping from off the edge of the quarter panel trim sections.
66   Remove the screw located in about the center of the lower quarter panel in the small recessed pocket.
67   Starting in a corner, using your flat trim tool, work your way around the edge of the panel to release the pressure clips.
68   As the panel comes loose, disconnect any electrical connectors that are attached to the quarter panel, (rear lighting, accessory power plug, etc.)
69   Remove the panel.
70   Installation is the reverse of removal.

Sun visor

71   The sun visors are held in place with two screws at the base. The inner visor catch

21.54a The seat belt bolt is below the trim cover

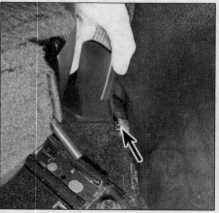

21.54b Slide the trim cover up the belt to expose the anchor bolt

21.55 Work your way around the outside edges to release the pressure clips

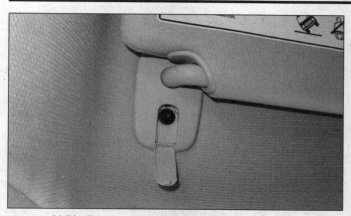

21.72a Flip down the cover concealing the screw, then remove the screw

21.72b If equipped with a lighted vanity mirror, disconnect the electrical connector

uses a single screw securing it to the roof support bracket.

72 Remove the screw securing the visor pivot to the roof support bracket. If equipped with a lighted vanity, pull the visor down about an inch to expose the wire connection. Disconnect the connector and remove the sun visor **(see illustrations)**.

73 To remove the support catch of the visor, remove the single screw securing the catch and pull it straight down for removal.

74 Installation is the reverse of removal.

Overhead grab handle

75 Carefully pry the plastic clip covers up **(see illustration)**, then remove the screws and detach the handle.

76 Installation is the reverse of removal.

Overhead console

77 Using a flat trim tool, pry between the edge of the overhead console and the headliner to free the pressure clips.

78 Once the pressure clips are free, lower the console down and disconnect the electrical connections.

79 Installation is the reverse of removal.

Headliner

80 Disconnect the cable from the negative battery terminal (see Chapter 5).

81 If applicable, remove the overhead console (see Section 21).

82 Remove the A-pillar trim, then pry out and position aside the upper B and quarter trim panels accordingly to allow for headliner removal (see related Steps in this Section).

83 Remove the sun visors, sun visor support catches, and grab handles (see related Steps in this Section).

84 Remove the interior rearview mirror (see Section 17).

85 Disconnect the electrical connectors at the left and right side A-pillars, then free the wiring harness clips running up the pillars.

86 Open the liftgate and remove the push-pins securing the rear of the headliner. Pull down on the rear of the headliner and disconnect the dome light electrical connector. Also disconnect the rear windshield washer hose, if equipped.

87 If equipped with a sun roof, carefully pry out the headliner and sun roof opening trim from around the sun roof to release the retaining clips to the trim panel and headliner.

88 As the headliner is lowered, check to see if the rear washer hose (if equipped) is secured by any remaining clips that will need to be detached.

89 Slowly lower the headliner and keep an eye out for any electrical connections or harness clips that may still be attached, then guide the headliner out of the rear of the vehicle.

90 Installation is the reverse of removal.

Instrument panel upper and lower trim covers

91 Disconnect the cable from the negative terminal of the battery (see Chapter 5).

92 Remove the A-pillar trim panels (see Step 33) and the door sill plates (see Step 41). Unclip the electrical connectors from each end of the instrument panel (through the openings where the end caps were).

93 Remove the defroster vent grille (see Step 12).

94 Remove the under-dash close-out panels.

95 Remove the center console (see Section 24).

96 Remove the heater and air conditioning control assembly (see Chapter 3, Section 11).

97 Remove the radio (see Chapter 12, Section 11). Also remove the radio support bracket.

98 Remove the center speaker cover and the screws underneath. Also remove the storage bin from the upper trim cover.

99 Working through the glove box recess, remove the two bolts from the passenger's airbag mounting bracket **(see illustration)**. Also disconnect the airbag harness electrical connector.

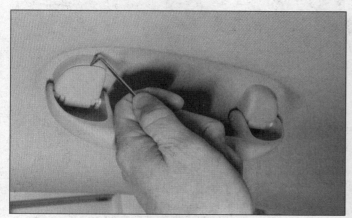

21.75 Use a small pick or screwdriver to pry the covers up

21.99 Passenger's airbag-to-instrument panel bracket bolts

21.100a Remove the screws from the right side . . .

21.100b . . . and center of the lower instrument panel trim cover

100 Remove the screws securing the lower trim panel **(see illustrations)**.
101 Using a plastic trim tool, carefully pry the lower trim cover from the instrument

panel carrier.
102 Remove the screws retaining the upper trim cover **(see illustrations)**.
103 Remove the screws securing the heater/

air conditioning ducts to the HVAC housing.
104 Detach the instrument panel upper cover from the instrument panel carrier.
105 Installation is the reverse of removal.

21.102a Instrument panel upper cover screws - right side

21.102b Instrument panel upper cover screws - left side, lower

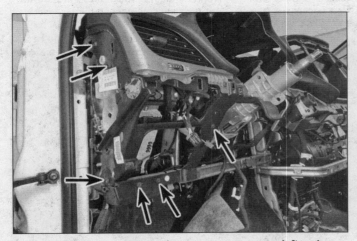

21.102c Instrument panel upper cover screws - left end

21.102d Instrument panel upper cover screws - behind instrument cluster and radio

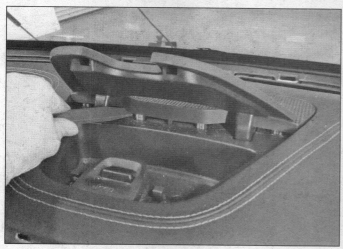

22.8a Open the center storage area and pry the trim cover up with a flat trim tool

22.8b Remove the screws hidden by the trim

22 Instrument panel - removal and installation

Warning: *Models covered by this manual are equipped with a Supplemental Restraint System (SRS), more commonly known as airbags. Always disable the airbag system before working in the vicinity of any airbag system component to avoid the possibility of accidental deployment of the airbag, which could cause personal injury (see Chapter 12). Wait approximately two minutes after disconnecting the negative battery cable before proceeding.*
Warning: *Wait until the engine is completely cool before beginning this procedure.*
Note: *The instrument panel removal and installation procedure can be very difficult to perform and is not recommended for the novice mechanic - make sure you are comfortable with your mechanical abilities before attempting to start this procedure.*

1   Have the air conditioning refrigerant discharged by a licensed air conditioning technician.
2   Disconnect the cable from the negative battery terminal (see Chapter 5).
3   Drain the cooling system (see Chapter 1).
4   Disconnect the heater hoses at the firewall.
5   Disconnect the air conditioning refrigerant lines at the firewall. Plug the ends to prevent moisture and debris from entering the air conditioning system.
6   Remove both front doors (see Section 14).
7   Remove the instrument panel end caps, instrument cluster bezel, steering column lower trim, speaker covers from the instrument panel, defrost grille, center bezel trim, glove box, driver's knee bolster trim, passenger's close out panel, A pillar trim, and door sill trim (see Section 21).
8   Remove the center dash bezel trim **(see illustrations)**.

9   Remove the center console and floor shifter housing (see Section 24).
10   Remove the floor ducts and distribution ducting.
11   Remove the transmission shifter assembly (see (Chapter 7A).
12   Remove the HVAC control assembly/radio assembly (see Chapter 3).
13   Remove the steering column (see Chapter 10).
14   Disconnect the radio antenna connector from the passenger's side kick panel area.
15   Detach the center wiring harness from the retaining clips.
16   Working in the driver's side kick panel area, disconnect the main wiring harness connectors, hood release cable from the hood release lever, as well as the on-board diagnostic (OBD II) connector port from the bracket **(see illustration)**.

22.8c Remove the rubber mat to expose the hidden retaining screw, remove the screw

22.8d Lift the center dash bezel and storage compartment out of the instrument cluster

22.16 Unclip the OBD connector from the dash, as well as the hood release cable. They will not be part of the instrument panel removal

1 Hood release   *2 OBD-II connector*

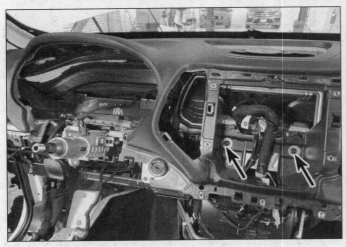

22.17 With the radio assembly removed, remove the center mounting bolts

22.18 The instrument panel side mounting bolts are only accessed with the doors removed

22.19 There are four bolts total for the lower center support

23.2 This is a Motorq® Super Drive bolt, which is used on these models. It will require the use of a special driver to remove these bolts

17   Remove the instrument panel center mounting bolts from the radio opening **(see illustration)**.

18   Remove the instrument panel side mounting bolts, which can only be accessed with the front doors removed **(see illustration)**.

Note: *The instrument panel side mounting bolts will require a 9mm deep socket with a full cut interior section to slip over the bolts.*

19   Remove the lower-center support bolts from each side of the center console area **(see illustration)**.

20   Remove the instrument panel upper bolts.

21   Remove the wiper arms and wiper motor (see Chapter 12).

22   Remove the two dash carrier to plenum fasteners located under the wiper linkage and motor assembly mounting area.

23   Disconnect the electrical connections that are involved with the removal of the instrument cluster. There are connections on both sides and in the center area.

Warning: *The manufacturer makes note that you should mark the location of the instrument cluster in relationship to the door sills*

and windshield by applying tape to the two surfaces and marking the two pieces of tape. This will insure the instrument panel will be re-located back into its original position. Failure to do so could make reinstalling certain trim impossible or to fit improperly.

Note: *Have an assistant in the vehicle supporting the weight of the dash center section from here on out. The dash is not that heavy, but can distort very easily if not handled with care.*

24   With the help of an assistant, carefully guide the instrument panel out from the vehicle - double-checking that all electrical connections have been disconnected and wiring harness clips have been detached.

25   Installation is the reverse of removal.

23 Seats - removal and installation

Warning: *Models covered by this manual are equipped with a Supplemental Restraint System (SRS), more commonly known as airbags. Always disable the airbag system before working in the vicinity of any airbag system component to avoid the possibil-*

ity of accidental deployment of the airbag, which could cause personal injury (see Chapter 12).

Note: *Some models will have more electrical connections and more features added to the seats. Be aware of the components and avoid damaging them when the seats are being removed.*

1   Disconnect the cable from the negative battery terminal (see Chapter 5).

2   On some models, the seats have been installed using Motorq® bolts. This will require the use of this special socket in order to remove the bolts **(see illustration)**.

Front seat

3   Slide the front seat all the way rearward and remove the mounting fasteners at the front **(see illustrations)**.

4   Slide the seat all the way forward and remove the seat mounting fasteners at the rear **(see illustration)**.

5   Tip the seat up to gain access to the electrical connections. Disconnect the connections **(see illustration)**.

Note: *Do not handle the seat by the adjuster release bar, as the bar is spring loaded.*

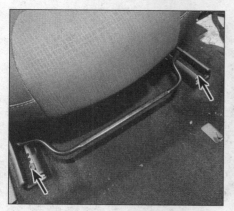

23.3 Remove the two bolts securing the front of the seat to the floor

23.4 Location of the seat mounting bolts (rear)

23.5 Disconnect the electrical connections

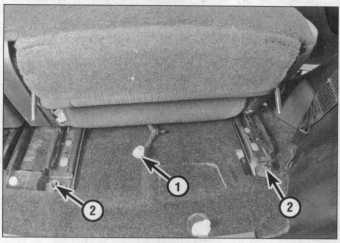

23.8a Rear seat mounting and electrical - right side

1   *Electrical connector*   2   *Mounting nuts*

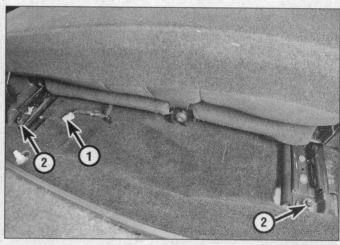

23.8b Rear seat mounting and electrical - left side

1   *Electrical connection*   2   *Mounting nuts*

6   Fold the seat back forward, then tilt the seat outward. Now hold onto the underside of the cushion and carefully guide the front seat out of the vehicle.

7   Installation is the reversal of removal. Tighten the seat mounting bolts and seat belt anchor bolts to the torque listed in this Chapter's Specifications.

Rear seats

8   Fold the rear seats down, then locate the nuts securing the seat rails to the floor for both the driver's and passenger's seats (**see illustrations**). Remove the nuts and disconnect the electrical connections from both seats.

9   Locate the front bolt trim covers. Use a trim tool or small screwdriver to pry open the trim covers (**see illustration**).

10   Remove the front bolts.

11   Disconnect any remaining electrical connections.

12   Tilt the folded seat forward, then guide the seat assembly out of the vehicle (**see illustration**).

13   Installation is the reverse of removal. Tighten the fasteners to the torque listed in this Chapter's Specifications.

23.9 Pry the trim covers off of the bolt access areas, then remove the bolts (not all of the front bolts are shown)

23.12 Guide the seat out of the vehicle (the use of an assistant is recommended)

24.4a Slide the trim tool under the edge, then work it around the outside of the bezel

24.4b Lift the bezel trim up and out of the way if you are just going to remove the console, otherwise remove the shifter knob to remove the trim bezel

24 Center console, shifter knob and bezel trim plate - removal and installation

Warning: *Models covered by this manual are equipped with a Supplemental Restraint System (SRS), more commonly known as airbags. Always disable the airbag system before working in the vicinity of any airbag system component to avoid the possibility of accidental deployment of the airbag, which could cause personal injury (see Chapter 12).*

1   Disconnect the IBS (Intelligent Battery Sensor) and the negative battery clamp from the battery negative post.

Note: *Always disconnect the IBS first to allow the IBS to discharge.*

Shifter knob

2   To remove the shifter knob, pull down on the chrome ring and trim leather to expose the two screws. Remove the screws and pull the shifter knob off.

3   Installation is the reverse of removal.

Shifter bezel trim

Note: *Alternatively, you do not need to remove the shifter knob. The shifter bezel trim will fit through the opening in the center console as you remove the console.*

4   Remove the shifter bezel trim by using a flat trim tool to pry up the outer edges **(see illustrations)**.

5   Use the flat trim tool again to lift the shifter console bezel trim by prying up on the retaining clips **(see illustrations)**. Disconnect the electrical leads once it has come free of all the clips and remove it.

6   Installation is the reverse of removal

Center console

7   Using a flat trim tool, remove the forward close-out panels on either side of the console **(see illustration)**.

8   Remove the center trim panel (small panel), and remove the two screws securing the front section of the console to the dash panel **(see illustrations)**.

9   Check for any obstructions caused by wire harnesses or connectors that may interfere with the removal of the console.

10   Disconnect the electrical harness connectors that may hinder the removal of the console that you can reach with the shifter to console bezel removed.

11   Slide the front seats forward as far as possible to gain access to the outer screws in the rear portion of the console **(see illustration)**.

12   Grasp the front edges of the console with both hands and pull out to release any of the remaining pressure clips.

13   Lift the rear section up to release any remaining rear retaining clips.

14   Lift the console up high enough to gain access to any additional electrical connections. Disconnect the electrical connectors **(see illustration)**.

15   Remove the center console.

16   Installation is the reverse of removal.

24.5a Shifter-to-console bezel trim is held down with retaining clips. Work your way around the outside edge to avoid damaging the bezel trim

24.5b Lift the trim up, and if necessary, work the boot bezel trim through the opening of the console to shifter trim and remove it from the vehicle

24.7 The close out panels are held in place with pressure clips. Use a flat trim tool to release the clips

24.8a Use a flat trim tool or a small pocket screwdriver to remove the trim cover

24.8b Remove the screws securing the console to the dash

24.11 With seats in the farthest forward position, remove the trim cover to gain access to the bolts (on either side) then remove the bolts

24.14 You can reach this main electrical connection with the side access panel removed

Notes

Chapter 12
Chassis electrical system

Contents

1 General Information

Warning: *A battery contains corrosive acids and chemicals. Avoid direct contact of battery acid with skin, clothing, or any painted surfaces. Use the appropriate protective gear such as eye protection, rubber gloves, and protective clothing. Immediately rinse any acid spills with water. Do not smoke or have any open flames near a battery - explosive hydrogen gas forms around a battery which, if ignited, can cause personal injury.*

1   The electrical system is a 12-volt, negative ground type. Power for the lights and all electrical accessories is supplied by a lead/acid battery, which is charged by the alternator.
2   This Chapter covers repair and service procedures for the various electrical components not associated with the engine. Information on the battery, alternator and starter motor can be found in Chapter 5.

3   It should be noted that when portions of the electrical system are serviced, the negative battery cable should be disconnected from the battery to prevent electrical shorts and/or fires or accidental airbag system deployment.

2 Electrical troubleshooting - general information

1   A typical electrical circuit consists of an electrical component, any switches, relays, motors, fuses, fusible links or circuit breakers related to that component and the wiring and connectors that link the component to both the battery and the chassis. To help you pinpoint an electrical circuit problem, wiring diagrams are included at the end of this Chapter.
2   Before tackling any troublesome electrical circuit, first study the appropriate wiring diagrams to get a complete understanding of what makes up that individual circuit. Trouble spots, for instance, can often be narrowed down by noting if other components related to the circuit are operating properly. If several components or circuits fail at one time, chances are the problem is in a fuse or ground connection, because several circuits are often routed through the same fuse and ground connections.
3   Electrical problems usually stem from simple causes, such as loose or corroded connections, a blown fuse, a melted fusible link or a failed relay. Visually inspect the condition of all fuses, wires and connections in a problem circuit before troubleshooting the circuit.
4   If test equipment and instruments are going to be utilized, use the diagrams to plan ahead of time where you will make the necessary connections in order to accurately pinpoint the trouble spot.

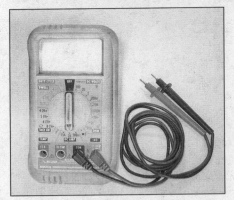

2.5a The most useful tool for electrical troubleshooting is a digital multimeter that can check volts, amps, and test continuity

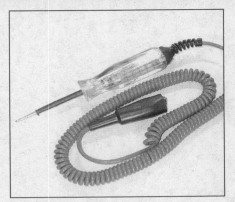

2.5b A simple test light is a very handy tool for testing voltage

Ground check

8   Perform a ground test to check whether a component is properly grounded. Disconnect the battery and connect one lead of a continuity tester or multimeter (set to the ohms scale), to a known good ground. Connect the other lead to the wire or ground connection being tested. If the resistance is low (less than 5 ohms), the ground is good. If the bulb on a self-powered test light does not go on, the ground is not good.

Note: *A lot of problems with electrical circuits can be attributed to weak or faulty grounds. Pay close attention to ground leads and their connections. A weak connection can result in a voltage drop across a given circuit. This voltage drop can cause some systems to become slow or not work at all. An example would be headlights that appear dim or have a low intensity. In this case, connections - or the ground itself - can be the cause.*

Continuity check

9   A continuity check is done to determine if there are any breaks in a circuit - if it is passing electricity properly. With the circuit off (no power in the circuit), a self-powered continuity tester or multimeter can be used to check the circuit. Connect the test leads to both ends of the circuit (or to the power end and a good ground), and if the test light comes on the circuit is passing current properly **(see illustration)**. If the resistance is low (less than 5 ohms), there is continuity; if the reading is 10,000 ohms or higher, there is a break somewhere in the circuit. The same procedure can be used to test a switch, by connecting the continuity tester to the switch terminals. With the switch turned On, the test light should come on (or low resistance should be indicated on a meter).

Parasitic battery drain

10   Parasitic drain (sometimes referred to as a parasitic load or ignition off-draw) is the term used to describe the condition of the electrical system to drain down its usable energy over a certain amount of time while the ignition is turned off. The small amount of current draw

5   The basic tools needed for electrical troubleshooting include a circuit tester or voltmeter (a 12-volt bulb with a set of test leads can also be used), a continuity tester, which includes a bulb, battery and set of test leads, and a jumper wire, preferably with a circuit breaker incorporated, which can be used to bypass electrical components **(see illustrations)**. Before attempting to locate a problem with test instruments, use the wiring diagram(s) to decide where to make the connections.

Voltage checks

6   *Voltage checks should be performed if a circuit is not functioning properly. Connect one lead of a circuit tester to either the negative battery terminal or a known good ground. Connect the other lead to a connector in the circuit being tested, preferably nearest to the battery or fuse (see illustration). If the bulb of the tester lights, voltage is present, which means that the part of the circuit between the connector and the battery is problem free. Continue checking the rest of the circuit in the same fashion. When you reach a point at which no voltage is present, the problem lies between that point and the last test point with voltage. Most of the time the problem can be traced to a loose connection.*

Note: *Keep in mind that some circuits receive voltage only when the ignition key is in the Accessory or Run position.*

Note: *In the modern vehicle, the computers are the main controller for a lot of systems. They utilize several different types of electrical signals to accomplish these tasks - from multiple data lines (CAN - Computer Adaptable Network) to communication data lines at various speeds (depending on the need of each system). Most of these signals cannot be read with a basic test light or multi-meter and require an oscilloscope or scanner to properly read these voltage signals. If you are unsure as to which method of testing is appropriate, seek professional help from a qualified mechanic for any electrical repairs.*

Finding a short

7   One method of finding shorts in a circuit is to remove the fuse and connect a test light or voltmeter in place of the fuse terminals. There should be no voltage present in the circuit. Move the wiring harness from side-to-side while watching the test light. If the bulb goes on, there is a short to ground somewhere in that area, probably where the insulation has rubbed through. The same test can be performed on each component in the circuit, even a switch.

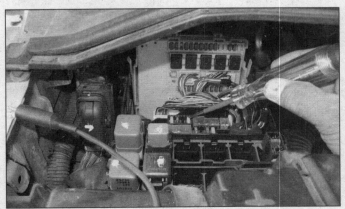

2.6 In use, a basic test light's lead is clipped to a known good ground, then the pointed probe can test connectors, wires or electrical sockets - if the bulb lights, the circuit being tested has battery voltage

2.9 With a multimeter set to the ohm scale, resistance can be checked across two terminals - when checking for continuity, a low reading indicates continuity, a high reading or infinity indicates high resistance or lack of continuity

is described in milliamps (mA). On Chrysler vehicles, this draw should not be more than 30 milliamps (0.030 amps). An amp meter is placed between the post and the battery clamp to obtain the readings. Each model, and each model type (what type of accessories have been added or were factory equipped with) will have a different acceptable parasitic drain that is allowable.

11 Parasitic load is different from an open or a short in the system. This parasitic load is supposed to be there to allow certain modules, computers, and other devices to gain the necessary voltage to maintain internal requirements. Some modules will power down after a few minutes, some can take up to 45 minutes or more to completely power down (sleep mode). Some of these parasitic draws will fluctuate with time, temperature, and motion. For example, if you touch the car near a door handle (on some models) the system will activate the interior lights or even sound the alarm. This requires a small amount of electrical energy to maintain this "alertness" which is acceptable and designed into the vehicle's parasitic load. However, excessive current draw is what you are looking for when determining whether or not the parasitic draw is within specifications. Checking for a battery drain on these models takes a highly trained technician with the proper equipment. It is not advisable to attempt this without proper training.

Finding an open circuit

12 When diagnosing for possible open circuits, it is often difficult to locate them by sight because the connectors hide oxidation or terminal misalignment. Merely wiggling a connector on a sensor or in the wiring harness may correct the open circuit condition. Remember this when an open circuit is indicated when troubleshooting a circuit. Intermittent problems may also be caused by oxidized or loose connections.

13 Electrical troubleshooting is simple if you keep in mind that all electrical circuits are basically electricity running from the battery, through the wires, switches, relays, fuses and fusible links to each electrical component (light bulb, motor, etc.) and to ground, from which it is passed back to the battery. Any

3.1a The engine compartment fuse and relay box location - depress the 2 retaining tabs and lift off the cover for access

electrical problem is an interruption in the flow of electricity to and from the battery.

Note: *When you are using a test light or any other sharp instrument to probe a wiring circuit, avoid stabbing directly into the wire. Use the back side of the connector to gain access when at all possible. If you do have to expose a section of wiring, be sure to insulate and protect the exposed section from corrosion after your testing is completed. This will avoid future problems from oxidation, wire rotting, and short circuits.*

3 Fuses and fusible links - general information

Fuses

1 The electrical circuits of the vehicle are protected by a combination of fuses, circuit breakers and fusible links. The main portion of the fuses and relays are located in the Power Distribution Center (PDC) located in the left side of the engine compartment next to the battery **(see illustrations)**. The interior fuse box is part of the Body Control Module (BCM) and is located behind the left side of the instrument panel **(see illustration)**.

2 Several sizes of fuses are employed in the

3.1b The underhood fuse box contains relays, fuses, and circuit breakers - the fuse layout is printed on the underside of the fuse box lid

fuse blocks. There are small, medium and large sizes of the same design, all with the same blade terminal design. The medium and large fuses can be removed with your fingers, but the small fuses require the use of pliers or the small plastic fuse-puller tool found in most fuse boxes.

3 If an electrical component fails, always check the fuse first. The best way to check the fuses is with a test light. Check for power at the exposed terminal tips of each fuse. If power is present at one side of the fuse but not the other, the fuse is blown. A blown fuse can also be identified by visually inspecting it **(see illustration)**.

Note: *Not all fuses are energized with the key in the Off position. Turn the key to the On position, then check those fuses for voltage.*

4 Be sure to replace blown fuses with the correct type. Fuses (of the same physical size) of different ratings may be physically interchangeable, but only fuses of the proper rating should be used. Replacing a fuse with one of a higher or lower value than specified is not recommended. Each electrical circuit needs a specific amount of protection. The amperage value of each fuse is molded into the top of the fuse body.

5 If the replacement fuse immediately fails, don't replace it again or use a larger amperage fuse. More damage can occur until the cause of the problem is isolated and corrected. In most cases, this will be a short circuit in the wiring caused by a positive feed wire lead reaching ground potential before it has reached its module or component. Internal component failure or computer failure can also be a cause of a fuse to blow. Look for obvious signs of wire harnesses rubbing against metal components or near a hot exahust. Abrasions to wiring harnesses are the most common electrical failures.

Caution: *Avoid using cheap aftermarket fuses in your vehicle. A lot of places will sell bulk fuses or fuses from unknown manufacturers that do not meet the specifications of the factory fuse. They can either carry far more current than they are rated for or not enough current. Be sure to use the correct fuses from a reliable source.*

3.1c The interior fuse box is integrated with the Body Control Module (BCM) behind the left side of the instrument panel

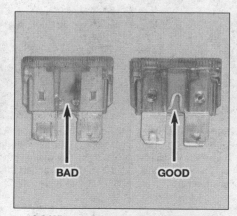

3.3 When a fuse blows, the element between the terminals melts

Fusible links

6   On these models, large, high-amperage fuses are used instead of traditional fusible links. They are located in the underhood fuse/relay box.

---

4 Circuit breakers - general information

1   Circuit breakers protect certain circuits such as the power windows, power seats, windshield wipers, and seat heaters. Usually any high-amperage and voltage system will have a breaker instead of a fuse as their protection device. Depending on the vehicle's accessories, there may be one or two circuit breakers, located in the fuse/relay box in the engine compartment.

2   Because the circuit breakers reset automatically, an electrical overload in a circuit breaker-protected system will cause the circuit to fail momentarily, then come back on.

Caution: *Circuit breakers tend to have a silver casing and are typically much larger than the standard plastic type fuses. If you suspect the breaker is the problem, be very careful touching the actual breaker. An electrical short generates a great deal of heat, so the breaker itself can be very hot to the touch. If the breaker circuit is too hot, disconnect the battery and allow the breaker to cool down before removing it.*

3   For a basic check, pull the circuit breaker up out of its socket on the fuse panel, but just far enough to probe with a voltmeter. The breaker should still contact the sockets. With the voltmeter negative lead on a good chassis ground, touch each end prong of the circuit breaker with the positive meter probe. There should be battery voltage at each end. If there is battery voltage only at one end, the circuit breaker must be replaced.

4   Some circuit breakers must be reset manually.

Electrical connectors

Most electrical connectors have a single release tab that you depress to release the connector

Some electrical connectors have a retaining tab which must be pried up to free the connector

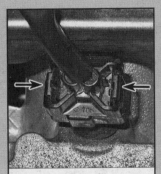

Some connectors have two release tabs that you must squeeze to release the connector

Some connectors use wire retainers that you squeeze to release the connector

Critical connectors often employ a sliding lock (1) that you must pull out before you can depress the release tab (2)

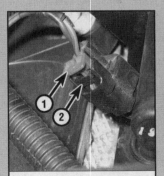

Here's another sliding-lock style connector, with the lock (1) and the release tab (2) on the side of the connector

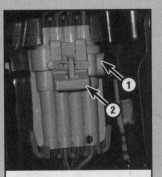

On some connectors the lock (1) must be pulled out to the side and removed before you can lift the release tab (2)

Some critical connectors, like the multi-pin connectors at the Powertrain Control Module employ pivoting locks that must be flipped open

5   Relays - general information

1   Several electrical accessories in the vehicle, such as the fuel injection system, horns, starter, and fog lamps use relays to transmit the electrical signal to the component. Relays use a low-current circuit (the control circuit) to open and close a high-current circuit (the power circuit). If the relay is defective, that component will not operate properly. Most relays are mounted in the engine compartment fuse/relay box **(see illustration 3.1a)**.

Note: *Some relays are energized by a computer using a negative or positive feed. Do NOT bypass a relay from these connections unless you are sure of the source of the signal. Refer to the wiring diagram for the routing and exact location of these input voltages.*

6   Electrical connectors - general information

1   Most electrical connections on these vehicles are made with multiwire plastic connectors. The mating halves of many connectors are secured with locking clips molded into the plastic connector shells. The mating halves of some large connectors, such as some of those under the instrument panel, are held together by a bolt through the center of the connector.

2   To separate a connector with locking clips, use a small screwdriver to pry the clips apart carefully, then separate the connector halves. Pull only on the shell, never pull on the wiring harness, as you may damage the individual wires and terminals inside the connectors. Look at the connector closely before trying to separate the halves. Often the locking clips are engaged in a way that is not immediately clear. Additionally, many connectors have more than one set of clips.

3   Each pair of connector terminals has a male half and a female half. When you look at the end view of a connector in a diagram, be sure to understand whether the view shows the harness side or the component side of the connector. Connector halves are mirror images of each other, and a terminal shown on the right side end-view of one half will be on the left side end-view of the other half.

4   It is often necessary to take circuit voltage measurements with a connector connected. Whenever possible, carefully insert a small straight pin (not your meter probe) into the rear of the connector shell to contact the terminal inside, then clip your meter lead to the pin. This kind of connection is called "backprobing." When inserting a test probe into a terminal, be careful not to distort the terminal opening. Doing so can lead to a poor connection and corrosion at that terminal later. Using the small straight pin instead of a meter probe results in less chance of deforming the terminal connector. "T" pins are a good choice as temporary meter connections. They allow for a larger surface area to attach the meter leads to.

7   Steering Column Control Module (SCCM) - replacement

Warning: *The models covered by this manual are equipped with a Supplemental Restraint System (SRS), more commonly known as airbags. Always disable the airbag system before working in the vicinity of any airbag system components to avoid the possibility of accidental deployment of the airbags, which could cause personal injury (see Section 27).*

Note: *The multi-function switch cannot be serviced separately. Any problems that arise with the external part of the switch or the internal components are only serviced by replacing the SCCM.*

Removal

Warning: *Tha manufacturer states that if the clockspring has become uncentered, the entire Steering Column Control Module (SCCM) must be replaced.*

Note: *The function of the SCCM is to carry the various data signals from the wiper switch, the multi-function switch, headlamp beam selection, telescoping and tilt for the column, the horn, steering angle sensor, as well as incorporating the clock spring as part of its internal makeup to link between the driver's airbag and the airbag control module. It also serves as the turn signal canceling cam. The SCCM should not be disassembled or internally serviced - it should be replaced as a unit.*

1   Rotate the steering wheel until the front wheels are pointed in the straight ahead position.

2   Disconnect the cable from the negative terminal from the battery (see Chapter 1).

Warning: *Wait at least two minutes before any components are removed.*

3   Remove the steering wheel (see Chapter 10).

4   Remove the steering column covers (see Chapter 11).

5   Remove the SCCM electrical connection.

6   Remove the screw on the collar band that secures the SCCM to the steering column shaft **(see illustration)**.

7   Firmly grasp the SCCM on both sides and using a quick short tug rearward, disengage the tab securing the SCCM collar band on the detent **(see illustration)**.

8   Remove the SCCM from the steering column **(see illustration)**.

Installation

Warning: *Before installing, make sure the clockspring is centered properly. Do not attempt to rotate the clockspring. If the clockspring has been rotated and you are unsure of the centering position, replace the SCCM with another unit.*

7.6 Remove the screw to the SCCM collar band

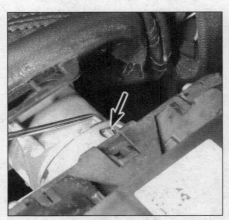

7.7 Notice the tab in the window slot of the SCCM collar band. This is the installed position of the collar band. Here we used a thin 90-degree pick to help lift the collar band off of the tab, but it can sometimes just pull straight off with a little effort

7.8 There are no serviceable components inside the SCCM. Replace the entire unit as one piece

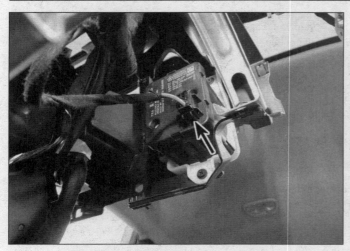

8.5 Remove the electrical connection from the ignition switch node module

9.5 Instrument cluster mounting fasteners

9   If a new SCCM is being installed, remove the lower gap hider (if equipped) from the original SCCM and install it onto the new one.

10   Slide the SCCM onto the steering shaft far enough to reconnect the electrical harness.

11   Align the notch (tab) on the steering column to the collar band of the SCCM. Position the collar band slot at about 12 o'clock as you slide it onto the steering column. Then align it to the projection tab on the steering column which is at about 1 o'clock. The tab needs to align to the slot in the SCCM collar band (**refer to illustration 7.7**).

12   Press the SCCM into position. Confirm the locking tab has engaged at the 1 o'clock position. The locking tab should be within the window slot of the collar band for the SCCM.

13   Install the screw to the collar band of the SCCM and tighten it securely.

14   The remainder of the installation is the reverse of the removal procedure.

Caution: *If you are replacing the SCCM with a new one, the clockspring will have a yellow safety catch keeping it from moving. Break off the yellow tab as indicated in the procedures that come with the replacement SCCM.*

Note: *A lot of squeaks, rattles, and strange noises coming from the upper steering column area are associated with the SCCM not being secured properly. Be sure to follow the installation procedure completely to eliminate any of these problems.*

8   Ignition system - key type and keyless type

Key type ignition

Note: *Today's vehicles are not connected directly to the engine start motor or for that matter to the engine electrical system that provides the spark and fuel pump power. Everything is a module that sends and receives electrical impulses from one compo-*

nent to the other. The keyed ignition system looks like an ordinary ignition switch but in fact is an individual module responsible of sending and receiving those same electrical impulses.

1   Disconnect the cable from the negative terminal of the battery (see Chapter 5).

2   Remove the HVAC/radio control head (see Chapter 3).

3   Remove the instrument cluster bezel trim (see Chapter 11).

4   Remove the knee bolster trim from below the steering wheel (see Chapter 11).

5   Disconnect the electrical connector from the back side of the ignition switch node (**see illustration**).

6   Remove the ignition switch node module from the instrument panel.

7   Installation is the reverse of removal.

Keyless type ignition

8   The individual wires and connections of the keyless ignition system can be diagnosed and checked with conventional testing

methods. However, anything beyond that will require the use of the proper type of scanning equipment and should be left to a professional service center.

9   Instrument cluster - removal and installation

Warning: *The models covered by this manual are equipped with a Supplemental Restraint System (SRS), more commonly known as airbags. Always disable the airbag system before working in the vicinity of any airbag system components to avoid the possibility of accidental deployment of the airbags, which could cause personal injury (see Section 27).*

1   Lower the steering column to its lowest position.

2   Disconnect the cable from the negative battery terminal (see Chapter 5).

3   Using a flat trim tool disengage the

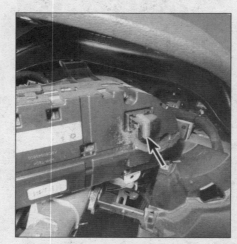

9.6a Depress the tab and move this orange lever to release the electrical connector

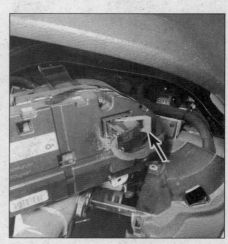

9.6b The orange lever should be in this position before you pull the connector from the instrument cluster

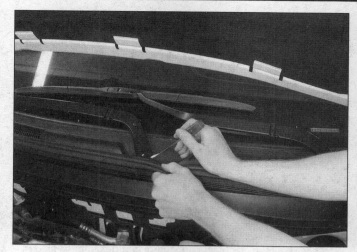

10.2a Pry off the caps, then remove the wiper arm nuts

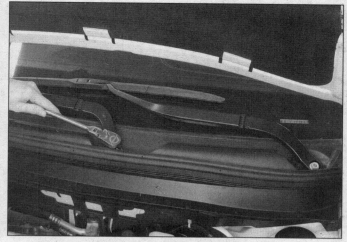

10.2b Remove the retaining nuts holding the wiper arms to their shafts

retaining clips of the instrument cluster seal. Move it out of the way to expose the remainder of the fasteners.

4   Remove the instrument cluster bezel trim (see Chapter 11).

5   Remove the instrument cluster mounting fasteners (see illustration).

6   Disconnect the electrical connector and remove the cluster (see illustrations).

7   Remove the instrument cluster.

8   Installation is the reverse of removal.

10   Wiper motor - removal and installation

Front

Caution: *Do NOT remove the crank arm nut from the motor output shaft.*

1   Place the wipers in the Park position. Mark the location of the wiper arms before removing them. Disconnect the cable from the negative battery terminal (see Chapter 5).

2   Pry off the protective caps covering the wiper arm nuts, then remove the nuts that attach the wiper arms to their spindle shafts (see illustrations).

3   Remove the wiper arms. If the arm is difficult to remove from the shaft, use a small two-jaw puller to loosen the arm, then wiggle the wiper arm free.

4   Remove the cowl cover (see Chapter 11).

5   Disconnect the wiper motor electrical connector, then remove the wiper transmission linkage assembly mounting fasteners (see illustration).

6   Using two large flat tipped screwdrivers, disconnect the ball sockets for the wiper arms at the crank arm connection. Place the screwdrivers on either side of the ball socket and pry evenly to disengage the ball socket.

7   Remove the screws securing the motor to the linkage bracket. Remove the wiper motor.

8   Installation is the reverse of removal.

Before installing the cowl cover, reconnect the negative battery terminal temporarily, then operate the wiper motor and linkage without the wiper arms attached to ensure correct operation. Return the wiper motor to the Park position, then disconnect the negative battery cable and proceed with the rest of the installation.

Rear

9   Disconnect the cable from the negative terminal of the battery (see Chapter 5).

10   Lift the wiper arm/blade off of the window, then remove the rear wiper arm. It is removed essentially the same as the front wiper arm (see related Steps in this Section).

11   Remove the liftgate trim paneling (see Chapter 11, Section 18).

12   Disconnect the electrical connector from the rear wiper motor, then remove the three bolts securing the wiper motor to the liftgate (see illustration).

13   Installation is the reverse of removal.

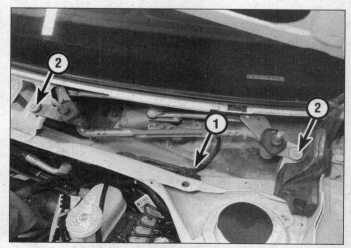

10.5 Disconnect the electrical connector (1), then remove the two mounting fasteners from the wiper motor assembly (2)

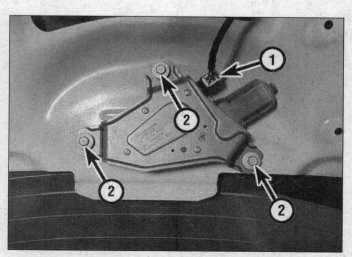

10.12 Disconnect the electrical connector (1), then remove the wiper motor mounting bolts (2)

11.3 To detach the radio from the instrument panel, remove these four mounting screws

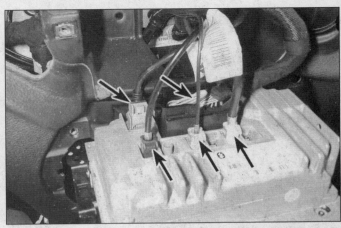

11.4 After pulling the radio out from the instrument panel, disconnect the electrical connectors and the antenna lead from the backside of the radio

11   Radio and speakers - removal and installation

Warning: *The models covered by this manual are equipped with a Supplemental Restraint System (SRS), more commonly known as airbags. Always disable the airbag system before working in the vicinity of any airbag system components to avoid the possibility of accidental deployment of the airbags, which could cause personal injury (see Section 27).*
1   Disconnect the cable from the negative battery terminal (see Chapter 5).

Radio
2   Using a trim tool, remove the radio trim bezel/HVAC control module (see Chapter 3, Section 11).
3   Remove the radio retaining screws **(see illustration)**, then pull the radio out of the instrument panel.
Note: *When disconnecting the connector(s), only pull on the connector body - do not pull on the wire itself or damage could occur.*

4   Disconnect the electrical connectors and the antenna lead from the backside of the radio **(see illustration)** and remove the radio.
5   Installation is the reverse of removal.

Speakers

Door speakers
6   Remove the door panel (see Chapter 11).
7   Remove the fasteners securing the speaker to the door **(see illustration)**.
8   Remove speaker from the door panel, disconnect the electrical connector and remove the speaker **(see illustration)**.
9   Installation is the reverse of removal.

Door tweeter speaker
10   Remove the door panel (see Chapter 11), then turn the panel over to gain access to the speaker.
11   Remove the fasteners and then remove the speaker from the panel.
12   Installation is the reverse of removal.

D pillar - upper quarter panel speakers
13   Drop the rear section of the headliner down (see Chapter 11).
14   Remove the upper panel trim (quarter panel) (see Chapter 11).
15   Remove the fasteners from the speaker, then disconnect the electrical connector and remove the speaker.
16   Installation is the reverse of removal.

Instrument panel speakers
17   Remove the instrument panel speaker grilles by prying up at the corners of the grille.
18   Remove the speaker mounting screws **(see illustration)**.
19   Pull out the speaker, disconnect the electrical connector and remove the speaker from the instrument panel.
20   Installation is the reverse of removal.

Subwoofer (right-rear quarter panel area)
21   Remove the right-rear quarter panel trim (see Chapter 11, Section 21).

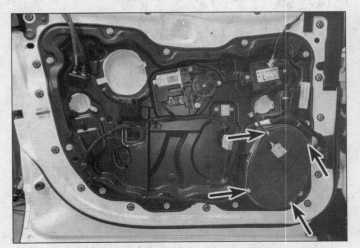

11.7 Speaker retaining screw locations

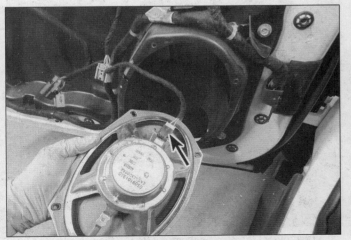

11.8 Speaker electrical connector

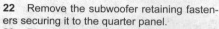

11.18 Use a short socket to remove these small speaker screws

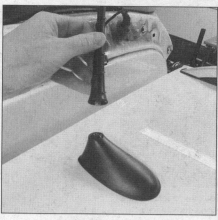

12.2 Remove the antenna from the antenna base

12.4 Antenna cable and wire connections shown

22   Remove the subwoofer retaining fasteners securing it to the quarter panel.
23   Disconnect the subwoofer electrical connector and remove the subwoofer.
24   Installation is the reverse of removal.

EAM (Emergency Assist Module speaker) - Center console speaker
25   Remove the driver's side cover from the center console.
26   Remove the wire connection to the speaker.
27   Remove the fasteners that secure the EAM speaker to the driver's side console side cover.
28   Installation is the reverse of removal.

12   Antenna - removal and installation

Note: *The AM/FM radio antenna is incorporated into the the satellite radio antenna.*
1   Disconnect the cable from the negative battery terminal (see Chapter 5).

2   Unscrew the antenna from the base (**see illustration**).
3   Lower the rear section of the headliner (see Chapter 11, Section 21) to gain access to the underside antenna dust cover.
4   Disconnect the wire harness (**see illustration**).
5   Remove the antenna mounting fastener.
6   Using a flat trim tool press in on the plastic flange tabs securing the antenna to the roof as you push the antenna base upward.
7   Remove the antenna.
8   Installation is the reverse of removal.

13   Rear window defogger - check and repair

1   The rear window defogger consists of a number of horizontal elements baked onto the glass surface.
2   Small breaks in the element can be repaired without removing the rear window.

Check
3   Turn the ignition switch and defogger system switches to the On position. Using a voltmeter, place the positive probe against the defogger grid positive terminal and the negative probe against the ground terminal. If battery voltage is not indicated, check the fuse, defogger switch and related wiring. If voltage is indicated, but all or part of the defogger doesn't heat, proceed with the following tests.
4   When measuring voltage during these tests, wrap a piece of aluminum foil around the tip of the voltmeter positive probe and press the foil against the heating element with your finger (**see illustration**). Place the negative probe on the defogger grid ground terminal.
5   Check the voltage at the center of each heating element (**see illustration**). If the voltage is 5- or 6-volts, the element is okay (there is no break). If there is not voltage, the element is broken between the center of the element and the positive end. If the voltage is 10- to 12-volts the element is broken between the center of the element and ground. Check each heating element.

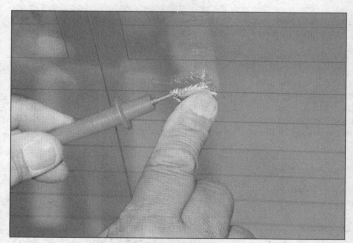

13.4 When measuring the voltage at the rear window defogger grid, wrap a piece of aluminum foil around the positive probe of the voltmeter and press the foil against the wire with your finger

13.5 To determine if a heating element has broken, check the voltage at the center of each element. If the voltage is 5- or 6-volts, the element is unbroken; if the voltage is 10- or 12-volts, the element is broken between the center and the ground side; if there is no voltage, the element is broken between the center and the positive side

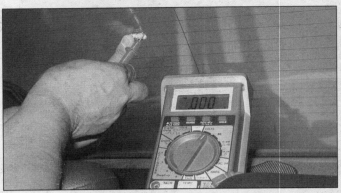

13.7 To find the break, touch the voltmeter negative lead to the defogger ground terminal, place the voltmeter positive lead with the foil strip against the heating element at the positive terminal end and slide it toward the negative terminal end. The point at which the voltmeter reading changes abruptly is the point at which the element is broken

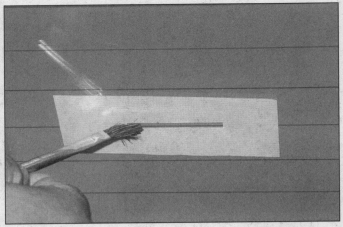

13.14 To use a defogger repair kit, apply masking tape to the inside of the window at the damaged area, then brush on the special conductive coating

14.3 Headlight housing bolt locations

14.4 Headlight housing electrical connector

6   Connect the negative lead to a good body ground. The reading should stay the same. If it doesn't, the ground connection is bad.

7   To find the break, place the voltmeter negative probe against the defogger ground terminal. Place the voltmeter positive probe with the foil strip against the heating element at the positive terminal end and slide it toward the negative terminal end. The point at which the voltmeter deflects from several volts to zero is the point at which the heating element is broken **(see illustration)**.

Repair

8   Repair the break in the element using a repair kit specifically recommended for this purpose, available at most auto parts stores. Included in this kit is plastic conductive epoxy.

9   Be sure to have adequate ventilation and that the glass be at a moderate temperature. Do NOT try this repair on an extremely hot or cold glass. Glass should be at or near 72 degrees F (room temperature).

10   Prior to repairing a break, turn off the system and allow it to cool for a few minutes.

11   Lightly buff the element area with fine steel wool, then clean it thoroughly with rubbing alcohol.

12   Use masking tape to mask off the area being repaired.

13   Thoroughly mix the epoxy, following the instructions provided with the repair kit.

14   Apply the epoxy material to the slit in the masking tape, overlapping the undamaged area about 3/4-inch on either end **(see illustration)**.

15   Allow the repair to cure for 24 hours before removing the tape and using the system.

14   Headlight housing - removal and installation

Warning: *These vehicles are equipped with halogen gas-filled headlight bulbs, which are under pressure and may shatter if the surface*

is damaged or the bulb is dropped. Wear eye protection and handle the bulbs carefully, grasping only the base whenever possible. Do not touch the surface of the bulb with your fingers because the oil from your skin could cause it to overheat and fail prematurely. If you do touch the bulb surface, clean it with rubbing alcohol.

1   Disconnect the cable from the negative battery terminal (see Chapter 5).

2   Remove the front bumper cover (see Chapter 11).

3   Remove the four bolts securing the headlamp housing to the vehicle **(see illustration)**.

4   Pull the housing away from the vehicle to gain access to the electrical wiring harness **(see illustration)**.

5   Installation is the reverse of removal.

15   Parking light/turn signal housing (front) - removal and installation

1   The front parking lamp and turn signal

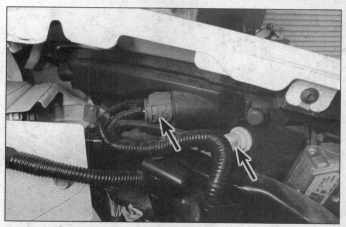

15.4 Bulb and wire connections located on the back side of the parking light housing. Three bulbs in total, not all are shown. These can be reached from under the hood

15.5 Two fasteners locations shown, four fasteners total. The remaining two are on the other end of the housing

16.2 The seal cap can be rather stubborn at times. Use both hands if necessary to release the seal cap from the housing

16.3 Rotate the bulb about a quarter of a turn counterclockwise, then pull straight out to remove it

16.4 Disconnect the electrical connection, but don't touch the glass part of the bulb. Any oils or debris on the glass will intensify the light at that point and can burst the bulb over time.

are contained in their own separate housing from the headlamps.

2   Disconnect the cable from the negative terminal of the battery (see Chapter 1).

3   Remove the front bumper cover (see Chapter 11).

4   Disconnect the electrical connections from the back side of the light housing **(see illustration)**.

5   Remove the fasteners securing the housing to the vehicle **(see illustration)**.

6   Pull the housing out to release the alignment pin. The alignment pin is located in the lower rear corner of the housing. The pin is set into a plastic socket and might take a bit of force to free it from the socket.

7   Remove the housing from the vehicle.

8   Installation is the reverse of removal.

Parking light/turn signal housing bezel - removal and installation

Note: *A (new) replacement parking light*

housing does not come with the bezel. The bezel will need to be transferred to the replacement part.

9   Follow the procedures for removal of the parking lamp housing.

10   Turn the housing upside down.

11   Remove the three screws securing the bezel to the housing.

12   Separate the housing from the bezel.

13   Installation is the reverse of removal.

---

16   Headlight bulb - replacement

Warning: *Halogen bulbs are gas-filled and under pressure and might shatter if the surface is scratched or the bulb is dropped. Wear eye protection and handle the bulbs carefully, grasping only the base whenever possible. Don't touch the surface of the bulb with your fingers because the oil from your skin could cause it to overheat and fail prematurely. If you do touch the bulb surface, clean it with rubbing alcohol.*

Halogen headlight

1   Disconnect the cable from the negative battery terminal (see Chapter 5).

Note: *The right headlamp can be accessed by removing the air filter housing. The left headlamp can be accessed by removing the battery, but either headlamp can also be reached by pulling back the front section of the inner fender for the appropriate headlamp, far enough to access the headlamp housing seal cap.*

2   Rotate the headlamp housing seal counterclockwise to disengage the seal cap from the housing **(see illustration)**.

3   Rotate the headlight bulb counterclockwise, then pull the bulb from the housing **(see illustration)**.

4   With the bulb and holder removed, disconnect the electrical connector **(see illustration)**. Do not touch the glass part of the bulb.

5   When installing the new bulb, align the tabs on the bulb socket mounting flange with the slots in the housing. Installation is otherwise the reverse of removal.

17.1a Vertical adjustment screw location (right headlight shown, left headlight identical). The adjustment can be reached from under the hood using a long Phillips screwdriver

17.1b In this illustration you can see the gear mechanism that will turn as you adjust the screw that is located at the bottom of the cone shaped access port

Xenon (HID) headlights

Warning: *Some models use High Intensity Discharge (HID) bulbs instead of conventional halogen bulbs. According to the manufacturer, the high voltages produced by this system can be fatal in the event of shock. Also, the voltage can remain in circuit even after the headlight switch has been turned to Off and the ignition key has been removed. Therefore, for your safety, we don't recommend that you try to replace one of these bulbs yourself. Instead, have this service performed by a dealer service department or other qualified repair shop.*

Note: *The HID headlamp system consists of a bulb, igniter, and a ballast. The HID system is not compatible with the halogen type bulb system nor is the halogen system compatible with the HID system. They are completely different and operate in a totally different manner.*

17   Headlights - adjustment

Warning: *The headlights must be aimed correctly. If adjusted incorrectly, they could temporarily blind the driver of an oncoming vehicle and cause an accident or seriously reduce your ability to see the road. The headlights should be checked for proper aim every 12 months and any time a new headlight is installed or front-end bodywork is performed. The following procedure is only an interim step to provide temporary adjustment until the headlights can be adjusted by a properly equipped shop.*

1   The vertical headlight adjustment screw, located on the inside corner of the housing **(see illustrations)**, controls up-and-down movement of the beam.

2   There are several methods of adjusting the headlights. The simplest method requires a blank wall 25 feet in front of the vehicle and a level floor **(see illustration)**.

3   Position masking tape on the wall in reference to the vehicle centerline and the centerlines of both headlights.

4   Measure the height of the headlight reference marks (in the centers of the headlight lenses) from the ground. Position a horizontal tape line on the wall at the same height as the headlight reference marks.

Note: *It may be easier to position the tape on the wall with the vehicle parked only a few inches away.*

5   Adjustment should be made with the vehicle sitting level, the gas tank half-full and no unusually heavy load in the vehicle.

6   Turn on the low beams. Turn the adjusting screw to position the high intensity zone so it is two inches below the horizontal line.

Note: *The adjustment screw is located in an oblong slot in the upper close-out panel just above the headlamp assembly for each side.*

7   Have the headlights adjusted by a dealer service department at the earliest opportunity.

High-Intensity Area

Floor to Center of Headlamp Lens

Center of Vehicle to Center of Headlamp Lens

Vehicle Centerline

25 FT

Front of Headlamp

17.2 Headlight adjustment details

50029-12-19.3 HAYNES

Bulb removal

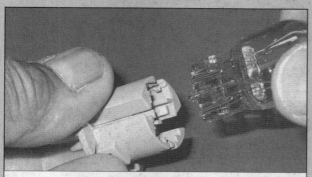

To remove many modern exterior bulbs from their holders, simply pull them out

On bulbs with a cylindrical base ("bayonet" bulbs), the socket is spring-loaded; a pair of small posts on the side of the base hold the bulb in place against spring pressure. To remove this type of bulb, push it into the holder, rotate it 1/4-turn counterclockwise, then pull it out

If a bayonet bulb has dual filaments, the posts are staggered, so the bulb can only be installed one way

To remove most overhead interior light bulbs, simply unclip them

18   Bulb replacement

Bulb removal
Exterior light bulbs
Note: *Disconnect the cable from the negative battery terminal (see Chapter 5).*

Front park and turn signal bulbs
1   Open the hood.
2   If necessary, remove the air filter assembly to gain access to the bulbs.
3   Disconnect the electrical connector from the bulb (**see illustration**), then rotate the bulb holder counterclockwise and pull it straight out of the housing.
4   Remove the bulb from the bulb holder.
5   Install the new bulb into the bulb holder.
6   The remainder of installation is the reverse of removal.

Fog light bulbs
Warning: *Halogen bulbs are gas-filled and under pressure and might shatter if the surface is scratched or the bulb is dropped. Wear eye protection and handle the bulbs carefully,* grasping only the base whenever possible. Don't touch the surface of the bulb with your fingers because the oil from your skin could cause it to overheat and fail prematurely. If you do touch the bulb surface, clean it with rubbing alcohol.
7   Loosen the wheel lug nuts. Raise the front of the vehicle and support it securely on jackstands. Remove the wheel for the side of the bulb being replaced.
8   Remove the fenderwell splash shield front fasteners (see Chapter 11, Section 11), then move aside the splash shield enough to access the fog light bulb.
9   Disconnect the bulb electrical connector.
Note: *Some models may have retaining screws that have to be removed from the fog light bulb housing, as well as latches to be disengaged.*
10   Using a wide-bladed screwdriver, carefully pry between the fog lamp housing and retaining latch to unlock the latch. Repeat this for the remaining bulb retaining latches, then pull the bulb out of the fog light housing. The bulb and bulb bracket should come out of the fog light housing together as a unit.
11   Installation is the reverse of removal.

Center high-mounted brake light
Note: *The high-mounted brake light LEDs are an integral part of the housing and are not available separately.*
12   To remove the light you will need to remove the spoiler from the liftgate.

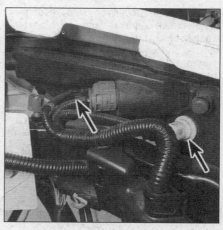

18.3 Rotate the bulb socket to remove the socket and bulb from the housing

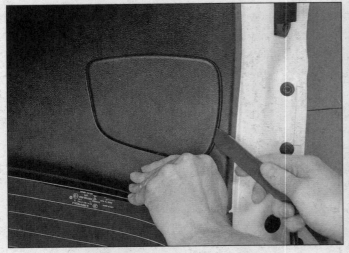

18.15a Inner taillight housing: Open the liftgate and pry off the access panel trim plate.

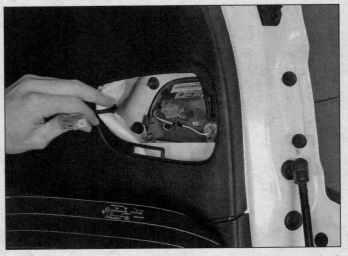

18.15b The marker bulb and electrical connection can be reached from the access panel. To remove the lens, remove the four nuts securing the housing

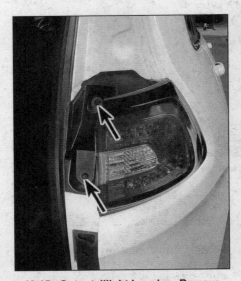

18.15c Outer taillight housing: Remove these two fasteners, pull the housing outward . . .

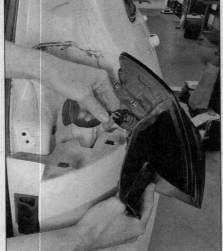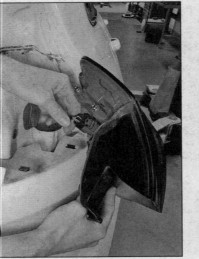

18.15d . . . then disconnect the main electrical connector

18.17 Insert a small screwdriver to remove the housing

13   With the spoiler removed, disconnect the electrical connector and rear windshield washer hose, then remove the five screws to the center high-mounted brake light assembly to separate it from the spoiler.

14   Installation is the reverse of removal.

Taillight bulbs

15   For the replacement of the taillight assembly and marker lamp, follow the accompanying photos and captions (see illustrations).

16   Installation is the reverse of removal.

License plate light bulbs

17   Carefully pry the light housing from the liftgate (see illustration).

18   Separate the bulb holder from the lens housing by rotating it counterclockwise.

19   Installation is the reverse of removal.

Interior lights

Instrument cluster illumination bulbs

20   The instrument cluster LEDs are an integral part of the cluster and not separately serviceable. If the LEDs stop working, the cluster must be replaced (see Section 9).

Front dome light bulb

21   To remove the dome/reading light bulb, pry the lens cover off with a small flat bladed screwdriver. With the lens removed reach in and pull the bulb straight outward.

Note: *There should be a tiny slot imprinted to indicate the correct end for prying out the lens cover.*

22   Installation is the reverse of removal.

Front dome light assembly - removal and installation

23   Using a trim panel removal tool pry the

light assembly from the headliner, then follow the illustrations on replacing the bulbs (see illustrations).

24   Installation is the reverse of removal.

Trunk light bulb - replacement

25   Open the liftgate and gain access to the trunk light bulb fixture (see illustrations).

26   Installation is the reverse of removal

---

19   Horn - replacement

Warning: *The models covered by this manual are equipped with a Supplemental Restraint System (SRS), more commonly known as airbags. Always disable the airbag system before working in the vicinity of any airbag system components to avoid the possibility of*

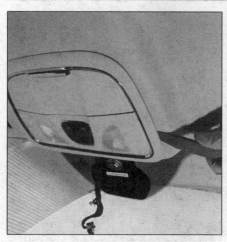

18.23a Carefully pry the assembly from the headliner, starting from this end

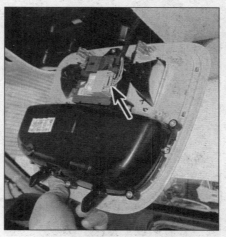

18.23b Rotate the lens assembly downward to disengage the hooked end, then disconnect the electrical connector

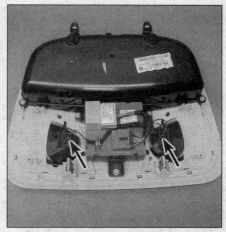

18.23c Lay the assembly on a flat surface

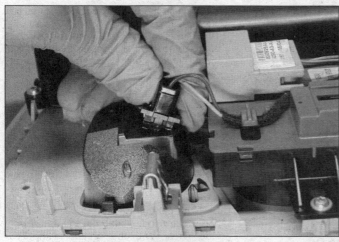

18.23d Release the clips holding the bulb socket into place. On occasion, these clips will become weak or brittle from an extended amount of time the bulb is on. Taking the entire dome lamp housing off like this is the only way to snap them back into place

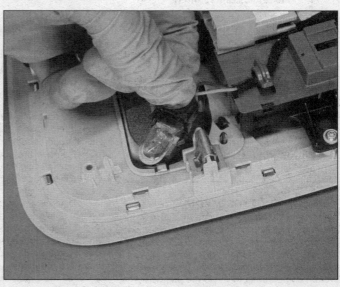

18.23e Now pull the bulb straight outward from the bulb socket

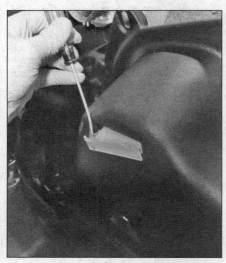

18.25a Pry the lens fixture out with a small pocket screwdriver

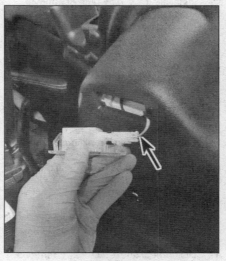

18.25b Disconnect the electrical connection

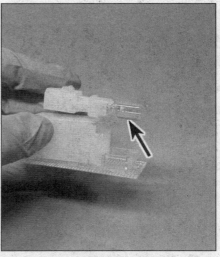

18.25c Pull the bulb straight outward from the fixture to remove the bulb

**19.2 Disconnect the fastener (1) securing
the horns, then disconnect the
electrical connector (1)**

20.4 Reservoir upper mounting bolt

**20.8 Locating the screws securing the
washer bottle to the frame**

accidental deployment of the airbags, which
could cause personal injury (see Section 27).
1   Remove the front bumper cover (see
Chapter 11).
2   Disconnect the electrical connector, then
remove the horn mounting fastener and horn
assembly **(see illustration)**.
3   Installation is the reverse of removal.

20   Windshield washer fluid reservoir and pump - replacement

Washer fluid reservoir

Warning: *The models covered by this manual
are equipped with a Supplemental Restraint
System (SRS), more commonly known as
airbags. Always disable the airbag system
before working in the vicinity of any airbag
system components to avoid the possibility of
accidental deployment of the airbags, which
could cause personal injury (see Section 27).*
Note: *Although it is not absolutely necessary,*

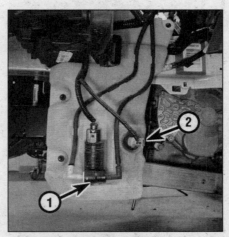

20.17 Washer fluid reservoir details

1   *Pump motor*   2   *Fluid level indicator*

it may be easier to first remove the washer
reservoir prior to replacing the pump, if greater
access is needed.
1   Rotate the steering wheel all the way to
the left.
2   Disconnect the cable from the negative
terminal of the battery (see Chapter 5).
3   Siphon out (or use a suction gun) to
remove as much fluid as possible from the
windshield washer fluid reservoir. If the fluid is
still in good condition, it can be reused.
4   Remove the bolt attaching the reservoir
to the radiator core support **(see illustration)**.
5   Raise and support the front of the vehicle on jackstands.
6   Disconnect and lower the inner fender
splash shield (see Chapter 11).
7   Disconnect the electrical connections
and hoses from the washer bottle.
8   Remove the screws securing the reservoir **(see illustration)**.
9   Lift the reservoir upward slightly to clear
the plastic hooks securing it to the frame rail.
10   Maneuver the reservoir out of the vehicle.
11   Installation is the reverse of removal.

Washer pump

Note: *Although it is not absolutely necessary,
it may be easier to first remove the washer
reservoir prior to replacing the pump, if greater
access is needed.*
12   Rotate the steering wheel all the way to
the left.
13   Disconnect the cable from the negative
terminal of the battery (see Chapter 1).
14   Siphon out (or use a suction gun) to
remove as much fluid as possible from the
windshield washer fluid reservoir. If the fluid is
still in good condition, it can be reused.
15   Raise and support the front of the vehicle on jackstands.
16   Disconnect and lower the inner fender
away from the area of the reservoir (see
Chapter 11).
17   Disconnect the electrical connections
and washer hoses from the pump **(see illustration)**.

18   Wiggle the pump back and forth as you
pull the pump outward.
19   The grommet can be replaced with the
pump removed. Be sure the inner edge of
the grommet is entirely on the inside of the
reservoir.
20   Installation is the reverse of removal.

21   Electric side view mirrors - general information

1   The electric rear view mirrors use two
motors to move the glass; one for up and
down adjustments and one for left-right
adjustments.
2   The control switch has a selector portion which sends voltage to the left or right
side mirror. With the ignition in the ACC
position and the engine OFF, roll down the
windows and operate the mirror control
switch through all functions (left-right and
up-down) for both the left and right side
mirrors.
3   Listen carefully for the sound of the electric motors running in the mirrors.
4   If the motors can be heard but the mirror
glass doesn't move, there's probably a problem with the drive mechanism inside the mirror. A loud but distinct clicking can be heard
with most failures associated with the drive
motors failing to move the actual mirrors.
Power mirrors have no user-serviceable parts
inside - a defective mirror must be replaced
as a unit (see Chapter 11).
5   If the mirrors don't operate and no sound
comes from the mirrors, check the fuses (see
Section 3).
6   If the fuses are OK, remove the mirror
control switch. Check the continuity of the
switch with a multimeter, or if in doubt, have
the switch continuity checked by a dealer service department or other qualified shop.
7   Check the ground connections.
8   If the mirror still doesn't work, remove
the mirror and check the wires at the mirror
for voltage.

9   If there's no voltage in each switch position, check the mirror and control switch for a disconnected (open) lead. It should be noted that a weak or loose connection is often overlooked as the problem. Be sure to check all electrical connections as well.

10   If there is voltage and grounds at the leads on their respective positions and the mirror still does not respond, replace the mirror assembly.

11   For removal and installation instructions, see Chapter 11 for details.

22   Cruise control system – description and check

1   The cruise control system maintains vehicle speed with the Antilock Brake Module (ABM), Powertrain Control Module (PCM), instrument cluster, throttle actuator control motor, brake switch, wheel speed sensors, control switches and associated wiring. There is no longer any mechanical connection, such as a vacuum servo or cable. Some features of the system require special testers and diagnostic procedures that are beyond the scope of the home mechanic. Listed below are some general procedures that may be used to locate a common problem.

2   Check the fuses (see Section 3).

3   The brake light switch deactivates the cruise control system. Have an assistant press the brake pedal while you check the brake light operation. This still does not eliminate the brake switch as the fault; further testing of the brake switch wiring and connector will need to be done.

4   If the brake lights do not operate properly, correct the problem and retest the cruise control.

5   Check the wiring between the PCM and throttle actuator motor for any obvious opens or shorts and repair as necessary.

6   The cruise control system uses information from the PCM, ICM, SCCM, BCM, TCM, and the ABS systems for verification and operation of the cruise control. Refer to Chapter 9 for more information on the wheel speed sensors.

Note: *If the ABS warning light is on, and it is due to a faulty wheel speed sensor, this can cause the cruise control system to not function.*

7   If after a few basic tests as described or a test drive does not determine the problem, then take your vehicle to a dealer service department or a qualified independent repair shop for further diagnosis.

23   Power window system - description and check

Note: *For window regulator (motor) removal, see Chapter 11.*

1   The power window system operates electric motors, mounted in the doors, which lower and raise the windows. The system consists of the control switches, the motors, regulators, glass mechanisms, the door module and associated wiring.

2   The power windows can be lowered and raised from the master control switch by the driver or by remote switches located at the individual windows. Each window has a separate motor that is reversible. The position of the control switch determines the polarity and therefore the direction of operation.

3   The circuit is protected by a fuse and a circuit breaker. Each motor is also equipped with an internal circuit breaker; this prevents one stuck window from disabling the whole system. However, it should be noted that each door module will reverse the window direction if the current flow becomes greater than its preset values.

4   The power window system will only operate when the ignition switch is On, and for a period of time after the ignition key has been turned Off (unless one of the doors is opened). In addition, many models have a window lockout switch at the master control switch which, when activated, disables the switches at the rear windows and, sometimes, the switch at the passenger's window also. Always check these items before troubleshooting a window problem.

5   These procedures are general in nature, so if you can't find the problem using them, take the vehicle to a dealer service department or other properly equipped repair facility.

6   If all the power windows won't operate, always check the fuses and circuit breakers first.

7   If only the driver's window is functioning, check to see if the master switch window lockout button - located on the driver's window switch panel - has been depressed.

8   If only one window is inoperative from the master control switch, check the wiring between the switches using the wiring diagram.

9   Window regulators can fail as well as the switches. If a motor is in question, remove the door panel and locate the wire connector to the motor. Check for voltage across the leads with the appropriate window switch depressed. If voltage is present and the motor does not move, chances are the motor itself has failed. Replace the window regulator assembly at that point.

10   Unusual noises from the door may indicate a problem not with the electrical side of the power window but with the track or guides. In most cases the track guide is sold as a window regulator assembly, which generally will come with a new motor as well. See Chapter 11 for window regulator removal.

Caution: *Keep in mind, the power windows in today's cars still use a reversing 12 volt motor to operate the window, but beyond that, the entire system has been developed to run on various low current, and low voltage signals. Improperly introducing current or applying higher voltages to these leads could result in some very expensive repairs.*

11   Today's window systems incorporate computer data signals for their basic operation as well as other duties such as telling the theft system the window position for example. These systems are getting more and more complicated as time goes on, which also means that for most diagnostic evaluations you will be required to have a scanner to perform those tasks.

Note: *If none of the basic tests yield an answer, see a dealership repair center or an independent repair shop and have it properly tested.*

Power window re-learn

Note: *Any time the window regulator is removed or replaced, or there is a question as to whether or not there is an issue with the door module the window needs to be re-calibrated (re-learned).*

12   The battery needs to be fully charged, all the doors must be closed before performing the re-learn pocedure.

13   Using the proper type of scanner, run the ECU reset for the appropriate door module, DDM (driver's door module) or PDM (passenger's door module).

14   This will set a missing calibration code into the ECU for that particular door module.

Note: *It is advised that you sit in the vehicle to perform this procedure.*

Note: *When depressing the window switch for this procedure be sure to push (or pull) the switch to the second detent position (express operation).*

15   Begin by lowering the window to the very lowest position using the switch.

16   Hold the switch for an additional two seconds once the window has reached the lowest position.

17   Raise the window to the fully closed position using the window switch.

18   Continue to hold the switch in the up position for an additional two seconds.

Note: *Have the stored code cleared from the ECU.*

24   Power door lock and keyless entry system - description and check

Note: *These models use input and output signals from various electronic components. These systems are linked to each other in several ways to the CCN (Cab Compartment Node), which allows simple and accurate troubleshooting, but only with a professional-grade scan tool. The door lock systems involve the ignition switch, wireless control module, instrument cluster, TIPM, door latches, door control switches and the respective door modules. Proper diagnostics requires special training and equipment. Have the vehicle diagnosed by a dealership service department or other qualified automotive repair facility.*

1   The power door lock system operates the door lock actuators mounted in each door. Diagnosis can usually be limited to simple checks of the wiring connections and actuators for minor faults that can be easily repaired.

24.10a Using the emergency key or small screwdriver . . .

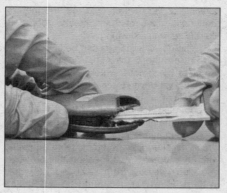

24.10b . . . carefully pry the halves apart

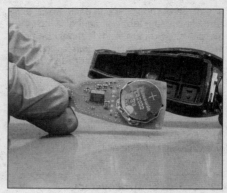

24.11a Remove the circuit board from the key fob housing

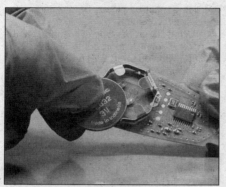

24.11b Remove the battery, noting which direction the battery faces

2   Power door lock systems are operated by bi-directional solenoids which are part of the door latch. The lock switches have two operating positions: Lock and Unlock.
Note: *If you are unable to locate the trouble using the following general steps, consult your dealer service department or qualified independent repair facility.*
3   Always check the circuit protection first. Some vehicles use a combination of circuit breakers and fuses. Refer to the wiring diagrams in this Chapter.
4   If all but one lock solenoids operates, remove the trim panel from the affected door (see Chapter 11). Using the wiring diagram, locate the positive voltage wire/connection that leads to the lock actuator and check for voltage (as well as the ground signal) while operating the lock. The lock actuator is an integral part of the door latch.
5   If the inoperative solenoid is receiving voltage and has a good ground signal, replace the latch assembly (see Chapter 11).
6   If the inoperative solenoid isn't receiving voltage, check for an open or short in the wire between the lock solenoid and the BCM (Body Control Module).
Warning: *Do not apply ground or positive voltage to any lead unless you are sure of its actual intent in the circuit. Some leads will show a ground at specific times when the circuit is not activated or a positive voltage when it is*

activated. *Sending a current or a ground at the wrong times could damage sensitive electrical circuits or computer systems. Do not assume anything. If in doubt, always disconnect the lead from both ends before testing for continuity or wire integrity.*
7   If the above tests do not pinpoint the problem, take the vehicle to a qualified dealership repair facility or qualified independent shop with the correct scanning equipment for proper testing and repair.

Keyless entry system
8   The keyless entry system consists of a remote control transmitter that sends a coded infrared signal to a receiver, which then operates the door lock system.
9   Replace the battery when the transmitter doesn't operate the locks at a distance of ten feet. Normal range should be about 30 feet.

Key remote control battery replacement
Note: *The key remote control replacement battery is a CR2032 battery*
10   Use the tip of the emergency key, a plastic trim tool or coin to carefully separate the case halves **(see illustrations)**.
Caution: *Do not touch the battery terminals that are on the back of the transmitter housing or the printed circuit board. The transmitter contains "perchlorate material" that may require special handling for disposal. See www.dtsc.ca.gov/hazardouswaste/perchlorate for more information.*
11   Replace the battery. The battery number is Panasonic CR 2016 or equivalent **(see illustrations)**.
12   Snap the case halves together.
Note: *A good battery should have a 66 foot range from the vehicle. If equipped with a factory remote start system the range is increased to about 300 feet. The exact range depends on a lot of factors such as the location of obstructions, interfering radio frequencies, and high voltage power lines.*

Transmitter programming
13   Programming replacement transmitters requires the use of a specialized scan tool and a PIN (Personal Identification Number).

Take the vehicle and the transmitter(s) to a dealer service department or other qualified repair shop equipped with the necessary tool to have the transmitter(s) programmed to the vehicle.

25   Daytime Running Lights (DRL) - general information

1   The Daytime Running Lights (DRL) system, which is required on new Canadian models and an option on models made for the United States, illuminates the headlights when the engine is running. The DRL system supplies reduced power to the headlights so they won't be too bright for daytime use, which also prolongs headlight life.

26   Power seats - general information and procedures

Warning: *Models covered by this manual are equipped with a Supplemental Restraint System (SRS), more commonly known as airbags. Always disable the airbag system before working in the vicinity of any airbag system component to avoid the possibility of accidental deployment of the airbag, which could cause personal injury (see Section 27).*
Note: *Front seat airbags are standard equipment on these models. The air bag is marked by a sewn tag with an embossed airbag logo on the outboard side of the seat back trim.*
1   The power seat system receives battery voltage from the PDC (Power Distribution Center) located under the hood. The power seat can be operated regardless if the vehicle is being operated or not.
2   The power seats can be operated in six different directions, not including the recliner (the recliner is on its own switch, incorporated with the seat switch).
3   Each seat has a seat module that incorporates the various functions of the seat including a voltage spike protection for the controller as well as the motors. On non-memory seats a self-resetting circuit breaker is part of the motor itself for overload protection.

Note: *Memory seat positions can only be adjusted when the vehicle is in park and no seat belt is attached.*
Note: *The MSM (Memory seat module) works in conjunction with the remote keyless entry (RKE) system over the computer data network (CAN) bus for setting the seat memory. If the seat memory system fails to respond check that the RKE system is functioning properly.*
Note: *The MSM will cease to move the seat into the position stored in its memory if the vehicle is taken out of park, the seat is manually moved, or the adjustable pedals are moved during the time the MSM is moving the seat to the required position.*

Power seat system check

4   If the power seat fails to function properly, follow these test procedures:
5   Check under the seat for any obstructions or anything that might have pulled the electrical connections apart. Secure all electrical connections. If the connections are good and the seat still does not move, go to the next Step.
6   With engine off (to reduce noise level), operate seat controls in all directions and listen for any sounds coming from the seat motors.
7   A grinding sound when the motor is on indicates either a broken gear (usually plastic gears) or the cable between the motor and the seat transmission (if applicable) has stripped. If you do not hear any noise or motor movement, this could mean there is no voltage/ ground to the motor assembly, or the motor/ seat transmission assembly has frozen. A quick check is to leave a door open and watch the interior lights as you operate the switch. If the lights dim as you move the lever, but the seat fails to move, chances are it is stuck in that position for some reason.
8   Check the power seat fuse in the TIPM. If the fuse is good, proceed to the next Step.
9   Remove the power seat switch, and check for positive and negative signals on their respective terminals (following the appropriate wiring diagram). If switch is OK, check the leads between the switch and motor assembly. If the wires are OK and no signal is leaving the switch when moved to the appropriate position, replace it with a known good switch and recheck. If voltage is leaving the switch, wire connectors and harness are good, the track assembly will need to be replaced.

Track assembly replacement

Note: *Any time the MSM (memory seat module) or seat track is replaced a scanner is needed to re-calibrate the track and seat operation.*
10   Remove the driver's seat from the vehicle (see Chapter 11).
11   Remove the seat side trim and the fasteners securing the cushion to the track assembly. Remove all wiring harness connections and leads from the track assembly. Remove the seat back and the track assem-

bly. Transfer any components that are going to be reused to the new seat.
12   Installation is the reverse of removal.

Power seat switch - replacement

13   Operate the seat to its farthest forward position.
14   Disconnect the negative battery terminal from the battery post and isolate the terminal away from the post (see Chapter 1).
15   Using a flat trim tool, remove the seat belt retractor trim plate.
16   Remove the screw hidden by the seat belt retractor trim plate to the seat cushion side trim panel.
17   Use the flat trim tool to work the side trim panel off of the seat.
18   Slide the side trim panel forward to disengage the panel from the seat.
19   With the flat trim tool, work the four tabs that secure the seat switch to the seat cushion side panel trim.
20   Disconnect the electrical leads from the switch.
21   Installation is the reverse of removal.

Heated seat system - general information and procedures

Note: *It is recommended to replace the Occupant Detection Sensor (ODS) when replacing the seat heater element(s).*
22   The seat heater circuit receives its power from a fuse in the PDC in the engine compartment. The seat heater system is controlled by the seat heater module mounted below the driver's seat. When the seat heater switch is depressed, a data message is sent via the LIN (Local Interface Network) to the instrument cluster (CCN - Cab Compartment Node). This message is then transferred to the seat heater modules. The module sends positive voltage from an internal solid state relay to the seat heater elements.
23   Both the seat heater module and the carbon fiber seat heater elements can be serviced by removing the seat. The seat heater module is bolted to the bottom of the lower cushion. To access the seat heater elements, the seat must be removed and the seat cushions must be disassembled. The elements can be peeled from the seat cushion and replaced separately, rather than having to replace the entire seat and/or cushions.

---

27   Airbag system - general information and precautions

Warning: *Before performing work near any airbag system components, disconnect the cable from the negative battery terminal (see Chapter 1), then wait at least two minutes for the back-up power supply to be depleted and discharged from the storage capacitor. During this two-minute interval, the SRS is still capable of deploying.*

General information

1   All the models covered in this manual are equipped with a Supplemental Restraint System (SRS) with both active and passive safety devices. Active systems require some action from the passenger, such as connecting the seat belt. The passive systems are automatically activated in the event of a collision.
2   The SRS is controlled by the Occupant Restraint Controller (ORC), which is mounted in the center of the vehicle, below the instrument panel. The SRS uses an array of airbags to protect the occupants. The driver's airbag, passenger's airbag, knee bolster, side curtain airbags, front seat airbags, and seat belt pre-tensioners are standard features in these models.
3   The airbag indicator light is activated at each start up. The light will remain on as it performs a self check on the system's components. If there is a failure, the airbag light will remain on until the fault has been corrected.
4   The SRS is activated by impact sensors in various strategic locations throughout the vehicle as well as an internal impact sensor inside the ORC. Impact sensors in the front of the vehicle concentrate on the AHR (Active Head Restraint), front airbags, and seat belt tensioners for a more precise activation during a direct frontal collision. Side impact sensors work with the same components as the front impact sensors, but in a different way than the front impact sensor does. The side impact sensors also include the side airbags, (curtain air bags) as part of their protection strategy written into the ORC software.
5   The clockspring is incorporated into the SCCM. The clockspring is a ribbon like coil of wire that delivers battery voltage to the steering wheel airbag.
6   A steering angle sensor is mounted in the SCCM and determines the actual position or angle of the steering wheel. This information is also used for airbag operation as well.
7   Seat belt pre-tensioners are incorporated into the seat belt retractor mechanisms. These are pyrotechnic (explosive) devices which when activated, retract the seat belts up to four inches very quickly holding the occupant in the seat long enough for the air bag to fully deploy.

Driver's airbag

8   The airbag inflator module contains a housing incorporating the cushion (airbag) and inflator unit, mounted in the center of the steering wheel. The inflator assembly is mounted on the back of the housing over a hole through which gas is expelled, inflating the bag almost instantaneously when an electrical signal is sent from the system. The airbag is a multi-staged release type, meaning it will deploy at various speeds and levels depending on the severity of the collision.

Passenger's airbag

9   The airbag is mounted beneath the instrument panel just above the glove box.

The passenger's airbag is considerably larger than the steering wheel-mounted unit. The trim cover is textured and painted to match the instrument panel and has a molded seam that splits when the bag inflates. Due to its size, the passenger's airbag deploys at a different rate than the driver's side does. Also, the windshield plays an integral part in the operation of the passenger's airbag. As the bag is deployed an upward as well as outward motion is carried out. This motion covers the major portion of the windshield to prevent any debris from coming in contact with the passenger as well as helping to shape and direct the airbag into the ideal position to protect the passenger.

Side-impact window airbags

10   Side-impact airbags, also known as curtain airbags, protect vehicle occupants in the event of a side impact and are a standard feature on these models. The side-impact airbags are located near the A and C pillars in the headliner. Each side can be deployed separately depending on the location of the collision. The airbag is not reusable. In the event of a collision the trim and headliner will need to be replaced as well.

Seat airbags

11   Seat airbags are standard equipment in these vehicles. The SAB (Seat Airbags) or also known as the AHR (Active Head Restraint) is built into the seat and is hidden by the trim. In the event of a collision the unit will be deployed, unfolding itself and enveloping the occupant in such a way to help prevent bodily injury. The SAB is a one-time use safety device. After deployment the seat frame will be compromised and the entire seat will need to be replaced.

Seat track position sensor

12   The STPS (Seat Track Position Sensor) is mounted under the front seats on the seat track. This sensor is used to determine the actual position of the seat so that the ORC can determine the strength and initial timing for the front airbag deployment.
13   This sensor is not adjustable, and should not be tampered with. Replace the sensor if it is damaged or are instructed to do so by any service bulletins or trouble codes information.
Warning: *Avoid jamming things under the seats to avoid dislodging the sensors or pulling electrical leads apart.*

Seat belts

14   The seat belt systems on these vehicles incorporate an inertia-type ELR (Emergency Locking Retractor) system. The front seats also include a CFR (Constant Force Retractor) system as well. The driver's seat belt system also includes an additional protection with an ALR (Automatic Locking Retractor) system. These systems are an integral part of the seat belt retractor mechanism and cannot not be adjusted or repaired. In the event of a collision the seat belt retractor assembly needs to be replaced.
Warning: *The airbag system should be disabled*

any time work is done to or around the seats.
Warning: *Never strike the pillars or floorpan with a hammer or use an impact-driver tool in these areas unless the system is disabled.*

Child seat anchors

15   The child seat anchors are located in the second seating area. They are considered part of the airbag system due to the fact it is a safety issue when adding a child seat. These anchor points are in fixed positions for ease of use. They are considered part of the active type restraint controls because it requires some action from the occupants to ensure it is being used correctly.
16   There are seven anchoring points: Three across the top of the rear seats, and four along the bottom cushion area of the seat.

Clockspring

17   The clockspring is the rotatable ribbon-like tape that attaches the steering wheel to the stationary steering column.
18   The clockspring when purchased, has a red molded locking tab on the top of it. This tab will be removed once it is properly installed. The locking tab ensures that the clockspring has not turned during shipping.
19   The clockspring is an integral part of the SCCM (Steering Column Control Module) and is not serviced separately. After a deployment, or any damage has occurred, or the centering of the clockspring has been compromised, the unit must be replaced. For SCCM removal and replacement (see Section 7).

Occupant Restraint Controller (ORC) or Airbag Control Module (ACM)

20   The ORC or ACM supplies current to the SRS in the event of a collision, even if battery power is cut off. The ORC/ACM checks the SRS every time the vehicle is started, and indicates that it is doing so by turning on the AIRBAG readiness light. If the SRS is operating properly, the ORC/ACM turns off the AIRBAG readiness light. If it detects a fault in the system, the AIRBAG readiness light will remain on. If this condition occurs, take the vehicle to your dealer or appropriate independent repair facility immediately for service.
21   The ORC is located in the center of the vehicle and can be identified by a large arrow pointing to the front of the vehicle on the top of the unit. There are no serviceable components inside the ORC. Any damage to the unit, or after a deployment, the ORC will need to be replaced.

Disarming the system and other precautions

Warning: *Failure to follow these precautions could result in accidental deployment of the airbag and personal injury.*
22   Whenever you are working in the vicinity of the driver's airbag in the steering wheel or any of the other airbags on your vehicle, DISARM THE SYSTEM. To disarm the system:

a) *Point the wheels straight ahead and turn the ignition key to the Lock position.*

b) *Disconnect the cable from the negative battery terminal (see Chapter 5). Isolate the cable terminal so it won't accidentally contact the battery post.*
c) *Wait at least TWO MINUTES for the back-up power supply to be depleted. Back-up power is supplied by a capacitor which needs those two minutes to fully discharge. During this two-minute interval, the SRS is still capable of deploying.*

23   Whenever handling an airbag, always keep the airbag opening (the trim side) pointed away from your body. Never place the airbag on a bench or other surface with the airbag opening facing the surface. Always place the airbag module in a safe location with the airbag opening facing up.
Warning: *Never measure the resistance of any SRS component. An ohmmeter has a built-in battery supply that could accidentally deploy the airbag.*
Note: *Never dispose of a live airbag. Return it to a dealer service department or other qualified repair shop for safe deployment and disposal.*

Component removal and installation

Warning: *Always disarm the airbag system before any components are removed or disturbed in any way.*

Driver's airbag

24   See Chapter 10, Section 18 for the driver's airbag removal procedure.

Clockspring

25   The clockspring is an integral part of the SCCM (Steering Column Control Module) and is not serviced separately. After a deployment, or any damage has occurred, or the centering of the clockspring has been compromised, the unit must be replaced. For SCCM removal and replacement (see Section 7).

Passenger's airbag

26   Remove the glove box (see Chapter 11).
27   Reach into the glove box opening and locate the two screws securing the airbag lower bracket to the instrument panel. Remove the two screws.
28   Disconnect the instrument panel wiring harness (clip or push fasteners) that secures the wiring harness to the passenger's airbag module housing.
29   Remove the top pad from the instrument panel and set it upside to gain access to the passenger's airbag module (see Chapter 11).
30   Detach the hooks on one side of the airbag housing from the underside of the dash pad.
31   With all the hooks detached from one side, rotate the airbag housing upward to release the hooks from the other side.
32   With the airbag free from the dash pad, disconnect the electrical connector from the airbag module.
33   Installation is the reverse of removal.

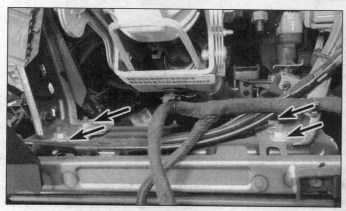

27.35 Arrows mark the position of the retaining nuts for the knee bolster airbag module

27.39 Knee bolster module mounting nuts

Driver's side knee bolster airbag

34   Remove the knee bolster close-out panel (see Chapter 11).
35   Locate the four nuts securing the knee bolster airbag module to the instrument panel support (**see illustration**).
36   Lower the airbag module and disconnect the electrical connection.
37   Installation is the reverse of removal.

Passenger's side knee bolster airbag

38   Remove the glove box (see Chapter 11).
39   Locate and remove the four nuts securing the knee bolster module to the instrument panel support (**see illustration**).
40   Rotate the module vertically to gain access to the electrical connector (**see illustration**).
41   Installation is the reverse of removal.

Other airbag modules

42   We don't recommend removing any of the other airbag modules. There are no serviceable components behind these airbags that would require them to be removed. These jobs are best left to a professional.

Seat belts

43   The seat belts are held in place with a large Torx bolt. The Torx size is unique to the seat belts.
44   Remove the bolt securing the seat belt to its anchor point. In the case of some of the seat belts some trim panels will need to be removed in order to gain access to the opposite end of the seat belt. Follow those procedures as needed.
45   Always torque the seat belt bolts to their proper specifications listed in the Chapter 11 Specifications.

Diagnosing, programming and re-calibrations

46   At any time the airbag light remains on after the initial start up cycle this is an indication of a fault in the airbag system. Basically, if the airbag light is On, the airbag system is Off. Any diagnostic work needs to be carried out with the proper type of scanner usually only

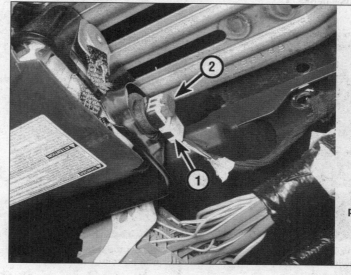

27.40 Notice the orange safety connector (2) is in the up position. This must remain up when the main connection (1) is being removed. The orange safety connection only is pushed into place when the main connection is properly seated into the airbag module

available to the professional mechanic.
47   Any component that is replaced, or for instance, you are removing and reinstalling the front passenger's seat, there will be some form of programming or re-calibration that will be required. These procedures should be left to the professional mechanic. The equipment and diagnostics that are involved are far more complicated than what is available for the average home mechanic.
48   As with any safety device in today's cars, the information and procedures are constantly being updated by the manufacturer, and direct contact with the manufacturer is essential in order to have the latest information available. These latest improvements and updates ensure your safety and can change many previous procedures completely. When you and your family's safety is involved, seek professional help and don't try this at home.

28   Steering wheel switches - removal and installation

1   Remove the steering wheel (see Chapter 11).

2   Find a flat, smooth (clean) surface that you can lay the steering wheel onto. Follow the illustrations for removal and installation (**see illustrations**).
3   Installation is the reverse of removal.

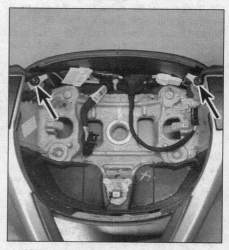

28.2a Remove these Torx screws . . .

28.2b . . . then remove these two screws. This will remove the main section of the steering wheel switches

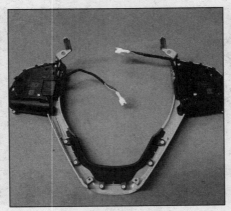

28.2c The main set of switches will come off in one large piece

28.2d To remove the switches from the rear side, start by prying off the trim panels

28.2e Remove the Torx screw from each switch . . .

28.2f . . . now the rear switches can be removed

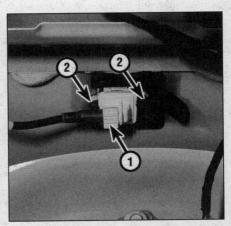

29.9 Rear view camera details

1   *Electrical connection*
2   *Mounting screws*

29 Camera systems

Forward facing camera

1   Disconnect the cable from the negative terminal of the battery (see Chapter 5).
Note: *Always disconnect the IBS (Intellignet Battery Sensor) first before disconnecting the main negative battery terminal.*
2   Separate the rear view mirror trim.
3   Disconnect the forward facing camera electrical connections.
4   Rotate the camera downwards as you disengage the attachment hooks. This will release it from the bracket.
5   Installation is the reverse of removal.
Warning: *Anytime the forward facing camera is moved, suspension has been altered, a windshield has been replaced, or tire size has been changed from factory specifications, the camera will need to be recalibrated. This will have to be done by a professional mechanic with the proper type of scanning equipment. Failure to recalibrate the camera could result in certain aspects of safety and operational duties of the vehicle to fail or not work properly.*

Rear camera

6   Disconnect the IBS and negative battery terminal from the negative battery post.
Note: *Always disconnect the IBS (Intelligent Battery Sensor) first before disconnecting the main negative battery terminal from the negative battery post.*
7   Remove the rear camera access panel from the lift gate.
8   Disconnect the electrical connection to the camera.
9   Remove the two screws securing the camera to the lift gate (**see illustration**).
10   Installation is the reverse of removal.

Rear camera cleaning procedures

11   Start off with compressed air blown across the lens at right angles.
12   Using a microfiber cloth, gently wipe the lens free of any debris.
13   Apply a small amount of lens cleaning solution onto a clean lens tissue (available anywhere glasses and contacts are sold).
14   Wipe in circular motions until the lens is free of debris

15   Let the lens dry and check the clarity of the image on the display panel.
16   Repeat if necessary.

30 Wiring diagrams - general information

1   Since it isn't possible to include all wiring diagrams for every year covered by this manual, the following diagrams are those that are typical and most commonly needed.
2   Prior to troubleshooting any circuits, check the fuse and circuit breakers (if equipped) to make sure they're in good condition. Make sure the battery is properly charged and check the cable connections (see Chapter 1).
3   When checking a circuit, make sure that all connectors are clean, with no broken or loose terminals. When unplugging a connector, do not pull on the wires. Pull only on the connector housings themselves.

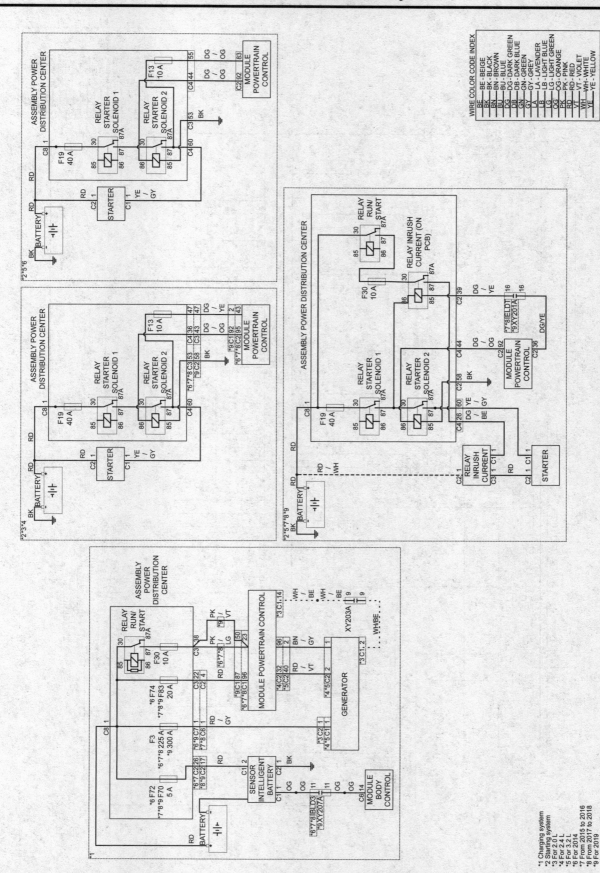

Starting and charging systems

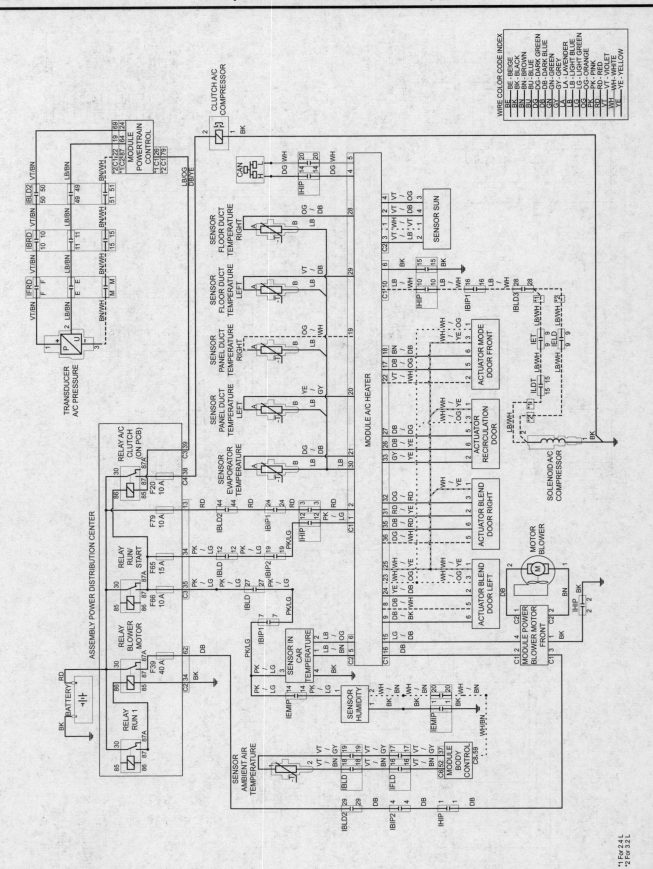

Heating and air conditioning systems (automatic) - 2018 and earlier models

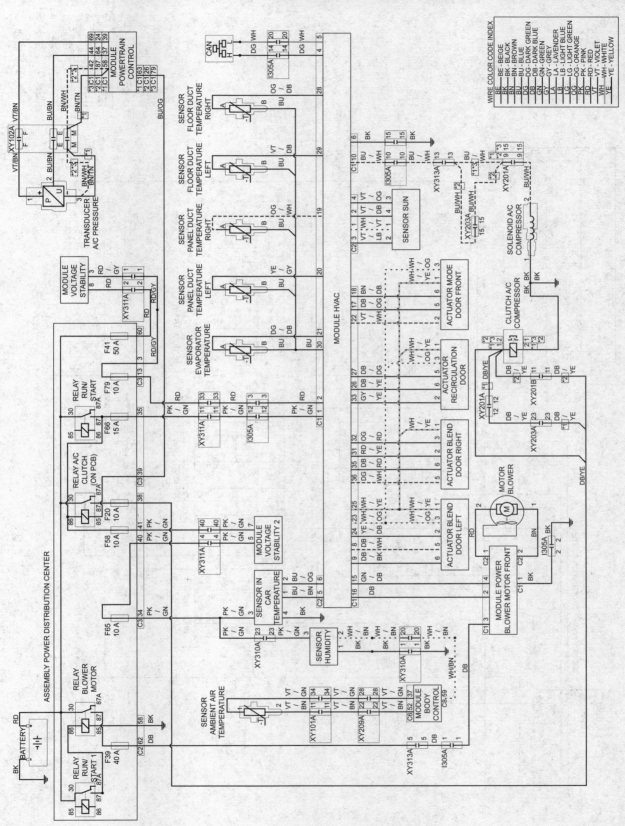

Heating and air conditioning systems (automatic) - 2019 models

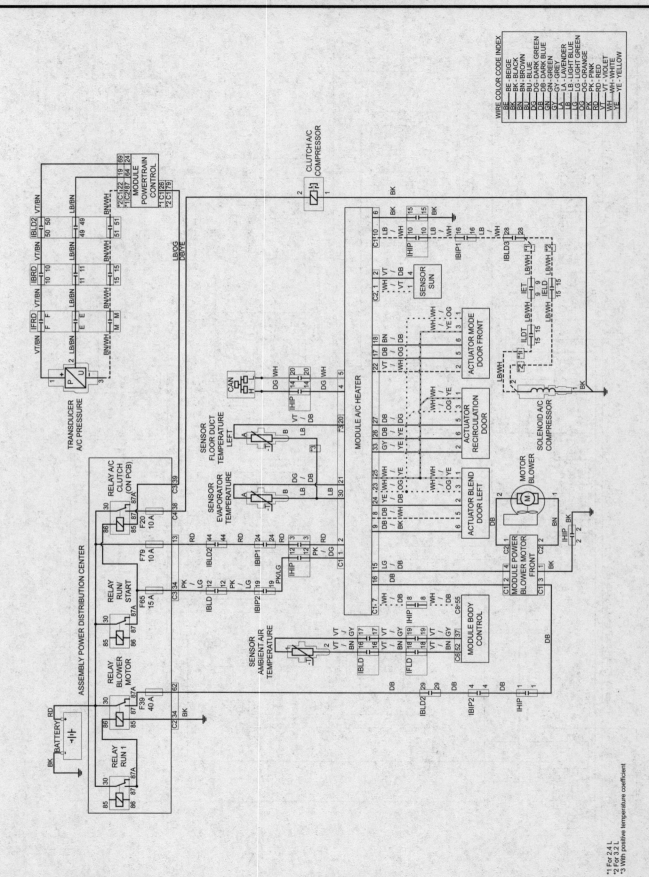

Heating and air conditioning systems (manual) - 2018 and earlier models

*1 For 2.4 L
*2 For 3.2 L
*3 With positive temperature coefficient

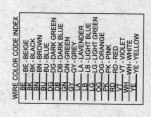

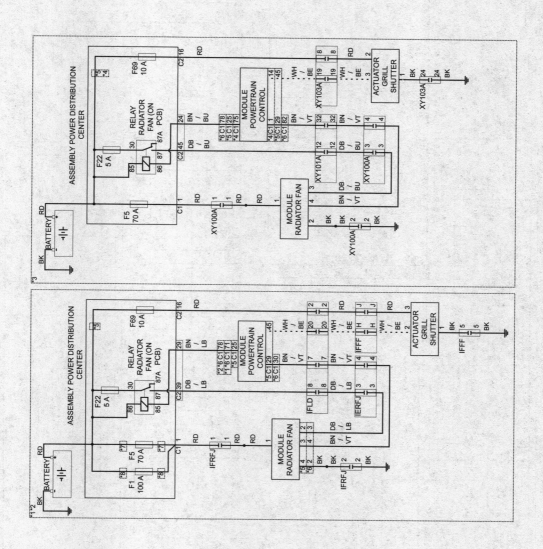

Heating and air conditioning systems (manual) - 2019 models

*1 For 2014
*2 From 2015 to 2018
*3 For 2019
*4 For 2.0 L
*5 For 2.4 L
*6 For 3.2 L
*7 Version 1
*8 Version 2

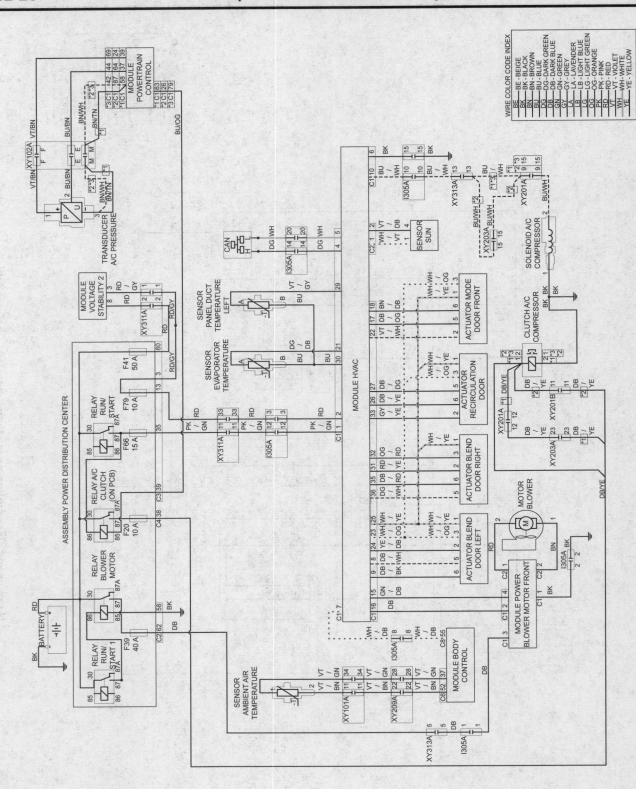

Engine cooling fan system

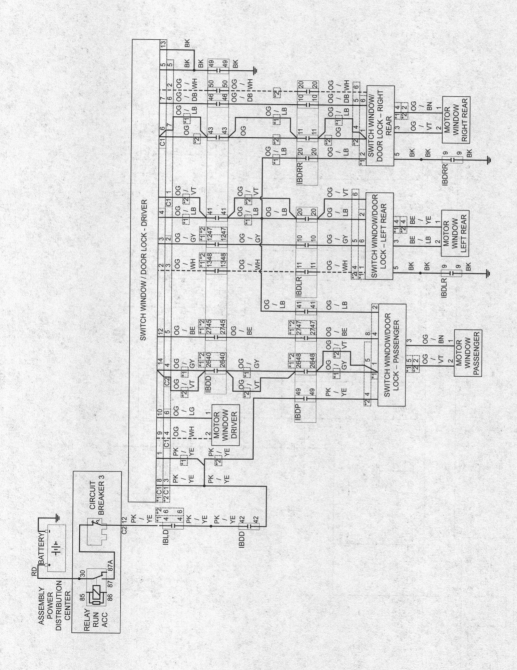

Power window system (base) - 2018 and earlier models

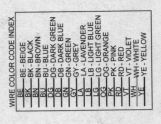

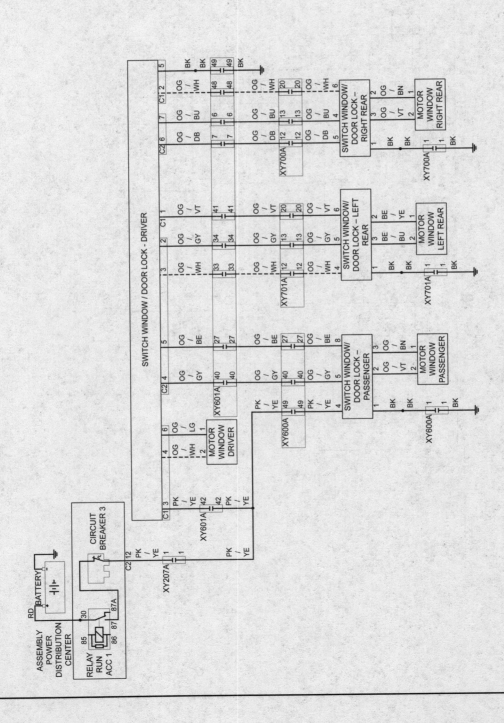

Power window system (base) - 2019 models

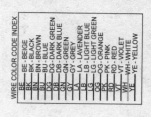

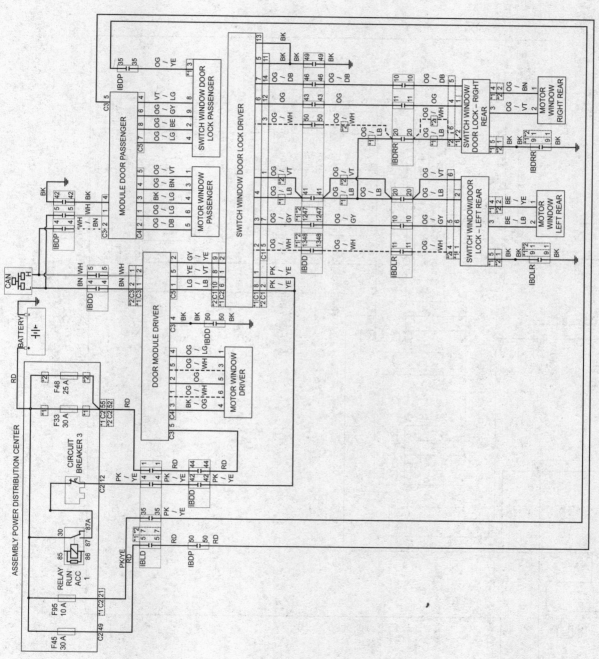

Power window system (premium) - 2018 and earlier models

*1 For 2014
*2 From 2015 to 2018

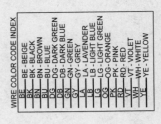

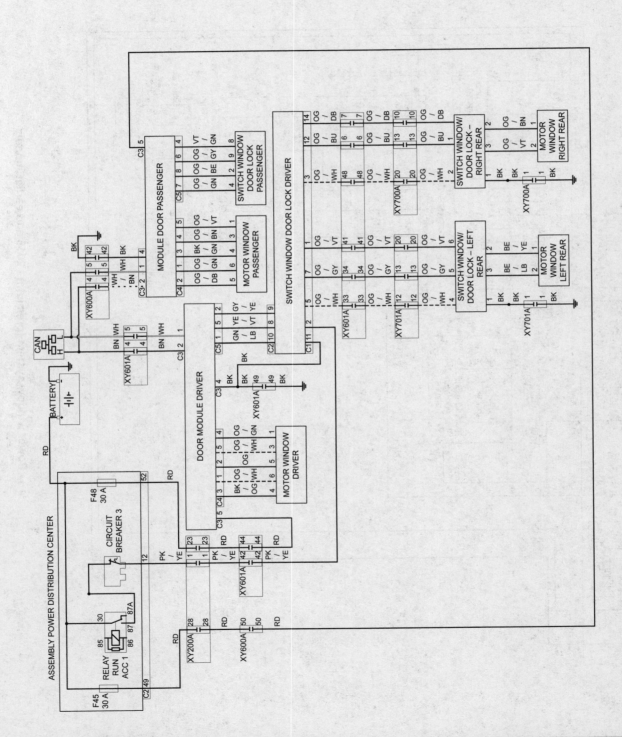

Power window system (premium) - 2019 models

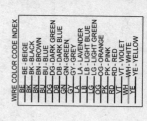

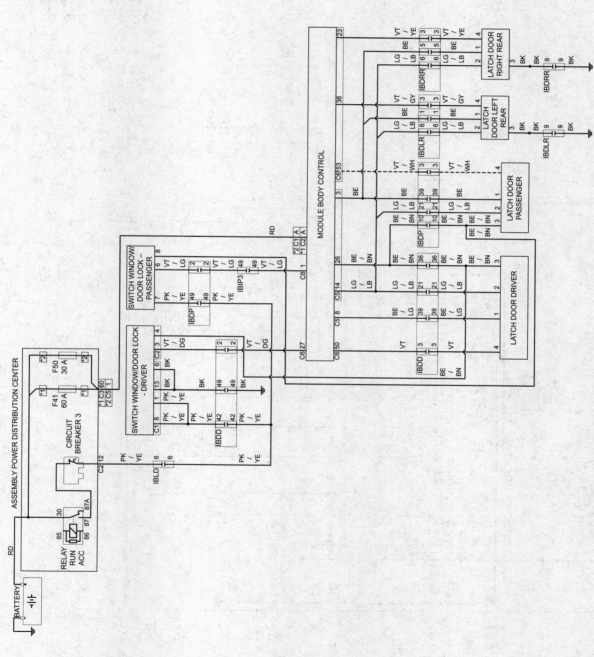

Power door lock system (base) - 2018 and earlier models

*1 For 2014
*2 From 2015 to 2018

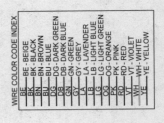

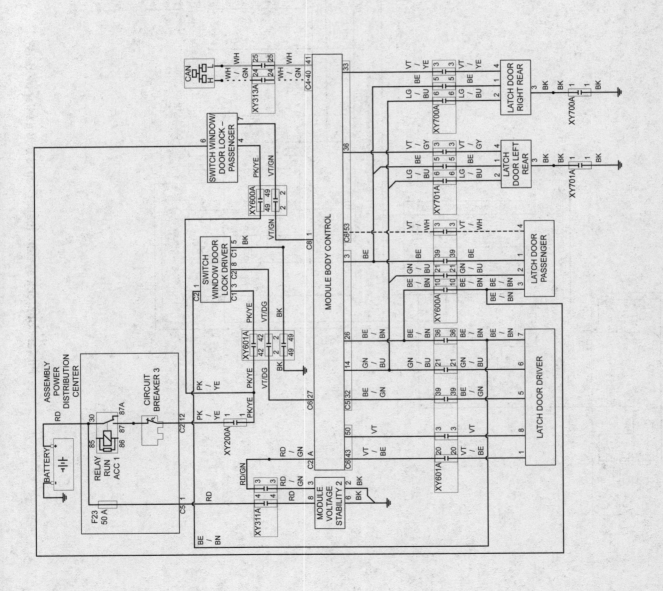

Power door lock system (base) - 2019 models

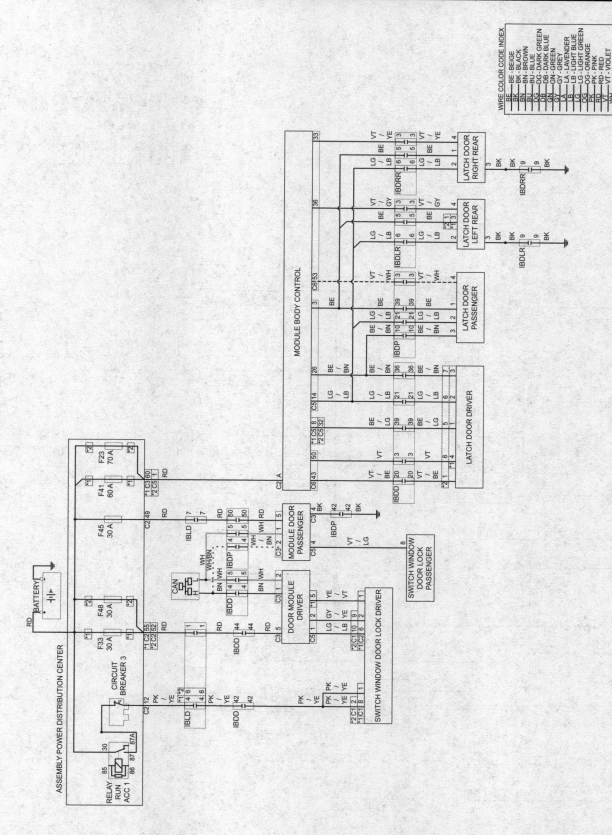

Power door lock system (premium) - 2018 and earlier models

*1 For 2014
*2 From 2015 to 2018

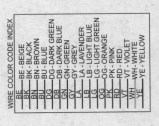

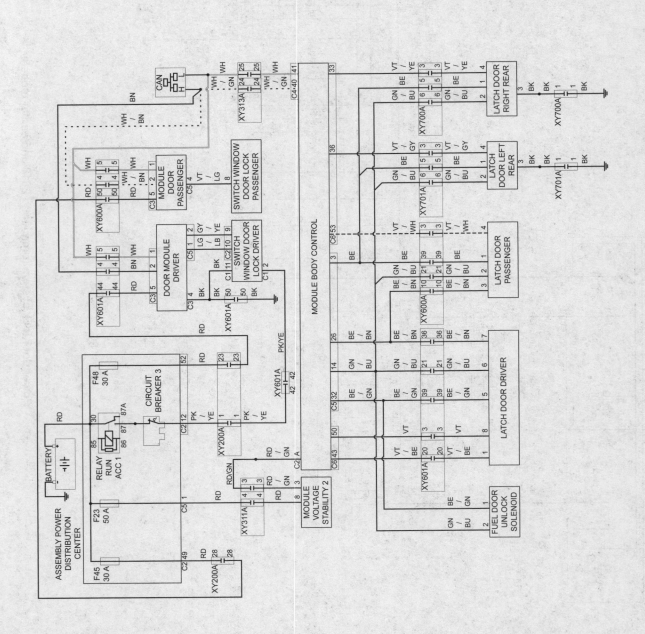

Power door lock system (premium) - 2019 models

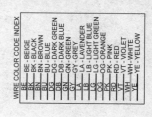

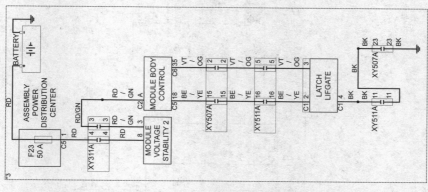

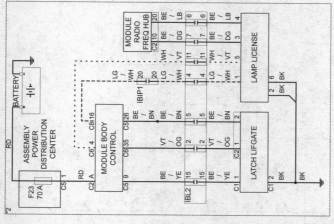

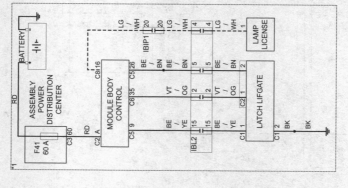

Power door lock system - liftgate

*1 For 2014
*2 From 2015 to 2018
*3 For 2019

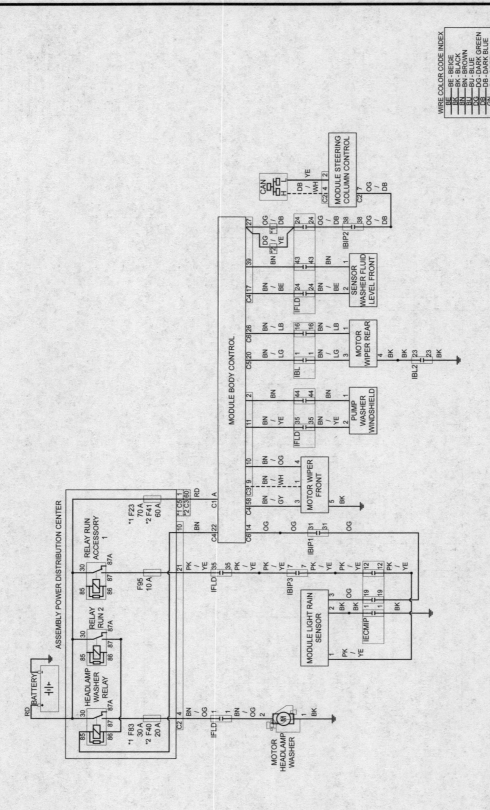

Windshield and rear wiper/washer systems - 2018 and earlier models

*1 For 2014
*2 From 2015 to 2018

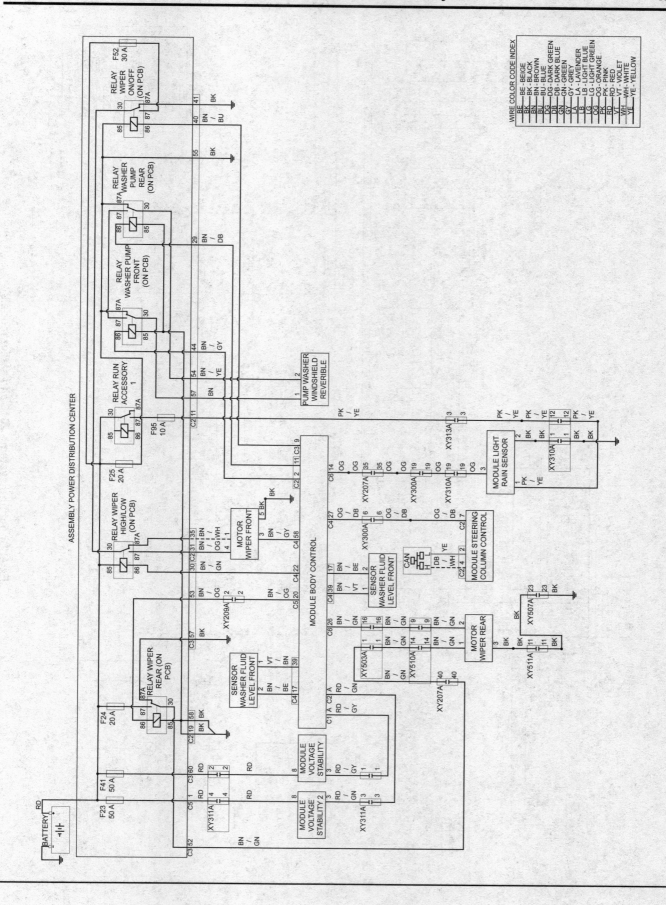

Windshield and rear wiper/washer systems - 2019 models

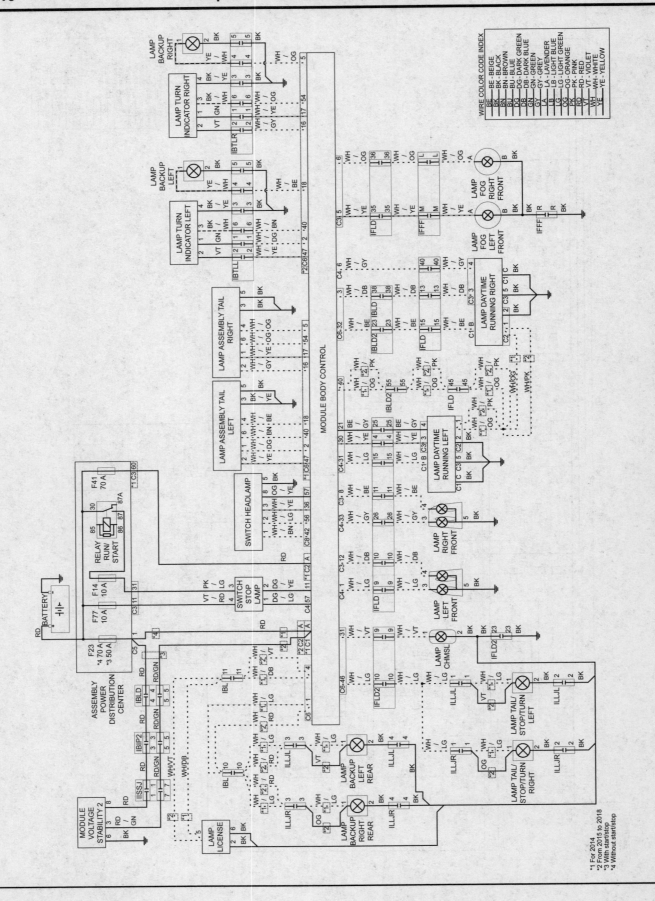

Exterior lighting system - 2018 and earlier models

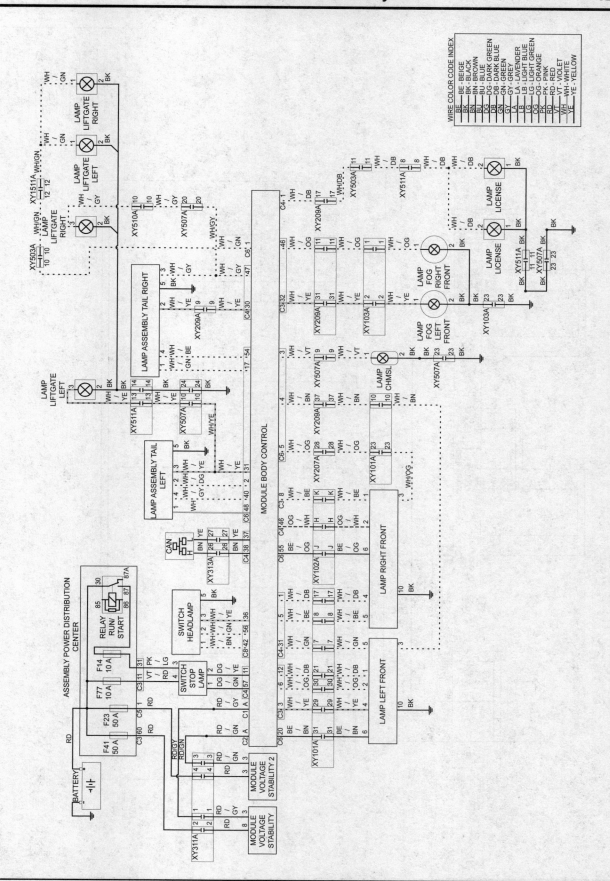

Exterior lighting system - 2019 models

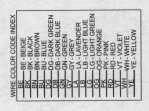

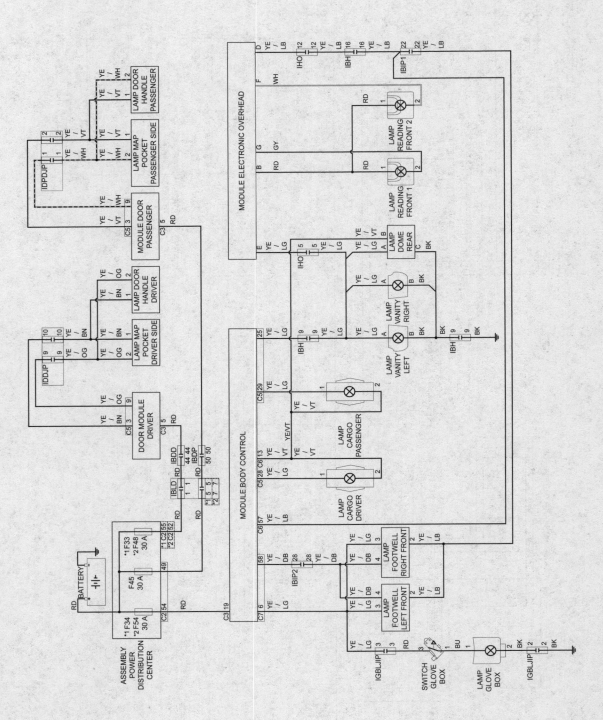

Interior lighting system - 2018 and earlier models

*1 For 2014
*2 From 2015 to 2018

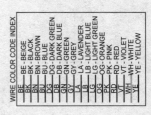

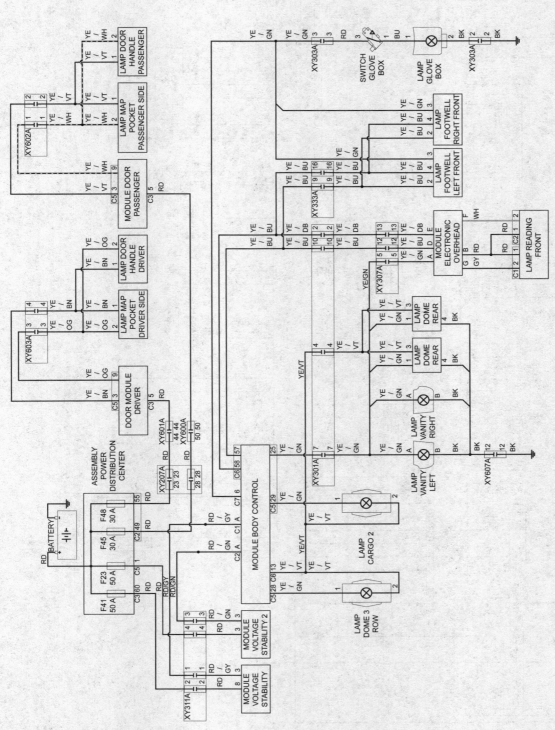

Interior lighting system - 2019 models

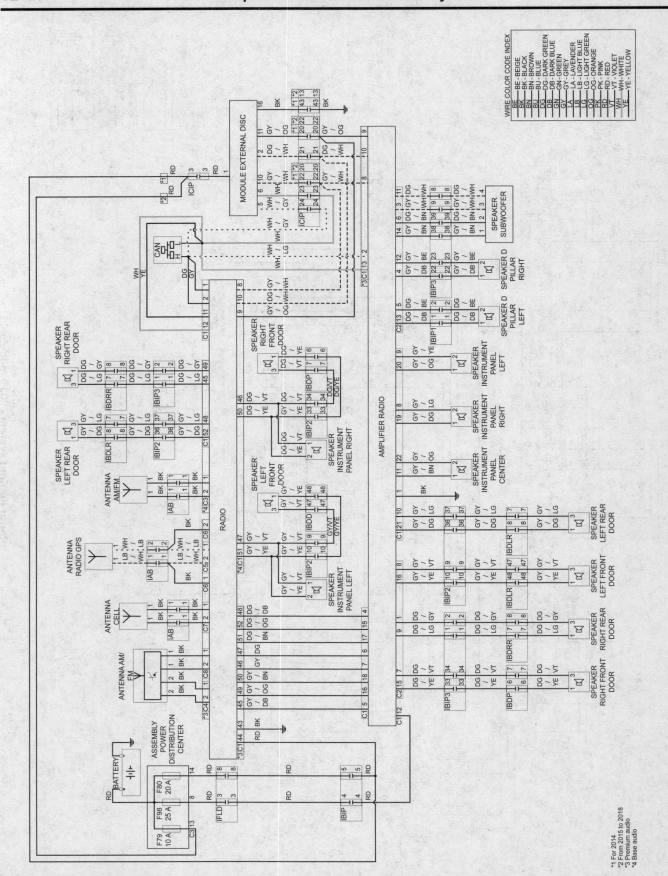

Audio system - 2018 and earlier models

*1 For 2014
*2 From 2015 to 2018
*3 Premium audio
*4 Base audio

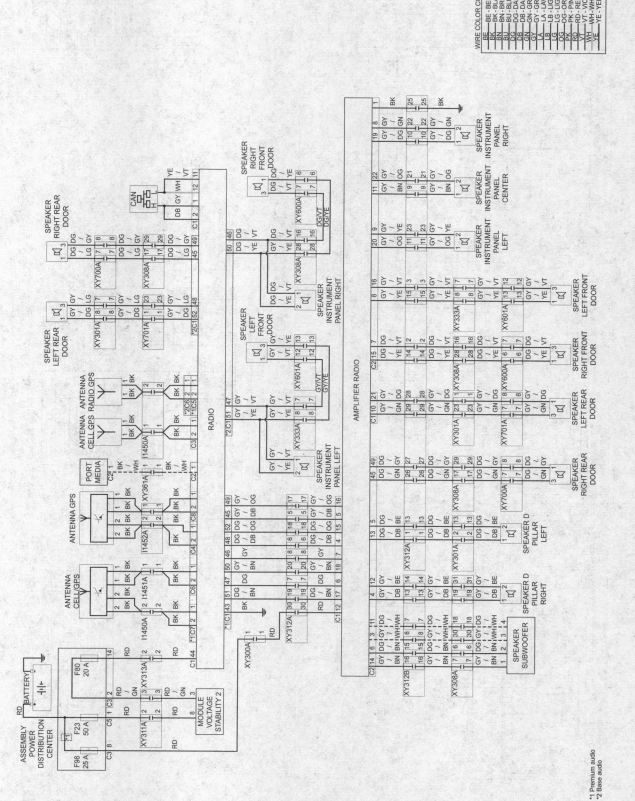

Audio system - 2019 models

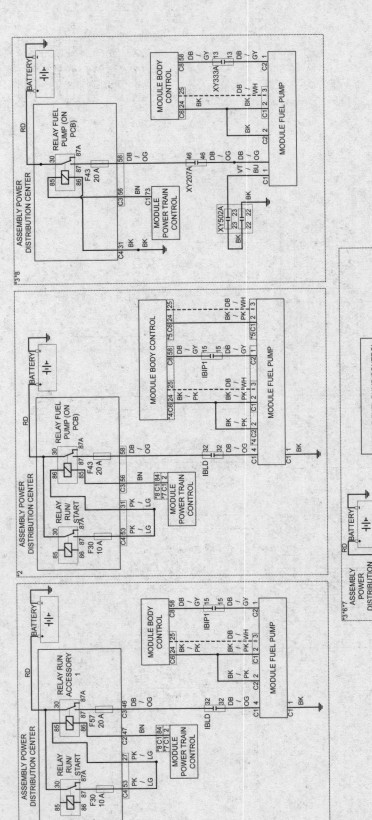

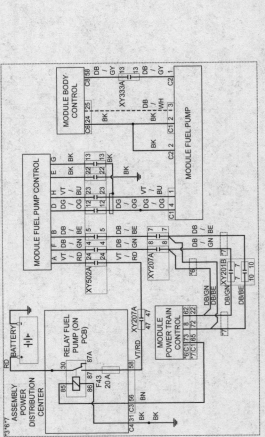

Fuel pump system

*1 For 2014
*2 From 2015 to 2018
*3 For 2019
*4 AWD
*5 FWD
*6 For 2.0 L
*7 For 2.4 L
*8 For 3.2 L

UNDERHOOD – POWER DISTRIBUTION CENTER

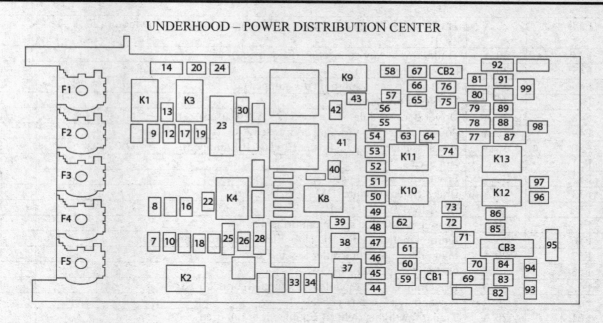

FUSES/RELAYS	VALUE	DESCRIPTION	OEM NAME
F1	100 A	EPS module	F1
F2	50 A	Battery Feed (B+)	F2
F3	300 A	Alternator (225 A also used)	F3
F5	100 A	Radiator fan module (70 A also used)	F5
F7	-	Not used	F7
F8	25 A	ECM and fuel injectors	F8
F9	15 A	Ignition or Coolant pump or not used	F9
F10	20 A	Power take off unit (PTU)	F10
F12	20 A	Brake Vacuum pump (If Equipped) or not used	F12
F13	10 A	ECM	F13
F14	10 A	DTCM, PTU, RDU, RDM, BSM, Brake pedal switch, EPB, Backup lamp switch	F14
F16	20 A	Ignition coil	F16
F17	30 A	Brake Vacuum pump or not used	F17
F19	40 A	Starter	F19
F20	10 A	A/C Compressor Clutch	F20
F22	5 A	Radiator fan enable	F22
F23	70 A	BCM feed 1 or VCM (50 A also used)	F23
F24	20 A	Rear wiper or not used	F24
F25	20 A	Rear wiper or not used	F25
F26	-	Not used	F26
F28	15 A	TCM (9 Speed)	F28
F30	10 A	ECM, EPS, Coil relay, Fuel pump	F30
F33	30 A	DDM (If Equipped) or not used	F33
F34	30 A	BCM feed 3 or not used	F34
F37	50 A	DC/DC Converter or not used	F37
F38	-	Not used	F38
F39	40 A	HVAC blower motor	F39
F40	20 A	Trailer tow park light (If Equipped)	F40
F41	60 A	BCM feed 2 or VSM feed 1 (50 A also used)	F41
F42	30 A	EPB-left or Trailer tow module	F42

Fuses and relays (1 of 6)

F43	20 A	Trailer tow left stop, Turn light (If Equipped) or Fuel pump motor (20 A also used)	F43
F44	30 A	Trailer tow 7-way connector (If Equipped)	F44
F45	30 A	PDM (If Equipped)	F45
F46	25 A	SCM single panel sunroof (If Equipped)	F46
F47	30 A	DTMC or not used	F47
F48	30 A	Driver door module or not used (25 A also used)	F48
F49	30 A	Power lumbar support, Power inverter A/C	F49
F50	30 A	Wireless charging pad, Power liftgate (If Equipped)	F50
F51	-	Not used	F51
F52	30 A	Front wipers or not used	F52
F53	30 A	Brake system module (BMS), ECU valves	F53
F54	30 A	BCM feed 3 or not used	F54
F55	10 A	Rear camera/Blind spot monitoring	F55
F56	15 A	Ignition module, KIN, RD Hub, Electric steering lock	F56
F57	20 A	Fuel pump motor or Trailer tow left stop	F57
F58	10 A	OCM, VSM, ESCL, TTOW	F58
F59	30 A	Drivetrain control module (If Equipped) or not used	F59
F60	20 A	Power outlet – centre console	F60
F61	20 A	Trailer tow lights right (If Equipped) or not used	F61
F62	10 A	Power mirror or windshield de-icer	F62
F63	25 A	Front heated/vented seats (If Equipped)	F63
F64	25 A	Heated steering wheel (If Equipped) or Rear heated seats (If Equipped)	F64
F65	15 A	HVAC, Instrument panel cluster	F65
F66	15 A	In car temperature sensor, Humidity sensor, DAS, PAM (10 A also used)	F66
F67	10 A	In car temperature sensor/Humidity sensor or not used	F67
F69	10 A	Transfer case switch (TSMB), Active grill shutter (AGS)	F69
F70	5 A	Intelligent battery sensor (If Equipped) or not used	F70
F71	20 A	Windshield De-icer (If Equipped) or Right HID headlamp	F71
F72	20 A	Trailer tow right stop, turn light (If Equipped) or Heated mirrors (10 A, 5A also used)	F72
F73	20 A	Trailer tow backup lights, NOX sensors	F73
F74	30 A	Rear defroster	F74
F75	20 A	Cigar lighter	F75
F76	20 A	Rear differential module (If Equipped)	F76
F77	10 A	Fuel door release, Brake pedal switch	F77
F78	10 A	SCCM/DTV/Diagnostic port	F78
F79	10 A	ICS/HVAC/ASBM/IPC	F79
F80	20 A	Radio/CD	F80
F81	20 A	Customer selectable location for power outlet or not used	F81
F82	5 A	Gateway module or not used	F82
F83	30 A	Engine control module (ECM) (20 A also used)	F83
F84	30 A	Electric park brake (EPB)	F84
F85	15 A	Heated steering wheel or not used	F85
F86	20 A	Horns or not used	F86
F87	20 A	HID headlamp left or not used	F87
F88	15 A	Seat belt reminder, smart camera (10 A also used) (If Equipped)	F88
F89	10 A	Auto headlamp levelling (If Equipped)	F89
F91	20 A	Power outlet D pillar or not used	F91
F92	20 A	Rear power outlet or not used	F92
F93	40 A	BSM pump motor	F93
F94	30 A	EPB right	F94
F95	10 A	Sunroof, Rain sensor, ECMM, Window switch	F95

Fuses and relays (2 of 6)

F96	10 A	Occupant restraint controller	F96
F97	10 A	Occupant restraint controller	F97
F98	25 A	HIFI-amplifier (If Equipped)	F98
F99	30 A	Trailer tow module (If Equipped) or not used	F99
K1	-	Starter solenoid 2	-
K2	-	ASD	-
K3	-	Starter	-
K4	-	Brake vacuum pump or not used	-
K8	-	Blower motor	-
K9	-	Run/Start	-
K10	-	Front defogger or rear defogger	-
K11	-	Ignition Run	-
K12	-	Ignition Run Accessory 1	-
K13	-	Ignition Run	-
CB1	30 A	Driver power seat	CB1
CB2	30 A	Passenger power seat or not used	CB2
CB3	25 A	Power windows	CB3
The following relays are integrated:			
K14	-	Headlamp washers	-
K15	-	Windshield de-icer	-
K16	-	Ignition Run Accessory 2	-
K17	-	A/C	-
K19	-	Vacuum pump	-
K20	-	ICR	-
K21	-	Fuel pump	-
K24	-	Trailer tow park light backup lamp	-
K25	-	Trailer tow park light turn left	-
K26	-	Trailer tow park light turn right	-
K27	-	Trailer tow park light lights	-
K28	-	Rad fan high speed	-

MODULE BODY CONTROL (FROM 2014 TO 2016)

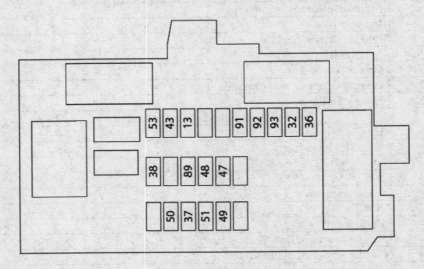

FUSES/RELAYS	VALUE	DESCRIPTION	OEM NAME
F13	15 A	Left xenon headlamp	F13
F32	10 A	SBMT	F32
F36	10 A	Intrusion module	F36
F37	7.5 A	USB and AUX	F37
F38	20 A	Passenger and rear door locks	F38
F43	20 A	Washer pump	F43
F47	5 A	110 VAC inverter	F47
F48	25 A	Horn, rear fog	F48
F49	7.5 A	Lumbar support	F49
F50	7.5 A	Wireless charging pad/Auxiliary switch bank module	F50
F51	10 A	Power mirrors or Window/Door lock driver	F51
F89	15 A	Driver unlock liftgate release	F89
F91	7.5 A	Front left fog lamp	F91
F92	7.5 A	Front right fog lamp	F92
F93	15 A	Right xenon headlamp	F93

MODULE BODY CONTROL (FROM 2017 TO 2019)

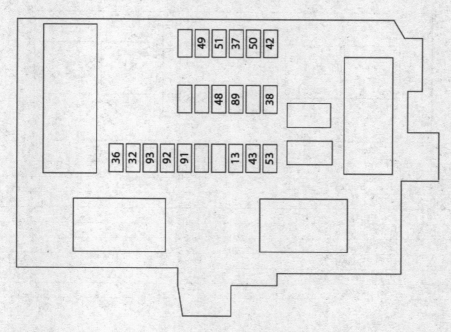

FUSES/RELAYS	VALUE	DESCRIPTION	OEM NAME
F13	15 A	Left headlamp or not used	F13
F32	10 A	Interior lights	F32
F36	10 A	Intrusion module siren	F36
F37	7.5 A	Media port	F37
F38	20 A	Passenger lock, Rear door locks	F38
F42	7.5 A	Passenger lumbar support or not used	F42
F43	20 A	Washer pump	F43
F48	25 A	Horn, Rear fog lights	F48
F49	7.5 A	Lumbar support	F49
F50	7.5 A	Wireless charging pad	F50
F51	7.5 A	Window, door lock driver	F51
F53	7.5 A	Instrument cluster or USB and AUX or not used	F53
F89	15 A	Driver unlock, liftgate release	F89
F91	7.5 A	Left front fog lamp or not used	F91
F92	7.5 A	Right front fog lamp or not used	F92
F93	15 A	Right headlamp or not used	F93

AUXILIARY POWER DISTRIBUTION CENTER

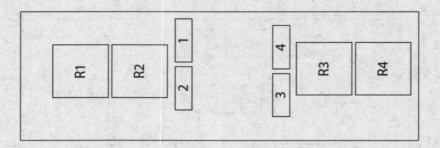

FUSES/RELAYS	VALUE	DESCRIPTION	OEM NAME
F1	50 A	PTC heater 1	F1
F2	50 A	PTC heater 2	F2
F3	-	Not used	F3
F4	50 A	PTC heater 3	F4
R1	-	PTC heater 1	R1
R2	-	PTC heater 2	R2
R3	-	PTC heater 3	R3
R4	-	Not used	R4

FUSE COLOR CODE INDEX

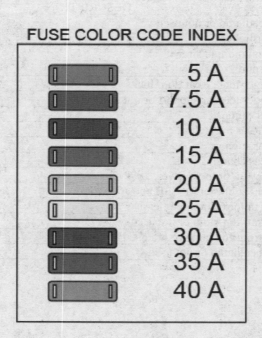

Fuses and relays (6 of 6)

Index

Haynes Automotive Manuals

ACURA
12020 **Integra** '86 thru '89 & **Legend** '86 thru '90
12021 **Integra** '90 thru '93 & **Legend** '91 thru '95
     Integra '94 thru '00 - see HONDA Civic (42025)
     MDX '01 thru '07 - see HONDA Pilot (42037)
12050 **Acura TL** all models '99 thru '08

AMC
     Jeep CJ - see JEEP (50020)
14020 **Mid-size models** '70 thru '83
14025 **(Renault) Alliance & Encore** '83 thru '87

AUDI
15020 **4000** all models '80 thru '87
15025 **5000** all models '77 thru '83
15026 **5000** all models '84 thru '88
     Audi A4 '96 thru '01 - see VW Passat (96023)
15030 **Audi A4** '02 thru '08

AUSTIN-HEALEY
     Sprite - see MG Midget (66015)

BMW
18020 **3/5 Series** '82 thru '92
18021 **3-Series** incl. Z3 models '92 thru '98
18022 **3-Series** incl. Z4 models '99 thru '05
18023 **3-Series** '06 thru '10
18025 **320i** all 4 cyl models '75 thru '83
18050 **1500 thru 2002** except Turbo '59 thru '77

BUICK
19010 **Buick Century** '97 thru '05
     Century (front-wheel drive) - see GM (38005)
19020 **Buick, Oldsmobile & Pontiac Full-size**
     (Front-wheel drive) '85 thru '05
     Buick Electra, LeSabre and Park Avenue;
     Oldsmobile Delta 88 Royale, Ninety Eight
     and Regency; Pontiac Bonneville
19025 **Buick, Oldsmobile & Pontiac Full-size**
     (Rear wheel drive) '70 thru '90
     Buick Estate, Electra, LeSabre, Limited,
     Oldsmobile Custom Cruiser, Delta 88,
     Ninety-eight, Pontiac Bonneville,
     Catalina, Grandville, Parisienne
19030 **Mid-size Regal & Century** all rear-drive
     models with V6, V8 and Turbo '74 thru '87
     Regal - see GENERAL MOTORS (38010)
     Riviera - see GENERAL MOTORS (38030)
     Roadmaster - see CHEVROLET (24046)
     Skyhawk - see GENERAL MOTORS (38015)
     Skylark - see GM (38020, 38025)
     Somerset - see GENERAL MOTORS (38025)

CADILLAC
21015 **CTS & CTS-V** '03 thru '12
21030 **Cadillac Rear Wheel Drive** '70 thru '93
     Cimarron - see GENERAL MOTORS (38015)
     DeVille - see GM (38031 & 38032)
     Eldorado - see GM (38030 & 38031)
     Fleetwood - see GM (38031)
     Seville - see GM (38030, 38031 & 38032)

CHEVROLET
10305 **Chevrolet Engine Overhaul Manual**
24010 **Astro & GMC Safari Mini-vans** '85 thru '05
24015 **Camaro V8** all models '70 thru '81
24016 **Camaro** all models '82 thru '92
24017 **Camaro & Firebird** '93 thru '02
     Cavalier - see GENERAL MOTORS (38016)
     Celebrity - see GENERAL MOTORS (38005)
24020 **Chevelle, Malibu & El Camino** '69 thru '87
24024 **Chevette & Pontiac T1000** '76 thru '87
     Citation - see GENERAL MOTORS (38020)
24027 **Colorado & GMC Canyon** '04 thru '10
24032 **Corsica/Beretta** all models '87 thru '96
24040 **Corvette** all V8 models '68 thru '82
24041 **Corvette** all models '84 thru '96
24045 **Full-size Sedans** Caprice, Impala, Biscayne,
     Bel Air & Wagons '69 thru '90
24046 **Impala SS & Caprice and Buick Roadmaster**
     '91 thru '96
     Impala '00 thru '05 - see LUMINA (24048)
24047 **Impala & Monte Carlo** all models '06 thru '11
     Lumina '90 thru '94 - see GM (38010)
24048 **Lumina & Monte Carlo** '95 thru '05
     Lumina APV - see GM (38035)
24050 **Luv Pick-up** all 2WD & 4WD '72 thru '82
     Malibu '97 thru '00 - see GM (38026)
24055 **Monte Carlo** all models '70 thru '88
     Monte Carlo '95 thru '01 - see LUMINA (24048)
24059 **Nova** all V8 models '69 thru '79
24060 **Nova and Geo Prizm** '85 thru '92
24064 **Pick-ups** '67 thru '87 - Chevrolet & GMC
24065 **Pick-ups** '88 thru '98 - Chevrolet & GMC

24066 **Pick-ups** '99 thru '06 - Chevrolet & GMC
24067 **Chevrolet Silverado & GMC Sierra** '07 thru '12
24070 **S-10 & S-15 Pick-ups** '82 thru '93,
     Blazer & Jimmy '83 thru '94,
24071 **S-10 & Sonoma Pick-ups** '94 thru '04, includ-
     ing **Blazer, Jimmy & Hombre**
24072 **Chevrolet TrailBlazer, GMC Envoy &**
     Oldsmobile Bravada '02 thru '09
24075 **Sprint** '85 thru '88 & **Geo Metro** '89 thru '01
24080 **Vans - Chevrolet & GMC** '68 thru '96
24081 **Chevrolet Express & GMC Savana**
     Full-size Vans '96 thru '10

CHRYSLER
10310 **Chrysler Engine Overhaul Manual**
25015 **Chrysler Cirrus, Dodge Stratus,**
     Plymouth Breeze '95 thru '00
25020 **Full-size Front-Wheel Drive** '88 thru '93
     K-Cars - see DODGE Aries (30008)
     Laser - see DODGE Daytona (30030)
25025 **Chrysler LHS, Concorde, New Yorker,**
     Dodge Intrepid, **Eagle** Vision, '93 thru '97
25026 **Chrysler LHS, Concorde, 300M,**
     Dodge Intrepid, '98 thru '04
25027 **Chrysler 300, Dodge Charger &**
     Magnum '05 thru '09
25030 **Chrysler & Plymouth Mid-size**
     front wheel drive '82 thru '95
     Rear-wheel Drive - see Dodge (30050)
25035 **PT Cruiser** all models '01 thru '10
25040 **Chrysler Sebring** '95 thru '06, **Dodge** Stratus
     '01 thru '06, **Dodge** Avenger '95 thru '00

DATSUN
28005 **200SX** all models '80 thru '83
28007 **B-210** all models '73 thru '78
28009 **210** all models '79 thru '82
28012 **240Z, 260Z & 280Z** Coupe '70 thru '78
28014 **280ZX** Coupe & 2+2 '79 thru '83
     300ZX - see NISSAN (72010)
28018 **510 & PL521 Pick-up** '68 thru '73
28020 **510** all models '78 thru '81
28022 **620 Series Pick-up** all models '73 thru '79
     720 Series Pick-up - see NISSAN (72030)
28025 **810/Maxima** all gasoline models '77 thru '84

DODGE
     400 & 600 - see CHRYSLER (25030)
30008 **Aries & Plymouth Reliant** '81 thru '89
30010 **Caravan & Plymouth Voyager** '84 thru '95
30011 **Caravan & Plymouth Voyager** '96 thru '02
30012 **Challenger/Plymouth Saporro** '78 thru '83
30013 **Caravan, Chrysler Voyager, Town &**
     Country '03 thru '07
30016 **Colt & Plymouth Champ** '78 thru '87
30020 **Dakota Pick-ups** all models '87 thru '96
30021 **Durango** '98 & '99, **Dakota** '97 thru '99
30022 **Durango** '00 thru '03 **Dakota** '00 thru '04
30023 **Durango** '04 thru '09, **Dakota** '05 thru '11
30025 **Dart, Demon, Plymouth Barracuda,**
     Duster & Valiant 6 cyl models '67 thru '76
30030 **Daytona & Chrysler Laser** '84 thru '89
     Intrepid - see CHRYSLER (25025, 25026)
30034 **Neon** all models '95 thru '99
30035 **Omni & Plymouth Horizon** '78 thru '90
30036 **Dodge and Plymouth Neon** '00 thru '05
30040 **Pick-ups** all full-size models '74 thru '93
30041 **Pick-ups** all full-size models '94 thru '01
30042 **Pick-ups** full-size models '02 thru '08
30045 **Ram 50/D50 Pick-ups & Raider and**
     Plymouth Arrow Pick-ups '79 thru '93
30050 **Dodge/Plymouth/Chrysler** RWD '71 thru '89
30055 **Shadow & Plymouth Sundance** '87 thru '94
30060 **Spirit & Plymouth Acclaim** '89 thru '95
30065 **Vans - Dodge & Plymouth** '71 thru '03

EAGLE
     Talon - see MITSUBISHI (68030, 68031)
     Vision - see CHRYSLER (25025)

FIAT
34010 **124 Sport Coupe & Spider** '68 thru '78
34025 **X1/9** all models '74 thru '80

FORD
10320 **Ford Engine Overhaul Manual**
10355 **Ford Automatic Transmission Overhaul**
11500 **Mustang** '64-1/2 thru '70 Restoration Guide
36004 **Aerostar Mini-vans** all models '86 thru '97
36006 **Contour & Mercury Mystique** '95 thru '00
36008 **Courier Pick-up** all models '72 thru '82
36012 **Crown Victoria & Mercury Grand**
     Marquis '88 thru '11
36016 **Escort/Mercury Lynx** all models '81 thru '90
36020 **Escort/Mercury Tracer** '91 thru '02

36022 **Escape & Mazda Tribute** '01 thru '11
36024 **Explorer & Mazda Navajo** '91 thru '01
36025 **Explorer/Mercury Mountaineer** '02 thru '10
36028 **Fairmont & Mercury Zephyr** '78 thru '83
36030 **Festiva & Aspire** '88 thru '97
36032 **Fiesta** all models '77 thru '80
36034 **Focus** all models '00 thru '11
36036 **Ford & Mercury Full-size** '75 thru '87
36044 **Ford & Mercury Mid-size** '75 thru '86
36045 **Fusion & Mercury Milan** '06 thru '10
36048 **Mustang V8** all models '64-1/2 thru '73
36049 **Mustang II** 4 cyl, V6 & V8 models '74 thru '78
36050 **Mustang & Mercury Capri** '79 thru '93
36051 **Mustang** all models '94 thru '04
36052 **Mustang** '05 thru '10
36054 **Pick-ups & Bronco** '73 thru '79
36058 **Pick-ups & Bronco** '80 thru '96
36059 **F-150 & Expedition** '97 thru '09, **F-250** '97
     thru '99 & **Lincoln Navigator** '98 thru '09
36060 **Super Duty Pick-ups, Excursion** '99 thru '10
36061 **F-150** full-size '04 thru '10
36062 **Pinto & Mercury Bobcat** '75 thru '80
36066 **Probe** all models '89 thru '92
     Probe '93 thru '97 - see MAZDA 626 (61042)
36070 **Ranger/Bronco II** gasoline models '83 thru '92
36071 **Ranger** '93 thru '10 & **Mazda Pick-ups** '94 thru '09
36074 **Taurus & Mercury Sable** '86 thru '95
36075 **Taurus & Mercury Sable** '96 thru '05
36078 **Tempo & Mercury Topaz** '84 thru '94
36082 **Thunderbird/Mercury Cougar** '83 thru '88
36086 **Thunderbird/Mercury Cougar** '89 thru '97
36090 **Vans** all V8 Econoline models '69 thru '91
36094 **Vans** full size '92 thru '10
36097 **Windstar Mini-van** '95 thru '07

GENERAL MOTORS
10360 **GM Automatic Transmission Overhaul**
38005 **Buick Century, Chevrolet Celebrity,**
     Oldsmobile Cutlass Ciera & Pontiac 6000
     all models '82 thru '96
38010 **Buick Regal, Chevrolet Lumina,**
     Oldsmobile Cutlass Supreme &
     Pontiac Grand Prix (FWD) '88 thru '07
38015 **Buick Skyhawk, Cadillac Cimarron,**
     Chevrolet Cavalier, Oldsmobile Firenza &
     Pontiac J-2000 & Sunbird '82 thru '94
38016 **Chevrolet Cavalier &**
     Pontiac Sunfire '95 thru '05
38017 **Chevrolet Cobalt & Pontiac G5** '05 thru '11
38020 **Buick Skylark, Chevrolet Citation,**
     Olds Omega, Pontiac Phoenix '80 thru '85
38025 **Buick Skylark & Somerset,**
     Oldsmobile Achieva & Calais and
     Pontiac Grand Am all models '85 thru '98
38026 **Chevrolet Malibu, Olds Alero & Cutlass,**
     Pontiac Grand Am '97 thru '03
38027 **Chevrolet Malibu** '04 thru '10
38030 **Cadillac Eldorado, Seville, Oldsmobile**
     Toronado, Buick Riviera '71 thru '85
38031 **Cadillac Eldorado & Seville, DeVille, Fleetwood**
     & Olds Toronado, Buick Riviera '86 thru '93
38032 **Cadillac DeVille** '94 thru '05 & **Seville** '92 thru '04
     Cadillac DTS '06 thru '10
38035 **Chevrolet Lumina APV, Olds Silhouette**
     & Pontiac Trans Sport all models '90 thru '96
38036 **Chevrolet Venture, Olds Silhouette,**
     Pontiac Trans Sport & Montana '97 thru '05
     General Motors Full-size
     Rear-wheel Drive - see BUICK (19025)
38040 **Chevrolet Equinox** '05 thru '09 **Pontiac**
     Torrent '06 thru '09
38070 **Chevrolet HHR** '06 thru '11

GEO
     Metro - see CHEVROLET Sprint (24075)
     Prizm - '85 thru '92 see CHEVY (24060),
     '93 thru '02 see TOYOTA Corolla (92036)
40030 **Storm** all models '90 thru '93
     Tracker - see SUZUKI Samurai (90010)

GMC
     Vans & Pick-ups - see CHEVROLET

HONDA
42010 **Accord CVCC** all models '76 thru '83
42011 **Accord** all models '84 thru '89
42012 **Accord** all models '90 thru '93
42013 **Accord** all models '94 thru '97
42014 **Accord** all models '98 thru '02
42015 **Accord** '03 thru '07
42020 **Civic 1200** all models '73 thru '79
42021 **Civic 1300 & 1500** CVCC '80 thru '83
42022 **Civic 1500 CVCC** all models '75 thru '79

(Continued on other side)

Haynes North America, Inc., 859 Lawrence Drive, Newbury Park, CA 91320-1514 • (805) 498-6703 • http://www.haynes.com

Haynes Automotive Manuals (continued)

NOTE: If you do not see a listing for your vehicle, consult your local Haynes dealer for the latest product information.

42023 Civic all models '84 thru '91
42024 Civic & del Sol '92 thru '95
42025 Civic '96 thru '00, CR-V '97 thru '01,
 Acura Integra '94 thru '00
42026 Civic '01 thru '10, CR-V '02 thru '09
42035 Odyssey all models '99 thru '10
 Passport - see ISUZU Rodeo (47017)
42037 Honda Pilot '03 thru '07, Acura MDX '01 thru '07
42040 Prelude CVCC all models '79 thru '89

HYUNDAI
43010 Elantra all models '96 thru '10
43015 Excel & Accent all models '86 thru '09
43050 Santa Fe all models '01 thru '06
43055 Sonata all models '99 thru '08

INFINITI
 G35 '03 thru '08 - *see NISSAN 350Z (72011)*

ISUZU
 Hombre - *see CHEVROLET S-10 (24071)*
47017 Rodeo, Amigo & Honda Passport '89 thru '02
47020 Trooper & Pick-up '81 thru '93

JAGUAR
49010 XJ6 all 6 cyl models '68 thru '86
49011 XJ6 all models '88 thru '94
49015 XJ12 & XJS all 12 cyl models '72 thru '85

JEEP
50010 Cherokee, Comanche & Wagoneer Limited
 all models '84 thru '01
50020 CJ all models '49 thru '86
50025 Grand Cherokee all models '93 thru '04
50026 Grand Cherokee '05 thru '09
50029 Grand Wagoneer & Pick-up '72 thru '91
 Grand Wagoneer '84 thru '91, Cherokee &
 Wagoneer '72 thru '83, Pick-up '72 thru '88
50030 Wrangler all models '87 thru '11
50035 Liberty '02 thru '07

KIA
54050 Optima '01 thru '10
54070 Sephia '94 thru '01, Spectra '00 thru '09,
 Sportage '05 thru '10

LEXUS
 ES 300/330 - *see TOYOTA Camry (92007) (92008)*
 RX 330 - *see TOYOTA Highlander (92095)*

LINCOLN
 Navigator - *see FORD Pick-up (36059)*
59010 Rear-Wheel Drive all models '70 thru '10

MAZDA
61010 GLC Hatchback (rear-wheel drive) '77 thru '83
61011 GLC (front-wheel drive) '81 thru '85
61012 Mazda3 '04 thru '11
61015 323 & Protogé '90 thru '03
61016 MX-5 Miata '90 thru '09
61020 MPV all models '89 thru '98
 Navajo - *see Ford Explorer (36024)*
61030 Pick-ups '72 thru '93
 Pick-ups '94 thru '00 - *see Ford Ranger (36071)*
61035 RX-7 all models '79 thru '85
61036 RX-7 all models '86 thru '91
61040 626 (rear-wheel drive) all models '79 thru '82
61041 626/MX-6 (front-wheel drive) '83 thru '92
61042 626, MX-6/Ford Probe '93 thru '02
61043 Mazda6 '03 thru '11

MERCEDES-BENZ
63012 123 Series Diesel '76 thru '85
63015 190 Series four-cyl gas models, '84 thru '88
63020 230/250/280 6 cyl sohc models '68 thru '72
63025 280 123 Series gasoline models '77 thru '81
63030 350 & 450 all models '71 thru '80
63040 C-Class: C230/C240/C280/C320/C350 '01 thru '07

MERCURY
64200 Villager & Nissan Quest '93 thru '01
 All other titles, see FORD Listing.

MG
66010 MGB Roadster & GT Coupe '62 thru '80
66015 MG Midget, Austin Healey Sprite '58 thru '80

MINI
67020 Mini '02 thru '11

MITSUBISHI
68020 Cordia, Tredia, Galant, Precis &
 Mirage '83 thru '93
68030 Eclipse, Eagle Talon & Ply. Laser '90 thru '94
68031 Eclipse '95 thru '05, Eagle Talon '95 thru '98
68035 Galant '94 thru '10
68040 Pick-up '83 thru '96 & Montero '83 thru '93

NISSAN
72010 300ZX all models including Turbo '84 thru '89
72011 350Z & Infiniti G35 all models '03 thru '08
72015 Altima all models '93 thru '06
72016 Altima '07 thru '10
72020 Maxima all models '85 thru '92
72021 Maxima all models '93 thru '04
72025 Murano '03 thru '10
72030 Pick-ups '80 thru '97 Pathfinder '87 thru '95
72031 Frontier Pick-up, Xterra, Pathfinder '96 thru '04
72032 Frontier & Xterra '05 thru '11
72040 Pulsar all models '83 thru '86
 Quest - *see MERCURY Villager (64200)*
72050 Sentra all models '82 thru '94
72051 Sentra & 200SX all models '95 thru '06
72060 Stanza all models '82 thru '90
72070 Titan pick-ups '04 thru '10 Armada '05 thru '10

OLDSMOBILE
73015 Cutlass V6 & V8 gas models '74 thru '88
 *For other OLDSMOBILE titles, see BUICK,
 CHEVROLET or GENERAL MOTORS listing.*

PLYMOUTH
 For PLYMOUTH titles, see DODGE listing.

PONTIAC
79008 Fiero all models '84 thru '88
79018 Firebird V8 models except Turbo '70 thru '81
79019 Firebird all models '82 thru '92
79025 G6 all models '05 thru '09
79040 Mid-size Rear-wheel Drive '70 thru '87
 Vibe '03 thru '11 - *see TOYOTA Matrix (92060)*
 *For other PONTIAC titles, see BUICK,
 CHEVROLET or GENERAL MOTORS listing.*

PORSCHE
80020 911 except Turbo & Carrera 4 '65 thru '89
80025 914 all 4 cyl models '69 thru '76
80030 924 all models including Turbo '76 thru '82
80035 944 all models including Turbo '83 thru '89

RENAULT
 Alliance & Encore - *see AMC (14020)*

SAAB
84010 900 all models including Turbo '79 thru '88

SATURN
87010 Saturn all S-series models '91 thru '02
87011 Saturn Ion '03 thru '07
87020 Saturn all L-series models '00 thru '04
87040 Saturn VUE '02 thru '07

SUBARU
89002 1100, 1300, 1400 & 1600 '71 thru '79
89003 1600 & 1800 2WD & 4WD '80 thru '94
89100 Legacy all models '90 thru '99
89101 Legacy & Forester '00 thru '06

SUZUKI
90010 Samurai/Sidekick & Geo Tracker '86 thru '01

TOYOTA
92005 Camry all models '83 thru '91
92006 Camry all models '92 thru '96
92007 Camry, Avalon, Solara, Lexus ES 300 '97 thru '01
92008 Toyota Camry, Avalon and Solara and
 Lexus ES 300/330 all models '02 thru '06
92009 Camry '07 thru '11
92015 Celica Rear Wheel Drive '71 thru '85
92020 Celica Front Wheel Drive '86 thru '99
92025 Celica Supra all models '79 thru '92
92030 Corolla all models '75 thru '79
92032 Corolla all rear wheel drive models '80 thru '87
92035 Corolla all front wheel drive models '84 thru '92
92036 Corolla & Geo Prizm '93 thru '02
92037 Corolla models '03 thru '11
92040 Corolla Tercel all models '80 thru '82
92045 Corona all models '74 thru '82
92050 Cressida all models '78 thru '82
92055 Land Cruiser FJ40, 43, 45, 55 '68 thru '82
92056 Land Cruiser FJ60, 62, 80, FZJ80 '80 thru '96
92060 Matrix & Pontiac Vibe '03 thru '11
92065 MR2 all models '85 thru '87
92070 Pick-up all models '69 thru '78
92075 Pick-up all models '79 thru '95
92076 Tacoma, 4Runner, & T100 '93 thru '04
92077 Tacoma all models '05 thru '09
92078 Tundra '00 thru '06 & Sequoia '01 thru '07
92079 4Runner all models '03 thru '09
92080 Previa all models '91 thru '95
92081 Prius all models '01 thru '08
92082 RAV4 all models '96 thru '10
92085 Tercel all models '87 thru '94
92090 Sienna all models '98 thru '09
92095 Highlander & Lexus RX-330 '99 thru '07

TRIUMPH
94007 Spitfire all models '62 thru '81
94010 TR7 all models '75 thru '81

VW
96008 Beetle & Karmann Ghia '54 thru '79
96009 New Beetle '98 thru '11
96016 Rabbit, Jetta, Scirocco & Pick-up gas
 models '75 thru '92 & Convertible '80 thru '92
96017 Golf, GTI & Jetta '93 thru '98, Cabrio '95 thru '02
96018 Golf, GTI, Jetta '99 thru '05
96019 Jetta, Rabbit, GTI & Golf '05 thru '11
96020 Rabbit, Jetta & Pick-up diesel '77 thru '84
96023 Passat '98 thru '05, Audi A4 '96 thru '01
96030 Transporter 1600 all models '68 thru '79
96035 Transporter 1700, 1800 & 2000 '72 thru '79
96040 Type 3 1500 & 1600 all models '63 thru '73
96045 Vanagon all air-cooled models '80 thru '83

VOLVO
97010 120, 130 Series & 1800 Sports '61 thru '73
97015 140 Series all models '66 thru '74
97020 240 Series all models '76 thru '93
97040 740 & 760 Series all models '82 thru '88
97050 850 Series all models '93 thru '97

TECHBOOK MANUALS
10205 Automotive Computer Codes
10206 OBD-II & Electronic Engine Management
10210 Automotive Emissions Control Manual
10215 Fuel Injection Manual '78 thru '85
10220 Fuel Injection Manual '86 thru '99
10225 Holley Carburetor Manual
10230 Rochester Carburetor Manual
10240 Weber/Zenith/Stromberg/SU Carburetors
10305 Chevrolet Engine Overhaul Manual
10310 Chrysler Engine Overhaul Manual
10320 Ford Engine Overhaul Manual
10330 GM and Ford Diesel Engine Repair Manual
10333 Engine Performance Manual
10340 Small Engine Repair Manual, 5 HP & Less
10341 Small Engine Repair Manual, 5.5 - 20 HP
10345 Suspension, Steering & Driveline Manual
10355 Ford Automatic Transmission Overhaul
10360 GM Automatic Transmission Overhaul
10405 Automotive Body Repair & Painting
10410 Automotive Brake Manual
10411 Automotive Anti-lock Brake (ABS) Systems
10415 Automotive Detailing Manual
10420 Automotive Electrical Manual
10425 Automotive Heating & Air Conditioning
10430 Automotive Reference Manual & Dictionary
10435 Automotive Tools Manual
10440 Used Car Buying Guide
10445 Welding Manual
10450 ATV Basics
10452 Scooters 50cc to 250cc

SPANISH MANUALS
98903 Reparación de Carrocería & Pintura
98904 Manual de Carburador Modelos
 Holley & Rochester
98905 Códigos Automotrices de la Computadora
98906 OBD-II & Sistemas de Control Electrónico
 del Motor
98910 Frenos Automotriz
98913 Electricidad Automotriz
98915 Inyección de Combustible '86 al '99
99040 Chevrolet & GMC Camionetas '67 al '87
99041 Chevrolet & GMC Camionetas '88 al '98
99042 Chevrolet & GMC Camionetas
 Cerradas '68 al '95
99043 Chevrolet/GMC Camionetas '94 al '04
99048 Chevrolet/GMC Camionetas '99 al '06
99055 Dodge Caravan & Plymouth Voyager '84 al '95
99075 Ford Camionetas y Bronco '80 al '94
99076 Ford F-150 '97 al '09
99077 Ford Camionetas Cerradas '69 al '91
99088 Ford Modelos de Tamaño Mediano '75 al '86
99089 Ford Camionetas Ranger '93 al '10
99091 Ford Taurus & Mercury Sable '86 al '95
99095 GM Modelos de Tamaño Grande '70 al '90
99100 GM Modelos de Tamaño Mediano '70 al '88
99106 Jeep Cherokee, Wagoneer & Comanche
 '84 al '00
99110 Nissan Camioneta '80 al '96, Pathfinder '87 al '95
99118 Nissan Sentra '82 al '94
99125 Toyota Camionetas y 4Runner '79 al '95

Over 100 Haynes
motorcycle manuals
also available

7-12

Haynes North America, Inc., 859 Lawrence Drive, Newbury Park, CA 91320-1514 • (805) 498-6703 • http://www.haynes.com